FOLLOW
THE MUSIC

The Life and High Times of
Elektra Records in the Great Years of
American Pop Culture

Jac Holzman and Gavan Daws

elektra®

FirstMedia Books, a unit of
F.M. Group Inc.
2034 Broadway
Santa Monica,
California 90404

Library of Congress Catalog Card Number: 97-77539

Library of Congress Cataloging-in-Publication Data:

Holzman and Daws
Follow The Music: The Life and High Times of Elektra Records in
the Great Years of American Pop Culture
p.   cm.
includes photographs, discography and index

1. Jac Holzman 1931-   2. Elektra Records   3. Music Business
4. Rock Musicians-United States 5. California- Social Life and Customs

ISBN   0-9661221-1-9

First Edition

Printed in the United States of America

Distributed by Publishers Group West

Website address: www.followthemusic.com

Book and cover design by Kurt Triffet

1 2 3 4 5 6 7 8 9 10

for

Estelle Sternberger and Paul Rothchild

and the people of Elektra

Table of Contents

List of Illustrations

Foreword

I get to say a few words up front.

Jac Holzman started his own record company when he was all of nineteen. His total assets amounted to a handful of dollars, a brain fizzing with ideas, and a heart pumping with naive late-teenage hope. He christened his label Elektra

The first album he produced sold a swift zero copies, the second a few hundred over twelve months. Not great numbers. But Jac kept at it, Elektra survived, and the rest is, as they say, history. Twenty years later, Jac had brought five hundred albums into being. He built the hippest, most advanced studio in the known world, its walls lined with gold and platinum records. More than a hundred people were working with him out of offices in New York, Los Angeles, and London; and Elektra's reputation was global.

Elektra was Jac's reason for being, his work and his play, his professional and personal garden of delights. It gave him a box seat on life.

He saw, close up, the United States going through its amazing cultural transformation from the Fifties to the Sixties. Music was the beating heart of that change: from acoustic to electric, from folk to rock, from "protest" songs to the music of the late Sixties, when for the first time a popular art form had become a universal medium of expressive yearning for a whole generation—making it possible to believe, as one young American put it, that if you sang long enough and loud enough you could change the world. Millions believed; and at Elektra, Jac was leading the chorus and turning up the volume. In the creative social turmoil of the times, Jac Holzman was a significant agent of change.

Jac was a player. For him the sport and pastime of watching the great procession of American pop culture winding from coast to coast, New York to LA, Greenwich Village to the Sunset Strip, was an endless fascination, and Elektra was a prime place to be, a sweet spot. Andy Warhol, at exactly the seven and a half-minute mark of his own fifteen minutes, was more than pleased to be invited to Jac's party. And any number of others, from the justifiably celebrated to the obsessively heat-seeking, to the notoriously scabby and worse, were attracted to the radiance of Elektra on their way to finding their own place in the sun: from Harrison Ford when he was a journeyman carpenter to Jann Wenner as he was setting out to become Mr. Rolling Stone; David Geffen before he was even the babiest of moguls; Marlon Brando as a fan of bizarre sound effects; Jackson Browne, teenage troubadour; Iggy Stooge, premature father of punk; Jim Morrison, rock icon, darkly romantic, lethally intelligent, forever testing the locks on the cage doors of American cultural and sexual taboos; Nico, an apparition, a disapparition, a naked dancer, a waver of guns, a death-talker; and a wannabe guitar player named Charles Manson, casing Elektra just weeks before he announced to the world his true vocation. And a cast of hundreds more . . .

How to get down on paper those years in all their richness? When Jac and I first talked about trying, we weren't sure we would be able to recover the substance, the style, and the flavor of those lives and those times. The Fifties have been gone long enough to seem almost a different world—the past as another country. And of course there is the famous one-liner that if you remember the Sixties you weren't there. (Who said that? David Crosby? I don't remember.)

Jac does remember, though. He and I spent uncounted hours together over a period of more than three years, Jac talking, me listening and asking questions, with the tape recorder running. But we made an early decision not to do the book as a first-person "as told to." For my money, and Jac's too, that kind of celeb autobio is a bastard art form, and neither of us has any interest in fathering yet another such literary illegitimacy upon the world. On his own, Jac fired up the word-processing program and labored endlessly to make sure of saying exactly what he meant, exactly the way it needed to be said. And when I went out to do reconnaissance among others who were there, what I came back with was wonderful: the uproarious sound of life as it was lived, harmonies and discordancies, the rich and complex music of memory. Such a range of recall, and such different takes on experience, in so many distinctive voices—Rashomon in stereo. It was a natural choice to arrange and orchestrate the book so as to give full play to all these tonalities, people speaking for themselves, with Jac's voice soloing over the chorus.

At Elektra, any number of interesting things happened while Jac was out of the room. But in or out of the room, Jac was the dominating presence, an object of fascinated study and endless discussion. All testify to that, and with reason. Professionally, there had been no one before in the record industry (and there has been no one since) with his outstanding combination of business smarts, technical expertise, vision, and pure intelligence, all put passionately at the service of music. The greatest American record men agree on this. In personal terms, of course everyone sees Jac from the particular angle of his or her own vision. And Jac, for his part, knows that he does not see himself as others see him. He has been more than willing to allow others—Elektra artists and staffers, friends, lovers, competitors, adversaries, everyone—full candor in what they say about him. The portrait of Jac Holzman in these pages is imperfections-and-all, and the more true and human for that.

We see him stumbling from his late teens into his twenties, gaining his footing, striding through his thirties into his early forties. He had to thread his way through minefields of power plays and mazes of elaborate pretense. He had to learn to deal with sensitive artists and sellouts, to detect and deflect opportunists, and to appreciate loyalty. He met with triumphs, and with disasters, some of his own making. He lost his way and found it again. And—central to his life and being—he was present at the creation of some of the most remarkable music of his remarkable times.

Would he have predicted any of this? Not for a moment. The next voice you hear will be Jac, recounting his awkward and unpromising beginnings, his first steps on the road to Elektra . . .

GAVAN DAWS

Cast of Characters

MARK ABRAMSON. Elektra producer from the early Sixties on, with a gentle touch and an appetite for encounter. In the late Nineties, running a crisis center near Woodstock.

BILL ALEXANDER. A Marin County therapist.

DAVID ANDERLE. The incarnation of Elektra in Sixties LA. Beloved of artists. Later senior VP for A&R at A&M Records.

ALAN ARKIN. A Tarrier, later a movie star.

ARS NOVA. Classically trained musicians going medieval on the ars of rock.

MOSES ASCH. An obsessive, invaluable chronicler of world folk music on his Folkways label.

K.O. ASHER. The "Scroogiest" and most honest independent record distributor in the Midwest.

TED ASHLEY. Former chairman of Warner Brothers Inc.

OONA AUSTIN: A lady of the canyon.

EVE BABITZ. A Sixties LA watcher and writer. Sister of Mirandi.

MIRANDI BABITZ. Sister of Eve. Measured the inside leg of Jim Morrison for his custom-made leather pants.

PETER BARTÓK. Early genius audio engineer. Son of the composer.

PAUL BEAVER. A Moog man who departed this earth on a UFO . . . Strange days.

THEODORE BIKEL. Actor, folk singer, conscience. Recorded sixteen LPs for Elektra.

MIKE BLOOMFIELD. Guitarist. For sheer skill and passion, a white Hendrix. Died of drug overdose in 1981.

BRUCE BOTNICK. Boy wonder recording engineer for Love, Tim Buckley, the Doors, and co-producer of "LA Woman." In the Nineties, a producer of movie soundtracks and Disney cast albums.

BONNIE BRAMLETT. As in Delaney & Bonnie. A great white blues singer.

DELANEY BRAMLETT. Husband of Bonnie. Put his name ahead of hers and blacked her eye.

OSCAR BRAND. Folk interpreter with an encyclopedic repertoire. Recorded non-stop for Elektra in the Sixties.

MARLON BRANDO. A fan of bizarre sound effects.

DAVID BRAUN. Music business attorney and wit.

BREAD. A sweet-harmony soft-rock group.

BERTOLT BRECHT. A lyricist for the Doors.

JACKSON BROWNE. Signed to Elektra's publishing unit as a teenage songwriter.

LENNY BRUCE. Once called a "sick" comedian; died of dope and genius.

LORD BUCKLEY. Before Lenny Bruce there was Lord Buckley.

TIM BUCKLEY. A doomed angel with a four-octave voice and a bad habit. ODd at 27.

ERIC BURDON. An Animal, with war stories of Jim Morrison's night tripping.

PAUL BUTTERFIELD. White electric blues man. Knew the South Side of Chicago, made a noise at Newport. Died in 1987 after years of poor health.

EDWARD TATNALL CANBY. An early enlightened stereophile and music critic.

HARRY CHAPIN. The last artist Jac personally produced and sent on his way— 'Taxi!' Killed in an auto accident 1980.

CIGAR PAIN. Burned his throat so his voice would sound like Jim Morrison's.

ERIC CLAPTON. A fan of Delaney & Bonnie.

JOE COCKER. Another fan of Delaney & Bonnie; a Mad Dog and Englishman.

ALAN COHEN. Executive VP for Warner Communications, Steve Ross's right hand until he allegedly tried to bite it.

HERB COHEN. Castro "freedom fighter," sky diver, LA coffee house pioneer, partner of Theo Bikel, manager of Judy Henske and Tim Buckley.

LEONARD COHEN. A poet in his youth.

JUDY COLLINS. Began as a folk maid of constant sorrow, became an artist of taste and constantly refreshing inventiveness.

STAN CORNYN. Head of creative services for Warner Bros. Records.

PAMELA COURSON. Emotional partner in crime of Jim Morrison, till death did them part.

CROSBY, STILLS AND NASH. Sat on Paul Rothchild's couch in Laurel Canyon and sang.

MARIA D'AMATO. Singer with the Even Dozen Jug Band; later Maria Muldaur.

ALLEN DAVIAU. Camera store clerk in his youth; later a cinematographer with five Academy Award nominations.

CLIVE DAVIS. Highly talented record company president who threw a demo tape of Carly Simon across the room. In the Nineties, well-thought-of chairman of Arista Records.

DOROTHY DEAN. The Spade of Queens. Famous doorperson at Max's Kansas City.

JOHN DENSMORE. The Doors' drummer. Suffered for his sanity.

MAYA DEREN. Haitian voodoo adept, avant-garde film maker.

DEADLY DIANE. Waitress at the Unicorn on the Sunset Strip. A barebreasted portrait is in the Herb Cohen collection.

JIM DICKSON. Producer, scene-maker in Sixties LA.

DIGBY DIEHL: Journalist, Doors observer, later wrote for Playboy.

ROGER DI FIORE. Cook, master joint roller, W.C. Fields admirer.

THE DILLARDS. The real bluegrass thing.

HENRY DILTZ. Photographer to the stars of rock.

CONNIE DI NARDO. One of the Three Graces of Paxton Lodge.

NED DOHENY. Teenage guitar wizard.

THE DOORS. *The* Elektra band—high musical intelligence and five gold albums in a row, on the way to platinum.

BOB DYLAN. The road not taken: signed to Columbia while Jac was out of town.

JACLYN EASTON. Daughter of Jac and Nina. In the late Nineties, an Internet business specialist.

CASS ELLIOTT. A Laurel Canyon Mama.

ALLAN EMIG. Helped design Elektra's LA studio.

AHMET ERTEGUN. Founder, with brother Nesuhi, of Atlantic Records. One of the greats.

NESUHI ERTEGUN. With brother Ahmet, founder of Atlantic Records. An internationalist in musical and cultural reach.

THE EVEN DOZEN JUG BAND. Count 'em. What you hear is what you get.

PAT FARALLA. Of Elektra West. Later the master baker of Santa Fe.

CYRUS FARYAR. The Persian minstrel of Barham Boulevard. Nearly a Sufi.

DANNY FIELDS. Elektra publicist, designated company freak. The hippest guy in New York. Close personal friend of Max's Kansas City.

MITCHELL FINK. On the scene then . . . and now.

HARRISON FORD. A carpenter in his youth.

MICHAEL FORD. A poet in his youth.

BARRY FRIEDMAN. AKA Frazier Mohawk. Laurel Canyon prankster, circus clown, fire eater, wearer of gorilla suits, escape artist. In the late Nineties, producing records in Canada.

DAVE GAHR. Folk and rock photographer with a discerning eye.

DIANE GARDINER. Publicist for the Doors, friend and long-suffering neighbor of Jim Morrison.

DAVID GATES. A civilized recording artist. Leader of Bread.

BILL GAZZARI. Sunset Strip club owner, auditioned the Doors.

DAVID GEFFEN. Once and future enfant terrible, baby mogul, billionaire rising.

BOB GIBSON. Washington Square folkie, traveling twelve-string guitarist, talent scout extraordinaire. Died in 1996.

TONY "LITTLE SUN" GLOVER. Of Koerner, Ray & Glover. A young white blues musician out of Minneapolis.

CYNTHIA GOODING. Tall, beautiful, intelligent, multilingual Village folk singer.

PEARL GOODMAN. Jac's soul-of-discretion secretary for three decades.

SAM GOODY. Big record store man in New York City.

JIM GORDON. Rock drummer on a Judy Collins album, later beat his mother to death with a hammer.

ARTHUR GORSON. Manager of singer-songwriters, Sixties activist.

BILL GRAHAM. Mr. Fillmore, West and East. Killed in helicopter accident 1991.

GEORGE GRAVES. Jac's driver. Played great pool, spoke softly, and carried a big switchblade.

ANTON GREENE. A stuffer of quail eggs.

JEANIE GREENE. Southern reincarnation of Mary Magdalene.

MARLIN GREENE. Husband of Jeanie. An Alabama State Trouper.

JOYCE GRENFELL. An English comedienne with a spy camera.

ALBERT GROSSMAN. The Jabba the Hutt of artist managers, sometimes referred to as "the floating Buddha." Represented Dylan, Peter, Paul and Mary, The Band, Janis Joplin. Died 1986.

WOODY GUTHRIE. Nonpareil folk chronicler of America: this land was his land.

JOHN HAENY. Elektra studio engineer of great virtuosity and Virgosity.

BRUCE HARRIS. A miniskirt-mesmerized freshman, later an Elektra publicist.

LARRY HARRIS. Music business lawyer at CBS who walked across the street to Elektra.

STEVE HARRIS. Elektra's good shepherd for Jim Morrison, Tim Buckley, and Carly Simon.

GEORGE HARRISON. A fan of Delaney & Bonnie.

BILL HARVEY. Elektra art director. Created and elaborated the label's visual identity. Died in early Nineties.

FRED HELLERMAN. A Weaver of wisdom, arranger for Theodore Bikel.

SUZANNE HELMS. Ran Elektra's West Coast office. Jazz aficionado, auto mechanic, chocolate lover, dog trainer, disciplinarian of Jim Morrison. Married a jazz bassist, lives in Switzerland.

JIMI HENDRIX. A jammer in a cabana, and a Plaster Castee.

JUDY HENSKE. Stood tall, sang strong, opened for Lenny Bruce and Woody Allen in a Louise Brooks wig.

THE HOLY MODAL ROUNDERS. On drums, Sam Shepard. Rockin' around on that belladonna cloud—Euphoria!

ADAM HOLZMAN. Son of Jac and Nina. Grew up to play keyboard with Miles Davis, Wayne Shorter, Chaka Khan, Grover Washington Jr.

JAC HOLZMAN. El Supremo of Elektra 1950-1973, from age 19 to 42. Continued with Warner Communications as Chief Technologist. In 1982, became chairman of Panavision Inc. In 1986, created FirstMedia, which acquired Cinema Products, makers of the Steadicam. Came back to music in 1991, establishing the Discovery family of labels, which in the late Nineties became part of the Sire Records Group, a unit of Time Warner.

KEITH HOLZMAN. Jac's brother and working colleague at Elektra and Nonesuch.

NINA HOLZMAN. Was Nina Merrick. Married Jac in 1955. Mother of Adam and Jaclyn. At Elektra, invaluable yin to Jac's yang. Later Nina Lamb.

THE INCREDIBLE STRING BAND. A trippy British group.

MICHAEL JAMES JACKSON. Stockboy-novelist-observer of the Elektra LA scene.

SANDY JACKSON. An escapee from Synanon. Second chair in an encounter group.

RON JACOBS. Boss Jock of Southern California rock radio.

MICK JAGGER. A fan of the Elektra studio in LA.

BILLY JAMES. Laurel Canyon hipster. One of the earliest record business company freaks. Saw the Doors as worth signing, managed the teenage Jackson Browne. Husband of Judy.

JUDY JAMES. Wife of Billy. Watched the Laurel Canyon creatures come and go. Theater and philosophy major, later a theater and movie producer, partner of Richard Dreyfuss.

DICK JAMES. Publisher of the Beatles' music.

JEFFERSON AIRPLANE. Toured with the Doors, sharing notes about the nature and quality of life and pharmacology in the Sixties.

DR. JOHN. A night tripper, a somewhat strung-out session musician for Judy Collins.

JANIS JOPLIN. Almost but not quite an Elektra artist.

SHERRI KANDELL. A high school Strip chick in bellbottom hip huggers. Danced in a go-go cage at the Whisky and on top of the deli at Canter's.

DAVE KAPP. Of Kapp Records. Made an offer that Jac could refuse.

KATHY AND CAROL. Joan Baez times two.

LENNY KAYE. Musician, writer, anthologist and thinker.

STACY KEACH. An actor encountered by Jac. Lover of Judy Collins.

SALLY KELLERMAN. A waitress at the Unicorn.

JANICE KENNER. Teenage beloved of the teenage Jackson Browne. One of the Three Graces of Paxton.

FRED KEWLEY. Manager of Harry Chapin.

CAROLE KING. A Laurel Canyon dog owner.

"SPIDER" JOHN KOERNER. Out of Minneapolis, a young white urban blues man.

KOERNER, RAY & GLOVER. Surprised and delighted Jac's ear—a new direction for Elektra.

SANDY KONIKOFF. Sal Mineo as Gene Krupa. A drummer for Dylan. Purveyor of the Sphincterphone.

BERNIE KRAUSE. With Paul Beaver, a pioneer of synthesizer music.

ROBBY KRIEGER. The Doors' guitarist. The Jackson Pollock of rock. Writer of 'Light My Fire.'

KRIS KRISTOFFERSON. Played with Carly Simon.

JIM LADD. A Doors true believer.

BOB LANDY. An anagrammatic piano player.

RHONDA LANE. Go-go dancer in a go-go cage.

KANDY LATSON. Leader of an encounter group. And a snorter.

TIMOTHY LEARY. Evangelist of the sacrament of LSD.

ARTHUR LEE. Early into psychedelic eyewear. Leader of Love. Emblematic of the mid-Sixties west coast scene.

JOHN LENNON. Fan of Koerner, Ray & Glover.

HAROLD LEVENTHAL. Grand old man of folk artist management, from the Weavers to Judy Collins to Arlo Guthrie.

HARRY LEW. An Elektra distributor.

MONSIEUR L'HÔPITAL. An immaculately clad Frenchman whose word was good.

THE LIMELITERS. Jac's first chart group: Lou Gottlieb, Alex Hassilev, Glenn Yarbrough.

FRANK LISCIANDRO. A Morrison watcher.

ALAN LOMAX. Like his father John, a great white folk collector.

THE LOS ANGELES FANTASY ORCHESTRA. It seemed like a good idea at the time.

LOVE. Jac's first West Coast rock and roll band.

THE LOVIN' SPOONFUL. One that Jac missed out on. John Sebastian was his friend.

THE LOWER EAST SIDE. David Peel's stoned band—"Have a Marijuana."

LONNIE MACK. A wham of a Memphis man, later a Rock and Roll Hall of Fame guitar player.

CHARLES MANSON. Wannabe Elektra artist, mass murderer.

RAY MANZAREK. Doors keyboardist and keeper of the flame.

PHIL MANZINI. Threw Manzarek, Morrison, Krieger and Densmore out of the Whisky onto the Sunset Strip—"This is the end!"

MC5. Revolutionary rockers out of Detroit.

PAUL McCARTNEY. A recommender of bespoke boots.

PAT McCOY. A fan in the radio business.

ED McCURDY. Village folkie. Recorded for Jac in the Fifties. Big baritone voice and sharp tongue.

BROWNIE McGHEE. Vintage black folk singer.

GEORGE McGOVERN. Fan of 'Amazing Grace.'

BARRY McGUIRE. The voice of God in Laurel Canyon.

BHASKAR MENON. Head of Capitol Records, later Chairman of EMI.

FREDDIE MERCURY. Glam rocker, lead singer of Queen. Died November 1991.

BETTE MIDLER. Judy Henske was what Bette wanted to be when she grew up.

RUSS MILLER. Ran Elektra's publishing, produced, was Elektra's man in Nashville.

JONI MITCHELL. A beginning song writer and lady of the Canyon..

FRAZIER MOHAWK. AKA Barry Friedman. Practitioner of Laurel Canyon voodoo, inducer and producer of psychedelic albums.

JIM MORRISON. Lead singer of the Doors. Rock icon, lethally intelligent stoned explorer of the dark and the deep. Dead poet, July 1971.

VAN MORRISON. Jammed with the Doors at the Whisky.

CRAZY NANCY. Crazy for Jim Morrison. Hung out for love, broke in and stole for desperation.

FRED NEIL. Uniquely talented musician, prototypical flake.

PAUL NELSON. Founder of the Little Sandy Review, folk-friend of Jac.

MICHAEL NESMITH. Ex-Monkee. Produced for Countryside Records.

BOB NEUWIRTH. Hippest of the hip, sharpest of the sharp, hired gun of Bob Dylan, designated minder of Jim Morrison.

JACK NICHOLSON. Friend of a friend of Carly Simon.

NICO. An apparition, a disapparition, a death-talker, a waver of guns, a naked dancer with Jim Morrison. Also a member of the Velvet Underground. Died from heat exhaustion while bicycling in Spain 1988.

MICHAEL OCHS. The ultimate rock archivist. Brother of Phil.

PHIL OCHS. Protest singer second only to Dylan—but that hurt. Died a suicide 1976.

LOTTIE OLCOTT. One of the Three Graces of Paxton Lodge.

MO OSTIN. A recording industry legend. Chairman of Warner Bros. Records, and in the Nineties Dreamworks Records.

DR. PANGLOSS. Voltaire's philosopher. Would have made an enthusiastic radio promotion man.

CHARLIE PARKER. A night visitor.

VAN DYKE PARKS. Backup musician for Judy Collins.

PAUL BUTTERFIELD BLUES BAND. White and black electric blues. Blew the house down at Newport.

TOM PAXTON. A singer-songwriter, endlessly productive.

RICHARD PEASLEE. Composer of the music for "Marat/Sade."

DAVID PEEL. Voice of the Lower East Side.

MICHELLE PHILLIPS. A Mama.

GEORGE PICKOW. Photographer. Did early album covers for Elektra. Husband of Jean Ritchie.

THE PLASTER CASTERS. Cynthia and Diane. Performance artists ahead of their time.

PLATO. An urban music critic.

POMPEO POSAR. Photographed album covers for Jac and later Playmates for Hugh Hefner.

MEL POSNER. A boy from Brooklyn. From stock boy to president of Elektra, later head of international division of Geffen Records.

THE PSYCHEDELIC STOOGES. Iggy's band.

ANN PURTILL. Brought Jac to listen to Harry Chapin.

QUEEN. The ultimate British glam rock band. Jac's last major signing.

IAN RALFINI. Ran the London office of Warner/Elektra/Atlantic—WEA—which was like juggling chain saws.

DAVE "SNAKER" RAY. Of Koerner, Ray & Glover.

SUSAN REED. A redhaired folk singer.

JACK REINSTEIN. Elektra accountant, king of the adversary audit.

RHINOCEROS. A supergroup that staggered under the weight of talent and expectations.

FRITZ RICHMOND. Mr. Jug Band. His washtub bass is in the Smithsonian. Famous Cambridge folk scene viper. Studio engineer at Elektra LA. Brother of Marty.

MARTY RICHMOND. Brother of Fritz. Saw it all, from Paxton Lodge to Tranquility Base to Lahaina, Maui.

PAUL RICKOLT. Jac's first Elektra partner.

JOSHUA RIFKIN. Kazoo and piano player with the Even Dozen Jug Band, arranger for Judy Collins, wunderkind musicologist for Nonesuch Records, revitalizer of Scott Joplin rags.

LEONARD RIPLEY. Mustachioed playboy. Jac's Elektra partner, bought out in 1958. Husband of Alexandra, who later wrote *Scarlett*, the sequel to *Gone With The Wind*.

JEAN RITCHIE. Classic early folk singer from Viper, Kentucky. Wife of George Pickow.

SUE ROBERTS. Elektra business affairs supervisor. One of the first female record company executives.

ROLLING STONES. Heard and appreciated by Jac during an audition taping in London, but not available for signing.

PHIL ROSE. Record executive who ate more cake than he ever thought he would have to.

WESLEY ROSE. A Nashville music publisher.

STEVE ROSS. The charming conglomerateur of Warner Communications and then Time Warner. Died 1992.

ARLYNE ROTHBERG. Manager of Carly Simon.

DAN ROTHCHILD. Son of Paul and Terry, grew up to be a musician-producer.

PAUL ROTHCHILD. Jac's high-powered producer all through the big years of the Sixties. With the Doors, had five gold albums in a row, and platinum rising. Died of cancer in the spring of 1995. Jac was with him to the end.

TERRY ROTHCHILD. Wife of Paul, mother of Dan.

ROBB ROYER. A member of Bread.

TOM RUSH. A singer-songwriter-guitarist with commanding presence.

IRWIN RUSSELL. More than corporate counsel, a wise personal counselor to Jac.

LEON RUSSELL. Heavy-duty keyboard player.

SABICAS. Fast-fingered flamenco guitarist.

BOB SACKS. At St. John's College, had a record player and a collection of folk 78s that turned Jac on.

ELLEN SANDER. Rock journalist, immortalizer in print of the Plaster Casters, Jac's lover, mother of Marin.

MARIN PAUL TAJ RAIN SANDER-HOLZMAN. Son of Ellen and Jac, born in Bolinas. Grew up to be an actor-dancer in San Francisco.

JOE SARASINO. Record executive who told the Doors to get out of his office with their insane songs.

AL SCHLESINGER. A gentlemanly music business attorney-at-law—and that is not an oxymoron.

JOHN SEBASTIAN. Session musician for Elektra, later a Lovin' Spoonful, later again lived in a tie-dye tent.

PETE SEEGER. Traditional folk music's voice of conscience.

CLIVE SELWOOD. Elektra's man in England. Released 'Amazing Grace' as a single.

MAURICE SENDAK. A West Village bathroom muralist.

SAM SHEPARD. A drummer, a Holy Modal Rounder.

BILL SIDDONS. Teenage manager of the Doors, grew to maturity and acquired wisdom on the job.

PAUL SIEBEL. Sixties singer-songwriter. An Elektra favorite who never found a big audience.

PETER SIEGEL. A producer with an ear for real folk.

JEFF SILVERMAN. A teenager with a camera, in the right place at the wrong time.

SHEL SILVERSTEIN. Hairy jazz man, later a famous cartoonist, versifier, and writer of children's books.

CARLY SIMON. Singer-songwriter, Woman of the Seventies, class act.

PAUL SIMON. Almost but not quite an Elektra artist in his youth.

JOHN SINCLAIR. A White Panther.

GRACE SLICK. Would not be wooed away from Jefferson Airplane to solo at Elektra.

HARRY SMITH. Folk anthologist, formative for Bob Dylan.

JOE SMITH. One of the fastest minds and mouths in the record business. President of Warner Bros. Records and then Capitol Records.

MAYNARD SOLOMON. With brother Seymour, founder of Vanguard Records, friendly competitor of Elektra. Later the renowned biographer of Beethoven and Mozart.

SEYMOUR SOLOMON. With brother Maynard, founder of Vanguard Records.

ABE SOMER. Pit bull lawyer, and that's not an oxymoron.

ROGER SOMERS. Wild man of Muir Woods, Pied Piper of the hot tub, design genius.

EDWARD SOREL. An album cover illustrator for Nonesuch Records in his youth.

JOSEPH SPENCE. Guitar wizard of the Bahamas.

GEORGE STEELE. Played celebratory trumpet in the office when Elektra had a hit.

ESTELLE STERNBERGER. Jac's much loved maternal grandmother.

TERESA "TRACEY" STERNE. Presiding intelligence of Nonesuch Records.

CAT STEVENS. On the bill at the Troubadour with Carly Simon.

STEPHEN STILLS. A lover of Judy Collins.

IGGY STOOGE. Teenage father of premature punk.

JONATHAN TAPLIN. Roadie for Dylan, later a movie producer.

JAMES TAYLOR. Sat at the feet of Carly Simon.

STUDS TERKEL. A writer of liner notes for early Elektra, later a famous Chicago broadcaster and author.

SONNY TERRY. Vintage black folk singer.

THEM. Van Morrison's band. Jammed with the Doors at the Whisky.

THE TRAVELERS 3. Multicultural folk trio.

VINCE TREANOR. Sound man for the Doors tours. The King of Loud.

JOHN VAN HAMMERSVELD. Observer of the LA scene.

DAVE VAN RONK. Village folkie, white blues man, jug band leader.

PAUL VENEKLASSEN. Acoustical engineer for the LA Elektra studio.

VITO. The old man of the Whisky dance floor.

ELLEN VOGT. Second chair to David Anderle at Elektra LA. Found Jim Morrison face down in the bushes.

KIM VON TEMPSKI. A ship's purser bearing an aromatic sealed envelope.

ANDY WARHOL. Artist famous for more than fifteen minutes. Gave Jim Morrison a gold Louis XIV phone.

ANNE WARNER. Fed Jac Brunswick stew in his hungry Village days. Wife of Frank.

FRANK WARNER. Husband of Anne. Folk song collector and singer. Recorded 'Tom Dooley.' Owned a famous autographed banjo.

THE WEAVERS. A founding folk group.

KURT WEILL. Song writer for the Doors.

GEORGE WEIN. Founder of the Newport Folk Festival.

J. MAX WEIS. Jac's grandfather. A rebel rabbi.

JANN WENNER. The once and future Mr. Rolling Stone.

DOUG WESTON. Owner of the Troubadour in LA.

JERRY WEXLER. Mr. R&B. With the Ertegun brothers, made up the Atlantic Records triumvirate.

JOSH WHITE. Black folk singer, virtuoso guitarist, charismatic showman. Died September 1969.

TIMOTHY WHITE. Teenage Elektra fan from the Jersey 'burbs. Later a writer of fine books about music and musicians, editor of Billboard.

THE WHO. Shared the bill with the Doors more than once.

FRED WILLIAMS. On the scene down on the Farm.

PAUL WILLIAMS. Founder of Ur-rock magazine Crawdaddy; godfather of Marin Sander-Holzman.

STEVIE WONDER. In pursuit of a Number 1 record.

JERRY YESTER. Guitarist for Judy Henske, later produced Tim Buckley, and later again Tom Waits.

IZZY YOUNG. Proprietor of the Folk Center in the Village, intermittent bill payer.

BOB ZACHARY. Elektra producer-executive.

FRANK ZAPPA. Father of the Mothers of Invention, patron of the Plaster Casters, passionate advocate of free speech in rock lyrics. Died 1993.

WARREN ZEVON. An excitable boy in Laurel Canyon.

Chapter 1

Opening bars ...
Fugue of an Upper East Side kid ... Maryland Avenue ...
Narrow streets, some of cobblestone ...
With Sister Anne in the Vistadome

JAC HOLZMAN: I was not raised, I was lowered.

As far back as I can remember, I was sure that I had been born to the wrong parents. The family showed its best face in public; in private there were powerful currents of dissatisfaction and unease. My mother was not uncaring, but my father was a silent dominator. He ruled house and home, marriage and family. Everyone served at his pleasure—my mother, my younger brother Keith, and me. Especially me. Many times and in so many ways my father told me that I, his firstborn, had not bred true to his high standards. With my father I rarely did anything right. He withheld communication, controlling the emotional temperature, and he kept the cold turned up. The unstated message: I was not worth much.

My father was a successful doctor, a graduate of Harvard Medical School who had interned at Mt. Sinai and was a strong diagnostician much in demand for consultation. Working frequently with gentile doctors, he was tagged with the tolerant WASP designation of the time—"white Jew."

Money was the measure of my parents' wellbeing. We lived in a big apartment, with high ceilings, on the Upper East Side of New York, on 84th Street between Park and Madison. I was born in September 1931, and all through the years of the Great Depression we had servants, a live-in couple, the wife doubling as maid and cook, the husband as butler and chauffeur. My parents were at the fringe of café society, and I recall my mother in evening dress, my father in top hat, tails and spats, sporting an ivory-tipped cane.

Yet, for all my "advantages," I wanted to be anyone but who I was, anywhere but where I was. Every year from age five I ran away, pedaling my fancy Schwinn bike as fast and as far as I could from the Upper East Side, to sell on the street for train ticket money. On Mother's Day of my twelfth year I made it all the way to Trenton, New Jersey, on my own at last in Bleaksville, independently miserable in a hotel room with smudged cream-colored walls and a tiny moon of a dusty light bulb dangling from a frayed wire.

From these escape attempts I was always dragged home. My only other escape was far more to my liking—the movies. The images on the screen showed characters of stature, grace, and romance: the world the way I wished it could be. From my bedroom window, if I craned my neck just so, into view would come the Trans-Lux theater, which changed films weekly and gave you a free pass on your birthday. I haunted the place. I must have seen eight out of every ten Hollywood movies made every year of my young life. If not at the Trans-Lux, then along 42nd Street, which was lined on both sides with theaters. I fondly remember "King Kong," Errol Flynn swashbuckling in "The Sea Hawk," and I was mesmerized by Orson Welles in "Citizen Kane," which I saw four times in two weeks, totally absorbed in the cinematography and the scale of the drama.

Movies jump-started my emotional life. And music was my emotional soundtrack. My parents had bought a 1939 state-of-the-art console, an Ansley Dynaphone with the legendary Garrard turntable, the pickup weighing close to half a pound. Included with the Dynaphone was a library of classical music on fragile shellac 78 rpm records. I was introduced to the great warhorses of the symphonic repertoire—nothing like the climax of Tchaikovsky's Fourth Symphony to stir the blood.

Nearly all of my emotional life was passed cocooned in music, blocking out the discordancies of life; or in the dark of movie houses, absorbed in fantasy more real to me than reality. Home and family seemed jagged, hazy, often treacherous.

School too. I was never a conventional student and had no patience for anything the way it was taught. I absorbed what I needed to know by osmosis. Once, during a math test, I submitted the answers but not the proof and was accused of cheating. Why the rigor of proof if I could get to the answer without any effort? I sassed my teachers, first at PS 6 and then at a private school, Pennington, from which I managed to get myself expelled.

I went through my childhood making a general pest of myself, troublesome, not filially dutiful, uncomfortable in my own skin. My father thought child psychiatry would be helpful, but the psychiatrist told him he was the one who should make an appointment.

With psychiatry out, I was shipped off to the Peekskill Military Academy, "confined to barracks" for two years.

If it had not been for my grandparents, Estelle Sternberger and J. Max Weis, I would have been a basket case. Long after I had grown to adulthood I came across a line by Margaret Mead that expressed my situation perfectly: "Children and their grandparents have a common enemy." Estelle and Max gave me a sense of perspective and balance, and from them I felt my first unconditional love.

Estelle had grown up in Cincinnati. From her earliest years she was a crusader for women's rights, and in the mid-Twenties she was brought to New York to head the National Council of Jewish Women. She moved on to political commentary on WABC (CBS's flagship New York Station in the Thirties) and WQXR, the voice of the New York Times, and to writing speeches for President Franklin Delano Roosevelt. Estelle held a Saturday afternoon political salon, where I met Jim Farley,

Holzman Family Archive

**Jac's grandmother,
Estelle Sternberger**

postmaster general of the United States and head of the Democratic Party. Also Mary McLeod Bethune, a world-famous educator. Mrs. Bethune was the first black person I had ever seen up close, and she was jet-black, the ebony pigmentation that brought out the worst of American prejudice—"If you're white, alright. If you're brown, stick around. If you're black, get back." When I was introduced to Mrs. Bethune I shook her hand, for once a model of small-child good manners, and then to the horror of my liberal grandmother I furiously tried to rub the color off her wrist. Mrs. Bethune, who had the carriage and speech of a queen, kidded Estelle about that episode for years.

I loved to be with Estelle when she did her

radio broadcasts. I would sit in the control booth, watching the sound mixer move the knobs for the different microphones. Precision and control were words I would not have known, ideas I could not have formulated, but that is what impressed me.

Everything about radio was fascinating. Somehow a transmitter agitated the airwaves, and out of a box came words and music. I was a big CBS fan, rising early to listen to the 8am world news: Winston Burdett or Eric Sevareid or Ed Murrow from London.

I began to experiment, building rudimentary crystal sets. At Pennington, after lights out at ten, when all electricity was cut off in the dorm, I would listen under the blankets. And at military school in Peekskill I built myself a tiny battery-operated heterodyne receiver which I connected to the spring support of my mattress. With this oversize antenna I could pick up all the New York stations.

I fed my appetite for electronics knowledge by devouring the wonderfully illustrated catalogs of Concord Radio, Lafayette, Newark, and especially Allied out of Chicago. If you read the Allied catalog carefully it was an education in itself. You could infer how equipment worked, and how one component could be hooked together with others. I studied till the pages came loose from their binding.

JAC: My father enjoyed the old Washington food market, downtown. On a Saturday afternoon he might take Keith and me with him, and we would gravitate to the Cortland Street area. Collected there were all the stores selling surplus electronic gear from World War II, chaotically spilling out of cartons onto the sidewalk: Navy fighter gunsights, vacuum tubes, radio transceivers, radar antennas, walkie-talkies, B-17 intercoms, black boxes with odd connectors I had never seen before, all at prices even my meager allowance could afford.

Our favorite stop was Digby's, which offered the most amazing range of overstock inventory, remaindered and unloved. But to a Digby's auctioneer nothing was an odd lot, everything was special, with a value only Digby customers were intelligent enough to recognize—a bargain never to be repeated. When someone eventually rose to the bait, the auctioneer would throw in two extra as a bonus, and everybody would crowd around, begging to get in on the deal. The art of the spiel.

One Saturday afternoon in 1946 I fell in love with a machine which fundamentally changed my life: a Meissner semi-professional disc recorder with a built-in radio, an integrated machine with glowing tubes and crystal (piezo) devices for microphone, record and playback transducers. It would look and sound neolithic now, but then . . . To be able to record, and then manipulate time, to hear repeatedly, on my own schedule, the fascinations of radio! It was $120, but I had to have it.

My fifteenth birthday was coming in two months. I lobbied my father with the energy and duplicity of a Washington pol. Think of all the ways I could use the Meissner profitably: record weddings and bar mitzvahs; do air checks for celebrities (we knew a few minor ones); save his favorite programs if he was out on a house call. I made a classic Jac pest of myself, but I was more singleminded than my parents had seen me in years, and they ultimately caved in.

That same year I scored another coup. I persuaded my mother and father to let me live by myself for the entire summer in the city (my grandparents were only ten blocks away), and take a job. My parents' custom was to spend the summer months aboard their cabin cruiser, the Omar, a 42-footer moored off Glen Island in Long Island Sound, within earshot of the big bands that played the Casino. The boat was an Elco, made by the Electric Boat Company, which had been building submarines for the United States Navy since the turn of the century. With military orders scarce in the Twenties, they began to build luxury cruisers. Ours had a large pilot house, windows on all sides and a 360-degree view of the harbor, a galley, a cabin aft which was the private domain of my parents, and a forward cabin where Keith and I were stashed. Unhappy with the isolation from the city, I would lie on my bunk for hours, reading comic books or electronics catalogs, prompting my father to dub me "Horizontal Holzman."

My first real job was sorting invoices in the office of a doll manufacturer. Then I worked as a statistician for Picker X-Ray, keeping track of film shipments. Another summer I went to Cincinnati to work for my uncle Saul in his waste materials business. One lesson from that adventure was that I did not ever want to work to someone else's timetable, and never for anyone but myself

My father refused to believe that I had any imaginable business or professional future on my own merits. In his view the very best I could hope for was to be a pharmacist: he would send me his patients, I would fill their prescriptions, and we would share the profits.

At sixteen I graduated high school (smart enough to want to get it over with), and when it came time to contemplate college, my first choice was my father's alma mater, Reed College in Oregon. The driving motivation was not filial devotion but a hunger to get as far away from home as possible. My father had two reactions. First, he was flabbergasted that I was admitted. Second, he was concerned that my talent for mischief might tarnish the family name. So Reed was crossed off a very short list. The next option was Bard. It was closer to home and required an interview. The appointment was set for a weekend when I had a promising date, so I just didn't show. Almost as an afterthought, St. John's, an unorthodox liberal arts college in Annapolis, Maryland, was mentioned. For whatever reason, they were open to the idea of an unteachable Holzman as a freshman, and they were so delighted to have a paying student that they waived the interview. I returned the compliment by not reading their catalog. Assured that it was not a rigid Catholic college, but knowing nothing else about it, I turned up a few days after my seventeenth birthday, over six feet tall and still growing, weighing perhaps one hundred forty pounds, in jeans, with the bare minimum of sports coats, slacks and sweaters, some electronics reference books, a few tools, and my treasured Meissner disc recorder.

JAC: St. John's was never a big college, and in the fall of 1948 it could not have been much smaller. The student body was a strange mix of dedicated bookworms, intellectual dilettantes, World War II veterans on the GI Bill, parental escapees, and a sprinkling of well-off, mentally undernourished preppies with grades so indifferent that only a St. John's could see any possibility of redemption.

The curriculum was organized around the Great Books of Western civilization, the Top 100 classics. My only connection with great books had been a dumb devotion to Classic Comics, which I read for the stories. I did not know that the glory of the classics was ideas. Heavy on philosophy, the well-reasoned argument, the elegance of language, subtlety of expression, the symmetry of music and mathematics, St. John's opened my eyes and mind. There were no electives; we all studied the same material. We wore jeans during tutorials, but the ritual of the Friday night lecture and the twice-weekly seminar commanded higher respect, so ties were sponged and the dust shaken from sports coats that had never seen a dry cleaner. We argued over Aristotle, Plato, Herodotus, Dante, Newton, Descartes, Kant . . . I was plunged in at the deep end, simultaneously attracted and overwhelmed.

The other overwhelming attraction of St. John's was an electronics lab, a quonset hut crammed with army surplus. For me it was a personal Cortland Street. I would hang out for hours, exploring the possibilities and permutations of oscillators and amplifiers, power supplies, test and measurement equipment, exciters. I was in love with that stuff. I could get lost in the lab, in reverie, fondling the odd shapes and making my ideas work.

JAC: Down the hall from me in the dorm was Bob Sacks. Bob was bright, with an educated musical intelligence and a wonderful record collection. He also had cerebral palsy, which occasionally made it difficult for him to position those breakable shellac 78s on the thin metal spindle of his changer. Usually Bob managed fine, but sometimes I might hear an extended screech like a cat being run over—Bob trying to get his changer going. He would call for me, tell me what he wanted played and in what sequence, and I would sort and load the records.

Bob's dorm room was where I first really listened to and really heard folk music. Burl Ives and his unrelenting 'Blue Tail Fly.' John Jacob Niles, a channeler of the purest Anglo-American ballad tradition, who played dulcimer and gushed his songs in a thin high voice that sounded like the cry of an electronic theremin, if a theremin could sing. Susan Reed, an art singer with a silky voice kissed by Irish mist. Richard Dyer-Bennet, a troubadour who sang the classic English ballads accompanied by his own very elegant guitar. Woody Guthrie, the American wanderer, socially conscious, wary-eyed, feeling injustices, chronicling them in human outrage, yet sensitively, and always in love with the immensity and potential of his country. Josh White, a black man who had earned his right to sing the blues the hard way and had become an interpreter with tremendous guitar technique. And Huddie Ledbetter, Leadbelly, another black man, jailed for murder but given early parole from a state prison farm by an about-to-retire governor who just happened to like his singing. I never heard this kind of music at home, or anywhere in New York, and I quickly fell in love with the simple directness of melodies and words.

JAC: I don't know when the idea of starting a record company first hit me, but it was moved along in the early fall of 1950, when the soprano Georgianna Bannister performed a lieder recital at St. John's featuring new musical settings of poems by Rilke, Hölderlin, and e.e. cummings, accompanied by the composer, John Gruen. Bannister had a nicely rounded, muscular voice, and Gruen's architectural and very apt musical settings struck me as worth recording. So without thinking much about it, and with an impulsiveness that was to become characteristic, I simply asked them to record for a label that existed only in my mind—a label without a name, experience, distribution, and until I raided my bar mitzvah bank account, no money.

Being a genetic loner, I wanted to avoid partners, but with only $300 to launch this venture I asked Paul Rickolt—a classmate who was a few years older, had served on an LST in the navy, was a nice guy and who didn't have a whole lot else to do—to put up his $300 veteran's bonus as matching money.

October 10, 1950 is the date on which Elektra became real for me. School had started in late September. I was in my junior year, slogging through the middle of the Hundred Great Books and simultaneously looking for a label name. I recalled a Greek demi-goddess, one of the Pleiades, who presided over the artistic muses: Electra. Electra with a C struck me as too soft. I had always admired the use of Ks as brackets in the Kodak trademark; I liked their solid bite. So I chose a Germanic form and substituted K for C. Much better. Unable to afford special graphics, much less a logo, I turned two Ms on their side to create a distinctive E for the label and the jacket logo.

When I was working for my Uncle Saul in Cincinnati, he said, "If you ever have a company of your own, pick a name early in the alphabet." He himself did business as Cincinnati Waste Materials. Not too clever but very practical. Why? "Because invoices are most often processed alphabetically, so your chances of getting paid are much better." A lesson worth remembering. Elektra was safely in the first twenty percent of the alphabet.

I was in business, or at least I had a business identity, so I went looking for an off-campus mailing address. Wally of Wally's Tobacco Shop on Maryland Avenue in Annapolis was student-friendly. In exchange for a free copy of the inaugural Elektra album (still no more than a gleam in my imagination) he allowed me to place a discreet sign in his window.

In December 1950 I recorded "New Songs By John Gruen" in one three-hour session at Peter Bartók's small studio in New York. Peter was the son of the composer Béla Bartók and one of the most instinctively ingenious engineers I have ever known. Even the term "engineer" seems too confining. Peter paid scant attention to what was written on the science of recording and, except for the immutable laws of physics, conjured his own rules and constructed his own equipment to standards so exacting no one could afford to manufacture his elegant designs.

We recorded directly onto tape, without the interposition of mixing consoles or equalization, just two mikes, astutely placed, feeding the tape recorder direct, a technique which thirty years later would be resurrected and hailed as organic.

I sequenced the songs and took the tapes to Marjorie Tahaney of RCA Records to be mastered and custom-pressed. The first test pressings arrived the following February. Not knowing any better, I had trusted the prestigious RCA to get it right. But the sound was a mess, thin, with very low level, the music barely audible above the surface noise. RCA, wearing its cloak of corporate infallibility, insisted that the pressings matched the level of their calibration disc. "No," argued I, and borrowing a friend's car, drove five hours through a bitter winter night to RCA's studios in New York to supervise another transfer. This time I brought a Scott pre-amplifier, which had a wide variety of equalization, compression and companding controls, and inserted it into the recording chain between the tape recorder output and the mastering amplifier to achieve a warmer, fuller sound. It worked.

On a wet and wintry March day in 1951, EKLP-1 arrived at St. John's in twenty damp boxes of twenty-five LP records each. They were hefted up to the third floor of my dorm and piled into an empty adjacent room which became my shipping department. I felt as if I had just given birth, both thrilled and fearful.

There was no how-to book for running a record company. I'd just have to figure it out. Immediately I contracted with Jay Wesley Smith, a "national distributor." Jay Wesley took a hundred albums and demanded fifty more for "promotion." I later learned that what he meant by national distribution was that he would take an additional discount of twenty percent and resell his inventory to his distribution buddies in other parts of the country. Hmmm. I could have done that if I had his list.

"New Songs" received fine reviews in little-read music publications, but it sold fewer than the hundred "bought" by Jay Wesley. Evidently the combination of oblique poetry set to avant-garde music by a new composer and sung by an unknown soprano on an absolutely unheard-of label needed rethinking.

"New Songs"— new label **EKLP-1**

Of the original $600 investment, $500 was gone, and then Jay Wesley returned a hundred records for which I had to credit him. Whatever records he sold came out of his promotional stash. Here was a lesson to remember: it was possible to get back more records than you sold.

By the fall of 1951 I was at a decision point. Elektra was smelling like a failure. I could stay in college and not deal with it, but having tasted the joys of working on a project of my own, I did not want to remain in school. I could leave and get a regular job. That was something I could never see myself putting up with. Or I could regroup and try again. And this is where the genius of the St. John's program made the decision for me.

At the end of three years an "enabling exam" was required, to confirm that the student had absorbed enough to be enabled to move on to the fourth and final year. I had read three-quarters of the Great Books, but I was notoriously absent from lectures, seminars, and tutorials, much of that time having been spent experimenting in the quonset hut. I devoted a month to boning up, and passed by the merest smidge.

The acting dean, Dr. Jacob Klein, a well-regarded philosopher, summoned me into his office on a day grey with rain and misery, the kind of weather of the soul which can move people to kill themselves if they are at all so inclined. Dr. Klein's "suggestion" was that I take a year to get my bearings, then decide if I wanted to come back for my senior year.

I agreed. But what would my parents say? Especially my father: he had been an exemplary student and frequently reminded me of that fact. I asked Dr. Klein to call my grandparents, Estelle and Max, and explain the situation. Estelle told me later that Dr. Klein thought I had some kind of genius but no tolerance for or interest in anything not of my own choosing. An accurate assessment. I then gratefully let Estelle and Max explain to my parents, who wondered, in the way of parents, what was to become of me.

JAC: I moved back to New York with my books and an avalanche of LPs, to camp out temporarily and uncomfortably under my parents' roof on the Upper East Side.

Greenwich Village was the symbol of free living and free loving. I longed to live there. I walked the narrow streets, some of cobblestone, and found a room for $5 a week in a walkup at 40 Grove Street in the residential part of the West Village.

Estelle, who had been supportive of all my choices, came unglued. "You are going to leave your parents' house?" she said in old-world disbelief. To her it seemed a major mistake, leaving me nothing to fall back on, but that was exactly what I wanted: no outs.

My weekly $5 entitled me to one of five small rooms on the fifth and top floor, less than two hundred square feet of rotting wood and cracked plaster, with a single black Fifties sling chair butting up against a well-worn bed that I sprayed repeatedly to ward off all sorts of bugs, real and imagined, and a grungy shared bath that required major disinfecting every time I used the tub. I installed extra door locks, scoured the place down, put together book cases from boards and glass blocks, and painted the walls—I was now entering my dark period, so I slathered on a semigloss battleship grey.

At nineteen, I was, at last, living on my own, in the heart of the Village. I was thrilled.

But how was I going to live? What did I know about business? Not nearly as much as I didn't know. Still, I knew I loved music, was an early member of the Audio Engineering Society, and a facile electronic tinkerer. There were other people like me, and they were inventing high-fidelity sound, puttering around in little store fronts trying to improve the breed with new amplifiers, better tuners and odd speaker designs. I created some small cash flow for myself by designing and building the earliest compact bookshelf speaker with a tiny ducted labyrinth, and assembling full-on systems for a very tiny roster of particular clients, some of them friends of the family. I survived.

From a broader perspective, it was clear to me that the convergence of early hifi, the rapid refinement of the tape recorder, and the LP album—long-playing, and unbreakable too—were going to change the way we listened to music. The concert hall and live performance had been the ideal, but as people slowly transitioned to listening in their homes they began to pay closer attention to the quality of sound. As the recordings improved, more listeners were attracted. The availability of static-free FM radio in the early Fifties, and stereo discs in 1957, were part of an ongoing line of evolution that continued over the horizon. Already I could see—the view from five flights up on Grove Street—the dawning of an opportunity. As the Chinese political philosophers might have said, the hegemony of the major labels could be broken.

This was not my vision alone, but also of several hundred other people who decided to start their own personal record companies almost at the same time, and for the same reasons. It was truly a revolution of the musically undernourished and disenfranchised. They could not find what they wanted on the major labels and so created it themselves.

Atlantic was begun by Ahmet Ertegun out of his deep devotion to jazz and blues>. (By coincidence Ahmet was a St. John's boy, seven years before my time—and he graduated.) At Vanguard, Maynard and Seymour Solomon's primary interest was classical. There were tiny folk labels: Tradition, Riverside, and Moses Asch's Folkways, which was very ethnically oriented, very esoteric, with a small but ferociously loyal audience.

I adored both classical and folk, but decided to avoid the classical repertoire because of the large-scale musical forces involved, and because there was no chance of exclusivity on a Haydn symphony or a Beethoven sonata. I was much more comfortable with folk music. It fitted my one-to-one approach and my almost nonexistent budget. The equipment and recording techniques were straightforward, mistakes would not be catastrophic, and I could create a label with a stylistic niche.

In those years we independents made it up as we went along. The sense of shared risk took the edge off natural competitiveness and made for camaraderie. We would exchange horror stories and grumble over dinner. We traded information and experience freely, about recording equipment, acoustically good halls, the best distributors, what dealers were up and coming, and most important, who was not paying their bills. There were advantages to knowing what everybody was doing. We helped each other because whenever one was successful, it made it easier for all—it showed what the independent labels could do.

It was a benign, fun kind of business to be starting out in. The innocence was sweet, the pace agreeable. There was nothing cutthroat about it. You were only struggling to keep your own head above water, not to push the other guy under. People treated you honestly; you treated them with similar consideration. Everyone cared deeply about what they were doing, and as a secondary consideration you might even be able to make a living.

JAC: One day I ambled into a sheet music store at 189 West 10th Street, next to an archetypal Chinese laundry where you could get shirts done for a quarter. The sheet music lady wasn't doing very well. I convinced her that to attract customers she needed records. I had a few hundred dollars, and I bought a startup inventory. After two months during which her sheet music still didn't sell, I took over the lease—very inexpensive, $100 a month, and re-named my store the Record Loft. It wasn't a loft, it was at street level, but Loft sounded folksy.

The designer look I gave the place was Salvation Army Living Room, with a few chairs, and oak tables against the walls stacked with wooden bins of LPs. In back was a little curtained-off area with a sink, a drawing board for a table, and a hopeful cigar box for attracting cash. Across the front window I stretched chicken wire to display record jackets, and I showcased my Elektra E, the M turned on its side. Instead of conventional business cards I printed record labels with all the pertinent information. If a customer wanted to audition an album I would play it on my store system: a Rek-O-Kut turntable with a Pickering arm and a GE variable reluctance cartridge, an Electronic Workshop pre-amp, a McIntosh 250-watt power amp that came in two very heavy metal cases with tubes sizzling on top, and an infinite baffle speaker system, huge, about twice the size of a late twentieth-century Sub-Zero refrigerator. In 1951 that added up to about fifteen hundred dollars worth of serious equipment.

With five thousand dollars you could have bought me out of everything, and my suppliers would have been thrilled, since much of the time I was living off the cash from their inventory, buying my records on thirty-day open terms.

My stock was less than a thousand albums, perhaps four hundred folk titles, the rest baroque and what these days would be called world music: African rhythms, Indian music, and Flamenco, to which I was powerfully attracted. Both Flamenco and Indian were indigenous musics with a rich tradition, classical precision, and dramatic intensity. My Flamenco titles came from the Westminster catalog. Most of my folk titles were from Moses Asch at Folkways, with a smattering from other independent labels.

The Record Loft

The Record Loft was open seven days, and my plan was to clear enough each day to meet my nut and have enough left over for a meal and a movie. Rent and electricity averaged five to six dollars a day, so twenty dollars would cover necessities and anything over that a few indulgences.

People came into the Record Loft as much to talk as to buy, and that was one of my first big lessons in business: Listen to your customers. They were mostly white, teachers, social workers, students, bohemians, a leftish fringe, and professionals living in the Village. The Village was an appealing walking area, and people would come from all over the city for a taste of bohemia.

One very rainy night, I saw two eyes boring in through the chicken wire of my front window. It was a black man, clearly drenched. I invited him in out of the wet. We sat and talked. He was a jazz musician, charming company, and the soul of politeness. He was playing at the Village Vanguard, just a few blocks away. He played uptown too. Then he told me his name: Charlie Parker.

JAC: Sooner or later everyone in the very narrow world of city folkdom came into the store, singers, guitar players, collectors, aficionados like George Pickow, a photographer, whose wife was from a family of Kentucky mountain singers. Ken Goldstein dropped by, and that was the start of a long friendship. Ken was far more knowledgeable than I about traditional folk music—he knew all the Folkways titles, advised me to get an index of the Library of Congress collections, and generally pointed me in useful directions.

GEORGE PICKOW: Ken used to hang around Jac's store and give him information.

He was an accountant, and he saw folk music in an accountant's way. He knew the number of every song in the Child collection of folk ballads. It used to amuse me that the two of them would chat in numbers. "Oh, Child 793." "No, 792."

JAC: Edward Tatnall Canby was another fascinating character and a strong influence. He was the son of Henry Seidel Canby, founder of the Saturday Review of Literature. Ed was an early hi-fi enthusiast, rare in that he understood and was thrilled by new technology but always in the service of music. He wrote an article for Audio Engineering magazine titled "Binaural Rats," analyzing problems inherent in two-channel recording—what was eventually to become stereo. It was a knockout, prescient piece. Ed and I became friends and I learned a great deal from him about broadcasting and recording technique. In 1951 I offered him a chance to buy into Elektra. He turned me down. Years later he said it was the stupidest thing he had ever done.

My meeting with Ed, following on my enjoyment of Bob Sacks' folk music collection at St. John's, pointed me toward my first folk record, my second release: "Jean Ritchie Singing Traditional Songs Of Her Kentucky Mountain Family." Jean was George Pickow's wife.

GEORGE PICKOW: Canby wasn't really interested in folk music. His interest was totally classical. He just felt that what Jean did was, in a way, classical.

JEAN RITCHIE: I was born in the Cumberland Mountains, at Viper, Kentucky. We were kind of shut away there in the hills, didn't have much of the outside world coming in. Music was something you did, like walking and talking and breathing and working. There were no instruments, even, for a while; people just sang, and maybe made music with their clapping or patting their foot or dancing. When Mom and Dad were little, they did everything by singing. When I came along there were fiddles and dulcimers and banjoes.

Jean Ritchie

First talking machine we ever had, my dad sent away to a mail order company. And then he had to take a mule and wagon and go about sixty miles to the nearest freight office and pick it up. Along the way home he'd stop at people's places and stay the night, and to pay for his lodging he'd play them some music on the talking machine. It was one of those record players with a big horn in front, and you cranked it up. They'd all run around, look behind, to see what was making the sounds. They all thought there must be a little man in there making music.

PAUL RICKOLT: Ed Canby got Jac together with Jean, and we decided to bring out our second record. We each invested another $200.

JEAN RITCHIE: We recorded most of it in Ed's living room, in his apartment on West 4th Street. His walls were full of records, and you know how heavy 78s can be. He kept saying, "Tread lightly, because my floor is very unsafe. One more record and the landlord is going to ask me to move out."

Ed was propping the mike on books and sometimes moving it back and forth to get the instrument and the voice. The funny thing was that the tape recorder was running slow. Jac corrected it somewhat, but never got it perfectly right, so I sound like I'm about twelve years old, very young and my voice very high, whereas it really was a little bit lower and more serene.

JAC: Total recording cost was about twenty dollars, for tape.

JEAN RITCHIE: I still have a copy of my contract with Jac. Two pages, five clauses. Jac is "a minor," represented by his guardian, his father. "The party of the second part"—me—"as self-accompanied singer will perform the folksongs before a recording machine and the party of the first part"—Elektra—"will provide such recording machine and studio including services for the recording, manufacturing and commercial distribution of such recorded songs." I got twenty-two cents per record sold and three copies free.

JAC: It was a 10-inch LP, a grand size I thought for albums of less than thirty-five minutes, which seems so short by current practice. George did the cover, and he drew an improved logo, yet still preserving my stylish E. The retail price was $4.45.

We were working now through a new distributor, Harry Lew, who was a bit more aggressive than Jay Wesley Smith. And we actually sold about a thousand units.

Jean's first album... Jac's second

JEAN RITCHIE: When George and I went to England for a year, we sub-let our apartment to Jac.

While we were away Jac wrote us several letters, typewritten, that I still have. "The apartment is in fine shape and shall be spic and span for your return. It has been so well cleaned that you will not recognize it . . . Your record has received magnificent reviews and should do quite well. Our distribution is wider and we have sold about 600 so far. It will sell 2000 before it is through . . . By the time you return we shall have twelve LPs on the market, which will further solidify our status as a top-flight record manufacturer . . . Business at the Record Loft has steadily advanced. We are doing triple what we did last year at this same time. I have a weekly program on Folkmusic over WNYC. It's been going on since last November and has been very successful. I am writing articles; have been asked to teach at New School and am also working on an outline for a book. In addition I have written some technical articles that have been published . . . "

Jac knew everything. He was the genius in the room, and you knew it at all times. Very young and green, smoking a pipe in order to look older. And pushy, a little bit. He wanted to get things done in a hurry, and he wanted to do a lot. He wanted the whole world to fall in for him. And it did. After a while.

We got to be very good friends, but you had to get by the first impression he made on you—here's a pompous person who knew everything. Once you got to know him you came to like him. But we all thought it was kind of funny, because he was a different personality than any other I had run into before.

Jac used to love to have me come and sit in his shop with my greyhound. We had a beautiful brindle that we named Lady Gay, after a ballad, and Jac said, "Come sit with your greyhound in my shop so that people will be impressed."

You know, the folk world was very small. We sort of helped to bring Jac into the scene. I introduced him to Frank Warner—

Peter Carbone in his instrument shop

JAC:—At Peter Carbone's Village String Shop. If you sat there long enough, you could meet every person of any celebrity who ever played a guitar, from Carl Sandburg on.

ANNE WARNER: Frank walked in and this tall lanky young man was sitting there, and that's how he met Jac.

JAC: Frank was the traveling secretary of the railroad YMCAs. He and his wife, Anne, were diligent and talented collectors, mining the Appalachians for material, collecting hundreds of songs and variants.

ANNE WARNER: The first time Frank and I went into the mountains was 1938, and the first song we collected was 'Tom Dooley.' We learned it from Frank Profitt, and Frank—my Frank—put it on one of his Elektra recordings. He sang it across the country, because he did a great deal of traveling, and the Kingston Trio must have heard it.

JAC: The Kingston Trio released 'Tom Dooley' in 1958, at the beginning of the first wave of popular interest in folk music. It charted at Number 1, sold a million, and earned a gold record. We were years ahead of our time with it.

JEAN RITCHIE: Frank was from Alabama. A very fine man. Very ethical, very formal, dressed like a preacher does. But he was full of fun and a love of life. He could imitate any performer he ever heard, sing a song to sound just like that person. He would have big photo blowups of each person, he'd say the name and sit the photograph on the chair and say, "Charley will sing the

Frank Warner, Carl Sandburg and Jean Ritchie

song. Now, don't listen to me, listen to him."

Frank was like everybody's uncle. As soon as he took a liking to you, you were his friend for life. Anne was a very good cook. She was one of those women who would come into the kitchen and put on a great big apron and be there all day. She'd make old dishes from the South, and Jac loved it.

ANNE WARNER: When we met Jac he was living on Grove Street in a hole in the wall. We sort of adopted him. He spent a great deal of time with us. He usually came at dinner time, because he was very low on money.

NINA MERRICK: Anne made a dish called Brunswick stew that Jac was crazy about, an old Southern recipe, with chicken, originally with rabbit or squirrel, and corn, and Jac ate it up. Jac was very close to the Warners. He met them way before I met him, when he was sort of bumming around the Village, not getting on that well with his family, and they really became very emotionally supportive to him.

ANNE WARNER: My two sons were small. Jac would baby-sit for us, and the boys and he would wrestle, and it was great fun. He spent the night several times, went to bed by an open wood fire, and that was a new experience which he loved. He had his first traditional Christmas with us, because he hadn't been brought up with a real Christmas, and he was thrilled.

Frank's first album after years of collecting. **EKLP-3**

We were very devoted to him. We saw an awful lot of him for years. We always knew that he was bound for some kind of great career because he had all the earmarks. He was totally convinced that he was capable of doing anything he put his mind to. I said to him once, jokingly, "Do you think, Jac, there's anything you can't do?" And he considered it seriously and said, "No."

JAC: Frank's banjo head was graced with the signatures of the great folk singers and folklore preservationists. Years later, when he thought my accomplishments were sufficient to add my signature to those of Leadbelly, Woody Guthrie, and Alan Lomax, I signed and inwardly wept for the joy of being included, accepted, recognized.

JAC: I knew Susan Reed's voice from Bob Sacks' collection. She owned a shop a short walk from my place, on Greenwich Avenue, dealing in English and American antiques. Susan was in her thirties, with the rosy complexion of an Irish lass crowned with the most vibrant red hair. We talked about recording and she was willing to consider it, but she had previously been on Columbia, and it was emotionally difficult for her to move to a fledgling label. But no one else was asking her.

George Pickow

Susan Reed

PAUL RICKOLT: Susan was a union musician, which meant we had to have a union contract. Jac wouldn't have anything to do with the union. He said, "You go." I walked in, and I felt like I was in the stevedores' hall, guys sitting around with their hats on, smoking big fat cigars: "Whatcha want, kid?"

JAC: We recorded in a small Village church in the evening, when the city quieted down. If traffic noises intruded we stopped and waited for the last tremor to fade away. Susan was easy and gracious to work with. Most songs were recorded in less than three takes. Total recording costs were under a hundred dollars, plus the church rental of $50, and we came away with astounding quality. Musically the record was like the finest crystal. The New York Times reviewer called it the best vocal recording he had ever heard—which was considerable acoustic bang for practically no bucks. I began to feel that I knew what I was doing.

JAC: Cynthia Gooding was the first artist I had a crush on. She was Amazon-tall, dark-haired, slender, with long legs you could just die for. And piercingly intelligent.

JEAN RITCHIE: We met Cynthia through Bill Pressman, who took us to hear her in a little tiny hole in the wall in the Village. It was where Leadbelly used to sing. She was so tall her head touched the ceiling. Jac and Cynthia were a funny pair, both so long.

CYNTHIA GOODING: Jac wasn't half as attractive as he was later on. He used to be built like a conga, with the narrow part on top and the wider part in the middle. He looked not at all physical, like a sweet roll, and he shambled when he walked.

JAC: Cynthia was married to Hassan Ozbekkan, a Turk who was a strategic planner for General Electric. He beat me every time we played chess because he could think many more moves ahead. I hated to lose. I was so desperate to develop the skill that I took several months of formal training. Our games improved but I never did beat him.

CYNTHIA GOODING: Jac and Hassan got along very well because I don't think either of them thought what women had to say was terribly important. I don't think Jac would have recorded me except that my husband was a very good talker, and the two of them talked a lot. I think Jac liked what I sang but not necessarily what I said.

JEAN RITCHIE: Cynthia sang songs from different countries, but highly arranged and very elaborate. Great sort of flamenco licks on the guitar. She didn't sing them like a peasant, but they were ethnic songs to begin with. And she was very good as a singer.

MARK ABRAMSON: A commanding presence. Nothing prima donna about her, but very dignified. Later on I saw her at the Newport Folk Festival, which was always kind of bedlam and chaos, and when Cynthia performed everybody quieted down, like, "Oh, we'd better pay attention."

Cynthia Gooding

JAC: At parties the guitar would be passed around and some young girl would do a lovely little song, and Cynthia would look down the bridge of her very regal nose and say, "Well, that's sweet, dear."

CYNTHIA GOODING: Jac never really put me at ease, though he tried a lot. But I always trusted him when he recorded. He hears well. The artists really sounded like themselves, and that's saying a lot.

JEAN RITCHIE: Jac was a very good businessman even in those days, and very honorable. He consistently paid royalties on time. They weren't very much, but at least I'd get a little, and at least he gave accountings. If I didn't make anything, he'd send an accounting anyway. No one else did that.

JAC: Recording contracts were delightfully simple. They stated the length or term, outlined the territory, detailed how royalties would be calculated, when paid and what offset deductions were permissible, the royalty rate for overseas (always lower), the number of option periods, and the amount of the advance, usually a token sum, never more than a few hundred dollars.

Artists generally signed the agreements without question. In the case of a female artist, the husband might look the documents over. Rarely a lawyer—lawyers were not the growling gatekeepers they are today. Our relationship was always direct and with the artist and we insisted on keeping it that way. We put out solid records, the artists were paid, if not very much, and we were generous with free copies.

It was gloriously uncomplicated. The only big deal was the music.

PAUL RICKOLT: Our fifth record was "Voices Of Haiti," from wire recordings that Maya Deren had made in Haiti. Maya was a famous avant-garde film maker. Her father was a Russian psychiatrist. She wrote *The Divine Horsemen*, which is considered by many to be the best book ever written about Haitian voodoo. She was very striking looking—short, redheaded, long wiry hair. She ate at Simple Simon's in the

Village, and I spoke to her there. I think she thought I was trying to make a pass. Then, seeing her a number of times, we got to know each other and she told me about her trip to Haiti and the recordings. And this led to our idea of bringing out a record

The sessions with Maya were horrendous. Maya was a strong character and she could be very difficult. And she had all these voodoo things, supposedly. In the kitchen the light often wouldn't go on, and Maya would just snap her fingers and it would go on.

Everything had to be transferred from wire to tape, and the wire had a tendency to stretch. Jac souped things up a little bit, adjusting the bass and so on. We brought out the record, and people, including critics, thought it was high-fidelity.

We did things that we didn't know we couldn't do, we just went ahead and did them. And—we felt very adamantly about this—we made the very best recordings we knew how. Our recordings, compared to most, were ten times superior.

OSCAR BRAND: Jac has a very good ear. He knew when something didn't ring right, and he would say so. A lot of people would stay out of it—if the beat is wrong, well, that's folk music. But Jac brought requirements to recording. He wanted people to live up to high standards. Ergo, he got better recordings.

JAC: Life in the Fifties was not a constant rush. The fast lane hadn't been invented. But eating took valuable time away from work, so I decided that one well-balanced meal a day was enough. My refrigerator held the bachelor's minimum: the odd piece of fruit, cheese, crackers, fruit juice, milk, beer, week-old bread. I certainly didn't need coffee to get started in the morning, but I might grab some juice for breakfast. Around noon at the Pam Pam I ate my daily quarter-pound of grilled ground sirloin, with peas and a baked potato, and cobbler for dessert, pretty much the same thing every day, and I got out for under a buck, including the afternoon paper.

The most excitement in the air was the Army-McCarthy hearings on TV, centering on the publicity-hungry anti-communist witch-hunting Republican senator. My sense of fair play was deeply offended by McCarthy. So as not to miss a moment of him getting his, I would ride my bicycle to the office balancing my TV set under my arm. It was an old 8-inch Motorola which weighed about twenty-five pounds, but somehow I made it back and forth without once dropping it.

The McCarthy hearings had more inherent drama and were more compelling than anything on radio, a lot of which was Elvis Presley. My folk inclinations just did not include hip-swinging, yet-to-be-revered, neo-rock icons. I thought most rock and roll had nothing to say. It didn't seem like real music to me. I was in my head, and rock and roll totally missed my gut.

My day was defined and circumscribed by the Village. My friends were there, and most everything that was happening in my kind of music, or of any interest to me, occurred south of 14th Street, the Village's official northern boundary.

In 1952 I bought a motor scooter, which extended my range considerably. It was an early Vespa (meaning "wasp" in Italian), privately labeled for Sears. Mine was the first Vespa in New York, which meant problems getting it registered. I kept it chained outside my house, or I could wrestle it inside. One of its great blessings was that it could be parked anywhere, and it proved to be amazingly ticket-proof. Even the cops thought it was cute. It attracted so much attention that I printed a little information flyer giving detailed specs. Everyone wanted to know how fast it could go. Answer: with a gentle wind at your back, close to fifty miles per hour.

The tires were 3 1/2 inches thick, the legal minimum, just wide enough to get me over the bridges and through the tunnels. I rode it everywhere and in all kinds of weather. I would drive in the snow without chains, my thick boots a half inch above the pavement, sort of a protective outrigger balancing act if I were to skid or slide.

Most significantly, the Vespa extended my territory for going to the movies. Along with music, movies were all I cared about. They were still my primary connection to my emotions, and my life was calibrated to seeing as many as possible. I would go four or five times a week. I hated taking the bus anywhere, but especially up to the Thalia Theatre at 95th Street and Broadway, a tedious hundred blocks by city transport. With the Vespa, a hundred blocks was a song.

The Vespa was also a great dating vehicle. The lady could choose to ride sidesaddle or astride. Astride was less genteel but more promising. If a woman wouldn't mount the scooter, there was no future to the relationship—the young Holzman's elementary version of sexual triage. With the juices burbling, my priorities were Elektra, the movies, and getting laid. The ratio of movies to getting laid was about thirty to one.

I wasn't a drinker and certainly not a doper. Once in college I had gotten dead drunk and threw up so long and hard that my abdominal muscles cramped for days. My drinking stopped before I had really started. My bar-hopping around the Circle in the Square was mostly to pick up women, which was very tough to do in the Fifties, at least for me. There were women I'd meet, some who were customers of my record store. After I moved out of that cell-like walkup on Grove Street and sublet Jean Ritchie's apartment, I could bring them home without embarrassment—the place was neat, and I made the bed.

JAC: In 1954, with seven or eight records released, I decided to close the Record Loft and move Elektra around the corner to larger offices at 361 Bleecker Street. The shop plus the label was just too much, and I wanted to zero in on Elektra. In 1955 I bought out Paul Rickolt's interest for $1000.

Financing expansion was a continuing problem. New releases were paying for themselves out of moderate sales but not much more. Elektra needed cash to grow. I talked another St. John's schoolmate, Leonard Ripley, into buying a piece of the company.

Over two years, Ripley invested $10,000. I was drawing a meager salary, $100 a week; Ripley, who was born to money, I think oil, was living off family largesse. He was a fun guy, debonair, with a bristling mustache, a dilettante in record land, ambling in and out of the office on his own schedule, always taking excellent care of his personal life.

Ripley (no one ever called him by his first name) had a natural flair for engineering and good musical ideas. It was Ripley who suggested we record the amazing Flamenco guitarist Sabicas. Sabicas had fingers so fast you could barely see them move for the blur. They galloped over the strings and riveting Flamenco poured into your ears.

Sabicas was distrustful of record companies ever paying royalties and insisted on receiving a flat sum, in cash—for his first album on Elektra it was $1000, the largest advance we had ever paid. For the cover we did a photo of his hands in motion, a Gjon Mili time-lapse knockoff. The album sold wondrously well, so we recorded another. Sabicas could sell between fifteen and twenty thousand units, which was a bargain for us. If he had accepted royalties he would have earned four times his cash fee.

Ripley had gone to school at Le Rosey in Switzerland, an institution for the young royalty of Europe and America, and he was always jaunting back and forth to the Continent. In Paris he recorded two American expatriates, Gordon Heath and Lee Payant, who were the rage among Americans taking the hip summer tour to France. They performed at L'Abbaye, a semi-basement club on the Left Bank near St. Germain des Près. The local gendarmes had forbidden the audience to disturb the tenants upstairs with the noise of applause, so you snapped your fingers instead, which started that whole beatnik finger-snapping affectation. Heath and Payant were so popular that fans returning from France would leave the boat and cab directly to Elektra on Bleecker Street to pick up their commemorative copies of "An Evening At L'Abbaye."

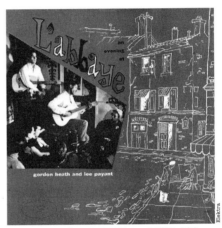

"An Evening At L'Abbaye" EKL-119

After Ripley started working with me, a Parisian friend introduced him to a true belle of the old South. Mother and daughter go after Ripley. They get him to commit to the altar. The bride-to-be goes through his address book, sending out invitations, and discovers that Ripley is a former classmate of the Aga Khan. A florid postscript to the invitation urges the Aga to attend the ceremony. There is no response. As Ripley told me the story, three months later a call comes from US Customs: there is a package from a Mr. A. Kahn that must be picked up personally. So, with visions of her weight in diamonds, Ripley's wife sends him down to customs. Ripley is led to the Aga's wedding gift—a baby elephant, four hundred fifty pounds of the thought that counts. What to do? Send it back, what else? First the animal has to have its immunization shots, and then be crated and freighted, and on landfall Sabu must be hired to return it to the jungle.

Years later the Ripleys are divorced, and years later again the ex-wife's Southern belle charm finds perfect financial and cultural expression: Alexandra Ripley writes *Scarlett*, the sequel to *Gone With The Wind*.

JEAN RITCHIE: The Village was a very exciting place. I used to go everywhere at night by myself, as a young girl, to the Country Dance Society, or to do a concert. I never had the slightest worry. A few of us used to go down into the subways and sing, because the acoustics were so good; we'd sing rounds and madrigals and things down there. And we'd have parties at each others' houses; all the people lived in lofts, you know.

OSCAR BRAND: That was the scene from the end of World War II, before Jac's time, when Leadbelly lived in the East Village, and Pete Seeger was living on MacDougal Street, and Lee Hays was staying with Will Geer, and Woody Guthrie was living on Coney Island but coming in all the time, usually not going home.

THEODORE BIKEL: Folkies would meet with cheap wine and beer and no eats, in smallish rooms, just large enough to have some elbow room so you could play a guitar or banjo, and most everybody played and sang. Sometimes there were people who neither played nor sang, and one wondered what they were doing there. Jac was one of those.

OSCAR BRAND: He was out of place in the folk scene. His looks, his language, his attire. He was definitely a WASP, even though we knew he wasn't—he was WASPish anyway. We were chipping at his exterior a lot, but there was always something different about Jac. My feeling was that he was always apart.

THEODORE BIKEL: Jac took me aside and said, "I think you're very charismatic. But I have no idea how much of what you do is visual and the impression of your personality. I make records, and personality has to translate itself only in sound and nothing else. Would you be willing to come to my apartment and do a tape of two or three songs? I'd like to play it for people who can't see you while you're singing and get their reaction."

It wasn't a career move for me at all. I was an actor, brought over here to do a Broadway play. I had always sung, in England, everywhere, but I'd never thought of wanting to make records, or making money from making records. America's a strange place—they won't tolerate your doing anything well without forcing you to accept money for it. But I was intrigued by the notion that what I did was so tied in with how I did it.

So I remember going to Jac's place, walking up all those flights of stairs, and recording some songs. Several weeks later he called me and said, "I played this tape for quite a few people and they're all very taken with you and would you like to make records?" I said, "What do you want to record, because I'm kind of eclectic in my taste and I know a lot of music of many countries and languages." He says, "Why don't we do a record of what you know best?" At that time Jewish music, Hebrew music, Israeli music was very big in the United States. There was a hunger for it, suddenly a market for it, he felt. And so we made an LP, 10-inch, "Folk Songs Of Israel," and it did very well indeed.

JAC: That was the beginning of a long and satisfying association with Theo who became a close friend, neighbor and star artist with his rich repertoire of unusual material in many languages. Theo was born and raised in Vienna, then moved to Palestine before World War II, studying drama. He was to become our principal musical—and financial—mainstay from 1956 to 1961.

JAC: In 1955 I flew to the West Coast to visit my distributors in San Francisco and Southern California. They were mom-and-pop at best, and I was planning to abandon so-called national distribution and sell to the regional independents directly. It would cut out the middleman profit and give us more direct control, and we needed both the improved marketing and the additional gross margin of about thirty cents per album to expand the label.

On my United Airlines flight to San Francisco one of the four prop engines caught fire, belching smoke into the cabin, and another began to sound asthmatic. Serious trouble. The priest next to me began fingering his beads at just under the speed of light. Mothers were running up and down the aisle lamenting, "I'll never see my baby again." From the cockpit, not a word.

We were twenty minutes from Denver. I sat staring at my watch as the second hand moved very s-l-o-w-l-y. We were far enough out that they had time to foam the runway. We jounced to an OK landing, but at that point I had serious problems with flying. I cashed in what was left of my ticket and took the train, a Vistadome streamliner where you could perch in a bubble top and view the world passing by, and at night curl up in a sleeper.

On that train I met a Catholic nun, a Maryknoll sister from New York State, transitioning to her new convent in Stockton, California. She was a bright and wise lady in her early thirties, and I was attracted to her wisdom and gravitas as well as to the fantasy aspect of nuns. We talked, shared a table in the dining car, and entered that zone of quick and deep intimacy, so easy when you know you will probably never see that person again.

Sister Anne (not her real name) had the bottom berth and I the top. In the middle of the night she thrust her head between the curtains and said she hadn't had a man in ten years and wasn't likely to have another, so I joined her. You don't make noisy love in a Pullman, but very quiet, very sweet love. And the next morning she was off the train before I awoke.

In San Francisco, my Uncle Dick took me aside and said, all mock-seriousness: "There are three things I want to tell you. One—if a woman asks you and you like her at all, never say no. Two—don't ever talk about her afterwards." And here I've talked about Sister Anne. What was three? "Never eat brown gravy you haven't cooked yourself."

Aside from the train ride, the West Coast visit didn't amount to much. Musically, California was very sleepy except for pockets of contemporary jazz.

I took the plane home, white knuckles all the way. And for several years after I was too scared to fly.

Chapter 2

Music is heard in the Village ...
A marriage made on Bank Street ...
A dissolution on Bleecker Street ...
The sexy Sabra of Long Island ... Dalliance

JAC: I was living in a railroad flat on Bank Street in the West Village when I met Nina.

NINA MERRICK: In the summer of 1955 I was fresh out of college. I found a sublet at 119 Bank Street.

The West Village was bohemian. There were coffee places, and a bar nearby called the White Horse, a big literary hangout. The whole district had a spirit of its own, a vitality. You could talk to strangers, not feel you had to avoid eye contact.

Across the street from my apartment was an ice factory, and there would be men hacking on these huge blocks of ice way into the wee hours of the morning; and I remember—this tells you how different it was at that time—coming home at midnight, taking the subway, walking down the street by this ice factory, and feeling perfectly safe. It never occurred to me to be afraid. It wasn't naiveté, life just was like that.

My apartment was $69 a month. It was a walkup, very old, a railroad flat, with the rooms one after another, like a train. You came into what was a living room, then a little sort of bedroom, and beyond that the kitchen, and the bathtub was in the kitchen—you had a piece of wood on top of the bathtub so you could use it as a dish drain—and beyond that a little toilet-shower thing.

Early Sendak EKLP-6

JAC: My apartment featured original art painted directly onto the wall. Ed Canby had a friend struggling to make it as an illustrator, and I commissioned him to do several album covers. He created wonderful pen and ink drawings, an unusual, very special style. In exchange for one each of our records, about fifteen albums, he agreed to paint the wall above my tub, a little bathing scene with childlike figures happily gamboling. So that was my Maurice Sendak original. I hope no one painted it over after I left .

I was entertaining a lady one evening and I went next door to borrow some paper napkins.

NINA MERRICK: I had been there maybe three weeks. A knock comes on the door, and there stands Jac. "Oh," he said, " who are you?" And he stood there and he chatted and chatted. I didn't know he had a lady literally next door.

JAC: I went back a few days later on the pretext of returning the napkins—

NINA MERRICK:—And he invited me out. On our first date, we went on the motor scooter. I was horrified. I had never been on one of those in my life. We went up to somewhere around Radio City and saw a Japanese movie, "Rashomon." On the second date he asked me to marry him.

I said, "No way, I have a career." I was working at Dance magazine, as assistant to the editor. Remember, it's 1955—it never occurred to anyone that you could be married and have a career. But he said, "You are going to marry me, and I will be a millionaire by the time I am thirty-five."

I thought, "Isn't that wonderful, to have a dream." He was twenty-four, living in this little funky apartment, and his favorite meal was tomato soup, potato sticks out of a can, two vitamin pills and a glass of water. And Elektra Records was a storefront on Bleecker Street. To me, his million by thirty-five was a complete fantasy. I admired it and I respected it, but that's all it was to me. I grew up without money, and the scripting I created on myself was, I never want to be poor, but I never said I want to be rich or that I aspired to it.

We kept going out. About a month after his first proposal I invited my mother and one of my sisters to come for dinner with Jac. I love to cook, but I had never even let on to Jac that I could, because I didn't want him to be interested in me because I could cook. Anyway, that night I cooked and Jac was flabbergasted.

So things were going along. The main problem over the next few months was his family. I was only half Jewish; my mother was Russian Jewish, my father was Spanish Catholic. I did not have money. And I was myopic, I wore glasses—this was a big consideration.

When Jac told them we were getting married, they were not thrilled.

JAC: We decided on Columbus Day.

NINA MERRICK: Jac was marvelous. He was very strong. He said to them, "We would love to have you there, but if you're not there, we're getting married anyway."

Our wedding was on Christmas Eve, at my family home out in the country, by Jac's grandfather who was a rabbi. Not very many people, our families and a few friends. Ripley was best man. Jac's family did show up, and it was pleasant enough. It wasn't my dream wedding or anything. We didn't have a honeymoon right away, not for four months. The whole business thing prevented our going right away, and then we went on a little cruise.

JAC: Now into my life came Josh White. My only experience recording black music had been two 10-inch LPs of folk and city blues with Sonny Terry and Brownie McGhee.

Josh did not have a recording contract and couldn't get one, because his politics and some past connections were suspect during the ugly years of the blacklist and the anti-communist witch hunt of the House Un-American Activities Committee.

OSCAR BRAND: The blacklist period was a deadly business.

JEAN RITCHIE: It was a very egg-treading time. You didn't dare say anything. We think of the KGB in Russia—it was like that in our country for a while. So you had to—you did—watch your step.

THEODORE BIKEL: Folk singers went to the source, not only to rural sources but to urban sources, and that had to do with the labor movement, with songs of the Depression, hunger, social unrest, oppression by the very rich of the very poor, exploitation. And that's why I hardly know any folk songs written by right-wing conservatives.

JAC: Josh was born in Greenville, South Carolina, the son of a preacher who tried to bring Josh up as befits a preacher's son. As a boy Josh went on the road with wandering blues singers like Blind Lemon Jefferson. It was a hard-scrabble life, scratching for pennies. He was threatened by white sheriffs and he saw lynchings.

In the Forties he made his way to New York and became a celebrated cabaret singer, a charismatic performer and a stunning guitarist. He was a close friend of Libby Holman, who had created a sensation with a song called 'Strange Fruit,' telling of blacks lynched and left to hang for days from trees with blood staining the leaves and spattering the roots.

During World War II Josh did benefits for Russian relief and other organizations later said to be communist fronts. He was a friend of Eleanor Roosevelt, whom he accompanied to Scandinavia in 1950. Josh played to huge crowds but refused to sing 'Strange Fruit' overseas; he took the view that it was wrong to sing ill of his country on foreign soil.

The FBI had a dossier on Josh that ran to 473 pages. The mudslinging witch-hunting publication surveying the entertainment business, Red Channels, offered to "clear" Josh if he would denounce Paul Robeson, the much admired black singer-actor-athlete-activist. Josh refused. He was subpoenaed by the House Un-American Affairs Committee, where he read a prepared statement but never named names. That left him on the outs with those who controlled media access and jobs in entertainment—just about unemployable. Like too many others.

OSCAR BRAND: Woody Guthrie couldn't work. The Weavers were knocked off the air. Harry Belafonte was attacked. Susan Reed was attacked. Cynthia Gooding dropped out, didn't record any more. I had been blacklisted by the other side, the Communist Party, and the House Un-American Activities Committee wanted me to cooperate with them, but I didn't, though everybody thought I had. Then there was the question whether Josh had named names.

ED McCURDY: Josh was working Café Society Downtown when I was working the Village Vanguard. He'd come around and talk to me between sets because no one else would speak to him. His leftist friends were a bunch of shits and didn't have the courage of their own decency.

JAC: My upbringing and my own sentiments were liberal. The witch hunt would have no effect on my musical judgment. I was impressed by Josh the musician and performer: compelling personality and terrific guitar chops.

Signing Josh gave me an artist with a broad reputation who might actually sell some records. And more importantly, it was my first contract as a professional with an artist who had inspired me to record folk music when I was DJ-ing at St. John's for Bob Sacks.

THEODORE BIKEL: Josh took simple musical forms and brought them into a club format.

He played stuff on guitar that people in the fields obviously didn't play in that form—those chords, that slide up and down. He had a great regard for authenticity, but he was also a showman.

ED McCURDY: God, he was one of the most magnetic performers I ever saw. He was my friend. When I knew where he was appearing I used to wire him, "Dear Mr. White, please sing 'Swanee River,' and if you can't sing it, it makes a nice sand dance. Signed, Ratford P. Brown." And he introduced me one night at Café Society: "My motherfucking friend Ratford P. Brown."

JAC: Josh was nearing the twenty-fifth anniversary of his first recordings in 1931 and he had this notion to create an assemblage of railroad songs, tied together with a short narrative which we called "The Story Of John Henry." It sold close to twenty thousand, a big hit for us.

Though Josh was compelling in concert, I thought he was at his very best late at night, in a small club crowded with great-looking ladies. There were Josh White groupies, stunning females, usually white, and he would seduce them musically. Every woman in the room thought he was singing just to her. And he was.

That was the mood we tried for on "Josh At Midnight," just Josh and his bass-playing pal, Sam Hall, recorded in the dark of evening, at a church that had been converted into a studio. Nina wrote the liner notes from a woman's perspective. It did very well.

NINA HOLZMAN: Josh would record with a cigarette behind his ear, like some people would put a pencil. He had a lot of style.

BILL HARVEY: We were shooting an album cover one night, with a model, very romantic mood, and underlying that very sexual, because everything about Josh was sexual. He kept chasing this girl all over the studio, and it wasn't very big, about the size of a living room. He'd get her in one corner, another corner, while the photographer kept lighting the different areas, trying to create a mood. I was

Josh White (right) with Sam Hall, bass. "Josh At Midnight" sessions, 1955

interested in getting a good shot of him, but I wanted to imply that she was there. She had ample bosoms, so that in the haze of the silhouette you could very definitely make out that this was a lady. We got all the pictures, but Josh didn't make out with the girl.

NINA HOLZMAN: Josh was very charming, unpredictable, irresponsible. We'd get midnight calls from his wife wanting to know where he was, which was the part I didn't want to know about.

OSCAR BRAND: Josh was my close friend. He was tough, exacting, prickly, especially with white college boys. Jac handled him very nicely, not presumptuous, supercilious, all the kinds of things Josh despised. Jac wasn't political with Josh either. Josh had taken awful bites from both sides. All he wanted was recognition as a musician and as a man. To him, Jac did what he was supposed to do. And it was so great to find a record producer who paid you.

NINA HOLZMAN: The thing about Jac in those early days was that I knew even then that this was a very, very special person. There were a lot of gaps in his personality that I did not totally understand. But my feeling was, first of all, I very much loved him—

JEAN RITCHIE:—Nina and Jac were very much in love when they married. They couldn't stay two inches away from each other, they always had their arms around each other—

NINA HOLZMAN:—And at the same that this was a very gifted person. He wasn't just a wannabe businessman. He had the marks of an artist. In his own way he was a genius. He had a vision that very few people ever had. Because of that, I felt that he had to be excused for many things that would be expected of more ordinary people.

One day he said, "OK, now it's time that you come and work with me." So I left Dance magazine, way west on 57th Street, for Elektra, at 361 Bleecker Street.

Bleecker Street was very ethnic, which is probably why the rent was so cheap. Little restaurants, wonderful food stores, bakeries, places where you could buy cheese and salami, the best. Lots of Italian ladies sitting out on the doorsteps.

The office was a funny little place, very Bleeckerish. It was old, but we thought it was wonderful. It looked like the front of a store, with windows where Jac would always have posters or the newest releases. Jac used the front part as a sort of shipping area, and then you walked up a few stairs, so there was a little balcony where we worked, and in the back there was a kitchen, where I would make coffee in the morning.

We sat across from each other, face to face. We each had a phone. I took typing in high school, and I was trained on an electric typewriter—Jac would always want state-of-the-art in whatever he could afford at the moment. And I did everything. I was the secretary-receptionist, I did the books, I paid the royalties, I wrote letters, I listened to everybody, and I made the coffee.

JAC: Nina was the first Elektra staffer. I paid her the same as Dance magazine, $55 a week. I was paying myself $100, so between us we were making $8,000 a year, adequate for 1956.

NINA HOLZMAN: In the morning we got on the motor scooter and went to work. We worked all day together.

JAC: We would stay until 7pm, then go to a little restaurant nearby for dinner.

NINA HOLZMAN: There was a place down the street called La Palette, $2.69 for a complete dinner.

JAC: We'd split a dish. Beef stroganoff was a splurge.

NINA HOLZMAN: Jac felt free to invite people home for dinner. I was a good cook, so there were plenty of people always wanting to come over. There was no separation between the work life and the other life. There were recording sessions at night, and concerts. It was very exciting.

JAC: After Jean Ritchie's first album I had decided to buy my own recording equipment, a Magnecord PT-6 tape machine, carryable in two cases, plus an Electro-Voice Hammerhead mike with a collapsible stand and a bag for tapes. For playback I modified a set of World War II tank commander's headphones.

We did our recording on location, and I'd drive there on my motor scooter with the equipment nestled between my legs and strapped to the rear luggage rack.

We avoided conventional studios, most of which were former broadcast studios, deadened with perforated, square acoustic tile. They were sound-neutral, neither adding to nor detracting much from what the microphone heard. Neutral is like beige, it lacks character. I preferred rooms with a fatter, more opulent sound.

One evening I was listening to Ed Canby's choral group, the Canby Singers. It was soon after we had made the first Elektra record of Georgianna Bannister in Peter Bartók's little studio on 57th Street. I had been vaguely dissatisfied with the overall sound and thought it would have been better to record her in a more spacious environment, but I was not yet sure of my opinion. Now the Canby Singers were performing Monteverdi in the armor room of the Metropolitan Museum of Art, a tall vaulted thirteenth-century cathedral-like nave. It sounded so full and godlike, but to sing Bach or

Jac recording on location, 1956

other baroque music in that same room—highly filigreed, contrapuntal music—the subtlety and clarity of line would be confused. It hit me that Bach composed consciously for the acoustics of a North German Protestant church, wood and plaster with modest ornamentation. The sound was relatively dry and the details of his music would be heard in sharp relief. At the other end of the spectrum are Gregorian chants, where each sung phrase floats on top of the preceding phrase, like a multi-layered, Catholic Jell-O. What I learned from that evening was to match the singer to the recording environment.

For folk music we shunned the Catholic cathedrals and went for Lutheran churches. Or we rented a recital hall in the Columbia Artists Building where we could flavor the acoustics with panels—reflective on one side, absorptive on the other—that rolled on rubber wheels. The miking was trickier, less forgiving, and we frequently had to stop for an airplane overhead or the subway below, but we were able to make it all work.

A fine way to record a folk artist—usually a single self-accompanied singer—was in their own home, an ambiance where they would be comfortable. Wood walls were ideal, reflecting responsively and adding timbre. We would hang heavy blankets to subdue over-reverberant corners. Always we would have to stop for passing trucks or neighboring domestic arguments. I recall a Frank Warner session on Long Island where Frank competed with a chiming clock, a noisy water heater, a parakeet, a duck, several children, numerous chickens, and the Grumman jet air base.

Our records were easy to make. It was rare to spend more than three days in sessions. And they were inexpensive, usually under a thousand dollars. The sound was uniformly good. Although we didn't know it at the time, we were recording at a quality far above our ability to play it back. Listening to those early tapes now, with improved playback equipment, thinner-gapped heads, and the more sophisticated conductive materials of the last ten years, I am finding a richness of detail I never knew existed.

I did my own engineering and editing, cutting into the master tapes with Gem industrial single-edged razor blades, a hundred to a box, further honed on a well-worn whetstone. I never would do traditional fades or insert white plastic tape between tracks for silence, which was the normal practice; I preferred to separate songs with the natural sound of the room itself.

Our lacquer masters were cut by Peter Bartók. I would motor-scooter to his apartment in Riverdale with the tapes secure in a backpack. Peter would align the tape playback head with the high frequencies on my tape. Whenever we needed a level change or a slight equalization tweak, we did it on the fly. I prepared elaborate cue sheets and knew exactly when each adjustment was coming. We never dubbed the

Jac in his home electronics lab

changes down to a second generation as most every other label did, because it added noise and lessened quality.

Manufacturing was a constant battle. I was looking for a combination of quality and price. Samples from pressing plants were highly suspicious, and with long production runs of LPs there was tremendous variability between pressings. Even though the re-cut was from the same tape, somebody might flavor it differently, or the cutter head would act up, or a tube in the final amplifier stage might be weak. In the analog world consistency was difficult to achieve—which was part of its

Mastering lathe circa 1959

charm and made it a craft. To be a good mastering engineer was an exalted skill.

Quality control—trying to get records that didn't have skips, pops, clicks, or distortion—was a headache. We were infamous for rejecting test pressings. We couldn't compete with the major labels in paying advances, but we could and did compete in giving the artist and the audience an album of quality.

For album covers we hired excellent photographers, such as George Pickow, Jean Ritchie's husband, and knowledgeable and witty writers for the liner notes, the ones we didn't write ourselves. For an album Bob Gibson did with Hamilton Camp, the notes were by Shel Silverstein, and they were very hip. On another of Bob's albums the notes were by Studs Terkel and the photo by Pompeo Posar, who went on to shoot a thousand Playboy Playmates.

Other labels occasionally provided notes and lyrics. We did full booklets consistently and conscientiously. If songs were in a language that did not use the Roman alphabet, we would have the original typed on a special keyboard, whether it be kanji or Cyrillic. There would be a transliteration so that you could follow along with the words as well as an English translation. I wanted our listeners to have the deepest experience of the music and reasoned that it would create a greater appreciation for the material and for Elektra. Heightened satisfaction, in turn, might encourage more people to talk about the record, and word of mouth was the engine for reputation and sales.

Raw pressings were delivered to the Elektra office, the printer/fabricator would supply jackets, and we would do the assembling, slip the record into a protective glassine sleeve and then slide it plus the booklet into the jacket. Shrink wrapping was still unheard of.

Orders would be boxed and lashed to the motor scooter and I would drive to freight forwarders on the West Side. For office pickup there was a surcharge of $1.25 per box of about fifty albums, so it was much cheaper to deliver them yourself.

We were now selling directly to independent distributors. Immortal in memory is K.O. Asher. He was headquartered in Chicago, claimed the Midwest as his realm, and defined "Midwest" with a scope and sweep worthy of a Roman emperor: if a state didn't have an ocean on one of its borders the territory belonged to K.O. He was the most careful person with a buck I ever met, including me. He refused to spend money on printed stationery or order forms. K.O. would take a sheet of hotel stationery torn in half, or a free color postcard, handwrite his order, then rubber-stamp his name and address. For Christmas in 1957 I had some special stationery designed as a gift for him. He never acknowledged receipt and no trace of the elegant design ever crossed my desk. He kept on being K.O.

His one massively endearing quality was that he paid his bills on time. You always knew that, come the first of the month, K.O. would pay up. In 1958 I sent him a notice dropping him as our distributor because I wanted to break his huge territory into five or six smaller distributorships. Immediately I received a telegram—an expensive first from K.O.—with a gigantic order. It totaled almost a year's supply of Elektra albums, for which I thought I was never going to be paid, but I was contractually obligated to ship. K.O. paid, right on the nose.

In retrospect, independent distribution was not efficient, but it worked for me at the time. Even though some distributorships in the big East Coast cities were reputed to have unsavory connections, I quickly found that if you treated these customers with a sincere respect to which they were unaccustomed, they reciprocated and paid their bills. Nina and I would invite them to our home for artist parties, and they were pussycats.

Our ad budgets were small. Promotion was centered on getting reviewers interested enough to write about an album or getting it played on whatever station or program would air folk music. Generating word of mouth was critical, people telling other people, or a clerk in a record store guiding a customer.

Inventory control and accounting were primitive. If we had an invoice with thirty different records on it, one or two or ten of each title, these all had to be posted to a card. That card would indicate what you received, shipped, were paid for and, by derivation, what you owed in royalties when you multiplied it all out.

In the beginning I did the bookkeeping myself, with no experience or training. I kept track of the cash that came in and the cash that went out, cigar-box accounting. The economics were very simple. If I sold four or five thousand copies of an album I broke even on that project, paid for the overhead, and even made a little money, over time. For the first five years I never had a financial balance sheet because I had never heard of one; and since there were no profits there were no taxes.

It became our accounting practice, and it remains pretty much the standard industry practice to this day, to write off the value of newly released masters to zero. Once the record had been initially shipped it was no longer carried on the books as a financial asset, although it had value and we continued to work it energetically. This quick write-down minimized short-term profits which meant that more cash remained in the company.

Our suppliers carried us. In effect I was borrowing from them rather than the far more rigid banks. As long as I kept my commitment to pay agreed-upon installments, all was well. The first year Elektra could be said to have made even a small profit was 1956. Unexpectedly, and to the delight of our suppliers, we began to catch up on our bills, bringing most everyone current by late 1958. Suppliers who stuck with us, like our printer, Peter Strauss, continued to be our vendors when we entered our period of steeper growth.

The transition from red ink to black had resulted from a happy convergence of events. Clearly the most important were our artist signings, but I was also searching for a way to take our specialized and distinctive catalog and have it heard by more people. As a fanatical moviegoer, I knew the value of the film trailer. I translated that to the record business. My concept—I have always been big on concepts—was a sampler LP: a collection of musical trailers, a compendium of carefully assembled material, with lyrics and notes, all on a 10-inch LP that would sell for a bargain price unheard of in 1954: $2.00.

The first Elektra sampler featured a new logo, a drawing of a musician sitting on a conga-shaped barrel playing a guitar. My intuition was that samplers could become permanent marketing tools, so I inserted a "sampler clause" in all new

The very first sampler

artists' contracts, allowing me to use one track from any album, royalty-free.

In 1956 we produced our first 12-inch sampler for sale through retail. The normal pricing structure wouldn't allow for any profit margin to us, so I engineered the "short discount," reducing the dealer's unit profit but convincing them that if they displayed the samplers prominently and pushed the concept, it would result not only in more sampler sales but increased visibility of records by the featured artists. The dealer margin was lowered to 25 percent and the distributors worked on half their usual markup. We received $1.25 per record against our direct costs of $.55 plus the cost of special point of sale marketing tools. With no royalty obligation and only the raw cost of manufacturing to consider, a good sampler could net between ten and twenty thousand dollars.

This was the best of all possible worlds. We were actively promoting our records, the public was paying for the privilege and getting good value in return, and Elektra was being fertilized by the profits. We were making our garden grow. Dr. Pangloss would have smiled.

One large American company was not thrilled. The word "sampler" had a folk connotation as a piece of sentimental needlepoint to be framed and hung on the wall, but it could also be construed as referring to the famous Whitman's Sampler of boxed chocolates. After our first sampler was released, Whitman's white-shoe lawyers sent me a threatening "cease and desist" letter on their ogre stationery, so thick it cracked when fold-

First 12" sampler to be sold at retail

ed. My reply was to type up the definition of "sampler" from various unabridged dictionaries and send it back to them. After two years of sporadic correspondence they gave up.

JAC: Theodore Bikel continued to be our main prestige name. Theo was fluent in many languages and at home in an international repertoire that seemed endless. In another part of his professional life he was a marquee-name actor, starring in films and on stage in London and on Broadway. He was a total entertainer. As a performer and recording artist he was respected, intelligent and much loved, especially by Jewish mothers who could fantasize a match for their comely daughters. The more Theo was seen, the better his record sales. His back catalog moved with happy regularity and with his endless repertoire and quick learning skills he could put out two new albums a year.

THEODORE BIKEL: In my case the concept was language—Russian, Hebrew, Yiddish, or international, going from one language to another. A couple of times Jac teamed me up with other people, like Cynthia Gooding or Geula Gill. Jac had a good nose for talent in the first instance, and secondly, not just to take what the talent was doing at the moment, but to see the potential of what that talent might do and encouraging them in that direction.

JAC: Theo's first album, "Folk Songs Of Israel," had been originally issued in 1955 as a 10-inch LP with the title prominent and Theo's name in much smaller type, almost an afterthought. By mid-1956 Theodore Bikel was a name that, by itself, generated attention, so we took our 10-inch LP, recorded additional songs, and reissued it as a 12-inch.

Theo Bikel's debut album 1955 EKLP-32

The new version hit you in the eye with a knockout cover—a field in Israel, the crops poking their little green sprouts above the rich soil of the promised land, and a busty Sabra with an olive tan, a shirt with rolled-up sleeves, and khaki shorts over long slender legs, proudly striding the plowed furrows, a hoe resting on her shoulders, a jaunty kibbutz-type cap perched on her head, her eyes fixed on the future. The authentic spirit of Israel. And sexy.

New and Improved "Folksongs Of Israel" EKL-132

THEODORE BIKEL: Everybody was so impressed that we had gone all the way to Israel to photograph a real kibbutz person. Actually, I don't think this girl had been out of the country, or even out of New York. The art director found her in Manhattan and had her march through some green fields on Long Island.

JAC: We must have answered a hundred calls from eager young men desperate to meet that girl. Letters from Israel begged for her name and her kibbutz. It was a film fantasy brought to record covers, and a lesson I would never forget about the power of album cover art.

JAC: Ed McCurdy was a character around the Village, tall, taciturn and lantern-jawed, with an orotund voice, in which he pronounced more than talked.

Records and occasional concerts weren't sufficient to feed his family, so weekday afternoons Ed metamorphosed into Freddy the Fireman, hosting a local television show for kids in New York. Ed's landlord liked to see Freddy on the tube. It meant Ed was working and able to pay the rent.

OSCAR BRAND: Ed was a tough nut. A couple of drinks and he could be nasty. When he was not in his cups, he was a doll, a funny, clever guy.

MARK ABRAMSON: His voice had that whiskey depth. We would be on 14th Street, across from the armory, with those crenellated towers, and he would yell out as loudly as he could: "Who's manning the battlements? Someone should be manning the battlements!" Everyone stopped and stared.

Ed McCurdy

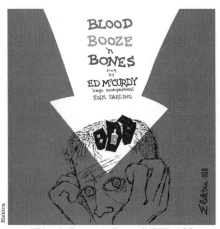

"Blood, Booze 'n Bones" EKL-108

JAC: We recorded several virile McCurdy folk albums with testosterone titles like "Sin Songs Pro And Con"—one side in favor, the other against—and "Blood, Booze 'N' Bones." One day Ed dropped off a batch of Elizabethan lyrics from Tom D'Urfey's "Songs Of Wit And Mirth, Or Pills To Purge Melancholy." The words were great but there were no melodies, so Ed adapted them to traditional melodies of their time, or wrote new ones.

Ed played robust, dexterous guitar, and we brought in Erik Darling, later of The Rooftop Singers, to play banjo, and Alan Arkin of the Tarriers (and eventually of Broadway and Hollywood) to play recorder.

Ed and I anguished over a title. The word "dalliance" popped up and he said, "Well, maybe we'll call it 'When Dalliance Was in Flower,'" and I said, "Yeah—'And Maidens Lost Their Heads.'" Very racy.

The album was an instant smash in college dorms, not six years after the birth of Elektra in a similar dorm. Students would be heard humming snatches of 'Go Bring Me A Lass'—"Let her body be tall, let her waist be small, and her age not above eighteen, Let her care for no bed, but here let her spread, her mantle upon the green."

The original cover was line drawings of buxom maidens. After the album took off I decided to switch to a color photo. We shot a photo of saucy wenches, featuring some nubile Playmates of the Month and some horny dallying dudes, of whom Leonard

First of the "Dalliance" series

Ripley was one and I was another, to save the cost of male models. The record company president on his own record cover, in jerkin and tights—certainly a more fetching vision than my out-of-focus guitar-playing Cossack on Theo Bikel's "Songs Of A Russian Gypsy."

The first "Dalliance" sold so well that follow-ups were inevitable. Fortunately, "Pills to Purge Melancholy" was stuffed with adaptable lyrics and so "Son of Dalliance" was born, with the cover shot featuring a maiden being banished for having an out-of-wedlock baby.

Follow-up in the "Dalliance" series

Over time the four albums of the Dalliance series probably sold over one hundred thousand copies. These were numbers big for any record company and gigantic for us.

JAC: In mid-1957 Nina and I got pregnant.

NINA HOLZMAN: That was great. It was what we wanted. I can remember one of the first days I wore a maternity dress. It was at some incredible audio show that took place every year, at 38th Street and Seventh Avenue. Jac was demonstrating his records on certain equipment, somehow involved with small speakers. One of the trademarks of Elektra Records, and what propelled him into the business in the first place, was that he wanted to have the best possible sound. He felt that Columbia LPs didn't sound that good. So hi-fi and the whole idea of the best sound possible was a driving force. And when this stuff was demonstrated at audio shows, it really sounded terrific.

I was wrapped up in getting ready to be a mother, even though I continued to work with Jac. We were not on such great terms with Jac's family at that point. But our obstetrician was a family friend. He had delivered Jac and his younger brother Keith. There were phases where we went in and out with Jac's parents. There did come a time when I could do no wrong with them, though Jac continued to have a hard time with his father.

I rode on the back of the motor scooter right up until the day I went to the hospital to give birth, much to the horror of the Italian ladies on Bleecker Street. Our son Adam was born in February, 1958.

MEL POSNER: When I got out of the army in April of 1958 I couldn't shake two nickels together. I went to an employment agency and I was sent out on an interview, and it was at Elektra Records. I didn't know anything about Elektra. I was going to take the job for the summer and go back to school at CCNY in the fall.

NINA HOLZMAN: I always adored Mel. He was as close as I could get to having a brother, because I never had one. He was just very loyal, he was sweet, he was good, and if he wasn't all that capable initially when he walked in the door, it was because he was very young, and he did develop.

JAC: Mel was eager to learn, quick to ask questions, didn't have to be told things twice, was quite disciplined and was willing to work hard for not a lot of money—it couldn't have been much more than fifty dollars a week—and if he resented working in the deep dungeon of our subterranean stockroom he was smart enough to keep it to himself.

One thing Mel did was to take over the assembly and packing of records from me, a blessed relief after eight years of personal pick and pack. I would still transport the boxed orders to the freight forwarders on the West Side. The poor Vespa—if I suddenly got off when it was loaded it would tilt dangerously backwards, so Mel would strap the boxes to the carrying rack while I cautiously mounted this unruly beast, careful not to upset its delicate balance.

And Mel and I went on the road, doing presentations.

MEL POSNER: In Cleveland the Elektra distributor was also the distributor for RCA white goods, and one time, to show them the covers of our albums, we actually set the slide projector up on a dishwasher and projected against a refrigerator.

MARK ABRAMSON: Mel had a lot of friends in Brooklyn, people he grew up with, policemen, firemen. Once I went with him to a place out there euphemistically called "the pigpen," a place to pick up women. This was pre-singles bars. It was an indescribable scene. I will describe the indescribable. It was this big hall, with some band playing that you didn't want to hear, and when the band wasn't playing, the piped-in music was so distorted you couldn't hear, and there were people milling about, all these hungry, predatory people of both sexes. Mel had himself beautiful women all along. He was very attractive to women. I think it was because he was genuine. He didn't make fun of people, he wasn't one of those ha-ha guys, he wasn't the guy in the corner going, "Hey!" He had a good heart, good soul, and I think women sensed that. A lot of the women there knew him. You could tell that he had a place in the group.

NINA HOLZMAN: Years later, when I saw "Saturday Night Fever," I thought of Mel, because there's something about that commute from Brooklyn into Manhattan. It was way more than a subway ride. Especially to the Village.

MEL POSNER: Working in the Village was a strange kind of thing for me. Every day was an adventure.

I was never aware of this huge homosexual contingent in the Village. I knew about homosexuality, but I didn't know there was a large community down there. I would take my lunch to the park, and I suddenly found myself in a strange situation, and I would just say, "Thanks, but no thanks," and that would be the end of it. But I suddenly became aware of things that I would not have been conscious of in Brooklyn.

And not only from that point of view, but from the artistic point of view. I suddenly recognized that where I thought it was important that people go out and earn a living and have a certain kind of lifestyle, now I was confronted with artists who were giving everything for their art, and they were more talented than I was, more willing to expose themselves, more willing to say things publicly that I was shy about, and that's when I got my respect for that community. I really became enamored by the whole creative process.

One evening Jac said to me, "Would you like to go to the studio?" I said, "Great, who?" He said, "Josh White." I got on the back of the Vespa. I had the microphone boxes on my lap and Jac had the cables and everything, and we went up to Judson Hall and recorded Josh White. And that was the kind of thing that started happening more and more, so that while I was learning from the business standpoint and the shipping standpoint, traffic and so forth, there was another element that I had never thought about, the association with the creative aspect of it, which in the end becomes the most exciting. At that stage, I'm twenty-two years old. And that summer job lasted twenty-six years.

JAC: In the spring of 1958, our financial nose was just a whisker above water when trouble began to brew with Mr. and Mrs. Ripley. Ripley's wife had insinuated herself into what had been a relaxed and friendly working relationship. She was convinced her husband should be running Elektra because he had invested more cash than I, but I owned more than half the stock and was drawing a modest salary. In her opinion I was bleeding Elektra.

She urged Ripley to tell our artists about the problems he was having, and that the company might not survive unless they supported him. I should have guessed that he would lobby the artists, but when I found out it stunned me.

It didn't have to become a contentious or vitriolic situation. Ripley had been best man at my wedding and we had always gotten on well. When he met this woman, that well-balanced equation changed, and I was so wrapped up in what I was doing that I didn't notice. Then they sued.

NINA HOLZMAN: That was a tense time—Adam just a baby and a lawsuit looming. It was the only blight on that whole period.

JAC: My regular lawyer evaporated, because he knew both Ripley and me and was uncomfortable representing either, so he turned me over to a partner in his office named Irwin Russell.

IRWIN RUSSELL: When I started to handle Jac's work he had his twenty-foot storefront on Bleecker Street. If we had to go through some contracts I'd come around, and we'd finish packing up the records and make the shipment for the day, then we'd sit down and do the contract paperwork.

JAC: It was fortuitous casting because Irwin and I quickly became friends and he helped me navigate through the Ripley situation, for which I was totally unprepared.

There is always a lot of posturing in the opening phases of any lawsuit and this one was no exception. We met with Ripley, his lawyer and, of course, the wife. The lawyer did all the talking, fanciful tales about how I was bankrupting the company with my $100 per week salary plus the clear nepotism of having Nina also work for Elektra. I kept my mouth shut, which is never easy. I just stared at Ripley, who was trying to project firmness but looked sheepish instead.

IRWIN RUSSELL: It got to the point where it seemed that either one or the other side would have to buy the other out. And we decided that they really didn't understand the business, so we would let them set the figure.

JAC: The beauty of Irwin's plan was that we retained the critical option to either buy Ripley out at his figure, or sell to him for that figure plus an additional sum representing my control of the majority stock.

It all boiled down to one number. If they set it right, it would represent a bargain for him but a figure too rich for me.

IRWIN RUSSELL: Ripley was no businessman, and his lawyers didn't comprehend the whole thing. They just assumed we didn't have any money. They set a very low figure, quite a bit lower than we would have been prepared to pay.

JAC: That figure turned out to be $25,000. The minute I heard the number I knew it was a bargain. My twenty-seventh birthday was coming and I decided to buy all of Elektra as my birthday present to me.

The Ripleys were surprised when we opted to acquire rather than sell—they were convinced I didn't have the cash. And they were absolutely right. I had thirty days to come up with the money. I slept fitfully for two weeks until I figured it out: Sam Goody was the key.

Sam was the king of New York's largest record store, west of Broadway, about twenty thousand square feet—gargantuan for a music outlet. Sam tried to keep every worthwhile LP of every label in stock, and he filled orders for customers worldwide.

Sam was short, thick, balding, fast-talking, a lover of fine deli, with a scrappy personality and an eye for the ladies—you never walked into his office without first listening at the glass door. He and I were friendly. One day I was visiting him and slipped off my loafers, and for years after, if I didn't remove my shoes, Sam thought I was uncomfortable.

Sam had filed for bankruptcy in the mid-Fifties. I wangled a seat on the creditors' committee as representative of the smaller independent labels. Although I stood to lose almost five thousand dollars I was strongly on Sam's side, because the independents couldn't afford to lose the outlet—at one point Sam was doing five percent of all the record business in the country. So I was very supportive and vocal in his defense.

With the Ripley buyout on my horizon it was time for Sam to return a favor, and he did. With an exaggerated flourish, Sam wrote me a check for $10,000 for records yet to be delivered. I gave him a big hug. Irwin found the other $15,000 for me by way of a friend.

IRWIN RUSSELL: I had to guarantee the signature.

JAC: Irwin's $15,000 was short-term money, to be paid back within ninety days. I had no idea how I was going to do that, but I managed to borrow $7,500 from my father on a six-month note and the other $7,500 from my bank, where I had been running smallish balances. The collateral was merely all my master tapes.

Now I owned Elektra. It was by far the most daring thing I had ever done. And I was deeply in debt. Not only did I have the Ripley buyout money to pay off, I still owed $90,000 to my suppliers. But I didn't worry much about this larger, looming debt. It never occurred to me, having suffered through the lawsuit with Ripley, that Elektra was going to be anything other than success-ful. When one hundred percent of Elektra was my responsibility I threw myself into fifth gear.

Theo Bikel's "Songs Of A Russian Gypsy" turned into an immediate hit. We sold over thirty-five thousand copies within the first four months. That was big cash flow for us, and there were no copyright payments on

**Theo's breakthrough album,
"Songs Of A Russian Gypsy" EKS-7150**

folk songs, which at $0.24 each for thirty-five thousand units meant an extra $8,000 for the company to reduce debt.

Ninety days after the Ripley buyout was completed, in the late fall of 1958, I was up to date with all my suppliers.

THEODORE BIKEL: A few months after Jac bought Ripley out he said to me, "I really feel I owe you, because you were with me from the beginning and you have done well for me. If you want five percent of the company, I'll let you have it for $20,000." At the time, that was a pretty piece of change for me, or for anybody, to come up with. But five percent of Elektra was already worth far more than twenty grand. And Jac really didn't have to do that. He could have walked away from buy-ing Ripley out and said, "I own all of it and I earned it and that's it." But he did make the offer. And I accepted. The investment was later returned twenty-five-fold.

Chapter 3

Brando and the stereo car crash ...
Flying solo ... A maid of constant sorrow

JAC: The year I bought the part of Elektra I didn't own, 1958, was also the year that we moved the company from 361 Bleecker Street to new and bigger offices at 110 West 14th Street, next to the Salvation Army. Some wag called it "The House That Theo Built."

We had managed to stay alive by fancy footwork through the kinds of problems that plague most small companies: inexperience, lack of marketing know-how, no credit rating, shortages of money, and a sawtooth revenue line. But I felt confident. Once I took full control, my sense of the possibilities expanded. We were selling more records, and we were selectively adding to our staff, now up to seven souls. We signed a five-year lease for five thousand square feet: three thousand for storage and shipping, the rest for offices. Record companies still stored and shipped their own records; they were not yet drop-shipped from the manufacturing facility.

Elektra now occupied the entire fourth floor of an old loft building. The main entrance was always locked at night, and tenants were given only one key, stamped DO NOT DUPLICATE. If we worked late and someone had to leave, they would walk downstairs with the key and re-lock the main door from the outside, and we would drop a fishing line with a hook and reel the key up again.

At 14th Street I had my first experience building a studio. My thought was to use it for solo artists or small groups of up to three musicians. With studios you design carefully and you pray. The space was too small to do very much, but we designed it as well as we could. No one was yet making mixing consoles for the record industry and the ones in use were mainly modified radio control room boards, so we commissioned a recording console with equalization, sliding level controls, plug in pre-amps, limiters and remote tape handling to be custom-built by Jan Syrjala. Now we could easily handle spoken word, voice-overs, sound effects, and overdubbing, such as it was in those days, which was very infrequent. The studio turned out to be less than successful for recording but very valuable as a mix-down and listening room. We hired our first fulltime engineer, David B. Jones—

MARK ABRAMSON:—The epitome of a techie. He was the one who hired me. I knew nothing. I spent the first week rewinding reel-to-reel tape. I hadn't met Jac, and then, the second week, in came this tall stooped person radiating energy.

After a while they took me on recording dates. We were going to record the Oranim Zabar Israeli Troupe in concert at Town Hall, and the biggest snowstorm of the year happened, the night before and all day. The streets were closed, you couldn't drive on them, but the subways were running, so David Jones and I, with two hand trucks, took all the equipment—and those Ampexes were heavy, the mixer and everything—and took the subway all the way to 42nd Street, and pulled them through these streets piled with snow. We were treading our way, tromping down the snow to get to Town Hall. We were sure that we would be the only ones there—we weren't even sure Oranim Zabar would show up. But they did, and they had a full house, and they were moved because everybody had come. It was a great recording, because everybody was so proud to have gotten there. The worst part was trundling everything back in the subway at two in the morning. But that was part of the fun.

Back at 14th Street we would listen to the tapes, and I started to learn how to edit and put things together in the studio. There were basically no record producers in those days. The engineer was essentially the producer, and everybody who was around listened. I started to do more and more of the editing and remixing. I had a knack for it. Somehow I could hear.

Jac was Production Supervisor. He was at the recording sessions. If we were talking about covers he was there. He was on the telephone. He was always part of everything that went on, with immense energy. I never felt him looking over my shoulder, but his energy was so nonstop—having a quiet moment with Jac was not something that was going to happen.

We started to get close, when I started supervising recording sessions.

JAC: I spent a lot of time with Mark, teaching him tape editing, mike technique and a bit about acoustics. He had a natural musical and dramatic sense and absorbed the practical aspects of engineering rapidly. He was an artist himself, with an even temperament, able to get along very well with the artists, and he became a hybrid recording engineer/producer— our first.

JAC: Once we had the space, it was time to bring in Bill Harvey fulltime, as art director. Our release schedule was based on the number of records that seemed worth doing, and that number was increasing. Bill had done fine work for us as a freelance, including the new logo which debuted on our first sampler. Graphics were becoming increasingly important, and I wanted consistency, speed and immediate input to artwork in process.

BILL HARVEY: The first time I came across Jac, it was back when he was still working in his record store. He was a strange dude, about six foot four, and I'm six foot two, and we were both skinny, and I didn't like tall skinny guys. He looked too much like me and I looked too much like him, and I thought, "I'm not going to get along with him."

He takes me to his apartment, which is one room, and he puts on a tape and plays the most god-awful music I ever heard: "O' Lovely Appearance Of Death." I had never been subjected to this kind of music before. Everything a cappella, no guitar, just this girl, and she sang and sang, and I sat there for forty minutes, and it was July, he had a skylight in this room and the sun was pouring down, it was like five-thirty in the afternoon—you know the Village, sweat was pouring off me. Jac says, "It's exciting, isn't it? Can you do something with this?" I needed the money, I have kids, and it's fifty bucks. I said, "Well, let me work on it, you know."

In those days there was no such thing as four-color process for record covers. Everybody did one-color, two-color jobs. No photography, or very little, except at CBS and RCA; the little companies couldn't afford that. But "O' Lovely Appearance Of Death" was a perfect black-and-white job—mostly black. So I did some very ghoulish-looking line drawing of a face with the eyes closed. And that's how I met Jac.

I did more covers for him. I was always paid on time. I could see there was a market here, and I seemed to have an ability to do something with this ten-inch square.

Any money I could make this way I could use, so I did some work for another record company. Jac found out about it. He said, "I want to take you to lunch." I said, "There's a very nice restaurant on Fifth Avenue, right around the corner from Fairchild where I work." Well, to see Jac go into a restaurant like that in those days, it was kind of funny.

O' LOVELY APPEARANCE OF **DEATH**

**The first William S. Harvey cover
EKLP-10**

I think he found it hard. I mean, he usually ate standing up. But I figure, "What the hell, Jac, you're buying." We sit down, we have lunch, and suddenly he comes on with this tirade about the nerve I had, doing this work for this other company. I said, "Jac, you don't own me. I like working for you, everything's fine. But don't tell me who I can work for or who I can't. Besides, I've got three kids and another coming, I've got to get all the money I can." So nothing comes of it, and I went home and told my wife, "I think we just lost an account—Jac Holzman is very angry with me."

I still had some work to deliver to him, and I took it to 14th Street, and he presented me with a portable phonograph. I thought, "Gee, that's very nice of you, Jac. Obviously I didn't lose the account." A few months later I was delivering him a brochure and he said, "How would you like to come and work for me?" He gave me a big room for my studio and my art department, with a drawing board in the middle of it, and a chair, and art supplies, and a wastepaper basket. And we went to work.

JAC: Even through Elektra's expansion in the late Fifties I still longed for the simple life: make a good record, and if it sold enough to recoup costs and a bit more, use the bit more to go to the movies, and if there was a big enough bit more left over, make another good record.

Yet when I told Nina I was going to be a millionaire by thirty-five, I meant it. Part of me wanted to make money, the only scorecard of success my family recognized, and by saying the words out loud I was committed, strict timetable and all. I wanted desperately to succeed, but do it my way.

Day by day Elektra was surviving. Inch by inch we were moving forward; but in the driven part of me, inch by inch wasn't fast enough. To this day I am like a dog who throws his own stick. Chase the stick, grab it, then throw it again, chase it, grab it, throw it, chase it—each time faster, each time farther. And trying to be faster than the next dog.

I was moaning about my slow progress to Fred Hellerman, an original member of the Weavers and a close friend of Theo's and mine who had arranged some of

Dressing for success Fifties style

Theo's biggest albums. Fred had a constructive cynicism wed to a Talmudic wisdom. His advice was to keep at it. "One of these days," he said, "you will be standing in the right place at the right time, and you're smart enough to recognize it." I badly wanted to believe him.

I was taking myself more seriously, dressing better—sports jacket, quite frequently a tie, a handkerchief tucked into my breast pocket. I didn't own many clothes, but I bought good ones, generally Brooks Brothers knockoffs.

I was spending more time at the office, out listening to artists three nights a week, and weekends there would be hootenannies. All other evenings I worked at home, in a sanctuary off the living room for my photographic, amateur radio and audio equipment, to which I would retire after dinner, listen to records, edit tapes and experiment with equipment, until it was time for bed.

The volume of work was turned up for everybody, not just myself. The gradient level at which Elektra people handled work always had to expand because the workload would get heavier and more was required of each of us. If your people are fragile and likely to buckle under pressure, find out early and replace them.

MARK ABRAMSON: Jac would write me memos about coming in to work on time in the morning.

BILL HARVEY: At the other end of the working day, it got later and later, to where I would be packing up trying to make the 7:30 home to my wife and family in the dark, and Jac would look at me as if I was betraying him.

MEL POSNER: I had a military obligation. They had a thing called Active Reserve. I was responsible for going to meetings in the evening once a week and then two weeks in the summer. I said to Jac, "I have to go away on my summer camp for the Army." He said, "That's fine. Have a nice time on your vacation." I said, "No, no, I have to go—" He said, "That's your vacation."

JAC: By 1957 I had repackaged all my 10-inch LPs as 12-inch. The record stores had revolted against the 10-inch album, complaining that it took just as much depth to store a 10-inch as a 12-inch, and they didn't net as much money. I was a holdout. For folk music I preferred the compactness and the thirty-minute playing time of the 10-inch. I hated to see it go. The last Elektra 10-inch was released in 1955, Josh White's double-LP set, "The Story of John Henry."

When we re-packaged for 12-inch, we either recorded additional material or combined two records, one on each side. Suddenly Cynthia Gooding had Mexican folk songs on one side and Spanish and Turkish songs on the other. New recordings were now conceived for 12-inch, which was another animal entirely. With up to twenty-two minutes per side, more and better material was needed to give the album vector and shape. And more tunes demanded even greater care to assemble a program that worked dramatically and musically. Assuming twelve selections, the number of sequencing possibilities was in the millions.

I also experimented briefly with musical genres other than folk. In 1956 I became attracted to jazz and made some solid albums, with Art Blakey and the Jazz Messengers, Herbie Mann, Anita Ellis, and "Hairy Jazz" with Shel Silverstein. Vanguard, on the other hand, contracted with John Hammond, a legendary jazz connoisseur, producer and concert promoter, to supervise their jazz series, superbly produced albums that just flew out the door. If you're going to

**Early jazz release,
"4 French Horns Plus Rhythm" EKL-134**

do genre music, you have to know it cold. Although I enjoyed the free flow of the music and the collaborative back and forth between musicians, I recorded only six jazz albums because I didn't understand or love the music enough.

JAC: In the early years my competition had been Moses Asch at Folkways. Moe resembled a rumpled Josef Stalin in build and facial structure, and his politics also leaned to the left. Moe considered me an upstart, an encroacher, but the Record Loft was a good customer, and eventually we became friends.

Folkways was headquartered on West 46th Street between Sixth and Seventh Avenues, across from a wonderful Mexican restaurant, Xochitl, easily the best in New York. Their combo platter was a work of art and you could make substitutions if you were a regular. Xochitl had been a favorite of my family for over twenty-five years and I was weaned on their molé. Moe and I would meet every few months for lunch to discuss the state of the business, which meant dissing just about everybody but ourselves.

Folkways was really just Moe and his associate, Marian Distler. They were devoted to the company and to each other and worked the kind of crazy hours we all did. Theirs was one of the world's great folk and ethnic music libraries.

In the early Fifties Moe issued a compilation by a filmmaker and folklorist named Harry Smith of three volumes of American Roots music titled "Anthology Of American Folk Music—Ballads (vol.1), Social Music (vol.2) and Songs (vol.3)." Each of the two-record sets chronicled different tributaries of American music, from blues and hollers, to fiddle tunes and the Anglo-American ballad. These were "desert island discs." If you could have only three folk albums to listen to for the rest of your life (or until rescued) these were the ones with which to be marooned. Much of what would become ingrained and important in British and American pop music can be traced back to the material in Harry's Smith's soundings. I still treasure my original copies, dogeared and scratched as they are.

A Folkways album resembled no other. Rather than print individual sleeves they stockpiled a standard, very sturdy, pebbled jacket—blue, maroon or black— onto which Moe would hand-glue a modest descriptive label with photos, or graphics, sometimes commissioned from top-flight artists like Ben Shahn. It was a method of self-supplying "just-in-time" jacket inventory with minimal dollar out- lay. The thoroughly researched Folkways booklets were inserted along with the disc and the album was complete. Except for his Pete Seeger records, Moe would press just a hundred at a time, and sell primarily to educational institutions, scholars, a select group of retailers or devoted collectors willing to pay $5.95 for a record of wedding dances from the Sudan.

Collectors would submit field recordings from their travels, and Moe would respond with a small check and then release the album. Or musicians would come by, and Moe would push some boxes aside and record direct onto his Presto disc recorder or his tape machine, pay them a very modest fee and off they would go.

Moe Asch in his tiny Folkways studio

OSCAR BRAND: At Folkways there wasn't much attention paid to record quality. I taped something for Moe on an Ampex 300 with a Telefunken microphone, one of the best, and I got good quality. When I got the record it sounded like a field recording made in Louisiana seventy years ago.

ED McCURDY: They used to say Moe mastered through a gravel filter. Jac was the first person who put folk songs and folk music on records of good quality.

JAC: As Elektra grew, my competition changed. In size and presence we had moved beyond Folkways, Tradition, and Riverside, and by the late Fifties we were nosing level with Vanguard.

Vanguard's offices were just down the block from Elektra on West 14th Street. They were a bigger label with more presence and larger facilities, a fully staffed and beautifully equipped engineering department, and considerably higher revenues. When the Weavers recorded a reunion concert in the early Fifties, Harold Leventhal offered the tapes first to Vanguard, and that was instant cachet for the label. They had classical cachet too, a fine series devoted to baroque and other classical music and the works of J.S. Bach on their Bach Guild series.

Vanguard was owned and operated by the Solomon brothers, Maynard and Seymour. Seymour was brash, emotional, with great enthusiasms. Maynard was more contained, exceptionally literate and somehow didn't seem to belong in the same play pen as the rest of us. Later he wrote elegant and authoritative biogra- phies of Beethoven and Mozart.

I admired Maynard. He had taste, intellect, focus. And he was his own man. Seymour was the violinist of the family, but Maynard looked it, with a shock of hair like a Chia Pet that had sprouted wire. He was the first person I ever knew who wore sneakers with a suit and tie and made it look stylish. He was soft of speech and manner and I never felt the iron fist in the velvet glove, though I suspected it was there. His wife, Eve, was equally gentle and contained, and Maynard had a lovely, sweet way with her. Nina and I enjoyed going to dinner with them, and it was Maynard who in 1960 introduced us to Japanese cuisine, at the Kabuki restaurant near Wall Street.

I envied Maynard his range and his self-image. And Maynard might have wished for more of my energy and willingness to take risks. When I thought of it, and I did, we might have made a terrific team.

Yet deep down—in fact from the top down and the bottom up—I really didn't want a partner. Not Paul Rickolt, not Leonard Ripley, not even Maynard. One aspect of my solitary individual drive was to prove that I could succeed by my own efforts. And as my own boss, doing things my way, I would work my ass off.

JAC: Ever since my frightening experience on United in 1955 I had been wary of flying. If I was going to travel and build the company I had to get over the fear. In the summer of 1959 I took myself across the Hudson River to Teterboro airport in New Jersey and nervously signed up for ten basic flying lessons.

The instructor stuck my ears between a headset and helped me maneuver my long legs into the front seat of a Piper J-3 Cub, built of doped fabric over a frame of aluminum tubing held together by wires that seemed frighteningly fragile. The entire aircraft, without occupants, weighed just about a thousand pounds.

We called the tower on a very rudimentary aircraft radio, taxied out and took off, with me following the instructor's coordinated hand and foot movements on the controls. I was surprised at how little effort it took to guide the plane and soon I was so involved in the process of flying that my fear just vanished . . . as long as I was in control.

I learned that it took a lot to make a plane fall out of the sky. The instructor, having been briefed about my white-knuckle concerns, put the plane in slow flight, the nose pointed skyward, hanging on the prop. Then he intentionally stalled, pulling the stick back so that insufficient air was flowing smoothly over the wing and the lift was bled off. Kicking in a little rudder, we began to spin gently downward, in a maneuver that terrifies most fledgling pilots. A little opposite rudder to correct the spin and some gentle back pressure on the stick with the throttle simultaneously moving forward—and we were flying comfortably straight and level again. I wasn't scared. The airplane wanted to fly!

As I got further into flying, an interesting thing happened. I had been having stomach cramps from internalizing my problems. Elektra was coming up to its tenth birthday, I felt behind schedule in my ambition and I was running out of clarity. At first I thought it was an ulcer, but it turned out to be a severely spastic colon. I tried all kinds of drugs and nothing worked. After six weeks of flying twice a week, my internal body began to relax and my symptoms vanished.

Holzman Family Archive

Jac's first plane

I earned my private pilot's license in 1960, and that same day bought a Cessna 172, single-engine, four-place, high-wing, fixed-gear, new, for $10,700 cash. The moment it was delivered I took Nina up. We flew over the slow-moving midget autos crowded bumper to bumper, winging toward Montauk at the tip of Long Island, enjoyed a leisurely picnic, and returned home the same afternoon.

Two years later, with 250 hours in my logbook, I was aching for a more com-

Holzman Family Archive

Jac's longer-range Beechcraft Debonair

plex aircraft, so I upgraded to a Beechcraft Debonair, high-performance, single-engine, low-wing, retractable gear, new, $26,000. I had it configured to my requirements, with a wing leveler autopilot and dual navigation and communications avionics.

If road traffic from the Village was light, it was only twenty-two minutes through the Lincoln Tunnel to Teterboro. From 1960 to 1962, I flew several days a week and left all my concerns on the ground while I enjoyed the freedom and fraternity of the air. In this plane I was to fly all over the United States.

JAC: In a funny way, my flight path crossed my recording path, by way of Oscar Brand.

ED McCURDY: Oscar and I were strange friends. He's not my favorite singer. He knows that. He called me up once and said, "Don't you think I'm singing better?" I said, "I hope so."

But we all owe Oscar a great deal. He has a filing system in his house, and an additional one in his brain, and if ever I want to know anything about a song, I call Oscar.

OSCAR BRAND: I had plenty of songs—folk songs, working songs, game songs, silly songs, political, bawdy, dirty.

I was on radio in New York, WNYC, every week, prime time on Sunday. I got letters from all over the world. I put out a book called "Singing Holidays For Children." When I got to Armed Services Day I had a Navy song, Army songs, Marine Corps songs, and I didn't have an Air Force song. So I wrote one, based on an old Army song.

I started getting sheets of songs from all over the country, all over the world. Fighter pilots, bomber pilots—"What, you never heard this?" or, "Interested in these songs?" One of the collections I got was about two hundred forty-six songs.

JAC:—'Save A Fighter Pilot's Ass,' 'Cigarettes And Sake,' inspired titles like that. And I decided to make the record.

OSCAR BRAND: We got six musicians I had worked with. No rehearsals, we just sat in the studio and did head arrangements.

JAC: We chuckled and charged our way through sixteen songs and recorded the entire album over three evenings.

OSCAR BRAND: For the cover, George Pickow put me in a studio, hung me from the ceiling. Then he had the idea of putting a bird on my cigarette holder, which meant my mouth kept drooping. He had me pouring champagne, and I'm a temperance man.

"The Wild Blue Yonder" EKS-7168

At that time I weighed about a hundred sixty-eight pounds. I just hung there, and after about six hours I started to settle, my ass sticking out, dumpy and fat, looking like a hundred ninety-two.

JAC: We called Oscar's album "The Wild Blue Yonder, Songs Our Fighting Air Force, Sung By Oscar Brand And the Roger Wilco Four" released it with a modest promotion to the AAFES (Army and Air Force Exchange Service, the PX) and. . . nothing happened.

Oscar Brand

Then one Monday morning as Mel and I were opening the mail we came upon a thick envelope from the AAFES. A bundle of papers in quintuplicate tumbled out with an order for ten thousand units. I was in shock. I called the AAFES office in Texas and cautiously asked, "Did you slip a zero or two? Is that a hundred or a thousand?"

Keenly amused, the AAFES told me what had happened. The staff had listened to our promotional sample record and decided it was perfect for their hundreds of PX locations. Starting in Texas, the album caught on at barbecues, in officers' clubs and enlisted men's beer halls.

We had never received an order for ten thousand pieces of anything. We shipped them, cracked a bottle of champagne, and kept on shipping, by the thousands.

OSCAR BRAND: Jac said, "Let's do more." So we did a Navy album, then "Tell It To The Marines," and another Air Force album—

JAC:—And then we did them for civilians: golfers, skiers, boaters, sports car enthusiasts, you name it, we did it.

JIM DICKSON: Jac discovered that there weren't modern sound effects albums in stereo. He did the classic smart American thing: find a need and fill it.

"Sound Effects" ...13 volumes in all

JAC: We produced a set of thirteen LPs of freshly recorded sound effects. It was a first in 1960, the only encyclopedic library, and it became one of our most successful projects.

High-quality portable battery-operated stereo recorders were nonexistent, so we kluged our own, using a transportable, conventionally powered Ampex connected to a special inverter to operate from a duplicate set of car batteries. A young engineer named Mike Scott actually did most of the recording, from a list of sound effects I had developed over a dozen evenings of watching TV till my eyes ached, writing down every effect I heard and then prioritizing them. Boiling water, escaping steam, door buzzers, body falling down stairs, Good Humor truck, whip cracks, railroad crossing bell, sonar pings, shotgun blasts, heart beats, hospital waiting room, bank interior, lumber yard, building demolition, earthquake tremor, avalanche, strafing from low-flying fighter plane, Geiger counter, A-bomb. There were five hundred of them.

JIM DICKSON: I made several hundred dollars without leaving my house. Drill going through wood, drill going through metal, door closing, door opening, faucet running, faucet dripping. I could sit around the house, and Jac was paying five or ten bucks apiece for them.

JAC: One of the most spectacular—and popular—was our car crash. We drove to Long Island and slicked down an out-of-the-way dead-end street and repeatedly skidded a junker car. Then we hauled what was left to a junk yard where we spread a layer of old car parts under a huge magnetic crane. Our junker was lifted and dropped over and over, with metal clanking, glass shattering, and very important-sounding destruction. The tape edit made it much bigger than life, and it was perennially licensed for TV and radio.

SUZANNE HELMS: Marlon Brando, for some reason, loved those sound effects. His secretary would call up and say, "OK, we need Volume 8." God knows what he did with them.

JAC: In time, we sold over a million units and there were no artist or publishing royalties to pay.

JIM DICKSON: Jac was very wise. It was a bonanza. It turned out they were a backbone of Elektra's financial stability during the folk period. It allowed him to do things that the other labels just couldn't afford.

JAC: After a decade making records I enjoyed my first chart album, with the Limeliters—Lou Gottlieb, Alex Hassilev, and Glenn Yarbrough. Glenn had been at

St. John's with me. When I bought my first decent tape recorder in 1949, Glenn's was the voice I used for experimentation, and later I had recorded him as a folk artist.

HERB COHEN: I knew Lou from San Francisco. And I had hired Alex and Glenn both to work at my club in LA, Cosmo Alley, and then when Lou called me to say he was looking to put together a group, I told him to come down and I introduced him to Glenn and Alex.

The Limeliters EKS-7180

MEL POSNER: They came up with a folk album that had pop potential, more mainstream. Suddenly we were getting on the radio. The album sold fifty or sixty thousand, enough to get us on the charts—at the low end, but still . . .

JAC: In October of 1960, on the tenth anniversary of Elektra, I bought Nina a pearl and gold necklace at Tiffany's and threw a party at the Maisonette Room of the St. Regis. We invited our artists, distributors, reviewers and the suppliers who had carried me for so many years. It was black tie, quite soigné, and I was given a lovely statuette of the Elektra logo. It was nervy to throw ourselves a party, but it had been an eventful ten years and the label was beginning to solidify. The party was by way of closing out one phase in anticipation of another.

Nina and Jac at Elektra's Tenth Anniversary Party

JAC: I first heard of Judy Collins from Bob Gibson, an Elektra artist who was an uncanny judge of talent as well as a terrific guitar player and banjo picker. In 1959 Bob had introduced Joan Baez to the world at the Newport Folk Festival, not long after Paul Rothchild had seen her at Club 47 in Cambridge, still in her larval state. Paul's one-line take was: "Bare feet, three chords and a terrified attitude." By Newport, the chrysalis was unfolding; she was an instant sensation. Coming onstage with a brief introduction from Bob, Joan humbly and very smartly waited until everyone quieted down and then unleashed her astonishing voice in an a capella ballad. Albert Grossman snapped her up for representation and made a swift deal with Maynard Solomon at Vanguard. When the record was released Vanguard had difficulty pressing them fast enough. In 1960 Joan returned to the festival a star, ceremonially chauffeured in a hearse with motorcycle escort. Not having an artist as exquisite as Joan rankled me.

MARK ABRAMSON: Jac would say, "We'll find our own." And he did. I saw him do that several times over the years.

BOB GIBSON: I suggested to Jac that he listen to Judy and look at her very favorably. Because, good as Joan was, I thought Judy had more depth and life, and I told Jac so.

JAC: I listened to a tape of 'The Great Silkie,' pure folk, recorded at a coffee house in Denver, the Exodus, where Judy was a regular.

JUDY COLLINS: A funny little record.

JAC: Judy was still a step away from serious recording—promising but not ready. I saw her again in 1961 at the Village Gate and it was clear that she had made enormous progress.

JUDY COLLINS: The Solomon brothers and Harold Leventhal and Manny Greenhill and John Hammond were always around in the same places, Jac too, hearing the same music, talking with the same people. Everybody kind of knew everybody; this wasn't a huge group.

JAC: In the late Fifties and early Sixties there was still time to watch an artist evolve without rushing to sign them immediately. It was some months before I stepped up.

JUDY COLLINS: It was a dark and stormy night in the basement of the Village Gate, Art D'Lugoff's wonderful place. Jac loomed up, a tall, slender, attractive, very clearly businesslike man, put his hand on my arm, and said with absolute conviction, "Dear"—which he continues to call me even today—"you're ready to make your record." And I said, "What are you talking about?"

He seemed to know what he wanted, and he seemed to know what I was doing. But I didn't know him. And making records wasn't foremost on my mind. I was very involved in my own family situation, a personal life that was very different from the folk scene. I had a husband who was teaching literature, I had a baby, I had a life in Connecticut in the countryside to which I was very devoted but from which I had to go out into other places and make a living doing my work.

I don't know how Jac heard what he heard. A storyteller, yes. He heard the stories, most definitely, and I think he heard the eclecticism of the material even then, roaming in a lot of directions. Gutsy songs like 'The Bullgine Run,' and sea songs, which were a real passion of mine. Railroading songs—I loved railroad songs. Truckdrivers—give me a truckdriver song and I'll sing it. I think Jac liked the choice of material, and I think he saw this twenty-one-year-old with a guitar singing 'The Greenland Fisheries' and thought, "This is what I want to do next." I think he saw that it was very commercial and viable, and he might have heard the singer through whatever else was going on.

A week after Jac, John Hammond of Columbia came to see me and said, "You're ready to make a record." And I said, "Well, you're a week too late, because I've already made a verbal agreement with Jac Holzman." We often laughed about that,

John and I. He was another great music man. Perhaps John and Jac had a singular gift in that they saw the artist and the talent and they said, "I want to work with that." They didn't say, "I wanna lay such and such on this artist."

JAC: What I saw in Judy was a captivating voice, a good story sense, but still unsure of herself and lacking authority.

JUDY COLLINS: What I saw was a man who could float around as many clubs in the Village as he wanted, and he would never lose the look of somebody who was thinking and reasoning and filtering everything through that brain of his. He was not a hanging-out kind of laid-back kind of drifting mindless folkie by any means. There was no vagueness around him. He was very, very clear, always articulate, very determined about what he wanted to do. No ambivalence. And I need that and want that from people. It was just a meeting of minds.

JAC: We recorded Judy's first album at Fine Sound on 57th Street, within whispering distance of Carnegie Hall. The studio itself was a hotel ballroom, very live, with a wide open, slightly echoic feel, but a natural echo. Robert Fine, who owned and managed the facility, was an excellent technician who had engineered the famous Telefunken U-47 miked sessions of great bombastic classics for Mercury Records, albums that were routinely used by audiophiles to show off their equipment. For Judy's session we had Fred Hellerman on second guitar, with Erik Darling (a Weaver at one time, and later of the Rooftop Singers) on banjo. Fred had also played on Joan Baez' debut recording.

Judy was new to studio work. There were many false starts, and it took longer than I would have liked. I pushed her very hard, bringing her close to tears: "You can do better. Try it again." Deep down Judy understood that I cared about getting it right.

JUDY COLLINS: Then we fought over sequencing the tracks. Jac generally won. He was usually right. He had a big-picture idea about how things worked. He knew

how to take things that were wonderful and make them work in a sequence that was even more so.

Linda Moser took my picture, a very blue picture, and I had sung my saddest of all songs, 'Maid Of Constant Sorrow,' and that was what the album was called, and I was thrilled when this actual record arrived at my home in Connecticut.

"A Maid Of Constant Sorrow"

JAC: The record sold about five thousand copies with the expected comments citing Judy as a Baez clone. I shrugged it off, having learned during our sessions that Judy and I shared a mania for getting it right. Immediately, we began planning her follow-up album, "Golden Apples Of The Sun."

My thought was to co-produce with Mark Abramson, but as we got into the first evening and I watched Mark bonding with Judy, I decided to let him solo. He was gentle, they were getting on terrifically, so I just turned them loose with each other.

MARK ABRAMSON: Judy looked like a skier. She was blond, athletic, strong forearms, that kind of snub-nosed freckled look, she looked like definitely a product of the West, and there was a certain fresh-air feeling to her, which was not really too much in evidence at Elektra, with people like Dirty Ed McCurdy. There was Jean Redpath from Scotland, also a breath of fresh air, and Jean Ritchie, who was from the South, but she was more homespun. Judy wasn't really homespun, she was more that kind of fresh Western energy folk singer. Very fresh voice, powerful guitar player. And on top of that she was a pianist, classically trained.

With Judy there was a feeling that now we had somebody who could break out into the general market, really the first person who was seen as someone to get Elektra on the map on a larger scale, who in that sense could be a star.

JEAN RITCHIE: I was very excited when Judy Collins came along, because she was more pop than the rest of us. Somebody asked Jac about her, and he said, "Oh, she's just great. She's Jean Ritchie with balls." And that got back to me and I was so mad. But Jac was always thinking ahead.

THEODORE BIKEL: Jac said, "You have a Carnegie Hall concert coming up. Why don't you introduce Judy?" I listened to her at the Bitter End, and she was lovely, with a gorgeous voice. So I said, "Sure."

JUDY COLLINS: Theo gave me a very big break, because that was an important concert. He was very sweet to me always. He's a very good man.

THEODORE BIKEL: That was very shrewd of Jac. It gave Judy a push upward, it married her for a brief time to a big artist, and it helped the label and the records and everything.

JAC: As the Sixties began, Elektra had issued a steady stream of folk albums, most of them worthy, some of them notable.

"Music Of Bulgaria," originally released on EMI, had never found its audience. Sales had slipped below an acceptable level, and the record had gone to the boneyard where superb albums that don't sell sadly languish. After a few phone calls, EMI agreed to license the masters to us, and it was a gratifying success. Its vocal layers, with their soaring harmonies and open-throated exuberance, turned many sets of ears towards the richness of world music, though that term was not yet in common use. The album was so hip that its release on Elektra further burnished our image. Artists and producers from other labels were forever asking for free replacement copies. It echoed all the way through the Sixties and beyond—David Crosby told me that it influenced the harmonies of Crosby, Stills and Nash.

Other excellent ethnic folk records were Jean Carignan, a Canadian fiddler;

"Music Of Bulgaria" EKL 282

Saka Acquaye's highlife album, "Gold Coast Saturday Night", a first in the US; Jean Redpath's "Scottish Ballad Book" and "Laddie Lie Near Me;" plus several albums of Japanese music featuring shakuhachi and koto. None were significant sellers but the music was so worthy that I felt a happy commitment to record them.

During this period, Elektra continued to enjoy substantial success with Theo Bikel. Theo could do his regular two albums per year. Good as they always were, that was a lot of times to be going to the well, so we exercised Theo's acting muscles with readings from the Bible, passages from Genesis, the Song of Songs and others, set to music composed by Dov Seltzer of the Oranim Zabar Israeli Troupe, and played by the Vienna Opera Orchestra.

Oscar Brand's concept albums were good for a chuckle and ten thousand units, but neither Oscar nor I would ever claim these as substantive. They were fun to plan and record, but we were doing them to death.

What it was coming down to was that the Elektra catalog of the late Fifties and into the early Sixties was missing a thematic direction. There was no arc to it, and the music I was hearing in clubs, audition tapes and on the radio yielded no clues.

To keep the label active while I awaited the muse, we recorded whatever struck me as reasonable, or that interested or amused me. Children's folk songs. Flamenco guitarist Juan Serrano. Renaissance music. "Catches And Glees Of The English Restoration." "Bobby Burns's Merry Muses." "Four French Horns + Rhythm." An audio test record for professionals to calibrate their pickup cartridges and playback system. A Morse Code LP, for which I had the neat notion that one could vary the speed of the code by playing it at 33 1/3, 45, and 78 rpm, and selecting a pitch low enough so that when the LP was played at two-and-a-half times its normal speed it was still readable. Folk banjo styles. The Greenbriar Boys. The Irish Ramblers. "Our Singing Heritage." Jean Shepherd, a radio personality who did quiet, idiosyncratic personal monologues.

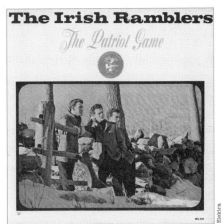

The Irish Ramblers EKS-7249

Adding to this odd collection, I released an album Jim Dickson had made several years before—Lord Buckley, the original hipster comedian. Buckley came out of the Chicago speakeasies, and how he got from there to a pith helmet and a waxed mustache and inventing The Church of the Living Swing, I have no idea. His riff on Jesus Christ as The Nazz was and remains a classic—this white aristocratic-looking figure with an absolutely black-sounding voice and a weird, antic wit.

JIM DICKSON: When I first put that record out, there were probably not more than three hundred people who could understand him. He was the first of a kind, before Lenny Bruce, before all of them. He was the first one to really capitalize on the language.

Henry Miller wrote about him, compared him to Rimbaud. Miller thought that he was black for years and years, and when he saw his photograph he was outraged: "My God, I've told everybody about this guy, thinking he was black!"

JAC: I had always been charmed by the English comic actress Joyce Grenfell, so I phoned her American agent. She was just back from a holiday in sunny Australia. She dropped by the office and showed me photos she had taken with a tiny Minox spy camera. The film negative was miniscule, and the photos were so grainy you couldn't tell the koala from the goanna, but I loved the absurdity of it, and I thought it would be wonderful to have this toothy, funny woman in the studio doing monologues that only the most rabid of anglophiles might understand. It was one of the nice things about owning the label; I could indulge my personal taste. The album cost under two thousand dollars, including her advance, and it did better than break even. Who else would be crazy enough to record her?

So many albums, some wonderful, a few dreadful. I was rudderless, less concerned about uniqueness and vision than I was about staying in the game.

The needle went deeper because Vanguard was just down the block, and they had the rights to record the Newport Folk Festival, plus Joan Baez who had risen to icon status. I was feeling second-rate and I hated it.

The company had to grow musically if we were to be taken seriously, but I didn't know what to grow it with. A hit would not be enough. I needed a breakthrough. I was bored, losing my way, and for the first time I could not see the road ahead.

JAC: In November 1961 our daughter Jaclyn was born. Jewish tradition frowns on the naming of male children after their fathers (as my father had done) but the rule didn't apply to females and I didn't care anyway. To preserve my full initials, JEH, Jaclyn was given a middle name, Estelle, after my grandmother who had been the most profound and supportive influence in my life. Estelle beamed.

Though I was a family man with two children we could all still fit on the motor scooter. I would drive, Nina would sit on the pillion holding Jaclyn, while Adam stood in front, protected by my arms and legs, peering over the handbars.

Chapter 4

Prematurely laid back in LA ...
Lenny Bruce on Cosmo Alley ...
A unicorn, a banjo in the rain, and a Louise Brooks wig

JAC: By 1962 the New York scene was looking very tired. Everyone was picking over the same turf. The major labels had wised up and were now sending people down to the Village. But looking for what? Nothing that I could see. It was all very gray. There had to be a lighter vision somewhere.

When the territory feels picked over I tend to pull up stakes. I started thinking about California.

There was a psychological as well as a continental divide between East and West. The West Coast was a world afar where life was defined differently. In New York nobody took California seriously, except perhaps San Francisco. Other than the four majors, no East Coast record companies staffed offices there. Records that were successful in the East tended to travel West but not the reverse. Television drama in the early Sixties was still New York-based, with most of the stories set in eastern locales. "77 Sunset Strip" was the beginning of a shift in TV consciousness from east to west. I had a hunch something was going to happen in California, and when it did I wanted to be there first.

JIM DICKSON: LA was a lot of fun then. There were only about a third as many people. In the winter time you could stand on the Sunset Strip, look down the end, and watch the moon, the full moon, come over the snowcapped mountains.

HERB COHEN: You could drive to Santa Monica and there was empty space. Westwood was a little village.

JIM DICKSON: It seemed more personal. Everybody knew everybody.

JAC: I was now managing Theo Bikel, who was very busy in television and films, many of which were shot in LA, and that brought me to the Coast often. Every few months I would jet out for a week.

LA worked its sundrenched charm on me. My routine did not vary much. In the morning I would head to Schwab's, have a relaxed breakfast with friends, drink an enormous tumbler of their freshly squeezed orange juice, and read the trades. It was a surreal Hollywood scene: all those wannabes with some tenuous connection to show business scanning the trades before they opened their newspapers—if they read newspapers at all. Movies were all anyone talked or cared about. Records weren't taken very seriously.

Elektra was growing and so were the West Coast distributors, and that relationship was important to nurture since we lived a continent apart. I was curious about what was selling, who were the best dealers, and since local radio was pretty much handled by the regional distributor, I came to meet the movers and shakers of the air waves. New York radio was by-the-numbers and predictably dull except for early morning comedy talent like Bob & Ray. The fresh, progressive style of LA radio alerted me to the major changes about to take place. It was smart, loud, full of itself and had a pulsing vitality. In three years they would be calling it Boss Radio.

Most of the independent record labels in New York got on well with each other and I wanted to extend that feeling to the companies based in California. Les Koenig owned and ran one of the sharpest jazz labels, Contemporary, doing most everything himself, including cutting his own masters on the same lathe that had cut the master discs for "The Jazz Singer." Fantasy, operated by Saul Zaentz, was based in Oakland and also specialized in jazz, and the "sick humor" of Lenny Bruce. Later they would be the home of Creedence Clearwater Revival, and Zaentz would become a major force in literate motion pictures, winning Best Picture Oscars for "One Flew Over The Cuckoo's Nest," "Amadeus" and "The English Patient."

My days were mostly spent working on Theo's career, calling on stores, visiting distributors and looking up talent managers. These connections might make it easier to find artists, which was my primary goal. Friends showed me around the clubs.

Having a hungry East Coast record company soliciting material in California was a novelty. Slowly the submissions began to flow. Jim Dickson turned me on to the Dillards.

JIM DICKSON: The Dillards were a bluegrass band. They were the real thing. Most of the people in folk music sort of learned a few chords on the street. But the Dillards were from Missouri. They'd actually grown up with the music and were much better players than anyone in folk music.

JAC: Len Grant brought me the Travelers 3, sort of a Kingston Trio knockoff, who were great fun. The banjo player was Japanese-American, the guitar player was Hawaiian, and the only regulation white American issue was the standup bass. They loved to challenge the $2.95 all-you-can-eat restaurants and wipe the buffet table clean.

My trips to California were becoming so frequent that Theo and I decided to share an apartment. Our place was moderately upscale, a two-bedroom duplex, a block south of Sunset, on De Longpré Avenue, in what is now West Hollywood.

I no longer had problems with flying and the jets would take you across the country in under six hours. I was shuttling back and forth, trying to give Elektra a West Coast presence without losing effectiveness in New York.

Underneath everything, and coming to the surface, I was tired of New York and wanted to experiment with a move to Los Angeles. In 1962 I decided to do it.

I flew my B-33 Beechcraft Debonair, hauling fragile recording and test equipment I did not want to leave to the untender mercies of transcontinental movers. Mark Abramson, always up for adventure, flew with me.

The first day out we came uncomfortably close to hammerheads—large, anvil-shaped clouds intimately associated with thunderstorms; so we put down at Cape Girardeau, Missouri, short of our first night's planned destination. Taking off the next morning at sunup, we scudded south under low-hanging grey clouds, following the gentle curve of the Mississippi Delta. From the air, the delta was exactly as I had imagined it and I started humming snatches of Robert Johnson. About a hundred-fifty miles north of New Orleans we hung a right and headed toward the broad expanse of Texas. We flew until our buns ached . . . and we were still over Texas. At El Paso we gave in, landed, and out of curiosity took a cab across the border to Ciudad Juarez. The third day we headed for California and touched down at Santa Monica as the sun was dipping into the Pacific.

We opened a small office, just east of where Santa Monica Boulevard meets Melrose Avenue, right across from the Troubadour. It was intended to be a West Coast A&R and marketing outpost with the main "get it done" responsibilities handled out of New York under the supervision of Bill Harvey and Mel Posner.

Nina and I and the kids took a one-year lease on a California ranch-style house on Edelweiss Drive, above Beverly Hills, about as high up as one could get, at around fourteen hundred feet. It was open to the sky and perpetually sunny. Driving down the hill to work in the morning I would hit a bank of low lying clouds that Angelenos referred to as the marine layer. It was gloomy weather for a summer day and hung over the city till mid-afternoon. Welcome to LA.

JAC: Theo Bikel collected a wide variety of interesting people to keep him amused when his film and TV shooting shut down. One was a former Castro "freedom fighter" named Herbie Cohen.

THEODORE BIKEL: Herbie was a kid from the Bronx, with those sleepy eyes. He was looking to do something, to open something that had to do with folk music and that would satisfy our own societal needs as well as the craving for the music. He said San Francisco had all those coffee houses, and it was all nice and structured, but LA had nothing of the kind.

HERB COHEN: I opened Cosmo Alley, by the Ivar Theater, jazz, with some folk on the side. Folk music was new, rock and roll was new, political comedy was new. Mort Sahl was very big. Lenny Bruce was just starting. He played three weeks at Cosmo Alley before he went to San Francisco and became very popular. Then Theo and I did the Unicorn.

THEODORE BIKEL: My name was quite well known, so I was sort of the shill, the come-on. Herbie was more of the entrepreneur.

HERB COHEN: We had Lenny Bruce at the Unicorn, and he got arrested. It was all about saying "fuck." You could say it offstage, you just couldn't say it onstage. The Unicorn stage was near the Sunset Boulevard side of the building. So Lenny used to open up the back door and walk out with a microphone with a thirty-foot cord and stand in the street and tell the audience inside, "If I say fuck onstage, the police who are standing there are going to arrest me. If I say fuck out here in the street they can't do anything." They arrested him anyhow. Then I took over the old USO canteen. We had Lenny there for a week, and the first night the cops arrested him and closed the place for health hazards, and then tore the building down.

JAC: I was a major Lenny Bruce fan and loved to hang out at the club. Through Theo I met Herbie, who managed a singer named Judy Henske . . .

JUDY HENSKE: I wanted to be a college graduate. Unfortunately, I flunked out of Rosary College in River Forest, Illinois, when I was a senior. Then they said, "Because we feel so sorry for you, we'll give you a chance to make up this theology credit." They said, "You could take a couple of courses at the University of Wisconsin summer school and then come back and graduate." But I got expelled from the University of Wisconsin. I had this boy friend and he was a lifeguard, this great big strong dare-devil kind of guy, and I lived on the third floor, and he used to climb up and in my window, smoking a big cigar.

Anyway, I got expelled, but I met a guy who played the banjo, so I followed him to Oberlin College in Ohio and we became engaged. Then he left for India and he left me his banjo, and that's how I became a folk singer.

So I came to Los Angeles, and I was just a total beatnik, and I wore these real weird clothes because I was a beatnik, a rubber duck-hunting jacket, and I had really long hair that hung down way below my waist.

I was living with this gay Flamenco dancer friend and we didn't have any money, so I went down to this place and they said, "Oh, there's this little club called Cosmo Alley and it has jazz and folk music sometimes and you should go and audition there."

So I went down in my horrible clothes and my long stringy hair, and I was sitting outside on a rock in the rain with my banjo, and Herbie Cohen came walking up, and he stopped and looked at me and he said, "Can you play that thing?" Because there weren't any chick banjo players. And I said, "Sure." So after the jazz act came off, I got up on stage and sang, and Herbie said, "You're hired."

I had some songs that really used to make jazz people pissed off because they only had, like, two chords. It was the opposite of jazz, honka-chonka kind of music, and I hit my foot and played in my hideous clothes and my horrible hair. And the waitresses would come by—they were jazz chicks with big long fingernails and real beautiful eye makeup and little form-fitting outfits, and I was just this terrible beatnik, so they wouldn't talk to me. They would drop trays on purpose during my show. But I never took it personally. I thought, "Well, they have their lives and I must live mine."

Herbie said, "I have another club up on Sunset Boulevard, called the Unicorn." He took me up there, 8907 Sunset. It was a very funky coffee house. Everything was black and they had female nude paintings hung upside down.

HERB COHEN: I have a painting in my office now of Deadly Diane, barebreasted, with very big dark eyes and shadows under the eyes and flowers. The waitresses all wore black. The freak scene hadn't started yet. Sylvia, Angie, Joanne, Sally Kellerman—an odd collection.

JUDY HENSKE: Herbie said, "I'll give you ninety bucks a week—fifteen a night, six nights." I performed in my duck jacket sitting on a closed-up player piano. I sat on the top of it and my feet were down where the keyboard was. I only had to do twenty-minute sets, but I only knew like maybe eight songs, so I would talk in between. "Well," I'd say, "how are all you jazz fans out there?" And needle them a little bit. Oh, yeah. I appeared with Lenny Bruce there. I opened the show. The Lenny Bruce audience were the hard-bitten Hollywood habitués. They were so hip, so mean—come on, the meanest audience on earth! And my parents came to hear me, from Chippewa Falls, Wisconsin, when I was opening for Lenny Bruce. Not good.

Ah, Unicorn nights. There were these horrible fights, where like drunken sailors would come in and start throwing chairs against the wall.

HERB COHEN: We had this Mexican waitress, tiny, four-foot-six, with her own deadly tray, steel, not plastic—if she hit you with the edge of it she could take your head off.

JUDY HENSKE: If you wanted class, you went up the street to the Golden Violin, same side, maybe three doors up. Or if you really had to have a drink, they would agreeably sell you like a giant malted milk in a plastic cup, with gin in it, and you could take it to the Unicorn. The Golden Violin had these big grayish plastic booths with pink and artificial gold accents. But when you went in it smelled. But it looked OK when you saw it at night. Like so many of us do . . .

Here's what happened. I did good at the Unicorn, the crowds liked me and Herbie said, "Well, I'm going to be your manager now."

HERB COHEN: I decided to manage her because she was incredible. She was so weird that I knew it was going to be a lot of fun.

NINA HOLZMAN: She was Bette Midler before Bette Midler. Bette Midler says that.

JAC: Mama Cass Elliott of the Mamas and the Papas modeled her persona on Judy.

NINA HOLZMAN: Judy was one of my favorites. She was very smart, with this wild sense of humor.

JAC: The great one-liner about there being three kinds of singers—male, female, and chick—that was Judy's.

PAUL ROTHCHILD: An absorbing entertainer. A very powerful personality. And the tallest woman I ever stood next to.

JAC: Taller than ninety-nine percent of record executives.

JUDY HENSKE: Herbie said, "You better go on the road." OK. So I took my banjo and I went on Trailways buses, playing all these little coffee houses in my duck-hunting jacket. I always had the money I made in my pocket, the rubberized pocket, it was perfect for money carrying.

I think it was, in a way, the most fun that I ever had. In those days they used to have places where the folk singers lived, going from town to town, like a theatrical boarding house. It was really fun because of the people that you met and the artists that you met. It wasn't like the music business is now, which is big bucks. It wasn't big bucks then. It was totally mom-and-pop.

I did great in Tulsa, I did great in Oklahoma City, I did great in Boulder, I did great in Chicago. Here's where I didn't do well. Indianapolis. I didn't do so well in Canada. I played once in Biloxi, Mississippi, and they were practically spitting at me as I left the stage. But I did great in Cleveland.

MICHAEL OCHS: I remember seeing her in New York at the Village Gate, opening for Woody Allen, who was relatively unknown. She was an incredible show person. One of the smartest women I've ever met. Some of her raps were as good as the singing, and her singing was unbelievable. She was trying to learn how to play the guitar, and she is like fiddling with it, and she would go, "Damn, I wish they'd make these things bra cup size."

JUDY HENSKE: After I had been out on the road for a while I came back to LA. I was singing at the Unicorn. Jerry Yester was playing guitar for me. That was a step up from just my banjo playing.

JAC: That's where I first saw her. That raunchy humor, that outsized voice—forget about breaking genteel crystal wine goblets, Judy could shatter tempered wind-shields in the parking lot. She banged her foot so hard, keeping time, she punched a hole in the stage. I wanted her for Elektra.

JUDY HENSKE: Jac came in and said, "Oh, we'd really like to sign you up." He was very white-skinned, dark hair, a good haircut, horn-rimmed glasses. And he seemed like a natural aristocrat. He wasn't your regular beatnik, let's put it that way, he wasn't a funky guy. Everything seemed to matter to him and he was very focused. He had on a nicely pressed pair of Levi's. And a T-shirt with a collar that was nicely pressed, maybe like a Lacoste shirt. As a matter of fact, I think he had his T-shirt tucked in. He came in the next night and he had this contract and he said, "We will give you an advance of $2,000," and $2,000 was written in. I don't know that I've ever had more than that in the bank since then. I've always lived on the brink of extinction. Certainly of monetary extinction.

Nina was just so well-behaved. They were both extremely well-behaved people, in a group of people who were not well-behaved. A lot of the artists they had were people who were not well-behaved, they were misbehaving all the time. But that's part of being a well-behaved person—you don't have to do it, but you can produce records from it.

Jac said, "Well, you can't have that long stringy black hair," because he thought, "Hey, she's too much of a beatnik, let's make her into more of a cocktail singer." So Nina said, "Come here, we're going to make you look just fabulous."

NINA HOLZMAN: I had a designer friend, and I kind of got Judy together, clothes-wise.

JUDY HENSKE: But I was a troubled beatnik, remember. I wasn't going around in dresses. Most of the time I had a broken collarbone from motorcycle accidents and stuff. I mean, I was on the other side.

My parents were very clothes-conscious and I had beautiful clothes at college. They bought me the best of everything. I had beautiful shoes, I even had hats and stuff. But then I got tired of always—it's like being in a monkey suit, and I was a monkey anyway, so why be in a monkey suit? So I got out of it, then Nina got me back into it again.

She was just wonderful. She would say, "Well, when I look at you I see a diamond in the rough." Of course, not knowing that's what I will always be, and that's my charm. She said, "Oh, well, we'll make her into a Julie London." She said, "We're going to make you look really beautiful," and they did. They spent all this money giving me this image. All these dresses from really fine stores.

Now I had the clothes but I still had the long stringy hair. The black wig was the final thing. Nina got it at Saks. This gay guy doing styling of all the models says, "I know how you'd look good," and he goes cut, cut, cut—"Tada!" Complete transformation. I looked like a cocktail singer.

Jac spent tons of money on my first album. It was one of his most expensive albums. And Jac himself was unfailingly wonderful to me. He was very encouraging and said, "Oh, I know you're just going to be our greatest act." He knew what he wanted and what he thought I should do. His idea for my first album, he found this African-American disgruntled jazz guy and got him to arrange a whole bunch

Judy Henske

of cuts, all my funky songs, 'Low Down Alligator' and 'Good Old Wagon,' but with a big band. A really big studio, with a big audience invited. We had one night live with this big orchestra, and then they went back and worked on the tracks. It was, like, sixty thousand dollars, really a lot of money, honey. Or no, I think one of my tracks was sixty thousand takes. Jerry Yester was leading the orchestra, and he was so jealous of my getting this record deal that during 'The Salvation Army Song'—my big song, regardless of how icky it is—he was conducting and he pretended to faint. He was lying on the floor in this gigantic studio, they had to stop all the recording, and I bent over him and I said, "Jerry, this isn't fair." And it wasn't.

On the first album cover they had me all dressed up, pearls, beautiful white dress with drapery around the bosom and beautiful stockings and shoes. And the wig. And it said on the cover, Judy Henske looks like this . . . But she sings like THIS, and there I am, still with the Louise Brooks wig but screaming, hollering. Which was the way I really was. Under all those clothes I was a very funky human, I was still the person in the duck-hunting jacket with the big rubber pockets so the blood wouldn't soak through from the killed birds.

I didn't care about the wig. I would wear it performing, but I never put it on its styrofoam form head. I would put it on a box instead. So that when I got on stage, instead of looking like, "Now we can make some money with her," there was something wrong. There was real mean sniping at me by critics. They would say, "Her hair looked like a mortar board on top of . . ." But the album was very well reviewed.

MICHAEL OCHS: Judy was probably the first superstar in the whole movement. She was the first to make Newsweek, this big article about this six-foot-one singer, and she'd stomp her feet so heavy on the floor that she'd go through the floorboards. She was this real Bessie Smith type gutsy singer, but white. And at this point everyone is going, "Is it ethnic or is it real?"

JUDY HENSKE: "Hootenanny" was happening, which was a TV show, and I was on that a whole lot.

MICHAEL OCHS: Herbie Cohen puts her in this movie—

JUDY HENSKE:—"Hootenanny Hoot"—

MICHAEL OCHS:—And they have her singing 'Wade In The Water,' in a Beverly Hills swimming pool.

JUDY HENSKE: Please don't search for it, and you must promise now to never ever watch it if it comes on television. Thank you. I try to exact a certain loyalty.

I didn't know what I was doing. I didn't want to be involved in anything. When I had to get dressed up in a little thing with a leopard collar and go in and audition for a television game show, I didn't feel right. Once they said in this nasty TV guide thing, "Judy Henske just acts like a befuddled housewife."

What I was interested in was the life of being on the road. It was really fun. And I loved being in the studio, because I got to sing all the time. Just singing, that was all I was interested in. I just wanted to come in, sing, and then go back to my life. I liked drifting. Other than that I was at a complete loss, didn't have a clue. I lived with different men at different times. I was one of those women, willy-nilly, blown through the world. The thing is, that although some people are aggressive enough to be an artist on the stage, they also have a deep bovine passivity. I would say I have. I wanted someone to tell me what to do. It's like I wanted to be dependent all this time, and all of these men, Jac included, and Herbie, were very much men who would take over. I mean, they would take over people who didn't want to get taken over, and I wanted to get taken over, so I was like a big plum. They'd say, "You're gonna do this and you're gonna do that." So I just said, "Oh, OK."

You have to be very smart, very canny, as a girl singer to get anywhere. You have to be very seductive to the right people, seductive on stage and also in a way backstage, to make it work. Everybody says, "You've got to take control of your life and you've got to take risks." Well, I always took risks and I never took control. My assemblage, the people that accompanied me, I let it go completely out of my hands, and it was wrong, completely, utterly wrong. You can't be there by yourself with one musical sensibility and then everybody else is going off on their own. Regardless of how good their musical inten-

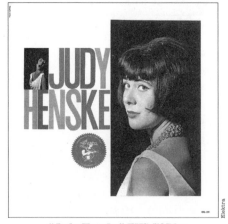

"Judy Henske" EKS-7231

tions are, it's not gonna work. They meant well, and they wanted to make a beautiful presentation. But it's like presenting a chocolate cake on a mirrored catapult drawn by fox terriers. I mean, do you really want that cake? It's dessert, for Christ's sake, let's just put it on the table.

They had brought me out one way, and then they went, "Whoa, we better cut back." So "High Flying Bird" was a better album. It was a smaller band, more banjo and guitar stuff. It sounded more like a human being than, you know, a chanteuse. We got really great reviews. Because I was unusual, I guess. Except for Crawdaddy. It said, "Judy Henske continues to wallow in her own bizarre brand of musical jelly." And I read it and I thought, "Sounds like me, alright." And I was very pleased that at least someone understood me, and there's an insult that was great. All of the stuff that was written that was good I didn't really agree with. But I liked "her own bizarre brand of musical jelly. "

NINA HOLZMAN: It's a shame it never did quite work with Judy.

JUDY HENSKE: It wasn't anyone's fault. Certainly not Nina's. Nina was wonderful. And Jac was unfailingly good to me. You had a sense that he was really excited about what he was doing and that it was really fun. And that's it—if it isn't fun you shouldn't do it. Instead of like now. What's happening now is, if it tastes good, spit it out. It was just that Herbie and Jac didn't know what to do with me. But then nobody did. They wanted Al Grossman to manage me, Dylan's manager. I had dinner with Albert, but that was all.

I have no idea why I left Elektra. That's business. I don't know anything about that.

JAC: LA was great for lifestyle. I wasn't much of a sun lover, but I was becoming more relaxed, dressing for comfort in jeans, tees and velour shirts. Nothing much was happening musically, and people still talked endlessly of movies and restaurants.

In retrospect I was a much duller person in Los Angeles. I wasn't challenged. Elektra was still without a clear sense of direction. I was paying bills and salaries, four people in LA, seven back in New York, but I didn't have my arms around anything solid on the West Coast to get excited about. What I hoped would happen in LA wasn't happening and I obsessed that my competitors in New York, the Solomon brothers at Vanguard and John Hammond at Columbia, were getting ahead of me.

Vanguard had Joan Baez, and she had been on the cover of Time. Soon after, the label fell into a hit single with 'Walk Right In' by the Rooftop Singers, absolutely perfect for the moment—an American skiffle tune with pre-jug band overtones. And was I ever right about John Hammond. While I was lifestyling in LA, he was signing Bob Dylan.

I didn't hear Dylan until I bought his first album, prematurely in the cutout bins at Wallach's Music City, the major Los Angeles record retailer. Music City stayed open through the wee hours and you would meet all kinds of offbeat people strolling through their fluorescent-lit aisles. They stocked everything: Latin, jazz, big band, classics, pop and folk. And now Dylan in the cutout bin. Whatever my New York office had been doing about A&R, they hadn't picked up on Dylan. We missed him totally. It made no difference that his debut album had stalled; he was astonishing, and that was obvious from the first track.

This was the summer of 1963. After a year of waiting to surf the perfect music wave in LA, I realized that it wasn't happening, and I had better return east. Sometimes I dither about making changes, putting off decisions that need to be made until I suddenly switch gears and do them. I called Bill Harvey and told him I was coming back; then shut everything down and moved, all within a few weeks.

Chapter 5

A tree grows in the West Village ...
Paul the pistol ... The great jug band party of 1963 ...
Uptown, uptempo, urban blues

JAC: Searching for someplace to live, Nina and I lucked out on our first try—a love-ly co-op, at 37 West 12th Street, in a part of Greenwich Village that was tree-lined, well-bred, and in striking contrast to my old five-dollar-a-week walkup on Grove Street. It was new, tastefully modern with bronze exterior framing, very few owner-tenants, a twenty-four-hour doorman, and a garage where I could keep my scoot-er. The building was in bankruptcy, so we could have our apartment for $37,500, with a fresh coat of white paint and no monthly maintenance fees till legal own-ership could be transferred many months down the line. I wrote myself a bonus check for many years of back pay and made the fifty percent down payment.

The apartment was blessedly quiet. You could actually hear a bird sing, which for New York was amazing. With three bedrooms we could subdivide the master unit so that each of the kids would have some privacy. Nina and I took the second, smaller bedroom, opening onto a court with one glorious tree that mirrored the seasons. The third bedroom, also facing the court, was my study, and there I assem-bled all the tools needed to critically edit and evaluate music. The living room was paneled in rosewood, with soft, velour-covered maroon couches that surrendered willingly to the shape of your body. Just before the walls were painted, I ran thick, multi-wire cable from my power amplifiers to play master tapes for our guests.

ADAM HOLZMAN: My dad had great stereo equipment. I had a little record play-er in my bedroom, but I couldn't use the main stereo. I wasn't allowed. Are you kid-ding?—you needed a pilot's license to use that stereo. He piped sound out of his office. He played a lot of stuff he was working on, loud, loud.

JAC: A year of LA had left me torpid. New York re-energized me—the pace of the city, the sharpness of people, the very air I breathed. I regained my panther walk and honed my edge.

My first major decision was to move Elektra uptown. The Village was comfort-able, it was where I lived, it was where the clubs and the artists were, but I want-ed—needed—to ratchet up, to put myself and the company at a higher level of risk and reward.

The 14th Street lease had a few months remaining, but I was already mentally uptown. I wanted to be fully set up in new offices by the next big selling season, the fall of 1963. With great good fortune, I found the perfect location, in the Sperry-Rand Building on Sixth Avenue, between 51st and 52nd Street.

Sperry-Rand was one of those tall towers with metal mullions that had sprung up on a street of mixed use, fancifully renamed the Avenue of the Americas. The old Sixth Avenue was block after block of clustered walkups, a jumble of old world shops, some tenements, and an elevated rail line that bisected the street and overwhelmed the neighborhood with the thunder of rattling metal and the screech of straining rails. Anyone who ever lived near an El line would never forget it. Stripped of the El and the tatty collection of buildings struck down by the swing of a demolition ball, New York had grown itself a brand new commercial business corridor, one upscale block west of Fifth Avenue.

JAC: In my new offices, after thirteen years making records, I had the single most important conversation of my professional life up to that time. Paul Rothchild came to see me.

I knew Paul from Bleecker Street days, when he would drop by, browse, and occasionally buy records. He had moved to Cambridge and was into the folk scene there, a director of Club 47, a remarkable little folk outpost from which blossomed all sorts of interesting artists: the Charles River Valley Boys, Bob Neuwirth, the Jim Kweskin Jug Band, and Joan Baez.

Paul's bread and butter had been selling for the Boston record distributor who handled Elektra, and when we ran a national sales competition, Paul was the hands-down winner.

PAUL ROTHCHILD: At one point Jac came out with a special incentive program. For every X number of records you sold you would get a certificate worth one book of green stamps. My wife and I needed a refrigerator. I went out and sold my ass off, I got a pile of these books, and we got our refrigerator free. When I mentioned it later to Jac—"You know, you were personally responsible for us having our refrigerator," he said, "You sold more than anybody in the country by a factor of two."

JAC: Now Rothchild the pistol was back in New York, doing A&R and producing for Prestige Records, primarily a jazz label but with folk aspirations. On the "street" I would see him doing his highly intense hang in the Village clubs and on the sidewalks out front.

In his early days with Prestige, Maynard Solomon was looking at an act that Paul was interested in and sharply warned him off, claiming that Paul had broken one of the cardinal rules among record companies, namely that once an act is talking to a label it was hands-off for everyone else. One evening Paul offhandedly asked me about this unwritten law. I looked at him with astonishment and then burst out laughing, "Paul, you've been had! You can talk, negotiate, do your dance, sing your song, until the moment the pen hits the contract." Paul never quite trusted Maynard again.

Paul had come to me to release one of my artists for a project at Prestige. I hesitated, wanting Elektra artists to build their careers at Elektra, with Elektra (meaning me) calling the shots. But, as people with similar interests and passions are wont to do, we began to talk of other things, and I was increasingly impressed. Paul had obvious energy and a hip hustle, coupled to superior intelligence and acute perceptions about music and the business of music.

PAUL ROTHCHILD: I was raised on classical music; my mother was a singer at the Met. We lived in Teaneck, New Jersey. Growing up, I used to run off into New York, to the jazz clubs, Birdland, Eddie Condon's on 52nd Street, catching old and new jazz. I started working in record stores as a salesman, and found out about early blues and their connection with jazz. And I studied conducting with Bruno Walter. He said I had a great heart for music, but others had much more talent, and I would probably wind up conducting a high school orchestra in Sheboygan, but that my passion for music would show itself later in life. I cried for years, but in a strange way his prophecy came true.

The way I was seeing things when I talked to Jac, there had been a blending of traditional music into the urban scene, a kind of mulching of all these different idioms that came before: Appalachian ballads, Child ballads, bluegrass, and all versions of the blues, up to and including electric. It was all the truth, by people who sang from the heart. And when you add to the equation Dylan and the Beatles, there lies the explosive element. It's all primed and ready. There are all these people who have the talent, and then there are these breakthrough writer-artists who change the way popular music can be made.

Dylan did it first through Peter, Paul and Mary, when they hit with 'Blowing In The Wind,' and of course his own success came after that. And the Beatles did it with their first album. I don't know anyone who didn't love that first album. Everybody from the hardest core Appalachian singer to Roger McGuinn, they all loved it. McGuinn one day said to me, "Paul, what should I do? I'm a banjo player, but I sense this new thing happening." I said, "Go get an electric guitar." So he went out and bought a twelve-string and started singing Beatles songs, and with that he was headed in the direction of the Byrds. This was a story you could tell a hundred times over. The first week the Beatles were on the radio, the possibilities changed—the world changed.

JAC: As Plato said, "When the mode of the music changes, the walls of the city shake." The Sixties weren't the Fifties, across the board, from politics to music, from Eisenhower to Kennedy, from Mitch Miller to Dylan and the Beatles.

Paul and I were breathing the same heady air of New York. We talked for two hours, and the more I listened the more I loved the way Paul thought and felt about music. We both shared a conviction that record making was, like the church, a calling rather than a career.

PAUL ROTHCHILD: I got up to go. We were shaking hands, and Jac said in parting that any time I was unhappy at Prestige to just let him know. When I hear this, I immediately sit down again. I debrief him about my complete and total anguish with my boss, who was an amazing boor. And my overwork. And my poor pay.

JAC: I said the obvious: "Why not come work alongside me at Elektra?"

PAUL ROTHCHILD: Jac had the elite, he had the cabaret folk acts, the coat and tie folk musicians, he had put out two Judy Collins records and she was getting a lot of notice, but Theo Bikel was still the biggest selling act he had. Jac said, "I want you off the street for other companies and on the street for me. I want you to bring street music to this company."

JAC: Paul was on the street more than me, and there was no doubt he was better with certain kinds of artists than I was. I was stuck in the office and couldn't go into the studio as often as I wanted or the label needed. I had Mark Abramson producing, but Mark couldn't do it all himself, simply as a matter of work load.

Paul Rothchild

PAUL ROTHCHILD: Jac said, "Can you produce ten albums a year?" At Prestige, in slavery, I had done thirteen in five months. I said, "No problem."

JAC: We were averaging about twenty records a year and I figured that Paul and Mark would split the production responsibility. Paul would broaden the reach of Elektra, and being respected and appreciated at work would encourage Paul to become fully himself. I was sold on him.

PAUL ROTHCHILD: He said, "I'll triple your salary, I'll give you a car."

JAC: Actually I said I would double his meager Prestige salary and give him a car allowance.

Paul was eager but unsure. He had heard one of those untraceable rumors that Elektra was going broke. Of course we weren't. Irwin Russell, who was in the office that day, pointed out in his well-reasoned lawyer's logic that a company with a fresh lease in the Sperry-Rand Building needed a good credit rating, ergo Elektra had to be solid. Paul was hungry to make the change. He just wanted reassurance, which Irwin provided.

PAUL ROTHCHILD: The first group I worked with was the Even Dozen Jug Band.

JAC: Suddenly jug bands were hot. The strong pulse of well-played instrumental music propelled by washtub bass and a skillfully blown jug created a folky sound with an exuberant edge, new to this folk music generation.

One day there were no jug bands, then overnight there were three. The Jim Kweskin Jug Band was from Cambridge, Paul's old stomping ground. Kweskin was there first and clearly the best. The other two were newly formed in the Village: Dave Van Ronk's Hudson Dusters, and the Even Dozen.

PETER SIEGEL: The Kweskin Band was on Vanguard. Jac and Maynard Solomon were friends, but Jac didn't like it when Maynard got something before he did. He offered the Even Dozen an astounding amount of money to record for Elektra—I think it was $1,000, which among twelve people came out to $83 each, less our manager's cut. We took the money and made up little band uniforms, which on that budget was a pair of black jeans, a blue work shirt and a vest.

JOSHUA RIFKIN: Paul Rothchild came to work with us.

PETER SIEGEL: Paul genuinely loved the music, he was very ambitious, and he had a feel for what could be a hit, what kids would like, what was cool.

He knew how to work with musicians. He came in to the first rehearsal, and some people would say, "Well, I don't know if I want to do this," but he just looked at us and said, "Hey, you wanna make records? Groovy. You don't? Beautiful." And he just stood there like he was ready to leave. And we said, "Oh, we wanna make records." And that was it. Those terms, groovy and beautiful, sounded a lot hipper than they do today. But that was his attitude. He was always on top of the situation. He knew what to say.

JOSHUA RIFKIN: After a couple of sessions, Paul said, "You guys don't need a producer, you need a group psychiatrist." This was pretty much true. But it was also a rather interesting organization in its own right. John Sebastian played harmonica with us and went on to form the Lovin' Spoonful. Steve Katz went on to become a member of Blood, Sweat and Tears. David Grisman became well known as a mandolin player. Stefan Grossman had an interesting career, mainly in Europe. Peter Siegel became a producer at Elektra, with a specialty in serious ethnic music. And we had a singer named Maria D'Amato who later achieved renown as Maria Muldaur. Quite an assortment of talent. But there were a lot of us, and it was a kind of crazy world. And of course we were all puppies. We were most of us still in our teens—I think the oldest was twenty, twenty-one.

Rothchild was a tremendous presence. I had done the usual classical child prodigy route of early piano lessons, and then in my teens I drifted much more into composition and then studying older music. When I was seventeen I went to Europe and studied with Stockhausen. This is a rather curious background for playing kazoo with the Even Dozen Jug Band, and I had in some ways the snotty kid classical outsider sort of ambivalent view of this whole scene and this whole process. But Rothchild had a very impressive classical background himself, and that gave him an instant kind of credibility with me. He had tremendous smarts, tremendous musical knowledge.

He was also someone then to whom all of us looked up. He was our great authority figure. To us he seemed the very embodiment of hip. He was well positioned already and married and had a kid, and knew more than all of us about dope and sex and everything else.

PETER SIEGEL: He always had dope and knew how to spread it around. It was part of his getting things done, part of his being a producer in the broadest sense, ambitious, getting things done that way. He was immensely talented, and as a record producer myself I can tell you that having a manipulative mind doesn't always hurt. He used language well in the service of what he wanted to accomplish. If that meant talking a lot, it meant talking a lot. If it meant not talking that much, he could do that too. He was a smart guy. I think you're talking about somebody who always had good pot, who would lay it on his friends. It was part of the way he would impress people. Just as he had the coolest suede jacket, he had the best dope.

JOSHUA RIFKIN: If Paul played all this as a card—if he did, and I'm questioning that—I'd have to say that he played it very generously. He shared the knowledge, he shared the dope. I remember stories of him and John Sebastian going out one night and getting laid together; so he didn't build barriers. He never pulled rank, never separated himself from us. He wanted to see us do our best, make the best possible record.

It was tremendously exciting, a real adventure. There we were in the record business. There we were performing, starting to do shows. There we were discovering groupies, discovering dope. It's a very heady thing when you're nineteen. We had all these expectations of great success, fame and fortune, Carnegie Hall coming up—we were going to conquer the world. I might say in parentheses that none of us had really paid much attention to these reports coming from Britain about something called the Beatles. Jug band music was supposed to be the next great thing. So it was a marvelous summer. We worked very hard, morning till night, five, six days a week, we went out, we did concerts, we hung together a great deal, and Paul was with us.

Jac, too, dropped in. He wasn't there as much, because obviously he had a company to run, and Paul was our point man. And Jac was also that much older again than Paul, so to us he seemed an absolute patriarch—

JAC:—I was thirty-two—

JOSHUA RIFKIN:—But a very hip patriarch. He, too, although he was a little bit above the fray, never set himself apart, any more than Paul did, and we had the feeling that we could relate to them easily and that we were kind of all sharing a common enterprise.

We would go to the Elektra office, to visit, just to say hello, to get records, and I could go in, as a nineteen-year-old kid, admittedly a member of one of the house acts, but I could just walk into the place, say hi to everybody, and then walk into Jac's office, and Jac, president of Elektra Records, would not be too busy, and he would say, "Come on in, sit down," and we'd just talk for an hour or so. That seems like a vanished world . . .

PETER SIEGEL: At the same time, Jac ran a tight ship. I only realized how tight later on, when I went to work at other record companies and found out how comparatively sloppy they were.

Paul in his professional life was extremely disciplined, too. He had studied classical music. He was a great one with jazz. He was a great one with folk music. It was the first time we had ever met a record producer, and he really tightened things up quite a bit for us. Our music was full of stop breaks and little starts and stops that were sloppy as hell, and he worked with us and cleaned it up. He was able to point out things that were out of rhythm, that were out of tune, that didn't make sense, that were too busy. He actually came close to conducting the band.

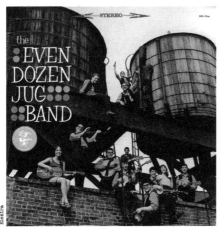

"The Even Dozen Jug Band" EKS-7246

JOSHUA RIFKIN: We finished recording, and there the tapes were, ready to be edited. I worked a lot on the editing with Paul, which was a wonderful experience for me. I had written one of the tunes, 'The Even Dozens,' and Paul invited me to join him for editing it, putting the tapes together. This was in the days of analog tape editing, where you cut and spliced it, which did seem like an awesome skill. Looking back from our digital perspective, there was something rather heroic about it. It was a kind of high-wire act. I remember one particular cut, right near the end of a little piano solo, a slow downward arpeggio, and I remember our having to join two takes there, and Paul cutting right in the middle of it, sort of off the beat, on a note that you'd never expect, and my just being dazzled by this.

Paul certainly seemed to me someone who had the secrets. He was in the temple, and yes, he certainly opened it up to all of us, and here to me. It was very generous. So was Mark Abramson. And so was Jac.

What I realize, looking back, is that these people were having great fun doing what they were doing. It was still sort of a cottage industry, folk music leading into pop music—an enjoyable business. Everybody was having a good time. There were clearly, even then, people to whom rank and everything was important, but to these people at Elektra it wasn't. The headiest thing about this experience was at nineteen or twenty to become a colleague of these people, be taken into the circle, become one of them.

JOHN SEBASTIAN: There was an interesting moment that gave me a feeling of solidarity with Elektra, and by extension with Jac. This was the party for the closing of the Elektra offices on 14th Street.

What it was—and I think it was conceived partially by Rothchild—they decided to have a jug band party, that included all the jug bands known to this younger generation of old-time music enthusiasts: the Jim Kweskin Jug Band, who came down from Boston, the Even Dozen Jug Band, and Dave Van Ronk's Hudson Dusters.

FRITZ RICHMOND: That was a famous party.

JOSHUA RIFKIN: It was a great wonderful mob scene. There wasn't much furniture left, but lots of food was set up and people sat on the floor and lounged against the walls, et cetera. They brought in kegs, huge barrels of beer.

JOHN SEBASTIAN: It was the first time I had ever attended a party that had more than one keg.

JOSHUA RIFKIN: The beer, the pot, everything flowed very freely. I don't know where they stuffed the ganja, but everything was available and we were all super mellow.

Our girl singer, as they were called in those days, Maria D'Amato, was living on the Lower East Side with a harmonica player, and they weren't getting on so well.

FRITZ RICHMOND: John Sebastian had been trying to get next to Maria. But when Maria saw Geoff Muldaur from the Kweskin Band, this blue-eyed, Waspy, breathy singer with that warble in his voice, her heart went bumpety-bump for him, and it was all over for John.

JOSHUA RIFKIN: Geoff was the most laconic, lackadaisical character you could ever hope to find, and I remember walking into some room and there's a bunch of people sort of hanging on the walls in various stages of far-goneness, and Geoff is slouched down on the floor, his head butting the wall, totally blotto-eyed, and I see Maria kind of stretched out across him, looking into his eyes and starting to sing in this very, very drunken voice, "Oh, Geoff Muldaur, Geoff Muldaur, I want you to walk through my door, Come and give me some more, Geoff Muldaur"—and with that, she barfed all over his chest. Geoff nodded his head a bit from side to side and looked at her and she looked at him, and two days later she was on the train up to Boston, and she eventually became Maria Muldaur.

Much later in the night there was an early proto-groupie who was hanging around and was interested in the Even Dozen Jug Band and had gone through some of it, and it was my turn, and I remember our doing it standing up on the fire escape outside and thoughts coming into my mind: "My God, it's four o'clock in the early dawn in Manhattan, and I'm outside on the fire escape with my ass bare."

JOHN SEBASTIAN: The great jug band party—there was something about the attitude of the people at that party that spoke to me of the power of this good-time music hybrid of rock and roll sensibilities and jug band instruments that would later become the Lovin' Spoonful and other strong bands.

But I would also say that party simultaneously marked the end for a slightly earlier genre of folk music and folk singer, the end of the earliest folk scene.

JAC: John whiffed that sense of change. So did Paul, and so did I.

JAC: Our new offices were right in the hard-core center of happening Manhattan. From Park and Madison avenues, across to Sixth or Seventh Avenue, and from 42nd Street up to 57th Street, there was a concentration of the hungriest people in New York, working, scheming, fighting each other for rungs on the ladder, and I was one of them.

FRITZ RICHMOND: I saw Jac's office. He had all these jazzy toys on his desk. Do you know what the Archimedes Devil is? It's a tall glass cylinder, liquid-filled, and in it are little figures, also liquid-filled, and depending on the temperature these things are either at the bottom or at the top or split. It's a very simple scientific principle why they do what they do, but it has always escaped me. Jac had one of those, a nice big one. I was impressed. It was definitely a nicer office than Maynard Solomon's over at Vanguard, which looked like a movie set for a poverty-stricken accountant. Maynard smoked, and there was an ashtray on his desk. Jac didn't smoke, and there wasn't an ashtray on his desk. It might have been the nicest office I had ever been in.

JAC: From my perch on the twenty-eighth floor I could see to Central Park, the playground of my early years. The breadth and clarity of the view said to me that I had made it partway, but I was poised for more. Elektra was my instrument and I was tuned and ready.

Within a month of moving, I was invited to lunch at the Friars Club by Dave Kapp, the owner of Kapp Records. Dave was one of the founders of Decca Records, a company that had been launched at the height of the Depression as a low-cost singles label and was best known for its early recordings of Bing Crosby.

The conversation was amiable. Dave wanted to acquire Elektra, but he wasn't quite sure why. We didn't talk numbers, we tried to talk about music, but the world of Kapp wasn't the world of Elektra. The Kapp logo was a bandmaster's hat, all tassels and polished brass; the Elektra logo was a folk musician, sitting on a barrel, playing his guitar.

Like a kid who likes to count the change in his piggy bank, I was curious to find out what someone experienced in music business values might offer. I called Dave a week later, after they had looked at some very rudimentary numbers, and the offer was $1,000,000. At thirty-two, I was three years ahead of my schedule.

I graciously turned it down. For starters, I didn't think it was nearly enough. I believed in my own ability to build the company into something far more substantial. Our offices were classier than Kapp's. And never, ever, did I want to work for someone else.

On reflection, I noticed that when I first tasted success, on the cusp of the Sixties, I had been able to save perhaps a hundred thousand dollars. That was real money then, and I found myself acting more conservatively, frightened that I might blow it. But the music spoke to me with greater urgency than the business ever could. As I did with flying, I finally just let the fears go. Not risking was a worse risk in itself. If I blew it, at least I knew I was talented, had some reputation, and could land a job that would take care of survival. So I said to myself, "I'll just pretend I'm right and move ahead—follow my ears and my heart more, and my analytical mind less."

Nina and I discussed the offer, but agreed that having our own company was so much more satisfying. Still, knowing that it was worth a million to someone was comforting.

JAC: Paul Nelson and friends put out a home-brew music magazine in Minneapolis called the Little Sandy Review, quite influential in the tightly-wound folk world of the time. The magazine had caustic opinions, and often took me to task for making albums they considered insufficiently ethnic.

Elektra

Josh White's "Chain Gang Songs"
EKS-7158

PAUL NELSON: It was either Elektra or Vanguard who put out a chain gang album with banjoes and strings and heavenly choirs, and I wrote this review that said, "Instead of sending your kid to summer camp this year, why not send him to the chain gang, because it really sounds pleasant, these records make it seem like so much fun."

JAC: Our only chain gang album was by Josh White, so I wrote to Paul about the piece, as I wrote to so many supporters and critics of Elektra. I wanted them to know that I was reading their stuff and paying attention. I never once complained about what they said, just wanted them to hear our side.

PAUL NELSON: If we panned one of his records he'd always write a funny little note back, and I sort of felt I knew him through the letters.

JAC: One day I received a record from Nelson: three beardless, rumpled white kids calling themselves Koerner, Ray & Glover, on the Audiophile label, a one-man operation somewhere in the Midwest. I shoved it to the bottom of the "To Listen" batch. Four or five days later it floated to the surface, I put it on, and absolutely fell in love with it. It was gutsy, down home in the holler, totally unselfconscious roots music, and those guys could stomp and play their asses off.

PAUL NELSON: "Spider" John Koerner, Dave "Snaker" Ray, and Tony "Little Sun" Glover—

PAUL ROTHCHILD:—One doing almost perfect incarnations of Leadbelly twelve-string guitar, another writing his own songs in an uneven bar style that blew your mind, and one guy on the moon who played the strangest harmonica you ever heard.

TONY GLOVER: The Audiophile guy wouldn't give us any comps, but he'd sell us records at cost. Big-hearted guy. We bought three, sent one to Billboard, one to Cashbox, and Paul Nelson sent one to Elektra, to Jac Holzman, because he thought he might be into it. I thought that was kind of dubious, because at that time they had like Josh White and Oscar Brand and to me kind of ersatz people. But I thought, "What the hell, a couple of bucks, if we lose it we lose it."

So we sat around and nothing happened and nothing happened, and finally somebody, I think Paul, got a letter or a phone call from Jac saying, "Holy shit, what's the deal with these guys, can we talk?"

JAC: The Audiophile owner had recorded them very simply, which was absolutely right, and he was fanatical about sound quality, which I also appreciated. The music got to me, and within forty-eight hours I hopped a plane to Minneapolis.

TONY GLOVER: My first impression of Jac was that he was kind of a young dapper Ivy League sort of guy. In a way he was a yuppie of that day, but it was really a more elegant kind of style, almost literary, East Coast literary kind of style, the kind of guy that carried an umbrella and a briefcase. I didn't know how well we were gonna get along with him, but he seemed pretty enthusiastic, and I figured we didn't have a damn thing to lose, so why not, you know?

We had a meeting over at Dave's dad's office—he was an insurance salesman—sat down and worked out a contract which then got reworked at dinner.

JAC: I had to pass muster with both parents. They were nice, solid Midwestern people, slightly bemused that someone would fly in from New York because he liked what these three kids were playing.

TONY GLOVER: Over dessert, Dave's old man played Jac a good Minnesota rube routine and ended up getting us a much more favorable deal.

JAC: We agreed that I would buy the masters of the Audiophile album, and we'd cut some additional tunes in New York.

TONY GLOVER: Jac put us up at the Hotel Earle.

JAC: It was an old music scuffler's spot, close to where I lived and to the Sixth Avenue bus line, easy for the boys to move around without a car.

TONY GLOVER: The thing I remember about it was there were a lot of strange chicks, and spikes and orange peels in the elevators.

Jac was living in this kind of staid co-op, with a doorman who looked horrified at the sight of us. One time Jac and his family were all out of town and he said we could stay at his apartment. The doorman practically had shit fits, he'd see us walking up with our suitcases and had to be held back. We had orders not to hassle the maid, because they were hard to find, so we should clean the bathtub after ourselves.

I still have this mental picture of Jac riding down the street on his motor scooter with his black suit, white shirt, tie, umbrella, and white gloves. Actually I'm not positive about the white gloves. But a very dapper sort of New York looking cat. He also kept unpaid parking tickets in his car that he would carry around, different kinds, like rainy, dry, mud-splattered, and ones that had been rained on and dried. He'd pull out the appropriately weathered parking ticket, slap it on and go about his business. Sort of a crazy guy, but very straight looking.

When it came to recording, he went out and bought a pair of jeans so he could do the group better. Brand new pair of Levi's.

JAC: I put the three of them into the studio with Paul Rothchild and me, at Mastertone on 42nd Street.

TONY GLOVER: It was like coming in out of the carnival. This is before the days of user-friendly recording studios. I mean it's a square fucking room, rectangular, with high ceilings, bare walls, and fluorescent lights, and the lights were either off or on, no in between, and it was driving me nuts, I couldn't record with fluorescent lights, too bright, too green, so Jac went out and bought a couple of candles and labeled them Elektra Illumination Unit #1 and #2, which I thought was a real Holzman kind of thing to do.

JAC: I took some back cover pictures, including one of a trash can overflowing with beer cans and whiskey bottles. It was appropriate for the sessions.

TONY GLOVER: One time I was giving Jac some shit about Oscar Brand and all those kinds of guys, and he got uppity and said, "It's guys like those that give me the money and the time to record guys like you." Which I thought was a pretty good comeback.

When Jac signed us he expected to lose money on us. He was really surprised when we sold enough records to pay back the thing. He was just doing it because he liked the music and thought it was good.

Tony "Little Sun" Glover and "Spider" John Koerner at Newport

JOHN SEBASTIAN: It was raggy, it was bluesy. Good-time music. It was played a little bit faster than the original guys did it. That was because they were excitable young white boys who sped up.

PAUL WILLIAMS: That first album had a terrific energy and freshness. Koerner had a tremendous personality. In the early writings about Dylan, the people in the Minnesota scene, the Minneapolis scene at that time, expected Koerner to be the one who would make a national impact. Dave Ray, to me, during that period, was creating an incredibly powerful music, often a closer identification with Leadbelly than I can remember anybody else trying, and yet it was something that was just totally relevant to me, a seventeen or eighteen-year-old white kid. And the music still sounds good to me now. There's some extraordinary art in the performances.

JOHN SEBASTIAN: It was a step along the path towards what became a style that the Lovin' Spoonful drew upon, and so did a lot of people—Tim Hardin, and Fred Neil, of course.

ADAM HOLZMAN: Koerner, Ray & Glover were one of the few bands I appreciated as a little kid. They had the hippest tunes and they threw in a lot of

(L. to R.) Koerner, Glover and Ray

tricky little musical riffs, weird time changes.

Snaker Ray would come and stay at the apartment, in my room, and I had to move into my sister's room. I remember he had these huge boots—

JAC:—Black shit-kicker motorcycle boots with a strap across the instep and thick no-nonsense heels, clearly made for stomping bad dudes—

ADAM HOLZMAN: And he was always fixing them.

NINA HOLZMAN: I really loved Koerner, Ray & Glover. They were very dear to me. Adam got very sick at one point, and Dave Ray was staying at the apartment while Jac was off somewhere, and Dave went with me to take Adam to the hospital.

JAC: I thoroughly enjoyed KR&G as friends and as artists. Over the years, music people would tell me about records that had influenced their lives, and Koerner, Ray & Glover always came up.

Their music helped me decide what I wanted to do at Elektra. If I asked myself whether I would rather have recorded Koerner, Ray & Glover or Peter, Paul and Mary, the answer was clear. I just wanted to make records I genuinely loved and believed in.

PAUL ROTHCHILD: One of the directions I was guiding Elektra towards was an exploration of root American music as performed by new urban interpreters. There was so much talent out there. I didn't think we could justify a whole album of each of them. I wanted a catch basin. So I went to Jac and said I wanted to do a series of what I called project albums: blues, urban blues, string bands, solo banjo, singer-songwriters.

It gave Elektra something the label needed badly. Which was an association with not just the most commercial aspects of folk music, but the roots of it and the people who were actually the progenitors, the germinal ideas and where they came from. I wanted to start with the blues.

JAC: I said to Paul, "This is the prototype. Make it great. And keep the costs reasonable."

PAUL ROTHCHILD: I brought in the best white urban blues interpreters. Spider John Koerner and Dave Ray, of course; Geoff Muldaur, Dave Van Ronk, Eric von Schmidt, Ian Buchanan, Danny Kalb, Mark Spoelstra, John Sebastian. They were sitting waiting to go on next, barbershop style. I got Bob Dylan to come down and play piano—we wrote him in on the liner notes as Bob Landy.

I did all the tracks in a single twelve-hour

"The Blues Project" EKS-7264

session at Mastertone. It was a brilliant session. Jac was just back from one of his trips. I called him, woke him at two in the morning and said, "I have an album completely recorded. I'll have it edited within a week."

Another "Project" album EKS-7276

JAC: "Wonderful," I said, and went back to sleep.

PAUL ROTHCHILD: No song royalties, and total recording costs were $996.00. Try that today. Within the first three months it sold about thirty-five thousand copies. For a record with no star artist on it to become, in a short period of time, such a street buzz was unheard of at Elektra.

JAC: Or anywhere else.

PAUL ROTHCHILD: So here Jac Holzman is prepared for the new urban blues era.

JAC: On the back of our album we did something we were always happy to do—we plugged an artist on another label: "No survey of the urban blues scene would be complete without calling to your attention the debut album of JOHN HAMMOND on Vanguard Records (VRS-9132). The New York Times hailed John as a 'young giant of the blues.' We at Elektra concur."

JAC: When Judy Collins performed at Carnegie Hall with Theo Bikel, it moved her forward professionally, but in her personal life things were rough. Her marriage was breaking up and she was fighting for custody of her son. She went into therapy. She also had her first experience with psychedelics—in the East Village, with John and Michelle Phillips (still a few years away from being a Mama and a Papa), and it was not an idyllic trip. And then she was diagnosed with tuberculosis.

The best treatment was at the Jewish National Hospital in Denver, Judy's home town. I called Theo, who was hugely influential in the Jewish community, and he helped smooth her admission. Judy had no insurance and I recall giving her advance checks on albums yet to be made.

In addition to first-rate medical care, Judy needed visitors who could help keep her connected with her career, so I went to visit her. It was seventy-five degrees when I left LA and twenty below when I hit Denver wearing only my wool sports jacket. A stockman's convention was in town and it took two hours shuttling between hotels before I could find a room.

The immediate good news was that Judy could leave the hospital for the day to visit with me and her family, including her father Chuck, well known in Denver for his long history on local radio.

Judy had been told she would be finished with her treatment within six months. I never doubted that she would be coming back to Elektra.

Among the gifts I brought her were LPs by Jacques Brel, recorded in concert at the Paris Olympia.

JUDY COLLINS: What attracted me to Brel, one, he was writing his own songs, and two, he graduated from a guitar to working with a symphony.

JAC: Judy was a classical pianist, and she appreciated the progression. The Brel records were what started Judy moving beyond the boundaries of conventional "folk." On her next album, "Judy Collins #3," she began her interpretations of new songs written by her contemporaries.

MARK ABRAMSON: Before that, if you were a folk singer you did folk music. If you happened to write stuff, you would do that. But only your own. It was a tremendous time of transition, and Judy was the first to make the transition to being an interpreter of contemporary folk-oriented songs.

JUDY COLLINS: That's where my real strength was, as an interpretive singer.

JAC: "Judy Collins #3" is where it starts to show for the first time. Judy was back and in better vocal shape than ever. Her interpretation of Dylan's 'Masters of War' was edgy and unsettling, a mother's lament over man-made stupidities that murdered the young.

Everyone involved with the making of that record was rooting for her. The gods smiled. It was a knockout album.

JUDY COLLINS: Bill Harvey did the art work. I did all my covers with him. We sweated, we argued, we had scenes, we tore our hair out—you know, we really cared about how the album was going to look.

JAC: The 12-inch LP was a great format visually. You would do a lot with its size. Compared to the limited 5-inch square of the CD, it had grandeur.

Bill Harvey knew how to present an artist. For Elektra, compelling covers were essential to capture the eye of the browser and convey the drama of the music to people forced to buy on faith, because we had very little radio support, and retailers no longer provided listening booths. Elektra graphics— by intention and hard work—were a key part of our identity.

I always thought that Vanguard's graphics for Joan Baez failed to do her justice. With the album cover for Judy's "#3" we hit a home run. A whole square foot, 144 square inches of four-color—it just leaped out of the rack at you. It was a simple close-up, but with those challenging, intensely piercing blue eyes staring directly into yours. A knockout.

"Judy Collins #3" EKS-7243

JUDY COLLINS: Jac knew how to make records go out into the world. He was very singleminded about business, and so was I. I was working. I was always in the clubs. You did the routine. You go to a club and sing for a while, and you get a phone call from somebody in Boston: "You wanna come to the Golden Vanity?" You say, "Sure," they give you the money and you buy your ticket and you go and sing for a couple of weeks, then off again. That's what all of our lives were on the folk circuit. I was slowly coming on the concert circuit. I did Newport in 1963. It all worked together. I could have been as gifted and interesting and talented and intelligent and musical as you would like, but if I'd chosen to lock myself up and not tour, I don't think it would have worked. But I was a worker. That's how I was raised. And for Jac, that's what made sense from a business point of view. He could tailor things around the planning of the tours. There was always a lot of dialogue with Jac about where I was, what I was doing.

NINA HOLZMAN: Judy depended on Jac a great deal. Jac was and is one of the best career counselors. He's always very, very perceptive. His advice to people, when they're stumped, is usually right on the money. Jac was really guiding her career in a lot of ways, choice of material, choice of tour, musicians playing with her, that kind of thing.

JUDY COLLINS: Slowly the different professional pieces came into play. After the third album, Jac and I talked.

JAC: We decided she should have a serious manager.

JUDY COLLINS: I went with Harold Leventhal.

JAC: Harold was top of the line in the folk world. He was a former song plugger for music publishers, knew the folk music scene from the beginning as friend, adviser and manager for Pete Seeger and Woody Guthrie, the Weavers, then Theo Bikel, and later Woody's son Arlo. Harold had a droll sense of humor that could

Harold Leventhal

come at you from the most unexpected angle and delivered deadpan from a roundish face framed by a fence of sideburns. And he was the Rock of Gibraltar of honesty.

JUDY COLLINS: We did promotion by the seat of our pants. In Cleveland we set up in the college cafeteria at lunch time, while all the students were eating. Then the college audiences were there for me, and once a year I did a big college tour. "Oh, good," Jac would say, "you're in Boston, we'll be sure that the Harvard Co-Op has plenty of records."

JAC: The "#3" album began selling immediately at the Co-Op, which was the record mecca for every college student within a ten-mile range of Cambridge, the best concentration of audience for Judy and for Elektra. The "coop," as it was called, was reordering almost daily. A box lot of twenty-five one day, two boxes the next. That's when we were sure that something important was happening, and we stepped up our promotion. We even managed some limited airplay.

HAROLD LEVENTHAL: You begin to knock off city after city. By the mid-Sixties, Judy was primarily a concert performer.

JUDY COLLINS: All the festivals began to hire me. There was a lot of opportunity for radio, just not in the mass doses that became a habit later. I was singing all over the country. Jac knew that I would be out in such and such an area, and he got the right people to work with.

All my education as far as making, producing, mixing, programming, and then marketing, collaborating in everything, making the whole thing add up to more than the record and the concert separately, was very much tied up with the Elektra people. It's as though I had gone away to college and the college that I landed at was Elektra. That was where I got my higher degree.

Maybe we get into our lives the people that we need. Maybe we attract the people who are going to fundamentally help us to shape who we are. I always think of Jac as one of those people.

That's why the collaboration was so important. That's why it was always so exciting. And so difficult. I don't think you have relationships like that, that just go along smoothly through the daisies. That was a time when a lot of people wanted to prance through the daisies. I was not a daisy prancer. I was raised studying, I was raised cogitating, meditating, searching, and that was where Jac and I came together.

We come from very different points of view, but there is a similarity. We're very particular, both of us. And we have a strong, strong sense of ourselves—we're inner-directed people, who deal with the outer world. We did differ. We could argue about anything—we would argue about what to order at a Chinese restaurant. In the music, Jac always pushed for what he thought was best. But he also respected the people that he chose to work with, or else he wouldn't have been involved with them in the first place. So whatever the argument might have been about, whatever he might have been in disagreement about, his original decision to involve himself with the person would be the thing that carried the day. He let you have your honorable place in your own decision—not to feel pushed around as an artist. Very valuable. I took up the space that was given to me at Elektra, and I was given a great deal of room, and I always felt supported.

MICHAEL OCHS: Judy Collins earned her way up. She just kept getting better and better, album after better album.

JAC: There were other Elektra folk artists whose careers faded away like a morning mist, for a variety of reasons, and none more poignant than Kathy and Carol.

Elektra

"Kathy & Carol" EKS-7289

PAUL ROTHCHILD: Ah, Kathy and Carol. The most beautiful Renaissance ballad record I ever heard. It's just perfect. If you like Joan Baez, here's Joan Baez times two, with gorgeous harmony, singing purist songs like angels. Angels. And they meant it. It was real for them.

JAC: Just read Kathy's liner notes for their first album, all about how she and Carol sing in harmony, how they even laugh in harmony, how in a way they feel sorry for people who sing by themselves. She tells us how their music is intricately interwoven with everything good and healthful—sunshine, fresh air, mushrooms, lichens, mold and rain, love and laughter, birth and death—as a part of a kind, serene world, which none of man's follies can ruffle.

PAUL ROTHCHILD: They were both virgins. I prayed to my God every day, "Please don't let these girls get porked." We went back almost a year later to make the second album, and Kathy had gotten porked. The innocence was gone. It all went away.

Chapter 6

The hired guns of Bob Dylan ...
Basket house cases ... The politics of lyrics ...
How can we tell the singer from the song?

JAC: What had begun with Judy Collins was beginning to spread. Folk singers turned to writing their own songs, and those who didn't looked to those who did.

It was John Sebastian's observation that the overwhelming success of the big commercial folk acts following the Weavers—the Kingston Trio, Peter, Paul and Mary, the Limeliters, the Brothers Four—had used up the traditional material. All their imitators (and there was truly a tidal wave of five-string banjo players, a hundred-year flood) meant too few traditional songs being worn out. The umpteenth time you hear 'Wake Up, Wake Up, Darlin' Cory,' it puts you to sleep. Here was where Paul Rothchild's insight made so much sense: the crucial importance of new songs.

Folk singers writing songs was not new. The early modern creators, Leadbelly and Woody Guthrie, wrote from life. That was their power. Even the folk purists who clung to the belief that any truly "authentic" folk song sprang from unknown traditional sources were caught up by 'Goodnight, Irene' and 'This Land Is Your Land.'

Singer-writers like Richard Fariña and Ian and Sylvia Tyson were adding to the growing body of new music. Then Bob Dylan arrived in New York, barely into his twenties, without the life experiences of a Leadbelly or a Woody Guthrie, upon whom he clearly modeled himself. But he did have—and in depth—the power of his beliefs, a burning itch to set the world right and a prodigious gift for couching his truth in language of power and felicity. Dylan forever ended the argument about who wrote folk songs. Pete Seeger had it right: Folks did. And Dylan nailed it.

JAC: The Village scene was a few square blocks of clubs, bars, red-sauce Italian restaurants that had been family-run for generations, and, of course, the coffee houses.

Izzy Young's Folklore Center, a few steps above MacDougal Street, was a storefront with a rough assemblage of records, sheet music, instruments, strings, capos, and the odd-lot necessities of the urban folk singer, displayed according to Izzy's cockeyed logic. Izzy was one of those unforgettable characters of whom everybody was fond but also wary. Maynard Solomon and I pretty much kept him in business by granting him ridiculously generous

Izzy Young in his Folklore Center

terms of payment. "Izzy," we begged, "if you sell it, please pay for it." The rent would come due and Izzy would be just a bit short of cash, and you know who got paid first. But Izzy knew all of folkdom and the Center served as Musician's Central Station.

Just a few doors south was a heavy hangout bar, the Kettle of Fish. The Kettle was sawdusty, dimly lit, comfortable, and much beloved for its turmoil. It did not have live entertainment, so it was uncontested terrain, and it became a community watering hole. I remember one night when Dave Van Ronk, John Sebastian, Richard Fariña, Tom Rush, Albert Grossman and Bob Dylan all showed up. At the Kettle you could always find out what was or might be happening, and to be on the safe side you checked in, like knocking on wood.

The Kettle was the hub, and from there you fanned out and sampled the action. The Gaslight was directly downstairs, it was just a short walk to Gerde's Folk City, the Village Gate, the Bitter End, and on and on.

PAUL SIEBEL: I lived in a walkup at 139 Thompson Street, just below Houston, right next to the Catholic Church; I remember those church bells going off. I was from Buffalo, which was a closed scene. I thought I'd just better get out of there with my guitar. I headed for New York. For a while I worked in a baby carriage factory in Brooklyn, but I gravitated to the Village. I was making forty-some dollars at the baby carriage factory, and I would save my money and go see a double bill in the Village, which would be, like, Ramblin' Jack Elliott and Mississippi John Hurt, and that would be a magical night.

I would be wearing Levi's, a lot of denim. I couldn't afford good boots. Definitely a wide belt with the Levi's, though. Fancy buckles were a problem because they scratched the back of your guitar. I have a picture of myself wearing a belt with the buckle on the side, around my hips, so it wouldn't scratch. I think Jerry Jeff Walker actually gouged a hole in the back of his guitar because of heavy buckles. Another thing that was worn—I didn't, I'm proud to say, and I won't mention any names—but guys would wear a little leather pouch with a drawstring hanging from the belt, and they would keep finger picks and guitar picks and sometimes dope paraphernalia, a little pipe and some Zig-Zag rolling papers.

I was a folkie, but there was a lot of overlap. When a Dylan album came out, or a Beatles album, the kids would line up outside the record stores. If they heard that it was coming out on Thursday, they'd start on Wednesday night, and there'd be thousands of them. Reporters would be down interviewing them.

Being in the Village was kind of the epicenter of all that. In fact, it would get so crowded on the streets at night that the police would block off Bleecker Street and West 3rd and MacDougal and not let cars drive through.

There was dope on the streets. You could be pretty casual about it. I can remember the cop on the beat, Jack, and the other good-looking one, looked like a movie star, asking us, "Please smoke a little farther down the street"—if the captain went by they'd get in trouble. The stuff was just all over. In everybody's apartment. All the girls used it, just about everyone I knew, they would have the fixings in some wooden bowl sitting on the coffee table, with posters on the wall. In fact the mothers of MacDougal Street were protesting, "Do away with the coffee houses," because it was corrupting youth. Well, it was. You bet. Why else would anyone be there?

When you're in your early twenties, it was nice. It wasn't crazy dangerous like today, between the dope and the violence. Then it was just pretty much kids. It was us, and what we'd snobbishly refer to as the uptown crowd, people slumming or just trying to hang out in the Village, some people who were closet guitar players: "I know a few chords, listen to this," and they'd go into 'They Call The Wind Maria' or something.

BOB GIBSON: The guys who originally got involved in running the coffee houses were not altogether savory. One of these reasons they opened coffee houses was to avoid the police department cabaret permit ban on those who had been convicted of felonies or drug arrests or things like that. They did not have to have a police permit to sell coffee, tea or mulled cider.

PAUL SIEBEL: You could go down the street and hear singing several houses away because there was a rickety kind of amplification. They had guys who would stand outside, usually quite colorful characters, some of them had done some time, and they were called drags, because they dragged the streets to get people to come in. They would usually dress quite spectacularly. They were the first guys I remember wearing extremely long hair, shoulder length or longer, earrings, tattoos, that sort of thing.

These places were called basket houses. The performers weren't paid. You would do a set and do a basket pitch: "This is my last song, and at the end of the song we're gonna pass a basket. I would appreciate anything from a joint to the color green, I like the color green."

I was hired at the Four Winds by Charlie Chin, a Chinese-American guy. I quit my job at the baby carriage factory the next day. I worked at the Four Winds for more than a year, five or six sets a night. Of course you fought for the spot, and to hold it. You didn't want to lose it, but on the other hand you wanted other good players to share the night, to help pull people into the place. I worked through the lean times, which was the winter when it snowed and blowed, and sometimes you and your girlfriend and the other performers would be the only ones in the club, and you'd maybe only get two or

**Paul Siebel "Jack Knife Gypsy"
EKS 74081**

three dollars in the basket, maybe make five dollars a night. But other times we would do very well. Sometimes the girls would make a hundred in a night, and I can remember making sixty and seventy, and my God, that's all we were paying a month for rent.

Richie Havens, I remember seeing him in a place called the Zig-Zag. I also worked with Peter Tork—he played a long-neck banjo and sang kind of silly things, like this thing called 'Elmo,' which was an alligator that went down the drainpipe. He said he had to get out of New York, nothing was happening for him, he was gonna go to California, and he did, and he turned into a Monkee.

MICHAEL OCHS: Everybody was in this ten-block radius. It was dirt cheap. It didn't cost anything. Almost any kid could afford it. Most places there was no cover charge, maybe a two-drink minimum.

The Pete Seegers, the Oscar Brands, the Ed McCurdys would still be playing, and it would usually be a mixture. Ed McCurdy would be the headliner and Patrick Sky would open for him, or Oscar Brand would be the headliner and they'd have Phil Ochs opening for him.

The old Night Owl Café, everybody used to hang out there a lot. It used to be Tim Hardin singing, and behind him would be Freddie Neil playing guitar, Peter Childs second guitar, John Sebastian playing harmonica; he wasn't a singer yet. They would go from a Bo Diddley tune to a Freddie Neil tune, back to some classic rock and roll. I saw Hardin play four hours straight one night and he didn't open his eyes once. Talk about heroin—

PAUL SIEBEL: As far as shooting heroin, no, not me, but it was around us, we had to wade through it, and we knew junkies.

ARTHUR GORSON: Freddie Neil was a junkie, unfortunately, but still those Freddie Neil records were incredible.

JOHN SEBASTIAN: Fred was an interesting cross. He went around the South with his father, who was stuffing jukeboxes. I think Fred was essentially a pop songwriter. Remember, he had Number 1 songs.

PAUL ROTHCHILD: He was on Elektra. For my sins I had to produce him. He was a brilliant songwriter and a total scumbag. The forerunner of the unreliable performer, the original rock flake. We'd book recording sessions and he'd show up or not show up. I mean, here's a guy who wrote 'Candy Man,' which Roy Orbison had a hit with, and the day he finished writing it he went to the Brill Building and sold it to about twenty different publishers for fifty bucks each. This is not a nice man. Here's a guy who would go to Izzy Young and say, "Izzy, I've got a gig tonight

Fred Neil "Bleecker & MacDougal"
EKS-7293

and I don't have a guitar." Izzy would say, "Freddie, you owe me for about twenty guitars, but I love you, here's another twelve-string." And Freddie would go to the club fucked up, he was always fucked up—I've watched this on about ten occasions—couldn't get the guitar in tune, pick it up and smash it to smithereens on the stage. A guitar he didn't own.

JAC: Elektra signed many singer-songwriters, some of whom were kinder and gentler, others more strenuous and political. It was the nature of the times. The world was in the Village and the Village was the world.

ARTHUR GORSON: It had to do with social protest, Malcolm X, civil rights, and then the scene around MacDougal Street and the people that come and go.

I had been working in the civil rights movement in the South as a field organizer, and then with striking coal miners in Hazard, Kentucky. It was romantic, Robin Hood-like. There was a lot of turmoil, violence. We ended up raising money to support the movement by doing concerts, mainly in Greenwich Village, and then we were bringing folk singers down to Hazard—Tom Paxton, Phil Ochs, Bob Dylan, Judy Collins. And people started writing songs about all that.

Tom, Phil, and Judy were all on Elektra. So Elektra had a good share of the energy of the time. It was one of the leading companies that captured that moment in New York that generated fabulous singer-songwriters.

In a way these newer artists were folk singers by default now. I mean, there was the traditional Woody Guthrie, but a lot of them wanted to be Buddy Holly. Phil Ochs's favorite songwriter was Merle Haggard. And there was something in the air that was common among all these people. The singer-songwriter movement was a radical break, both in substance and philosophically, just like rock and roll was a radical break with soft music of the Forties and Fifties. It was also a radical break in terms of how the artists viewed themselves—as the source of everything, no longer the slaves of the record company and the publishers and all the rest. Certainly the idea of a songwriter having his own publishing company was very radical, it wasn't something that had really happened before. They all wanted to control everything, down to what the album cover looked like. Everyone thought of themselves as geniuses, and as very broadly talented. They read the newspaper, they were involved with talking to politicians. It was a very lively time. And they were very much a part of that time. So it was a revolution in more than one way. The artists desired to control their destiny.

Which made traditional record company dealings more difficult. And now here is Elektra, which wasn't a traditional record company, which was also finding its way. Jac, musically and philosophically, was a risk-taker. He was facing forward. Elektra was the label of choice to be on; in terms of energy and spirit, it was the place to be.

JAC: We had quite a singer-songwriter stable: Phil Ochs, Tom Paxton, David Blue, Fred Neil, Mark Spoelstra, Hamilton Camp.

The "Ramblin' Boy" LP, EKS-7277

JOHN SEBASTIAN: Tom Paxton was a strong writer from the get-go, who was drawing on an older tradition. In other words, he really came more from the Woody Guthrie, Pete Seeger tradition than someone like Fred Neil.

OSCAR BRAND: Tom, in the creative world, is one of the best. One of the sharpest ears. He wrote beautiful songs. And a really charismatic figure. You'd look at him and say, "That's not charisma," but you'd feel it. You'd feel the kind of brightness, sharpness, that he had right from the beginning.

ED McCURDY: Ha. I used to think that if Paxton had three hands, one would be over his ears. I used to refer to him as the young Narcissus. He came to me once and asked me what I thought of his singing, really. And I said, "For a young man who considers himself a cocksman, you sing with less balls than anyone I know." And that shocked him. But he's probably the best writer-singer, not singer, but certainly the best writer-singer in the business. I put his creative capacity over almost all of them. Because he's continuous, he does it all the time.

JAC: Tom Rush was not yet into writing. Like Judy Collins, he was a fine interpretive singer with superb taste, an ear for great new songs, a warm engaging voice, and a killer guitar.

ARTHUR GORSON: Tom's album "The Circle Game" represented a certain moment in history, because we had a scene of singers and songwriters. There were songs everywhere and everyone trading songs, and Tom was able to draw from that material. So the "Circle Game" album has the first Joni Mitchell songs recorded, the first Jackson Browne songs recorded, and James Taylor. Brand-new material, never heard, by songwriters that weren't really known, beautiful songs.

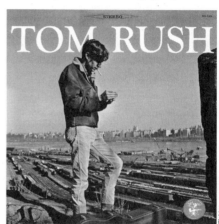

"Tom Rush" EKS-7288

JAC: You always want to know how your artists are going down with live audiences, and what you could be doing to get them more exposure. I was forever in the clubs, checking the action, looking for inspiration. One night when Tom Rush was playing the Bitter End, the plumbing in the men's room failed and we had to use the women's john. On my visit to the stall I came across this graffiti: "Tom Rush is an easy lay." And right below this fascinating revelation, in a different hand, some disappointed groupie (or, who knows, maybe a defender of Tom's virtue) had written "Oh, no he's not."

JAC: One of the most promising, puzzling and troubled of Elektra's singer-songwriters was Phil Ochs. Phil was a committed folkie and became an extremely effective political voice. His songs were bold and to the point.

STEVE HARRIS: He went for the jugular.

LARRY HARRIS: Tom Paxton was like a velvet blanket, like a tropical balmy breeze. He could make you think about issues without standing up and coming to attention. Phil made you stand up and come to attention.

MICHAEL OCHS: Phil was a great organizer. He was the first person to try to organize all the musicians, try to organize strikes to get them paid an actual wage, instead of just passing the baskets.

ARTHUR GORSON: I managed Phil.

MICHAEL OCHS: Arthur was heavily involved in the civil rights thing. He got really badly beaten up, almost got killed a couple of times. And Phil really respected Arthur because he had the courage to do that.

ARTHUR GORSON: Phil and I formed a publishing company called Barricade Music. "A Revolution In Songwriting" was our campaign. We were ambitious, we were political, but we weren't greedy. It wasn't about money yet, it was all about doing anything to reach a new audience.

And it was all about the competition between our office, meaning the Ochs office, and the Dylan office.

PAUL WILLIAMS: Ochs was in a league by himself. With Tom Paxton, he was the most important topical songwriter. After Dylan, I mean. Everything was after Dylan.

GEORGE PICKOW: I have some film that I shot at a party at Alan Lomax's house. Clarence Ashley is in it. Doc Watson. The New Lost City Ramblers. Mike Seeger. John Cohen. Ramblin' Jack Elliott and Peter La Farge and Muddy Waters. Roscoe Holcomb. Maria Muldaur—Maria D'Amato at the time, you see her dancing. And Bob Dylan was sitting there getting high on marijuana through the whole evening, but he had just signed with Albert Grossman, and Grossman told him, "Don't let anybody record you or take your picture at all unless they talk to me," so he's not on film.

ARTHUR GORSON: In the Village you had an art scene, a rare art scene. Dylan and Ochs and David Blue and Eric Andersen and a whole bunch of others were writing songs about similar topics. They weren't imitating each other, they were coming from a similar inspiration, a similar cultural moment, it was blowing in the wind. It was like Paris at the turn of the century, and yet it wasn't. In Paris there were a lot of equals. The Village was a scene where there were a lot of equals and one giant. Everyone was braving a new path, but Dylan and his output stunned the rest of the world.

Dylan at Newport 1963

JOHN SEBASTIAN: Suddenly here was this great new songwriter, and it was like everyone else was all ready made to receive his work and get it out there. Would I credit Dylan with the hybridization of folk song and rock and roll? No. It wasn't, like, if you didn't get it from him and then go on, you didn't receive the Holy Cross or anything. But this is not to minimize his importance to songwriters as a songwriter. In this, he loomed absolutely the largest. The strength and breadth of his writing during that period, it just eclipses everybody.

ARTHUR GORSON: I don't think Dylan stole other people's ideas from around the table. He stole Woody Guthrie, he stole traditional ballads—

JAC:—Listen to Harry Smith's "Anthology of American Folk Song" on Folkways, and then to the collected works of Dylan—

ARTHUR GORSON:—But the one complaint that Phil Ochs and other people never voiced was, "Dylan just stole my song." What Dylan was writing about was experiential things about people on the street. I mean, "You've got a lot of nerve to say you're my friend," all those lines, and everyone would sit around and think they knew everybody in the song, a song that they might be thinking about writing, and they would say, "Damn, he wrote it before me."

We would be at the Kettle, and David Blue and Eric Andersen would be there, and the Gorson office would be there, me and Phil Ochs and Tom Rush, and in comes Albert Grossman and Bob Dylan, and this is like the killers coming in, with Bobby Neuwirth, who was the hired gun of Albert Grossman and the cutting edge of Dylan, like Dylan's hired killer with words. Neuwirth was a singer-songwriter, but not developed at that point. He was so sharp and so recklessly brilliant, and also so frustrated. So there they would be, and everybody would go at each other. They called it rapping. It was a very clever scene. Mainly sitting around being really tough on each other, tearing each other's songs apart: "Man, you can't use that word, I use that word"—that type of thing. And everyone would go away and the next day come back with new songs, and be criticized and torn apart again.

BOB NEUWIRTH: It was pretty much dog eat dog, heavy fire.

PAUL NELSON: Phil told me this story. He had spent weeks writing 'Changes,' which was sort of away from his usual topical themes, and he was pretty proud of this song. Dylan dropped over to his apartment and Phil wanted to play it for him, and Dylan said, "Oh yeah, here's something I just knocked out in ten minutes, tell me what you think." And it was 'Like A Rolling Stone.' Phil worked on his song for two months, and this guy bashes out 'Like A Rolling Stone' in ten minutes on the way over to your house. That was the position they were all in.

PAUL SIEBEL: Yes, Dylan was the center, and everyone watched and followed him. I was at the Gaslight one night to see Judy Henske when Dylan walked in. The Gaslight had a strange seating arrangement, with benches. I was sitting facing the stage, and one of the dishwashers who was into the folk scene was sitting facing me, facing the back, and we were sitting there talking quietly, and all of a sudden he said, "He's here." His words: "He's here." Dylan came in with Al Grossman and sat in one of the booths, and I remember Judy Henske asking him to come up on stage and sing with her, and he wouldn't. And a few minutes later she got off, and Dylan was there a while, and within twenty or thirty minutes that little club was just stuffed, packed, jammed with people. All the Who's Who of the folk scene. And Dylan went up on stage and sang two songs that he hadn't recorded yet, 'It's

Alright, Ma (I'm Only Bleeding)' and 'Tambourine Man.' None of us had ever heard those songs before, and he was like twenty feet in front of me. The most electrifying moment, I think, ever. And after he got through he just got up and everyone left . . .

MICHAEL OCHS: Phil always wanted to be as good as Dylan, but I don't think he ever believed he could be better, because Dylan was the Shakespeare of the Sixties, and Phil was always in Dylan's shadow.

BOB NEUWIRTH: And Dylan had enormous drive and energy and focus. I mean, he didn't get there by accident. He was career-oriented.

JONATHAN TAPLIN: Phil definitely had a Dylan phobia. And Dylan, and some of the people who were around Dylan, who were very tough, like Bobby Neuwirth, would put Phil down. They were very competitive.

JAC: It didn't do to criticize Dylan's songs to his face. Phil said 'Can You Please Crawl Out Your Window' wasn't going to be a hit, which it turned out not to be.

**Phil Ochs "I Ain't Marchin' Anymore"
EKS-7287**

But with Dylan, truth in criticism was no defense. When Phil gave his opinion, he was riding in Dylan's limo, and right then and there Bob ordered him out onto the streets of Manhattan. That's a diagnostic story in more than one way. It could have been a verse in a Dylan song—or in a song by somebody else about Dylan. Or it could have been a chapter lead in a biography of Phil.

ARTHUR GORSON: Phil was an artist who wanted to be a star, and he had a tremendous degree of ego, and felt that he had a message. He was insanely driven.

JAC: He was very confused about what he wanted to do, who he wanted to be, and, most poignantly, who he really was.

OSCAR BRAND: The one thing he wanted was to be a national hit. But this he couldn't be, because his songs themselves preempted a small area and therefore precluded a large audience.

JAC: Every time Phil came to the office, he would inquire about his sales figures, as if they could give him validation.

STEVE HARRIS: The man did sell out Carnegie Hall.

ARTHUR GORSON: Phil would sing anywhere. He would go and play even if it cost us money. He would put every penny into getting to another town or another country. Then he would lose his tickets before he'd get to the airport and then get to the airport and lose his contact lenses, and then lose the piece of paper which told him what hotel to go to.

MICHAEL OCHS: He was very ingenuous. And he treated his fans that way, too. I mean, we'd be racing to catch a plane and somebody would stop him to ask a question and he'd stop and start talking to them. And it wasn't star to fan; if somebody was saying something that was interesting to him, he would stop and discuss it. He always came off as a guy you'd really like.

He couldn't stand his own company, couldn't stand solitude. He always had to be around people. He would come back from a grueling six-month tour, drop his bags off at the house, run out, call Judy Henske, go visit Judy in Pasadena, then go visit someone in Hollywood. He just would never stop.

ED McCURDY: Ochs was a horrible singer, but with great charm, a very honest straightforward approach. He was a very nice man until he got hung up. I had a heart attack in Bryn Mawr and he happened to be in the neighborhood, so he came and finished the date for me, came out and visited me. We became quite friendly. Then he got into the booze and became very nasty.

JAC: We kept him on Elektra for three of the six albums we could contractually claim, and then he asked to be released because he felt we weren't doing enough for him. In a way that was true, because by then—and this is getting ahead of the story by several years—the whole music scene was shifting away from what Phil did, or at least what he did best, which was the topical political song. With fewer people listening, his personal devils took over.

MICHAEL OCHS: He was your typical person who can't face their own problems, so wants to live for the problems of others. I think his greatest wish would have been to have been shot on stage. To become a martyr for the cause. He was very depressed. There was a family history of manic depression, and basically, I think, Phil egged on the manic-depression thing, because he thought you have to suffer to create—the old artistic thing. I think he egged it on worse than it had to be, frankly.

TOM PAXTON: Phil was one of the most tortured people I have known personally. I think there was real disease there. For one thing, alcoholism, in a rampant stage. And clinical depression.

The last time I saw Phil, he was sitting on the stoop outside the Bitter End, and I had just come to work, and he called my name and we talked for a minute. He had some portable radio that he had

Phil Ochs leans on the Establishment

obviously just bought and clearly would lose before the night was over. He said, "Let's go get a drink." I said, "Great, let me go put my guitar away." But I never came back out, because he was in terrible shape, and I just didn't want to be involved in what the rest of that evening was going to be about. Besides, I had to work.

OSCAR BRAND: I saw Phil the night before he died. He'd been up and down, but he said, "I'm really in the groove, I'm working like a dog, writing hundreds of new songs, I'm going back to California." And the next day he hanged himself.

MICHAEL OCHS: The last four months, I talked to him at least once a week, and he kept saying, the same question over and over again, "Will the songs survive, Michael? Will my songs survive?" And I would say, "Of course they will, Phil."

ARTHUR GORSON: For some years there was an annual Ochs tribute in New York. It was interesting to see all the young folk singers singing Phil Ochs songs. And Sean Penn wanted to play Phil in a movie.

Chapter 7

On a paper tablecloth a baroque label is born ...
Johann Sebastian, meet the Beatles ...
Ode to an Ondes-Martinot

JAC: Those singer-songwriter years were filled with change and challenge, both political and personal, and Elektra was in the thick of the movement. But I could feel the need for something more, to make a bold move unrelated to what the label had been doing, and I had absolutely no idea of what that might be. Then, without notice or ceremony, it hit me.

No experience in life goes wasted. I recalled when I was an indifferent college student at St. John's. Music was a key element of the Great Books program, but it went beyond the "harmony of the spheres" that permeated our celestial mechanics and math studies. Music would pour out of the windows of the dorms, which were really very large, post-colonial houses. And no junk. Walking across campus, you would hear folk music, music for ancient instruments, Haydn, Vivaldi, Beethoven's "Grosse Fuge," Johann Sebastian Bach and all his progeny, and a glorious helping of Mozart, the patron saint of St. John's music junkies.

There was only one record store in Annapolis, Albright's, on Maryland Avenue. It had a few cramped listening booths, and I would go down and graze among the classical records, especially the baroque offerings, which were stocked only because St. Johnnies were serious music people.

The Westminster label recorded with care and offered a broad range of music that fit my taste. In the early days of LP's, Westminster albums cost $5.95 each. I wanted two, but I could only afford one, and I would drive myself nuts choosing. Buying only one album was like trying to satisfy your craving with one potato chip.

Fast forward fifteen years. All that time I had been keeping detailed notes on classical records issued in Europe, subscribing to a large number of overseas record magazines, clipping reviews of whatever looked interesting and pasting them onto loose-leaf pages by label and genre of music. I had three notebooks full of information and no idea what I was going to do with it.

By late 1963 we were set up in our new offices adjacent to Rockefeller Center. Paul Rothchild was on board. Koerner, Ray & Glover were becoming known. The singer-songwriters were an established genre. And now . . . what? My mind was searching for something to get interested in.

Nina and I were at a restaurant on 57th Street for dinner with Harry Lew, our New York distributor, and his wife, and they were late. Perhaps because Carnegie Hall was right across the street, I was struck by my recollection of having to choose between two records I wanted so badly when I was a student. In 1963 classical records were $4.98, and quality paperback books, trade paperbacks, were $2.50. "Wouldn't it be neat," I mused, "to have a line of fine records at the same price as trade paperbacks?"

What kind of music? Unusual, baroque-oriented, with a very focused sense of audience—meaning essentially me as I was in 1948-1950. In sum, adventurous repertoire for music lovers with more taste than money.

Package the line intelligently. Fashion liner notes that would not only discuss the music, but also—and this was important to me—the social context, because music, sports, reading, and I assume sex, were the prime entertainments of that day. And I knew Bill Harvey could come up with some clever cover ideas that would showcase the music, with all fustiness brushed away.

The whole idea came to me so fully realized that I couldn't find the words to express it for a minute or two. I diagrammed the basic shape of it and wrote out the critical details on the paper tablecloth.

Harry Lew finally arrived. He heard me out, and thought I was crazy to try to compete in classical music with the majors and the knowledgeable established independents like Vanguard.

That was not about to slow me down. Next day I boarded a jet to Europe, my carefully assembled classical notebooks in my carry-on—this was the raw material of the idea and I wasn't taking chances with lost baggage.

Paris and London were my first stops. I cold-called everyone, introduced myself and booked appointments. Being president and owner of Elektra was enough to get me in the door to make my pitch. I wanted records the European labels never thought would or could be released in America, and here is a guy offering a $500 advance per album plus a royalty. I brought very simple licensing agreements and a raft of blank checks which were clearly visible and aching to be filled in.

I creamed seven quite nice albums from these sources, and spent many hours in further research at London's Gramophone Shop, which stocked everything worthwhile in classical recordings from Europe. I returned to New York with the certainty that if we could bring the whole concept together I could easily acquire many more albums, and I had already targeted the most likely sources of repertoire.

We gave the project a code name, Nonesuch, so that if we were ever asked we could truthfully say there was no such project—what in government is called "plausible deniability."

I had asked Bill Harvey to mock up a few covers, and I contacted Ed Canby to write the liner notes. Bill thought the best approach to create an identity was original artwork in a well designed frame, with the label's logo prominently on top, for instant recognition as people flipped through the record racks.

Once we had the first releases looking good, and about sixty days from initial launch, I decided to tie up the richest lode of material available from a single source, Club Français du Livre et de la Disque in Paris, which had a fine music division (also a major book club reprinting European classical literature in complete sets, handsomely bound, much beloved by the French). My reasoning was twofold. If the idea caught on, I would have to move fast to build a catalog, because I didn't have one of my own to draw from as did Vanguard, Vox, and the majors. Anxious to preempt anyone else from accessing the riches of Le Club, I telexed the owner-president, M. L'Hôpital, and followed up with a visit.

BILL HARVEY: Jac learned his French from Berlitz. A forced education—a guy would come in every day, I think for a couple of months, and Jac had the door closed, and he learned French, you know. Like anything else Jac did, if he put his mind to it, he was going to do it.

JAC: Le Club did business from a formidable stone mansion on a prestigious street in central Paris. Outside M. L'Hôpital's office door were two lights, one red, one green, so his secretary would know when she could enter. The door was tufted brown leather, and when it was opened there was an identical door reset about eighteen inches, forming a leather airlock.

The office was in elegant Empire style, and behind a gold leaf desk was M. L'Hôpital, a cultured, quite handsome gentleman in a blue pinstripe suit, the most perfectly ironed shirt with a collar to envy and an immaculately knotted tie. He spoke excellent English, but had never heard of Elektra. I showed him preview samples of the first Nonesuch releases, and told him I was willing to commit immediately to twenty albums, and that I wanted three years exclusivity to comb his list. And I just happened to have a check with me for $10,000 for a contract to be negotiated. My hunch about M. L'Hôpital was that he could make the deal and that his handshake would seal it. He gave his commitment to twenty masters which would be air-shipped to me as soon as they could be duplicated, and I left with him a sample agreement that Irwin Russell had prepared. Then we went out and had a civilized French lunch of several courses and wine. It's a good thing we got the business done first.

IRWIN RUSSELL: The way Jac went about it was really clever. We drafted up a very simple form, and he would go wandering around Europe picking up this quartet and that master.

JAC: I was doing this all very quietly, but still there were rumors around the office about some new record label. I would deny them, saying there was no such thing.

One evening as I was driving Judy Collins home, she asked me what was going on and I gave her the basic outline of the project. She asked what I was going to name it. I was undecided between "Caravelle," a lovely-sounding word meaning a light, agile ship, and our code name, "Nonesuch." Without hesitation, Judy said, "Oh, call it Nonesuch, it has such a positive ring to it."

BILL HARVEY: When I started on the covers, I used to read the liner notes very intensely and absorb as much as I could before I did anything. The first two or three, I was feeling my way. Then suddenly I got this idea.  Jac is pitching to the college audience, trying to get to young people who like this music but can't afford the full-price records. So I said, "Why don't I bring some humor, some fun to this stuff?" And I went to a sort of stylized drawing that I used when I was doing promotional illustration for Fairchild Publications. It's common in album artwork now, but you never saw it then. I did the first couple, and then I started to hire guys that I'd used when I worked at Fairchild. It gave them an opportunity to work in full color, and with a sense of humor. My main idea was to get

Bill Harvey's Nonesuch logo

a multi-range of styles, in the sense of the illustrations, but I wanted to keep one format that would stamp Nonesuch as Nonesuch. And it really worked.

JOSHUA RIFKIN: Edward Sorel is an illustrator I first came across through Nonesuch; he did a lot of the earliest covers. The point to be made is that Jac was maybe one of the first post-modernists, liberating classical music from solemnity.

JAC: The covers became so commented upon that seven years and many hundreds of albums into the label, we mounted a traveling art show of the originals and toured it to colleges around the country, to great enthusiasm.

SUZANNE HELMS: Those Nonesuch covers, the original art, are collectors' items now, very valuable.

JAC: On February 14, 1964, we formally launched Nonesuch at our new Sperry-Rand offices, more or less combining an office warming with a defined musical purpose. Originally we had planned to have a big party between Thanksgiving and Christmas of 1963, but JFK was assassinated and I lost all heart for celebration just then.

We released the first ten records with a simple ad campaign in the monthly Schwann catalog and High Fidelity magazine. The copy read, "Quality Recordings [not "Records"] At The Price Of A Quality Paperback." The ads were full-page, in my most convincing prose, describing what the label meant to us and the care and consideration that would be lavished on each release, despite the low price. For emphasis and specificity there was an adjoining one-third-page column listing the initial releases. I thought my copy was great. It spoke to everything I felt when I was too impoverished to buy all the music I craved as a student.

So much energy had gone into the creation of Nonesuch that I was astounded when there was absolutely no discernible public reaction. For six whole weeks.

MEL POSNER: I was having a tough time introducing Nonesuch.

JAC: Mel couldn't convince our distributors that this was a serious, ongoing effort.

MEL POSNER: That $2.50 price—everybody in the industry said, "Who needs it? Who wants to be involved in another bastard price?" In Washington, DC, the only way I could sell this one account, Discount Record Center, was to buy the rack. I said, "OK, I'm buying this space. Now let me put my Nonesuch records in on consignment. If they don't sell, I'll take them out." That was OK with Jac.

JAC: Placing Nonesuch records with retailers on consignment was a major concession because, except for singles, when records were shipped in 1964 they were sold with only a modest exchange privilege allowed the distributor.

At the beginning of the sixth week after release, the re-orders began, first a trickle, then a downpour. Thousands of albums by composers no one, except musicologists, had ever heard of, so obscure that they weren't even listed in the Schwann catalog. The Decca plants, which we had contracted to press Nonesuch, could not fulfill orders fast enough.

I quickly realized that I had better set up a very aggressive release schedule before everybody figured out what I had tumbled onto. Vanguard, especially, had a huge library, and they could kill us. By April 1966 we were pouring them out at the rate of about ten a month, especially milking the riches of the Club Français du Disque catalog.

Seymour Solomon of Vanguard came by the house one evening for drinks before dinner. He looked sagely through the early titles and commented knowingly about the origin of many of the records. He couldn't believe that anyone would try such a crazy stunt, especially a folkie like me. He tried to convince me (and himself) that I was in over my head. I allowed that he might be right, but why not indulge me and see what happens.

I was actually much better prepared than he knew, and I had Josh Rifkin squirreled away in the back room giving me guidance when I was unsure of myself. Josh was the Even Dozen's kazoo and piano player, but he was also a full-on musicologist who could tell you in what library and on what shelf in Europe you might find a particular composer's "lost" work.

JOSHUA RIFKIN: Many of my interests, virtually all, in fact, coincided with Jac's. My generation and the generation immediately before, which was Jac's, were the first to really grow up musically through recordings. When I was a kid, a teenager, records were the medium through which in many ways we thought about music, which gave them a special cachet, and which also meant that already well before I ever came to Elektra, I was very keen somehow to be involved in the record world. That was the coinage, in the sense of status, of achievement.

I was interested in out-of-the-way repertoire, particularly Baroque and Renaissance music and so forth, so I started telling Jac about labels and records that might interest him. Certain records that were submitted to him for licensing, Jac gave me to take home and check out. I started doing that informally, and pretty quickly I said to Jac—I was kind of brash in those days—that the information, the titles, the artist listings, were really not up to snuff, that they were taking too many things from the French original releases, which were very sloppy. I would get these

things from France, "The Greatest Hits Of The Renaissance," with everything completely misidentified; you didn't know what the hell it was.

JAC: I was impressed. This was an important talent of Josh's. Since he was of an age with our college audience, why not have one of their own write the liner notes?

JOSHUA RIFKIN: I can remember the first set I brought in to Jac. He copy-edited them, and did a very skillful job. He's terrific with words, and not only that, he knew the mechanics of seeing things through the press, which I hadn't yet learned. The guy was an all-around pro.

Before long I was overseeing most of the printed copy on Nonesuch. I edited people's notes, I wrote notes, I did the research on the titling, I helped work out details of the covers. Where I learned my musicology, my music history, and where I learned to write well, was all at Nonesuch—the discipline of writing something about music that is understandable to people and yet does say something, and fitting this all into a ten-by-eight inch square area: the greatest possible training.

So there I was, at twenty, twenty-one, helping to run a record company. Doing stuff like this, being involved in production and having been an artist, meant that you'd crossed the threshold between "us" and "them." You were now what you had always considered "them," and now you were part of a new "us."

JAC: Nonesuch turned out to be a bulletproof concept. For $500 I was able to audition the record first, and if I didn't like it, it went unreleased and the advance was applied to the next album. The all-in cost of production was low. We were paying only 11 cents in royalties, 25 cents for pressings. That totaled 36 cents. Add another 20 cents for the elaborate covers and the full cost was somewhere between 56 and 60 cents per unit. And there were no copyright royalties on baroque music. We were getting $1.10 per unit, so our profit margins, percentage-wise, were close to normal.

I had the contracts worked out to pay royalties on a $2.25 list price rather than on $2.50, because I would be giving dealers and distributors an additional ten percent discount to carry the line. This was known as a "functional" discount, origi-

nally intended to provide extra margin to rack jobbers, an intermediate layer of distribution supplying large drug chains and discount stores. Our regular dealers, who in the normal run of things were shut out from the "functional," thought the extra margin was great incentive. They were getting something for nothing, and they responded by displaying the line prominently. It was all rather symmetrical and graceful, and in the quantities they were selling, hugely profitable.

By the early winter of 1965, reports began coming back from the field that Nonesuch was a winner, but few in the classical record world put much credence in those reports—at first. The numbers proved real, and inevitably others began releasing their own similarly priced classical lines. Vox launched Turnabout; their ads screamed, "Turnabout Is Fair Play." Vanguard countered with their Everyman series. But by that time it was too late to bump us. Nonesuch was there to stay.

MAYNARD SOLOMON: Every major classical label had to scramble to catch up.

"Brandenburg Concertos" gatefold HB-73006

JAC: The New York Times ran a very complimentary feature on Seymour Solomon of Vanguard that heralded him as "The Baron of Baroque." I dropped Seymour a note of congratulations, signing it "Jac Holzman, Pretender to the Throne," and he got a big chuckle out of that. We rooted for each other, if with some wariness. Deep down, I think Maynard always believed I was more interested in the money than I was in baroque music.

MAYNARD SOLOMON: I was afraid of upsetting the balance between budget lines and high-priced LPs. Jac said, "I couldn't care less, as long as I make money on it." I was impressed with his boldness. Nonesuch was great packaging. Bill Harvey was a brilliant artistic director and thus a brilliant packager. And that's what made Nonesuch the forerunner of all budget labels. I was impressed by the shrewd moneymaking clever effort, but I also thought of the overall long-term welfare of the record business.

KEITH HOLZMAN: Jac had been after me to come and work at Elektra. I joined the company after I left the army. They were just getting ready to ship the second Nonesuch release, five records. The company was starting to do music that really intrigued me.

JAC: It was excellent timing, to have Keith come on board when he did. Nonesuch was perfectly suited to his training and his musical instincts. It was something solid for him to sink his teeth into.

KEITH HOLZMAN: We went on shipping five to ten albums a month.

JACLYN EASTON: I remember a lot of Nonesuch music in the house.

KEITH HOLZMAN: Nonesuch was hugely profitable. It was the tail wagging the Elektra dog.

MEL POSNER: At one point Nonesuch was fifty-five percent of our business.

JAC: In Nonesuch's first year we issued sixty records, selling in excess of a million units, and earned about $550,000 net, doubling our profitability. It's one of those rare instances in the record business where success in the classical music area was so enormous that it could fund popular music.

JAC: By the early fall of 1965 the Beatles songbook had grown so large that it dominated Top 40 radio and had spilled over into the MOR (middle of the road) format for easy listening. It was in the elevators, it was everywhere. From this sprang an idea.

I called Mark Abramson and Steve Harris together and asked them about doing Beatles songs that would lend themselves to baroque interpretation, as a serious musical exploration, but packaged with humor and an eye toward the Christmas season.

The gating issues were who would do the arrangements, and could I get permission from the Beatles. Their publisher, Dick James, had a platoon of lawyers protecting the sanctity of the copyrights. Early on, Brian Epstein, the Beatles manager, had given Dick the publishing which he guarded like the golden goose it was. I didn't want to start an album and have problems. Better to find out immediately.

"Baroque Beatles Book" EKS-7306

I asked Josh Rifkin to give things a try before I took off for London. My thought was for Josh to write a trio sonata arrangement of 'Ticket to Ride' for us to evaluate. Josh did a wonderfully inventive job and I headed for London leaving Josh and Mark to draw up a list of other tunes and ways of adapting them.

Dick James was a music publishing legend—tall, thickly set, up from the streets, with an accent that George Bernard Shaw and Lerner & Loewe must have meant with the line from "My Fair Lady" that an Englishman's speech absolutely classifies him. Dick was midway between Cockney and Mayfair.

Dick was heading over to the studio to see the boys and I tagged along in his Silver Cloud Rolls. Dick went in first while I waited. In a few moments he came and got me, and I made my very simple pitch. John Lennon's first comment was, "You did Koerner, Ray & Glover." I nodded a proud "Yes." "Well, that's alright then. Anyone who records Koerner, Ray & Glover is OK with me." The others thought it was a cute idea, and that was it, plus an autographed picture: "For Adam from The Beatles." He adored it. And Paul McCartney took me over and introduced me to his bespoke boot maker.

The album was completed in good time for the holiday season and Steve Harris managed to get WMCA, the crucial Top 40 station in New York, to feature it on Cousin Brucie's morning show.

STEVE HARRIS: They played it twenty-eight times in a row! Unheard of! All that radio play for an Elektra album—also unheard of! I remember Jac striding up and down, beaming, saying, "Fuck 'em, we'll beat 'em at their own game."

JAC: Flushed with success, we sponsored a Baroque Beatles Book concert at Lincoln Center. And nobody came. It was one of those nights where there are more on stage than in the audience. But the album sold very well.

JAC: My paternal grandfather Harry Holzman, who was born in Liverpool on his family's way to America from Lithuania, was a good-natured charmer. His business interests included bits and pieces of hotels, pawn shops fronted by his relatives, and the buying and selling of precious metals. He died when I was six, but he imprinted on my young mind something which at the time had no meaning for me, but over the years proved to be one of the verities. Grandfather Harry hoisted me onto

Three generations.
Harry (Jac's grandfather) top,
Dr. Jacob (Jac's father) center,
Jac at five years old

his knee and told of calling on potential customers without an appointment, a normal practice in days when not everyone had a telephone. When asked who was calling he would reply, "Tell Mr. So-and-So that CASH is calling." And then he pressed a silver dollar into my hand. Point taken, lesson learned: Get liquid and stay liquid.

Elektra, together with Nonesuch, had grown to a critical mass where the company's financial needs could be met from current cash flow without ever requiring interim loans from banks. My personal concerns about money were now past. I loved the comfort of knowing I could "write the check."

Late in 1964, in a rare vagrant moment with not much to do and nothing on my mind, I strolled Park Avenue and was drawn to a Mercedes showroom. The window displayed an immaculately crafted four-door sedan, which appealed to my aesthetic sense. In California my car had been a crummy Ford Falcon that kept dropping parts along the freeway. Without a moment's thought I signed up for a new Mercedes four-door sedan, burgundy with tan leather interior, very smart-looking, $4500. Two months later it arrived and I hired a driver.

JAC: Nonesuch was bringing in over half a million dollars per year in retained profit, and that money was recycled into our expansion program. We could staff up a bit. Nonesuch had been me, working with Josh Rifkin and Ed Canby as primary consultants, but I needed a knowledgeable assistant who could handle the routine daily matters with precision and class. I found her in Teresa Sterne, who had worked with Seymour Solomon at Vanguard.

I would never have raided Vanguard, but Tracey had already quit and spent a summer in Italy. I was primarily looking for someone to assist on Nonesuch in the way she had been assisting at Vanguard, but I soon found that I could give her substantial autonomy. Tracey was immensely savvy, had great sensitivity to the music, and was tight with music publications, reviewers, university music departments and the like. She would bring a formidable range of contacts to bear on what we were doing.

TERESA STERNE: Jac was very busy, involved with his Elektra doings and making original records, and he immediately left a lot to me. I said, "I'll be very honest, I haven't run a label before. I've been around it, I've helped to do it, but I haven't taken full responsibility." He said, "Well, it's really on wheels, the thing is going. You'll see for yourself what needs to be done."

JAC: And if there were any snags, we would work our way through them together.

TERESA STERNE: Josh Rifkin was coming in a couple of times a week, and this had been going on for several months when I came to work. I remember Bill Harvey telling me, "Watch out, Josh is a pretty arrogant kid. He really almost knows too much. If you don't get along with him, or he doesn't serve your needs, just change it. It's up to you. You have to be the boss here." Of course, I very quickly found that Josh was invaluable, and it was wonderful. He had the musicological scholarly knowledge which I didn't have. I mean, I was a trained, very educated musician, but there's a different level of knowledge when you get into early music.

None of us was paid very well. Josh was getting a token honorarium. I came on a secretarial salary—

JAC:—Executive secretarial.

TERESA STERNE: It took years to fight my way out of that. And there was no budget for help; I couldn't have a secretary. I went to work on October 25, 1965, and it was way into 1968, the late

Teresa (Tracey) Sterne

summer, that I finally sat down and wrote Jac a memo. I said I couldn't go on without at least a part-time secretary. I'm doing everything. I need help. I mean, three years. I had lots of energy, but I couldn't do it any more.

JAC: Yes, she was taking on the world and not getting much money for it, but her visibility in a field she loved had risen remarkably. She was able to green-light records swiftly, and this was real power in a musical arts community always begging for scraps.

Tracey was releasing forty to fifty albums a year. Each week we would have a long sit-down and review all problems and repertoire issues, considering how each proposed record would fit into the catalog. To me a catalog was not an agglomeration of records, there had to be a certain symmetry. Our weekly sessions were always a pleasure because we got so much done and they were enormous fun.

Tracey prepared well and I rarely turned her down on any request. At the end of each meeting we always gave each other a huge hug. There was that kind of affection.

If Tracey drove people up the wall—and she did—it was because someone had not come through and it impinged on the rhythm of her work. If she got testy— and it was rarely more than that—I was thrilled. Tracey was just doing her job and I was well served. Because she handled Nonesuch so well, she provided me the freedom to run Elektra. She gave Nonesuch a hearty, full-throated voice, and for me it was great that the voice belonged to a woman. Tracey was a jewel.

JAC: In Nonesuch's second year we introduced the Explorer series. I knew a number of ethnomusicologists doing field recordings who could be enticed to release through Nonesuch if we could demonstrate that we would treat the material with reverence and attention to detail.

To prime the pump and give the Explorer series some shape, we deleted our Flamenco, Japanese, Indian and African music from the Elektra catalog and switched them to Nonesuch with new covers, some re-editing and better mastering. With Elektra moving toward pop music, these specialized records deserved a new life in a more nurturing environment.

TERESA STERNE: They were called the Explorer International Series. When I came, there were already about five or six such records. It wasn't yet a big focus.

Peter Siegel played a major role with Explorer. He came to work the same day that I did, as a producer.

PETER SIEGEL: Over the next few years I recorded something like fifteen or twenty albums. The stuff was low profile, relatively non-commercial, and inexpensive to produce, so that I was pretty much able to do what I wanted. I would say to Jac, "I think we should record this," and he would say, "Fine, just do it."

TERESA STERNE: Peter had a great love for this music. Asian music, Indian music, was becoming very—not to use the word fashionable, but people were tuning in to it, and it was a part of the Sixties and meditation and all that. Peter treated it very seriously.

David Lewiston called up soon after I came to work, before I was taking responsibility, this guy with an English accent—

JAC:—A very winning English accent—

TERESA STERNE:—And he said he had some tapes he'd made in Bali of gamelan music and would we be interested to hear them? I said, "Well, you know, before you

"Music From The Morning Of The World"
H-72015

even get involved, let me switch you to the head of the company." Jac set up an appointment for him to see Peter Siegel. And the next thing I knew, I heard this great sound coming out of the studio and Peter dashed out, saying, "Oh, my God, this is fantastic." And they made a deal with him.

JAC: A $500 advance against a royalty for the use of the tapes which included liner notes to please the fussiest world music fanatic. David's notes were so fulsome we had to set them in eight-point type to fit them on the back cover, readable only by owls with magnifying glasses.

TERESA STERNE: And he was on his way almost immediately to do more, to South America. In the Sixties, for goodness sake, you could take a thousand dollars and do a whole field trip. So David would get a little licensing money from us and make another trip. He came back a year later with the makings of four magnificent records. He ended up doing a lot of recordings for us.

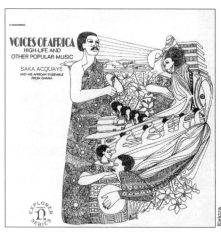

"Voices Of Africa" H-72026

But the Tibetan stuff—when he handed me that first tape, I didn't know what to make of it. I said, "My God, it sounds like everybody's groaning." I talked to a couple of musicians who were more into this and they said, "This is great stuff." And you know, somehow I zoomed into it. I listened and I listened, and I began to hear what it was about. One night, it just hit me suddenly. I was listening to it and I was sort of half falling asleep and it got into my soul.

PAT FARALLA: A chorus of monks chanting at dawn. It was musical nirvana. It was the temple. It was Holyville. It was our friend that soothed our fried brains. Everybody was addicted to that music. We listened and understood, and Jac made it possible . . .

FRITZ RICHMOND: When I was in the Jim Kweskin Jug Band, one of my favorite tapes was one that Jim had, by Joseph Spence, a Bahamian singer and guitar player. We'd listen to it over and over. There was never anyone quite like him. Ry Cooder is maybe like him, Taj Mahal a little, but really no one. Joseph played finger-style guitar, based on church music, shaped note hymnals, highly complex. He taught himself how to do it, and it was so complicated that it seemed no great guitarist could even play it.

I had to get down to the Bahamas and see this guy do what he did before I died. Down I went to Nassau and went around the bars and music clubs. I found Blind Blake, a famous local player there—he wrote 'Sloop John B'—and he knew Joseph. His bass player wrote down "St. Thomas More." It was a church, and at the church they knew how to direct me to Joseph. First to a little grocery store, and they sent me across the street to his house. His wife answered the door: "Come back at nine." I was so happy. I cabled Elektra for some recording gear—

JAC:—Which I happily sent.

FRITZ RICHMOND:— And I recorded him. He was marvelous. I got a camera and shot the front album cover pictures. And when the record came out I took some to Joseph.

JOHN SEBASTIAN: That album was radically different. For New York City finger-pickers, it was required reading.

Jac, Bill Harvey, Josh Rifkin and Tracey Sterne

PAUL ROTHCHILD: It was done in Joseph's living room. Total production costs were under a thousand dollars, including air fare, cheap hotel down there, tape stock, paying Joseph, guitar strings. It was called "Happy All The Time." It was probably the best, the purest Explorer record of that time. And it sold ninety-three copies.

JAC: It actually sold a few thousand, but the point was, Elektra had recorded and proudly released Joseph Spence's album because it was tremendous music.

PETER SIEGEL: We recorded Joseph again for Nonesuch, and those albums were deeply important in the long run. You can hear his musical influence in many places, from the Incredible String Band to Ry Cooder to David Byrne to the Grateful Dead.

JAC: I wanted to keep Nonesuch moving in interesting new directions. Open mind, open ears—and it continued to pay great dividends, musically and culturally, long-term.

JOSHUA RIFKIN: I had known some of Scott Joplin's ragtime music in my pre-teen years, and I then forgot about it for a long time. Then I became friends with a composer and critic named Eric Salzman, who was starting to get interested in ragtime, largely through his friendship with another musician, William Bolcom, who later did a lot of recording for Nonesuch. Talking with Eric and Bill reawakened my interest. I would sit with Eric and play endless rags. I started playing ragtime publicly. For Nonesuch I was doing nice little finely produced records of Baroque and Renaissance music and at some point I said, "You know, Joplin is great stuff. We ought to record this music. Instead of selling five hundred copies as we did of my last recording of fifteenth-century French secular music, we might sell fifteen hundred." Tracey liked the idea. We took it to Jac, and he liked the idea—and that it would be cheap because I would be the performer. So we just went into the church and recorded.

JAC: I had heard of Joplin but knew very little about him except for 'Maple Leaf Rag.' That he was a serious classical composer who had written operas, ballets, marches and songs was all new to me. Joplin's struggle as a black man to overcome a general indifference to his music piqued my interest, and I quickly agreed to do the album with Josh performing and the recording to be done at a church that Josh thought would give the music the right acoustic frame.

JOSHUA RIFKIN: It was a labor of love. Joplin rags were known in those days, if at all, to a fairly small coterie, and known as kind of fast, loud music. Our intention was to present it on Nonesuch, on a classical label, with a dignified cover and literate notes, as music to be taken seriously, not honky-tonk or catchy.

At Elektra and Nonesuch it was all music-driven, not market-driven. It seems like another world now. We knew absolutely zero of such things as marketing or promotion. We did with the Joplin record what we did with every Nonesuch record, which was, put it on the market and see what happens. But within a few weeks we began to sense that something was afoot. Journalists started writing about it: "I'm going to have So-and-So do a feature review of it." Radio stations started playing it: "God, I love this record!"

JAC: And the rest is, as they say, history: a robust revival of ragtime, a special and uniquely American kind of urban folk music, cresting in a Joplin craze; and in terms of direct popular culture influence, a straight line from Josh's recordings to Marvin Hamlisch's Academy Award-winning score for the immensely successful Paul Newman and Robert Redford film "The Sting," to the production of a new musical of E.L. Doctorow's novel, "Ragtime."

The album that rebirthed the music of Scott Joplin. Nonesuch H-71248

JAC: On Nonesuch we could bring the musical and cultural past back to life in the present, and we could project music and culture into the future. Nonesuch was the first American label to seriously address electronic music.

BERNIE KRAUSE: Jac introduced me to Paul Beaver. Paul had a place in LA, on Hyans Street, a one-story red brick warehouse, pretty funky, falling apart more with each earthquake. Inside he had the largest collection of Novachords, the first synthesizer, built by Hammond in the Thirties, with many presets—

JAC:—It had a hundred sixty-nine tubes and weighed a quarter of a ton.

BERNIE KRAUSE: Paul had an Ondes-Martinot too, a little French synthesizer, also from the Thirties. He built all kinds of other instruments. He was doing a lot of effects work with "Creature of the Black Lagoon"-type B movies—on the sound stage he would have a series of oscillators and other devices on a table thirty feet long and scurry back and forth. He did the effects for "War Of The Worlds," "Invasion Of The Body Snatchers," movies all through the Fifties. He had quite a reputation. Paul was also a conservative Republican. He wore blue serge suits with dandruff on the shoulders. He was one of the world's greatest Wurlitzer theater pipe organists—his big dream was to build a restaurant in the round where he would come up with his organ through a water fountain and play all night. He was also a Scientologist and a believer in UFOs.

I was a folkie—I had been a banjo player in the Weavers, the last replacement for Pete Seeger. I was looking for a different musical voice to express myself. At Mills College, at the music center, they had early prototypes of the modular synthesizer, and I got very excited about the potential of the instrument, the medium of electronic music.

Paul and I bought a synthesizer, a Moog, but we couldn't get Hollywood interested in using it, and we couldn't get record companies interested in electronic music. We had something like a hundred rejection letters from all around the world. We were almost broke.

I had done some consultant producer work for Nonesuch with Tracey Sterne, and I knew of Jac's proclivity for experimentation. He was the only one with the vision to see what this instrument, the synthesizer, could do.

JAC: It didn't take much genius to figure out that the record was the ideal medium for electronically generated music. I had been aware of the possibilities for years. My dad had a lawyer named Abe Frisch whose hobby was creating tapes of music, synthetically generated, only Abe did it with a massive inventory of tiny magnets which he pressed, one by one, onto the tape, re-arranging the ferrous oxide tape particles into something resembling a sound.

BERNIE KRAUSE: Jac took the risk, got behind it, and gave us a contract to record a guide to electronic music as a boxed set with LP and detailed booklet. The album was on the Billboard charts for twenty-six weeks, one of Nonesuch's best-selling records to that time. It was the key to introducing the synthesizer into pop music and film. This was something really important, something that broke down all the walls in the music business.

More broadly, Jac's vision gave a voice in the world to a new musical instrument, in effect the first to be successfully introduced since the saxophone a century before.

JAC: I decided to take a leaf from seventeenth and eighteenth-century musical life and be the patron of an electronic album.

First Nonesuch commission for
electronic music to Morton Subotnick
H-71174

After talking it over with Tracey, we decided that Morton Subotnick would be an ideal recipient for the first-ever commission of a piece to be created for the medium of home stereo. Subotnick was not only a gifted composer, he also helped design the Buchla keypad on which the album was created. "Silver Apples Of The Moon" was honored with numerous prizes.

Chapter 8

Buttering up the blues ...
Power dives and re-recordings ...
From the south side of Chicago
to the Newport electric blowout of 1965

JAC: Paul Rothchild was doing everything I had hoped for, and more. He wasn't just complementing me, he was greatly extending my reach, and was doing it with the same kind of manic energy I saw in myself.

We were talking one day about what was happening on "the street," and I said, "Paul, you don't have to go to the street. You're in a position where you can make the street."

What I meant was put Elektra out front. Paul could and did. He could gossip, schmooze, cajole, wheedle, beg, and orate—plus that most critical ability: he could "close." It was fine to romance artists. Getting them signed to Elektra, and for a modest advance, was an order of magnitude more difficult. Paul could do that.

PAUL WILLIAMS: Paul was a hanging-out guy. He almost invented something we totally take for granted now, which is that the secret of being a successful producer in the rock and roll world, especially in the drug-soaked Sixties, was the ability to hang out with the musicians and have them feel that you were one of them and that you were part of this incredible campaign that we were all on to turn the world upside down with our music and the great ideas we had when we were stoned last night and so forth. Well, Paul could run with you as fast as you were running, and talk with you as fast as you were talking, and he was just as into it as anybody.

JAC: One of Rothchild's first independent signings was the Paul Butterfield Blues Band. This was yet another beginning, and where it would take us we could never have imagined at the time.

PAUL ROTHCHILD: I'm at a party in Cambridge, Massachusetts, New Year's Eve of 1965. Fritz Richmond is just in off the road with the Jim Kweskin Jug Band. He says, "Hey, Paul, you remember that harmonica player, Paul Butterfield? Well, I've got to tell you, I've just heard the best music I've ever heard in my entire life. He's got a full-on electric blues band, and he's playing in a bar in Chicago. You should go there right away."

I got on a flight to Chicago, got off the plane, walked into Big John's about three in the morning, in time for the last set. And I heard the most amazing music. It was thrilling, chilling—changed my entire genetic code.

At the end of the set I talked to Butter and told him I wanted them to make a record with Elektra. Paul always had to have an argument. This one lasted about ten minutes over pizza. Then he said, "OK."

Then Butter said, "Are you tired yet?" I said, "No, I'm on fire, I'm ready." He says, "Great. I've got this buddy playing at an after-hours club over on the South Side. Pepper's Lounge." I walk in and it's Muddy Waters. Those guys were playing at the clubs every day then. So Paul showed me the last of the great era on the Chicago South Side.

Towards dawn he says, "One more stop." We walk into a luncheonette kind of place, and there's another band playing, and it's like a pale reflection of Paul's band. But there was a guitar player that just tore my mind apart. About four tunes in I turn to Paul and say, "Who is that?" He says, "Oh, that's Mike Bloomfield. That's his band." I say, "Wow, how come he's not in your band?" He says, "Nah, he's got his own." I say, "How would you feel if he was in your band?" He says, "Wow, it would be great. Two guitars. Amazing. Nah, it'll never happen." I say, "Do you mind if I give it a shot?" He says, "No, but I've tried it twenty times." Michael comes and sits down at our table. We shake hands. We then do a half hour of intense intellectual Jew at each other. He found a kindred soul, I found a kindred soul, it was wonderful. Finally I said, "Michael, how would you like to leave your band and join Paul's band? We're going to New York to make a record." He said, "Sure." Butterfield is sitting there with his jaw on the table.

MARK ABRAMSON: It was the first electric music Rothchild had ever recorded. I was helping him in the studio, and I didn't know any more than he did. They were loud. Nobody on Elektra had ever been that loud before. We were a folk music label. If there were drums it was somebody going tchk, tchk, tchk, and we would do it in Judson Hall and it didn't make any difference if it bled all over the place. The Butterfield Band, though, with Sam Lay—big black man, huge arms—the way he laid into the drums, it scared the daylights out of us technically. We had to figure out how to record loud, by trial and error.

PAUL ROTHCHILD: I recorded, edited for five weeks, put the album together, sequenced it, lacquered it. Then I waited.

And an important thing happened. Jac had discovered long ago that if he put out these little promotional records, his samplers, he could introduce the hungry folk world to new talent and new albums. He did one in the spring of 1965 that was called "Folk Song 65." Tom Rush was on it. Dick Rosmini. Judy Collins. And one of the cuts was from the Butterfield sessions, 'Born In Chicago.'

JAC: Normally we would expect a sampler to sell twenty-five thousand copies.

PAUL ROTHCHILD: By the third or fourth week, sales had skyrocketed past a hundred thousand!

JAC: Actually sixty thousand—which was still an amazing number.

PAUL ROTHCHILD: Jac got on the phone and called the stores to ask what the hell was going on. He finds out that people have been asking for the record with 'Born In Chicago' on it. Big sales for Elektra. Especially for something that was not standard rock and roll and not standard rhythm and blues. It was white people performing black music. Butterfield was the first electric person besides Elvis to do this successfully.

Bells go off in Jac's head. He realizes that this is a hit act. For the album, he goes for an initial pressing of ten thousand. He had never done an initial press of anything like that—

JAC:—Not of a new artist.

PAUL ROTHCHILD: So the album is jacketed and boxed, ten thousand copies, ready to go out into the world—

JAC:—Paid for—

PAUL ROTHCHILD:—And I'm going through hell. Because from a producer's point of view, after listening to the record I realize, "Rothchild, you didn't get it. You did not get that act on tape."

In the middle of this anxiety I get a call from Jac. "How would you like to fly up to Martha's Vineyard and visit Tom Rush at his aunt's house and eat some fresh zucchini?" So we're up in the little Elektra plane—and somewhere over Long Island Sound I say, "Jac, I got a problem." He says, "What is it?" I say, "I want to re-record the Butterfield album."

I thought he was going to have a coronary. The plane goes into a power dive. I thought we were headed all the way into the drink. He says, "You want to do what?" I say, "We should junk it." He says, "Paul, it's packed, ready to ship! It's going out on Monday!! You're insane!!!" I say, "Jac, there's all those people out there waiting for a great album, and I didn't get it." He says, "'What about 'Born In Chicago?'" I say, "That's the only track we can salvage." He says, "Oh my God, what do you want to do?" I say, "I want to recapture that first moment I felt when I walked into Big John's in Chicago. We don't have that on tape. We have a pale facsimile. I want to record them live for a week." He thinks for a moment, then he says, "Not a bad idea." And he brings us out of the power dive.

JAC: We ate zucchini on the Vineyard, and never discussed it on the way home.

MARK ABRAMSON: That shows the persuasive power of Paul Rothchild, to get Jac to dump thousands and thousands of those first pressings.

JAC: The voice of reason told me I was crazy, but Rothchild had my artistic sensibility convinced. There was much more than a single album at stake, there was everything else Paul could do in the future. To say "No" would have been to neuter Paul as an Elektra producer.

PAUL ROTHCHILD: So—we essentially four-walled the Café Au Go Go, across from the Bitter End, one of the major high-tone folk clubs, and brought in the recording trucks. And that's when the union showed up, and that's when our costs quadrupled over our budget projections.

JAC: We had already paid the band their advance, gone to the expense of scrapping the first album, and now the union was asking for more.

PAUL ROTHCHILD: We thought we were just going to be paying recording costs, but all of a sudden there's the union threatening to fine us for not reporting sessions, and a guy in the club every night clocking it—huge dollars.

JAC: They recorded over several nights.

PAUL ROTHCHILD: I started going through the tapes, carefully, and about three weeks later I went into Jac's office and said, "Jac, you're going to love this. It sucks beyond your wildest expectations. We have nothing." He said, "Oh my God!!! What are you going to do now????" I said, "I'm going to go back into the studio and get it right."

JAC: And I said, "OK." For all the same reasons.

Paul Rothchild (center) rehearsing the Paul Butterfield Band

PAUL ROTHCHILD: The band came back to New York. I put them in a musician's hotel, the Albert, in the Village. They drove up in a truck and unloaded the equipment out front. I said, "One of you stay here, I'm going to go in and register you all." I'm at the desk about five minutes and I turn around and they're all standing there behind me. I say, "Who's watching the equipment?" They say, "It's just right outside." We run out and it's all gone, down to the last drumstick.

JAC: So we rented equipment, and Paul took them to Mastertone and recorded for a week.

PAUL ROTHCHILD: Three productions for the release of a first album! Our costs got up to fifty thousand dollars, which in those days was enormous. But that album is golden.

FRITZ RICHMOND: It was the sort of an album you could take to a party and the mood of the party picked up when you put that record on, just as well as if you brought in a keg of beer or a bottle of whiskey.

PAUL ROTHCHILD: It still sells. Far more than that, certainly all through the Sixties and Seventies, I didn't meet a guitar player who wasn't influenced by that album. Most of them have one comment: "The first two Butterfield albums taught me how to play guitar and changed my life."

Butterfield was the genuine article. He was blessed with really being a blues musician, feeling the blues. And his instincts about musicians—I believe he was one of the

First Butterfield album ...
on the third try EKS-7294

greatest band leaders this country has ever had. He's right up there with Benny Goodman or Nelson Riddle. He had the ability to pick personnel who are great players, and who you know will join with your concept. Some of the greatest musi-

cians in the world up through the mid-Eighties were ex-members of one version or the other of the Butterfield Blues Band.

MARK ABRAMSON: The original band were a very intelligent group of fellows. Butterfield was very laid back, very quiet. The dynamo in the group was Mike Bloomfield. He was hilarious. We would go on a trip, he would have us rolling on the floor. We never knew what exactly he was saying. He was in the genius category. And I think he couldn't handle the world. He was on everything. How somebody that nervous can be on speed without destroying himself in five minutes, I

Butterfield Blues Band's classic "East West" EKS-7315

don't know.

PAUL ROTHCHILD: Bottom line, the Butterfield Band opened another door to American musicianship. It made the electric blues a viable form for popular music, made it possible for hundreds of American performers to play electric music.

JAC: In the mid-Seventies I was living on Maui. The phone rings. It is the two Pauls, Rothchild and Butter. It's late in Hawai'i, so God knows what time it is wherever those two characters are. They had been hanging, talking of old times, and suddenly Butter says, "Let's call Jac." They both got on the phone and said that if they had ever given me any trouble, any grief, they wanted to apologize, because once they were gone from Elektra they had both discovered what a swamp the rest of the record business was. They never fully appreciated who I was and what the label meant to them, and they just wanted me to know.

In late 1994 Paul was asked by Rhino Records to locate the masters of the original (pre-power dive) Butterfield tapes for release under the title "The Long Lost Original Paul Butterfield Blues Band Album." Paul and his son Dan eventually located the original tapes and prepared the masters. If Paul was unhappy with those sessions in 1965, thirty years later he was thrilled. They were rough, gritty and real—everything a blues record should be. What Paul considered inferior recording quality was actually much better then either of us remembered, giving the music a growling authenticity we would not have recognized or understood in 1965. Paul turned out to be very proud of that album.

JAC: The event of the folk year was the Newport Folk Festival. It was launched in 1959 by George Wein, who was also founder of the Newport Jazz Festival and an accomplished jazz pianist himself.

At the folk festival, Elektra was always well represented with performers on stage. I went every year from the first. You'd see all the people you normally would run across in New York or LA, but out of the city there was time for relaxation that transcended business or party loyalties. For me it was a mini-vacation. I loved just wandering around, catching the workshops and the impromptu get-togethers of musicians showing off their licks and trading songs.

THEODORE BIKEL: We brought artists from all over the world. From Hawai'i, from Fiji, Maoris from New Zealand. We brought a penny whistler from South Africa, a black man, at a time when people couldn't even get a passport.

We were non-profit. If there was any money left over, we'd give it to folklorists to get proper equipment to record songs, or to resuscitate Cajun music, or we'd sponsor smaller regional festivals, or give money to indigent musicians for good instruments.

Each year at Newport we were not only presenting artists, we were housing them, we were feeding them—there were tables laden with food. It was a nightmare to be a director, because we had to be everything. Caterers. Counselors. We had to place people for gigs, we had to be apologists for the presence of the cops. But it was the place to be. There was an extraordinary spirit in the air.

The "Folk Mafia" (left to right) Jac, Theo Bikel, Pete and Toshi Seeger, Harold Leventhal, Fred Hellerman, Maynard Solomon

JAC: Every year there was something fresh to catch my interest. Newport is where I met Paul Williams, an eighteen-year-old college dropout with an armful of his homemade, very perceptive rock magazine, Crawdaddy.

PAUL WILLIAMS: I started Crawdaddy before Rolling Stone. In the first year it was a few mimeographed pages, with aspirations. The time Jac is talking about, I was walking around selling it by hand, me and two girls. We had brought four hundred copies, and we sold them for a quarter. And one of the people who bought was Jac. Jac being Jac, he took an interest in it, and in me. We hung out and had a good talk. He was very willing to meet me as an equal, very enthusiastic about what I was doing. I had brought my three back issues with me, just one of each. Jac being Jac, he wanted to see them all, and he bought them, and the current issue, for $1 the lot—the first person to acquire a complete set. And Elektra was the first record company to take out paid ads in Crawdaddy.

JAC: Newport was set up with formal concerts in the evening, and during the day workshops based on a variety of themes: guitar and banjo picking, Delta blues, city blues, ballads, every kind of folk-tinged music. Each workshop was overseen by a moderator to move things forward. Perhaps Pete Seeger and fifty young, dexterous and very ambitious five-string banjo pickers. Or Delta bluesmen, Mississippi John Hurt or Sonny Terry and Brownie McGhee, sharing songs and licks with eager, scrubbed, predominantly white faces.

THEODORE BIKEL: We had anywhere from twelve to twenty areas where things were happening—under a tree, in a corner, on a tennis court, in a gym. Mouth organ, Appalachian, Slavic, ballads here, storytelling there, work songs there, songs of protest there, international songs there. It was like a smorgasbord of folk music.

JAC: On the Saturday afternoon of the 1965 festival there was a blues workshop. Alan Lomax was hosting the black traditionalists. Alan was the son of John Lomax, two great white collectors, for whom traditional music seemed to freeze-frame about the time of the Tennessee Valley Authority. Alan was the last protector and refuge of the lone voice from Mutton Hollow.

The second segment of the workshop was slated to be white urban blues, featuring the Butterfield Band. Due to the amazing sales of 'Born In Chicago' on the Elektra sampler, and the buzz that went with it, I had arranged for them to perform at Newport. Albert Grossman, the manager of Bob Dylan and Peter, Paul and Mary, was in full hover over them as future clients.

PAUL ROTHCHILD: I had introduced Butterfield to Grossman.

Butterfield and band wailing at the Newport Blues Workshop

JAC: The crowd at the blues workshop was enormous. Instead of a few hundred this one had nearly a thousand.

PAUL ROTHCHILD: Lomax was loaded for bear. After the traditionalists and ahead of the Butterfield set, he got up and said something like, "Today you've been hearing music by the great blues players, guys who go out and find themselves an old cigar box, put a stick on it, attach some strings, sit under a tree and play great blues for themselves. Now you're going to hear a group of young boys from Chicago with electric instruments. Let's see if they can play this hardware at all."

JAC: Lomax was so condescending, I was embarrassed for him.

PAUL ROTHCHILD: Grossman took it the worst way. Lomax comes down from this little stage and Grossman coldcocks him. And for about the next five minutes these two leviathans, monsters, both kings in their own right—

JAC: —Dueling behemoths. Two big growlers, overweight, unfit, far from agile—

PAUL ROTHCHILD:—Groveling in the dusty dirt of Newport over the Paul Butterfield Blues Band. It was wonderful. Holzman was laughing his ass off.

JAC: Al 'If I Had A Hammer' Grossman versus Alan 'Mighty Defender of the Status Quo' Lomax. One very short round, split decision. And this was only the preliminary bout. The main event was the following night when Dylan went electric—

THEODORE BIKEL:—To the delight of some, to the dismay of most.

JONATHAN TAPLIN: Grossman, upon hearing that Bob wanted to play electric, hastily put a band together. And the only guys who had electric instruments were Butterfield's band.

JAC: Albert had Al Kooper flown in by charter from New York to play organ. Al was always a reluctant flyer, and winging to Newport in a tiny plane with one engine was not his preferred mode of travel.

DAVE GAHR: I knew what was coming, because in the afternoon I was the only photographer allowed in to shoot Dylan with Butterfield's band.

JONATHAN TAPLIN: We kicked everybody out of the stadium and did a short sound check, which Peter Yarrow was mixing. The problem was the rhythm section. They were great blues players, but Dylan didn't play twelve-bar music. He played very bizarre music in terms of its structure. So they didn't really understand what was going on at all. And Bob refused to do much of a rehearsal—

JAC:—Ten or fifteen minutes. Let's say that musically, Dylan's electric set was not going to be tightly wrapped.

That evening I was standing next to Dave Gahr in the photographer's pit, below and in front of the stage. Peter Yarrow introduced Dylan for the very special artist that he was, and from the moment he launched into 'Maggie's Farm,' now fleshed out with an incredible electric intensity, it was clarity and catharsis.

I could feel the tickler go up on the back of my neck, the hairs rising in happy resonance. My friend Paul Nelson of the Little Sandy Review was standing alongside, and we just turned to each other and shit-grinned.

This was electricity married to content. We were hearing music with lyrics that had meaning, with a rock beat, drums and electric guitars, Mike Bloomfield keening as if squeezing out his final note on this planet. Absolutely stunning. All the parallel strains of music over the years coalesced for me in that moment. It was like a sunrise after a storm, when all is clean . . . all is known.

Then suddenly we heard booing, like pock-

Dylan goes electric at Newport 1965

ets of wartime flak. The audience had split into two separate and opposing camps. It grew into an awesome barrage of catcalls and hisses. It was very strange, because I couldn't believe that those people weren't hearing the wonderful stuff I was hearing.

PAUL ROTHCHILD: I was at the console, mixing the set, the only one there who had ever recorded electric music. I could barely hear Dylan because of the furor.

JAC: I looked directly into Dylan's face as he squinted into the darkness, trying to figure out what was happening.

PAUL ROTHCHILD: From my perspective, it seemed like everybody on my left wanted Dylan to get off the stage, everybody on my right wanted him to turn it up. And I did—I turned it up.

JAC: Backstage, an un-civil war had broken out. Alan Lomax was bellowing that this was a folk festival, you didn't have amplified instruments. Pete Seeger was beside himself, jumped into a car and rolled up the windows, his hands over his ears.

PAUL ROTHCHILD: On one side you had the old guard, George Wein, Alan Lomax, Pete Seeger. Pete, pacifist Pete, with an ax: "I'm going to cut the cables!" The other group is Peter Yarrow, a festival director, Albert Grossman, not a director but on the other side. There were about eight people on each side of the cable, and more gathering, one group trying to defend it, the other trying to cut it. Seeger's a tall thin guy, and Yarrow's a short thin guy, and they are nose to nose, screaming at each other.

JONATHAN TAPLIN: Out front it was turning into a disaster.

JAC: Crazier and crazier.

JONATHAN TAPLIN: Bob was getting booed and he walked off.

JAC: Dylan left the stage hurt, angry and shaken. Peter Yarrow took the stage again, very rattled. Like a wounded cheerleader, he attempted to rally support, urging the audience on until there was enough positive emotion that Dylan could return with dignity.

JONATHAN TAPLIN: I saw Dylan backstage from a little bit of a distance, and he seemed to be crying. Johnny Cash came up and gave him a big Gibson guitar, a jumbo, much too big for Bob, and told him to go back out there.

JAC: His face set with determination, Dylan walked back onto that stage and stared down ten thousand pairs of eyes.

JONATHAN TAPLIN: He says, "Does anybody have a D harmonica?" And all these harmonicas were being thrown from the audience. The audience thought they'd won—here was Dylan, no band, back into acoustic folk stuff. And then he sang 'It's All Over Now, Baby Blue' and walked off.

JAC: And Dylan and folk music and Elektra were never the same again.

JONATHAN TAPLIN: It was unbelievably dramatic. At the party afterwards he was pretty much by himself. I mean, all the other singers and everything were very supportive of him, but it was clear that he didn't like what had happened.

I ended up working with him, touring, all over the country and then all over the world, for two years, and he was booed everywhere. Every time. He would play the first half folk, with just harmonica and guitar, and the second half rock and roll, and get booed.

PAUL ROTHCHILD: To me, that night at Newport was as clear as crystal. It's the end of one era and the beginning of another. There's no historical precedent. This is a folk festival, *the* folk festival, and you couldn't even say it's blues and the blues has moved to an electric format. This is a young Jewish songwriter with an electric band that sounds like rock and roll.

There were two very big passions happening here. And it was an election. You had to choose which team you were going to support. I expected Peter Yarrow to join with the future, because of his peer group and his dedication to Dylan, whose songs had made Peter, Paul and Mary's success so resounding. At the same time it changed Peter's professional life. Peter, Paul and Mary were acoustic folk singers, and Peter had to know that their moment had passed; but personally, Peter's commitment was to the future. Albert Grossman, that was an obvious one. And Jac. Jac could just as easily—more easily—have joined with the Newport board of directors, the Weins, the Lomaxes, the Seegers, and said, "No electric music." But he didn't. I was very proud of Jac at that moment, watching him choose the unknown rather than the comfort of the known.

JAC: I followed my instinct and my heart. I followed the music.

Chapter 9

The Strip ... The trip ...
Love those psychedelic eyeglasses ...
Inhalations and incarcerations

JAC: I loved the singer-songwriters for their originality and point of view; they were an integral part of the Elektra identity. I was fond of jug band music too, and understood the logical progression from field recordings, to folklorists singing the songs they had collected, the solo and group interpreters, singer-songwriters, and the jug band emphasis on well-played instruments. What was going to be the next unfolding, the next link in the progression? I would know it when I heard it.

Actually I had heard it in London in 1963, on a bleak winter afternoon. I was visiting with David Platz of Essex Music, the Elektra affiliated music publisher. The Essex office was upstairs in a very old but well-kept building on Denmark Street, catty corner to Foyles, the famous bookstore on Charing Cross Road. The building was from a period that predated indoor plumbing. Kitchens and bathrooms had been added, either at the rear wall or cantilevered over the alley, with a profusion of black pipes crawling up the building's backside in a rather odd geometry.

I had to go to the loo. Sitting suspended tentatively above the alleyway, with my buns freezing, I first felt and then heard a throbbing blues-rooted rock and roll—'I'm A King Bee,' as I recall—from the Regent Sound Studios a few floors below. I pulled my clothes together, rushed downstairs and slipped into the control room to find out what was going on. It was a band cutting their audition demo for the London Records division of the English Decca Record Co. I introduced myself as from Elektra, inquired about their availability, and was told that the Decca deal was almost certain. I left my card anyway, but I never did hear from the Rolling Stones.

When Dylan went electric at Newport, I definitely knew what I was hearing. Energy! And that meant electric music. I just gut got it. Going electric didn't mean falsifying anything (any more than acoustic music was a guarantee of integrity), and going electric carried an emotional wallop. There was greater tonal flexibility, a wider range of shadings. It made an order of magnitude difference. And it was new.

John Sebastian was putting together a new "electric" band. Paul and I were close to John and often used him as a session musician, so we knew early on about the Lovin' Spoonful. We went to hear them. In the dark around us were record people that one normally didn't see in Village hangouts sipping hot cider with cinnamon. Either word had gotten out or the band's management had made a lot of phone calls.

The Spoonful played their entire repertoire, including 'Do You Believe In Magic,' a song that echoed my own feeling about music, about being young with all the possibilities open before you. Four richly schooled musicians with overpowering electric intensity—this was better than twenty jug bands in a row. I wanted them for Elektra, badly.

PAUL ROTHCHILD: Their manager, Bob Cavallo, came to me and said, "Listen, everybody wants you to produce them. They want to be at Elektra. I need to have a certain amount of money to get this thing together and work right. We need an advance of $10,000." I went to Jac and he said, "No way. I have never given an artist $10,000 and I can't start now." I went to Cavallo and everybody was just destroyed.

JAC: That's not how it looked to me. The $10,000 was a bit of a shocker, not so much because the money was so large for that day and time, but this was 1965 and we could only break the Spoonful through singles. I

John Sebastian (right) with Lovin' Spoonful

was sure the Spoonful had a great album in them, but FM radio had yet to take up the cause of rock music, so Top 40 singles were it, and Elektra had no experience in this area, where special relationships meant everything and some of those relationships were less than savory.

The Spoonful had already recorded some demo sessions on multi-track. I said to Paul, "Make sure those tapes are safe, because I have a hunch they will never do 'Magic' any better." I spoke from experience. Demo sessions often produced music that was more spontaneous and joyful than formal sessions.

Paul and I met again the next evening. Paul was hungry for the Spoonful and made an eloquent case. I spelled out my concerns about Top 40 radio and singles, but I agreed. Elektra would pay the $10,000.

Paul immediately phoned John, who rushed over to the house, thrilled that the family would stay together. Asti was uncorked, and when the evening was ended we all went to sleep thinking that the band was now on Elektra.

But—to raise seed money, the Spoonful had already taken an advance from a publishing company with a record arm, and these people interpreted the contract to include both publishing and recording. Or so we were told. Personally, I didn't believe it, but the Spoonful were informed that their manager had made the deal and they were bound by it. Furthermore, what did Elektra know about singles? This was a fair point. We had never had a single on the charts.

John came to see me, all apologies, feeling trapped between an obligation he had not fully understood and his affection for Paul and me. Elektra probably had some kind of case, but I liked John and chose not to pursue it.

The reality was that the Spoonful would be several generations down from any income stream. In fact the Spoonful received very little money for all their talent and great songs.

DAVID BRAUN: How much came off the top before the kids in the Spoonful got their money, between the producers and the managers and the middle guys, we'll never know.

JAC: Most of their realized income was from performances and publishing. Years later I saw John in a summer concert at the Wollman Rink in Central Park and went backstage to say hello. He ran over, gave me a gigantic hug, and said, "If we had gone with Elektra it would have turned out so differently. We would have been paid." And they would have.

That was how I missed the Spoonful, a group that I saw as an electrical extension of what Elektra had been doing. A year later, when I heard 'Summer In The City' all over radio, with its pulse and urgency, that gritty New York rooftop feeling, it was exactly the kind of powerful music I wanted. It hit Number 1, was ten weeks on the charts, and I came very close to putting my fist through the window.

JAC: I was on a quest for a band, and now my search area was expanded by my first experience with drugs.

In my business at that time I couldn't help but be around grass, yet I was still on the straight side of the equation. It's not that I wouldn't, it was just that no one had asked me, possibly out of concern for how I might react.

At Esalen on Big Sur, Nina and I would spend time with our friends Richard Fariña and his wife Mimi, Joan Baez's sister. We had met at Newport, and when they visited New York they would often stay with us, bringing their dog Lush, ferociously large but mild-mannered due to his vegetarian diet, a true Sixties counterculture canine. Mimi did not get loaded, but Richard was always going into small rooms by himself or with friends, and you knew what was up.

I was also sure that Paul Rothchild was a "viper," but he wasn't being obvious about it.

FRITZ RICHMOND: When I met Paul, which was when he was on the board of directors of Club 47 in Cambridge, he was a businessman-looking guy who was often in a jacket and necktie, but he seemed like a guy that I was going to be able to get along with. And it seemed we had some unspoken interests.

One of the things that went on in Cambridge was paranoia about marijuana. Almost everyone who was a player got high to one degree or another, but there was always, "This is illegal, you can get arrested and do jail time for this."

Well, I began to get the feeling that Paul Rothchild might have got high in his life once or twice. But you didn't open up the subject of pot with another person that you weren't positive got high, or unless someone had given you the word, "This guy is OK." It was a secret society .

I think Paul knew I turned on, just from the way I dressed, long hair, helicopter pilot boots, and a suede jacket, well-worn—I bought it in a used store, and I always carried in the pocket a comb and a toothbrush, because I never knew where I'd end up.

So one night I'm at Club 47 with Paul, in the basement, which was for the in-group and the musicians. It's about fifteen minutes before my show, and he complimented me on my boots and jacket, and that was like code words, I knew he was telling me he was a viper.

We're sitting in the middle of Marijuana Paranoia Central, and he said, "You know, if we were quick about it we could have a toke right here." My paranoia went right off the scale and said, Ring-a-ding-a-ding! Paul Rothchild, member of the board of Club 47, is inviting me, this nefarious dope-smoking washtub bass player, to get high right here?

He was gonna roll a joint. I said, "Well, I don't know if we've got time to have a joint. But dig this." And I pulled out my little thimble pipe. I had bought a little tobacco pipe, very short-stemmed, and I said to myself, "You know, you can't smoke pot in this kind of a pipe because it gets sucked up the stem because the pieces are too small. It's not like tobacco. Tobacco is wet and gooey and stays there, and pot is dry and tiny flakes. It needs a holder." So I take a thimble, and it's got dimples, and I drill about a dozen holes through these dimples, and I had a perfect holder and it was a nice tight fit in the pipe. It was very convenient. If you had the pipe in your pocket it just looked like a pipe, and in your other pocket you had a dirty thimble, and it wasn't immediately obvious what it was. Except to other dopers. Every viper that saw it sort of slapped themselves on the forehead and said, "Wow! Why didn't I think of that?" And it became quite popular; everybody made their own variation.

Paul instantly knew what it was, and what a great idea it was. He loved toys, nice little toys. He had antique toys in his apartment. He had a cigarette lighter that probably had fifty-seven little machine parts. Then he'd have a nice little something or other to keep his stash in. Anyway, the significance was that we bonded over this pot thing.

JAC: By the rules of proximity and probability, it would figure to have been Paul who turned me on, but it was Arthur Gorson. Arthur thought I needed loosening up, and I'm sure I did. But, then again, I never met a temptation I didn't like.

We were at Arthur's house in the country, and it didn't take long to figure that his mission was to bring me into the fraternity of hemp. I suspected that smoking dope was something like losing your virginity, you never could get your innocence back, but Arthur was a trusted friend, Nina was with me, and the setting was beautiful.

Arthur gave me the crash course: Take a long drag, inhale and hold it for at least ten seconds, then exhale. I did. Nothing happened for about a minute. Then my head felt like a bottle of Mumm's had been uncorked. Whatever reserve I still clung to, the dope vaporized. I felt relaxed, happy, transmogrified—Doctor Jac, meet Mister High.

The following week, Arthur's friend, the "founder of the feast," swapped me a generous stash in exchange for a one-foot stack of Nonesuch albums.

After that first happy inhalation, Nina and I would get loaded most every weekend, lying on the bed, ears wrapped in Koss headphones. I thought I heard deeper into the music, the layers, texture heaped on texture, discrete but reinforcing each other. I understood the parts and their relationship to the whole so much better, not as an observer but embedded in the cellular structure of the material. My already intense feeling about music as essential to my life and wellbeing was strengthened. I went "Wow," which I did a lot while smoking.

After that, I would rarely commit to a record unless I heard it loaded. The normal and reasonable procedure was to make up my mind without outside influence, but once the decision was taken, to give it a final check through a cannabis filter. There was a time when I jokingly said that some of our records should only be heard if you are loaded.

Nina and I shared the wealth. Dope was the classic communal sacrament and we gave parties built around the experience.

NINA HOLZMAN: If nothing particular was happening on a Saturday night we would invite people over, and I would make a wonderful dinner and a fabulous dessert—

JAC:—Nina's famous parfait pie, a combination of ice cream and fruit-flavored Jell-O neatly molded inside a homemade, brown-sugar-laden graham cracker crust—

NINA HOLZMAN:—And we would sit around listening to music. I mean, what else?

JAC: I assembled "head" tapes, great stoner songs like Jefferson Airplane's 'White Rabbit,' Beatles psychedelia, anything trippy, an hour of music collated on 10-inch reels running at 7 1/2ips, excellent quality. I had rigged a box with six headphone jacks for the living room so we could listen together—everyone loaded on cannabis cookies, or smoke, people floating away in their private reverie, head soirées.

The perfect stoner's album.
Incredible String Band's "5,000 Spirits
Or The Layers Of The Onion"
EKS-74010, 1967

Grass was cheap. We're talking $150 a kilo, though it didn't have the potency of today's product, but it certainly cooked up well. Nina put together clever recipes which began: "First, take a pound of grass . . . " I had heard about grass as an ingredient of haute cuisine. You boiled it in water and threw in a half pound of butter, and eventually a green-yellow viscous mixture formed at the top, and you poured it through a strainer to sift out the seeds and stems, and put what was left in the refrigerator to cool. Four hours later a greenish buttery fat would form at the top which you skimmed and stored in the freezer. If a recipe called for butter, and didn't they all, you would whack off a slab—of course, no one in the mid-Sixties had heard of cholesterol. My contribution to the art, devised in the Holzmanian drive for aesthetic perfection through technology, was to simmer the mixture in a *pressure cooker* for several hours, squeezing every last measure of oomph from the weed, forcing every mote of cannabis into the butter. One batch yielded months of high good times. Our buddy Bill would come over almost every weekend, get loaded, and sleep till Monday, sprawled on the floor, until he was awakened by the housekeeper vacuuming around him.

I could never get my brother Keith loaded, but I kept trying. One evening Nina made him a special batch of enriched cookies. He kept nibbling away, and I was beginning to worry that we were going to have to get him some Thorazine, or take him to the hospital. When I called the following morning, Keith said, "Thanks for the party. I can't recall ever having slept so soundly."

JAC: I was getting antsy about finding a breakthrough act for Elektra. I had no Lovin' Spoonful, and New York was being picked over by record business players with lots of pop experience. I thought I'd try the West Coast again.

By now there were dozens of clubs in the heart of Hollywood, near Vine, and on the Sunset Strip, from La Cienega on the east to Doheny on the west.

PAT FARALLA: You could just cruise. We walked the Strip from club to club. We really felt like we owned it, that it was our street. It was our town, and we were inventing it as we went along.

MARK ABRAMSON: Every other building was a club, but it had no name, and you'd figure somebody just hired it for Saturday night, and they had beer and Coke and that was it. And all of these California girls, everybody just grooving for hours. The police were always coming to break it up because there were too many people. But just the band, completely relaxed and at home, in that groove—ah, it was wonderful. That was the best part, the music live, and being in those places.

JAC: In LA I would check all the music listings in the Los Angeles Free Press, one of the first freebie alternative newspapers. I spotted a club I had never heard of, Bido Lito's, and a band with an intriguing name, Love. I asked Herbie Cohen to join us that evening.

NINA HOLZMAN: Bido Lito's was this funky little place off Hollywood Boulevard. We walked in and it was tiny, very congested, wall to wall people.

JAC: The Black Hole of Calcutta with a door charge.

NINA HOLZMAN: We really didn't know what we were going to see. Arthur Lee got up, and he had these boots with the tongues hanging out, no laces, and his eye glasses had one blue lens and one red, and a funny shape. He was the most bizarre person I'd ever seen in my life, by far.

HERB COHEN: For the time and place, only average. You want real bizarre, there's five thousand of them on the Strip any night.

MARK ABRAMSON: Love were definitely not the folk musicians that Jac had been dealing with. He was very intrigued with them. I mean, he really liked it. I think Jac is a teenybopper at heart.

JAC: I was fascinated. It was a scene from one of the more amiable rings of Dante's inferno. Bodies crushing into each other, silken-clad girls with ironed blonde hair moving the kind of shapes you didn't see in New York, to a cadence part musical and all sexual. The band was cranking out 'Hey, Joe' and 'My Little Red Book.' Inwardly, I smiled. 'My Little Red Book' was by Burt Bachrach and Hal David, and featured in the Woody Allen movie, "What's New, Pussycat?" Hip but straight. And here were Arthur Lee and Love going at it with manic intensity. Five guys of all colors, black, white and psychedelic—that was a real first. My heart skipped a beat. I had found my band!

Elektra

Love assembled... more or less

We met with Love after the show, and I committed to signing them without cutting a studio demo. We agreed to get together the next day, Herbie assisting with the negotiations. Although I wasn't sure of Herbie's role, he seemed to have a relationship with Arthur, and I needed someone to watch over the band when I wasn't around.

HERB COHEN: They're all living in one hotel room, starving, and Arthur says, "I want a $5,000 advance to sign the contract—cash. " Jac says, "OK, meet me at the bank." Jac cashes a check. Arthur says to the band, "Go back to the hotel. I have to pick up something." And about four or five hours later Arthur shows up with a gold Mercedes 300 gull-wing that he paid $4,500 for. "Well," he says, "we need some transportation for the band, so we can get around to the gigs."

JAC: The Mercedes gull-wing is a two-door two-seater. Arthur plus four in the band makes five, not to mention equipment. Arthur was not strong on the realities of cubic content.

HERB COHEN: Arthur had also bought a harmonica. He gives each of the guys a hundred bucks, and there goes the five thousand.

JAC: I hadn't recorded in an LA studio for years, and wasn't taken with the few I had used. I wanted a funky studio, preferably with a live echo chamber, and, at the top of the list, an experienced engineer who knew electric music, to avoid our painful learning curve with the Butterfield Band.

We had heard good things about Sunset Sound. There was no likelihood that Arthur would be ready to record before 7pm, so I decided to check out the facilities early, look into the mixing board, four-track Ampexes, available mikes, and schmooze with the engineer assigned to Mark Abramson and me. I sauntered in and saw this kid, whom I took to be no more than nineteen, deftly moving his fingers over the console and generally looking like he knew what he was doing. He told me his name was Bruce Botnick.

MARK ABRAMSON: At Elektra we didn't know anything about recording this kind of music. I think that we did folk music as well or better than anybody. Butterfield-type blues we learned from scratch. When rock and roll came in, we had to start all over again. A mike here, a mike there, ten mikes on the drum, all these baffles around the drummer, people in the studio with earphones on. We watched Bruce with our mouths open. Wow! He saved our asses.

BRUCE BOTNICK: Recording Love went quickly. It was very fast in those days.

JAC: Bands had yet to get into their bad habits in the studio.

BRUCE BOTNICK: Love came in already prepared. They'd been playing live. And whether they were straight or whether they were smoking hemp or doing acid or whatever, they came in and they just played it. Jac had seen the band, he knew the songs, he had made his notes, who had the lead vocal, where the chorus was, who was going to take a solo. He knew the music almost as well as they did. And because he knew a lot, the group worked with him real well.

JAC: We were completing three fine tracks a day. Arthur frequently played someone else's instrument if he thought he could play it better, and he always could. Once, we had completed a take using up all four of our available tracks. Arthur still wanted to add a harmonizing vocal on track #3. With no tracks available, I asked Arthur if he was sure he could get it on the first take. He stared at me over his glasses as if I was some sort of alien bug. Bruce Botnick pulled the erase head on track #3 so we could record to the track without obliterating the material already there. We gave Arthur his cue and it was perfect. It was a one-week album.

BRUCE BOTNICK: Jac left the masters with me and I mixed the album and sent it back to New York.

JAC: Mark and I reviewed the mixes, made some corrections, and it was done.

We had the music—music that was new to Elektra. The album cover deserved a visual style unlike any other Elektra album that had gone before.

Elektra, now an established label in 1965, was besieged by hungry suppliers eager for business they would have turned down in 1955. It became such a drag on Bill Harvey's time that I asked him to restrict salesmen's calls to Thursday mornings.

A printing supplier showed Bill a new process. A standard jacket was normally printed front and back on paper, then the paper was cut and glued to reinforced cardboard. With this new, entirely automated process, the jacket could be printed both sides at once, directly onto board, in four-color. Full color front and back was a first, and it was cheaper as well as better, the ideal combination.

I liked to watch people in record stores. If they were at all caught by the look

"Love" EKS-74001 Front   Back

of an album they would pull it from the rack, scan the cover, and instinctively flip it over to check contents and basic information. I thought that having different photos of Love on each side would increase the visual impact—and hopefully sales.

I also asked Bill to design a distinctive logo for the group, to appear on the album and all promotional materials: advertising, T-shirts, and the like. These days they call it "creating a brand identity" but at the time it just seemed like common sense. My thinking was twofold: create a logo for each group that the public could easily recognize, and since the logo was our design and our trademark, it was a negotiating point at contract renewal time.

For Love, Bill devised an elaborate psychedelic design, with male and female symbols. Seen large, it looked great. But when it was reduced for small ads, it was so busy that it didn't hold up well. Lesson learned: Future logos not only had to look good large but be legible and impactful when reduced.

Bill Harvey's Love logo

In every way Love was a fresh beginning and an experiment—in repertoire, recording technique, packaging, marketing, and the behavioral sciences of rock and roll.

KEITH HOLZMAN: With the Love LP we started a new cataloging system: the 4000 series, our new pop line. "Love" was EKL-4001 (mono), EKS-74001 (stereo).

JAC: The first time I ever had a single on the charts was 'My Little Red Book.'

KEITH HOLZMAN: We were always an album label. We couldn't get arrested with singles.

JAC: Before 1965, Elektra had released less than thirty singles, primarily as calling cards for albums, not knowing what to do with them. "Marketing" sounded very Madison Avenue and un-folky, and I couldn't define it very well. Our music had pretty much sold itself, tying it in with artist appearances. We spent some money on advertising and publicity; we lavished our time getting the covers right and cadging radio coverage on the few stations that played our kind of music.

Elektra did not have its own radio promotion people. We relied instead on our distributors who maintained a minimal staff to cover their immediate territory, so we piggybacked on their capability, hoping that in the process we might learn the ropes.

Singles required specialized promotion and the ethics of a polecat. It was not clean. Stories abounded of money and favors passing hands. I didn't want to know about that. I had a private chat with Sid Talmadge, the owner of our LA distributorship, Record Merchandising. We were not the biggest of his labels, but we were growing the fastest. We had done well together and there was no point in moving Elektra away if he could deliver. We weren't asking him to perform miracles; Love already had a solid local following. Others were asking to distribute us, and I laid it out for him.

To supplement our distributors' efforts we hired local radio promoters on a project-by-project basis. They would report in frequently and send in Top 40 reports which we tabulated, gradually acquiring a more national sense of the Top 40 radio world. We learned the stations and introduced ourselves to the DJs, who could often choose their own music. I was surprised at how many of these Top 40 jocks knew and cared about Elektra and Nonesuch. Our past successes and our fifteen years' track record helped to make us more real. Although many were amused by my pop aspirations, no one said it couldn't be done.

Now that I was committed to pop music, I listened to Top 40 stations wherever I went. They were all AM, usually with very powerful signals that covered a wide footprint—you could tune in one station and follow it over several states.

I was driving to Annapolis, to St. John's College, where, fifteen years after being tossed out at the end of my junior year, I was now a member of the Board of Visitors and Governors. I tuned to the local Baltimore station, and out of the Mercedes speaker blew 'My Little Red Book.' It was the first time I ever heard one of my singles on Top 40 radio, a small but sweet triumph, a validation. My world sang. I pulled over to the side of the road with the joy of it.

The single struggled onto the bottom of the charts. The album sold steadily and in solid numbers. Within nine months it had reached a hundred fifty thousand units, which in those days was mighty impressive, and our biggest record to that time.

We had signed a three-year, six-album deal with Love. After the first flush of success, Arthur told me that he was no longer recording for Elektra and he could walk away from his contract because he was a minor when he signed.

To look at Arthur, it would never occur to anyone that he was a minor. He was a heavy ingester of substances and he wasn't Dorian Gray. I didn't know Arthur's age, and Al Schlesinger, the attorney who represented Arthur and Love in the formal contract negotiations, didn't suspect either. Al, an honorable man, was beyond embarrassed.

I was urgently trying to keep the door open, because I needed the group and it would look like hell if I lost them. In the music world, perception is often confused with reality. Al indicated that Arthur might re-sign for a higher royalty, ten percent, because he was considering having ten members in the band. I said to Arthur, "By that logic the Mormon Tabernacle Choir gets a one hundred-ten percent royalty."

With Al's help we worked out a resolution, increasing Love's royalty from five to seven percent, plus other reasonable adjustments. Love stayed on Elektra.

After the dust had settled, Al said to me, "Jac, I'm sorry, I honestly didn't know, but you handled it like a gentleman. If something good should ever come my way that I feel would be right for Elektra, I promise to give you an early shot at it." And he would be true to his word.

By the time we had gone through all these machinations, Arthur had finally turned twenty-one. I asked to see his driver's license, Xeroxed it, and attached an initialed copy to the contract.

BRUCE BOTNICK: Came time for the second album—

JAC: —"Da Capo"—

BRUCE BOTNICK:—And Paul Rothchild was made producer. Jac was going to produce, but things were starting to hit on all cylinders and he couldn't do it. He did produce 'Seven and Seven Is,' where I put an atomic bomb explosion at the end. That was a pretty cool recording.

JAC: Side two was all one cut, 'Revelation'—the first full-sided track in rock history.

MARK ABRAMSON: Love, the whole band, was just about as strange as you could get. And Arthur—what an incredible guy. He was this kind of brooding, dark presence. He wore these jeweled glasses that he obviously couldn't see through, low on his nose. He always looked at you over them, so he had this look of a kind of berserk intellectual or teacher or a judge or a guru of some sort. He would sit back and talk, and it would make a lot of sense until you tried to figure out what he was actually saying, and it didn't scan. But it didn't make any difference, he would just go on. 'Your Mind And I Belong Together'—once he explained that title to me for about five minutes.

BRUCE BOTNICK: I've never heard anybody talk the way Arthur did. He was on acid twenty-four hours a day, or smoking hemp—something. But he was so high all the time that he wasn't high. He had achieved what they call clear light.

I have a fond spot in my heart for Arthur, because he's a very, very gentle human being.

MARK ABRAMSON: I loved Arthur's house, up in the Hollywood Hills. Everything was kind of sunken and covered with furs. And he always had a couple of white girl friends around.

ADAM HOLZMAN: Arthur took me up to his place. I was nine. He drove really fast and I was scared to death and I thought it was the most exciting thing in my life, I just knew I wasn't going to get in a car accident. He had one of those houses where the swimming pool comes into the living room. We sat around and listened to the new Jimi Hendrix "Are You Experienced" album. Arthur and Jimi were supposed to have formed a band a long time before Love ever happened. I think Hendrix would have liked to have someone like Arthur write the lyrics and sing so he could just play. That would have really been one of the all-time bands. But it never happened. Arthur loved Jimi Hendrix, and he played that record over and over again. He kept getting up and saying, "I'm going to have to listen to that one more time." And he would put it back to 'Purple Haze.'

Arthur was real nice to me. One Christmas he gave me a present, a little box you look into with lights that blink on and off.

Love "Forever Changes" EKS-74013

JACLYN EASTON: Adam emulated whatever Elektra artists he liked at the time. He dressed like a mini-Sixties person—the fringed jackets, the striped pants. There's a great photo of him looking exactly like a mini-Arthur Lee, even down to the pink sunglasses.

JAC: Arthur was phenomenally talented, probably more talented than anybody in town, and he knew it. He hungered for success, always reaching for the brass ring, but it would just pass him by. In his career and his relations with the company he was a basket case. We did four albums with him, each different. "Love," "Love Da Capo," and most famous of all, "Love Forever Changes," which was—and remains—a classic, and finally, "Four Sail."

Yet Arthur was only famous in a very narrow neighborhood. It's not that Love wouldn't play, it's that Arthur wouldn't travel. I finally insisted that he come to New York to meet the East Coast staff who had worked so diligently for the band. He stayed less than thirty-six hours. We could never tour him anywhere, and the result was that his records were mainly popular on the West Coast, and in England, where he had a big reputation precisely because he was so mysterious and refused to travel.

Deep down, I have always believed that Arthur's refusal to travel was because he wanted to stay close to his connections. Which is not to minimize the importance of connections . . .

ADAM HOLZMAN: I remember once my dad and Arthur had these little chunks of hash that they were checking out in my dad's study. Arthur's chunk was really dark, and he said to my father how he'd heard that it was stronger if it was darker, the darker shit was better. And my father said something about how the light shit was pretty good too. I was looking over and I said, "What is that?" My father said, "It's a special kind of tobacco, Adam."

JAC: I knew people in California, or somebody would know somebody, and you would go and connect up, and I would bring the grass back to New York on the plane. This was long before baggage inspections and sniffing dogs. I flew into JFK once with a kilo destined for the pressure cooker neatly Saran-wrapped in my suitcase, and that suitcase was not among the baggage being offloaded. Everyone else's tumbled onto the conveyor, and I'm still standing there. Finally this lonely little suitcase comes trundling off, and I thought long and hard if I should pick it up or just get out of there. I nonchalantly retrieved it and went to my car. No one followed. But I was scared.

And then Paul Rothchild got busted.

TERRY ROTHCHILD: Paul of course considered himself a big wheeler-dealer in whatever he did. He liked the idea of big money, and he was a big record producer, and I suppose he was thinking he was a big drug distributor. I was his wife, and I loved him, and I had no idea what he was doing, and I didn't want to know most of it.

I was never much of a one for smoking weed. Marijuana made me hungry and put me to sleep. I liked the other psychedelics—acid, mushrooms. But I was getting very tired of the drug scene anyway. We had a baby at that point, and I was thinking family, I was thinking stability, I was thinking neighborhoods, schools, stuff like that, the nesting instinct.

But Paul was in the music business. He was traveling back and forth to LA. I don't know who he knew, who he ran into, but somebody there sent a whole trunk full of marijuana to our house in New Jersey. Huge, like three feet by about a foot by about eighteen inches.

JAC: Reflect for a moment. Having a trunkload of dope delivered to your home, addressed to you, would be the ultimate in uncool, and Paul was not uncool. This did not compute. There were rumors about a setup. Others suspected that someone in Dylan's entourage had done it, for what reason I would have no idea. A third story, by the way, had Paul turning Dylan on to acid, and if that's true it's a significant moment in the history of American pop culture. Anyway—

TERRY ROTHCHILD: This package shows up at the door. I didn't know what it was. The guy says, "Sign here, lady," so I signed, and all of a sudden there are cops everywhere, police cars all over the place.

MARK ABRAMSON: I was with Paul at the office when they came and arrested him.

TERRY ROTHCHILD: It was photographs and fingerprints and it was just dreadful, being treated like an object, totally dehumanizing. It was an awful experience and something I don't ever want to have to repeat.

They dropped the charges against me. But not Paul.

FRITZ RICHMOND: It was the thing that we all dreaded to hear about our friends, because it's being eaten by the lions.

JAC: Paul was released on bail just before the weekend. We usually went to the Sunday hootenanny at the Village Gate, but Paul felt so ashamed he couldn't bring himself to go. I told him that he was going and that I would be at his side, confirming Elektra's support. I almost had to drag him, but he went, and the moment we walked in there was an excited hubbub and then silence. A friend came over and gave him a big hug, others crowded around and, in that moment, Paul was transformed from contrite doper to outlaw folk hero.

PAUL ROTHCHILD: When I went on trial, Jac testified for me. He was a brave man, because in those days no one aligned themselves with anybody who was on a drug charge.

JAC: At least no one who cared what the straight world thought.

PAUL ROTHCHILD: One joint could ruin your public life. Albert Grossman testified for me too, and so did a New Jersey state senator, Matthew Feldman. I thought

I had plea-bargained my way to probation, but I was sentenced to two and a half years, and—a fascinating moment—I watched the Butterfield Blues Band album make the charts from the New Jersey pen.

TERRY ROTHCHILD: The thing I remember about Jac is his incredible compassion. He stuck with Paul the whole time.

PAUL ROTHCHILD: Whether I was guilty or not, what my involvement was, didn't matter to Jac—

JAC:—I never knew, and I never asked.

TERRY ROTHCHILD: All the time Paul was in jail, Jac kept him on the payroll at half salary. And Jac also provided me with work, things I could do from home, typing names on mailing lists and so on.

MARK ABRAMSON: Jac and I would drive down to see Paul.

JAC: I'd bring technical publications and Xeroxes of articles I thought he might find useful or amusing. It kept us connected and reassured him that his job would be waiting.

MARK ABRAMSON: He was working on the farm. He had gained about twenty pounds eating potatoes. He had been listening to the radio and he was all excited, he had all these ideas about what he was going to do when he got out. He says, "This is great, I can just listen. Boy, I really got all these great ideas about things. I know what's next, I know what we need to do." That was Paul.

JAC: Worse than jail, Paul hated his isolation from the street. He had a very hard time imagining how the world could get on without him. That thought resonated for me too.

Seven months into his sentence there was an automatic parole hearing at which I spoke with eloquence about his importance to the company and to his artists. I vouched for him and guaranteed his job.

PAUL ROTHCHILD: I was released on parole. I walked out of prison, went home, had a good night's sleep, and went to work at Elektra the next day.

JAC: John Sebastian called and asked when Paul would be at the office. This was during the peak week of the Spoonful's huge hit with 'Summer In The City.' John was in demand everywhere, yet he came to the office and sat in reception, waiting to welcome his friend and mentor home. Paul didn't arrive till midday, so John helped out in the mail room, doing grunge work. I remember that with great affection. People mattered to John.

PAUL ROTHCHILD: Jac gave me a big welcome hug and said, "Tom Paxton needs a record made right away." And I said, "That's good. Because while I was in there I think I invented a new concept for recording vocals in my mind."

I went into the studio with Tom, tried it out, and it worked. I was back in the record production business.

JAC: Judy Collins had come a long way from being a folkie maid of constant sorrow. Her first two albums had been traditional. By the third she had been listening to Jacques Brel and was opening to European influences. I was happy recording all kinds of music: folk, singer-songwriter, pop, or classical, so long as it was distinctive. Quality mattered. And Judy, in her choice of American writers, was uncannily perceptive: Dylan, Pete Seeger, Richard Fariña, Shel Silverstein, Mike Settle, John Phillips, Randy Newman. You can hear all this emerging on her third through fifth albums. Underpinning everything was her classical background. Judy was a gifted pianist who debuted, in Denver, at thirteen playing a Mozart concerto.

JOHN HAENY: Every record Judy did was courageous, and I've always admired that part of her artistry. I guess others can talk about her long hair, and her big blue eyes, and the special quality her voice had, because it did. But there was something else going on. I think you look at her earlier life as a classical pianist, and later on her great skill in working on her documentary film about Antonia Brico, and some of the other things she's done in her life, and you maybe get a sense of where the real artistry was in her career.

JAC: The risktaking and the sensibility were parts of the same artistry.

JUDY COLLINS: One of the nice things about Jac was that he was always willing to explore those directions. His openness was paramount to their getting done. He could have said, "No. I can't afford that. Don't do that." But you know, if I walked in to him and said, "Look, I want to go climb Everest and I'm planning to take a sound crew with me and I'm going to sing all these a capella songs up there in the wind," he would find something positive about it, and he would make sure that it happened. And the interesting thing is that he would have found a way to sell it. Jac is brilliant about how to figure out how to make his taste everybody else's taste.

MARK ABRAMSON: The greatest thing about the Sixties, I think, even more than the wonderful stuff that got created, was the possibility that you could do anything. There were no inhibitions. You didn't any more have to make a folk record that had twelve folk songs on it. You could do almost anything and it was possible for it to be a giant hit. The Beatles probably had more to do with that than anybody. Who knew what they were going to do next? And I think in her own special way that was what Judy was onto—no boundaries. It was exciting.

Judy chose all her own stuff. There was never any filler on her albums. Every song was meaningful in some way. It was a very serious kind of thing. It was always a long process, and eventually it got to be real agony, not from a personal point of view, but because the level of selection got to the point where only a few things would filter through her consciousness to where she really wanted to do them.

JUDY COLLINS: Mark and I had our steamy moments over various issues. We fought and wrestled one another to the ground.

JAC: In 1966 we were preparing Judy's sixth album, "In My Life."

JUDY COLLINS: Mark and I wanted to break rules. We were sitting around thinking up what to do to make trouble, start the next fire, change the world. We wanted to be very dramatic, very theatrical, and we said that out loud. Jac was one hundred percent behind us. He was very interested in where his people wanted to grow. If he gave you a record contract and you had an agreement, he was really depending on that. These days—maybe I'm wrong, but I think the viewpoint is narrower, the goal is to make money. That was not really our goal. Our goal was to make something fantastic.

So Jac would be saying, "Where can we go? Let's start listening to things, talking about things." He would take me to a Dylan concert, and we would agree that such and such was the best song of this new batch. We would sit around at Jac's place and he would play records. He would dig things up from his very esoteric and eclectic past. Mark would do the same, I would do the same. Going to classical concerts. Ploughing through your record collection. Woodshedding. I was living in the Village, seeing people in the clubs, and one would call another and somebody would call me and say, "Have you heard Eric Andersen's new song? He should come and sing it for you," and he would. Lennon and McCartney's 'In My Life' came into the picture because I fell in love with it. 'Pirate Jenny' came from me listening to Kurt Weill and Bertolt Brecht's "The Threepenny Opera." I'm a theatergoer, I see "Marat/Sade," a revolutionary piece of theater, I flip out over the music. I call the composer, Richard Peaslee, just as years later I called Hal Prince about 'Send In The Clowns.' I get a reel-to-reel tape. I play it. I call Jac right away, and Mark: "Oh my God, I can't wait to tell you what I've found! " And they were all excited.

Now for a wonderful coincidence of artistic matching. Jac had a wonderful label called Nonesuch, run by Teresa Sterne, and Josh Rifkin did a lot of work for Nonesuch.

JOSHUA RIFKIN: During the course of editing and mixing "The Baroque Beatles Book," Judy Collins was a frequent visitor. Mark Abramson and Judy had a relationship at the time. I remember her stretched out on a sofa in front of the mikes, nuzzling up to Mark a bit, or just talking. That she's a beautiful woman goes without saying, and that certainly made its impression. And how unobtrusive she was. She was very, very nice, very gracious, well spoken, very articulate and very engaging, but in no way drawing attention to herself, in no way the grande dame. And she was very musically alert, interested and curious.

I was invited down to Jac's house in the Village, to meet with Mark and Judy to talk about arranging her next album. Which was a total surprise to me. But I think, seeing what I had done with "The Baroque Beatles Book," they were all kind of looking me over. And I was up for anything.

JUDY COLLINS: Josh was young, cute, darling, sweet, great sense of humor, and very much the scholar, the Nonesuch musicologist. He knew his stuff. Very intense. And a wunderkind orchestrator. The main thing he had was musical intelligence.

He made wonderful suggestions. So here we have this great music from "Marat/Sade." I had it in the shape that I wanted. I had cut it, interspersed it, and put songs together, made it into a sort of suite. Obviously it was going to be orchestrated. So who can do that? Josh. And he's in the family. I asked Teresa, "Do you think he'd be interested in doing something like this?" And she said, "By all means."

And then I meet Leonard Cohen. My friend Mary Martin calls me and says, for about the tenth time, "I've got this friend who's a Canadian"—she grew up with him—"He's just written his first songs. He's written poetry before, he's got a novel out, but these are his first songs, and I really want you to hear them, because they're great." She brings him to the house, and the first song he plays is 'Dress Rehearsal Rag.' Very dramatic, into something new; it fits right in. I call Mark and say, "You'll never believe what I found! I can't believe this song. It's exactly what we want." And then Leonard sings 'Suzanne'. . .

JOSHUA RIFKIN: We recorded in London. This was the summer of 1966, which was a wonderful summer to come to London. I hit the city the day the Beatles' "Revolver" album was released. I walked straight to HMV on Oxford Street and bought it. I was taken to all of the shops on Kings Road; I was buying Mod clothes. It was a wonderfully exciting time. To be getting a foothold in the pop world was musically very thrilling. And this was perhaps the most exciting period in pop music.

There was nobody with whom I would rather have done this sort of thing than Judy. Judy's voice and her style of singing, her delivery, that very cool, to some people's way of thinking understated, but to my way of thinking very subtly inflected manner that she had—it fit my stylistic predilections at that time hand in glove. In a certain way I banked on her just singing them in that very fine straight silvery way of hers, and then embedding that into everything else that the instruments were doing, creating a very fine line through which she was to thread her singing. I could have wonderfully outlandish combinations. On 'Sunny Goodge Street' we had two harps, two pianos, guitars, everything that could make strumming and banging sounds, a kind of gigantic music box effect. I was turning to use everything that I had known as a high modernist classical composer, in fact using a lot of the colors, a lot of the sense of spacing, a lot of other things that had gone into my knotty, miserable, unlovable serial music, turned to this much more approachable and accessible language.

There was a genuine feeling of excitement at what we were doing. And we were doing it pretty well. Mark as producer was always extremely calm, extremely relaxed, appreciative; his job was to get beautiful balances and thus transparency. We knew we were making a good record, something living up to what we had hoped for. So it was an enormously happy project.

JUDY COLLINS: 'Suzanne' was the song that jumped out of the "In My Life" album in a big way. And I formed this wonderful bond with Leonard.

DANNY FIELDS: Judy attached herself to him. "This is Leonard Cohen, you must know Leonard Cohen, you must appreciate and love Leonard Cohen, he's my friend, my idol, my muse."

Elektra

Judy Collins "In My Life" EKS-7320

JUDY COLLINS: I brought him to Newport. I was on the board of the folk festival foundation at that point, and I said, "You've got to open up to new things here. You've got to stop living in a very isolated mode, in Lomaxland." So I structured a singer-songwriter workshop. Leonard was on it, Joni Mitchell, Mike Settle, Janis Ian. It was wonderful. People still talk about that afternoon and all those songs.

DANNY FIELDS: There was also a weekend at Newport when Albert Grossman had Janis Joplin before her show in a pig pen backstage. It was after Monterey Pop, and there were so many people pestering her that Albert put her in a pen—police barricades, like fifteen by eighteen, and she could stand in this thing and people couldn't get that close to her. If anyone wanted to speak to her, they would have to speak to Albert first, and he would call her over. After the show she was perfectly mingling with the crowd. In fact she was screwing my assistant. I had to fire him for fucking her when I needed him to work for Judy. I had to go up to Janis's room and the door would be open and her legs would be flopping up in the air, and there was my little assistant humping away. I'd say, "Judy needs us." And he'd pull out, and she'd go, "There's your boss again. Aw, shit."

JUDY COLLINS: At Newport, Leonard and I also got Danny through an acid trip, which was very exciting for him—

DANNY FIELDS:—Watching the rug turn into the universe—

JUDY COLLINS:—Going out to the ocean and watching the mussels and staring for hours at the rocks. I took two serious acid trips in my life, and this wasn't one of them. I think I was trying to stay on the planet so that I could be present for Danny. But of course in my usual manner I drifted off with some young man. Leonard was sitting on one bed writing songs, and I was in the other bed with somebody I can't even remember, writing my erotic history, I suppose. But the sign of how much I trusted Leonard was that was OK with me; I mean, he could sit on the other bed and write songs all week, all month.

DANNY FIELDS: Judy was very glamorous to me. She was very wise and wonderful and warm and she was a big star. She wasn't like these rock and roll bands that they throw together in a studio that had to prove something about themselves. She was my muse. I loved her. She was to me the essence of upper bohemia. She made pots and she was in all these movements and she slept with who she wanted to.

JUDY COLLINS: The fall after the singer-songwriter workshop, I put Leonard on stage at a Town Hall benefit. He was articulate, but very shy, and he couldn't sing his way out of a paper bag. I pushed him out on stage to sing 'Suzanne.' He got

FOLLOW THE MUSIC • **141**

halfway through it and went dead cold, couldn't sing it, and walked off. It was wonderful! I said, "You've got to finish this song," And I came on and sort of picked up the pieces and brought him back and sang with him. So I like to think that I encouraged him at least as much as he encouraged me. Because he made the difference for me. He sent me things that he was writing, and he allowed me after a ten-year hiatus of not writing to start writing songs again. He was very powerful. And his work, in the next fifteen years, kept me on the planet, because his work is so deeply spiritual. I recorded a lot of his songs, great songs: 'Dress Rehearsal Rag,' 'Suzanne,' 'Sisters of Mercy,' 'Bird On A Wire,' 'Take This Longing,' 'Famous Blue Raincoat,' 'Story of Isaac,' 'Hey, That's No Way To Say Good-bye.'

Chapter 10

Business as performance art ...
Chinese banquet as metaphor ...
The clause that refreshes

BRUCE BOTNICK: My first-ever trip from LA to New York was with Jac, overnight on the red-eye—Jac never wanted to miss a business day. But he also wanted his sleep. In those days on a 707 they had a little settee just outside first class, for the stewardesses. Jac commandeered it and slept on it, all six foot three of him, no matter what the stewardesses said. Jac was a firm believer that he was who he was, and this was the way to live it, and he did.

BILL SIDDONS: He was always clearly the guy in charge. He kind of put his shoulders back and lifted his chin and walked in a way that you went, "Who the fuck is that guy? He thinks he's somebody." And he was somebody. He was regal. Not many others were.

DAVID BRAUN: He was seen as pompous by some, but I saw him as just acting out the way he felt about himself. He felt good, he was strong, he knew he was a leader.

PAUL WILLIAMS: He was the sort of guy you would think, "If I had to pick one of my friends to be the president of the United States," well, Jac would come to mind.

PAUL NELSON: I voted for him for president once, a write-in vote. And Norman Mailer for vice-president, to write the story.

DAVE GAHR: Jac had style, mystique. He was mysterious. You couldn't put your finger on it. Most people didn't know where he was going, but he always knew.

BHASKAR MENON: Constantly an explorer. He is a man who will never have the peace of being content with the mediocre. There is no frontier or threshold that he would not wish to cross, and that's what makes him a fascinating fellow, a wonderful influence. He maintains a capability for stimulating vitality, a driving passion for the consequential. He is a man who improves you, because he does not rest.

DIANE GARDINER: With Jac it is all up, up, up, build, build, build. Life to us looks like this, but I sometimes think that life, to Jac—he can shrink it down and move around trees and countries. He does it all the time.

PAUL ROTHCHILD: He was an amazingly rapid assimilator, and in the process he could become a leader rather than a follower. I watched him study what it takes to be an executive, and that's when Elektra got into its big stride. I watched that growth and it was miraculous. Jerry Wexler and John Hammond, for two, were more spontaneous. Jac had a lot of spontaneous invention too, but he covered both sides. He'd go after it methodically, try to become the leading expert in whatever it was that he was chasing down. He was a student of life. In his way he attempted to become the impossible renaissance man, to know more about a subject than anyone else, to be the ultimate authority on dozens, hundreds, of details of complex living in the modern world.

THEODORE BIKEL: I was always intrigued by the fact Jac that got himself one of those novelty store pens that light up, with a bulb on the end that you pressed. I said, "Why?" And he said, "Because I wake up in the middle of the night with an idea, and I'm afraid I'm going to forget it by the time I wake up for good in the morning. So I have this pen." It's very telling about Jac, that he couldn't afford to let go of an idea, even if it came in the middle of the night or out of a half sleep or half dream. Which indeed is where many good ideas come from. Except how many of us have a lighted pen?

BILL SIDDONS: Twenty different ways during my relationship of working with Jac I always thought he got the big picture, he really knew what he was doing there, he knew what was important in any particular scenario.

MARK ABRAMSON: Completely right in his thinking—thought out before it was said.

TERRY ROTHCHILD: He talked fast. His mind would make a leap; you could see it.

SUZANNE HELMS: One of the four quickest people I know, and one of the others is David Geffen.

SUE ROBERTS: I never saw Jac procrastinate about anything. Very decisive. He wouldn't say, "I'll think about it and get back to you, dear," or "Well, dear . . . " There was always an answer.

JAC: I take upon myself a high level of responsibility for everything, because it heightens my enjoyment when things go well. Being a confessed responsibility junkie has made me something of a perfectionist and demanding of others.

PEARL GOODMAN: From the time I started working for Jac as his secretary, he had an extreme way of looking formidable. Most people were scared of him. I have had many bosses in my life, some very impersonal, but Jac seemed to me to be the most formidable of all. His standards were way up there. That may be one reason people were afraid of him, they couldn't meet his standards. He would give you a hug, but at the same time he could be a frightener.

PAUL WILLIAMS: Visiting Jac at his office, you could feel the intensity of business being done, and when you talk about Jac's presence in a room—even when he wasn't there you could feel his authority. Fear would be too strong a word, perhaps, but everybody was aware of him looking over their shoulder all the time.

DAVID ANDERLE: He's somebody you didn't want to have mad at you.

PEARL GOODMAN: He was a good boss in many ways. He was not a good boss in his stinginess with salaries. His raises were very meager.

MEL POSNER: After I was at Elektra for a few years I said, "Jac, it's great, it's wonderful being here, but how do I make some money? "And Jac said, "Well, we're going to create a bonus system." And he created a really nice situation for me, that in addition to my salary I would have a bonus of a certain percent of the sales over wherever the sales were last year. It wasn't a lot of money, but it was a signal to me that he was willing to allow me to participate in the success and the growth. At the end of every year I would prepare a document which would detail, this is our sales on this thing, this is the returns, this is the net, this is where we were, this is what I earned over here. It went on for a couple of years, and one year the growth was really stronger, and Jac said, "OK, now you have a ceiling." That was Holzman.

MARK ABRAMSON: Jac had me intimidated. He would have me over the barrel. It's like Lyndon Johnson saying, "You don't know the facts here, you don't know what's going on. If you knew all the facts, you would see that there's no way of not bombing Hanoi," or whatever he was bombing—"There's this and this and this, you don't know that, so this is how it has to be." But I have to say that it was very seldom that Jac had to do that with me, because I kind of would go along with anything. He had the right person in me for that, in that I dealt with everything like, "Oh, thank you." But inside I was seething because I felt disempowered so much of the time.

FRITZ RICHMOND: This was a subject of much debate, why people liked to work for Jac. Well, he's just the kind of guy who seemed to appreciate what you did, noticed what you did. He was a very aware person, and word would get to him when his people had made an extra effort—he could tell in the sound of records, and in other ways. And even if he didn't tell you in money, you knew that he was glad that you had gone the extra yard.

JAC: I gave a lot of thought to finding the exact right present for people. I would begin my Christmas shopping months early, to have time to carefully match the gift to the givee.

IAN RALFINI: He remembers people's names and wives and birthdays. And odd little things that he will throw into a conversation. I thought he must keep lists, there's no way he could remember all this.

CARLY SIMON: He gave me my first pair of boots, from the Chelsea Cobbler. I still have them.

SUE ROBERTS: I remember an incredible enamel cigarette case that he brought back to me from Europe, kind of a take-off on the Naked Maja, but with these two Arabian-looking guys leering at it. It was wonderful, except it was a little too small for cigarettes, and it took me a long time to understand what Jac was giving it to me for—just right for a joint.

BILL SIDDONS: The only weakness that any of us ever saw was that Jac could not take us out to dinner without counting up and double-checking the restaurant tab.

JAC: I still check the tab. Over twenty percent of the time it's wrong, and usually in the restaurant's favor.

IRWIN RUSSELL: Jac had a combination of business skills and musical taste. I always used to describe him as close as you could be to being an attorney without the formal credential, to an accountant without the formal credential, to an engineer without the formal credential.

SUZANNE HELMS: He took a lot of pride in his engineering. He knows a lot more than most, and he was very interested and supportive of his engineering staff. I've known several other heads of record companies, and Jac had more all-around knowledge. He knows about color transparencies and separations and those kinds of things, that an awful lot of guys who ran record companies didn't know diddly about. He's an all-around person.

Counselor Irwin Russell (left)
and Jac, in Aspen 1968

NESUHI ERTEGUN: A perfectionist. Uncompromising. These are not common qualities.

JAC: I applied a film producer's sensibility to record making: to creatively bring the best elements together, to keep the process running smoothly and to assure the result.

I would have much preferred to call record producers "recording directors," and tried to do just that on several releases, only to get them upset and demanding their conventional credit back. As Production Supervisor I was ultimately responsible—overseeing and tying together the many and varied aspects of record making; approving the material, making sure the record was sequenced properly, the artwork appropriate, the label copy correct, the record well mastered, all to achieve a harmony to the finished album with no distracting elements.

Following the music means more than tracking a trend line in the business. Whenever I have been stumped about how to set up or launch a recording, I have always found the answer by listening to the music until it tells me what I need to know.

ANN PURTILL: Jac used to say, "The first song on an LP should make you want to listen to the next song, the last song on side A ought to make you want to turn it over, and the last song on Side B should make you want to hear more from that artist."

IRWIN RUSSELL: He would predict what he would sell of each upcoming record, saying, "This is the way I think we'll come out at the end of the year," and he was usually right.

PAUL NELSON: He had this thing, even when Elektra got very big—at Christmas time, other times too, he'd go down to Sam Goody's or Tower Records and work as a clerk for a few days, because he wanted to keep in touch, not to lose the feeling of what the kid buying the record was asking for, and he did it for years and never told anybody.

BRUCE BOTNICK: He would allow himself to be a voyeur of the whole music scene and the whole music business scene, but only to a limit. If he didn't want to participate, if he felt that he was going to be out on his own and lose control, he wouldn't do it. Which I think is a responsible thing to do. He's always been a very responsible person. I've done it with my own companies. What's good for you is good for your company, what's bad for you is very bad for your company—which is in turn very, very bad for you in the long run. Jac always knew that he was on the edge of danger. He could walk that line and kind of put his foot in the water and see if it was safe and see that there were no sharks there. There are always sharks. But Jac never got his foot bitten off. Not that I ever saw.

MARK ABRAMSON: He took a lot of risks, but they were well calculated. So many of them paid off that probably for him they weren't risks. He really saw the possibilities and the consequences of what he did. He knows how to steer his course. He has the ability to think through every situation like a chess master.

BRUCE BOTNICK: Jac always signed acts with his stomach and his heart, acts that he would listen to at home at night with Nina.

JAC: I wanted to take musical and artistic risks that would stretch our opportunities. But I also needed to stay in the game, so I tried to avoid stupid things—

MEL POSNER:—But he took risks all the time that a weaker person might not have taken, I mean risks in the sense that Jac put himself on the artistic line all the time. He said, "I believe in this artist. Whether he sells ten records or not, I believe in this artist." Jac was willing to stake his reputation all the time. And that's what people respect him for. Yeah.

IRWIN RUSSELL: A business-oriented mind, and an understanding of cultural tastes. An organized mind. In touch with reality. And a driving ambitious guy.

MEL POSNER: The whole premise was that one day we were going to be gigantic. The thought that Jac had instilled was that Elektra was going to go public, make a lot of money in the public offering, and we were going to share. The whole theme of our scrimping and saving and not doing for ourselves was that it was going to affect the multiple, and therefore let's not do that. And we did without for a long time—profit sharing and pension plans and all those other perks—because it was in our interest, based upon the promise that one day there would be a payoff, a big upside for us.

BRUCE BOTNICK: I remember the first time Jac and Elektra came to record on the West Coast, they had brought their own tape because they knew that the studio would add a markup. He saved money that way. It cost less to make the album. When it recouped, the artist got his money sooner, Jac got his money sooner. It was just good business.

JAC: When there was enough money to fly first class I still flew coach, because I knew that if I saved the few hundred dollars difference, I would get it back manyfold in a public offering or merger.

Irwin and I thought that a potential public offering might be more attractive if we diversified the company. We bought a radio station in Hartford, Connecticut and made a sizeable investment in a speaker company, but both became time-consuming distractions and more than I could responsibly handle. So I returned to the core, which was always records.

I needed to produce albums that made my heart sing. Music was where I lived and I was driven to get it right, not only for myself but for all who would listen.

JANN WENNER: The first time I became aware of the Elektra name was before I started Rolling Stone, when I was at Berkeley. The first Butterfield Blues Band album said, "This Record Is Meant To Be Played Loud," and I just thought that was a neat thing. That one little line always made me aware of Elektra Records. You felt that it meant something special, there would be something intelligent there, and indeed it was the case. Later, with Rolling Stone, Jac cared about it. He was an adamant supporter, placing his advertising, building up the print medium. There was something valuable about his presence. What he did mattered to us. Whoever was signed to Elektra de facto was considered an important artist. They didn't just sign anything that came along and throw it out.

JAC: I always tried to see how few releases we could issue and still get the most out of them.

STEVE HARRIS: I noticed how careful everything was. If it wasn't right, it would go back and be listened to over and over again.

People that knew music, and had full libraries of music, would buy Elektra records unsolicited—they would walk out of the store with it in the shrink wrap.

TIMOTHY WHITE: Elektra was part of the new seriousness of rock. It was OK if something failed, because Elektra tried for reach—if the reach exceeded the grasp, at least there was reach.

PAUL ROTHCHILD: Jac was on the perimeter of the American music scene which would become mainstream within three to five years. We had stuff on record and out years before the rest of the world got onto it. So the Elektra image of being very avant garde, very hip, was maintained.

LENNY KAYE: At college I started noticing that a lot of records that I was gravitating towards were Elektra releases, especially after the first Love album. Any record I bought on Elektra would prove interesting. I found their signings to be fascinating. Definitely intellectually challenging. No other label was like that. They were cutting edge.

JAC: David Mamet talks about the culture of Chicago when he was a teenager—a mixture of the populist and the intellectual, the model being the autodidact, the self-taught, what Mamet calls people who so loved the world around them that they were moved to investigate it further, either by creating works of art or by appreciating those works. He and his friends would gravitate to "Midnight Special" on WFMT on Saturday night, a mix of show tunes, satire, folk, blues. His heroes were those with what he called "vast talent and audacity and no respect"—and the interesting thing is that so many of those who stood out for him had an Elektra connection: Shel Silverstein, Lord Buckley, Bob Gibson and Hamilton Camp, Studs Terkel.

TIMOTHY WHITE: Elektra always had an identity for me. Growing up in Montclair, in the New Jersey 'burbs, smart friends of my parents would have Theodore Bikel records, and that was a sign that this was a hip household, it would be cool to think out loud here and not get your knuckles rapped. I remember Judy Collins records, I think through a girl friend of my older brother. I liked the Butterfield Blues Band; I was aware that what they were playing was between Muddy Waters and rock and roll, between black and white culture. There was a lot of cross-pollination between electric blues and ethnic folk, and Elektra had these hybrid qualities. Elektra would take on things like "The Blues Project." Paul Rothchild was a name associated with interesting music; if I had been in a good viable band I would have wanted to sign with Elektra, and maybe Paul Rothchild would have produced. Vanguard was dry, in a way not heavily involved in pop culture, like a service organization. Folkways was ethnically funkier, because Moe Asch was obsessive. Elektra could strike a balance. Elektra took a lot of acts out of the coffee houses and gave them an audience they wouldn't have had—take someone out of left field, graft existing things onto one another. I went to college at Bensalem, part of Fordham, in the Bronx. Bensalem was Catholic anarchist, experimental, free-spirited, a hippie bordello. Arthur Lee and Love was a big album there, everybody played the fuck out of it. Love was also part of the refined hipness of the time—black and white hippies in a hip band, and Elektra calling no attention to the black and white. And they had Nonesuch too, a very cool, hip classical label. Elektra was a very canny label. It was always a literate label, contemplative, a world apart. It did a lot of good helping people understand the roots and capillaries of pop music. It was a sweet spot, the place to be.

MO OSTIN: At Warner Records, I always looked at Elektra as some kind of model.

I liked their repertoire. The thing you could not escape was the quality of the music—a bunch of wonderful artists—and the quality of the look. And I certainly thought Jac was as smart a record executive as I'd come across.

LARRY HARRIS: Artists loved to be at Elektra, and would sometimes take a lesser deal up front, because it was instilled that we would pay them on the hits, and pay them fairly, and they had a better chance of winning here, and they would buy that, because the alternative is shitting up against a wall.

GEORGE STEELE: The part of the business I had come from exploited artists—at independent record companies, take some black artist and do a blues album and give them a bottle of whiskey.

DAVID ANDERLE: There were companies that would pay artists in heroin.

GEORGE STEELE: The attitude of Elektra toward an artist was something I'd never witnessed before. It was warm, nurturing. The artist was not a property. The label was for the artist, not the artist for the label. That was what was different, and that's what struck me so hard. I think about it now, it almost brings tears to my eyes.

JAC: Over time our recording contracts had taken on weight and complexity and I felt we should try to simplify them. Most contracts were worded like insurance policies and it was the record company that was protected. The language was stiff, intimidating and open to wide interpretation. Just the sheer heft of the documents would alarm any new artist. Irwin Russell, Sue Roberts and I decided to recast the agreements, to write them so that an artist could readily understand them.

SUE ROBERTS: Irwin and I spent a couple of days drafting.

JAC: We divided the agreement into two documents. The first was a straightforward letter to the artists, signed by me, telling them how gratified we were that they had chosen to record with us; and then in plain language we outlined the term of our arrangement, amount of the advance, number of albums to be recorded and the royalty rate. This is what the artist really wants to know. And we got it all on a single page.

Attached to the letter was a pre-printed form which covered the many special conditions necessary in such agreements, with bold headlines for easy reference. In a fit of candor, I called the attachment "The Small Print," which is what it was, and had those words printed large at the top.

If a lawyer read it carefully there were little drolleries in the text, the most famous of which was our "love and affection" clause. It read: "Label agrees to treat artist with love and affection. Artist in turn agrees to treat executives of label with a modicum of respect." Lawyers being lawyers, some objected, and inserted their own language to the effect that a breach of this paragraph by either side was not to be construed as a material breach of the entire agreement. Ah, lawyers . . .

SUE ROBERTS: The love and affection clause was meant to be humorous and it was meant to be serious. It certainly took everybody by surprise. People sat up and noticed: "Wait a minute, there's something about this guy."

DANNY FIELDS: Jac always wanted to do the right thing for the right reason. I never saw hypocrisy or venality or political ambition.

NINA HOLZMAN: In a business where you have epidemics of lawsuits, Jac almost never got sued. And I can't think of a suit that prevailed on the merits. Jac would always say, "I'm not in the suing business, I'm in the music business."

BILL GRAHAM: I'd trust him with the combination of the safe. When I first got into this business, I talked to agents and managers, and I didn't care for many of them. If you're a businessman, fine, but don't try to convince me that you care for the artists. Jac was the first one in the industry that I met who not only had the power to effect positive things, he ran his label in a much more humane fashion.

TONY GLOVER: He was the first rich guy I met that wasn't an asshole.

JANN WENNER: There came a time when Rolling Stone had gotten into very perilous financial straits, like at the edge of bankruptcy, for several reasons, most of them having to do with immaturity and hubris. Jac was one of the people I went to borrow money from. He said, "Sure," in a second.

DAVID BRAUN: And he was not just a friend in business to get a better deal, he was a friend in need for people who worked for the company.

ANN PURTILL: It went beyond that. My first job at Elektra was to review tapes that came in, give them a fair listen and comment on them, more than a "Thank you, we're not interested," a wonderful all-purpose rejection letter that says nothing. What Jac said was, "They're sending us their life, their song, because they like and trust Elektra. We have to respond to them in kind."

ARTHUR GORSON: Jac was not predictable.

PETER SIEGEL: He would change from time to time, sometimes warm, sometimes cold and steely. At times the company would be like a total freakout, at other times Wall Street.

ARTHUR GORSON: You couldn't read him. He had mood swings. Sometimes he was a nice guy, sometimes he was very cold. That's not unusual in business. But Jac would surprise you with a curt answer when he's supposed to be your friend—and then come back and feel badly about it, and try to make amends.

JAC: I did have mood swings, but if I was not always even-tempered it was usually due to pressure, trying to do too much and do it well when you had really bitten off more than you could chew. Yet, at the still center of things, there was a conviction that even though I had my problems you could still trust my word, and if things got really tight people would be taken care of. This emotional shorthand was expressed in a heartfelt hug, a smile and the understanding that we were all in it together.

IRWIN RUSSELL: Basically, Jac wanted to do the right thing. He probably treated people better than they treated him.

DANNY FIELDS: He was nicer than the people who worked for him.

SUZANNE HELMS: Give him a show of trust and admiration, and Jac's more vulnerable than many people. I think he's not sophisticated in those relationships.

PEARL GOODMAN: He had a certain kind of naiveté—not about business, but about people. I don't think he knew the darker side of people. For example, I don't think he sensed that Paul Rothchild was a bit of an operator. He took to people or he didn't take to people, but I never felt he had a sharp eye for people as people, rather a sharp eye for people as useful to him in the work.

JAC: We were looking for people who could handle a variety of tasks, and we sometimes hired more by instinct than anything else. I mean, this whole thing was done by instinct.

SUZANNE HELMS: Jac's consistent in the things that he loves in people. We're all difficult or unique or something.

MARK ABRAMSON: Jac was a Virgo, and it wasn't just Jac. So many people at Elektra were Virgos—I think every recording engineer.

FRITZ RICHMOND: Jac was always personable. He came around and said hello to everybody. He wasn't one of those guys that comes in the side door to his own office and you never see him. You saw Jac.

BRUCE BOTNICK: There wasn't anything that Jac didn't know about. Which is the way it should be—when you've got a company that's manageable, you want to keep a pulse on everything. Down to who's dating who, what ménage à trois is happening in what department. Jac was up on it. He knew it all. He loved that intimacy with the employees. And he could smooth things out. He could be a friend to everybody, in their own way, because everybody's truly different. I know he did with me.

ARTHUR GORSON: Jac was a real guy, he had emotions, he had feelings. You could go through things with him. He seemed very tall, but you never felt he was looking down. And he was vulnerable himself.

MEL POSNER: People liked the idea of taking care of Jac, I think. He's not a person who projects that kind of thing, but they do want to take care of him.

JAC: Especially women. I've been blessed with a number of women in my life who have been caring and protective. Certainly Nina, and most of the ladies with whom I worked, made a real effort to make sure that I didn't get hurt.

What I'm about to say now comes from another time. The Sixties attitude towards women feels at a longer distance than almost anything else from my Elektra days—certainly further than the music. What follows comes from that era.

The people who could most upset an office were the women. If they were unhappy or working their way through problems, everyone could feel it even if they did not hear the words—there was a kind of off-kilter, high-frequency hum in the air, a vibration in the floorboards. I knew that women did the hard, routine work without which nothing happens, so I made an effort to keep them involved and happy. Women who were content, who found emotional satisfaction in their jobs, tended to settle in and it took a lot of outside influence to steal them away.

I would go round to each of the offices in the morning and speak with the girls and give them a hug. I just loved the warmth.

You could send women out on specific assignments, and when they were on business, they were on business. When the men traveled they were looking for chances to score. We even tried a woman in radio promotion but the world wasn't that enlightened; sexual favors were solicited, and I just felt it was unfair to put anyone in that position.

I noticed that women tended to work co-operatively, with less destructive ego. Men were very sensitive to turf and pecking order. This was not an issue with the women, or at least not so much of an issue. They were pleased to be recognized for what they contributed and they knew how to get the job done.

I am comfortable with women and have never been edgy about them, so promoting a woman to an executive position wasn't a big deal. We had more women in positions of real responsibility than any other record company—and most other businesses.

So there were large areas of the company I no longer had to be concerned about because I knew the ladies were taking care of it. They genuinely liked each other, and I knew they were fiercely loyal to the company and to me.

PEARL GOODMAN: I was proud to be Jac's secretary. I would go to record industry meetings where he'd speak—he was a marvelous speaker—and I'd say to myself, "That's my boss."

SUE ROBERTS: Such a sense of pride. I guess it's got to be geared directly to Jac, for having such an ability to sense real talent, real genius, real success. You'd go to an Elektra artist's concert, or you'd come into the office and the new album would be out and you'd listen to it, and you really awaited that. All that was part of a sense of, "We're all doing this together, and we're all part of why this is a success, a feeling of family." And that was all Jac-driven.

ANN PURTILL: We would have a hit, get something on the charts, and George Steele—he looked about twelve—would march up and down the hall blowing a bugle. It was lovely.

JANN WENNER: Those were great days, about the time I met Jac. Everyone was involved. Elektra wasn't a business, it was an ongoing drama of a kind, very meaty artistically.

DAVID ANDERLE: And all of us were brought together by Jac. We loved working with each other, we hung out with each other even when we weren't working.

JAC: Good Chinese food was a staple of the Elektra diet. All I ever had to do was yell, "Anyone for Chinese food when we get done?" and all hands would eagerly sign on.

I was musing one evening about the size of the perfect company, that fit my way of doing things, and concluded that it would contain fourteen people, no more than could comfortably be seated around a large, family-sized Chinese banquet table.

DAVID ANDERLE: Now, was Jac a father figure? No, he was too young. But he was somebody who you wanted to please, you were very aware of wanting to please Jac, so therefore he becomes like a father figure in a way.

SUZANNE HELMS: I don't think I'd call him a daddy. He was a lovable tyrant. Tyrant may be a bit strong, but maybe not.

BILL HARVEY: Slowly but surely we all came around to Jac's way. It was Jac's life, but it wasn't my life. It was my vocation, but that was about it. But the company started to grow. Things got more complicated. There were more responsibilities for a guy like Mel or me. Anybody who worked for Elektra Records, they ate, slept, breathed Elektra.

JAC: Most everyone considered me a control freak and I was. The careers of artists are an awesome responsibility, and the traces came together in one set of hands, ultimately.

At the same time, over the years I learned to trust my closest associates, most especially Mark, Paul, Tracey, Suzanne Helms, David Anderle, Clive Selwood, Keith, Russ Miller and a few others. They were happily allowed all the room they needed, but each of them knew when I should be consulted.

PAUL ROTHCHILD: When I first came to Elektra, my arrival time at the office would get later and later and later, until I was arriving at about quarter to five. Jac called me into his office and said, "Paul, I love your work, but you've got to get here earlier, we have a business to run, you have telephone calls to answer, there are conversations I have to have with you." I was a night owl, I did my best work at night. I would vanish at six o'clock and actually do my production work. I would leave at four or five in the morning go home, crash, get up, come back and do the same thing. Jac said, "I want you to be here when we open, every day." I said, "Jac, if that's what you want, fine. I will do my best to deliver. I can put out a lot of product, but my work is going to suffer. But I'm going to try to prove myself wrong."

After about two weeks he called me in and asked for a progress report on a project I was working on. I told him I had made virtually no progress: "I'm on the phone all day long. The phone rings and I get involved with managers and agents and the artists and their day to day problems, and I'm exhausted, and I leave at about seven o'clock and I've accomplished about ten percent per day of what I used to." And Jac said, "Paul, you come to work whenever you feel like it. I like it your way better." And that's something I saw throughout his entire career—understanding what it is that a specific creative person in his milieu needed, and he gave it to them. Go for it, just deliver—that's all that Jac ever asked of people, to deliver, because he expected it of himself, and what he expected of himself he expected from the people around him.

JAC: Paul was the exemplar of the multi-talented person able to do more than one thing well, which is something I looked for in all our people. I wanted to retain Elektra's compactness and agility, so one person able to wear many hats well was a real plus. It kept the overhead down, it minimized the number of necessary personal interactions, which is always a problem in any company. It gave us all a bit more freedom and we could fill in for each other. And it made a more exciting game for everyone.

If there was one thing I think I was good at, although I didn't realize it at the time, it was setting up a good game. You were never bored when you came to work. You might forget to go home, but you knew your day had been interestingly spent.

MEL POSNER: I start thinking about all of those wonderful memories of Jac and my growing up, and I realize that all of those experiences were learning experiences. He was very good at that, he had the patience and the ability to see beyond what your talents were today and look at the future. He was an excellent teacher.

ARLYNE ROTHBERG: Jac took us by the hand and walked us out to the end of the pier and showed us the ocean.

PAUL ROTHCHILD: I had a particularly fascinating relationship with Jac. He was only my senior by four or five years, something like that, but he and my father could have been brothers. My father was an Englishman, an English Jew, stern, cold, demanding. Closed, brilliant, logical mind. Taught me the whole logic side of life. I never really knew Jac's father, I only met him once, but I would suspect a very similar thing. I think Jac has to be father to mankind because he had to be his own father. He had to deny the fathering he had, create another person in himself, give himself the rules of the world.

JAC: Paul, as usual, is on target. Though my dad tried, he wasn't able to break through his own emotional shell, and I unconsciously mimicked some of his less endearing qualities. I hated that part of me and began to re-create myself as a kinder, more caring person. At first it felt like an act but after a while it came naturally.

PAUL ROTHCHILD: Here's something that I don't know if Jac ever picked up on. I was working in the control room, it was way after hours, around eight o'clock, and we had a conversation, and my mind was on the project, and I said, "Well, listen, Dad . . . "

It was one of those great Freudian slips. It embarrassed me, and I covered it. I don't know if Jac heard it, if it registered.

JAC: Oh, I heard it, and took it for the kind of endearment that had to slip out because Paul wouldn't have been comfortable speaking those words more directly.

PAUL ROTHCHILD: Jac became my surrogate father. I did things for him I never did for my father. I mean, I gave to Jac the things that my father would so dearly have wished for. There have only been three men in my entire life who taught me how to live a full, productive, meaningful life, that I have admired to the extent that I would literally do anything for them. All three I met in Greenwich Village in the Fifties, and Jac is one.

Chapter 11

Brecht and Weill at the next whisky bar ...
Diaghilev to the Doors ...
Days of Morrison, nights of Warhol ...
Eve of destruction at Delmonico's 1967

JAC: I never forgot Fred Hellerman's advice to me in the late Fifties when I was complaining to him about running like crazy and only inching forward. Keep at it, Fred told me, and I would find myself standing in the right place at the right time.

For me any time could be the right time. But where was the right place? New York was under an A&R microscope from competing labels. To multiply my opportunities I traveled constantly between the coasts.

In San Francisco, Paul Rothchild and I tried to recruit Janis Joplin for Elektra. On a spring afternoon in 1966, she brought her guitar and sang for us at a mutual friend's apartment—incredible power, the room was too small to hold her, she just about pushed you against the wall. Paul and I knew she deserved a better backing band, but Janis insisted on sticking with Big Brother and the Holding Company, and she was equally reluctant to let us talk to her record company about buying out her contract. I think she liked the idea of being signed to a local San Francisco label. Her ambition was very much in check.

LENNY KAYE: It strikes me as funny that Jac never really participated in the San Francisco scene. You'd figure that would be a really natural place for Elektra to make its stand, but they never really signed any of those bands. But he did love LA. Maybe that's where the millionaire part comes in.

JAC: The San Francisco scene was charming but chaotic. No one seemed serious and I didn't get that this was the reason people loved the place. I was not at the center; I felt like a voyeur.

LA was where I finally found what I was looking for. The time was the summer of 1966, and the place was the Sunset Strip, which had suddenly morphed before everyone's astonished eyes into the hippie navel of the universe.

BILL GAZZARI: Out of nowhere popped all these guys and girls with long hair, and they just started hanging out.

EVE BABITZ: One minute there was beatniks and then the next minute some guy introduced himself to me as a hippie and from then on there were just hippies.

JAC: I remember Jackson Browne saying that the first time he heard the word hippie, he thought it was an affectionate term for a small, hip person.

EVE BABITZ: A hiplet! There were millions and billions of them.

RAY MANZAREK: People who had let their hair grow long, people who saw the Beatles and the Stones and the English invasion and thought that was definitely the way to look. And the Strip was a safe haven for that kind of person, the freaks, the outsiders, the different people.

SHERRI KANDELL: It was definitely the dawning of the Age of Aquarius.

BILL GAZZARI: I guess you could describe it as a zoo.

ROBBY KRIEGER: Every night in the summertime it was just one big street scene. Cars lined up bumper to bumper.

JIM DICKSON: It had the exciting feeling of carnival. People were coming into Ciro's to see The Byrds, dressed in a new costume every night that they made that day.

SHERRI KANDELL: By day I was a high school girl from Bel Air, by night I was a Strip chick, hip huggers, bell bottoms, with my belly button showing. Sixteen years old, and I had a job dancing in the window at Mad Man Muntz in a leotard and fish net stockings, to attract people to buy car stereos and cassettes, to help me buy an Austin-Healy convertible. I danced at Gazzari's, I was a featured dancer and I had a picture of myself outside—my picture on the Strip! Once at Canter's I got up on the counter and danced on top of the deli.

ROBBY KRIEGER: We hit all the clubs. The Sea Witch, an underground kind of place. Pandora's Box, the Unicorn, the Trip, The Galaxy, next to the Whisky, Brave New World, Bido Lito's.

BILLY JAMES: Frank Zappa did a little map of Hollywood freakout hotspots for the edification of travelers.

MIRANDI BABITZ: My shop was right next door to a shop called the Psychedelic Conspiracy, so we had a hot little corner, right where Holloway runs into Sunset. My husband was in a band, and the shop was full of musicians. We had a drum kit set up in the back for anybody that dropped in.

John Densmore's band at the time and my husband's band were sharing a set of equipment. I had this big old Cadillac, and we would load the band stuff in the trunk and drive back and forth on Sunset, unload it on the stage and they'd play an early set, and then we'd truck it all down to the other end of the Strip for the other band to play a late set.

ROBBY KRIEGER: Gazzari's was where the local groups played, more or less.

BILL GAZZARI: The Doors were boys who kept sitting on the stoop and asking me if they could come in and audition. The one that did the most talking was Jim Morrison. I said, "Well, Jim, you got to wear shoes to come in here." So he turned around, went back out and sat out there on the ledge, just joined the hippies, as inside the Byrds and Buffalo Springfield and Ike and Tina Turner would play. And then he'd hit me up again a couple of days later: "We want to audition." And I said, "Well, Jim, we can work it out, but you gotta wear shoes." One day he said, "Bill, can we come in now?" I leaned over the counter and he had one shoe on. I walked around the counter and I seen that he didn't have a shoe on the other foot. I said, "Did you lose a shoe?" He said, "No, I found one, so I could get in."

JOHN DENSMORE: Our first real paying gig, if you could call it that, was at a little club called the London Fog.

ROBBY KRIEGER: Like a little dive, but it was near the Whisky, so that was good. This guy who ran it was named Jesse James. Like a hustler guy. A nice guy, though. Years later I saw him, he was driving a cab.

RAY MANZAREK: For our audition he said, "Come down and I'll let you play one entire night." We called everyone we knew, all the guys from UCLA, all the girls. The place was packed. Jesse was just delirious: "God, you guys, this is great. You're a really good band, and I haven't seen this place so crowded in a long time. You're definitely hired. Can you start tomorrow, Friday?" And of course Friday night came round and all our friends were gone, there were six or seven people in the club. Jesse said, "Gee, I can't understand it, there were so many people last night, it's Friday night, I thought the place would be packed. I wonder where everyone is." Of course we never said a word.

Next night, five people came in the club, the night after that four, the night after that six, and on the weekend all of ten or eleven. An occasional sailor would come in, two sailors, an occasional businessman. Most of the time there were about seven people in the club, the four Doors, the waitress, the bartender, who was none other than Jesse James, and Rhonda Lane, go-go dancer.

Now, Rhonda Lane, go-go dancer, was slightly overweight, but she certainly could shimmy. She was wearing a fringed outfit, she had go-go boots and sort of a discreet bikini, circa 1966. She go-goed to our music in her go-go cage, but it was extremely difficult for her. You could go-go to Johnny Rivers, do the Frug and the Watusi, but unfortunately Rhonda was attempting to dance those patterned, styled dances to the music of a group of acid-heads who had completely spaced out and gone into the ozone and were playing Miles Davis, John Coltrane, Muddy Waters and Igor Stravinsky rhythms all wrapped into one. I mean, we were in our own universe and our own floating, bobbing time structure and rhythmic structure, to which you could not dance the Frug or the Watusi or the Swim. Poor Rhonda. She was absolutely delightful, but Rhonda and the Doors never really had any kind of communication at all. We thought we were Dadaists, German surrealists. That was everything we had studied, that was the whole ball game, to be Brecht and Weill. Or if we couldn't be Brecht and Weill, we were going to be Stravinsky and Diaghilev and Nijinsky. We were going to do the "Rite of Spring" musically before your very ears. Listen while we play for you at the London Fog, and Rhonda Lane tries to do a nautch girl coochie dance to the Indian rhythms of 'The End.'

There's nobody in the club, but we knew that we were doing it for ourselves, we're preparing for the onslaught, the assault on the psyche of complacent, bourgeois America. We had been burnt by the fire of emptiness, the fire of vacuity. There was no one in the damn place, we had to create the fire within ourselves, to nurture ourselves and to create that spontaneous moment that we could be artists for the four of us.

We had made a demo. And we walked the streets of Los Angeles, record company to record company, saying, "Hey, we're a new rock and roll band, we're called the Doors." And we got turned down by everybody. We walked into Lou Adler's office and he put the first song on, played it for ten seconds, lifted the needle, on to the next song, five seconds, next song ten seconds, next song five seconds, last song two. It was like nnnnnnnnnn-nnnnn-nnnnnnnnn-nnnnn-nn. And at the end of it he said, "Sorry, nothing here I can use." Liberty Records—Joe Sarasino played the first couple of songs and didn't like them. He had a hit with some kind of rock and roll surf song with Twilight Zone stuff going on, and I said, "Play the one at the end of the demo, 'A Little Game,' " because I thought it had that same kind of tink-tink sound like outer space. And when he heard the lyrics, "Once I had a little game, I think you know the game I mean, the game called go insane," when he heard "Crawl back in my brain, go insane," he freaked and just ripped the needle off and said, "Get outta here! Take this record and get out! You guys are sick! Don't ever come back in my office again!" So we got rejected by everybody, except Billy James at Columbia Records.

BILLY JAMES: They had no appointment. Somehow they got into the building. Somehow my secretary took a liking to them. When I got back from lunch, there they were around her desk. They weren't falling all over themselves with eagerness to see me. If they were salivating over a possible record contract, they weren't showing it. Jim and Ray—right away I could see that they were smart, the intelligence behind the creative soul. Oh, UCLA film students? How interesting. Tell me more. They had their acetate with them. We had maybe a hundred acetates a week coming in. Their music was different. It had an insidious quality, not just moody, almost threatening, a quality of implied danger. "The game called go insane"— what an odd idea for a three-minute song that you want to get on AM radio and have little girls dancing to. "Go insane"—that's an option we hadn't considered in rock and roll.

RAY MANZAREK: Billy was great. At the time, you could tell a person who was turned on, shall we say, as opposed to a person who had not expanded his consciousness. I looked in Billy's eyes and I started to giggle. Jim said, "Shut up, Ray." And Billy said, "What are you laughing at?" And I said, "It's so good to see you, man." Finally, somebody who had expanded their consciousness. And Billy said, "I like what you guys are doing. You guys are now signed to Columbia Records."

BILLY JAMES: But Columbia did nothing. Weeks went by, months, and then they put the Doors on their drop list.

ROBBY KRIEGER: The funny thing is that we never doubted for a minute that we were going to be big. We knew immediately that we had the best material of any group, we knew that we had the best-looking singer of any group. What could go wrong?

RAY MANZAREK: Back to the London Fog.

JOHN DENSMORE: But the Whisky was the best club on the Strip.

RAY MANZAREK: Every other night we would stroll over and stand at the doorway and look in.

JOHN DENSMORE: Mario was the infamous doorman who, you know, loved everybody and knew everybody, all the bands, all the people. He sort of like ran the block. It was his ship. He loved the street. He saw it all. Kept the police happy, and loved the music, and loved to keep law and order. If there was a row, he loved that too. I saw him level folks that were out of line. "That'll show 'em!" Then, "How ya doin', John? Yeah, yeah, how's Julia?" Yin and yang.

RAY MANZAREK: The place was packed and people were dancing and rocking and singing, and boy, we would just look in there, knowing they would never let us in, you'd have to pay to get in and we didn't have enough money, because we didn't make enough at the London Fog. But we were dying to play the Whisky. If only we could play there then we would really have made it.

Jesse said to us, "We're not getting a lot of people in here, I'm going to have to fire you guys." On our last night, who comes walking in but Ronnie Haran, the booker at the Whisky. She had nothing to do, just came down the street, or maybe had heard something about the group, who knows, but came in, took one look at Jim Morrison and fell head over heels mad in love. She said, "I'm the booker at the Whisky, and I want you guys to be the house band."

We looked at each other and said, "Far out. Serendipity"—this is how things were construed in the psychedelic age. Ronnie said, "Can you start on Monday?" I of course said, "Yeah!" Jim said, "I don't know, I'm not so sure. Give me a call tomorrow and we'll see." Ronnie walked out and I said, "What are you doing?" And he said, "Of course we're going to take the gig. But, Ray, we don't want to appear over-anxious."

We were the house band. We'd play a set, the headliner would play a set, we'd play a set, the headliner would play a set. The Turtles and the Doors. Captain Beefheart and the Doors. John Lee Hooker and the Doors. Otis Redding and the Doors. Frank Zappa and the Mothers of Invention and the Doors. Buffalo Springfield and the Doors. And Van Morrison and Them and the Doors. Jim Morrison and Van Morrison on the same stage—what an incredible gig that was. That was a famous jam. We did 'Gloria,' and of course nobody taped it.

ROBBY KRIEGER: It's funny, because we never knew Van Morrison or what he was like until he came to the Whisky, and there he was stomping around, throwing the mike just like Jim would, you know—oh no, my God, another Morrison! You think of him later more as doing nice songs and stuff, but in the early Whisky days he was a terror. I mean you'd be afraid to come anywhere near that stage—drunk as hell, throwing the mike around, screaming and railing and stuff. He had some real devils inside.

PAUL ROTHCHILD: The thing that was so interesting to me was to learn how much chaos there was inside the group Them. It's almost as if Jim studied their chaos and brought it into the Doors.

DIGBY DIEHL: The Whisky was always a tourist place, but the local crowd that came was very much attracted to that darker side, the powerful weird thing that they were doing.

SHERRI KANDELL: There were Vito and his dancers, kind of a commune family that would come in and dance together. Very snaky Indian psychedelic dancing. Long hair, free-flowing diaphanous clothes, see-through, lots of skin showing, no body shame. I saw them once at a recording session, with all their commune kids crawling through everybody's legs, I couldn't tell if they were boys or girls. The Whisky would call me if someone couldn't come in to dance. I was a substitute go-go dancer, a substitute shimmyer, like a substitute teacher. I would come down out of my cage and dance on the floor, among the men doing their testosterone stomp. I always felt secure, never threatened. I remember Vito looking at me with that charismatic look, a wild look to him in the eyes.

JAC: Vito was famous for his conception of extended family. He was the old man of Szou and the father of a son, Godot, and a daughter, Groovee Nipple. And he was like the Old Man Of The Whisky, always poised to reach out and take hold of the slender ankle of some young dancer, all in the name of Sixties love. And it's only three years from there to the Manson Family . . .

ROBBY KRIEGER: Finally we started getting some nibbles. Zappa wanted to produce us. Terry Melcher wanted to produce us. But we didn't want a producer, we wanted a record contract.

RAY MANZAREK: And this is where Elektra enters the picture.

JAC: In May of 1966 I had flown to LA and was picked up at the airport by Ronnie Haran in her white convertible. Arthur Lee was playing the Whisky and expected me to drop by. It was 11pm LA time, 2am New York metabolism time. I was beat, but I went. Arthur urged me to stick around for the next band. Whoever they were, Arthur had a high opinion of them, and I had a very high opinion of Arthur's opinion, so I stayed.

It was the Doors, and they did nothing for me. There was another group that played the Whisky that I had fallen in love with and tried desperately to sign, Buffalo Springfield, but Ahmet Ertegun of Atlantic was far more convincing. We were a smaller label without Atlantic's amazing track record of hit singles. Love had gotten my foot in the rock door, and now I needed a second group to give Elektra more of that kind of credibility, but the Doors weren't showing it to me.

Jim was lovely to look at, but there was no command. Perhaps I was thinking too conventionally, but their music had none of the rococo ornamentation with which a lot of rock and roll was being embellished—remember, this was still the era of the Beatles and "Revolver," circa 1966. Yet, some inner voice whispered that there was more to them than I was seeing or hearing, so I kept returning to the club.

Finally, the fourth evening, I *heard* them. Jim generated an enormous tension with his performance, like a black hole, sucking the energy of the room into himself. The bass line was Ray Manzarek playing a second keyboard, piano bass, an unusual sound, very cadenced and clean. On top of Ray, Robby Krieger laid shimmering guitar. And John Densmore was the best drummer imaginable for Jim— whatever Morrison did Densmore could follow, with his jazz drummer's improvisational skill and sensitivity. They weren't consistent and they needed some fine tuning before they would be ready to record, but this was no ordinary rock and roll band.

In my folk days, I would mike voices and instruments very close up, and the records sounded fat and full, the voice popping out, right in front of your living room speakers. I thought that with equivalent miking and proper stereo spacing we could make a virtue of the group's sparseness. Kurt Weill's 'Alabama Song' was a surprise coming from a rock band, and their arrangement impressed me. And when I heard, really heard, Manzarek's baroque organ line under 'Light My Fire,' I was ready to sign them.

RAY MANZAREK: Someone said, "The president of Elektra Records is here to see you and he wants to talk to you about a recording contract." All right! We just started jumping up and down. Elektra was a very hip label from New York. We were very impressed with the roster.

ROBBY KRIEGER: Koerner, Ray & Glover being on Elektra—when I was in high school they were my idols, that band and that label. To be on Elektra was the greatest thing.

RAY MANZAREK: The Paul Butterfield Blues Band was on Elektra. Jac had Love. The Doors wanted nothing more than to be as big as Love. We thought it was absolutely marvelous that Elektra was a folk label that had gone electric and were now interested in the psychedelic Doors.

Fortunately that night we had played 'Alabama Song.' I think that pushed it over the edge—Jac said, "Aha! Kurt Weill, Bertolt Brecht. These Doors are not just California pretty boys, they actually have some brains." Finally, somebody's hip enough to understand what we're doing. And then up to the dressing room came this tall, distinguished-looking gentleman.

JOHN DENSMORE: He seemed a little strange, with those glasses. But kinda hip. Hearing how he started with a motor scooter and a tape recorder and recorded folk groups—we loved it. An incredible entrepreneur.

RAY MANZAREK: He talked in his very officious and very correct manner, and we thought, "Jesus, this guy is not only hip, he's smart too." Because, frankly, the people we'd met in the record business in Los Angeles were a little less than brilliant, a little less than bright. He was a bit pompous, but why not? The man was standing six-three and had a good brain in his head, had a good carriage and a good delivery. I was, frankly, very impressed with him. I thought, "This is going to be real, real good."

On the other hand, when he offered us the money and the points—

absolutely minuscule. $2,500 front money—oh. Five percent—heinous. And he keeps all the publishing—yiyiyiyi! Jesus, he sure drives a hard bargain! This was like a Brill Building deal.

JAC: Here are the facts. I offered what was slightly on the generous side of a standard deal in 1966 for an unproven group. Elektra would advance all recording costs plus $5,000 cash to the band against a five percent royalty with a separate advance against publishing, of which the Doors would own seventy-five percent and we would own twenty-five. And as a show of faith, I committed to release three albums. If the first album did less than well, the Doors wouldn't be out on the street, another disheartened and discarded LA band.

BILLY JAMES: Ray came up to my house to have me tell him what I knew about Elektra. I told him in confidence that Jac had asked me to come work at Elektra, that my job was to establish a presence on the West Coast, in LA, and I could think of no better group to support than the Doors. By all means sign with Elektra—I thought it was a terrific idea.

RAY MANZAREK: Jac wasn't offering much money. But a guarantee to record and release three albums—that was fabulous. We could create anything we wanted to, and Elektra would put it out. We had material for two albums. So we knew that all the songs we had would be recorded, and the records would be in record stores, and we also had the option of doing another record on top of that. So we felt incredibly secure.

Jac was fabulous that way: "We're signing you, because we want you to be creative." In effect, Jac Holzman to the Doors was like Diaghilev to Nijinsky and Stravinsky.

It had all gotten rather anticlimactic at the Whisky because we had gotten our recording contract. That was the important thing, to make records, and we had been playing there for quite a while. So Jim was getting a little lackadaisical about some of his performances. One night—

ROBBY KRIEGER:—Jim is late.

RAY MANZAREK: We expect him to walk on stage any moment, and he doesn't. We play a whole first set without him, some blues, some jazz, little Miles Davis imitations and Coltrane songs. The headliners come on, and Phil Manzini, one of the owners, grabs me and says, "You better get that Morrison boy. I got a contract here for four performers."

ROBBY KRIEGER: We were in trouble.

RAY MANZAREK: Maybe he's passed out in his room, maybe he's asleep. John and I go over to the Alta Cienega and pound on the door of his room. We hear a little scurrying around inside. "Hey, Jim, it's John, its Ray. Come on, open up." We hear boots rustling, we can hear movement, a body is moving in the room. "Jim, come on, man, you missed the first set. Phil is going to have a conniption fit. We're gonna be on in half an hour. We know you're in there, just open the door!"

Finally the door knob turns, very slowly, and the door opens, and there is Jim Morrison standing in his underwear with his eyes blazing. Totally zonked out. We looked at him and said, "Oh my God, what are you on?" He sat down on the bed and reached over and opened the bottom drawer of the night stand—and it was like when I entered that room I was no longer in reality, I had entered a strange kind of film noir movie, vaguely black and white, and it had a little bit of color to it, and when Jim opened that bottom drawer of the night stand, a purple light came out of there. There was no purple light, it was in my mind, but I could see purple—and what he had in there were thirty vials, purple vials, of liquid LSD. It's glowing and throbbing, whoom-whoom, and Jim reaches down and picks up one of these vials and holds it in front of us. "You want some?" I took his hand and put it back down, closed the drawer. "Not now, man. Come on, we've gotta be on stage."

Here he is in his underwear. He falls back on the bed, going mmmmmmmm. John and I start dressing him, we get his pants, put his boots on him, finally drag him out to the car, and off to the Whisky. He's humming like a generator, a dynamo or something, mmmmmmmm, you could feel the energy coming off him.

Phil Tanzini says, "You're lucky you got that Morrison. Alright, get on stage and play a great set."

We start to play, and Jim is sort of half there, half not there. Some of the songs he's singing, some he's mumbling, he's standing with his back to the audience, and the crowd is getting slightly restless. Then he wants to do 'The End.' The club is filled, people are drinking and dancing. 'The End' closes the evening, and Jim wants to do it in the middle of the second set.

But he wants to do it. So we started to play it. And we never played it so brilliantly. It was just great. Jim being on acid, it was like everyone was getting a contact high from him. It just became more and more hypnotic. Little by little the dancers stopped dancing, they were just standing there looking at us.

We got to the middle of the song and there's an improvisational area where Jim could do anything he wanted. We're playing very softly, just keeping the vamp going, waiting for him to come in. And he begins. "The killer awoke before dawn . . . He put his boots on . . . He took a face from the ancient gallery . . . And he walked on down the hallway." And I thought, "Oh my God, I don't know where he's going with it or what he's going to do."

But John and Robby and I were absolutely transfixed. He had us mesmerized. John was just accenting, chnk-boom, Robby was playing snaky Indian stuff, and I was just keeping that whole hypnotic thing going. When he said, "The killer awoke before dawn . . . He put his boots on," it just sent a shiver through the entire place. It froze the Whisky. I looked out at the audience and I could see that nobody was dancing. The waitresses had stopped taking drink orders. Now John and Robby and I don't know where he's going but we'll follow him into the jaws of the hell hound itself if we have to. This is Jim, our man, our main man, this is Dionysus, the wild, crazy poet who's free of all the chains. He's taking us on this psychic journey, we don't know where—"Driver, where you taking us?" So he begins to tell the whole story of the killer going down the hallway, his family, and finally—he gets to "Father, I want to kill you!" and "MOTHER, I WANT TO FUCK YOU!"

JOHN DENSMORE: Oh God, I didn't know we were going oedipal! I didn't know my Greek mythology! And oh God, my God, it's so intense in this band!

RAY MANZAREK: Jim screamed out, and John and Robby and I just jammed on our instruments, smashing, crashing, playing volume, and we shocked the entire audience, everyone, from this state of hypnosis to an absolute primal primordial scream shock of volume.

And then we went back into the song, and you could see the people taken out of their trance state, and the dancers began to dance again, and the waitresses and everyone began to go back to what it was that they were supposed to be doing. And we played the remainder of the song as we usually played it.

We finished the set and left the stage to a thunderous ovation. And there was Phil waiting for us, and he said, "You filthy foulmouth, Morrison, you guys are fired. You're disgusting, Morrison, nobody can say that about their mother, you're fired!" Like a fool, I said to him, "Phil, haven't you ever heard of Oedipus Rex?" He screamed, "Get outta here, you college-educated asshole! You guys think you're better than anybody, don't you? Get out, you're fired, don't ever come back here!"

The whole point of it is that Jac saved us. What did it matter that we were fired from the Whisky? We had signed with Jac Holzman and Elektra Records, and we were going into the recording studio in two or three weeks.

JAC: I toyed with the idea of taking them into the studio myself, but I wasn't the ideal producer for them. Paul Rothchild was. Paul was itching to sign a band of Albert Grossman's, the Paupers, but I had heard them and thought they sucked. At my insistence, Paul went to LA and watched one of the Doors sets, and told me I was nuts. I said, "I don't think so." I looked at other producers, but kept coming back to Paul. Paul was part martinet, which was fine, because the group needed a force they couldn't push around, someone who could earn their respect, and Rothchild was all of that. And once Paul made a commitment he stuck to it. Paul also owed me a favor, because I had stood by him during a difficult time. With great reluctance I finally said, "Paul, I never thought I'd say this to you, but you owe me. You've got to do this band. You are the only person for the job." And Paul said—partly out of relief that the books between us could now be in balance, plus my appeal to his pride that only he could record this band—"Well, if you put it that way."

ROBBY KRIEGER: We didn't know about producers. We saw the name Paul Rothchild on a Paul Butterfield record. We loved that record. Plus, the guy had just gotten out of jail, so we figured he couldn't be all that bad.

JAC: Paul was still on parole, and to leave the New York-New Jersey area required permission, some genuflecting, and mounds of paperwork. Paul's parole officer knew he wasn't a criminal but a person caught in circumstances. Still, if Paul didn't come directly from home to the office, or if he wanted to go out of state, we had to ask first. Now I was requesting that Paul be allowed to go it alone in California—

Sodom and Gomorrah West, for an extended stay. His parole officer interviewed me at our offices. I guaranteed Paul's good conduct, whatever that meant. I must have passed muster. Done.

BILL SIDDONS: Paul was the smartest guy about the business that I knew. And a kind of intense, consumed-with-passion-for-life kind of guy. Always an enthusiast, a real positive force.

BOB NEUWIRTH: He was an innovator, an instigator, and a motivator, very supportive, and he had the patience of an insect and the confidence of a rhinoceros.

BILL SIDDONS: He was also the only guy who could intimidate all the Doors. He could yell and scream in a very specific way. Where Bill Graham could throw a tantrum and you kind of went, "What's really going on here?" Paul was absolutely clear about what he was yelling at you for. He was a very well-equipped negotiator and fighter. He busted you point by point. He did not speak in generalities whatsoever. He was so detailed that whatever he went into, he knew every molecule in the structure of it. He had a very Germanic feel to him. He could always put you in your place. He was the leader, he was the producer.

BRUCE BOTNICK: Paul had plenty of time in jail to think about techniques and styles. He dreamed about it. He put a lot of that to work. He developed a lot of techniques that are standard today.

PAUL ROTHCHILD: I didn't want a Doors record to sound like anybody else's records, because that's like buying bread, it becomes stale very quickly. But if you create your own sound, if you've got something unique, the best thing you can do

Bruce Botnick Collection

Bruce Botnick at the Sunset Sound console 1966

is keep it as pure as possible, so that it's not copyable. For example, Robby Krieger was enchanted with the wah-wah pedal, which Jimi Hendrix is associated with. But you could buy that off the shelf, and it immediately made any guitar player sound like any other guitar player. Instead I said, "I prohibit you from using off-the shelf material. Create it. Invent it."

BRUCE BOTNICK: I was doing the engineering. We had gotten the sound the first day, and after that nobody touched anything. It was all live. We didn't do the effects afterwards. Even tape delays on the voice, we did at the moment.

JAC: The album was recorded in about a week.

PAUL ROTHCHILD: We could record four-track. Two tracks for the band, one track for the singer, leaving one glorious track for fucking around. We used that sometimes for Jim's voice, occasionally to bring another musician in, like we got Larry Knechtel to play bass on 'Light My Fire.' We stamped on a wooden floor to give us the very Nazi sound for 'Twentieth Century Fox.' Why we wanted to do that, I couldn't tell you today.

BRUCE BOTNICK: In the studio it was nothing to see them smoking grass. But acid—it wasn't obvious, somebody wasn't waving a flag saying I'm on acid. In the middle of 'The End,' they were really doing a very magical performance, the kind that you pray for, and that's when Jim kind of went sideways and I didn't know why. He went across to the Catholic church on Sunset, Blessed Sacrament, and I guess he was reading some vespers or something, and he peaked on acid and he had some kind of revelation.

We did two takes of 'The End.' One of them is where the acid started peaking. He had these vespers and he started reading from it and tearing it up and got into "Kill the father, fuck the mother." I just thought it was far out, you know. I figured it was part of the thing, because I had not heard the music before they recorded it.

PAUL ROTHCHILD: In my entire career in the studio, who knows how many hundreds of hours, I can count on two hands the true magic moments. And it happened once on that album. We were in the middle of recording 'The End,' a landmark composition. We had it choreographed. Sometimes Jim was leading the band, and at other times the band was full-out cranking rock-style and we couldn't have Jim in the room, so we had him in the vocal booth, and he'd be running back and forth between the booth and the mike set up out there, and Bruce Botnick, all of nineteen years old, making all the moves.

We were halfway through, and I got chills top to bottom. I said, "Bruce, do you know what's happening out there? That's history. Right at this moment. That's why we come here." It was one of those few times you can turn and say to somebody, "Pay attention, this is it." I remember it so vividly, and at the end of the take I was as drained as anyone out in the room from the experience.

Then in my true tradition—anyone who has ever worked with me has heard this phrase from me, and everyone has suggested it be my epitaph, on my tombstone—I got on the talkback and I said, "That was great! Let's do it one more time."

JAC: I edged into the studio control room during the second take and could tell by the beatific expression on the faces of Bruce and Paul that this was a blessed moment. The lights were dimmed and the mood flowed from the music and the intensity of Jim's inner light. I moved off to the side so that the boys wouldn't be distracted.

PAUL ROTHCHILD: On that take the front part wasn't as good but the back part was awesome. So we cut those two pieces together. And at that moment I knew the band was going to be famous.

ROBBY KRIEGER: When we did 'The End,' Jim was so strung out on acid that he was totally out of hand. I think he tried to throw a TV set through the control room window.

BRUCE BOTNICK: Supposedly. It was my portable set. He never threw it through the window, because the glass would have broken. It just bounced off, and we kept on recording.

ROBBY KRIEGER: He was on this Oedipus complex trip and he was saying, "Fuck the mother and kill the father! Goddamn it! Fuck the mother and kill the father!" and he would just rant on like that for hours. So we finally get him in to record and he did it great.

Then we decided he was too high to continue the session so we closed up and left. Jim didn't want to stop, so he climbed back in the place and he started having fun by hosing down the whole place with a fire extinguisher, including all the instruments.

BILLY JAMES: The sight of all that stuff on the harpsichord! Bad, bad boy.

ROBBY KRIEGER: Paul Rothchild jumped the wall and dragged him out of there.

BRUCE BOTNICK: The next morning I got a phone call from Tutti Camarata, the owner. "Get down here! What's goin' on?" This studio was built basically to do Disney records, which Tutti Camarata was the head of. So we'd be doing Mickey and Minnie and "Cinderella" in the daytime, and in the afternoon and night doing the Doors. It was really Disney's house, and to have a little madness in there kind of made things uncomfortable to Tutti. But Jac in his infinite wisdom was able to soothe the savage beast, I mean both savage beasts, Jim and Tutti. Jac's a great negotiator.

JAC: After Tutti and I settled the Morrison Misdemeanor Matter, Tutti draped a fatherly arm over my shoulder and said, "You're spending a lot of money on a band that can't behave itself. You've been a good customer and I'd hate to see Elektra hurt." The five thousand dollars I had spent in studio time seemed like a lot to Tutti who was used to bringing in a group of musicians who could knock out four tracks in three hours. I thanked Tutti for his concern and said I wasn't worried. Privately I took a deep breath and hoped I was right.

JAC: Did I believe, when I signed the Doors, that their music would last, for thirty years now and counting? Could I ever have imagined that album sales would be closing in on forty-five million units? No. I believed they were musically distinctive, and worth the effort—even to doing pick-up diplomacy with Tutti and writing a check for the studio damage. It wasn't until we were mixing that I knew we had made an album that was historic.

Recording is a very special art and far more than a sonic snapshot of a performance. Music must first be stripped of all its live ambiance to make it work in what is essentially a cool medium. People listening understand, at an unconscious level, that what is coming to them through recordings is another beast entirely, but it lets

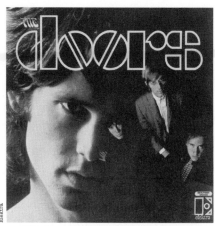

Elektra

The Doors debut album EKS-74007

them create their own excitement at their own pace. There is no chorus of agitated fans, no visual clues of any kind. It is just you and the music and you must create that experience for yourself with your only tools, great material, superb performance and willing ears.

And that is why Rothchild's production of the Doors is so brilliant. Rothchild did what I only understood much later. In physics there is a theory of the perturbation of systems—that evolution is not always well behaved and Darwinian, that occasionally a linearly developing system goes through a period of gigantic and unexpected upset, and from that upset evolution moves to a higher level, an order of magnitude beyond where it started. Rothchild perturbated the Doors. He really pushed them. He took enormous risks, and he was able to get them to want to perform for themselves and for their audience in a way that transcended "going into the studio," because they weren't just going into the studio, they were going into the soul of the music.

JAC: In October of 1966 we brought the Doors to New York and booked them into Ondine, a club cheek by jowl with the 59th Street bridge made famous by Paul Simon. It was the first time they had been east.

RAY MANZAREK: We played a month there. Terrific place. Everything very mod, very slick, very neat, very clean, very tight. Very sophisticated crowd. All the Andy Warhols and plastic inedible kinds of chicks and mod guys.

DANNY FIELDS: The uptown amphetamine crowd.

STEVE HARRIS: I went over in the afternoon before they opened. They were doing a sound check. Robby and John and Ray were on stage doing some instrumental work, and I introduced myself, and I turned around and this person slid off a bar stool and started sauntering over toward me. We met and we talked, and I called Jac and I said, "Jac, if he can read the phone book on key we're going to sell millions of records." He was that alluring and that demanding that he be noticed.

PAUL WILLIAMS: They did 'When The Music's Over' and 'The End,' and there'd be these musical brackets inside of which Jim would have these one-liners or these little raps and just take off with it, and the energy level was incredible. I don't mean coming just from him but from everybody in the room. This incredible thing shimmering out of the darkness while this band was playing. Just overwhelming.

BILL HARVEY: When we were shooting the album cover, we had the idea of overlapping the faces. Because at that time I didn't know who the star was. I mean, we really didn't, because they were all extremely good musicians, and the fact that Jim was the lead singer had nothing to do with it, except that he was absolutely beautiful. I mean, he was a gorgeous-looking kid. You began to realize that in front of the camera he was the one.

JAC: When it came to their visual image, the Doors knew what needed to be done—put their personal egos aside and Jim in front. They were smart about issues that had broken up other groups. For another—and very important—example, all monies from performing, writing and publishing were split equally between the four, and all copyrights were listed in the name of the whole band.

Originally I had promised to release the album in November of 1966 and now I had to talk them out of that. The record was so beautifully realized and important that I wanted to spotlight it free from the crush of year-end releases. Mid-to-late January was when albums would start being released again, after everything had been absorbed from Christmas. I wanted to slip it in on the first Monday in January, when there was a wide open window.

Initially they were disappointed, so I made a commitment that I would release no other album in January. We would focus on the Doors exclusively for that month.

I also promised to take a large illuminated billboard on the Sunset Strip. This was a new idea for the record business. No one in music had tried it before, but it was my way of saying to everyone in the music community of Los Angeles that Elektra had arrived, and we were big-time serious about a band that had a tenacious local following. It was a message to radio and our distributors that we were willing to spend to make it happen.

I also wrote an encouragement letter to my distributors saying that "The Doors" would be issued on January 4, 1967, our major push. "Theirs is the finest rock LP we have ever heard and the knowledgeable tradesters and insiders who have had the privilege of hearing their completed LP have been equally unstinting in their enthusiasm. Get behind the Doors. They are the most important sound in contemporary American music."

I took my LA distributor aside and insisted that the Doors were the best shot we were likely to have, a great West Coast band with an album that had no filler. If we could graft radio success in LA onto the rest of the country, we could break the Doors nationwide. He just had to deliver.

That first month the album sold ten thousand copies, which wasn't bad, although they were mostly sold into our West Coast distributorship.

Simultaneously with the release of the album we came out with a single, 'Break On Through.'

PAUL ROTHCHILD: Every one of us was positive that 'Break On Through' was going to be a hit record on some level.

JAC: It received polite but modest airplay, but didn't make it onto the Top 100. It "bubbled under" and stalled at Number 106. I did not want to lose even the slightest momentum. I decided to go immediately with a second single, 'Light My Fire.'

The full album version was seven and a half minutes long, way beyond the tolerance of Top 40 radio, but it was being played—and requested—on FM in a number of widely scattered stations in solid markets like New England, New York and of course, the entire West Coast, which is where FM rock really got started. This was enough airplay to give us a sure sense of spontaneous interest. The issue was— should we leave it at seven minutes plus and go on hoping? Or, if we shortened it, would that make the critical difference? Would that break it on AM?

Of course the Doors would be against cutting it and you couldn't blame them.

PAUL ROTHCHILD: They said, "Forget it. It can't be cut." The era of purity—when it's there, it's done. I defended that position for about ten minutes, and then Jac said, "Paul, you're a great editor. You can find something," And within half an hour I had a cut. I called the Doors up before I played it for Jac and said, "Listen to this." And amazingly, when I said, "Should we ship?" they said, "Sure, put it out."

PAUL WILLIAMS: I was in the Elektra office with Paul, and he showed me the splices in the tape. He had a little glass thing that allowed you to see the magnetic impulses on each of the four tracks on the tape. I had never heard of it anywhere else in my life, but Paul showed me and said, "I cut this right here, cut this out, and with this little device I could see how to link them up." He was so proud of these razor blade cuts he had made and that it worked so well. And he played it for me. So that's a little moment of history.

JAC: For extra punch in the monaural singles version, Paul and Bruce mixed through the Dolby noise reduction system and then elected not to "resolve" the tape, leaving it in its streched form. It sounded just right on AM radio.

JAC: 'Light My Fire' was like nothing ever heard before. And the Doors as a group were strange and dangerous. There were sections of the country that had no idea what to make of them. When they toured, no one knew what or who to expect.

RAY MANZAREK: We played a college town in Iowa. Beautiful old auditorium, held fifteen hundred. There must have been seventy-five people in the whole damn place. Seventy-five acid-heads, whatever they were—in Iowa, you know, mushroom eaters and cow pies. And they loved it. They were a great little audience. After the show the hall manager came up and said, "Gee, I don't understand why you guys aren't much of a draw here. We had the Association three weeks ago and they sold the place out." Thank you, thank you very much, we really appreciate that, that puts it all in perspective. The Association. 'Windy.' Right.

ROBBY KRIEGER: Another time in Seattle, nobody came. They didn't promote it right or something. It was like twenty people or something in this huge hockey rink. Jim was pissed and he wouldn't sing.

RAY MANZAREK: Detroit. We arrived at this theater in the afternoon to do a sound check, and it was very, very fucked up. This could possibly be the funkiest, worst place we've ever played, just really filthy and dilapidated, and the graffiti on the wall said it all: "You are now in the asshole of the world." But when the cover of night comes, and the lights are brought out and the people come into the place and the music starts to play, it's transformed. And nobody notices the rats and filth. So it was fine. The gig was fine, the people were fine.

JAC: Before the album was released I phoned Bill Graham in San Francisco and pleaded with him to book the Doors for the Fillmore before they broke wide. Though Bill and I trusted each other without question, selling him an unknown band was not going to be easy. After a heavy pitch, Bill finally agreed but extracted one option for a repeat date within six months of the first booking—and both gigs for scale, hardly enough to cover the air fares. Bill Graham was doing a Jac Holzman on me! I gulped hard but agreed. San Francisco was the heart of spacy, rebellious rock and roll and the Doors had to be seen there.

STEVE HARRIS: The album was not long out. The show was the Rascals, the Sopwith Camel, and opening, a new group—the Doors. When they went on, nobody was paying too much attention. It was a big ballroom, and everybody was kind of in the back, dancing and talking. Two or three songs into the set, people started walking up toward the stage. And by the end, no one was saying a word. The audience was completely mesmerized. There was a brief pause for them to realize what they had seen, and they broke into cheers and shouts and screams.

Jim came up to me in the dressing room and said, "There's something I really have to talk to you about." There was a storeroom above, with old mikes and furniture, with a ladder to get us up there. We climbed up and I said, "What is it, Jim?" He said, "I've got a great idea." I couldn't wait to hear it. He said, "Let's pull a death hoax. Let's tell everyone that I'm dead." And I said, "Great idea, Jim, except for one thing. Nobody knows who you are yet. Your album has just come out, so I don't think too many people are really going to care."

But people were starting to care. The Doors came at a time when there was a searching to find new things and good things. I think the audience became very possessive about certain artists, and when they first saw the Doors and heard the Doors, it had that cult feeling about it. Long, long songs like 'The End,' very poetic dark green kind of music. It became every listener's—every record buyer's—fantasy to say, "I've discovered this act." It's almost like the taste makers all woke up one sunny Tuesday morning and everyone discovered the Doors existed the same day.

JONATHAN TAPLIN: You couldn't turn on the radio anywhere without hearing 'Light My Fire.' I remember Geoff Muldaur, who was a very jealous kind of guy, being so pissed off that he couldn't avoid it.

BRUCE BOTNICK: I remember standing in the middle of the Village in the midst of a huge New York lightning storm, with Paul Rothchild introducing me to Jimi Hendrix, and 'Light My Fire' on the radio.

STEVE HARRIS: You couldn't go into a hip club that had a juke box and not hear the Doors. The hip place in New York at that time was Max's Kansas City, on Park Avenue at 18th Street—

DANNY FIELDS: Max's had an amazing confluence of creative types that you wouldn't find now. You would think that you were heirs to the Algonquin Round Table or something. To get in, you had to get past Dorothy Dean at the door. She was a brilliant, short, black Radcliffe graduate who ruled the world of gay culture. She was affectionately known as the spade of queens. She sat on a stool and gave the wrong people the You Are Not Welcome look. Her aura was ferocious. When you first walked in there was a large John Chamberlain crushed automobile on which all the women tore their stockings. At the bar were the original friends of the owner, Mickey Ruskin, the artists, the abstract expressionist heterosexual alcoholics. The waitresses were all beautiful. They all wore little black skirts and black stockings and black sweaters. They were all smart; you couldn't be a waitress at Max's and not be smart. A lot of them ended up marrying either Mickey himself or one of the up and coming artists, and many of those waitresses now rule New York left-wing society. There was a good juke box, a lot of Johnny Cash—'Ring of Fire,' I remember that. The famous back room, which really had the feeling of a club, was where the Warhol crowd gathered, Andrea Feldman showing her tits and all that, and Patti Smith and Robert Mapplethorpe hanging around the edges, knowing this is the society in which they want to be elevated. The musicians preferred this room, the gay people preferred this room. Germaine Greer came in with Sargent Shriver. People came in from a performance. You might see the whole Grateful Dead sitting there one night, or Janis Joplin might stagger in, with lots of feathers, or the Cockettes.

STEVE HARRIS: The way I knew that we had really broken through was, 'Light My Fire' came out, and immediately, about three or four days later, it was on the juke box at Max's. That was all you heard. And the funny thing was, I had come out of the john and I knew Jim was in there right before I was, and there was some graffiti just saying, "Ray's cuter."

JAC: 'Light My Fire' kept burning brighter and brighter.

STEVE HARRIS: I would always say to the boys, "Oh, the record jumped from this to this, and it's got a bullet," and they would act kind of amused. And they gave the facade, or at least Jim did, of I don't care: "Here you go again, Steve, telling us all these things about how great we are, and we really don't care." And so, with tongue in cheek, I would go a couple of days and never mention how the record was doing, and Jim cornered me: "Well, where did the record go? How much is it selling?"

ROBBY KRIEGER: Jim never thought we were big enough. He thought we should be at least as big as the Stones. It never happened fast enough for him. He kept saying, like, "Why isn't it faster? Look at the Beatles—swoosh, straight up."

JAC: 'Light My Fire' was moving from west to east like a slowly gathering blaze, receiving concentrated air play, but I was worried that it might not reach Number 1 nationally. We had already peaked in California, and by the time it was established on the East Coast it was no longer Number 1 in the West. And Stevie Wonder had a single nipping at our heels. Would we still have enough critical mass of airplay and sales to make it?

It went all the way. June, 1967, Elektra's first—my first—Number 1 single.

The moment I heard from Steve Harris that in Monday's Billboard 'Light My Fire' would be sitting on top of the Hot 100, my watch suddenly stopped. I shook it, rapped it on the desk—nothing. The next day, Saturday, I went to Tourneau, the most exclusive timepiece emporium in New York, and paid retail for a new Rolex. One era over, another beginning.

To have both the music and the label held in such high respect had me walking on air. I smiled so wide my face hurt. And to have your personal taste and judgment confirmed by the whole country was like flying a fighter jet on afterburners. The Number 1 single, and the album went gold on its way to platinum. Euphoria!

We celebrated with gifts to the boys. Ray and Robby got the very first Sony black-and-white reel-to-reel video tape recorders with a clock for off-air recording. John was into equines, so he received a horse. I gave Jim a gag "Get Out Of Jail Free" card.

I also ordered a gold record to be mounted on a plaque and sent to Paul's parole officer.

The Doors were booked on Ed Sullivan, absolutely the de rigueur prime time, nationwide television variety show, and live. Elvis, the Beatles, the Stones—all the bands that had "arrived" paid homage to Ed Sullivan.

I accompanied the group to rehearsal and we decided to grab a bite before air time. A crowd was hanging around the stage door. I was in my leather jacket. They screeched: "There they are! He's one of them!" We took off and they chased us until we dove into the protective cool of a nearby deli that had never heard of Jim Morrison or the Doors.

The Sullivan people were self-appointed guardians of the morals of America. When the Rolling Stones played the show, which was broadcast live, Ed and his acolytes didn't want Mick Jagger singing, "Let's spend the night together." Mick caved and sang, "Let's spend some time together," and concerned mothers everywhere could sleep easy. With the Doors, Bob Precht, the show's producer (and Ed's son-in-law) was going on about how much he loved 'Light My Fire,' but Jim mustn't sing "Girl we couldn't get much higher"—"high" being a drug word that would contaminate the purity of the CBS airwaves. Morrison promised to be a good boy, and in rehearsal he was. But then on the air, of course he not only sang "higher," he leaned on the word. There was apoplexy in Edville, and the Doors were banned from the Sullivan show.

PAUL ROTHCHILD: The four Doors took it all on various levels of cool, Ray being the coolest and most careful of the career from that moment on. John and Robby, the two transcendental meditators, I don't think ever recovered from the awesomeness of it all. And it gave Jim Morrison access to excess.

DANNY FIELDS: He instantly loved New York, the darkness of it, the intrigue, the possibilities.

EVE BABITZ: I ran into them in Washington Square, so I took them over to meet Andy Warhol, and from then on they didn't need any more introductions in New York, because they had the right introduction.

STEVE HARRIS: Jim had a way of knowing who was important and who was going to be important in his life, and conquering that person—man or woman. My wife made a comment too: "When he looks at me, he really looks at me with the idea he wants to conquer me." I mentioned it to Nina and she said, "He looks at me the same way." He had a way of looking at you and talking to you and listening to you that said, "Whatever it is that you do, you'd better do it right and you better do it for me, because I'm going to be a big star." For all intents and purposes, he was a star within himself before he was a star for the public. We'd be flying somewhere, he would get a magazine at the airport that he had given an interview, and he'd look at me and say, "How come I'm not on the cover?" Yeah, I remember watching him getting in and out of a limousine for the very first time and it was like he had been doing it all his life.

MIRANDI BABITZ: When I opened my store—very near the beginning—he came to me. This was by appointment. Nobody ever walked in, because all we did was custom. He asked me if I would design some stage clothes for him. He had ideas of what he wanted, and that was exactly what I did, was work with people on their concepts. He wanted a double-breasted suit in black leather with silver buttons and a broad green suede lapel and a navy-front pant. That was the first suit I made for him. He loved it and he looked great in that suit. I made a lot of just pants for him. Heavy silver conch belts, and sometimes with a conch on the flap of the leather that was actually the fastening. I think he was one of the first stage performers to really go for that leather look, solid leather. It wasn't fringes and it wasn't western or medieval. A lot of people wore suede or multi-colors, intricate design work, going more for the hippie medieval look, and Jim was not a hippie. That was not his thing. He wanted something that was sleek. Something that looked totally different, didn't look like what anyone else was wearing. The flap around those pants is something that he came up with. There is no fly. He wanted that smooth piece of leather across the front instead of a fly. It's a sailor front. But that was never done in leather.

BRUCE BOTNICK: This Adonis in black leather, right? They had never seen anybody—I mean, in those days black leather was associated with bikers and gays.

RAY MANZAREK: An intellectual poet rock star. He knocked New York on its ass.

BRUCE BOTNICK: Oh, he destroyed them. He swept them off their feet.

RAY MANZAREK: New York had the intellectuals, San Francisco had the soul, and LA was a plastic place, it couldn't possibly have an intellectual. And how could anybody in leather pants possibly be a poet? How could anyone that handsome be a poet? A poet was a scraggly guy with a scraggly beard who would scratch the side of his face a lot. A poet didn't look like Michelangelo's David, for God's sake, with ringlets of hair and a Steve Canyon jaw—

BRUCE BOTNICK: New York, that reception, definitely changed Jim. That whole thing created a major shift in his demeanor and attitude. Because he started to believe it. And they, like vampires, bled him. There are groups of people, the intelligentsia, that are literally like vampires. They take anything young that's coming along and they will suck them dry and corrupt them.

EVE BABITZ: Oh, well, everybody does that in New York. That's what New York is for. That's what innocence is for—to be ravaged.

STEVE HARRIS: I set up a gold record party for 'Light My Fire' at Delmonico's wine cellar. A wonderful place. The usual suspects were there—you know, the Warhol crowd, DJs and press people, some people who owned record stores.

Steve Harris and friend in
Delmonico's wine cellar

RAY MANZAREK: Jac really outdid himself. Here's the Number 1 in the nation, probably Elektra's first Number 1 anything, certainly our first. We were all as pleased as punch with each other, feeling awfully smug and great.

We're in the wine cellar. Mistake. Morrison proceeds to get rip-roaring drunk. He's reaching behind and pulling bottles out of the wine rack, calling the waiter over to open them, having a sip—"I don't like this, forget it." He was, like, blind tasting, alternating between pulling out twenty-dollar bottles and fifty, seventy-five, hundred-dollar bottles.

STEVE HARRIS: He just banged them open and drank them right out of the bottle.

RAY MANZAREK: People are toking, the smell of marijuana is in the air. People are just like kinda crawling over tables, laughing, joking, screaming.

JAC: I contemplated the scene in its entirety and decided that it was a good place to be absent from.

RAY MANZAREK: Jac was gone. The rest of the Elektra people were gone. The photographers had disappeared. The people from Billboard had disappeared. I looked around the place and thought, "This is like seventy-five to a hundred hippie animals, and there's not an adult in the whole goddamn place. This is absolutely insane." The manager walks in, the cops walk in: "That's it. The party is over. Everyone out." So we all stumbled and bumbled out of the place.

STEVE HARRIS: We headed for Jac's apartment. The intention was to listen to some new tracks.

Andy Warhol had given Jim a present, a sort of Louis XIV gold phone in a box. The car stopped at a light, there was a bum on the sidewalk, Jim rolled down the window and handed him the box, and as the light changed and the car rolled away into the night, the bum is standing there opening the box.

JAC: This is the famous night when Jim allegedly came hammering on our apartment door, and when we wouldn't open up, peed in an empty wine bottle and left it. Or, in another version, peed in the corridor. Or peed on the wall and the fabric peeled off in sympathy. The sensitive artist and the insensitive record company president, creative rage delivering righteous judgment on the crassness of commerce, or something. The stuff of rock legend.

Leaving aside the certainty that Jim would not have got past the doorman, especially at that time of night and even more especially in his condition, we wouldn't have been there to fail to come out, because from Delmonico's we went to check out an act at a downtown club. Furthermore, the forensic evidence does not support the urinary testimony. There was no bottle of pee outside our door, not even a carpet stain.

A year later I returned to Delmonico's wine cellar. The racks were happily full of bottles, intact and properly displayed, but they contained no wine. They were just for show. For the Delmonico management, one Morrison wine festival was enough.

The Doors receive plaque certifying 'Light My Fire' as Billboard's No. 1 single, June 1967

Chapter 12

The squire of West 12th Street, his good wife and family, and his switchblade chauffeur ... The music business as firstborn

JAC: With a hot, hot group and a Number 1 record, Elektra was now moving at warp speed. My dance card was filled and my life was busier than I had ever known it. I traded up from my four-door Mercedes to a Cadillac limo, slightly used, that could carry up to eight people if we squeezed, plus boxes and recording equipment—everyone and the lawn mower.

My driver, George Graves, was from Harlem, in his middle fifties, about five foot six and the color of burnished mahogany. George was very friendly but didn't say much unless you began the conversation. The entire office adored him. While waiting for me he would read—mostly paperback novels—or do personal chores: cuffing a new pair of trousers or giving himself a manicure. He would hold court at the pool table in the art department, casually pool-sharking the Elektra guppies.

I envied George's capacity to catnap and then re-awaken in an instant, fully alert. He moved with an air of understated bravado. His quiet dark suit and tie with a white shirt could not hide a ragged, bloated scar from a knife wound that almost bisected his neck, clearly not stitched by any surgeon. Once I asked about it and he said, "You don't want to have seen the other guy."

According to our gas receipts, the limo was getting about three miles per gallon. My guess was that George was filling up his neighbors' cars or getting a cash kickback. I mentioned my puzzlement over the poor mileage and it magically improved, to about seven. That was reasonable, because George paid his way in reliability, always there when he was supposed to be.

The limo was my only car, and if I traveled on a weekend I would drive it myself. One wet Saturday I braked suddenly, and from under the seat spun out a flick knife with an eight-inch blade spring-propelled from a wooden handle. I slid it back. Some weeks later when a Village lout hassled me about the limo, George burst from his seat, his right arm bringing the blade to the guy's throat, and that was that.

JAC: Elektra's three years in the Sperry-Rand building were great times. Paul Rothchild and Mark Abramson were turning out fine albums. Bill Harvey now had help in the art department, their offices enhanced with light from the east and south. My brother Keith was automating our accounting, with three on staff busy with billing, payables, and best of all, accounts receivable. Steve Harris was supervising radio promotion. Pearl Goodman was my super secretary. We had grown to fourteen, my fantasy Chinese banquet table magic number.

ARTHUR GORSON: Jac was a host. He set a table, and the table was Elektra Records. He created an environment, and he invited you in. It was like, "Come into my world."

DIANE GARDINER: I think that Jac Holzman is simply the ultimate performance artist. You have these performance artists who do their little set pieces in museums. I think that for Jac it's the world. He creates it and he gets to watch. Each set piece is ongoing, and because they're so big and they make money, people call it business. Jac knows how to make money, but it's just a small piece of his whole performance art. If you were to say, "What is Jasper Johns's most famous sequence?"— then with Jac, Elektra would be that.

PAUL ROTHCHILD: Jac was very well raised, well reared, and at the earliest opportunity he equipped himself and Nina and their lives with the tools of the yuppiedom of the day. You know, a nice apartment—the first co-op I'd ever been in in my life in New York—great kitchen, great food on the table, well thought and bought stuff on the walls, good collections of this, that and the other thing.

It's just a new name for a very old concept—tradespeople who have accumulated enough money to compete in the buying market with the wealthy. The arts have always needed their burghers. You can't support art without burghers, you can't do it just with kings and queens and princes, you need the burgher class to support the arts, and Jac's company addressed the burgher class.

So Jac was like a friendly representative of money with good taste, much like a supporter of the arts would be, understanding of the arts, sympathetic to the arts. And Nina was a woman of great innate taste.

JAC: Nina was our special events coordinator, planning listening parties for new records, artists' events, and all with sumptuous food.

PAUL ROTHCHILD: She introduced Jac to haute cuisine. You know, the ubiquitous cheese parties at Jac's house, and at Elektra, which Nina staged for events—the release of a record, visiting dignitaries.

JAC: Nina was an accomplished cook. The French conductor and gourmand, Roland Douatte, pronounced her roast breast of duck the best he had ever tasted. Everyone looked forward to Nina's theme parties. They were scheduled after a concert, with the artist's favorite food—for example, Greek food and green Hungarian wine for Tom Rush. Nina would spend weeks nervously planning and then cooking, sneak out of the concert half an hour before the end, hurry home, do the final touches and greet the first guests while I was backstage with the artist.

NINA HOLZMAN: Very big parties. Never less than a hundred people. I have files of exactly what I served. I never truly realized how hard it might be to pull it off, but I always managed. I always felt let down when it was over, like a theatrical production when you go through post-partum blues.

JAC: These events extended Elektra's sense of family beyond the office. Nina's quiet grace and fine food showed another dimension. I was mostly business. Nina added a softness.

PAUL ROTHCHILD: I think that Nina was a very important part of Jac's emotional development. She was the yin to Jac's yang.

SUZANNE HELMS: Jac couldn't have found anybody more perfect for that period of his life. Nina related well with the artists, she loved the music, she helped with the company.

NINA HOLZMAN: There was a point at which I totally and absolutely understood the whole business, and I don't mean just Elektra, I mean the whole record business. I mean, I knew everybody's phone number.

PAUL ROTHCHILD: From the first day I joined the company, Nina was an active part of the A&R department. Never in title, but she was always actively involved. Elektra was not just the business her husband was in, she was an integral part of it. She'd go out to the clubs during times when Jac couldn't. And once the artist was signed, she was very much involved in liaison, maintaining loving and positive contact. She was very bright, very giving. She was—what's the word I'm looking for?—the patron saint of A&R.

JUDY COLLINS: Nina was a good friend, just a good all the way through person. I remember the first time I did Town Hall, my very first New York solo concert in 1965. I got this beautiful long dress, and she said, "Don't cut it off, leave it long." And it was such a big deal to me, I mean, you don't wear a long dress. She said, "Wear it, it's beautiful." I said, "No," and I cut it off. So wrong. She was so right. Then she said, "The day of your concert, I want you to go to Elizabeth Arden's and have a massage and a facial." I had never been to Elizabeth Arden's. She paid for it. She gave that to me. (And introduced me to sin. I spent a lot of time at Elizabeth Arden's after that.) I thought that was so sweet. She was thinking about the way that you feel on the day of the concert, how nervous you are, how uptight, because it's your first time solo in New York, and oh my God how your knees are shaking. She was just there, and you really felt her presence. Great woman.

NINA HOLZMAN: Within Elektra, what happened over time was that I became a kind of buffer. If some of the artists had difficulty communicating with Jac, they would come to me. I was sympathetic and they would tell me the whole thing, and I would translate it for Jac and make it a little more palatable, or try to point things out to him. And if he wanted me to get a message to somebody, it worked in the opposite direction too.

Jac and I in the business got on extremely well. We were very complementary, with different strengths, and it just worked.

JAC: In the early days of Elektra and my marriage, my absorption with the business was matched by Nina's. Dinner talk was all business. Nina would let me ramble on. In most households the wife would have gone nuts, but not Nina. She hung on every word.

By the early Sixties—when I think back, as early as 1961—the terms of the equation were changing. We had two children, and the business was demanding more of me. The business was my first-born and it took a first-born's precedence.

In 1963 I even sold my airplane. No time.

What happened over the years was that the music portion of what I did could no longer be done in the office because of constant interruptions. Running any vital smallish business is like being a lone tennis player facing a hundred people, and they're hitting balls at you one after another, which doesn't leave you any quiet, contemplative time. So I'd deal with all the music at home. I would come home from work, play with the kids a bit, talk to Nina about the day, sit down for dinner, which was more record business talk, and then withdraw to my study. All my tools were there. I would work every night, head to bed about eleven-thirty, up the next morning at seven, and start all over again.

Business absorption was the same as self-absorption. I began to feel that every hour of every day I was president of Elektra and that was my job in life. It was more in my face than child-rearing, and whenever there were problems between me and Nina I'd retreat into whatever I was doing and not deal with it.

I undertook a project to edit all the Woody Guthrie Library of Congress recordings, transferring them scrupulously from acetate to tape, to be released as a three-disc boxed set on Elektra. Leadbelly too. I'd montage the music with short interviews, and after I finished I de-clicked everything, which meant finding every click, every imperfection, from the original acetate. We transferred to tape at 15 ips, which gave me room to edit, and I would just cut the click out of the tape manually. My cuts were undetectable. I think I got away with every one, and there were about a thousand of them. And I did this night after night after night.

NINA HOLZMAN: He was so focused, and so blind to everything but Elektra.

JAC: During the summers Nina would take the kids out of the city, to California, or to Connecticut, where I might visit with them on the weekends. I was happy to be by myself and cherished these quiet times when I stayed very busy and could focus exclusively on the only thing that really interested me.

Once, playing a mental game of What If, I posed the following question: "If I was forced to choose between my home life and Elektra, which would I choose?" And the answer was Elektra.

Chapter 13

Evolution of a bi-coastal life form ...
Other carbon-based structures ...
Standing on the corner of Broadway and La Cienega ...
Ten pounds of Hershey bar ... Goodbye and Hello

JAC: Once you bring a major group home everything gets bigger. There is more money and a heightened expectation by others. Drive and ego are yoked together to show the world that the Doors were more than a lucky fluke.

Finances, opportunities, needs, and risks all moved to a higher level. We were at the table now with the other big independents—Atlantic, A&M, Warner—and the major labels.

The decision to grow a company is often a choice not consciously made. Sheer momentum is carrying you along, and the time to reflect on future directions and personal costs whizzes by, usually without even being noticed. The negative repercussions of growth are easy to lose in the thrill of riding the tiger.

But what a ride!

JAC: By early 1967 Elektra had outgrown the Sperry-Rand building. Fortunately we were able to acquire one entire floor plus half of another, with almost twice the square footage, at 1855 Broadway at 61st street. It was not as central as 51st and Sixth, but it had the virtue of plentiful space. The crowding was relieved, at least for a while. Bill Harvey's art department still had eastern and southern exposures, and the odd geometry of the exterior wall gave my office an interesting angularity.

BOB ZACHARY: The twelfth floor of the building was A&R, the tenth was the offices.

BRUCE HARRIS: Elektra was the first record company office I was ever in. While at Hunter College, I reviewed a Love album, and Steve Harris invited me over. I was a freshman, and the place was impressive to me for three reasons: miniskirts, miniskirts, miniskirts. And it was a wonderful creative atmosphere, with people very intent on what they were doing, very ardent in their concern for the music.

KEITH HOLZMAN: A lot of our musicians—and staff—couldn't stand the fluorescent lights in the studio. I had worked in theater and I knew about lighting design. So, I bought colored theatrical gels, and people made collages of them, and laid them over the plastic diffusers, our own modern art.

JOHN HAENY: You walked through this door at the end of the hall, and all of a sudden the light changed to soft muted colors. There were Indian fabrics on the walls, and incense.

JAC: And other aromas in the air.

BOB ZACHARY: Floors two, three, and four were the New York state bureau of narcotics and addiction control.

KEITH HOLZMAN: It used to drive our musicians absolutely bonkers when they came in and saw the narc names on the sign by the elevator.

BOB ZACHARY: Also on the second floor was A&M Records. Down the street were Atlantic and Roulette.

SUE ROBERTS: And the ground floor had the best Chock Full O' Nuts.

JAC: This was the year we went to a new logo. Bill Harvey designed the Elektra butterfly, a beautiful thing with a sense of airy freedom.

I was flying too, but not like a butterfly, shuttling back and forth between coasts like a jet-powered badminton bird. I was still New York-based, but I had become a bi-coastal life form.

My West Coast reconnaissance in 1962 was ahead of its time, but from the mid-Sixties the scene was building. Both San Francisco and LA were hot. I was in LA often, dealing with A&R, marketing, recording, administration and, most importantly, keeping artists happy.

In 1964 Dave Hubert, a music publisher friend, had offered me a loaner office in his facilities in the Vine Tower on Sunset, but mostly my West Coast office was in my briefcase and my head. I thought Elektra deserved a West Coast presence of its own.

I loved New York's vitality, ease of movement around Manhattan, its air of self-importance and open ambition. It had everything but a feeling of expansiveness, room to breathe.

The most famous Elektra logo

LA was a city of low-rise buildings, offering reasonably priced space, an agreeable climate and a chance to be present at the beginning of something very new.

In addition to opening an office, I longed to build a studio. The studio would anchor our presence, give us a creative core and help us to more actively pursue the music. A good studio could be a draw, and I believed we could keep it busy with Elektra and non-Elektra artists. And this would be my chance to build a facility with the latest technology, always an irresistible impulse.

In 1966 I bought, for $69,000, a nondescript building and some land in the heart of West Hollywood, at 962 North La Cienega Boulevard, just south of Santa Monica Boulevard. This was the start of Elektra's permanent commitment to California.

JIM DICKSON: In LA you did a lot of giggling. There was a lot to giggle about. It had gone from a very poor, hardly getting along, bunch of people who just sort of had each other, to where everybody was just doing fine. And having a good time. It was a continuous party.

HERB COHEN: I never slept. Things were happening in Topanga, in Venice, nonstop. I made money, I spent money. I never bought clothes, or houses. I gave money to people hanging around to do things—people getting abortions, going to Mexico. Money wasn't an issue, it was a question of what else can we do, what else can we find?

JIM DICKSON: Right up to Monterey Pop in the summer of 1967 it was always exciting and fun.

JAC: Rock, as music or as a social force, could not be contained within four walls and a ceiling. In the open air of the Monterey Stadium it found its natural venue.

For impact, Monterey Pop was like ten Newports rolled into one. The Saturday evening highlights were Janis Joplin, who essentially repeated the high points of her afternoon set, and Otis Redding, in his first exposure to an almost entirely white audience. The explosive cappers were the Who and Jimi Hendrix, who outdid each other in volume, theatrics, and in multiplying the possibilities of what one could squeeze out of a guitar. Hendrix, who had flipped a coin with Pete Townshend to decide who would go on last, won, and played with such ferocious intensity that the line between man and instrument completely disappeared. Hendrix and his guitar blended into a frenzied rapture that pushed the guitar envelope in a hundred directions at once. And the future of rock and of a generation never seemed brighter.

JIM DICKSON: Monterey was about all anybody could handle. It was the most exciting thing I'd ever seen, and I think anybody who was there ever saw.

DAVID BRAUN: It moved the action to the West.

JIM DICKSON: Monterey was a mixture of two elements: people who thought it was a great new community happening, everybody excited and having a good time, and people who saw the commercial potential to it, to really score or promote with it.

DAVID ANDERLE: The LA club scene was so explosive. You could go for three days just naming LA bands starting to form, getting signed.

JAC: Judy Collins had hit for us in 1964 and Love in 1965-1966. By the spring of 1967, the Doors were smoking, and by Monterey the label was on fire.

LA was the place. Nailing down real estate on La Cienega was the easy part. I also needed people I could trust to oversee the West Coast operation.

My life has been blessed with great luck in finding the people I need just when I need them. Suzanne Helms and David Anderle both appeared on cue.

SUZANNE HELMS: I was working at Dave Hubert's office, where Jac was sharing space. Jac was in the Xerox room and I heard him call out to me, "There's a fire in the Xerox machine!" I went in to help him, and somehow in the middle of the smoke and getting his pieces out, he said, "I'm thinking of opening an office on the West Coast. Would you be interested? Think about it, dear."

DAVID ANDERLE: I had met Jac years before when I was working in LA at Auto Stereo, a company founded by Mad Man Muntz, duplicating record albums onto four-track cartridges for car stereos.

JAC: The Muntz proprietary four-track car stereo was a bulky device by today's standards, but the first. LA, being such a car-crazy, entertainment town, was the perfect environment to launch a music system for the automobile.

DAVID ANDERLE: One of the earliest companies we contracted with for music was Elektra. Jac came out from New York to negotiate the agreement. On a scale of one to ten for meticulousness about quality he was an eleven. Somehow he was impressed with my diligence, and he wrote a letter to the president of Auto Stereo saying he would allow his product—

JAC:—Selected releases—

DAVID ANDERLE:—To be put on our cartridges if I personally were to oversee quality control. After that I didn't see him for three years.

I worked in the record business, took time off to paint, then worked again. At the time of Monterey Pop, Al Kooper was staying at my house. He was looking to get his new band signed—Blood, Sweat and Tears. Al knew Jac from Newport, and Elektra was one label Al was interested in. I was at Monterey for a few days, came home, and Al and his friend Judy Collins were there. I loved Judy's work. We sat up all night talking and playing music, and she said, "You must come and work at Elektra." I had lunch with Jac, and—bingo.

JAC: I was looking for an attractive magnet to lure talent and keep our artists content and thinking kindly of the company. David could have been sent from central casting. Darkly handsome, with a jaunty Zapata mustache and a knowing air, he defined hip LA, laid-back and cool.

PAT FARALLA: Tall and lean, long-sleeve shirts, leather jacket, jeans, dark colors always.

JAC: There was much more to David than looks and leathers. He had a caring nature, and as a painter himself, he dealt with issues from an artist's viewpoint. His music experience had broadened considerably since the days of Muntz. Although we were both highly contained people, in our discussions of music we could get very excited. Music was my easiest portal to emotion, and I believe that was true for David.

SUZANNE HELMS: For the time being, David and I were working out of offices at 6725 Sunset. I was buying lots on La Cienega under different names with different brokers, because we didn't want it known that we were looking for contiguous property.

JAC: The building of a studio is a heavy responsibility, like creating a child. For me, the recording studio is a holy place. A studio is never turned off; perpetually powered up, it has a window on immortality. It is a galaxy of electronic variables and carbon-based elements flying in formation: integrated circuits, relays, transformers, motors, tape, capstans, coils, knobs, sliders, exotic materials, wood and glass, all in the service of music. It is the bridge of our own music-making starship, which it resembles to a remarkable degree. The studio controls us as much as we believe we control it. It is a living, breathing organism with a metabolism that is ever-changing, acoustically, electronically, psychologically. It can be a beast, benign or treacherous. It has a pulse, a voice, an opinion and a soul. Certainly, from the first moment it is switched on, a studio generates ghosts. It gets sick, tired, it makes funny noises trying to tell us what is wrong. It cries for a kind word or a gentle hand laid on its ailing insides. We nurse each other back to health and service.

I wanted our new studio and base of operations to reflect sunny energy, taste, and my belief that business, responsibly conducted, was an honorable pursuit, transcending mere work.

During my previous one-year tryout phase in Los Angeles, I had been charmed by Southwestern Mission-style architecture, so I decided to create our new studio and office facility from natural woods with beams, tiles, distressed wood floors, and very homelike furniture, tables instead of desks, rugs in lieu of carpet. The brightness, the color in the office would come from the fabrics and the people.

In practical terms, we needed a studio large enough to record groups, with an isolation booth to thwart loud or percussive instruments from bleeding into several microphones at once. Orchestras or large ensembles were not a consideration, but the room had to be friendly to small string and horn sections, of the type we had used so effectively on Love's "Forever Changes."

I was looking for a tight sound, meaning not a lot of uncontrolled reflections, but colorful acoustically and bigger than life. To pull it all together required a seasoned pro. Bruce Botnick thought he knew the ideal candidate, Allan Emig.

SUZANNE HELMS: Allan was a wonderful man, middle-aged, gay, odd, bizarre, but brilliant, kind and good.

JAC: He had worked for the majors, knew recording and mastering, and knew what he didn't know. Allan, in turn, recommended a noted acoustical engineer, Paul Veneklassen, who had helped improve the thin sound of Avery Fisher Hall at Lincoln Center in New York.

Paul constructed a three-dimensional paper model and began to shine tightly focused pinpoints of light through it, studying the reflective patterns and adjusting the splay of a wall to give the room more volume and better control. This was years before computer-assisted design software, which I believe often falls short of the older craft methods.

The door to the studio was to the right. You came from the outside world into a small, triangular air lock with thick windows, shut the first door behind you, then opened the next door, keeping all outside noise outside. The control room had double glass walls separated by a nine-inch air space for acoustic isolation. You looked from the mixing board to the long end of the studio with every corner in clear view. I wanted the walls to help create the Elektra sound: bright, clean, tight and in front of your face. On the left wall was a rack of moveable panels, pushed to one end of the studio along a large track. Panels could be unfolded and arranged to selectively deaden the sound. Each panel had two sides, one for greater and the other for lesser absorption. In contrast, the right wall was solid brick, rough-hewn and irregular. Behind the brick facade were floating walls, isolated from the floor and from each other, with concrete poured between many layers of plastered and impermeable dry wall. The entire studio was like a hand-crafted shell inside a thick concrete bunker.

For our floors, Mission style meant either tile or wood of some antiquity. Tile was hard on the feet and much too sound-reflective, so wood was the obvious choice.

SUZANNE HELMS: Two old Italian brothers did them.

JAC: Once the oak flooring was laid and had settled, the brothers began distressing it, hitting it with lengths of chains, gouging it with chisels, carving it with jack knives, stomping on it with hobnail boots. Suzanne was so entertained watching them that she could hardly find time to work. When they were finished, it looked as if Hannibal's army had practiced crossing the Alps in my studio—awful and grand at the same time. We sanded off all the dirt spots, gave it several layers of maple stain, and it glowed.

Lighting was critical. I wanted to be able to vary the mood and color of the studio from the control room. Sunset Sound, where we recorded Love and the Doors, had industrial fluorescent lights, which always struck me as too cold—to warm that room we had to kill the overheads and burn candles.

Nearby was the Home Silk Shop, owned by a Jewish family, with an inventory of thousands of square feet of the most beautiful imported fabrics. John Haeny, who had joined us in engineering, and Suzanne had a field day buying wild, wacky patterns. Nothing was too outrageous; after all, this was the flamboyant Sixties. The acoustic panels on the left wall of the studio screamed in paisley. There were Persian carpets, throw rugs and mounds of fluffy velour cushions, everything to make it seem less like a studio and more like a living room.

FRITZ RICHMOND: We had a famous piano, a Yamaha G-7. They didn't make very many of those. Allan Emig and John Haeny got together over at the piano store and said, "Listen, we want you to do something special—get rid of those cheesy Japanese bass strings and install these German bass strings, and it'll give the piano a unique quality." Which it did. You could have a rock band going full tilt and then you could have the piano take a solo live, which is very hard normally. Nobody had a piano that could cut through like this one.

JAC: I had found a mixing board in England with control features unusual for its day, great flexibility to fine-tune equalization at many frequency points. And we went for full Dolby noise reduction, a first. Plus four live echo chambers, isolated from the building structure and mounted on the roof. In the late Sixties, artificial echo devices were gaining popularity, and we had them also, but I always preferred the purity of live chambers, like the famous one at Sunset Sound that we had used to such good effect. We could gang our chambers together, or take an artificial reverberation device and run the output through the live chamber, and adjust the two in relationship to the primary tracks. That kind of arcane stuff always tickled me.

FRITZ RICHMOND: With Paul Rothchild or any other producer that I was going to work with, I always wanted to have the studio just right, and if it was the first session of cutting basic tracks, I would take three or four hours to set it up to where I would be quickly able to put a hand on any piece of gear that I might need, to move a microphone easily, or to take a setup out and put in a different one. If I knew we were going to be in there for a couple of weeks, I would set the lights so that everybody had a personal pool of light to sit in, because people often wanted the lights down, and when that happens in a studio, where you tend to have wires here and there, cables running, you don't want people tripping, so you arrange the lights in such a way that people can find their way around without an accident. I would get everything in the control room ready, make sure there were enough reels of tape ready

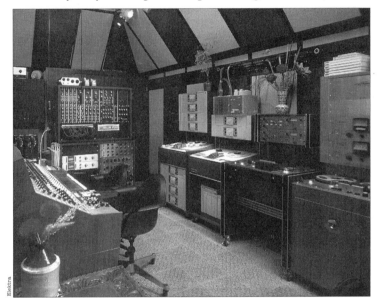

Studio "B" Elektra studio control room

to go, that the machines were aligned, and that no one had walked off with the rolling papers. There was a ritual that Paul and I would go through. Paul bought one of the first of the Mister Coffee-type coffee makers, and we'd have that sitting there, and you'd walk in and smell this fabulous coffee and you'd just want to have a cup and sit around smoke a cigarette and he'd want to clean some pot and roll a joint . . .

JAC: The studio was also very persuasive for product presentations. Each summer we invited our independent distributors for a mini-convention that lasted for two days. We'd blast the new releases through our studio playback system and wow that jaded group. And of course it was ideal for parties, great for dancing and general hanging out.

No other recording facility looked or sounded like it. It was the first from-the-ground-up hip studio. Artists ritually signed their names on the brick wall with indelible markers. As time went on, having your signature on that wall was a mark of having arrived.

To the outside world, the construction budget for the studio and office was $60,000, but knowing I would get carried away, my secret number was $100,000, without any equipment. It came in at $120,000, which would be $375,000 in late Nineties currency. I didn't care. It was the fulfillment of a dream.

JANN WENNER: A fantastic place. Before any of the other record companies, Jac built a headquarters in paradise. It's a model for what came after. Those

Studio "B" The Room

were great days, and Jac was one of the movers and princes of the business.

JAC: All a casual passerby on La Cienega might see was a Mission-style structure with no sign, and a wooden gate with an intercom leading into a small garden. The front door was set back twenty feet from the sidewalk.

FRITZ RICHMOND: You would come in, and there was a cloud of smoke and Pall Mall packs and piles of files, and Suzanne Helms.

JAC: Suzanne didn't go for this hip nonsense of sitting at a table. She insisted on a proper desk with lots of drawers, overflowing with important stuff to which only she was privy.

RUSS MILLER: All the other girls were running around in miniskirts or jeans or tie-dyes, and Suzanne was dressed as if she was working on Wall Street.

PAT FARALLA: Tight sweater and tight skirt always well matched and very nice looking, well coiffed, and stiletto heels.

JOHN HAENY: She had a mysterious position, never had a title, but you had better call her Mrs. Helms, and you had to go through her to get to anybody.

There was a wooden bench, the most uncomfortable bench in the modern world, and it didn't matter who you were, Jim Morrison, anybody—

SUZANNE HELMS: —I would always make Jim sit up straight. He liked to hunch his shoulders, and I hate that—

JOHN HAENY: —You had to sit on that bench, with Mrs. Helms glaring at you at point-blank range until you were allowed to go in.

BILL SIDDONS: She was physically intimidating.

GEORGE STEELE: She could be a terror. She would have people shaking in their boots. She never shouted or screamed. Her silence spoke. She said more with her eyes and the way she puffed on her Pall Mall. And no one ever raised their voice at her. Well, maybe once, but then you were never invited back.

RUSS MILLER: A great protector. The archangel of Elektra.

ROBB ROYER: She was the mama.

BILL SIDDONS: I thought she was a great lady. She was the source of all information.

MARTY RICHMOND: In the months before La Cienega was built, when there wasn't all that much going on, to occupy her time she took out the Los Angeles yellow pages and started with A and went through the listings, and anything she found fascinating, she'd call up and talk to these people about it. And she developed an encyclopedic knowledge of where you could get things in LA. You could ask her, "Who's got Japanese fans?" And she could say, "Well, this store has those, and if you want bigger ones they've got 'em, if you want green ones they've got 'em, but if you want the best—" It was truly amazing.

BILL SIDDONS: She knew what was going on everywhere. She had great wisdom, and direct access to the decision makers. She actually made everything happen.

PAT FARALLA: She was definitely the captain of Jac's ship. She was his right-hand barracuda. I think if it were not for Suzanne, in terms of books and money and finances and getting things done—who in hell would have done it? I think she's a queen. God bless her.

GEORGE STEELE: She was the vortex. She had to do a lot of tasks simultaneously. She had to marry and counter-balance dealing with a Paul Rothchild and a Bruce Botnick and a John Haeny and a Judy Collins from the artistic and administrative standpoint, administering all their contracts, and deal with the unions, and with contractors wanting to know where the plumbing should go, and city officials about ordinances, and copyright owners wanting to know about licenses. There would be miles and piles of paper, and if you didn't know the tributaries, where to get hold of a particular note or a particular file, there would be no way anyone else could ever do it, but she would be able to lay her hands on it instantaneously.

JAC: Suzanne would wave her hands over the disaster area that was her desk, either in blessing or in supplication, and then dive into it like a starved pelican, and, with forefinger and thumb, extract precisely the piece of paper she was looking for.

MICHAEL JAMES JACKSON: She was a polyphasic thinker and talker, extraordinarily intelligent, very streetwise, unshockable, and a pillar of self-strength. She took no shit from anyone. She did not need or seek approval even from Jac or David. She could deal with everyone on their own terms. She allowed Jac to be Jac and David to be David. She was the perfect player to sit between them. A chameleon—she could be on the phone with Jac, dealing with his Holzmanisms and having him trusting her implicitly, then do the same with David.

JAC: I absolutely loved Suzanne. Women of enormous energy and high capability were so much fun to work with. I had Teresa Sterne at Nonesuch on the East Coast. Now Suzanne managed the West Coast. They could not have been more different in style, but each in her own way was indispensable.

Suzanne was one of God's most wonderfully eccentric creations. She did her own automobile repair. And she adored dogs. David Anderle and John Haeny gave me a Siberian husky for my thirty-seventh birthday which I named Max, after my beloved grandfather. On a trip to Laguna, Max vanished. Adam and Jaclyn were heartbroken. I posted a $500 reward and Suzanne would field the reports of sightings, driving an hour and a half to Laguna, in the middle of the night, to check them out.

FRITZ RICHMOND: Some people you feel like doing little things for, and I felt like doing nice things for Suzanne.

MARTY RICHMOND: I knew that one of her biggest loves in the world was chocolate, and I conspired with the milkman to deliver a quart of chocolate milk every day to Mrs. Helms. It bugged her, trying to figure out who did it. I finally copped, and after that we were friends forever.

FRITZ RICHMOND: She seemed to have an incredible capacity for candy. She had a certain size and shape and she never changed, no matter how much she ate. Finally someone gave her a three-pound Hershey bar.

JAC: It was a ten-pound presentation bar which I had found in a catalog. The moment I spotted it I knew it belonged to Suzanne, so I gave it to her as a gag gift. Within a week Suzanne had polished it off. And ice cream—Suzanne could go through a half-gallon of Rocky Road a day. Once, when she needed to lose weight for some minor surgery, she shed thirty pounds in a month, and I calculated that she metabolized seventy-five hundred calories a day. She chain-smoked but stayed pleasingly Junoesque.

At a movie studio clearance sale, Suzanne bought the forest-green gown that Jane Russell had worn in "The French Line," and proudly confided that she had to take it in at the hips and let it out at the bosom. She sashayed into a company party tucked less rather than more into this dress. Fritz Richmond could not take his eyes off her cleavage. "Well, Fritz," Suzanne said, "I'm not Mrs. Bitch tonight, am I?"

ELLEN VOGT: On my first day at work, Suzanne pointed to a desk which was totally empty except for one piece of paper and one sharpened pencil, and said, "Your job is to take messages, that's all you do, you don't do anything else. David Anderle"—she explained to me who he was—"talks to three people, his wife, his lawyer, and Jac. And some artists. You're going to get a lot of phone calls, but he speaks to no one else." I never laid eyes on David for weeks. He was just through the wall, but I never saw him. He would drive his Porsche in back and come through the sliding glass doors to his office. His front door would be shut, and he never came out. And Suzanne never spoke to me. I thought, "This is the weirdest thing, I'm answering the phone for a man I never see, and a woman who doesn't talk to me all day long." Suzanne and David became my best friends, and have been forever. But it was very strange to begin with.

PAT FARALLA: Ellen was a great second to Suzanne. She was sweet, devoted to taking care of David in her own method and manner. In much the same way that Suzanne was to Jac, Ellen was to David.

ELLEN VOGT: David lived in that office, which was pretty much pitch dark, except for candles, and it was like a sanctuary.

FRITZ RICHMOND: He had like a tent, with pillows all over the floor and incense going, and he would sit there like a potentate and talk with artists.

DAVID ANDERLE: Sometimes on nothing, sometimes on joints, sometimes acid—

PAT FARALLA: —I remember getting lost in David's office one day shortly after lunch. As I recall it had something to do with opium, and the next thing I knew it was about nine o'clock at night. Those were the days, my friends.

FRITZ RICHMOND: It was Southern California, 1968, taken as far as you can take it and still do business.

RUSS MILLER: David was the best artist hanger-outer. Artists absolutely loved him, and for good reason, because he was an artist himself and a very lovable and very beautiful man.

PAUL WILLIAMS: Instant salon. His great gift was his ability to be a bridge between the people who are actually making the music and the people who are actually making the money.

DAVID ANDERLE: There was no such thing during those lucky years as work time and play time. It was Elektra time.

So much of the charm of Elektra in those days was that we didn't know what we were doing. Some of it worked and some of it didn't. If it didn't, good-bye, next. It was a real spirit and an attitude of no fear.

The company was growing so fast, the presence of Elektra was like fire. We did jillions of demos. I was demo-ing everything that could walk and perform. That's what the studio was all about.

I tried to steal Grace Slick away from Jefferson Airplane to be a solo act on Elektra. Crosby, Stills and Nash formed their band on my patio. We had the Holy Modal Rounders, trying to make an album with them, and that was about as bizarre as they come. Sam Shepard was the drummer. A great band of eccentrics, one doing speed, another doing smack, the producer doing both, and the only productivity is when the drugs balance each other out. We did an album with Freddy Engleberg, a great big husky good-looking guy, built like a football player, used to be the bouncer at the Unicorn. He wrote the most fanciful little poems, originally written to be performed in the dark behind a mime show. We did an album with Nico—

PAT FARALLA: She came in the back door like the veil of death. I didn't know squat about her, but she had things on her mind and she decided she would speak to me about whatever it was. I remember the line, "I like to sleep with dead men."

Nico "The Marble Index" EKS-74029

JAC: Nico was an apparition, a sprite with a spike, floating hazily in and out of focus. She would suddenly . . . materialize. Turn around and she wasn't there, turn back and she was filling the bench. Then she would . . . dematerialize. She'd call up and, in her low moan, tell you, "I'll be in on Tuesday, set up some interviews." Tuesday would come, and no Nico. Eight months later, she'd call again. "I'm back in town." You would say, "What about those other times?" "Oh, I couldn't do those, I had to go to Rome."

DAVID ANDERLE: Tim Buckley was already signed when I came to Elektra.

JAC: Herbie Cohen had sent me Tim's demo.

HERB COHEN: One of the great voices of our time. He had a four-octave range, five if he wanted to stretch it. Just brilliant.

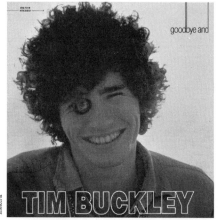

"Goodbye And Hello" EKS-7318

JAC: I listened to it over and over. If I was down I would play it and it would lift me. And as an artist to sign—so gifted, so original, the talent and the vision still unfolding.

DAVID ANDERLE: When I came, Tim had done his first album, and he was just finishing "Goodbye And Hello." I remember Jac and I listening to it together, both of us being so in love with that album—

JAC: The pain and purity of the songwriting, the plaintiveness of his melodies, the nakedness of his vocals, the artistic risks. I had believed in Tim from the beginning, and the enchantment of "Goodbye And Hello" exceeded anything I could have hoped for.

DAVID ANDERLE: Tim and I became very close. We just had a feeling for each other. It was like an instant thing. Sometimes when things would get too weird at the office, I would sneak out and go to the beach at Venice with him and just sit in the sand for hours and talk and watch the sunset.

ELLEN VOGT: I adored Tim. I had a big crush on him. I used to look out the window to see if he was coming. I was shy, I didn't know what to say to him. He would sit quietly, looking straight ahead, waiting for David. I think he was high every time he came in.

PAT FARALLA: A slightly slouching and shy young man, beautiful, hair like a halo, befitting yet another angel. I was in love with this young voice, those words, that torment, that frustration, that poet.

DANNY FIELDS: Brilliant, playful, prodding, alert, just wanted to swallow the world. He had no concept of age, race, sexuality, he was just free.

FRITZ RICHMOND: Tim had some very pretty groupies. He would pack the studio with groupies. He seemed to like to have them around as an audience, and they sometimes didn't even know each other. They'd be in there sitting around looking gorgeous and listening politely all day, and at the end of the day some would stay even after he left. They wanted to watch me clean up.

Buckley's band were the worst slobs. They would leave the studio and there would be wet garbage on the carpet. They'd order ribs and I'd have to pick bones off the carpeting. I thought that was inexcusably impolite. There were plenty of trash cans.

DAVID ANDERLE: There was a real push to get Tim popular. From our side, we just wanted everybody to know about Tim Buckley—

JAC:—To have the world hear him.

DAVID ANDERLE: But I had the feeling that if Tim didn't have to perform for an audience, it would be fine with him.

JACKSON BROWNE: Tim was in the Village, at this place Andy Warhol had put up, the Dom. A lot of uptown patrons, business people, stockbrokers, artsy, coming to the Village to get a glimpse of Warhol. He had a film loop of a sky diver falling endlessly, floating, and another one of someone eating a candy bar with this kind of intent look. Nico was on the bill. There were twenty-foot-high posters of her all over town, beautiful. She was always compared to Marlene Dietrich, with this deep voice and German accent, but less arctic than Dietrich. I was transfixed by her. She had this bunch of songs—songwriting was the event—a Tim Hardin song, an unrecorded Dylan song, a Donovan song, a James Taylor song, a Leonard Cohen song; Leonard Cohen used to come in and listen to her. Tim asked me did I want the job accompanying her, and I said, "Absolutely." Tim would back up Nico and play a set of his own and not take it very seriously. He didn't like this place or any of the people in it. He would sing a lot of Johnny Cash songs or whatever he felt like doing, and after a week he said "Hah," and he was out of there.

STEVE HARRIS: At his high point, Tim did a concert at Avery Fisher Hall at Lincoln Center. It was sold out. When he looked out he said something to me that was unintelligible, but it was almost like, "Oh, shit." He didn't want it. He didn't seem nervous, he just seemed pissed off, almost, you know, "OK, I've done this, now what do I have to do?" The concert was wonderful, it was fabulous. He had it all at his fingertips. And he had nowhere to go. After that, his whole musical outlook and his perception of what he was about and doing, changed. Almost the next day, changed.

Tim Buckley

HERB COHEN: Whatever success he had, he would try to avoid it.

JAC: On the Tonight Show he would insult the host, or he would refuse to lip-sync and walk out. At the Improv he would be onstage, snoring, and I heard about him once barking at an audience.

DAVID ANDERLE: He was poised all the time to become a major pop artist. Because he was so attractive and his voice was so beautiful, it was a natural tendency to say, "Come on, man, you could do this in your sleep and have everything you want." He had pressure from Herbie to do it more commercially. He had pressure from the label to try and make singles. He had pressure from everybody to do it a certain way. And he rejected it. He wanted so badly to do his own music.

I went to every one of his gigs at the Troubadour. A lot of times he would have a good audience for the opening show, but at the midnight show there might be only three or four people. It never bothered him. He would get into his experimental mode. Sometimes he would do one number for the whole set. He didn't give a shit, as long as he got to play what he wanted to play.

PAT FARALLA: The time I remember best with Tim was going down to Venice one night, and we cruised the bars, jazz bars, whatever, having the night I always wanted to spend with Tim. Just reaching into his mind. A lot of talk about jazz.

DAVID ANDERLE: I think he had the jazz demon. Certain guys—Charlie Parker, Thelonious Monk—they go after this unattainable thing. The music Tim was hearing was really different. And he had demons he could not control.

STEVE HARRIS: Tim was self-destructive, changing what he did, going into drugs. The last time I saw him was at a club in San Francisco. He was playing jazz and it was interesting. But all that went through my mind was how important an artist he could have been. He was so eager to talk about old times at Elektra. Elektra was Camelot, and people never realized it better than when, like Tim, they went elsewhere. I could see it in his eyes, talking about how well he was treated and respected.

CLIVE SELWOOD: The first time Tim came to England he was at our new house, and he went out in the back yard, which was still uncultivated, and played with our little daughter for an hour and came back in all covered with mud. The hippie child. The last time I saw him was at the Troubadour, and he was carrying a gun. I asked him why. He said, "The police, they see long hair, and they're going to arrest you or kill you, so I'm going to kill them first."

MICHAEL JAMES JACKSON: I saw him at the Chelsea Hotel, fucked up on heroin. A small, sweet, fragile guy, with wild hair. Why such a disastrous habit? It was trouble beyond my perception.

STEVE HARRIS: The day Tim died, I was at Madison Square Garden and Herbie was in town. He called me up and he could hardly talk. I said, "Herbie, what's the matter?" And he said, "Come right over. Tim died."

HERB COHEN: He OD'd. Twenty-seven.

Chapter 14

Thunder at the Hollywood Bowl ...
Fellatio Alger in the studio ... Amsterdam hash

JAC: Meanwhile the Doors earned their gold single, a gold first album, and were growing before the eyes of the whole country into a truly tremendous group. They were amazingly prolific. Ultimately we had five gold albums in a row with them, which may have been a record for an American band at that time.

The Doors embodied—incarnated—a major upheaval in popular culture. Their music was of the times and it shaped the times. Paul Kantner of Jefferson Airplane gave a TV interview in the Eighties in which he spoke of talking with Jim Morrison about the phenomenal moment in history they were living in the Sixties. Kantner described it as being swept along, like white water rafting—the swirling chaos of those days, a giant cultural explosion, the sexual revolution, the feminist explosion, the gay explosion, the civil rights explosion, the anti-Vietnam explosion, all in the space of a few years. He had this wonderful memory of the Airplane playing at a college in the Midwest, the students dressed in tuxes and prom gowns, and then going back a year later and the kids were all on acid, staging painted body ceremonies and nude love-ins. He had the perception that so many of us did—that music and politics and drugs were part of the same gestalt.

PAT FARALLA: There was an expansion, a growing, a sharing of our lives, our experiences, our pharmacology, and the manner in which we cohabited with each other. We were just totally involved in each others' lives and passionate about it. The power, the art, the transformation all of us were going through was a pretty potent aphrodisiac. We were addicted to the times.

JAC: And the Doors' music was both cause and effect of the addiction. If you want the essence of it in just a few words, look no further than Morrison's brilliant epigrammatic definition of himself and the group: "erotic politicians."

JIM LADD: We listened to this music in our parents' houses, or in our own rooms. We gathered in groups of two or three or four, smoking our first joint, taking the first acid together. This music was a sacrament to us—'The End,' or 'When The Music's Over,' about what have they done to the earth, stabbed her and ripped her and bit her and stuck her with knives in the side of the dawn. Those kinds of lyrics were unheard of at that time. They broke all kinds of new ground. I really believed that if we sang loud enough and long enough, we could change the world. And I believed that the Doors were certainly very responsible for changing the world.

RAY MANZAREK: What the Sixties, what the psychedelic revolution was to be all about, was giving up your individual ego, to create with your fellows—your brothers and sisters—something greater than yourself. The Doors had that symbiosis. We gave up our individual egos to the collective whole. We always had that give and take, that ebb and flow, so that the rhythm, the chord changes—nothing was ever perfect with the Doors, but we always attempted to attain a perfection, and perhaps we did attain a perfection within the ebb and flow that coursed between the four of us.

BILL SIDDONS: I think that Robby was, to put it in art terms, the abstract artist in the group. He was Jackson Pollock pouring paint on a canvas and saying, "What's it feel like?" Completely free form, kind of just bounced off walls—"Well, that's what's happening, accept it." My favorite quote of my whole history with the Doors came from Robby. Somebody asked him after a show, "Robby, what do you think of when you're playing your solos? You walk around without apparent focus or aim, you're obviously somewhere else, what are you thinking about?" Robby kind of smiled and said, "Well, I think about my aquarium a lot." And I thought it was the perfect description of his playing, floating around with his fish. While Ray was building chord upon chord, structure upon structure. Ray was not quite the cubist, more of a literalist. I always felt in Ray's playing, every next phrase was built on the one before, block by block. And he does that in conversation—he's a very structural person. Ray was the one who was always trying to see that control was maintained. Robby never cared about control per se, he cared about having enough order to get through what we were doing.

JAC: Robby's guitar playing looked so deceptively simple. Mike Bloomfield would eke out an E minor chord and go into spasm on stage with the sheer bravado of his own technique. Robby would be spinning incredible riffs and he might be watching an insect on the ceiling, or perhaps considering that in six months time he might buy another pair of jeans. And there was that very special Brechtian feel you got from Ray Manzarek's organ. Whenever Ray played, I saw two colors: earth brown and purple. So you have the uniqueness of Ray's keyboard platform supporting exquisitely precise, liquid guitar lines from Robby, given structural integrity by John's very inventive, staccato drumming.

VINCE TREANOR: John soaking wet with shot in his pockets probably weighed a hundred pounds at that time. But he'd make more music out of those simple bass and floor toms and two small toms and a snare drum with three cymbals than these guys with thirty-seven toms and fifty-one cymbals.

BILL SIDDONS: John wanted to be proud of his work. He didn't just step out and say, "OK, where do I play?" He was trying to read Jim, who was barely functioning in the same sphere. John was the guy who bore most of the weight emotionally. He was so overwhelmed with what was going on with the group, he left the band at least three times. John was the jazz player in the band. I thought he kept perfect time for Jim. When Jim slowed things down and changed tempo, John was right there with him. It gave the band more elasticity and fluidity than any other band—they would stretch and relax, stretch and relax, in ways that nobody else did, and that gave a dynamic tension to the music.

JAC: The band was so uniquely tuned into themselves and each other that Jim could wail in any direction he chose.

PAUL ROTHCHILD: Jim was blessed with a magnificent vocal instrument. His was one of the greatest voices I've ever had the delight to work with. He talked about being a crooner. He admired Sinatra's phrasing enormously. And he could do a great Elvis. But he was really an accidental musician. He couldn't play an instrument.

ROBBY KRIEGER: He could pound around on a piano pretty good. He could fake playing a harmonica. That's about it.

PAUL ROTHCHILD: His timing was terrible—whenever he picked up maracas or a tambourine, myself or someone in the band would try to take it away from him.

ROBBY KRIEGER: He wasn't really musical, not in a professional way. You couldn't say, "OK, Jim, hit a B flat." He was not like a Frank Sinatra who could read a chart and sing. He didn't have a whole lot of input on the arrangements. And lazy as hell. Would not practice. Loved to jam and sing blues songs, but never bothered to learn more than one verse.

PAUL ROTHCHILD: His talent was in creating dramatic situations with his voice and with his persona on stage, directing entire rock audiences into the drama in his mind. And he was very successful at it—more successful as a dramatic performer than he was as a singer, live, because his singing frequently failed him, but his sense of drama never did.

DIGBY DIEHL: The Doors, more than any other group I can think of, brought theater to rock and roll. When you see a video now, sometimes there's a whole intense little story told in there, and that's what the Doors used to do with one song. Morrison was a video performer before his time.

JAC: The short film Mark Abramson shot for 'Break On Through' helped us move the Doors around the country without transporting their bodies. It was one of the earliest pre-MTV clips aimed at the TV bandstand shows which were a staple of late afternoon programming. Groups might come and lip sync to the record, but no actual performance took place because the station, God forbid, would then have to pay union minimums. It was the easiest kind of show for a station, cheap and fast. Kids enjoyed seeing themselves and each other.

The live performance scene was equally sketchy. Except for well-developed venues in the largest cities, an act had to be really big to fill the converted warehouses and old movie theaters that were pressed into service in the smaller towns. And you couldn't tour unless you had a very big hit and could convince the local radio stations or key DJs to publicize the performance, for which they generally received a percentage. Aside from the Beatles and the Rolling Stones, the big arenas were in the future. But the Doors were getting there. They were a mesmerizing act, with Jim Morrison taking audiences to the very edge of the known world.

VINCE TREANOR: Incredible performances! The rocket's red glare of the Doors! Anyone that ever attended a Doors performance live, and you have the albums, every time you play a track, can you forget? Can it not bring to memory—vivid, absolute, almost hallucinatory memory—that hour and a half, two hours, that you spent in that hall, experiencing the Doors?

It's dark and it's humid, and there's this sound, this crowd out there, they're not loud, occasionally they'll whistle. "Yeah, let's do it!" Or "Where are the Doors?" And you look out, and there are these jewels in the night, the stars in the heavens—no, that's not a star, that's an exit sign, that's a joint being lit, and of course the place would turn into instant exhalations of everything smokeable. And that sweaty smell and that animal existence of thousands of people waiting for a cataclysmic event to occur. The trumpets are about to blow and St. Peter is going to walk on the cloud. And suddenly there's this stirring behind the stage. A door opens and there's a flash of light and you can see movement, in this dusky dull dark glow you can see these ghostly figures walk up on stage. And nothing. And then you hear from John's drums, datdat datdat, and then notes, dee, dong. Ray would have the volume on the organ way down, just a little signal passed between two musicians: "I have the note, Robby. Here, I'm going to give it to you—here, Robby, listen, catch it, catch it." And Robby gave it to the other five strings. Very quietly you can hear Robby, subtly tuning that guitar. And then there was silence. Time stopped. There wasn't any life. And suddenly that one person came across that stage, and there was a sound like crashing waves on a beach.

DIGBY DIEHL: Jim would work himself into these frenzies. I would arrive with him and sit backstage and watch him in an hour or so drink or toke himself up into the performer that went on stage. Often he'd arrive as the shy poet, and he would become that wild, theatrical sexual figure.

BILL GRAHAM: When you saw Morrison performing and then you looked at the audience, you realized there was something very rare. I saw it a few times, about four or five people that I've seen on stage and on the screen. Otis Redding. Perhaps Jimi Hendrix. On the female side, Ava Gardner, serpent of all serpents, panther of all panthers. She more than anyone on the female side had what Jim Morrison had. It exuded, like steam came out of there. Jim had that, a sensuality, an animal sensuality.

ELLEN VOGT: He was beautiful, like Elvis. He had that beautiful white skin, perfect features.

JAC: I remember a line from a story in Rolling Stone by Jerry Hopkins: "Morrison is so pretty he looks like he was made up on the phone by two fags."

EVE BABITZ: That whole thing with the hair and everything. And all of us women encouraged him to do it. His girl friend Pamela, my sister, all the women around him, we loved it when the hair was long and he looked so great and fabulous. He looked like a girl.

STEVE HARRIS: He knew how to look at a camera. Better than any rock star I've ever known. He posed. He wanted people to notice how terrific he looked. Jim had a degree in film from UCLA. He had seen classic movies. To see Jim on stage was really seeing the reincarnation of Marilyn Monroe, Greta Garbo, Marlene Dietrich. If he ran his hand through his hair, or shook his head like Monroe, if he posed like a Dietrich, and stared out like a Garbo, it would really have an effect with that tall, lean, mean masculine look of Jim's. When I mentioned that to him he did not disagree, he understood what I was talking about.

BILL GRAHAM: Keep your eyes on Jim, watch him just move, the way he goes toward the microphone, what he does with the microphone stand, but mainly how he gets from one space to another, how he prowls around the stage, and there's that, if you want to call it, snake, panther, slithery whispery movement to him that exuded sexuality, sensuality. Especially dressed dark, the black leather pants—

DIGBY DIEHL:—So tight they were like ballet dancer's tights, and they left no doubt as to his proportions—

BRUCE BOTNICK:—At least he wasn't stuffing a sock in there.

BILL GRAHAM: No underwear. Jim Morrison doesn't wear 'em. Very powerful statement. I think he had a far greater effect on young men's habits than when Clark Gable took off his shirt in a movie in front of a woman. Young women gave themselves to it willingly. When Jim took his shirt off, women seemed desirous of him.

He told me one of the turning points for him was in Cleveland. Must have been about ten thousand people, they did four or five encores and the crowd wouldn't leave, the house lights were on, and he said, "I went out and took a bow, and what scared me, Bill, I looked at all these women screaming at me, and I realized they all wanted to fuck me."

And men envied that attraction Jim had. I think he challenged them. For the men, this was Jim Morrison—"What does he eat, do, wear, think, I want to do that."

Adulation came on such a level, but it wasn't just bobby soxers screaming about Sinatra—that was just "aaaahh." People followed Jim across the country like the Crusades.

JAC: By the time we were ready to equip our studio at La Cienega, most everyone was moving to eight-track recorders using 1-inch tape. The logic was obvious: more command over the sound of each instrument so we could make changes later or sweeten by adding voices, effects or more instruments. We were approaching the holy grail of total control in both recording and mixdown.

When we were about to record the Doors' "The Soft Parade" album, 3M had just introduced a new recorder with an unusual arrangement of redundant tapes and amplifiers which took the excess signal at the top of its dynamic range and transferred it over to a second recording amplifier and tape. The cost was much higher but the results were noticeably better. Of course we had Dolby for every track and a very elaborate, home-brew relay switching mechanism to toggle them between record and playback. Our total studio bill for mixing console, tape recorders, Dolbys, playback amps, customized speaker cabinetry, microphones, et cetera, was $175,000.

From eight-track the industry moved to sixteen, then twenty-four, then thirty-two, and the only certainty was that the cost of producing an album rose in direct ratio to the numbers of tracks used in the recording.

In retrospect I doubt whether having more tracks would have made the first Doors album or Love or Tim Buckley any better. That was the technical road we were going down, but good sound by itself would never be enough. The success of any album would always be determined by the quality of the songs and the singers.

BRUCE BOTNICK: That was a really, really creative time. I had "Sergeant Pepper" a good three months before it came out. I remember playing it back in one of the mastering studios and absolutely flipping out. I brought the Doors in—I don't think Jim was there, but I brought them in and we listened, and our jaws dropped. And what it did for us, it said: "Let's not do it the same way we did before, let's invent new techniques of recording. No holds barred."

PAUL ROTHCHILD: It was the beginning of today's ferocious hunt after The Sound.

BRUCE BOTNICK: We developed a lot of techniques. In 'Horse Latitudes,' there's a sound of what sounds like ocean slowing down, which I did by hand on a tape machine.

PAUL ROTHCHILD: We were into exploring "organic" sounds. What happens if we take this guitar and put paper clips all over it—what kind of sound would that make?

ROBBY KRIEGER: And backwards tracks—it was fun.

PAUL ROTHCHILD: And we were inventing electronic sounds.

BRUCE BOTNICK: Paul Beaver had the very first synthesizers. He was an unique individual. Probably one of the brighter people around. He passed away at a very young age. In fact they say he didn't really die. Supposedly he knew people from other planets, and he went up to Mount Shasta, where the flying saucers came down and re-fueled and got energy, and went away with them. Anyway, Paul Beaver brought his synthesizer in. We set it up so that Jim played one key and it would put a real eerie edge on his voice on 'Strange Days.' This was our first use of a synthesizer.

JAC: During the recording of the first album the Doors were on their best behavior, which with Jim was a very relative term indeed. The album had turned out to be everything I might have wished for and the combination of Rothchild and the Doors worked as I was sure it would. Paul knew their psychology, and they had learned to trust each other.

The beginning of a session is usually slow, as the participants shake off the outside world and begin to adjust to the job at hand. Paul got them going as quickly as he could. When the Doors recorded, the studio was rarely broken down for another act, which made getting the mike balances a lot easier and kept the sound consistent. The Doors owned Studio B for the duration and at the end of each session we double-locked all the doors so nothing would be disturbed.

PAT FARALLA: Paul would come in the back door, briefcase, hair pulled back tight, always tight T-shirts, tight long shirts, and tight, tight jeans—I mean *bound*. He'd head for the studio, no chit-chat, no small talk, going straight for what he was going for. And he was ready for business. He was the briefcase.

JAC: The briefcase was famous. It held everything he might possibly need, pitch pipe, the latest gadgets, cigarettes, whatever drug was up for the evening.

MARK ABRAMSON: I used to marvel at it. Paul would open it and it was crammed, but everything was always perfectly in place and it always stayed perfectly in place. How did he do that? Everything about Paul stayed perfectly in place. His pants always looked perfectly pressed. How did he do that? And he'd smoke dope and only get more intense. How did he do that?

PAT FARALLA: He was an absolute loner in many ways, totally into himself, totally immersed in his work, into what he's in charge of, into what he's creating. His mind never stopped. His intelligence and his indifference, in a way, always attracted me, and I think attracted other people to him. Driven, powerful, the master.

JAC: Like all great producers, Paul was part actor, part chameleon, part broken field runner. He had a way of mirroring the space the artist was coming from, or a way to insert himself at exactly the artist's level, even to their speech patterns—he could do a "Hey, man" to the artist, though he didn't say "Hey, man" to me. And he was also a field general. Coupled to his deep knowledge of music was a pursuit of perfection and the militancy to achieve it. Paul was not an easy personality, but most recognized that he was usually right. And agree or disagree, as Paul went for Take 35 you always knew that he had the best interests of the album foremost in his mind.

BILL SIDDONS: Jac knew the right guy to work with the Doors. Rothchild was the perfect call. Because of Jim, it was Chaos Incorporated. Paul had to try to control the uncontrollable.

PAUL ROTHCHILD: Control is a word that didn't work around Morrison.

MIRANDI BABITZ: I don't think Jim was ever the greatest guy. I think he was a morose, depressed, moody, violent person. I just remember him being mostly furious at Pam about something, and her being on a rage at him, and the two of them duking it out and then making up and being happy and loving and then fighting. They brought all their problems and played 'em out in glorious Technicolor.

DIANE GARDINER: There was this swashbuckling thing going on, you know, the way swordfighters fight on the staircase, up and down.

JAC: We would continually receive Morrison storm warnings. Hurricane Jim and Cyclone Pam. Wherever they were was the epicenter. Pam has thrown all Jim's books out the window. She has shredded his clothes. She has scrawled FAG on the mirror. Jim has put a knife to her throat. The two of them have dropped acid and are playing chicken on the railroad track. Someone has to drive them to the UCLA neuropsychiatric unit. Again and again.

ROBBY KRIEGER: We were supposed to record 'When The Music's Over.' I got a call about 3am. This happened about once a week: "We're in trouble here, you'd better come over." He had taken acid with Pam the night before. I was going to take them to Griffith Park to cool out. Jim starts out the door and he doesn't have his pants on. "Jim, your pants." I told him to be sure to come to the studio by twelve. And he never shows.

JAC: Another bulletin—a mercy mission, to resuscitate Jim. This time he has made it to the studio, but in terrible shape, and he's not coming up with the vocal for 'You're Lost, Little Girl.' So they bring in a girl to go down on him. In one version of the story it's Pam bareass in the vocal booth, in another it's either a volunteer or a hooker.

DAVID ANDERLE: There was a deadline. Jac was getting antsy—you know how Jac can be. I was working at the office, came into the studio, and there was one of those crazy vibes, and Paul had a certain look he got when something weird was happening. Jim was barely able to stand, so they brought this girl in, and she was giving him a head job, and not only couldn't he sing, he couldn't get it hard.

JAC: They did get that vocal. Success. A Fellatio Alger story. Heroically, Paul finished the album, titled, not inappropriately, "Strange Days."

PAUL WILLIAMS: I remember Jac playing me the acetate at his apartment, and I said to him that it just felt like everybody involved would be in jail in six months. I meant that in a positive way—it was that revolutionary it was outrageous.

BILL HARVEY: For the cover, I didn't want to have to deal with the group, it was too difficult. I talked to them, and they agreed instead on something Fellini-esque, a troupe of strolling players idea. I shot at Sniffen Court, a mews between Lexington and 3rd Avenue, in New York. I gathered people from all over. I went up to this strange residential hotel, on Broadway in the Seventies. Very, very old place. Odd people were there. I was looking for these twin midgets. I knocked on the door and the door opens and I look down and there they are. I came in, and they had all their clothes laid out on the bed. They were as neat as pins, I mean everything was just perfect. They were

"Strange Days" indeed EKS-74014

just sweet people, awfully nice men. "Do you want us to wear this? Or do you want us to wear that?" I got a strong man from the circus. I found an acrobat guy. I got the photographer's assistant to put makeup on and I let him juggle some balls. I took a taxi driver and pulled him out of the cab and said, "For five bucks, will you stand over there and blow a trumpet?" Because he had on this battered old hat and I thought, "He's perfect."

JAC: The Doors had been briefly managed by two gentleman who, out of kindness, I will refer to as B and D. Their first strategic move had been to try and hijack the band off Elektra and into a label deal in which they—B and D—could participate. As close as I had been to the group, the arrival of these characters floored me. We had been so scrupulous in getting the boys the best of everything and, without telling us, they pick people who were the antithesis of class and with no demonstrated skill at career building for a rock act. I mentally gave the band six months to get wise and was relieved when Robby came to me in the studio one evening and confided that the group had decided to dump their managers and would I advance them $50,000 for anticipated legal costs. I never wrote a check with greater pleasure.

My investment in the Doors was as much artistic and emotional as it was financial. Elektra was on a solid footing, and though losing the Doors' record sales would make a horrific dent in our future revenues, the band wasn't critical to the company's stability. What was far more important was the longer view, a band that could make a string of great albums.

In addition to Elektra being responsible for Doors albums, we needed to coordinate their tours and club dates. Steve Harris was our designated ambassador and he would keep me posted on the band's mood. As long as Morrison was behaving I stayed in the background. Over the years I purposely held back from getting too intimate with the artists. I am not their best pal or hanger-on; I run their record company. To get too close erodes your objectivity and authority, and there may come a day when you will need both.

The Doors badly needed a wrangler who would get done what needed to be done, and they found the ideal candidate in Bill Siddons. He was still a teenager when he took the job, but he learned quickly and worked very well with us.

BILL SIDDONS: I was eighteen, and I had no idea what my responsibilities were, except to help with the equipment, and I didn't even know how to plug it in. I think it was my second weekend, we did a show on Long Island. We got there about four and they went on at eight, and Jim just hung out in the bar. By the time he went on stage he was completely dysfunctional. Fifteen minutes into the show, he started trying to take his clothes off. Densmore got up and walked offstage and was screaming in the dressing room, "I can't do this! I'm going home! I don't wanna do this any more!"

I went over to the bar, paranoid about what I had screwed up. I asked the bartender how much Jim had drunk. He said he didn't know, but a lot. I asked him to look at the tab. Twenty-six shots of VO.

Bill Siddons with Ray Manzarek

DIANE GARDINER: Jim would always get drunk. We were on the road, and we stopped somewhere, you know these god-awful places when you're touring. It was a bait store. They had cages and cages of crickets, big huge cages, and Jim bought every cricket they had and just let them loose. They were all over the parking lot.

STEVE HARRIS: There were a lot of reports coming in that Jim was drinking pretty heavily, so I went with him to Boston.

Here was the deal: I was going to drink exactly what Jim did, consume what he consumed, and if I felt, as if I were an artist, that I couldn't get on stage, then Jim's had enough.

We spent the afternoon walking around Cambridge, and went into Harvard Yard, and I was sitting there and Jim was sketching on a pad. I would say, "Gee, Jim, that's beautiful," and he'd crumple up the paper and toss it into a trash can. I read recently where some of his original lithographs went for ten thousand apiece . . .

Before the show, the two of us went to dinner at a sea food restaurant. Jim was pretty boozed up, but he was feeling well enough to perform. So I said to myself, "I think we've made it." We were waiting for a cab to pick us up to take us to the gig, and it was late. Some kids came by in a car, and they said, "Hey, we're going to see you! Want a ride?" So we jumped in the back of the car, and the driver turned around and said to Jim, "Hey, man, you want some acid?" I looked at Jim and said, "No, man, don't do it." And Jim looked at me with steel eyes and said, "Don't ever tell me what to do." But he did say to the driver, "No thanks." And the gig came off terrific. Jim knew he had to conquer them and he did. First thing he did after he came off the stage was come up to me and say, "Steve, thanks a lot for keeping me straight."

JAC: In December 1967, another Morrison communiqué, datelined New Haven—Jim had been busted for obscenity.

Before the show Jim was engrossed with a girl backstage, actually in a shower stall, and a cop came by and rousted them. Jim sassed back and the cop Maced him. Jim made a big thing of it during the performance, exercising his First Amendment rights on stage, and with cops posted throughout the hall, he was arrested.

That was a defining moment in pop culture: Jim Morrison, the first rock star to be busted while performing. Life magazine gave it a multi-page spread.

This and all the fuss that followed re-legitimized the Doors as a counter-culture group, and advance orders for their next album, "Waiting for the Sun," shot up to three quarters of a million units.

As this album neared completion the Morrison storm warnings grew in volume and frequency, including Jim passing out on the studio floor, peeing his pants. Fulltime care was indicated.

I talked about the problem with Paul. We reviewed the very short list of candidates who could get the job done and decided on Bob Neuwirth.

DAVID ANDERLE: Because that's what Bobby had done with Dylan.

PAUL ROTHCHILD: Neuwirth was someone Dylan could trust. He was a painter, street hipster, very bright, paranoid, big scene guy, the guy who is referred to as the star's star, America's guest. He was never Dylan, he was never Albert Grossman, he was never Jim. Bobby was second man. But he's also the guy who could get to the Number 1 man. And he was the only guy I knew who could outdrink Morrison, out-hip him.

BOB NEUWIRTH: I was living in New York and it was really cold that winter. In conversation with Paul on the phone, he said, "It's really warm out here," and I said, "Well, let's go."

We moved into the Landmark, on Franklin, right by the Magic Castle. Paul discovered the place. The only people staying there in those days were the Ice Capades, and Cannonball Adderley's band, and a lot of magicians. We had our own private phone lines installed. And it became Action Central. Everything was going in nine thousand different directions. The motel became like a zoo. Everybody started staying there, Janis Joplin, Leonard Cohen, Eric Andersen, members of the Committee, actors—it became another show business hotel, a contemporary one. And it became really pretty zoney.

Jim would hang out late at night, taking drunken dives into the swimming pool, waking everybody up. Luckily he was like a champion diver, he was very coordinated, athletic, so he didn't hurt himself, but it was pretty bizarre.

It became a matter of trying to keep him interested in making a record. It was a lot of cajoling. I represented the record company. Jim knew that I was there to try to bounce ideas around him, and he didn't want to be tricked into anything. He was his own man and he knew what he was doing. Even if he was giving the impression of being out of control, he pretty much knew what was up.

A great example is, one time he came into my room late at night and he picked up my guitar—which he didn't play—and he threw it toward the wall, in a typical irresponsible "I'll walk out this window and nobody will ever see me again"—and as he threw the guitar against the wall, I thought, "That's it, I'm gonna kill him," because it was of some value to me, this guitar. I was coming off the chair to punch him up, and I saw the guitar like a feather stop in midair and land on the sofa bed that was pushed up against the wall. So he had control.

There were lots of times when he pretended to be more out of control than he was. He had a method behind all of it, he had a great sense of his own image, and he played it. Scamp.

ROBBY KRIEGER: There was a lot of Jim getting drunk and bringing drunken friends into the studio and Paul throwing them out. Some heavy, heavy scenes. Heavy pill taking and stuff. That was rock and roll to the fullest, I would say.

BOB NEUWIRTH: Morrison had always been a hangout artist, basically. So there was a lot of socializing built into the job. In point of fact, the only way to relate to Jim was to drink along with him, so there were times when the both of us were pretty much in the bag.

JOHN DENSMORE: Bobby hanging around Jim got to be a real good mimic. One night we were recording 'Five To One,' and Jim was fucked up, inebriated, and we didn't know what to do. So Bobby did the vocal. And he had it all down. The way he was hanging onto the mike and slurring his words, "Heyyy, why don't you come over and get close to meee"—it was hysterical. Jim was watching. He laughed, yeah, he really laughed. I don't know whether we got the vocal that night. Probably the next day.

BOB NEUWIRTH: My favorite part of the record was 'My Wild Love.' Jim heard it as some kind of misty moors folk song. He wanted to record it with a banjo, and the rest of the Doors didn't. It became a real head-butting thing with Jim: "If I can't record it and do it the way I want, I'm not gonna record anything at all." I was casting around for an idea of how to solve this Irish Celtic dilemma. I said, "Let's try to do it a capella." Everybody went for it. Jac came in. He was, I'm sure, in such a state of relief to see that Jim was actually there and that the log jam had been kind of opened up, that he came out into the studio and took his place in the lineup. Yes, Jac Holzman did in fact take part in the a capella version of 'My Wild Love.' I think of Jac as a recording artist.

JAC: The two tracks on "Waiting For The Sun" that stand out—for very different reasons—are 'Hello, I Love You' and 'The Unknown Soldier.'

When I first listened to the Doors' original demo disc, recorded even before they were signed to Columbia, my son Adam loved 'Hello, I Love You,' which was about the second song Jim had written.

ADAM HOLZMAN: When the Doors first came out I thought that was just the end of the world. For years I did nothing but live, eat and breathe the Doors.

TONY GLOVER: I remember Nina telling me about Adam coming out of the shower naked with a teddy bear on his head. She said, "What are you doing?" He said, "I'm gonna be a rock and roll star."

ADAM HOLZMAN: I always tried to copy Ray. I tried to figure out his shit off the record. And from the little music books that were always wrong, always an awful transcription, never right. Jim showed me a couple of things. I was working on some little melodies on my recorder, and Jim said, "What have you got there?" And I played this stupid little melody, and he said, "Oh, that's kind of nice."

JAC: When they were doing "Waiting For The Sun," Adam reminded me about 'Hello, I Love You.' He said, "Dad, I think that's a hit single." He was all of ten at the time but so into their music that I called Paul. Paul reported that the Doors didn't want to do because it was one of their earliest tunes: "They think it's too ancient." I said, "Look, do it. If it doesn't come out right, I'll eat the studio costs." They recorded it.

ADAM HOLZMAN: And it was their second gold single.

JAC: 'The Unknown Soldier' emerged from the universal Vietnam consciousness of the time. Steve Harris and Paul Rothchild were present at the creation.

STEVE HARRIS: We were in New York. Jim was really drunk, in a good mood, playful, and out of his leather pants that he never seemed to take off he took a piece of paper, and showed me and Paul a song he had written called 'Unknown Soldier.' He handed it to us and laid back on the bed, face in the pillow, then raised up and just began retching into a wastepaper basket. Paul and I looked at each other and said, "America's Number 1 star, folks."

JAC: Here is America in the middle of the Vietnam War. Tens of thousands of protesters are marching on the Pentagon. Morrison is the son of a career Navy officer, a commander of a warship, and Morrison has managed to fail his draft medical. Grunts in Vietnam are playing the Doors, and Morrison is at home performing the anti-war 'Unknown Soldier' live.

As a stage performer no one is more dramatic than Jim, so much so that Rolling Stone is getting on his case for going over the top with his writhing and falling. I remember one of their headlines: "Much Ado About Nothing, or, Humpty Morrison's Great Fall." And 'Unknown Soldier' is the greatest fall—Morrison is "dropped" with a rimshot by John Densmore and he collapses "dead." They gave those performances all they had.

VINCE TREANOR: The Hollywood Bowl, right around July 4, 1968, unbelievable.

RON JACOBS: My radio station, KHJ, promoted that concert. Those were the days when things were (in alphabetical order) alright, bad, bitchen, bosco banana, boss banana, boss trip, burn, choice, clean, cool, crazy, fab, fantastic, fine, freaky, funky, a gas, great, groovy, happening, heavy, hip, hubba hubba, jeter neat, like wow, makakasaka, marvy, neat, neato-frito, noble, out of sight, psychedelic, raspy, righteous, sock it to me, something else, squishy, stock, super, swingin', terrific, too much, torpedo, total, tough, wild, wow, zunzabah. The Doors concert sold out, and it was the worst mob scene I had ever seen, worse than the Monkees or anyone, fans crashing through cops and all the football-player-size security to get backstage, get at them.

VINCE TREANOR: Unfortunately that performance was a little tighter than it should have been, nervous tighter. Nevertheless we blew the audience right out of the seats, right over the hill, right down to Sunset Boulevard.

ROBBY KRIEGER: Vince was into power. He loved to be the loudest one around.

VINCE TREANOR: When it was time for the 'Unknown Soldier' shot—there's a pause and then this shot rings out—the timing was to pace that moment, milk it for its theatrical best. I don't think a broadside from the battleship Missouri could sound more impressive. The noise was that great, people were calling in to find out what happened.

JAC: Mark Abramson did a film version, and of course the Doors were always up for that, because Jim and Ray had been film students at UCLA.

JOHN DENSMORE: I guess we had a loose idea that for the execution section we were going to tie Jim up and shoot him. Mark filmed us in Venice, walking down from the house to the pier, and he cut in World War II footage. It was sort of End The War, lyrically, not in reality—Vietnam was roaring along, so we decided to end it ourselves.

We had a giant argument with Bill Graham, trying to get him to play it at the Fillmore East in the middle of our concert. He took offense to it, you know. How did we twist Bill Graham's arm? Somehow. In the rideout, we played our instruments live, behind the film as it ended. We became like live stereo, and the whole audience stood up and started dancing around like the World War II victory folk in the film. And I mean, you know, we ended the Vietnam war at the Fillmore East in 1968. What a feeling.

DIGBY DIEHL: If Ray was the musical leader of the group, Jim was the emotional leader, and he carried them directly down the dark tunnel. A very ominous, threatening figure on stage, always seeming on the brink of something terrible, exploding in violence. He liked to think he was taking himself and the audience out to the edge of a new, new experience, out to the fringes, push it to the limits.

JAC: The Morrison alerts were a continuing barrage, including one at Force Five, from the Singer Bowl on Long Island.

JEFF SILVERMAN: I had gotten a really good 35mm camera for a high school graduation present. These were the days before press credentials. If you had a good camera you just went to where the action was.

I get up to the stage, and I'm standing there, literally using the stage as a place to balance my elbows, so I'm this close to the Doors.

There was some incredible eye contact going on between Morrison and this Hispanic girl. She and Morrison were most definitely playing to each other most of the night. In the break of a song, absolute silence on the stage, he just looks over to her—I'm actually standing right between them—and grabs his crotch with one hand, and says, "Mexican whore, come suck my prick."

I look back in time to see this big guy she was with. I had never seen—it was a combination of absolute shock and real hate. And he grabbed a chair, one of those wooden folding chairs, and just heaped it on the stage, and all of a sudden chairs start flying.

VINCE TREANOR: The place came apart so fast it was like watching a school of fish or a flock of birds change direction. Jim was delivering his message—be free, test the limits—and on that particular night in that particular place, instead of being seeds on fertile ground it was grains of black powder.

RAY MANZAREK: Kids were breaking chairs, throwing pieces of wood and chairs at the cops, the cops were running into the audience, beating on the kids.

JEFF SILVERMAN: The place is pandemonium. And Morrison is just dancing around, having the time of his life. The cops try to get him off the stage, but couldn't move him. At one point he laid down and the cops couldn't even lift him.

VINCE TREANOR: Kids behind the stage picked up this eight or ten-foot beam like a giant baseball bat and tried to knock us off the stage with it. They literally picked it up and swept the stage with it. People were hurt, equipment was stolen, a tremendous amount of damage was done.

After the audience was cleared out, there was just wood, like enormous tooth picks, laying crisscrossed, like pickup sticks, all over the ground, just shredded wood wherever you looked.

RAY MANZAREK: A sea of slats. One girl got hit in the head, and she was brought backstage, and Jim ministered to her, he was cleaning her wounds, ministering unto a girl with a little wound on her head.

JAC: That was the summer of 1968. In the fall, the Doors did a European tour with Jefferson Airplane, and from the other side of the world we received more Morrison communiqués, datelined Amsterdam.

Grace Slick and Paul Kantner recall the two bands walking down the street, Jim swinging a bottle like a gunfighter, kids pressing drugs on them—Amsterdam was a huge, open drug city—Jim downing everything on the spot, a big block of hashish, then a half a dozen beers before the show. The Airplane are opening, and in the middle of their set, on comes Jim, uninvited, gyrating to 'Plastic Fantastic Lover,' one of the Airplane's more up-tempo tunes. Mischievously, the Airplane begins to play ever faster, and to keep up Jim has to spin with greater speed, till he looks like a pinwheel, then collapses and is out of the Doors show. Ray has to sing the entire set. He does great.

BILL SIDDONS: Jim was hospitalized for two days because he ate so much hash it almost shut down his bodily functions.

Doors Photo Archive

Elektra publicity still

Chapter 15

How to orchestrate
a six-foot Southern California salad ...
Dolby delights ... Gathering wildflowers

JAC: In October of 1966, when I had a fully mixed first Doors album, I played it for Judy Collins. None of our artists had yet heard it but they were all very curious, and I wondered if Judy would get it. She surprised me with her all-out enthusiasm.

Judy understood that the Doors were a new voice for the label. Playing her the tape was my way of letting her know that Elektra was moving in new directions. She got that too, and it could not have been the easiest of acceptances. For several years she had been first in our hearts, with everything this implied in the way of support—musical, emotional, and financial. She had a great career ahead of her, with her musical best still to come, yet she could see that her record label—the company she had helped to build—was at another crossroad, and that, from then on, her direction might turn out to be the road less traveled.

ARTHUR GORSON: The game shifted. The singer-songwriters had been the royalty at Elektra, the heroes. But suddenly the attention went elsewhere, into the Doors and rock and what that meant. Rothchild came out West, Jac came out West. We had always been dealing with the "Circle Game" level, where we sold thirty thousand albums. Now suddenly Elektra is moving into a different game, which of course changed the history of Elektra. We were pissed because, as folk managers and artists, we were no longer the most important to the label, and attention, promotion, and all the rest of the things that we could always count on, even though they were small amounts of money, started drying up. It caused a philosophical problem and resentment. There was a line in a Phil Ochs song: "God help the troubadour who wants to be a star." Suddenly the whole skew changed. Elektra became a different company.

JAC: Yes and no. What I was doing with the Doors was following the music, as I had done all along—from folk to singer-songwriters, to Koerner, Ray & Glover, to the Butterfield Blues Band, to Love, to the Doors. But even at the height of Elektra's rock years I never stopped recording other kinds of music. Nonesuch kept going from strength to strength. In the area of Arthur's direct concern, I happily recorded Tom Rush all the way through the Sixties, and signed serious new folk-styled voices: David Ackles, Paul Siebel and Lindisfarne. And I kept on releasing pure ethnic material, from the Bauls of Bengal to "Crow Dog's Paradise," an album of Sioux Indian music.

As for Judy Collins, her new album, "Wildflowers," was another major landmark in her artistic development, and out of it came her first big hit single.

JOHN HAENY: "Wildflowers" was a large orchestral album. We recorded in LA, in Studio One at United & Western, which was a big room. Four-track. And Jac had discovered in England this thing called a Dolby box, for something called noise reduction. Pretty adventuresome. No one here had any real idea of what it was, how it operated, what its purpose was.

SUZANNE HELMS: It was another of Jac's firsts. We used the same Dolbys on both the east and west coasts, air-freighted back and forth in special crates that Jac ordered made. In LA I would meet them at the airport, they were so precious, bring them in by truck, tell the studio they were coming. One night we couldn't find any place to park on Sunset, and John Haeny and I had to drag them across the street, get the guard to sign for them.

JOHN HAENY: I recorded Judy with two four-track machines, one with Dolby, the other not, and used the Dolby as a reference. I'll never forget the first session, live, involving thirty or forty players. We had gotten a good take, and we said, "Well, let's play back the Dolby, see what it's about." Nobody knew what to expect. The Dolby was very confusing to plug in. I came up with an odd little harness to switch over from recording to playback. I had to crawl behind the machine and switch a bunch of stuff around. I did my major connections, rewound the tape to where I thought was the top, went to the console, and opened up the gains on the monitors wide, expecting to hear the shooop of the tubes and the tape hiss. In those days lots of noise told us the equipment was working. I heard nothing. Well, I assumed, this isn't working. I pressed the Play button. It turned out that I wasn't fully wound back through the tape, I was in the middle—and out jumped the first Dolby sound anybody had ever heard. It was a very large control room, Judy and the producer and probably half the orchestra were in it, and the monitors were wide open. Everybody had a stroke. It was a spiritual awakening for everyone present.

Original Dolby® audio noise reduction system circa 1964

JAC: That was a technical landmark in pop recording. Incredible clarity, no distracting noise, no veil between you and the music. And if ever an artist and a technology were made for each other, it was Judy and Dolby.

JUDY COLLINS: "Wildflowers" was the first completely orchestrated album of the genre. Not a folk guitar on it. And it had my writing. By that time I had started to write, so it has 'Since You've Asked' and 'Albatross'—and I sweated over those. Josh Rifkin did the arrangements, and he added a dimension of intelligence about orchestrations.

JOSHUA RIFKIN: In the studio Mark was very focused, but able to fool you completely; he could always seem so laid-back. John Haeny was more intense. He was a wonderful engineer with a fantastic set of ears. He could hear a run-through of my arrangements and know exactly how I wanted it to sound on the disk, and then could get that on the mikes. He got what was for those days a really beautiful, burnished, very rich sound quality that had a transparent sensuousness to it, if you will.

What I also remember John for is his hospitality. We went out a number of times to his small wooden house in Laurel Canyon, and one evening we spent there best sums up the whole style and spirit of the thing. Judy and some of the other women—I'm afraid it was still a society in which these roles were gender-determined—used to do our communal food shopping when we had meals together, hit the twenty-four-hour supermarket and come back with this absolutely mind-boggling produce. This evening they prepared this monstrous salad which I remember as being put into a bowl about six feet in diameter, and I recall that we smoked a lot of dope that night, and then the bowl was brought and laid on the floor, and we all spread out around it on our bellies, like the rays of the sun. John had this engineer's stereo system, huge beautiful speakers, and while we attacked the salad, he played us the entire Bach B-minor Mass, followed by "Sergeant Pepper." It was my quintessential California experience, and one of the most wonderful evenings I have ever spent. It was that evening that I first understood the B-minor Mass, really made the connection to it; and recording it myself later on, after that eye-opener, is in some ways a heritage of that evening. And that was all of a piece with what we were doing in the studio, and we just felt enormously happy, we felt we were doing something really worthwhile.

JOHN HAENY: Judy's particularly unique gift was song sense. Her whole purpose was to deliver the melody as straight as possible, with the lyrics as clean and understandable with as much emotional meaning behind it as she could impart, but without any vocal or dramatic tricks.

JOSHUA RIFKIN: Some things in the arrangements came from Judy. For example, although it's not literally so, the sort of harp figure that opens 'Michael From Mountains' was suggested by something she played on the guitar when she first sang the song for me. That put a certain image of sound in my mind which I took and reshaped. The keyboard figure that keeps going through 'Both Sides Now' may not be literally, but it's something like when she sat at the piano and played the tune for me. She's a very good pianist. When she'd sit and play something, I would pick up on it not simply because it was hers and because she may have wanted it, but because it sounded right.

Because the arrangements were being done at the last minute, Judy was in the unenviable position of having to do her studio work cold. And I threw a lot of complicated things at her. I took advantage of her musicianship, because she really knows what she's doing. I would have constantly changing meters—not starting in 4/4 and just keeping going, they keep shifting. Even with tunes you know, if you're faced with this at the last second, it's not the easiest thing. She did it, and did it terrifically and with great skill. I still have and cherish a couple of photographs taken at these sessions of our recording of 'Albatross,' this tune of Judy's, which is the most complex arrangement on the album. The meter is changing, every bar, from 4/4 to 3/4, 7/4, 5/4, et cetera. I'm conducting, and there is this lovely shot of Judy looking up at me very intently, very deeply involved, really focusing on what's coming next.

JOHN HAENY: Frequently there were large conflicts, not violent, but large creative conflicts between the importance of the vocal performance and the orchestral accompaniment, which was a push-pull between Josh and Judy that went on all the time.

MARK ABRAMSON: Judy always thought that Josh's arrangements would overwhelm her, or was fearful of them, and Josh always felt that everything had to be heard, and the voice was just part of that. Judy saw herself as the focus, and Josh saw the music as a whole as the focus. Very different.

JUDY COLLINS: I think Josh would have run off with it if he could have. But he couldn't.

JOHN HAENY: Mark sat in the middle and helped mediate. He was Judy's confidante.

MARK ABRAMSON: I was definitely caught in the middle, and I may not have been as strong as I should have been.

JOHN HAENY: We recorded everything live. You would look for the best orchestra performances and the best vocal performances and splice them together, bar by bar. Judy and Josh would sit there, and Mark would sit in the middle and try to figure out how I could physically edit the tapes to get Josh the best orchestral performance and Judy the best vocal performance. And sometimes I had to do almost impossible edits to accomplish that. I would just try to stay out of the conflict between Judy and Josh, waiting for them to decide who was going to win the battle over that particular few bars of music. That album had something like four hundred-fifty edits.

MARK ABRAMSON: We didn't have automated mixing then, digital processors. It was all manual. Some of these mixes were very complicated—three of us on the board at the same time, pushing buttons, mixing, changing equalization, because it took six hands to do.

JUDY COLLINS: One thing you don't want to do is walk away from a mix session. Ever, ever. You can't. One of the great struggles that I've had throughout my career is maintaining voice level to track level. They will drown you in their arrangement whenever they can. It's a natural thing, I think they come by it quite honestly, but every singer I've ever known in my life has to fight it. This is serious, serious stuff.

JAC: Josh and Judy were both right. Getting the balance between individual interests without wounding either is like performing the most delicate brain surgery, which it is. You don't want to lose the words, but those settings of Josh's were particularly exquisite and deserved equal weight. Judy's voice could sit comfortably in the arrangements—put some light but characteristically different reverb on her voice and balance it into the strings.

MARK ABRAMSON: Judy and I worked extremely well, I think, when the chips were down and things had to be done. She would be temperamental when we were mixing, or privately, but when everybody was there and there was work to be done, there was never any temperament that would get in the way.

Josh you put up with because of what he would contribute. Of course he was very young. I'm not sure he was fully aware that people were relying on him for more than just musical things. He could be a problem because of his own ego—his own sloppiness, frankly, where arrangements wouldn't be ready on the day. With 'Both Sides Now,' which we recorded in New York, we sat in the studio with the whole orchestra for an hour waiting for Josh because he hadn't shown up with the final copies of the score, and we were paying umpteen dollars an hour, going crazy.

Judy Collins "Wildflowers" EKS-74012

JUDY COLLINS: "Wildflowers" was released in 1968. That music was never an easy sell. But everybody was talking about 'Both Sides Now'—"By God, that's a single. But it needs remixing, or it needs something or other."

JAC: From the beginning I thought 'Both Sides Now' was a potential single but I wasn't sure about the timing. The world needed to settle down a bit for these wise and gentle words to be heard. Almost a year later there were rumors of an English group coming out with the song so I moved quickly.

JUDY COLLINS: He sent us back to the studio, and we remixed it and he re-released it—

JAC:—With great energy—

JUDY COLLINS:—Because he believed in it so strongly. And it hit. Top 10, Number 8, nine weeks on the charts.

JAC: And because it was so widely played on radio formats other than Top 40, it earned Judy the cover of Life magazine.

JUDY COLLINS: There was a lot of commitment on Jac's part to a project, whatever it was, but I never really felt that he was pushing me: "Quick, hurry up, get a record out." Because he respected the process, the time it took. There were times when it might have been a good idea for me to hurry and push and get a record out. But Jac never forced me to do anything I didn't want to.

Chapter 16

Creatures of the canyon, circa 1968 ...
The summer of incense ...
Turtle steak and brown rice in Lahaina ...
The Mexican rubber stamp dance

JOHN HAENY: Elektra on the West Coast was a record company where, when you got up, you decided if you were going to wear the denim shirt or the denim shirt or the denim shirt, and would the denim trousers be the bellbottoms with the roses embroidered on them or the ones with the gardenias? Those were the choices in life.

All of us were living on rock and roll time. We partied till the wee small hours, then slept until ten or noon or three. But of course Jac was in New York, on New York time. I think we suspected he would get up early, take a few uppers—

JAC:—I never needed uppers—

JOHN HAENY:—Have his chauffeur pick him up, and head to Elektra with his thousands of things to do. Jac has never been short on motivation. He always kept economic and office management on the East Coast, but we were the real creative people, the real hippies. So the phone used to ring an hour after we went to bed, and it would be Holzman from New York. He had to get those babies on the phone in California, with a thousand thoughts on his mind and yabadabadaba. He used to do it to all of us, and we all used to scream and holler and hang up on him. We were bratty children and he was the daddy, even though he was only in his mid-thirties.

JAC: The West Coast people thought of themselves as the elite, above the fray, while New York did the heavy lifting. The East Coast was a place to "do," and the West Coast was a place to "be." The West Coasters walked a fine line between doing business, being in the business, and looking cool. It was good to let them know from time to time that the world outside of hip LA still existed and was moving forward.

JOHN HAENY: Jac would make his royal visits and bestow his presence upon us. He was a big man, imposing, serious. If we had a tape to play for him he would give it The Big Listen—that's what we called it—face in hands, eyes closed, deeply concentrating on every nuance. At the conclusion of which everybody would wait for what was known as The Big Opinion. Jac would be listening as intently as possible, so that when it was finished he could say something that was as profound as possible—Jac, don't hate me for this, but I know the Virgo mind—some meticulous eloquent summation. We would sit there in rapt expectation, because he was the boss, he paid the bills, he held the keys, he had the power of life and death. El Supremo.

JAC: Those moments between the music's end and the expected words from my mouth were torture. If I loved it there was no problem. If not, I tried to find something I could single out for praise before sending them back to do it again.

JOHN HAENY: Record executives, especially from New York—they were suits, and that was that. Sometimes those people started wearing denims, but they still had business suits for minds. It could take a long time for the change to happen. But it wasn't fair to call Jac a suit, I mean just a suit. He was out on the streets of New York at nineteen, recording blues artists, ten, fifteen years before any of us were involved in the music business. There must have been a Jack Kerouac in him somewhere, to go out and experience it. And Jac was probably one of the first record company executives to show up in the office wearing jeans. So we all gave him denim points.

DAVID ANDERLE: The East Coast and the West Coast were totally different cultures. And there was the East Coast Jac and the West Coast Jac—it's almost like the classic case of the guy who's married to two women in two different ports.

JAC: California was seductive, and I was willing to be seduced. You didn't bring your briefcase to the West Coast, you left it in New York, where you had the administrative people to handle those things. In California, there was two to three times as much hang time. Hanging was a big part of getting things done in LA. And when in Rome . . .

DAVID ANDERLE: Jac would hit LA looking New York. He kept an apartment here, he'd go there, put on his jeans and his Indian shirts.

JOHN HAENY: He would always grace me with an evening, come to my little house in Laurel Canyon, which was very relaxed, laid-back—hippiedom. And being El Supremo, he would ensconce himself in the most auspicious place in the room, a double mattress in the middle of the floor, and it was like, "OK, make me feel good."

Jac always had a strong desire to be part of what we were, one of us. In 1968 it was important for everybody to love everybody. And Jac wanted to be loved.

DAVID ANDERLE: There were enormous preparations in my house to get ready for his arrival—there were enormous preparations for everything that's got to do with Jac. Paul Rothchild and I used to have contests about who could roll the greatest joints and give to Jac to blow his mind.

JAC: Rothchild rolled meticulous joints. If the Japanese were to manufacture joints, they would look like Rothchild's, not within spec but to spec, no slop tolerance. It defined Paul's hipness, rolling joints in front of artists, two-thirds the diameter of a cigarette and perfectly tubular. Works of folk art.

PAT FARALLA: And Jac loved maryjanes, hash or grass cookies. I remember making him some and wondering, "Too much? Or too little? Oh, what the hell . . . "

JOHN HAENY: My Laurel Canyon house was on Ridpath. In the living room was my stereo system, with big electrostatic speakers, extraordinarily exotic for then, and a five-foot hookah that I was keeping for my drug dealer whose mother wouldn't let him have it at home. I extended visiting privileges to him provided he brought the grass. He would show up from time to time with his friends, and I would invite my friends. We would lock all the doors and windows so the smoke would stay in the room. We were all into popsicles. I had the world's largest collection of popsicle sticks. We would fill the bowl of this huge hookah, a cup, cup and a half, and keep it lit by throwing popsicle sticks in, and pass the rope around till everybody passed out.

I woke up one morning to some chaos, and there was Judy Collins nude in my front yard. The yard had a high wooden fence and succulents, and there was Judy with her clothes off and a photographer. They were shooting the album cover for "Wildflowers." They ultimately came into the house. She was sitting on the floor, with some clothes on now, by a curtained wall with light coming through the window and one of my exotic brass vases with some dried flowers in it, and that became the back cover. The nude pictures were scotched.

Also at the Ridpath house I introduced Judy to Stephen Stills, and that resulted in their romance, and their romance resulted in Stephen writing 'Suite: Judy Blue Eyes.' Carole King was in and out of Ridpath—it was a dog owned by Carole and Gerry Goffin that sired my dog Niki's first litter of puppies. Neil Young was around. I was at some friend's house with David Crosby—we were all in a pack, you know, all buddies then—and somebody had brought a tape in of a young girl that nobody knew much about, except Judy had discovered her as a songwriter, and it was Joni Mitchell.

Joni was living on the next road up from Kirkwood. David Crosby was producing her first album. The people who recorded it were basically incompetent, and the tapes were a mess. David was having serious problems with the mix. I was exclusive to Elektra, but David came to me and asked would I sneak out and remix. We did it in the dead of night in a little studio at Sunset Sound. I didn't have a written contract with Jac, but it was a violation. Years later Jac told me he had always known I did it. There wasn't much going on that Jac didn't know about; he was a fox. He let it go because he knew Joni was important. David gave me a Swiss army knife. I still have it in a box out in the garage.

JACKSON BROWNE: I met John on Ridpath. A great guy, an interesting guy, very funny. He had these two white dogs, huskies, that he loved like they were his family. He was a genius engineer. Intensely talented. He made everybody sound great. Through his mind and his mike placements, he could shape things. And his demos sounded like completed records. He was sort of odd, a little goofy-looking, very sincere, not much of a hipster, probably a kid who had grown up taking apart Wurlitzer theater organs. Very anal retentive. In the studio he was fastidious beyond belief about how he wanted to do things, and he talked about it all the way: "I want to do this, I want to do that." Most people reserve a lot for the mix: "It'll really sound great when we mix it," and then you play this game, Beat The Demo. But John right there in the session could make it sound fantastic. He could hear it all at once.

BOB ZACHARY: He used to say, "Watch my hands, when you see them starting to sweat, we are only a take or two away from the best take."

JACKSON BROWNE: John was neurotic as hell, with little tics. "I've got a bladder the size of a walnut," he would say, and go to the bathroom. One time he nearly cut my thumb off in the middle of recording. He was doing an edit, he had the razor in his hand, I was reaching for a book of matches, and he thought I was going to step on the loops of tape cascaded onto the floor waiting for him to take up onto another reel. He screamed, "LOOK OUT!"—and he did like an umpire's safe motion with his hand and cut me right across the thumb, and the blood poured out, blub-blub-blub.

NED DOHENY: I met John on Ridpath too. We were all crashing on that street, in every sense of the word. The Incredible String Band was there. Gentle Soul. And Nico, talking about Dr. Hoffman on his bicycle.

JUDY JAMES: Around Ridpath was always an alternative area, with dirt roads, fire roads.

JAC: I remember someone saying the streets looked like they had been laid out by earthworms.

JUDY JAMES: It had gotten rundown and cheap before us, a lot of garages turned into one-room thises and thats, so there were always actors and musicians. There was a sense of hanging-outness, of finding out what was going on in the music business if you walked up and down Ridpath.

JACKSON BROWNE: There was amazing tribal life. There were houses supported by record companies, groups living with an account at the health food store.

JAC: Billy James' mailbox had listings for twenty groups, plus companies and artists.

JACKSON BROWNE: Billy was my manager, and he ran the Elektra office for a while. Sort of a hipster cat, something like a dancer. And he was very funny, very smart. Like somewhere in between a James Dean and a Mort Sahl. He was older than us, must have been in his thirties, but he was still one of us, he was a freak.

JUDY JAMES: No one owned furniture. People would be living on the floor, many of them on our floor. Runaways. Kids who were parentless. Groupies. This tremendous influx of kids from Orange County.

BILLY JAMES: Penny Nichols stayed in the laundry room downstairs for a while. Jackson slept over. Pamela Polland. Tim Buckley. Jimmy Spheeris, Greg Copeland, Steve Noonan, wonderful writers. All coming out of Sunny Hills High, Orange County. We were never alone. We had a dining room table made of three-quarter-inch ply with two-by-four legs. Seated a lot of people. Ray Manzarek came to dinner and told me it was the first time he had ever seen an artichoke.

Cass Elliott was living up the hill with Butchy. Tim Hardin was a couple of doors up. Leonard Cohen came calling. Frank Zappa was on Kirkwood, which is the street you take to get to Ridpath, and then he moved to a log cabin at the corner of Laurel Canyon, with a bowling alley downstairs. Lots of people lived in that house with Frank.

JOHN HAENY: Then there were Deering and Billy Howell, rich kids who liked to have stars around. They had a big house. We would head up there at midnight. David Crosby and Paul Rothchild and I ended up in the shower there with lots of Vitabath, which was very big in those days.

BARRY FRIEDMAN: And Jack the castle man, this guy who owned a bunch of castles. Different stars would rent them and move in with their entourage. They could make wonderful entrances down the stone staircases and they were good for practicing in and careening about on the parapets in various states of undress. I remember Nico with Jackson in tow coming down the stairs one day. That was quite a sight.

JACKSON BROWNE: Paul Rothchild lived on Ridpath too. Paul was like a superman. He knew about all sorts of things. He sat me down and had me listen to Kurt Weill and Bertolt Brecht, long before the Doors recorded 'Alabama Song.' He drove a Porsche and wore a velour hat, a Borsalino. These were things that denoted one's station, these were the people who had made a fortune or were on the way to making a fortune.

FRITZ RICHMOND: Paul's main room was one of the nicest music listening rooms that anyone knew of in Hollywood, and because of that people would come by with their tapes. I had my juke box there, and people would come over to check out what things sounded like on the juke box. The Doors would come up for playbacks. And Janis Joplin. I would wake up in the morning and hear her cackling away downstairs. She had a unique laugh, that woman.

DAN ROTHCHILD: My father had a story about a couch that Fritz eventually donated to a rummage sale in Portland in 1989. Among those who sat on the couch were Janis Joplin and the Full Tilt Boogie Band, Jim Morrison, Ray Manzarek, Robby Krieger and John Densmore, Joni Mitchell, John Sebastian, David Crosby, Stephen Stills and Graham Nash, Paul Butterfield, Glenn Frey, Linda Ronstadt, Jackson Browne, and another dozen butts of distinction. That couch should have great vibes.

JACKSON BROWNE: So there were interesting houses we could walk to. Or we would catch a ride to Peter Tork's house on Willow Glen. Peter had been a dishwasher at the Golden Bear in Huntington Beach and now he was a TV star, a Monkee. My friend Ned Doheny and I would say, "Let's go up to Peter's house, see what's going on." Sometimes you would walk in and there would be twelve girls in the pool, naked. And they were beautiful women, people of substance, not bimbos—not that we would have minded if they were bimbos. One time Jimi Hendrix was up there jamming with Buddy Miles in the pool house, and Peter's girlfriend was playing the drums, naked. She was gorgeous, like a Varga girl is gorgeous, this physically flawless creature. She looked like the drawings of Indian maidens that they airbrush on motorcycle tanks. I don't think she was as good a drummer as she was an object of desire, but she was something.

Barry Friedman was on Ridpath too, about a block from Billy James, two blocks from Paul Rothchild.

JOHN HAENY: Barry was one of Jac's little West Coast club of fanciful folk.

PAT FARALLA: Elektra on the West Coast was a real safe house for creativity and for eccentric people.

JACKSON BROWNE: Barry had this wonderful carny mentality. He had been in the circus, a clown and a fire eater.

NED DOHENY: Diablo the fire eater.

MARTY RICHMOND: He also had the amazing ability to get out of any ropes you could tie him up in. He wouldn't let us watch him doing it, but he could be loose in fifteen seconds or less.

NED DOHENY: He used to drive around town in a sports car dressed in a gorilla suit.

BARRY FRIEDMAN: It was a King Kong suit. It came to me by way of this Las Vegas hooker. Her husband Scotty was one of the original King Kongs, he did all the stuff on the Empire State Building. A great suit.

JUDY JAMES: Once, Barry phoned everyone and got us all to drop the needle on the new Stones album at exactly the same moment, so that the canyon would echo with music.

BARRY FRIEDMAN: One night it was full moon, we're all sitting around in various states of decomposure, and a voice is heard echoing over the canyon, "This is God speaking. I have a message for you." And He gave His message. Well, thousands of people throughout the canyon were somewhat freaked by this experience and talked about it for days. It turned out it was Barry McGuire, the 'Eve Of Destruction' guy, who had set up this huge sound system, I think at the Mamas and Papas' house up at the top of Lookout, and blasted this diatribe to the stoned minions below.

JUDY JAMES: Many times I sat on the steps of Paul Rothchild's house with Barry, talking. On a Saturday afternoon, before the night, before the music, before the drugs, if Barry was straight and into talking, it might as well be to me—I had a degree in theater and philosophy, and I didn't do drugs. Barry was a pretty interesting guy, a thinking, reading person, a watcher. And into sound, into how good the music could be.

JACKSON BROWNE: Barry produced Kaleidoscope's first album. Brilliant. Another very great record Barry did, on Elektra, was "The Moray Eels Eat The Holy Modal Rounders." The Holy Modal Rounders did extremely drug-oriented folk music. A lot of beautiful songs about being up for days and coming down—"Rockin' around in that belladonna cloud, euphoria." They were real freaks.

"The Moray Eels Eat The Holy Modal Rounders " EKS-74026

JUDY JAMES: I had an impression of Barry as a true hippie. In the way that Cass Elliott was a true hippie. They believed in what was going on. They believed in what Timothy Leary was finding out, and didn't yet know the danger of it, that it was only true for five minutes and then you could be lost to the acid experience.

Barry was at the center of a lot of stuff, drugs, recording, money spent on a loose, deliberate creation of that which the press was codifying as the Sixties, creating permission with money to go into the deeper darker side of the drug music culture. Bigger parties, more drugs, more permissions given, more permissions taken.

JOHN HAENY: Barry was in his late twenties. Most of the rest of us were younger, me for one, twenty-three. Some were much younger—Jackson Browne and Ned Doheny were still in their teens. Barry was sort of the leader of the pack.

MARTY RICHMOND: Undisputed leader of the band.

JOHN HAENY: There were social experiments at his house, where he pushed all the beds together in the living room, and all the people who were living at his house were going to start sleeping together.

JACKSON BROWNE: Orgies. Lots of bodies. The mechanics of that kind of arrangement are always problematic.

BARRY FRIEDMAN: One time Nico came in with a gun and grabbed some woman that one of the boys was in bed with by the hair and drug her out and made her run down the road, and we finally got the gun away from Nico and said, "Nico, why did you do that?" And she said, "Oh, some men like that."

JACKSON BROWNE: You'd meet all sorts of great people at Barry's house. That's where I met Warren Zevon. I met David Crosby there. He and Stephen Stills and Graham Nash would come over and play their demo. I played Barry some of my songs.

JUDY JAMES: This really was a moment when musicians had an enormous determination to communicate what they were feeling, whether in music or in lyrics. You could hear that at the hootennanies at the Troubadour, in living rooms all over town. On Ridpath, too. People were forming various groups and allegiances and alliances, and they all wanted to make a record.

JACKSON BROWNE: The Band came out with "Music From Big Pink." We had never heard anything like it. It was ragged, loose, but it was plugged into something so real. They recorded it where they were living, in this big pink-painted house at Woodstock—more than a year before what we know as Woodstock—and we all went, "Wow, they made their record in a house!"

My friends had made some slick records that didn't mean a thing to anybody. Producers were using the same musicians in the studio with very different artists, not finding what was unique about an artist and shaping the production around that. The session hack syndrome was looming, and it was the enemy. We were thinking, "How do you get in the studio and make something that sounds like itself?"

Jackson Browne in his early Elektra/Asylum days

We were taking Big Pink as a road sign. Being with all those guys in the canyon, around Ridpath, gave birth to the idea. So we were saying, "We want to make a record, in a house, in the country."

MARTY RICHMOND: One of Barry Friedman's many talents was the ability to assemble bands. He could take a bunch of untried kids, and after a little weeding put together a going band. He had done it before, with Buffalo Springfield. Then, while he was working for Jac and Elektra, he was wearing the cloak of a real exciting record label. He was able to attract many aspiring musicians. He was interested if they were competent; but if they were also young, and especially if they were pretty, his interests became more intense. His living room was one giant bed, where all of those crashing at his house could mingle. In some ways Barry's ideas had merit. He was convinced that any successful band contained a bond of love among all the players, which although not necessarily sexual was equally as strong. He was hoping to take a short cut, by introducing the sex and hoping that the love would follow.

NED DOHENY: Out of this snakepit of manic self-indulgence and general searching was born the Los Angeles Fantasy Orchestra.

JAC: Actually, it goes back to the Sunday morning of the Monterey Pop Festival. Nina, Barry Friedman and I were sitting in a coffee shop, infused with the heady good vibes of the festival, where flowers had been placed in the helmets of smiling motorcycle cops, and the lady mayor was making sure that everything remained peaceful and pleasant, because there was worldwide attention focused on her community.

I had been disappointed that the Doors had not been invited to Monterey, because wherever you went radios were playing 'Light My Fire.' Paul Simon, who was on the festival board, said to me that he was truly sorry they hadn't been asked. I know I cared, but 'Light My Fire' was Number 1, and that certainly softened the hurt.

With all of this euphoria and those incredible performances from The Who, Janis Joplin and Jimi Hendrix, there was this pervasive feeling, fueled by the haze of dope that hung over the festival, that the world was slowly shifting our way.

Barry had an idea, and he chose the final morning of the festival to lay it on me. He proposed a music ranch. Take talented kids out of the struggles of trying to make it in the city, give them fresh air, good food and the freedom to create whatever music came to them.

It just struck me as a worthy notion, and out of that enthusiasm came a "Yes." With the Doors and Nonesuch, Elektra was throwing off enormous amounts of cash, so money was not the issue. And I was much more inclined to be experimental if it made any kind of crazy sense whatever.

Barry had produced one of my all-time favorite albums, the first Kaleidoscope for Epic. He had been there early, trying to help me sign Buffalo Springfield. He had taste, and I knew that I would just have to give him his head and pray it would work. I also felt my presence during the project should be kept to the minimum. Elektra was too big for me to be everywhere at once.

JACKSON BROWNE: Jac went for the idea that we would have a repertory recording company, a loose aggregation of musicians that all responded to each other—the band, or the rock community, however large a circle you want to draw. We were all interested in making our own albums, and we were all going to play on each others' records.

MARTY RICHMOND: Jackson played guitar and piano and wrote songs. Rolf Kempf played piano, organ, guitar, and—oddly—accordion. He had had polio as a child, and he walked with a brace on his leg and a cane. Jack Wilce played banjo, mandolin and guitar. He had also written one song. Peter Hodgson signed on as the bass player. Ned Doheny, an heir to the Doheny oil fortune, was to play electric lead guitar.

NED DOHENY: It was a major adventure for a credential-less kid. I had originally auditioned for Barry before Ridpath, in some hotel room on Sunset Boulevard. I hooked up a little amplifier, played some Eric Clapton stuff, and was hired. At that time Barry was looking for somebody to play with someone named Jackson Browne, who I thought must be a huge black man. Imagine my surprise when I met him in Laurel Canyon and he was a small white person in his teens.

MARTY RICHMOND: All of the above had been spending a lot of time at Barry's house.

JACKSON BROWNE: The coolest thing we could imagine was being off where we could work on ideas and not have problems and we could get unlimited experience in recording and trying things. Cool. Pat Faralla, a very funny and astute woman who worked for Elektra, said to us: "Why should the world give you a house in the mountains? You have a problem with the clock? Are you, like, refugees from the rigors of studio life? Have you guys ever been in a studio?" Nobody appreciated her saying that. But it was true.

MARTY RICHMOND: Jackson had cut demos at Elektra. He knew the minimum basics of recording. The rest of them were going into it blind.

JACKSON BROWNE: We were all such whelps.

MARTY RICHMOND: The times were ripe for the plucking. The project was budgeted at around fifty thousand dollars and Jac approved it. Barry began scouting for a place.

NED DOHENY: Originally Barry told me he wanted to record Jackson's first album in a cave outside LA. So he was off to a flying start with bizarre methodology.

MARTY RICHMOND: Then he started looking in the San Fernando Valley. After several weeks he had nothing, and the search began to lead north.

JACKSON BROWNE: We drove up to Bolinas and looked around and didn't find anything.

MARTY RICHMOND: Finally, in some desperation, an ad was placed in the Los Angeles Examiner. A man answered, with a place for rent up in northern California on the Feather River, called Paxton Lodge.

BARRY FRIEDMAN: He was a bill collector, a guy about seven feet tall and a good three hundred-twenty pounds, and his son was just a little bigger.

JAC: Paxton was in beautiful mountain country—gold country—and, incidentally, on the stretch of Western Pacific railroad track where I had my adventure with the nun in 1955, so I already had an emotional connection with the place, a soft sweet memory.

MARTY RICHMOND: The only drawback was that it was five hundred miles from downtown Hollywood. Did they all want to stay in the Disneyland that is the Hollywood record world, or did they want to relocate to the woods and live in sylvan splendor? Barry took the plunge, and with Jac's OK the lease was signed for six months, with an option for six more.

JAC: The lodge was built by Western Pacific early in the century, as an overnight resort stop. When the railroad gave up on the place, it fell on hard times.

BARRY FRIEDMAN: It became a resort hotel for like little old school teachers, who would go to collect this rare kind of butterfly that was only found there. Then it became a brothel and a gambling place, with secret drops in the walls where they could hide the money when the sheriff came.

JACKSON BROWNE: Then a speakeasy. Then an alky dryout farm. Then nothing. Just this old empty hotel in the mountains. Small. Nothing as big as The Shining.

JACKSON BROWNE: About this time Barry changed his name to Frazier Mohawk.

BARRY FRIEDMAN: I think I owed American Express a lot of money and they kept coming around, and they sent someone to the door and asked if I was Barry Friedman, and I was very stoned at the time, and luckily Danny Kootch was there and he said, "No, no, he's Frazier Mohawk."

JACKSON BROWNE: God knows, in rock and roll we all have the right to call ourselves what we will.

JAC: I left Paxton to follow its fancy while I dealt with the growing enormity of Elektra and Nonesuch. I had an unbelievable number of things that needed attention.

PAUL WILLIAMS: Visiting Jac in his offices in New York, that was so fucking serious. You could see the sweat on his brow. Really a business environment. Not a stale, pathetic corporate environment like the Columbia office, the Black Rock, but you were very aware that business was being done here, on an extremely intense level.

JAC: And not just in New York. I had so much going on both coasts and with our A&R and distribution outpost in London that I was constantly in motion, yo-yoing back and forth. My marriage couldn't help but suffer.

NINA HOLZMAN: Jac had started traveling what I considered excessively, and I was constantly alone. I had the children, thank God. But I started living two lives, one life when Jac was home in New York, the other when he was traveling.

Jac had difficulties socially. He liked having people over to our house. But that was his turf. Otherwise, we would be going to a party, and it would be people he knew and liked, and I swear, as we were standing ringing the bell he would say to me, "What time can we leave?" I had other friends who didn't like Jac particularly, and I would see those people when he was out of town.

So things had started to fall apart. The business was fine, but his personal thing—I think there were major issues left over from his childhood that had never gotten resolved. And money doesn't resolve those things. It's only the beginning. In fact, it presented more problems. What's the next big deal? How am I going to live? It goes on and on.

I said to myself, "What do I have here that I won't have if I'm not here?" And I thought to myself, "I know that I'll get an OK settlement, so financially that's not an issue. I will still have my children, so that's not an issue. I'll still have my friends. So what is it that I won't have?" I wouldn't have Elektra, and Elektra was very important to me. But then again I knew I would move out to California, and there was an office out there, so I wouldn't be completely detached from it. And I wouldn't have Jac. But there wasn't enough joy at that point.

I decided that I would keep trying for another year. But there came a point—

JAC: To do more you need more people, and they bring people with them, and more artists, and the company just began to balloon. Though it put on more muscle, it also put on fat. And sometimes the fat and the muscle were on the same person. The problems were multiplied along with the opportunities and it was a strain to always be the good shepherd.

If your batting average in any field of endeavor is better than .500, everyone thinks you're a genius and wants to clip off a little piece of the hem of your garment as a talisman. To everyone at Elektra I was something different, because each one had needs that were different. In the sense of giving—or trying to give—everyone what they needed in the way of support, I lost my own center.

I felt reintegrated only when I heard music that justified the turmoil I was living through. It was a lonely existence.

This was far too buried for me to fully understand myself. Nina was the only person I could talk to, but by early 1967 we had begun to lead separate lives, hanging in there out of love for the company and a sense of responsibility to the children.

By the spring of 1968 I felt disillusioned, unable to articulate the problem, but knowing in my gut that I was at a profound dis-ease with myself and the company I had created.

There comes a point when you are no longer in control. Instead of riding the tiger, the tiger rides you. Elektra was getting away from me, and my reaction was to get away from it, to escape an organization in which I found my influence waning. So I said to Nina, "I don't want to do this any more. Why don't you try it for a while?"

NINA HOLZMAN: His intention was to go away for a year, go around the world or something, and he wanted me to run the company. That freaked me out. I didn't feel I was up to doing it. And I didn't want the responsibility. After all, I had two kids. I said, "What are you talking about? No way."

Looking back, I think Jac was probably having a nervous breakdown. He had worked so hard and in such a concentrated way for so many years, and he didn't know how to relax. That was not in his repertoire at all. So he just drove himself unmercifully, and took on all this responsibility, and he just broke. He was totally and completely emotionally burned out.

But right then I didn't understand his emotional state. To me it was a bit cavalier, to think that he could pull up, leave a company he had spent eighteen tough years building, and that he was in effect abandoning our family.

JAC: I don't think I meant a year literally, it was just something I blurted out, hyperbole to make my point, but it frightened Nina. She had never seen me come so unglued. I was acting wacko, and it scared her right down to her sandals.

Nina called our family friend and counselor Irwin Russell. By the time Irwin arrived I was calmer, but still feeling trapped in a zoo of my own making. I had to get away, find some perspective, clean my head.

We worked it out that I would take off for eight to ten weeks, traveling by sea as much of the time as possible. The vastness of the ocean has always had a quieting effect on me, so I decided to sail on the President Roosevelt from San Francisco to Yokohama, then to Hong Kong, then fly to my fantasy islands of Tahiti and the South Pacific, to walk the beach in quiet contemplation, and eventually return to New York.

JANICE KENNER: How did I get to Paxton? I'm in Laguna Beach with Connie Di Nardo, and Jackson calls.

CONNIE DI NARDO: We were in this commune that had something to do with Timothy Leary—

JANICE KENNER:—The Brotherhood of something. They had the first head shop in California, called Mystic Arts, incense and paraphernalia and clothes and beads. I didn't know I was on the cutting edge, all I knew is that I just happened to be there. I worked in the bead store. I took so many psychedelics—I mean I was just hallucinating. We had these little trays of beads, beautiful, they were constantly flying through the air.

So Jackson calls: "Come to Paxton." I said, "How am I going to get there?" Jackson says, "It's all arranged, your tickets. Just go to Elektra and pick them up." I said, "Well, I'm not coming unless I can bring Connie." He says, "Bring her, the more the merrier." So I say to Connie, "What do we have to lose? Let's go up there. This'll be fun." And I was so in love with Jackson.

I had fallen in love with him when I was just at the end of high school. I was obsessed with him. That's all I wanted to do, was be with him. I was living with my parents in Seal Beach and he would come down. He had nothing, just a Volkswagen bus. He had big holes in his shoes. He slept on our couch one night, and my mom was like, "Oh, the long hair, oh my God, what has she brought home now?"

We were just two people who fell in love very young. When we lived together he weighed about ninety pounds, wet, and he had his guitar, and he got his first piano and taught himself to play, and he stayed at home writing songs, from the moment he woke up to the moment he went to sleep. He was a musician, and I kind of feel that was his destiny, there was nothing else he could have done.

CONNIE DI NARDO: We would go see him sing in these little guitar shops, and there would be like twenty people, mostly women of course. Just Jackson and his guitar, and we would all be in tears, because he would be singing these sad songs that he wrote that would be just beautiful.

JAC: We had signed Jackson as a songwriter when he was seventeen.

JANICE KENNER: I always knew in my heart that Jackson was incredibly talented. To me that was such a special gift, magic, and I have to admit I was like a moth to a flame, before Paxton and again after Paxton. While he was writing I would draw all these pictures, and I wore these beautiful vintage Eighteen Nineties clothes, I got them at thrift stores, I had a real collection, and I would walk around like Greta Garbo, Jackson saying, "Take them off and throw them on the floor and draw nude," and he'd be there playing the guitar. It was so amazingly romantic.

We were on and off, off and on, but always passionately drawn to each other. When he called to say, "Come to Paxton," we were apart, but it took me about three seconds to decide.

JACKSON BROWNE: It was kind of like bringing in the dance hall girls for the miners.

CONNIE DI NARDO: They did their music, and we did our little housekeeping thing. They ate and we cooked.

MARTY RICHMOND: The first thing, when the girls got here they baked enormous batches of cookies which, when we went to town, we would hand out to the merchants, all prettily wrapped, and the sheriff wouldn't touch them, he was sure they had marijuana or acid in them.

JACKSON BROWNE: The girls liked to scandalize the people in Quincy by going into town wearing leopard-skin tights.

CONNIE DI NARDO: Leopard Capris, and aviator sun glasses and high heels. We didn't wear underwear, at least not all the time.

JACKSON BROWNE: They would go there in all their glory. Janice—really beautiful, incredibly kinky blonde hair like a lion's mane—looked like Jean Harlow just got out of the car and is now shopping in your mini-mart. Gorgeous open-faced beauty. A wildly exquisite girl. She imparted such goodness, like a Marilyn thing, this goodness-and-badness sexiness, but cleverly. She dazzled you. There was like a trail of open jaws as she left the market and got back in the car.

JANICE KENNER: They would cross the street not to pass us, because we were not the norm up there at all, we were an aberration.

JACKSON BROWNE: There was sort of a legend in Quincy about the goings on up at the old hotel.

CONNIE DI NARDO: A lot of us wanted to sleep with Ned. One time we told Ned his room was on fire so we could get up to his bedroom. I think he knew his room wasn't on fire.

NED DOHENY: After I moved out of a cabin and into the house, I selected one of the rooms in the attic because it had gables. We labored and dragged in a tub. We discovered that by moving several of the boards in my bathroom you could look down into the bathroom below. So not only did I have my own tub, I had a commanding view of the other tub. And I saw things that were real showstoppers.

WILLIE MURPHY: There were all these hippie girls and stuff that would wanna give guys baths.

CONNIE DI NARDO: Lottie Olcott was there when Janice and I came. Pale skin, blue eyes, turned-up nose, straight blonde hair. Small-boned, like a bird—she had the tiniest wrists in the world, you could put your finger round it. Real long legs, all legs, real ballerina-looking. She had always been a dancer. Her room was on the top floor, and they had fixed up a barre and a mirror for her. She was really just light and airy, sweet and gentle. Real hippie.

DAVID ANDERLE: I have a picture from Paxton, of a couple of the girls that were real friends, and they were, like, nude, posed and happy, and, you know, this is it.

WILLIE MURPHY: There were a lot of people's friends there, people I'd call hangers-on.

MARTY RICHMOND: Friends of Frazier's who came up from LA mainly on the lure of a free party.

FRAZIER MOHAWK: There were a couple of motel maids. There was one girl who wrote some of the strangest songs, who was a librarian.

JACKSON BROWNE: Annie the Junkie came up. She lived in Laurel Canyon. She was married to a jazz musician. He basically lived in New York and sent her money. She had these beautiful mulatto children. She was responsible, she always had someone looking after the kids. The kids didn't know she was a junkie. She was smart, so smart and good, a soulful woman, but strung out, a casualty of having been exposed to jazz and drugs, beautiful, soulful, with pancake makeup on the back of her hands. She was going to kick at Paxton.

NED DOHENY: It was the first time I had really been away from home. My parents probably pictured some sort of organized summer camp situation, people in cowboy hats and horses. It was definitely a lot more than that. It was a strange time for a human being to try and figure himself out. Most of us had the discipline of children. Our attention was grabbed by all sorts of strange things as we were seduced first in one direction and then another. Traditionally the late teens and early twenties are spent in college. We were in a very strange college. A big fireplace filled with roaring logs, nymphets dancing around, ferocious marijuana.

WILLIE MURPHY: In the middle of the living room table there was a great big wooden box that was always full of hashish and pot and stuff. It was a lot of fun hanging out, staying up to seven or eight or nine in the morning, talking to people, getting high.

MARTY RICHMOND: Roger Di Fiore was the champion joint roller as well as being the official chief cook. Roger was a friend and confidant of Barry Friedman throughout many of his early Hollywood exploits; at one point they had a direct phone line between their houses to eliminate the effort of dialing.

Roger was one of the great road managers for rock and roll bands. He could keep the group on the road, in the right city, at the right time on the right day—difficult—while keeping them out of jail after the destruction of a motel room—more difficult. The last tour had turned his hair prematurely grey. He was in early retirement. He came along to Paxton for the rest and relaxation he sorely needed, spending many a long hard day lying on his bed listening to his large collection of audio tapes of WC Fields movies over and over, laughing in the same places over and over. And he could and frequently did spend hours rolling joints, turning out as many as fifty at a sitting, each a perfect clone of the last.

The Paxton "inmates." (back, left to right) Lottie Olcott, Sandy Konikoff, Jack Wilce, Marty Richmond, Jac. (front, left to right) Steven Solberg, Jackson Browne, Ned Doheny, Rolf Kempf, Peter Hodgson. Frazier Mohawk on right holding rifle

He introduced us to the morning joint syndrome by each night placing two freshly rolled joints by each of our beds, one for before bed, one for upon waking. Often this meant trying to get up several times, each time smoking a little more and drifting off again. It's amazing that neither the lodge nor any of us were burned to the ground. Awaking in this way certainly does put a different light on the day. Following the morning joint, the after-breakfast joint, then the mid-morning joint, then the lunch joint . . . The day is in effect over before it begins. We went through a kilo and a half of grass a week.

JACKSON BROWNE: To tell you the truth, I don't remember making much music. I suppose we must have, but I don't remember. It wasn't wild drugs all the time, mostly just a daily haze, but I don't remember making much music.

JAC: For my getaway cruise, I had flown to San Francisco and boarded the President Roosevelt, one of the last passenger ships of the American President Lines, with stops in Honolulu, Yokohama and Hong Kong. Waiting for me in my cabin was a cable from Nina, wishing me a wonderful trip, with her hopes that I would find what I was looking for. To have her blessing, even though I knew she was in such pain, was the start of healing.

I had booked the largest cabin, the Lanai Suite, which, for all its trying for something approaching opulence, had a bunk too short for my frame and a lot of bad art. But it did have the loftiest cabin, opening to a tiny veranda—a lanai— where I would spend hours, quietly watching the ocean pass beneath our keel.

We were not long out to sea when I heard a knock at the cabin door. A young purser, Kim von Tempski, was standing there in his starched white uniform. He handed me a thick envelope that gave off a sensual crunch. "The crew and I thought that, of all the passengers, you might especially enjoy this."

Inside was some of the most beautiful dope I had ever seen or smelled, Thai Stick, the Courvoisier of smoke, neatly laid out in spindles of massive potency.

Later, when I asked Kim why I had been chosen as President Roosevelt cannabis honoree, he mentioned a recent issue of Life magazine, with a story about Elektra, photographed by Alfred Eisenstadt, following the fortunes of Paul Rothchild's latest discovery, a group called Ars Nova, made up of classical musicians, playing rock with medieval overtones. Viewed from mid-Pacific, all that seemed so far away, not of my world at that moment. Nothing was easier or more pleasurable than to let it drift away in a cocoon of Thai Stick. Ars Nova was not a success, but that article brought me the Thai Stick and, more importantly, a long friendship with Kim von Tempski that was to lead in several life-changing directions.

One evening, as Kim and I were lounging on the forward deck under a canopy of shimmering stars, he told me of growing up on the Hawaiian island of Maui. Kim was so enthusiastic for me to see Maui that I decided to leave the ship at Honolulu, fly to the island, and catch up with the President Roosevelt when it docked in Yokohama.

The morning of our Hawai'i landfall I was up on the bridge deck very early. With the sun just beginning its climb on the eastern horizon, the sky was cloudless, except for the far distance, where cottony tufts of white floated over a small mountainous area. As the ship closed the distance, the mountain defined itself as Diamond Head. I felt the same sense of wonder that every explorer who encountered these islands for the first time must have felt: beauty and peace and splendid isolation from my troubles.

When I jumped ship at Honolulu I took only the minimum of clothing. I caught a plane to Maui, less than half an hour by air but two generations earlier in time. Renting a small Toyota at Kahului airport, I began my drive across the isthmus of the island to Lahaina, through sugar cane fields bordered by clapboard houses, painted a weather-worn hint of what was once a leaf green, capped with rusted tin roofing. With only the sound of the trade winds, my head continued to quiet.

Kim's hotel suggestion was the Sheraton Kaanapali, northwest of Lahaina town, on the beach, built from the top down, the reception area two hundred feet above the sand and all rooms facing the ocean. In 1968 it was the only hotel in the area and the location and initial impact on a mainlander couldn't have been more dramatic. Everything seemed new and fresh, existing in a world quite different from my own. I lounged on my lanai, sniffed the lush vegetation, watched the sun dance over the repetitive roll of the ocean, and began to pull myself together.

Hungry, I drove into town for dinner, and found a charming restaurant, the Lahaina Broiler, half on land, half over the water, with a glorious and unobstructed view out to sea. The setting sun was turning a deep, memorable red. I looked out at the serenity of the ocean, the waves gently lapping against the boats in the harbor and the pilings under the restaurant and could never recall such a sense of equilibrium in myself or openness to nature. I took the first of many deep, cleansing breaths. Clearly, what was happening in the natural world was far more important and interesting than my self-absorption in business. There was real peace here, and I could effortlessly learn to love it. Waiting for my turtle steak and brown rice, I made myself a promise, "In five years, somehow, I'll be done, and I will move here to Maui and start over. This is my dream, my commitment, and my secret."

The Maui magic sunset of 1968

I took a photo of the sun in its final pause before being swallowed by the horizon, as a memento and a reminder.

NED DOHENY: If Frazier Mohawk had been smart, he would have broken the Paxton day up into a boot camp—nice, but a boot camp. He would have infused it with a sense of discipline. But Frazier was a campaigning loony who wanted to draw people into his orbit.

MARTY RICHMOND: We felt we were actors in a movie with a slightly deranged director.

JANICE KENNER: It was always kind of an amazing phenomenon to me. What is going on here, really? Occasionally you'd lapse into consciousness and you'd go, "Wow!"

NED DOHENY: Like the time Sandy recorded a percussion track with a microphone up his ass.

JACKSON BROWNE: Sandy Konikoff was a great drummer. He had toured with Dylan, he had played with Ronnie Hawkins and the Hawks, he hung around with the Band. This older, wiser, crazy, great guy. Probably the craziest and sanest of us all. Kind of like the Neal Casady hipster drummer—Sal Mineo as Gene Krupa. Always talking about a tailor he knew in Montreal or something Ronnie Hawkins had done. Those guys were famous revelers. We needed a drummer, and Sandy didn't have a gig, he was cooking hot dogs at a stand in Orange County. He was a handsome guy. Had a beard. His hair was thinning. He wore this great Nigerian police officer's helmet, almost like a Shriners thing. Around the lodge at midnight you would hear a knocking sound outside, and it would be Sandy naked except for his Ray-Bans, baying at one of the girl's windows.

JOHN HAENY: We used a very narrow microphone in a plastic bag. I put the Cornhusker's lotion on, and found the masking tape, and got Sandy to take his clothes off and go out in the middle of the studio and play hand jive while we recorded him with the microphone up his rear end. 'Los Stimulantos,' we called it.

JACKSON BROWNE: I had been to the movies in Quincy, I came back, and in the dining room they're doing an overdub on somebody's tune, they're motioning us to be quiet, and there's Sandy with a cord coming out of his ass, and he's hamboning—

NED DOHENY:—Slapping his leg and chest alternately. It's a rural American rhythm. Glen Campbell does it real good, Mac Davis does it real good. A most unusual sound, coming out of Sandy. He looked like an electric rat.

JANICE KENNER: Tape and hair and balls, and I'm thinking, "This is Dylan's drummer?"

JACKSON BROWNE: The playback sounded pretty good, actually. When Sandy went with the Joe Cocker tour, Mad Dogs And Englishmen, they put it on the poster, where they had a bit about each person: SANDY KONIKOFF—PURVEYOR OF THE SPHINCTERPHONE.

JOHN HAENY: I have the stereo mix. The track is called '?'. You can hear when the mike fell out and we put it back in.

JACKSON BROWNE: Of course it was Haeny's idea. Haeny was having the time of his life.

JOHN HAENY: Actually I believe it was Frazier's brilliant idea. Typically Frazier—came up with the idea and then went into his bedroom and locked the door.

JAC: After Maui I flew on to Japan, did a little business, and spent time in Hong Kong. I passed up Tahiti in favor of going back to Maui and began looking at raw land—when the time came I wanted a place waiting for me.

I also realized that I could no longer avoid the real world. Part of that world was my family. I wanted to call Nina, to ask her to bring the kids over for a short holiday.

But after eight weeks away, I couldn't remember my home phone number. I would have to call Pearl. But then I couldn't conjure up my office number either. Elektra would be listed—that much I did remember. I called Manhattan information, then phoned Pearl and said, "I know this is going to sound funny, but"—

NINA HOLZMAN: I was in California with the kids for the summer, and Jac called, anxious for us to join him on Maui for a few weeks. We went, but it wasn't a very happy time.

JAC: I knew Nina wasn't happy, and neither was I. She was such a special person, and she loved me, despite my inability to return the emotional support she deserved.

To begin a new life meant I had to complete the old one. Yet I couldn't bring myself to tell the truth about what was going on inside me. I just let it go unsaid, until one night when Nina and I were back in California, dining by candlelight at an outdoor restaurant. My birthday was just a few days off, and Nina asked me what I wanted. If ever there was an opening to tell the deep-down, painful truth, this was it. For what seemed like minutes but was probably only thirty seconds, I said nothing, and then with all the strength of will I could muster, I blurted, "I think I want a divorce."

It was finally out. I waited for her reaction. It was quite calm, which told me that she had come to the same place but by her own road.

NINA HOLZMAN: A California lawyer we knew told us about Mexican divorces, in Ciudad Juarez, just across the border from El Paso.

JAC: Within three days, we flew there from Los Angeles.

NINA HOLZMAN: As we were walking across the field to the plane, Jac said, "I don't think we should be doing this." And I said, "Well, I think we should."

So we went, and we had this wonderful couple of days, the best in a long time. Jac bought me a beautiful ring, turquoise and pearl, which I called my divorce ring. I still have it.

JAC: In 1968 Mexican divorces were a growth industry. It took just a few minutes. A lawyer, a judge, some minimal questions, and much rubber-stamping—Mexico was all carbon paper and rubber stamps, purple as I recall.

NINA HOLZMAN: Jac thought it would be a wonderful idea not to tell anybody we were divorced. He felt that if nobody knew, we could continue working on the relationship and maybe he could make it work. I really think it had a lot to do with my reputation in the business. I was very well liked, and Jac thought that if I told everyone we were divorced, it might cast a bad light on him, that he was in some way inadequate, not able to hold on to the marriage. So I said, "OK." We continued to live together. I told nobody, he told nobody. Nobody knew—not my sisters, not the children, nobody.

Chapter 17

Game hens and ganja ...
Tales of a rascally remittance man ...
A child of music is stillborn ...
Life crisis of a teenage troubadour

JAC: While all this deeply serious personal business was playing itself out in private, Paxton was heard from.

MARTY RICHMOND: The boys felt they were ready to record.

JANICE KENNER: The equipment was all in the dining room. Connie and I were the big cheerleaders, running up and down the dining room table. "Go, boys, go!" And they were all whang, whang, whang—

MARTY RICHMOND: Frazier decided to send Jac a telegram saying the time was ripe. We phoned the telegram in as a night letter to be delivered to New York the next morning. And the following afternoon, who should come strutting through the front door but Jac.

It was his first visit to the lodge, and for that matter most of the Paxton people had not the vaguest idea of who this overdressed dandy was. Someone actually challenged his right to come walking into our house. He replied that it was his party.

Frazier came to the rescue.

Welcome to Paxton. Jac at right, Jackson Browne (center) hiding in the trees

JAC: He handed me a brownie. I should have known better. It was tasty and loaded with grass.

JANICE KENNER: When Jac was coming—it's like, what do you do? Here the grownup is coming, you know. I only had one experience with him before this, coming back from a concert, and somehow it ended up that I had to be in this sports car with Jac. I was so uncomfortable, because he was— I had tons of respect for him, but it was impossible to know this man, he had this pale skin, this dark hair, these dark eyebrows, he had on this dark jacket, and he was just stiff. I was so intimidated. So now, do you try to impress him, or what do you do? I was really like beside myself. My role, being the Cancer that I am, I fell right into the mommy thing. "Oh, he's coming! We'd better serve something nice. Or should we serve bologna sandwiches so he doesn't think we're being extravagant? Nah—we're going to have Cornish game hens."

Cornish game hens—why this particular menu was chosen, I don't know. They just arrived. There were like a million of them, these little dead raw chickens, they were like frigging everywhere. All I knew was this better look good. It was kind of a groveling thing, almost, kowtowing. I've never been more intimidated or uptight in my whole life, than at that moment when I realized I had to serve a meal to this man who was paying for all this, and who I felt some compassion for, and guilt. I was probably one of the sanest ones there, I still had this little tiny sense of responsibility in my mind: "Somebody's footing the bill for all this, and I'm having too much fun. Something should be done. I should organize."

The kitchen was huge, hotel size, everything was Flintstone size. Three sinks like horse troughs. Every pan—if you fried eggs, you had to fry fifty eggs. The oven. So the Cornish game hens didn't take that long to cook. It was a timing thing. But I can't tell you the stress.

JAC: The cooking aroma that hit my nose was terrific. I looked into the industrial oven. Row upon row of Cornish game hens, like toy soldiers, browning away. A lot of them. More than should have been there, considering the fifteen or twenty people I thought were at the lodge. But by that time I was beginning to see doubles of everything, so I couldn't be sure.

JANICE KENNER: I think probably every one, by the time dinner was served, was too uptight to eat. I have a vision of Jac sitting there alone with this Cornish game hen, and twenty-five of them on either side, with no one sitting there because everyone was too fucked up to sit down, or too embarrassed, or no one wanted to explain what we had gotten done or hadn't gotten done.

WILLIE MURPHY: Frazier went all out, whole hog, put on this huge dinner. The understanding I got was that it backfired because Jac was rather taken aback at the way Frazier was spending his money. Jac seemed very quiet, didn't say a lot. That night he had a long private meeting with Frazier, with people going around, mugging, "They're in the next room," wondering if it was a big heavy thing.

MARTY RICHMOND: I found Jac on the second floor, leaning up against the wall. I said, "Is everything OK?" And he said, "Well, I'm kind of afraid to move."

JAC: I thought a bath might help, the healing power of water. Marty had installed me in a corner room upstairs which had a tub, and ten minutes later a young lady came in, climbed into the tub with me and started to wash my back with serious soap and a stiff brush.

JANICE KENNER: Let me just think if I can really recount what happened that evening. OK, here we go. We decided to ply Jac with drug-filled Cornish hens. There were dancing girls, then there was a bath, and there were women with no clothes on, and Jac was like, "No, I can't, I can't, wait, please, no," and they cajoled him, I swear to God he fought, he was so resistant, but somehow they managed to get him in this tub. Now, little did anyone know that Ned Doheny had a hole in the roof and was watching the whole time, peering down into this tub where Jac, completely naked, stoned on Cornish game hen, was being bathed by naked nubile young girls.

JAC: I have absolutely no memory of this, Your Honor.

JANICE KENNER: I was told it happened. It doesn't surprise me. Barry would have done it. Barry would have dressed up like a girl and bathed him, I swear to God he would have, and I swear to God I think that probably happened.

JAC: A few hours into the evening, I regained my equilibrium and finally got down to my purpose for being there. I wanted to hear some music.

MARTY RICHMOND: The boys sat down to play for Jac. It was in effect an audition, because Jac carried with him the ultimate veto power from which there was no appeal. Already impressed by the speed with which he had answered their summons—in fact Jac never did get the telegram, he was coming anyway—they played their hearts out.

JAC: Paxton was an extension, on a very grand and loopy scale, of early Elektra—recording artists in their own environments, in homes that looked similar to the lodge, old houses with stuffed furniture and lamps with their orange-brown shades askew. That's how I made my first records. This was not a foreign scene to me.

I sat quietly and listened deep, the Big Listen, with all the concentration I could muster. It was the kind of bravura performance that comes when artists are eager to please, and know in their gut this is make or break. I had to sign off on the music or it was over, the good times would no longer roll.

What I heard was extraordinary, and I was much relieved. Laurie Anderson once said that writing about music is like dancing about architecture, but here are some words for what I was hearing: a solid variety of music, good melodies wrapped around real poetry, and the performances, especially Jackson's, had sweetness, spontaneity and energy. Just terrific.

That evening was one of those moments when I felt deep down that I would have liked to be a musician, able to be in that room and play something easy, perhaps a bass, where I wouldn't make a fool of myself. The best thing I could do was stay out of the way. I wasn't their age, or living that life, and I wasn't a musician. But I could give what they needed, permission and support.

MARTY RICHMOND: Jac loved it so much that he fell down, literally. Victory! The boys were all aflutter with plans of how they were going to spend the millions that their music would generate.

JAC: I had nibbled on another cookie while listening to the music. Suddenly I realized that I hadn't called Nina in the last few days. The Paxton phone was a rotary dial, and I remember working very hard to recall my New York number, 1 plus the area code, plus the number. Putting those three elements together demanded concentration. There were some 8s and 9s in the number, and the springloaded rotary dial would return very, very slowly, each click, sharp and distinctive, taking f-o-r-e-v-e-r.

I had chartered a plane for the next day, and I had no idea if I would be in shape to crawl aboard and travel.

NED DOHENY: In the morning we got up and staggered down to breakfast, and Frazier decided he would eat fire for us, having been a fire eater in the circus. So he fashioned these batons out of coat hangers and wrapped them with twine and got white gas, which burns the coldest of any petroleum-based lighter fluid, and he put it out in his mouth. We were all hugely impressed. Then he walked out into the middle of the room, took an enormous mouthful, and blew a great ball of fire. Well, he had gotten too much in his mouth, and it came down the stream towards his face, and he was backing away with look of horror, and all of a sudden his face burst into flame. I was transfixed. When he came up from behind the couch, he looked like he had been out in the sun for an hour and a half, and his luxurious Pancho Villa mustache was singed down to a little triangle.

FRAZIER MOHAWK: Jac put me out. He threw something over me. It might have been a fat person.

NED DOHENY: Jac was so pale he looked bloodless. He was the color of powdered snow. He went out on the front porch for some time, while his composure returned.

Now I ask you, if you had just seen the producer of your recording project light his face on fire. . .

MARTY RICHMOND: I drove Jac out to catch his charter, to this tiny airstrip in the mountains. He was strutting around in a leather coat—he could strut great. It started to snow. There was a little office, locked. Jac got it open and went in and turned on the radio so he could talk to the pilot, who was wondering was anyone there. The mountains were socked in, and the pilot said he couldn't land unless he could see the runway. So Jac went out and stared at the clouds. And suddenly the clouds parted. The plane came down through the hole, Jac jumped in, they went back through the hole, the clouds smacked together and no one could land for another two weeks. I was impressed—this guy can part the clouds.

JACKSON BROWNE: I think Frazier was a flawed guy in that he resorted to manipulations and so forth that he didn't have to do. He was into being the guy that controlled the scene. It was all to do with some plan, but it didn't have anything to do with me. It was all about himself. He would give you a little bit of this, keep something back. Not good for anything that was organized around people's interactions. Music is a hard thing, and command in music is a hard thing to pull off, to put people together, but at the same time let it breathe.

FRAZIER MOHAWK: It wasn't very well organized. Everyone kind of decided where they wanted to go on their own, and the general consensus was everyone would just kind of go along with it. That was the concept. But everybody wanted to go to a different place at a different time. And there were a lot of people in different—a lot of creative people in a lot of different moods at different times. So it made it very difficult.

JANICE KENNER: There were all these little cliques. There was a Jackson team, each person had their team, either a musician who had bonded with them, or someone they brought up who was with them. There were moments when everyone would kind of go off in their own little groups, going, "I can't work with this person," or "This is not happening." But as far as everyone in the entire place sitting down and saying, "OK, what a joke, this isn't working, let's let him off the hook and get outta here and go home"—that never came up. Everyone wanted to stay. Because why wouldn't you stay? What young musician in their situation wouldn't have stayed in that place? And they were just blaming it on each other or on someone else.

DAVID ANDERLE: And it wasn't just about the music. There were certain hatreds, certain bitternesses, and people playing games with each others' heads. Multiple group situations where you put groups together, and there's multiple romances, and all those games start coming, and so much of the day is spent figuring out what you're going to do at night, and playing the games of position and possession and domination. It was just rampant. What was the blonde girl's name who was causing everybody the grief? Janice—oh, beautiful Janice. Everybody loved Janice. And Frazier Mohawk, who's like a master of the macabre, is in charge of this circus . . .

MARTY RICHMOND: Hanging on a thread of distant reality, life in the country began to take on its own shape and design, and more and more we all felt that we were caught up in events beyond our comprehension or ability to control. Time had flown away and we were in limbo. You had to hope that at any moment a little door in the hall would open and someone would jump out and yell, "Cut!"

FRAZIER MOHAWK: I don't know if it was any different than a health club is now. At that time it didn't seem like a bizarre idea, or a novel idea. To me, anyway. I mean, there were a lot of dentists taking acid then. It was a good place, maybe, to unwind and to puke out all of those things that you had been sort of saving up in the Fifties.

There were a lot of people who came up to kind of look at it. There was a guy, a psychologist who was a contributing editor to Psychology Today. We invited him up and he stayed for a weekend and just observed what was going on. We thought he might be interested in looking at it from the standpoint of—of whatever the creative hope of the place was. But we never heard back from the guy. He kind of fled in the night.

NED DOHENY: Winter was coming on. I was from LA. I had never seen snow. I watched the first snowflakes coming down and the snow banks piling up with my mouth wide open.

MARTY RICHMOND: We adopted a Christmas tree, a perfectly shaped fir, growing out of the hillside by the side of the road. We got icicles and some balls and decorated it, then got lights and hooked them to a car battery. We went back and forth into town, turning it on and off, till some trucker rammed it.

JANICE KENNER: When it snowed, the dogs would burrow in the snow. They were Alaskan, this is their instinctive thing, genetically. But these are LA dogs, what do they know? They're instinctively burrowing in the snow, but they're freezing their LA asses off, so we'd go find them, and they'd be like, "Brrr, we don't know why we're here, get us outta here."

MARTY RICHMOND: With the cold weather, more time was spent inside. Cabin fever made its appearance, and some had more severe cases than others.

Then there was a biblical forty-day period when it rained or snowed every day. And a ten-day period when, had we wanted to, we couldn't leave. A slide took out the railroad track, and it filled in so much of the river with rubble and rock that the river took out the road. And the phone was along the railroad, so it was down. And the electricity.

So we entered the winter of our discontent. Outside, days of great beauty. Inside, nights of dark dreadfulness.

MARTY RICHMOND: One of the conclusions I came to about Frazier was that he had a great fear of success. As soon as it looked like a project was destined to succeed, he began to throw up hurdles in its way, either bringing it down around him or having it slip through his fingers. After Buffalo Springfield was put together, they grew tired of his antics and in effect fired him. Frazier probably provoked them into it because he knew how good they were. This happened so many times as not to be the fates acting upon him. The law of averages is often fickle, but rarely perverse.

JANICE KENNER: Barry was always trying to be a professional in the music business, and do what was right, but he didn't have the talent of music, he had the talent of manipulation and fancy, and there was this side to him that was so down and dirty, and he could kind of keep them separate, but so often they meshed.

JOHN HAENY: I was up there to record, to do the engineering, and Frazier was up there to produce. But Frazier at this point realized he had bitten off too much, he could not chew any more, and he retreated to his bedroom. He is the producer, and he is abandoning the whole recording project. I go up there. I tell him, "They're saying, What'll we do?" He says, "Record." Many sessions he doesn't come down, doesn't grace us with his presence.

JACKSON BROWNE: If I tell you that was irresponsible, I would really mean it.

JOHN HAENY: Frazier would issue edicts from his room and you would come up. This meeting he was taking his bath. He said, "John, I want you to produce Jackson." I said, "No. You shit in this bed, you're gonna sleep in it. I would love to produce Jackson, but I'm not going to walk into a mess that's this screwed up, this late in the game. I refuse. I will not do it."

JANICE KENNER: Everyone knew it wasn't working. No one wanted it to end, but yet everyone wanted—it was like, shoot the dog and put it out of its misery, but yet—

NED DOHENY: On New Year's Eve Frazier had a nervous breakdown. I remember driving with Marty in The Mouse, Marty's old grey 1948 Chevrolet, blankets across our legs, snow coming down, blinding, hitting the windshield, making it to the doctor's to get a bunch of downers so Frazier could keep it together.

It was a pretty devastating period of time. Remove people from all things familiar and put them at the mercy of what was both a peculiar error and the company of eccentric people in a galaxy far, far away—there isn't a lot of reality in that. It had no center.

We all imagined that we were the Beatles on some brave adventure. That part became tarnished, because if Frazier was the captain, the ship was in trouble from the start. I just couldn't participate in it any more. And I was bounced from The Good Ship Lollipop. Jackson was sent by Frazier to ask me to leave.

JOHN HAENY: Jackson was thrown for a loop, everybody was thrown for a loop. Jackson and I used to have conversations. One night late, we sat up on the railroad track. An amazing experience. There had been an accident and they were having to redo a big stretch of track, and they were burning railroad ties, every fifty yards a pile of burning railroad ties in the night, as far as the eye could see. We were a little loaded, too. Jackson talked about his confusion in life and the mess he was in at Paxton, and what was my advice. It was a magical night.

JACKSON BROWNE: There was one time I sort of bolted. I split. I ran down this driveway, across the bridge over the river, down the highway. I got about three miles down the road and turned around, completely out of breath, and looked at this thing. Years later, I thought maybe I should have just kept on going to LA and told Jac, "I can't work like that. I'm part of the good people who had this smart idea, but this is not what anybody had in mind, and I don't want to do this." But I didn't keep going. I went back and toed the line.

JOHN HAENY: I couldn't see the album ever getting finished. It was pandemonium. I was through. I sat up for two days mixing down what was there, packed up the tapes and my dogs and went back to LA.

MARTY RICHMOND: Never to return.

JOHN HAENY: I was met at the airport by David Anderle. I fell into his arms in tears, went home, shut the doors, pulled the phones out, turned off the lights, and curled up in bed in the fetal position for about four days.

DAVID ANDERLE: I went up on a final fact-finding mission. It was a mess.

JAC: The music I had heard that night at Paxton was never going to make it onto a record, and if that was the case, it was time to put the wounded animal down.

Most of the recording equipment and lights came back, but I'm sure there were items bought and paid for by Elektra, the ownership of which, shall we say, was deemed ambiguous by the Paxton participants.

MARTY RICHMOND: Somebody drove Frazier to Reno. There were commercial flights to LA all day long. But he chartered himself a private jet.

MARTY RICHMOND: We were told the album wouldn't be put out.

JACKSON BROWNE: It was badly played and badly realized. We named it "Baby Browning," after a stillborn child's tombstone that we saw while we were walking around the local cemetery.

CONNIE DI NARDO: Janice and I saw the gravestone and thought, "Boy, what a weird thing." But it was old, and maybe that's what they did back then. So we wanted to take the others and show them. And we couldn't find it anywhere. We looked everywhere, the place wasn't that big, and we asked the caretaker. He was like a hundred-twelve years old, and he said, "I've been taking care of this place fifty years and I've never seen a Baby Browning." One night at the lodge they were recording, and when they played the tape back there was what sounded like a baby cry. I thought, was it the cat? And they're saying, No, no, the cat is in town—there were two cats, and they were both getting shots. We'd play it back, and there was the baby cry, and that's when they were going to call it "Baby Browning."

JACKSON BROWNE: Each of us was let go and given our publishing back. We all went down together, and Jac was out a lot of money—the lease on the lodge, months of food and drink and gasoline, the cost of building the studio and renting the remote truck, on and on.

JAC: Suzanne Helms had kept a running ledger. Still, it took almost a month to fully calculate the cost. We had to pay for repatriating people and shuttering the place.

FRAZIER MOHAWK: There was a bill for ten thousand in damages. I thought we had painted some of the rooms in a quite unique and colorful manner. One of the colors was Hashish Green. Truly. Imagine finding that in a store in Quincy. But I suppose for a hotel, an old hotel, they didn't think that was appropriate. That was part of the bill. And we had sawed their big pink neon sign down. The guy was really upset about that.

JACKSON BROWNE: It was humbling to be back on the street and not have a record deal. I hung around my art school friends down at Pico and Vermont. I hit the Troubadour, the Monday night hoots. I'd show up and play, maybe sit around a bit, but I didn't want to hang out. I wanted to be taken seriously.

My stopping smoking dope had a lot to do with my becoming serious as a musician. For many others, and lots of my best friends, it is not a factor in their musicianship. But for me, I think I had a huge identity crisis. It was after Paxton, after two or three years of walking barefoot around Laurel Canyon and sleeping in people's living rooms and smoking the best dope on the planet at the time. I had this huge self-conscious flash. It was in Paul Rothchild's house. Who the fuck are you, really? What are you doing? All these incredibly accomplished people here— Paul is one of the absolute best producers in rock and roll, Haeny is like this miracle engineer. And what do you do? What are you, some kind of hanger-on or something? This is bullshit. I haven't done anything apart from sitting here getting loaded. What am I to these people? They're nice to me, they think well of me, and they'll get me high. And so what? Who am I? And what am I going to do in this life? A terrible paranoid flash. It made it really hard for me to continue getting high the way I had been, which was to stay blitzed. Smoking a lot of dope is a way to avoid coming to terms with work. So Paxton was actually a very instructive time.

JAC: Before the roof fell in at Paxton, two fine records did get produced there. One was Dave "Snaker" Ray's "Bamboo," with members of the house band and Will Donicht sharing vocals, guitar and tack piano. The other became a classic of the slightly spaced-out stomping school of roadhouse music. With Frazier producing, "Spider" John Koerner and Willie Murphy created "Running, Jumping, Standing Still," named after a British short film of great charm that was a favorite of Spider's. Allan Emig engineered, with Jack Wilce and Sandy Konikoff of the house band beautifully integrated, The credits read: Recorded at Elektra's Paxton Lodge on the Feather River, Keddie, California.

**"Running, Jumping, Standing Still"
EKS-74041**

Barry/Frazier was like a rascally remittance man. You'd send him an ocean away, saying, "Never darken my door again," but there's a secret delight when he shows up unexpectedly at the old country estate, and you are forgiving, because he brings an excitement to life. What I admired about Frazier was his ability to set up a good game. That was my talent too: to provide the atmosphere, direction and support for people to play in a game of my devising, that worked for me and for them.

Paxton was a Potemkin village. Without honesty the music never could have worked. I was smitten with the idea and never saw the subterfuge. It was a form of arrogance from which I learned, and with time's passage the memory has softened.

The Paxton tab came to seventy-five thousand dollars, the equivalent of perhaps a quarter million in late-Nineties dollars. Not a huge amount and not very big considering what could have been the reward had it worked. My long-standing friendship and affection for Marty Richmond and Jackson Browne are not to be calculated. And there was some terrific music, if only for one evening.

Chapter 18

Guns of the White Panthers ...
Motherfuckers of the East Village ...
A Stooge in diapers, bleeding on Park Avenue ...
A loaf of Bread and a promise kept ...
And who knows where the time goes?

JAC: While Paxton was forming and fulminating and falling apart, Elektra was turning more and more into a corporation.

PAUL ROTHCHILD: I remember the day in 1967 Jac walked up to me in the hall and said, "Paul, this is the first year we're going to break five million, gross." There were about fourteen or fifteen of us on the payroll. And then all hell broke loose. The company got huge. Jac was running a corporation. The record part of it was tangential for a long time.

JAC: The company began to separate along tactical and artistic lines. Suddenly the tactical, which had always been there but had never had much visibility, acquired more people. Marketing, foreign licensing, music publishing, business affairs, accounting, inventory control, quality control—those departments began to grow. At the size we were approaching, without those systems there would be chaos. When the service aspects become blatantly visible, the creative people resent that they are no longer the princely constituency. But for every issue there was now a business component, requiring a business person to be involved.

GEORGE STEELE: Growing up, I was picking and packing records in a warehouse in LA, and I also had the opportunity of working the front desk. Mel Posner would come to town, and I always looked forward to when he would make a sales presentation, because unlike many of the other sales managers he would come well armed with a very sophisticated approach. His presentation was typically New York and bordered on getting one's attention in a rather loud way, always backed up with very specific hard reasons why certain things had better damn well happen based on certain criteria. Mel was a driving force. When he came into town, people came to attention. He was always incredibly sincere. The integrity of the associations was almost profound in the way that people would admire the man, the person. And when it came down to selling records, man, he was the best. He made the map.

When I finally came to work at Elektra, imagine me being able to sit in the conference room at La Cienega and being introduced to the data processing; how they planned to monitor sales, and be able to tie in the credits and debits and accounts payable and advertising scenarios and inventory control and management. As an independent company that didn't have the resources of a parent company—not an RCA Victor—to employ that data processing was not only cutting edge in terms of its sophistication in approaching a vision, but it was a huge marketing tool. If you made the sales, you made the money. You could do all the creative work you want, but ultimately you gotta sell records, because records generate revenue, which propels the system.

Mel was responsible for sales. And as someone working in sales, I felt I could never do enough homework, I could never be aware enough, I always had to work extra hard to ensure that I was very much up to speed on every one of the projects. I could only have one gear, top speed. And I had better be one hundred percent accurate one hundred percent of the time, because I'm gonna get a phone call from Mel. He's the driver. He's the taskmaster.

JAC: Mel could be tough. Whatever he's telling you and selling you, it comes through. His method was to get a little gruff and act disappointed with a staffer not doing his best. Mel conveyed his message with vocal timbre and gestures—he's investing a hundred percent of himself, you were his friend and you were falling short, and ultimately Mel was going to have to explain to me, and you wouldn't want to put Mel in that position.

Mel Posner with Jim

It was reassuring to have had Mel with me through the growth years, both of us learning on the job. And Irwin Russell, not on staff, but a calm outside intelligence to add wisdom and perspective. I also had my problem children within the company, most notably Bill Harvey among the old guard. Bill had been around since the scuffling days, and we shared history, but Bill was proprietary and assertive, not just about the art department, but about the whole company. His ambition far exceeded his skills. Bill had been able to keep his drinking within reason; now he began to drink at lunch. Alcohol was his enemy but none of us could convince him.

My brother Keith was an essential point person, smartly handling a wide range of administrative detail. He was in charge of less than romantic but sensitive areas like inventory control, which were critical to our ability to function. He knew about computers, had worked with them in the army. I knew we needed data processing, I just didn't know how to go about it. Keith was like a universal joint. He's the guy who's there earliest and stays latest and makes sure everything gets done. He took an appalling amount of abuse from people within the company because we shared the same last name; shit was directed at him that was meant for me. Of course, not to show even a hint of nepotism, I probably treated him less well than I did others. He was my brother, and I could trust him absolutely, and I think one of my greatest failings was not trusting more in his judgments of people.

To supervise business affairs, I hired Larry Harris from CBS, a seasoned music attorney who knew the ropes. When Larry told Clive Davis he was coming to Elektra, Clive called me and said, "If you're hiring people of Larry's caliber we all better be prepared for tougher competition."

Larry was needed because the music business was getting tougher. Early on I signed an artist directly. The contract was simple. As the music business starting making the financial pages, the deals got bigger, more byzantine, with higher

Elektra gang celebrates Judy's first gold album. Back row (left to right) Bill Harvey, Mark Abramson, Judy Collins, Jac, Larry Harris, Mel Posner, Keith Holzman. Front row, kneeling (left to right) Steve Harris, Paul Rothchild, Nina Holzman

demands and greater detail—read "nitpicking." Everyone wanted a piece and the piece came from the hide that was seen as the richest, meaning the record company. Some artists' lawyers were working on percentages. Managers took large slices. Producers came "attached" to projects. Suddenly there were demands to provide extras beyond the basics of a recording studio and musicians. We were asked for band equipment, living support before an artist ever made their first album, then tour support. It resembled the military at war. For every soldier in the field you needed five in close support.

This kind of swelling occurs whenever an industry comes of age. There was such an explosion of detail, that if I got too caught up, my perspective would be dulled. I'd much rather save myself for the broad-stroke decisions.

I had become a Swiss army knife. All the tools were there, but not the tools that I would have chosen to do every job on the scale the job now had to be done. I would need dedicated tools for that task. Larry Harris was that tool in the area of business affairs.

SUE ROBERTS: Larry was very steely, very aggressive of eyes, partly out of distrust, partly out of intelligence, partly out of quickness. You knew that he was not someone to fuck with. But just by his aggressiveness, his very nature, he got some really good things done.

LARRY HARRIS: Elektra went through the same kind of changes that any company goes through when it goes from being a small, family-type operation to a medium-size successful corporation. It became more of a job to run the company rather than to make the music. It was no longer a family. It wasn't six people, it was sixty. It became more fragmented, more political.

I was resented a lot when I came, because I had so much authority and freedom. People look back on Elektra and say, "What a wonderful place." But it wasn't Camelot. It was dirty, all that went on. Most of the artists never saw that. They were not the people on the inside who saw what was going on, including Jac, who fostered it. Mel Posner and Bill Harvey were very political. Bill was an artistic genius. Jac's genius was in recognizing that; his shortcoming was allowing that to get out of hand. Mel equally had an area in which he was very good. Jac's failing was the same there. Or in allowing the situation to develop politically. For all Jac's talent as a record executive—creative, business, marketing, et cetera—he could have been better with people.

GEORGE STEELE: I never knew what Larry did, other than help solve problems or create problems. My perception was definitely some of both. It was a phenomenon of the growth of the company. Larry had to put a harness around it, and he put his personality into making sure that the growth was proper, and that became Larry Harris-ism. My perception was that it was cumbersome, the arduous task of dealing with Larry.

DAVID BRAUN: Larry, I think, viewed it almost as a Talmudic duty to make a contract complicated. One I can remember—if Larry or I die, it will never be interpreted.

JAC: Jack Reinstein was another heavy-duty tool. When Jack switched from the outside accounting firm which audited our books to working full-time at Elektra, he was out of his suit and into size 44 jeans, beads and leathers in minutes. He could be charming around the lunch table, but he was ferocious on the job.

GEORGE STEELE: Jack was extremely hard about making us be disciplined on expense accounts, and there was no pulling the wool over his eyes. He would send out little memos about how we were buying too many felt-tip pens, about putting them in water overnight.

ANN PURTILL: A few people spent time on the phone exchanging records, and Reinstein said, "Are you giving away our records?"

JAC: One of Reinstein's many responsibilities was artist and publisher audits. Managers and lawyers would say they hated doing an audit at Elektra. An audit was always a grey area. The artist or publisher's representatives routinely threw in all manner of exaggerated claims to be used as tradeoffs in the final stages of give and take. The record company was where the money was and thus was always on the defensive. Reinstein was a master at dragging it out, making it uncomfortable. More than uncomfortable—with Reinstein an audit was scorched earth and minefields, to the point where the other side was happy to settle. This was no longer record company to artist, this was hardbitten gladiator matched against hardbitten hit man.

SUZANNE HELMS: I knew how many people waited for their royalty statements. Reinstein would say, "It must have been an accounting error." He wasn't stealing the money, he would invest it somewhere and get more return on it, so that the company would look better and he would look better, and some of the poor artists and producers would just tear their hair.

JAC: Jack and Larry did much of the dirty work while I retained my good-guy image. Every company needs a good guy to keep the communication flowing when things get tense. Larry was smart and tough and I didn't want to play Scrooge. I could float concepts in a negotiation through Larry that I would be uncomfortable doing myself, especially with lawyers with whom I had had excellent relationships over a long history. Larry got to loft the trial balloons, and if he was shot down, I was still the good guy, the court of last resort.

The problem was that Larry had eyes to run his own shop.

SUE ROBERTS: He was aware of his territory, very power-driven.

JAC: He tried to take greater control of Elektra, but he was never going to run my company. I knew that, and in time he knew it. Albert Grossman thought Larry was terrific, just the man to launch a new label for Ampex, and in the end that's where Larry went, to found Ampex/Bearsville Records.

I was relieved when Larry left. He had done some excellent work but I never fully trusted him. We needed a less contentious tonality in our business affairs department. I offered his assistant, Sue Roberts, the business chair. Sue didn't have Larry's legal experience, but she was blessed with good common sense and could sweet-talk people into things that Larry couldn't argue them into. Sue managed all business affairs and every contract, and she never dropped a stitch.

For our heavy legal work, we now cast outside lawyers. They could be our tough talkers. I chose counsel the way I would select record producers. And it was smart to have lawyers in the music business who owed you favors. There was always the possibility that they might bring us something good. Those were benefits we did not have with in-house counsel.

JAC: To deal with the whole culture of music in the late Sixties, the established record companies, which had always been run by suits, would, out of bafflement with the new scene, hire designated counter-culture types to be ombudsmen between the company and the artist. They were called "company freaks," the ones who interpreted the artist to the company and the company to the artist. If something new was beginning to surface, the CF's responsibility was to find out first and let me know. They networked voraciously. They listened to comments and criticisms about the label from Elektra and non-Elektra artists and fed that information to me. They were fertile sources of gossip and some gossip was of inestimable value. Our New York company freak was Danny Fields.

STEVE HARRIS: I loved Danny. He was a hippie yenta. In an hour he would fill me in on every bit of gossip. He would stay out late, and if he had copy due by three o'clock, he would stagger in at two, write this magical stuff and then leave. Nobody else had a Danny Fields working for them.

JANN WENNER: Danny was the hippest guy in New York.

ANN PURTILL: A legend in his own time. When Lillian Roxon did the first rock encyclopedia, Danny was one of her best friends, and he got every Elektra artist listed.

JAC: Elektra wasn't old-line, especially on the West Coast—in the La Cienega office just about everybody except Suzanne Helms and Ellen Vogt would have qualified as a company freak in a tie-dye T-shirt. New York was different. Put in the simplest of terms, there was a schism between inhalers and non-inhalers, ingesters and non-ingesters. I wasn't against inhalation, either privately or at the office. There were rooms where I knew the air was hazy behind closed doors, occasionally wafting out into the corridor. But some of the senior people were upset by my benign attitude and looked upon what they considered bizarre manifestations such as Danny with naked hostility.

DANNY FIELDS: They were suit and tie, martini lunch, old school, Madison Avenue, Fifties kind of people, and I was a Sixties kind of person. I had started out as a New York Weavers Jewboy, and now I was Andy Warhol and hard rock and revolution and march on Washington and marijuana galore.

PETER SIEGEL: One of the things Danny came upon in the streets was David Peel with his band, the Lower East Side.

Danny came raving, "You gotta hear this." I heard something completely different from what Danny heard. I heard a field recording of indigenous music of the Lower East Side. I didn't honestly believe it was the exact same thing as folk songs of Eastern Kentucky, but I modeled the production after that type of record. It was a documentary, it would be recorded on the street. I had a lot of nice ideas, like at the end of the record David shouting out the credits to the crowd: "Production Supervisor, Jac Holzman, yay!" We did it in Washington

Producer Peter Siegel (lower right) looks up at David Peel recording in Washington Square

Square with a portable tape recorder. We actually got a permit from the city, but that didn't stop some policeman from unplugging us. That was the climate at the time. Yeah, I had a permit in my pocket, but they were singing about cops being pigs. The light would go out, you'd look up and the cop would be right there with the plug in his hand, you'd show him the permit and plug it back in.

DANNY FIELDS: There had been an anti-Vietnam demonstration at Grand Central Station. Time reported on it, protesters storming in, led by a ragged singer chanting. It was David Peel. He was singing, "I like marijuana," but his teeth were sort of funny, so it came out "Have a marijuana." I saw this in Time, and I said, "There is the title of that album, we'll call it "Have A Marijuana." Bill Harvey growled, "This isn't what Elektra does."

"Have A Marijuana" EKS-74032

JAC: But we did. The album cover featured a massive marijuana plant, with "Have A Marijuana" in outsized letters. That cover and the photos of David singing to and with the crowd made it into newspapers, magazines and onto murals throughout the world as an example of what was happening in rebellious America.

DANNY FIELDS: We had another group called MC5, and they smoked a great deal. They would come into my office and close the door and puff away. The business people down the hall were raising hell. Bill Harvey and Larry Harris wanted to know what was going on. Harris called me into his office and said, "There'll be no more smoking marijuana in these offices." I agreed. I didn't think it should be smoked in the office. I allowed it to happen because they were artists, but I would never have done it myself. Or drink in the office, except at a Christmas party—I mean, I think that's not suitable. Unless you're Lou Grant and colorful and you keep a bottle in a bottom drawer. But I agreed that the halls should not be full with clouds of smoke. Anyway, Harris had me in his office, and he said, "There'll be no marijuana, there'll be no LSD." I said, "You mean I can't smoke any more LSD in this office, Larry?" He said, "No LSD in this office. You heard me, smoke it at home." I said, "Larry, if I can't smoke my LSD every morning with my coffee, I'm no good during the day."

JAC: Danny was responsible for bringing us MC5, a revolutionary (in the sense of "overthrow") counter-culture band. I found myself dealing with John Sinclair, chief factotum of the White Panthers.

DANNY FIELDS: John Sinclair was a friend of friends of mine, and they put me on their mailing list for all their marvelous graphic propaganda. Sinclair was a press release genius: "Last night three thousand people rioted and tore down the walls and screamed for more. The stirring and starting of a new world. This is it, the future." My friends persuaded me to go out to Detroit and have a look at MC5. I had started to assume A&R duties, as part of being publicity, because you would come across so many interesting people that the record company could sign cheap, like Nico. So out I went.

I stayed in Sinclair's house, in the commune. I loved the whole situation, the Minister of Defense with the rifle in the dining room, the men pounding on the table for food like cavemen, and all the women running in and out of the kitchen with long Mother Earth skirts on and no bras. In the middle of Ann Arbor, this totally middle-class college town. The men did everything but drag them by the hair. Who ever saw anything like it in New York?

I'd never met anyone like Sinclair. He would sit on the can, taking a shit with the door open, barking out orders, like a Lyndon Johnson smoking dope. I became great friends with him right off. I thought he was a fantastic man. He was funny, he liked good food, he liked to hang out, he liked to have plans, and he liked to talk. And he was a businessman. He was a promoter. He spoke the same language as everybody in the music business. I virtually signed him myself, gave him a handshake and assured him that getting Jac's approval was a mere formality.

JAC: Danny had immaculate taste for the arcane and he knew I'd go for it, so his commitment to Sinclair was in the bag before I knew what he had been up to. That probably did as much to piss off Larry Harris and Bill Harvey as the signing itself, but I was intrigued by how the MC5 maneuvered their music to drive their politics, like a loudspeaker assault on the established order: Who is on the inside, who is on the ramparts?—a rock and roll equivalent of storming the battlements.

Sinclair was no surprise to me, having cut my teeth with Phil Ochs. He was a hairier, heavier, wilier Phil; wild, woolly, intelligent, and easy to get on with. Sinclair wanted the band to be successful, and Elektra was a hip label. The signing was easy and immediate. Revolutions are things of the moment and I wanted to record them in the heat of the moment, which meant right away.

BRUCE BOTNICK: The first trip, just for listening, I took along a cassette machine, a little mono portable, with the speaker built in. They played in a ballroom, I sat in the middle, and I was amazed I could still hear afterwards, because it was the loudest thing I had ever heard in my life. I couldn't tell whether they were playing good music, bad music, or no music. But they were these poetical people up on the stage, waving and screaming and going through crazy gyrations, and it was incredible energy. I was blown away.

Jac felt that the only way to capture the MC5 was to record them live. I brought Wally Heider to Detroit from LA, the big macher of remote recording. He flew the equipment in and we rented a truck, into which we loaded a portable console and dual eight-track recorders. The day of the concert I went inside, I was hooking up my microphones, and I walked out and I see Wally and Jac standing there. They're both staring at the ground. And laying on its back is one of the eight-tracks. They had put it up on the truck and the truck was at a slight angle, and it rolled off and fell six feet to the concrete. We went, "Oh my God, are we going to be able to record?" We picked it up, turned it on, and it was fine.

We recorded for two days, the concert the first night, then the next day we recorded all their songs again, without a pause, just without anybody being there. This was another one of Jac's tricks, because a lot of times when bands are performing it's show time, they're not playing their instruments well. Jac was always thinking how to protect himself.

BILL HARVEY: We had a picture taken in their house. There must have been a hundred people in one room and the room wasn't very big. They were standing on each other's heads, practically. Jac and I, we weren't conservative, but we had jackets on, and we stood out like sore thumbs.

BRUCE BOTNICK: And I'm this twenty-three-year-old kid, married only weeks before, wearing a blue Sixties long suede jacket, black leather pants—I was a very mod dresser in those days. And, I mean, these guys are very funky. They're looking at us suspiciously, they've got guns and a printing press down in the basement printing revolutionary literature, and here's this kid looking very rich. I was scared shitless. I remember calling my wife and I was so nervous I started to cry over the phone.

We finished and I said to Jac, "Let's go home." He was feeling it too. He got on the phone, he arranged for the flight. And we bundled up the tapes and grabbed a cab.

There were three tunes where the performance was so much better the second day that we took the first note and the last note from the live performance and spliced it onto the so-called studio recording, and nobody was the wiser. You couldn't hear the audience anyway, the band played so damn loud.

JAC: The album was called "Kick Out The Jams," and the hook in their signature song was: "Kick out the jams, motherfuckers."

BRUCE BOTNICK: Inside the gatefold jacket it had the band standing there with "Kick Out The Jams, Motherfuckers" buttons, almost like in their skin, and a whole manifesto written by John Sinclair and his propaganda minister. We all thought it was kind of cool, because it's kind of fun to be in a position to taunt a little bit, but

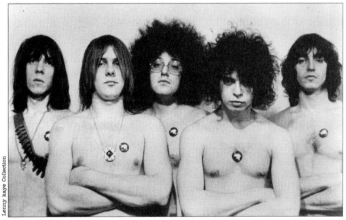

The MC5

still keep one foot in the establishment, never put yourself out there so you get hurt.

JAC: We actually had 'Kick Out The Jams' in two versions, one with "motherfucker," the other with "brothers and sisters." The single had "brothers and sisters." And with the album, stores could choose which version they preferred. Somehow, Hudson's, the retailing gorilla of the heartland, got the wrong version and reacted with the fury of a Midwestern twister. They instantly cleansed their shelves of the record, which mightily pissed off the MC5 who took out an ad in the local underground paper, saying "FUCK HUDSONS," signed MC5, with a very visible Elektra logo, and sent me the bill! In retaliation, Hudson's purged not only MC5 but every other Elektra album: Judy Collins, Paul Butterfield, Tom Rush, the Doors. And they didn't stop there. Nonesuch recordings of Bach, Mozart and Handel were piling back into our warehouse. I said to the MC5, "Hey, guys, you can't do that." They said, "Jac, we thought you were part of the revolution." I said, "I'm only interested in your music."

For MC5's first appearance in New York, we rented the Fillmore East on one of its dark nights. Bill Graham asked me to cancel but I didn't want to back down on a commitment made to the band. Bill was concerned about the potential for violence, especially from a bunch of East Villagers calling themselves the Motherfuckers—

DANNY FIELDS:—A "community group," meaning they didn't wash their feet.

JAC: Their credo was that music should be free to the people, meaning them. They demanded a free night at the Fillmore each week. Bill Graham was not amused.

DANNY FIELDS: My tragic, stupid error was bringing the band to the gig in a limousine—in New York, always if you have more than three people, you call a limousine, that was my Andy Warhol training.

JAC: Actually a limo was most efficient for the purpose, but we should have anticipated the reaction and hired a U-Haul, or better still a garbage truck..

DANNY FIELDS: The Motherfuckers are saying, "We want a free night," and this revolutionary band pulls up in a stretch Cadillac. The crowd went wild and broke down the doors and damaged the theater.

JAC: Here you have MC5, roaring out of a Detroit commune, guns stashed in their basement and obscenities on their album, billing themselves as dedicated to the overthrow of just about everything—and in the East Village they are trashed for being merely misdemeanor motherfuckers. Very late Sixties.

BRUCE BOTNICK: By the time we were going to record a second album, the band had gotten really gross. They were defecating on stage, as a cultural protest. Two of the guys bared their asses and took a dump and held it up. I mean, they had lost all sensibility. We recorded 'Call Me Animal' and a couple of other things, then—

ADAM HOLZMAN:—Someone turns their back in the studio for five minutes, and the next thing they know, MC5 has disappeared and all the equipment that Elektra had rented for the band has disappeared with them.

JAC: I sent a telegram granting them their release and suggested they find another label. Sinclair was very cool; he thought I handled it in a righteous manner. They went across the street to Atlantic and straight away got a $50,000 advance.

JAC: Though I wasn't part of the MC5 revolution, I was deeply concerned about the political direction of America. I had a strong liberal democratic upbringing. My maternal grandmother, Estelle Sternberger, wrote speeches for Franklin Delano Roosevelt, and my maternal grandfather was a rabbi who would marry Jews and non-Jews. Even—and this was truly radical for his time—marry Jews and blacks, for which he was forever banished to an obscure synagogue in Hoboken, New Jersey.

In my early Village days, I watched the McCarthy hearings with revulsion. The protest tradition in folk music appealed to me. In the Sixties, many of my singer-songwriters were protesters. I was bitterly opposed to the Vietnam war. At the time of the 1968 Democratic Convention in Chicago, when the infamous police brutality flashed from every TV set, I bought radio time to say in my own voice how disastrous I thought it all was: a corrupting war, an inquisition into what we read and smoked and saw and did with our lives. I did the same in 1969, supporting the anti-war Moratorium. In 1970, when four young people were shot and killed by the National Guard during anti-war demonstrations on the campus of Kent State in Ohio, Elektra took out full-page ads in the music trades and spots on radio decrying death by government violence. I thought Nixon was an abomination and financially backed George McGovern in the presidential election campaign of 1972.

THEODORE BIKEL: Jac was a middle of the road liberal, not extreme. He opposed blacklisting. But he would not demonstrate. For example, when the folk artists were opposing the cops in Washington Square who were prohibiting them from singing around the fountain, Jac was not there.

JAC: I was out of town for that one, but I did march on several occasions. Once in London, in a demonstration for nuclear disarmament, though my real motive was to get a closer look at Vanessa Redgrave. Another time I flew Judy Collins to Washington, DC, for a major demonstration. The police gave you a choice: be arrested or not be arrested. Judy chose to be locked up on a misdemeanor charge, as a badge of honorable commitment. I chose to return to New York.

DAVID BRAUN: Jac was a recorder, a chronicler. At the time of the American Revolution he would be making silver mugs for the soldiers to drink from when they came home from battle.

JOHN HAENY: We were recording Judy Collins at the War Memorial Auditorium in San Francisco, the day of the great peace march. I woke up that morning and stepped out on the balcony of my hotel and saw a quarter of a million people streaming down the street screaming "Peace!" and "Fuck Nixon!" It was an intense day. And that night the concert. Jac used to get real high seeing his children at work, you know. It's a beautiful hall and a beautiful night, full moon. Judy gives a wonderful concert, and Jac comes out to the van, it's a big gorgeous recording van and the sound is glorious, and you see it all in Jac's eyes, and he walks away two feet off the ground.

JAC: Though I wasn't on the picket lines, I did have an FBI file. Years later, under the Freedom of Information act, I read through my meager file and even I was bored. The most accurate description of me politically would be: founder and president of Elektra Records.

❧

DANNY FIELDS: The weekend I first met the MC5 they said to me, "If you like us, we have this other group, they're like this little brother group, friends of ours. You should see them." It was the Psychedelic Stooges. They were playing at the student union on a Sunday night. I never saw anything like it. I mean, not to be misunderstood, Iggy was the most incredible performer I had ever seen. He must have been about nineteen or so. The most wonderful dancer and inventive person I'd ever seen on a stage—but still I liked the music more than I liked Iggy's images, which I thought were magnificent. So I went up to him after the show and I said, "Hey, you're great," and he said, "Who are you?" and I said, "I'm from a record company," and he said, "Oh yeah, uh-huh." I found his manager, who was a sort of semi-partner of John Sinclair's, and I told him that I wanted to sign Iggy too. What a weekend. Two groups. And the Stooges only wanted $5,000.

JAC: Danny talked me into the signing despite my puzzlement as to what I was going to do with them. He had been right about David Peel and "Have a Marijuana" so I went ahead.

Iggy was this demonic spirit who kept falling all over himself. He looked like a spaniel with the saddest blue eyes; smaller than life but larger than life. Shocking and sweet. The Stooges were certainly unlike anything I had seen, but they were mainly visual, as in: Iggy is playing the Electric Circus, a major club on St. Mark's Place. Covered with peanut butter and glitter, he swan dives into the crowd. And they won't catch him. Iggy crashes ten feet to the floor. New York, New York, it's all heart.

Lenny Kaye Collection

Basic Iggy

But the Stooges could barely play their instruments. How were we going to get this on record? At least when we took them into the studio it wasn't going to be complicated, meaning expensive. Then Iggy and band arrived totally unprepared, with five songs, and I had to tell them to come back when they had better than an album's worth.

STEVE HARRIS: I saw something very interesting about Iggy. I was out in the field, working in the trenches, but it was just very, very difficult to make the people at the office to see the commerciality in all this.

JAC: He was beyond Jim Morrison. You had to be ready for something beyond stock outrageous.

LENNY KAYE: Driven, always unpredictable, touched by genius, star-crossed. Iggy was a psychodrama. He'd break the drumsticks off and jab them into his chest, and he wasn't fooling.

STEVE HARRIS: I saw him take "it" out in a club on West 70th and put it against a speaker. He took it out in front of the audience and they just watched the show, nobody went ooh and aah.

Another time he was working at Max's Kansas City, and at the end of the gig, it must have been about three in the morning, he says, "Where are you going?" I said, "Home." I lived on East 82nd. He says, "Well, I'm going to see this girl I know on Park Avenue in the 70s." I said, "Well, I'll drop you off."

Iggy was appearing on stage in a diaper, and he had cut himself up unmercifully, he was bleeding like crazy, and you'd think that he would change to go to Park Avenue and 72nd. But no. My attitude was, this is rock and roll—if Iggy Stooge wants to see some chick on Park Avenue in a diaper, bleeding from the waist up, that's his prerogative, he's the artist.

Mick Rock•Star File

Glam Iggy

He got out of the cab and said, "Come on up with me, have a drink." So there's this really lovely Park Avenue apartment building. The doorman's in full regalia. Iggy asks for this girl. The doorman is looking at him like he is absolutely out of his mind. "Who shall I say is calling?" Iggy says, "Tell her Iggy's here." And she says, "Send him up." All the way up, the elevator operator's looking at Iggy in his diaper, bleeding. We get there and it's this magnificent apartment, just like you see in the movies, and a girl answers in a negligee, slinky, a tall Lauren Bacall-looking woman. We had a couple of drinks, then I left, and Iggy stayed. The next day he called me at the office: "I can't work tonight, I had thirty-two stitches this morning."

DANNY FIELDS: Commercially, the music never went anywhere. Yet historically, those first Stooges records were way ahead of their time. They're avant garde still. The music was amazing. It was so beautiful to me. I thought that was the perfect group. The MC5 I loved for their vitality and their power, and their hold over large audiences, and that carnival kind of thing whenever they played. But I really loved the Stooges for the purity in the music and their songs and lyrics.

And the influence they've had on other musicians and around the world has been incalculable. Everything goes back to them. They were really the proto punk band of the world. There would have been no punk rock without them, no Sex Pistols, no Ramones or anything that was really important in the Seventies. It's like if there had been no Stooges, and no Velvet Underground, there would be nothing that is interesting now. The Stooges will be in the Rock and Roll Hall of Fame sooner or later.

JAC: It was fascinating, like an odd piece of art that someone strongarms you into buying, and years later it turns out to be of lasting importance.

I never knew what to say to Iggy. Danny Fields was a terrific filter, maintaining relationships between the company and the Stooges, but they offended Bill Harvey grievously. Bill could not fathom how I allowed them on the label. Mel Posner had not the slightest idea how he was going to sell these albums. I was relying on the large fan base of MC5 in Detroit, which has always been a great record area, plus the general political notoriety of MC5 to carry the Stooges forward. We did two albums with Iggy & the Stooges, couldn't get the public interested, and despite the honor bestowed by a teenage girls' club in Paterson, New Jersey, voting Iggy the World's Sexiest Man, I chose not to do a third.

JAC: Bread was at the opposite end of the performance and music spectrum. The story begins with a promise remembered.

When Arthur Lee of Love was renouncing his contract because he was a minor, his attorney, Al Schlesinger, an honorable man and as close to a rabbi as one could find in the record business, appreciated the way I had handled the situation. Al told me he would remember that I had been a mensch, and if anything ever came through his office that he thought would be good for Elektra, he'd be in touch. ·

One day I'm at my desk, 9am New York time, 6am LA time, and Al calls my private line, the red phone. He says he has a group for me. I only recognized one name, David Gates, from Captain Beefheart, but I quickly offered to have David Anderle cut a demo.

DAVID ANDERLE: They came and sat in my office and played, with acoustic guitars, and I said, "This is really good." I called Bruce Botnick, and we set up to cut a demo that night. I'm nervous about what Jac will think, because it's so pop, and Elektra is anything but pop.

JAC: The demo was couriered to me, and I thought it was great—utterly fresh and likable, harmonizing vocals that wove in, out and around each other; a softer, more considerate sound than the hard rock that was now everywhere.

DAVID GATES: Elektra did not have an act on its roster like us. Crosby, Stills and Nash had just gone with Atlantic, so we felt if we were on Elektra we might be unique in our style of music to them, and at the same time they would be unique to us.

JAC: Other labels were showing interest, especially Columbia, but Bread chose us.

DAVID GATES: Elektra was top of our list. The label and Jac had an excellent reputation of being music-oriented and worked good with artists. A nice home to be.

JAC: The way Bread went about recording was so civilized it attracted attention. Most groups would shuffle into the studio, if you were lucky, in the late afternoon, and nothing would happen until seven, and then you'd work until two in the morning. Bread would arrive in the morning at nine sharp, David with his attaché case, as if he was off to a downtown bank or Pacific Bell. They would record till lunch, break for an hour, work all afternoon, and David would go home to his family at five.

MARTY RICHMOND: Not all musicians are capable of that kind of discipline, and I'm not sure all of them want to be. And I'm not sure that his music wouldn't be better if he were a little more loose. But who can say?

JAC: The album was filled with winsome romantic songs; rich, layered voicings, enchantingly direct lyrics and fine acoustic playing.

ROBB ROYER: The day our album was released was the day we had our first performance, and it was the day the astronauts landed on the moon.

JAC: Two weeks after we released Bread, the first Crosby, Stills and Nash album appeared and essentially wiped Bread out. Bread still sold forty or fifty thousand copies, strictly on merit. I was mighty upset because I thought the group deserved better. I immediately picked up their option and began to prepare for their second album.

DAVID GATES: 'Make It With You' was about the fourth or fifth song that we were in the process of recording. Jac came in, and he absolutely flipped: "I must have this record out right away." Then the discussion began. "But the album's not done, and if you put this out and it does well, there'll be no album on the street." Jac says, "I don't care, that's a high-class problem." After the single was out just a couple, three weeks, someone in marketing called me and said, "David, we've got a smash." The record is being played on one station in Washington, DC, and people are coming into racked stores and asking for it, to drug stores and markets, and nobody could get it, because it was just barely out. And that does not happen unless you have huge runaway demand. It happened with 'Snowbird' by Anne Murray, and it happened with 'Make It With You.' And it was Jac who heard that thing, and it was his decision to put it out at once.

the best of bread

Bread's "Best Of" went multi-platinum
EKS-75056

He did it again on the next album. We had finished recording, and we had a playing session, all the Elektra people in the studio, twenty or thirty of us. I had sequenced 'If' as the fourth cut on side one. The whole album goes through, and Jac comes over to me and says, "Can I hear that fourth cut on the first side again?" Just like that he picked out 'If,' which has become the classic Bread song. He always honed in on the key track immediately.

Jac is a good music man. He would work with us to sequence our albums. We'd give him the twelve songs and he'd shuffle them around. I've never known anybody at his level that would get into that kind of minutiae. They're busy running the business. They're lucky to even hear the album their artists record, let alone help them organize the songs in the right order. But Jac was into that stuff.

Also, he's someone you could talk to if you had any problem within the band or the recording process. Really good. And to this day he's exciting, he's vibrant, one of the most—vibrant is the right word, one of the most exhilarating guys to be around.

He could also be brutally frank—not unpleasant, he just speaks his mind right there. But he does it because he's so positive in his thinking, and he's right nine times out of ten.

And Jac was certainly what an artist would want to have. You always felt he was really there for you, rooting and cheering and helping, and if he found out that something wasn't being done for you, boy, he'd get on the phone and take your case, call the radio station or the marketing guy or whatever. If he didn't think you were getting a fair shake, he'd go to bat for you.

MARTY RICHMOND: I asked David once, how he would know that he was a success? When he had a Number 1 hit song? He said, "No." He says, "The first time I walk into an elevator and hear one of my songs come out of the Muzak. Then I'll know." That was his goal, and he got there.

JAC: Judy Collins was ready for the studio again. "Wildflowers" had widened her audience considerably with songs like 'Both Sides Now' and her own exquisite evocation of love, 'Since You Asked.' Now she was looking for change. I recognized the signs.

MARK ABRAMSON: Judy began to feel that maybe Josh Rifkin wasn't the best arranger for her any more. That she wanted something simpler. Josh's arrangements are musically complex. When they work, I think—I still think—they are incomparable. And I think they work most of the time. But there were also problems of over-elaborateness, which I think Judy thought more than me, because I felt we could just deal with it in terms of how we would mix the records. But, you know, it was too competitive.

Judy and I would discuss it. I remember I called George Martin in London, and asked him if he would do some arrangements for Judy. He was very nice, said he was flattered, but no, he didn't arrange, he just produced. We thought of Randy Newman, a wonderful arranger, but he was doing his own stuff. It was really hard.

DAVID ANDERLE: Judy came out to LA to honor an old contract with Doug Weston at the Troubadour, four nights. I, as a good head of the West Coast office, went every night and watched her. People would totally fall in love with the Judy Collins show, especially that intimate at the Troubadour. And I saw this incredible warmth that she had, but that I never heard on any of her records. Live, she wasn't perfect, but she was real. So I started talking to her about, "You should make a record with a band, try to capture the spirit of a live performance."

She went back to New York and put a band together, came back out here, and went into the studio for two or three days with Mark Abramson and did these demos. Well, the band was rock and roll in structure, but all the players were classically trained, and instead of a drummer she had a percussionist. I just hated it. I said, "You would be best served to forget everything. This is awful. This is not rock and roll. This is, like, stupid." And she got very angry.

Elektra

Judy and David Anderle ponder a playback

We got into it a bit and along the way we became extremely close, and she said to me, "I want you to produce my record." Well, I had co-produced two records with Russ Miller, and that was the extent of my producing. She said, "I know you know what I should do, and I think you have the feel, and I want you." She calls Jac, and Jac basically says, "You're at the pinnacle of your career, and you want to what?" She says, "I'm not going to make the record unless David produces." And so Jac says, "OK."

I called one of my dearest friends, Stephen Stills, who was like a little brother, and I said, "Help, I'm going to produce a record and I know what I want but I don't know how to get it." I called Van Dyke Parks, another good friend, and said, "Would you come in and do some stuff?" And that was the beginning of my career as a producer.

I'm not a musician. I don't play, never have. I can't talk chords. I talk feelings, emotions, colors, shapes—maybe because I'm a painter. But I do have something about me that people like to rally around, or that they like to please. I don't know what it is, but I knew that from before, when I was in the theater and I used to direct; people like to use me as a focus. And I've always loved to be surrounded, no matter what I do, by the best people possible, because I'm not fearful. That's what I brought to the party. Plus Judy's trust.

So we had the best musicians I could get, and we picked the best songs we could find.

Judy taught me something which I haven't forgotten to this day. If you don't write a song, pick a song that either sounds like you wrote it or it was written for you. Period. At that time she was only just starting to write herself, and she was absolutely impeccable in choosing young songwriters. She talked to me about this young Canadian named Joni Mitchell, and she introduced me to Leonard Cohen.

Leonard came by, Leonard the poet, disheveled, but linguistically elegant. I didn't know who he was. He didn't want to play any songs. We had to, like, loosen up the thing. We went to lunch at Casa Cugat, about half a block down from Elektra on La Cienega, showy little Mexican restaurant, bright colors, wood, tile floor, and booths filled with straight people. We got blitzed on margaritas. When Leonard had to pee, he would leave the table from the sitting position, the same height as if he was on his knees, and he would go the bathroom like Toulouse-Lautrec. By late afternoon you could tell that they wanted us to leave. We were walking back to the studio to start listening to Leonard's songs, to pick a few. And as we were walking up the block, this very elegant woman was walking down, exactly the kind of woman you would see on La Cienega shopping for antiques, and she had a poodle with her. Suddenly Leonard broke away from us, dropped down in front of her, wrapped his arms around her legs and said urgently: "Madam! Madam! You must bring the dogs down from the throne!" I was in awe. I'll never forget that. I don't think she's ever forgotten it, either. So from there we crawled back to the studio, and the two songs we got out of that experience were 'The Story of Isaac' and 'Bird on a Wire.' Not a bad afternoon's drinking.

Anyway, the band was Stephen Stills, and Van Dyke Parks on keyboard, and Michael Saul on piano, Chris Ethridge on bass. And James Burton, who was Elvis Presley's guitar player, a great guitar player. James brought a pedal steel player named Buddy Emmons out from Nashville. I always loved the sound of the pedal steel, and we were going to do Ian and Sylvia's 'Some Day Soon' with a country feel, and there was a Dylan song we also wanted to record with a country feel. And Jim Gordon was playing drums. Jim became one of the greatest drummers in rock and roll and went to prison for beating his mother to death with a hammer.

Judy had never played with a band like that before. We cut it all live and very funky. There were things that were less than perfect vocally, but feeling-wise I thought it was great stuff. That album, "Who Knows Where The Time Goes," pretty much got rid of the folkie label attached to Judy.

In those days you had no outboard equipment to do any kind of acoustic effect. Everything had to be done by hand; you would hang pieces of tape all over the studio, labeled for editing.

JAC: That was delicate work. The tape-editing process was agonizing to Judy who would hover. She said those lengths of tape were like strips of her skin.

DAVID ANDERLE: And she was very concerned over the end result of the album. I think she got back to New York and a lot of her friends were giving her a bad time about the imperfection of some of the recording and some of her vocal performances, and I think it made her a little insecure, which Judy was wont to be in those days. Jac and Harold Leventhal were concerned too, because she was singing strange songs in a strange manner, and sometimes singing a little bit out of pitch, and the album had cost thirty thousand dollars.

JAC: Probably more.

DAVID ANDERLE: The album went gold, and quickly, so I must have been doing something right. But Judy didn't talk to me for a long time because she hated the record. Then she called and said, "I'm putting together my first 'Best Of' record, and I've been going through all the stuff, and the music from that album is remarkable." And I said, "Well, that really makes me feel good, but it's a little late." I was probably at that time not sophisticated enough as a record producer to know how to deal with that like I do now, so I took it very personally that I didn't have the response from her that I would have wanted.

But I got the producing bug. My first ever solo-produced album went gold, and I said, "Hey, this is easy, no problem." And only twenty albums later I got my second gold record . . .

JAC: Bread, Judy Collins—and then in that same year, 1969, Delaney & Bonnie.

DAVID ANDERLE: I saw them in Westwood. A white soul band. I'd never seen anything quite like it. I fell in love with them immediately and wanted to sign them. They finished their gig, I went down and opened up the studio, called John Haeny, brought them in for the weekend, and cut a demo.

JAC: Bonnie was one hell of a singer, the best white blues chick singer I'd ever heard. Blonde and fair-skinned but sounding so black. At seventeen she sang with Ike and Tina Turner in St. Louis, an Ikette for three days in a black wig and Man Tan skin darkener.

DAVID ANDERLE: White R&B was another kind of music for Elektra. A different discipline. And the first time that Elektra had been really exposed to that Southern white attitude. Elektra from the beginning had been this kind of intelligent, New York, folky label—bright boys from back East. Then after a while on the West Coast this insanity had started to happen, these scruffy urchins running the La Cienega office, trying to change things. And now here come Delaney & Bonnie. All of a sudden this weird Southern presence is around, like a band of gypsies.

GEORGE STEELE: Motorcycle boots and blue jeans and key chains hanging off.

JAC: I was wary of them as people. Something about Delaney made me itch. But I was attracted to their music. Several labels wanted to sign them, and I knew we weren't going to get them if we didn't deal. This was the first time I ever granted an artist any kind of say over the album cover. Bill Harvey took it personally and was appalled. And that wasn't all.

KEITH HOLZMAN: I remember being upset with Jac when I got a copy of the contract. He had given the artists control of the record. I said, "How could you do this? You just sold away your birthright. You will live to rue this deal. If this is what is going to happen, we're going to lose the music." I saw the handwriting on the wall.

JAC: My people bristled because of the way this signing was structured, but I knew that the entire record-making procedure and locus of control was about to shift. Artist's managers and lawyers needed to justify their percentage, which meant, inevitably, more interference in creative matters. Down the road I wasn't going to be able to hold the line. Why not offer this group, which sounded exceptional, some leeway?

KEITH HOLZMAN: It turns out I was absolutely right. That was symptomatic of the era of the artist becoming all-powerful.

JAC: David had John Haeny engineering the sessions. John wanted to record organically: basic band on two tracks, live, and sweeten on the remaining open tracks. Our Studio B was particularly well suited. It had a live quality that could be controlled. As for putting John with Delaney & Bonnie, I thought that it might lead to fireworks, but David was so laid-back he could probably keep them going.

GEORGE STEELE: The side band was just unbelievable. When you have Leon Russell playing keyboards for you—

DAVID ANDERLE: And Dr. John, Mac Rebennack, came in on a Saturday afternoon. We brought him in because Leon said he had this great song we had to record, 'Who'll Wear The Crown?' Dr. John was kicking a major heroin problem at the time. We explained that we didn't need him for the session, just to lay the song down on tape for us so we could do it. He'd sit at the piano, looking like death. We'd say, "OK, we're ready, Mac," and he'd play for a while and then he'd go out; he had this guy with him that would walk him into the bathroom to throw up or whatever.

DAN ROTHCHILD: My father had another story, of Dr. John bringing his wife with him, who would crochet right next to him in a chair. Dr. John was not connecting at all because he was so strung out, and then he went and shot up and came back and played the most incredible solo you've ever heard, and did this great gliss at the end, and with one great motion of his finger leaned over and threw up right on the floor, and his wife kept crocheting.

DAVID ANDERLE: We could control the amount of potential danger in the studio. But it was always Delaney & Bonnie "and Friends," the whole entourage, and it would spill out into Sue Helms's and Ellen's area. Or I'd open up my office, which was right across the hall. Or at the end of the hall was where the secretaries hung out, and everyone would just party in that back room over the weekend, beer and wine and Jack Daniel's and lots of smoke, pizzas all over the place, and then on Monday morning the girls would come in and there's trash cans overflowing, six-packs and wine bottles and little ends of joints, and all the papers on their desks would be covered with grease from barbecued spare ribs.

Later on, when I was recording Bonnie, it came down between her and John Haeny. The most painful studio time in my life. They got me so nuts I hadn't eaten for weeks, my stomach had turned into such a knot. John actually had me down twenty-five pounds. Finally I got to a point where I just laid it out to them. I got real clear and was feeling good enough that I could eat. So I order some ribs, and I'm beginning to eat, and Bonnie and John start going at each other again. It's like she could get him to be bitchy and crazy, and she knew that, and she would start grinding him, and the more she would grind him, the more effetely intellectual he would get, because he was so much smarter. They were going back and forth: "You bitch." "You whore." So I had to say, like a father to his kids, "Knock it off." And they wouldn't. So finally I say, "Get the fuck out of here." And they say, "We're sorry, we're sorry, OK? We won't do it again"—but they do. So I say to Bonnie, "Why don't you go out and practice?" She starts to go, and she stops at the door, clear across the room in the back studio. Everything is quiet, I'm eating my rib, and she says one thing to John, he immediately snaps back at her, and I went so out of my mind with anger that I took the rib from my mouth and I threw a bone at her so hard it just missed her head and stuck in the wall. She just stood there in awe, and John started crying. I said, "Bonnie, you're fuckin' out of here. And John, God love you, I cannot put up with your shit any more, you're fired."

JAC: And this was David Anderle, the sweetest and coolest soul in creation.

DAVID ANDERLE: Delaney & Bonnie were like a whole different people in Elektra's life. But they made this incredible record. And in a way it helped Elektra's international presence, because the English loved it. Bonnie singing her ass off, and Delaney being a great guitar player and coming from Mississippi, he really understood Robert Johnson, so he meant a lot to those English rockers.

It got out among them through Alan Pariser, who was on the Delaney & Bonnie management team, and he had major connections with the English rock scene. All of a sudden that record became a sensation. It was Mick Jagger's favorite, Keith Richard's favorite, Eric Clapton's favorite.

Then George Harrison fell in love with the album. He wanted Delaney & Bonnie for Apple Records, and they were just going to walk. He tried to take the record away from Elektra. In fact I have a copy of that record at home with the Apple label already on it. But they were still under contract to us. We said to them, "Excuse me, guys, this isn't Mississippi. You can't sign a contract with us and then, just because you fall in love with a Beatle, go off with Apple."

JAC: David and I flew to England to meet with Derek Taylor, the Beatles' publicist and close crony, and to talk with Apple management. Delaney and Bonnie had gigs back home and I didn't need them mucking around in very sensitive negotiations with people whose music I admired and who some years before had granted me swift and special permission to do the Baroque Beatles Book.

DAVID ANDERLE: The first night we went over to visit with Glyn Johns, who was mixing down "Let It Be" for the Beatles, and the next day we went to Apple Records—

JAC:—Which was falling apart. Chaos in the office. People in odd costumes running everywhere, preening because they were at Apple, but no work getting done. A lot of attitude without foundation. No clear chain of responsibility. Money spent recklessly. The Beatles themselves pursuing different paths. I had hoped for better. But we got Delaney & Bonnie back, as of course we should have.

DAVID ANDERLE: On the way out to the airport afterwards we stopped off at a Stones session. And then the Stones came over and finished "Let It Bleed" at Elektra.

All this is to say that Elektra in LA now became an international hip place, and it came through the Delaney & Bonnie record. And I got a huge reputation in England because of my work on that record. I started hanging out with the Stones whenever they came to town. You would go to Alan Pariser's house, and there would be Clapton. Harrison was always there, Keith, whoever was coming to town.

PAT FARALLA: The Stones were going to pay us a visit one day, or maybe Mick was going to come by, and there was lots of wheeoo-wheeoo over that.

JAC: To have Elektra so appreciated was heady stuff, but with Delaney & Bonnie we had crossed into the twilight zone. They charged through Elektra leaving a large and upsetting wake.

PAT FARALLA: Seems like Delaney was always drunk and Bonnie was most of the time mad.

JAC: Delaney was combative and surly. He was the only artist with whom I ever had major personal problems. I ran the company so I could make good records with people I respected. Elektra had much bigger stars who never acted with such callous disregard for the people who had gone out of their way to support them.

GEORGE STEELE: Their management group were very demanding.

JAC: In the guise of documenting the recording and release process, Barry Feinstein, their manager, would shove a microphone in my face and ask to what lengths I would go to promote the record. Would I pay off DJs? I mean—

DAVID ANDERLE: It would have been absolutely smashing if Delaney had been able to deal with his ego and just let the music be heard. But Delaney was about being Mister Big Guy of the whole world.

GEORGE STEELE: He was very arrogant, extremely demanding. "Get me this, get me that, this room sucks, the lighting sucks, the staging sucks, this is rubbish, fuck them, I'm not going to go on." He was demanding on his own musicians. He was demanding of Bonnie. She was really the big strength of that band, a focal point, but Delaney was jealous of the enthusiastic reaction of audiences to her singing.

JAC: Before they had a record deal they were Bonnie & Delaney, and then the moment Delaney thought he could see the big time coming, he insisted on putting his name before his wife's.

DAVID ANDERLE: Delaney used to beat the shit out of her. It was just awful. They were a white Ike and Tina Turner. Same story.

JAC: Bonnie would turn up in sun glasses on an overcast day looking embarrassed for having been the victim. Puffy and beat up and one of the saddest looking people I have ever seen.

DAVID ANDERLE: But the music—Clapton left Blind Faith to go with Delaney & Bonnie, and Clapton was on his way to becoming God. That's how good it was.

I have a handwritten note from Joe Cocker, saying it was the best album since Big Pink, it out-Atlantics Atlantic for THE sound, Joe saying he will do everything he can to make sure everyone hears it, don't let Elektra lose it.

After all that, the record didn't do that well. I'd have to say we didn't necessarily know how to market them. White soul music was new for Jac, it was new for Elektra. I'm not sure anyone ever figured it out. Everybody said it should have sold a lot more, but it didn't.

JAC: Delaney was hostile about his relatively weak sales, up around fifty thousand, nasty about everything. I was in England, staying at Claridge's, and he called. He was down in Aardvark, Texas, or wherever his father lived, and there were no

Delaney & Bonnie albums in the local store. He was smoldering: "If there aren't records in that store by tomorrow, I'm coming to England to kill you." I said, "You can put the records there yourself. Then you can go terrorize some other label because I'm releasing you as of now. It's as much a privilege to record for Elektra as it is for us to record an artist, and I won't be threatened."

I called David Anderle and broke the news. David was heavily invested in the band, but he had had his troubles with Delaney. There was about fifteen seconds of silence and then he quietly said, "Well, Jac, go look in the mirror and be proud of yourself." They had gotten to him too.

So Delaney & Bonnie went to Atlantic, new home of the MC5—

DAVID ANDERLE:—And drove Ahmet Ertegun and Jerry Wexler crazy.

JAC: After a couple of albums, Atlantic let them go. Then Clive Davis at Columbia made a very rich deal with them, six albums for a reported million-dollar advance.

Clive and I were flying to an industry event and I said, "That seems like a lot of money, Clive. You've paid $166,000 apiece for six albums, and these are people who, with the exception of the album Eric Clapton participated on, never sold

Delaney & Bonnie "Accept No Substitute" EKS-74039

more than about sixty or seventy thousand records." Clive gamely marshaled all his arguments as to why it was reasonable. D & B grabbed the advance, and about a month later they broke up. Under the contract, Clive was now entitled to six albums by Bonnie and six by Delaney. I sent him a telegram: "Now I understand the deal. You get twelve albums instead of six. You've cut your cost per album in half."

After that, Delaney made albums that didn't sell, and I heard that Bonnie became a born-again Christian.

Chapter 19

The evil triangle ...
The Plaster Casters, ahead of their time ...
Southern overexposure ...
Black leather pants and the great white shaft ...
The beard of the poet

JAC: Delaney & Bonnie at Elektra were a one-act melodrama that ended badly. The Doors were a full-on rock 'n' roll serial, and right on our doorstep.

JOHN VAN HAMMERSVELD: One thing that really flashes on me is how exposed Jim was. This exhibitionist kind of thing—the leather pants, the white shirt, the mane of hair. Being posed at the Players restaurant on La Cienega, down from Elektra Records, eating breakfast. A little vignette. You're driving by, and Jim Morrison is sitting alone in the sunlight, glistening, in this posture. And here he is a principal star in the media. No bodyguards, nothing, just totally exposed. It was like two dreams combined. He had his dream which he took down to the street, and ate, and my side of the dream is I'm walking by—and Morrison's a sound track, you know, 'Light My Fire,' or 'The End'—and why is he sitting in that ordinary space in the middle of that ordinary thing?

BILL SIDDONS: For the Doors office, I took a building on Santa Monica Boulevard, facing north, literally fifty yards from Elektra. It was a ramshackle, rundown duplex. The upstairs we made into the offices, and the downstairs was outfitted as a rehearsal room, ultimately as a recording studio, albeit a primitive one.

Freaks would show up. There was Cigar Pain, who wanted to be Jim Morrison, so he stuck burning cigars down his throat to make his voice real hoarse. He came in and sang demos for me. Crazy Nancy, one of those people who was crazy about Jim—she came by at all hours of the day and night to try and meet Jim and hang out with him. She might have been an acid casualty, but I'm not sure that it was even drug-induced. She was just someone who in most cases would be institutionalized because she was pretty dysfunctional. Harmless, though, and a very nice girl, so we were real kind to her and tried to give her a break. But she broke in a couple of times and slept there, and I think she stole a couple of guitars once because she was broke. So I put up iron gates, that stuff. We had a lot of crazies, a few that I just had to call the police and get rid of. But most of the time people came by who were completely giant Jim fans. He spoke to them in ways that nobody else did. He spoke to most people that way; they just took it more seriously than others. Sometimes Jim's girl friends, one night stands, would come by. It was an interesting time.

JAC: It was also the Warholian fifteen minutes of fame for the Plaster Casters, two teenage girls with a singular performance art specialty. They hung around rock stars, gave them head, then immortalized the erection on the spot by casting it with dental plaster.

Ellen Sander, one of the notable early rock journalists, wrote a wonderful article about them. Ellen normally published in the Saturday Review or the New York Times, but plaster casting was counter-culture news that did not qualify as fit for the Good Grey Lady's Arts & Leisure section, so Ellen's story appeared instead in Paul Krassner's sharp, funny and highly scabrous little alternative periodical, the Realist.

The Plaster Casters, in grand Hollywood style, acquired a manager, none other than Herbie Cohen, and a mentor in Frank Zappa, who was editing a collection of Groupie Papers. Zappa planned to have the exhibits bronzed and made into a permanent collection. Frank also came up with a mother of invention idea, making ice cream molds and marketing a line of flavors with the slogan, "Suck Your Favorite Rock Star."

Jimi Hendrix dwarfs the rock competition

Cynthia Plaster Caster and her industrious companion, Diane, amassed a unique collection of artifacts, spearheaded, so to speak, by Jimi Hendrix. I have been told that Fritz Richmond of our LA studio was also in that hallowed company. And of course the Plaster Casters wanted the Doors. Morrison was the most prestigious and eligible—or at least in his tight leather pants he was the most obvious. In or out of his pants he was generally available for all kinds of performance art, like prancing naked with Nico on the battlements of the venerable Hotel Chateau Marmont. But the Plaster Casters never did get Jim, or any of the other Doors.

SUZANNE HELMS: Jim hung around the Elektra office quite a bit. He would come in and sit on the bench. For hours he would sit there and write lyrics and bits of poetry on his yellow pad. And Jackson Browne would get a ride from Laurel Canyon into town, and sit in my office the whole afternoon. I typed both their lyrics endlessly, because I was teaching myself to type.

PAT FARALLA: Jim kept kind of slouching in in jeans, T-shirt, the leather jacket, rumpled, tousled boots, pretty much the same look night and day. He'd stroll through, usually around three or four in the afternoon, rather placid-looking, just shufflin' through, always serene, but with edgy waters inside. He'd be looking for somebody to talk to, or listen to, a warm body. He wanted to connect on some level. He'd say, "You want to go have a drink?" So we'd go down the street to this little French café and sit in the bar, and Jim would say a lot of nothing, to which I would say a lot of nothing, or he'd have something on his mind and just start to talk, free form, stream of consciousness. Who knew how much he'd had to smoke or drink or ingest before we got there?

BILL SIDDONS: Across Santa Monica from the Doors office was the Phone Booth, a topless bar. On the southwest corner, facing north, was the Extension, owned by the same people. The Alta Cienega Motel was around the corner, north on La Cienega, simple, clean, very small. The southeast corner was this decrepit run-down used furniture place run by an old couple who had stopped cleaning up twenty years before. The place was phenomenal in its trashiness, piles of stuff everywhere. I bought a file cabinet there that still has all my Doors memorabilia in it.

Across the fence from my back yard was an office building on La Cienega, facing east, in which David Geffen and Elliott Roberts had their office. And Pamela rented out the front for a boutique that she called Themis. She created a space that was full of snakeskin hides and feathers and the things you remember from those days, the Indian and Afghani garments, a lot of pretty far-out stuff.

Then a little bit east on Santa Monica was the whole subculture of Barney's Beanery, which was kind of a biker-beat-intellectuals crowd. And right across from Barney's was Rudy Gernreich, who designed the topless swimsuit.

So it was still primarily a busy business neighborhood, with four lanes of traffic, but with a bit of an artistic community. And a lot of freaks.

SHERRI KANDELL: Everyone was on drugs and I was kind of the hippie transport. I was driving my VW bus with the back seat taken out, huge Indian madras pillows and the roof draped in an Indian bedspread, and crystals hanging, and incense. I was working for the Moveable Feast, near the Troubadour, a company that made sandwiches and sent girls with baskets to office buildings at lunchtime. Avocado on whole wheat—that kind of health food consciousness was coming in. My Moveable Feast route in the VW bus was the anti-corporate hip route. Dick Clark's offices were on the Strip, way more corporate, very business. But Elektra was a freak show, which was why I loved going there.

EVE BABITZ: That Elektra-Barney's-Alta Cienega triangle—

BILL SIDDONS:—And of course there was the Tropicana, the flop house of the music business, the new rock generation and the hippies.

SUZANNE HELMS: Real seedy, seedy motel. They never repaired things or painted, there were fingerprint smudges on the walls. But they had a lot of things going on there.

BILL SIDDONS: Every rock star that came to LA for the first time had to stay there.

SUZANNE HELMS: A lot of famous people. It was a place of choice. Someone should write a book on the Tropicana. There was a wonderful old man running it that I used to lunch with about once a month. It was very important that I kept that relationship going, because we had a lot of people who really destroyed stuff.

MIRANDI BABITZ: Musicians, and people sliding down the bottom end of the scale. I think in those days it was really the core of the rock and roll scene and the drug scene.

BILL SIDDONS: Probably a dozen people had drug overdoses in the Tropicana.

DIANE GARDINER: Jim would take a room there when things were perhaps too intense at home with Pamela, when he needed to get away. That would be the office for all his bizarre stuff to come out.

PAUL ROTHCHILD: Morrison was two people. When Jim was sober, you couldn't want a better friend, you wouldn't want a dearer heart. A sensitive, aware, wonderful human being. Take him anywhere, take him home for dinner with Mom, take him to Ahmet Ertegun's party for senators and princes. Just don't give him a drink. If you give him a drink you end up with a taunting kid, looking to find your darkest weaknesses at all times.

Jim was a guy who tested the edges endlessly. And when he was drunk, tested them cruelly. With everybody. There were no exceptions. None.

There were a few hardy ones who could stand up under that and come right back at him. Myself as one. Bob Neuwirth. No one in the band. Lord knows they tried. Ray tried the hardest; he was the one who worked hardest at being the diplomat. But there were guys in Jim's drinking cadre—

EVE BABITZ: Jim would get himself into a sort of Hell's Angels group of companions. I mean, you can wallow on Santa Monica Boulevard if you're looking to.

VINCE TREANOR: On a Friday or Saturday night, when the Doors had finished rehearsing, or Jim had finished business, or he had come to get his weekly stipend, he was very close by the Phone Booth for a brief pause for refreshment. And he and his entourage, his followers who were followers as long as Jim was buying, would trek over there. Now, of course, if Jim had been drinking and wasn't feeling quite up to crossing the wide span of Santa Monica Boulevard, if he was a little unsteady or a little unsure how to get to the Phone Booth, he could always make it to the Extension, right next door to the office. But the Phone Booth was the resort of choice.

FRANK LISCIANDRO: I'd walk to the corner, and there would be Jim walking out of the Doors office, and the others might have been pulling up in an old car, and we would saunter across the street, and Tom Baker would already be in the Phone Booth, and we would order a round of drinks, and the next thing you knew we were moving on to another club.

You get a bunch of people like this together and there's going to be a lot of alcohol going down. You get feisty, you start challenging each other in boyish pranks, like—walk that ledge, or I can jump in front of the next truck that comes along, or jump on the freight, or bash that, jump on that typewriter with my boots on.

DIANE GARDINER: There was a side of rock and roll that Jim understood thoroughly—that people were utterly willing to make fools of themselves in the name of being close to a rock star, and he would do it, and he was a genius at it.

FRANK LISCIANDRO: I never really saw Jim necessarily initiate this kind of stuff, but when Tom or Babe Hill or I happened to mention, "Let's do this," I mean, Jim was volunteering.

VINCE TREANOR: There was another bar further west. The famous billiard table overturning incident occurred in that one. Jim and Babe and Paul Ferrara, you never knew how many, got down there and some controversy arose and the upshot was that this billiard table got upset and so did the owner.

FRANK LISCIANDRO: I never saw Jim hit anybody, I never saw him get into a fist fight, although Babe and I did save him several times from fist fights, in bars and around pool tables and things like that, mostly by ducking and dragging him out, or Babe wedging himself into a doorway and holding off all comers while I put him in the car and we made a quick getaway. Because Jim, if he got a little out of hand—I mean, he was not averse to insulting everyone in the bar. Could be bad, could be very bad.

DIANE GARDINER: I think he was fond of using that power, and at the same time, let's face it, it's pretty repulsive.

SHERRI KANDELL: I thought he was a dark character. I saw the depth, but it came across in a downer way—the charisma was anti-charisma. Sometimes late at night, after Gazzari's or the Whisky, I would be allowed to sit in a booth near Jim when he would be holding court at Ben Frank's. Unkempt, and his pants—god, can you see his short hairs? I was a high school girl, a virgin, and I was always worried and hopeful that I would.

MICHELLE PHILLIPS: Outside the Whisky one night, Morrison was tugging on Janis Joplin's braids. Actually it was kind of playful at first, but she didn't take very kindly to it, and she took the bottle of Southern Comfort that she had in her hand and whacked him upside the cheek with it, and then when he tried to apologize she whacked him over the other cheek.

DIANE GARDINER: He would just let it go and let it go until it got awful, dangerous, nauseating, horrendous.

ERIC BURDON: One night I was at the Whisky, and I had a very nice inoffensive girl friend who was a dancer across the road at the Body Shop, and I ran and got her after the show and brought her to the Whisky, and we were sitting having a drink and Jim slid in alongside of us in the booth. And I guess, in a way, to him, to impress the girl, he poured beer over her head. That really impressed her. You see, he orchestrated people, he wanted an immediate scene. And she was pissed off, but she maintained her cool, just, like, "Oh, no, what's with this guy?" And instead of getting crazed at him, I took him aside and I said, "Now listen, that's not on, Jim. You're moving among human beings here. This is not stage acting." And he was really upset at what he had done. It was like he came out of a trance and suddenly realized what he had done and he was very apologetic.

And then he clicked into madness again, because the next thing I knew, he climbed up on the stage with the band, a visiting band, young kids from the Midwest. When they saw it was Jim Morrison, they stood back in awe—"Wow, Jim Morrison's on stage with us!" But they were playing rock and roll, and he was grabbing the microphone and reciting poetry. So after a while the band ground to a halt and left the stage, it was just the bass player left, and it turned very sour. Jim started to rap about provocation and about revolution. "You've all had your revolution, and it's all over. And there'll never be another revolution, 'cause you're all niggers." If this act had been presented on the marquee outside as The Future Poets Starring Jim Morrison, Provocative Theater, there would have been applause. But it wasn't, it was out of time, he was out of time. He was trying to get in step with his own desire to create mayhem. He went on and on and on about, "You're niggers," and nahnahnah, and silence fell over the club. And then you could almost hear the hammer on this pistol from upstairs creak back. The old policemen, the private dick of the house, an old black guy, he put his head out and he drew a bead on Jim, and he said, "I'll give you niggers, you son of a bitch. Get off the fucking stage." And by that time somebody called the police and they were there in seconds. They were always patrolling that section. He was bundled out the door, his shirt ripped off. And I think he actually broke loose from the cops on the street and slipped past them and took off bounding over the roofs of cars into the night.

ROBBY KRIEGER: Jim ran into cops many times. He had a knack for antagonizing cops wherever he went. I'm amazed he never got shot by a cop, because he used to taunt them so.

MIRANDI BABITZ: He got so many drunk driving tickets they took his license away.

VINCE TREANOR: He piled up his Cobra, destroyed the damn thing. Bill Siddons got the tow truck to go get it before the police picked it up. I saw a picture of that car. Nobody could have survived it, and yet he walked away, stone drunk on his ass.

FRITZ RICHMOND: He'd get out in the middle of La Cienega with a bottle in one hand and the other hand waving in the air to keep his balance, stopping traffic and yelling at people, "You're all a bunch of niggers!" Can you imagine? Well, it's a cruel drug, that alcohol.

JANICE KENNER: He'd be staying out in the street, in his leather clothes, which he hadn't changed in probably a year, completely shitfaced drunk, trying to get girls.

ELLEN VOGT: Being around Jim scared me. You never knew his mood, you never knew what to expect. You'd be prepared for anything in the office when he walked in. A couple of times he'd get into it in the hallway with one of the Doors, there'd be a little pushing and shoving. Some mornings there would be a real mess. One morning I came in and my desk had been trashed and my typewriter had a malt poured down through it. You just picked up and went on with your day and you didn't really think about it. When we'd see him the next time, it was never mentioned.

SUZANNE HELMS: He got terribly drunk one night and destroyed my typewriter.

JAC: He grabbed the emergency fire ax from outside the studio door and took it to that innocent machine.

SUZANNE HELMS: I came in in the morning and the keys were all sticking up every which way, like one of those self-destructing sculptures by Jean Tinguely.

JAC: Suzanne Helms in high dudgeon is a fearsome sight. She was fond of that typewriter. In full sail, she thrust her arm out. "Look what HE did. " I agreed that this was indeed terrible. I told her to order a new typewriter and we'd charge it to his royalties.

MARTY RICHMOND: She calls IBM and sits there with her arms folded, refusing to work, until they deliver it.

ELLEN VOGT: One morning Michael James Jackson came in really excited and said to Suzanne, "There's a body laying in the bushes out front!"

MICHAEL JAMES JACKSON: Sprawled in a bizarre position, covered in leaves and mud.

ELLEN VOGT: Michael said, "He could be dead! Call the police!"

MICHAEL JAMES JACKSON: Suzanne said, "Put the phone down."

ELLEN VOGT: Michael was really upset. "Suzanne, he's not moving at all! He's just laying there, face down in the bushes!"

MICHAEL JAMES JACKSON: Suzanne said, "That's just Jim. He's just passed out. Don't touch him, don't talk to him."

ELLEN VOGT: She said, "Michael, just relax, go to work, everything will be fine." And a couple of hours later, Jim got up and dusted himself off—

MICHAEL JAMES JACKSON:—And strolled off to Duke's for breakfast.

JAC: The General Motors TV commercial may have been the flashpoint for some of the antics. General Motors asked to use 'Light My Fire' as the theme for a new model car. They were offering good money: $80,000 in 1969 dollars, which would be split, Doors $60,000, Elektra $20,000. During the negotiations, Jim was off and nowhere to be found, but the remaining Doors OKd it and so did Max Fink, Jim's lawyer. Personally, I didn't care one way or the other.

When Jim rematerialized he freaked. He was sure we had all taken advantage of his absence. The other Doors supposedly laid it on my doorstep. Jim phoned me in New York. I set out the sequence of events in typical Jaconian detail and he seemed mollified, or at least no longer blaming me. I said, "Jim, as far as Elektra is concerned it's not a matter of money. Elektra will contribute its full share to a film scholarship fund at UCLA"—an interest of his and Ray's—"if the Doors will match it. That will still leave $40,000, $10,000 each for the Doors." I was urging him to take the money and then turn around and do some real good with it. Jim thought it was a notion to consider, but after that conversation the subject never again came up.

A commercial was shot and aired, but very sparsely. Jim may have hoped to create such a furor that General Motors would be reluctant to use the tune. He once threatened to take his quarter share, buy a bunch of Buicks and smash them on Santa Monica Boulevard.

MICHAEL FORD: When Jim got out into public life and realized his imagination was being tapped into for a lot of the wrong reasons, a disenchantment became very marked in him. That disenchantment led to more eccentric ingestion of chemicals. His need seemed to me to be a quest, searching for a divine molecule that would give him what Ray, I think, once called The Ultimate Vision, a vision of himself exactly as he belonged in this dichotomous plane on which he found himself— the dichotomy of him being a visionary and a threat to cultural equilibrium, and a guy who jangled the cash register and got all the greedheads their fat wallets. Adulation and the money jones and the worship was a perversion of that vision, and then he realized that he had perverted everything that he in the beginning trusted about himself. What happens to an artist when suddenly he can't trust himself any more? "Wait a minute, I know I wasn't wrong, but this feels wrong. Buy me a drink, gimme a toke, gimme a shot, shoot me full of something."

JAC: Jim's reliability was a constant concern. Would he show up for a concert? What might he do on stage? 'The End' would bring out the fringe who would go crazy whenever there was a full moon, or who acted as if there was a full moon year-round. The off-the-wall types—the Andy Warhols and to the left of Andy Warhol—would cart him off. He would vanish for days.

ERIC BURDON: I had to run him out of my house once. For years I was into guns, a gun fanatic. I owned a .44 magnum which was given to me on tour as a gift so therefore I couldn't get rid of it—that's my excuse to keep it. There was a party at my house one night, and a crew of people didn't leave. It was Jim and his groupies. They decided to camp out in the entranceway to this villa that we had in Bel Air. Really an awful place, real Beverly Hills cream pie. Some woman had built this very feminine mansion, and the entranceway was a grandiose hall, with a massive chandelier, which I hated. I hated the place, but I was sharing it with a bunch of guys, and it was a good place to office out of. So I'd leave in the morning, and step by Jim's thin, half-naked body, black leather pants and this thin naked body and this group of girls. I'd step over them on the way out, I'd come home in the evening and they'd still be there. And this went on for days. On several occasions I said, "Just leave," and they didn't. So I went up and got the gun. I put one round in the chamber and came downstairs and I took the gunman's stance, legs apart, double hold, pulled back the hammer. Their ears perked up, they stood up. And it went click! Jim looked at these girls and went, "See, he's only joking." I spun the cylinder and went squeeze, click! and Jim said, "I told you, no problem," and they started sliding down the wall. I spun it again, squeeze, click! nothing. By this time their asses were on the floor. I went squeeze, click! again, and—POWWWW! I mean, like, the noise was horrendous. And a bullet went winging through the air, through the chandelier, didn't bring it down, but it chipped a few parts and spread glass all over the floor. And the bullet ricocheted around the room upstairs about five times and then disappeared through the roof. And they took off like a squadron of terrified bats! Desert bats in the night!

DAVID ANDERLE: One night Jim called me up and said, "I want to do a blues record." That's all he kept talking about. So I got hold of John Haeny, and without Jac and Rothchild and the other Doors knowing, we went in a couple of nights after hours and did this tape. Just Jim, playing piano, on which he was very bad, sketching some things. The sessions were fun and great, and the hanging out was great. Some of the most fun times I've had in the studio. When we finished, which was not real late, we went back to his house, and he walked in and said to Pam, "Hi, honey," and gave her a big hug and a kiss. He went upstairs and Pam said, "I just wish it could always be like this. He's doing what he wants to do musically, and he's with people who aren't putting pressure on him."

Then another day he came around the office, sort of the end of the day, and we got into a particularly good conversation about German theater, Brecht and Weill, which he knew all about. It was getting to be evening, and he said, "Let's go get something to eat," so we went to Casa Cugat. We had dinner, and he started drinking, beer and a little tequila, and he started changing a little bit. Then he said, "Let's go to the Whisky."

Elmer Valentine always had this special booth for Jim when he came in. If there were people sitting in the booth, he'd have them move. It was in the farthest corner, with no one at your back, and it's also where everyone had to pass by. So Jim and I were in that booth, and now we're starting to drink, and I'm into the show—it was a black act, Sam and Dave or someone—I'm into the audience, people are coming up, the girls are all over Jim.

And all of a sudden he is, like, gone. He is standing on the table and yelling, "Niggers! Fucking niggers can't sing! I can sing the blues better than you!" Thank God the music is loud. I grab him by the pants to try to get him seated, and I look up, and he's looking down at me, and it's the first time I ever encountered a schizophrenic, where a person's face actually physically transformed. Jim as a guy was so calm and soft-speaking, very gentle deep voice, beautiful eyes, very sweet face. But this was the Devil. Chiseled face, maddened eyes. Just hate coming out of that face, hatred. He resembled physically no one that I knew. I had no idea who that person was, and he had no idea who I was. In the truest sense, this was not just a guy who's blind drunk, but a person who actually went through a physical metamorphosis and became someone else.

I'd never been so scared. I just got up from the booth and split. I wasn't going to get killed for some guy I didn't know, this devil, this demon.

PAUL ROTHCHILD: Jim conjured—for his mad orgies with his cronies down in Mexico, or with a single individual, a girl who's been totally scarred by fire, head to foot, and he finds a day of great fascination with her. He does that also with the blues, where he looks into blues literature and tries to conjure up the darkness and the passion.

When exploring the underworld, sometimes you succeed in conjuring up the devil. And once you do, it's very hard to control the madness that such a conjure brings. Jim did that many times. He would conjure the dark forces and get swallowed by them.

But then again, that's what he wanted. He found that interesting. It's what he sought, really.

JAC: In March of 1969, Jim conjured the ultimate Morrison out-of-control experience. The word came that he had exposed himself in full view of a concert audience in Miami.

RAY MANZAREK: It was the first time we ever played in the South.

BILL SIDDONS: Our basic policy was not to work more than three days in a row, because by the third day Jim was pretty out of control. Miami was the first date.

JAC: If someone wanted to construct a bad scene, you could use this occasion as the template. I wasn't there, but I heard about it in infinite and intimate detail from people who were. The concert was in the Dinner Key Auditorium, a converted Pan Am hangar—

VINCE TREANOR:—An abandoned building. Dry-rotted, grayed-out, rickety, a concrete floor, and a wretched smell, the most godawful stench. It had been used by derelicts in every possible way for quite some time. A cesspool. They literally had to hose it out.

JAC: Bill Siddons said it was supposed to hold about eight thousand, and that was the agreed-upon limit negotiated with the promoter, but there were close to double that number. And no seats. It was hot, stinking, overcrowded, packed to the rafters and beyond. The promoter was ripping off the band and the audience. Bill had to get into it with him about the gate, the ticketing, the percentages—

BILL SIDDONS:—A promoter who was insane himself, and his karate brother who was threatening everybody with karate moves. I had my own security force, a number of black gentlemen out of Philadelphia, a former detective and all the people he used to arrest, and he is offering me that if I want anything done to the promoter he's got some friends, and he gives me an Italian name that I won't mention.

JAC: And all this is before the concert even started. Morrison turned up very late and very drunk, and then didn't want to sing. I heard the tape, and it is Jim rapping and ranting—about revolution, about needing love, someone to love his ass, alternately with the crowd being slaves, fucking idiots. He wants action. He says there are no laws. He taunts people to join him on stage.

VINCE TREANOR: There was a guy holding a lamb who jumped up on stage. Somebody else jumped up and poured champagne on Jim. Jim took his shirt off because he was soaking wet. He shouts, "Let's see a little skin! Let's get naked!" And clothes started to come off, shirts over the head and bras being thrown up.

JAC: On the tape Jim is taunting and provoking, shouting, crescendo. Now he says the crowd hasn't come for music, they want something more—they want to see his cock. The crowd goes wild.

RAY MANZAREK: It was like a beast—Wheeeuuuggghhh! Growwwlll! Some girls were screaming, "No! No!" Other girls were screaming, "Yes! Yes!"

JAC: Where had this come from? And why this night?

RAY MANZAREK: The week before, in LA, Jim had seen the Living Theater, Julian Beck and Judith Malina's group, every performance. They stripped right down, they were doing all kinds of stuff: "I'm not allowed to walk naked if I want to, I'm not allowed to travel without a passport." That sort of thing, and they did it brilliantly—

BILL SIDDONS:—Running through the audience, yelling things into your face. "I am not allowed to smoke marijuana!" They'd say that twenty or thirty times, and then they'd go, "I'm not allowed to expose my breasts!" and women would start taking their tops off in the audience. Jim was profoundly affected by how into the moment this brought people. It probably best reflected what Jim was really all about. From the time I knew him, he did things to provoke people, because he felt that's when they were most real.

RAY MANZAREK: Jim was doing his own mini-version of the Living Theater in the Dinner Key Auditorium. But he hadn't told the Doors. We had no idea what he was going to do. All we knew was that he was late to the gig, and we're in Miami, and he starts taking his clothes off.

JAC: But did he or didn't he expose himself? If it had happened it would have been a sight to remember.

BRUCE BOTNICK: The Great White Shaft.

RAY MANZAREK: The sheer heft! An avenger! A terrible object! The destroyer!

JAC: But no one with the best viewing angle actually saw the weapon being brandished. No one backstage. And no one on stage—not Ray, not Robby, not John.

VINCE TREANOR: Ray said, "Vince, Vince, don't let him take his pants down!" I came up behind Jim and put my fingers into his belt loops and tweaked, making his pants tight, so he couldn't unbuckle them or unsnap them if he was going to. I put my elbows on my hips and lifted his pants up. I think I lifted his pants hard enough so that he was choking on his whatzit down there. If he ever reached down there and pulled the thing out, that's a pretty long haul to pull it up over his pants when they're tucked up under your chin. I had him. I was literally curling him by his pants. Whether he opened his belt or not, whether he opened his fly or not, doesn't make any difference.

PAUL ROTHCHILD: With all those instamatic cameras, there's not one photograph.

VINCE TREANOR: Absolutely no pictures of any whimwham being seen.

PAUL ROTHCHILD: I think he created a mass hallucination. I'm sure he was making lewd moves. That was Jim. I think people chose to believe they saw what they didn't see.

JAC: With cops by the dozen all around, the show is not stopped, it lurches on. Jim continues to shout to the crowd to come up on stage. It turns into a mob scene.

VINCE TREANOR: The stage starts to collapse, the whole right rear quarter of it starts to come down, amplifiers are falling backwards, and we're talking about nearly a ton of amplifiers on each side of the stage. Plus one quarter of John's drum platform is on the collapsing side of the stage. The police start screaming to clear the hall.

JAC: The promoter's karate brother throws Jim off the stage—

VINCE TREANOR:—Stiff-armed him right off the platform.

JAC: Jim lands OK—that amazing physical control in the midst of chaos—and he snake-dances out, the crowd now transformed into Eve's serpent, following after him.

VINCE TREANOR: When the place is empty, people move in to start cleaning up. When they finished picking up the clothes there was a pile, my guess, twelve to sixteen feet in diameter and nearly six feet high with no wearers. Panties, bras, jockstraps, swimming suits, boys' underwear of every size, color and description, pants, dresses, shirts, jackets, shoes, socks, stockings, garters.

What did those kids wear home? How do you explain to Mom when you walk in without any pants or a dress?

JAC: Later, Jim said two things that were classic Morrison. First, he said he didn't remember even being in Miami. Second, when Pam asked him whether or not he did it, he leaned over and whispered, "You really want to know?" Pam nodded yes. Jim replied, wearing his sheepish, little boy look, "I did it." Why? "I wanted to see how it looked in the spotlight."

BILL SIDDONS: They issued an arrest warrant, a fugitive warrant for Jim.

JAC: Lewd and lascivious behavior, a felony. And five misdemeanors—one count of public drunkenness, two of public profanity, and two for indecent exposure, which always confused me since I thought he had only one set of genitals.

JACLYN EASTON: When Jim came to the house, I refused to come out of my room. My mother didn't know why I wouldn't come out and say hello, and I couldn't tell her why. I was afraid that Jim was going to pull his pants down.

Jim Morrison

PAUL ROTHCHILD: There were several ages of Jim, from the time I met him. And each one of them seems like a creation, a character that Jim seemed to actively create and manipulate in his exploration of the human soul—his experiments into the lowest common denominator, the wild edge of life. He was a driven person. He created these personae to explore places where you and I wouldn't go.

I think Miami freed him in a way: "I give my notice that this is not my medium and I'm bailing out." It took him a year and a half, two years to pull free, but in the old theatrical sense that moment was the denouement for Jim as a rock star. He broke the mold he himself had cast. He killed his James Dean.

JAC: A black cloud descended over the Doors. I felt badly for the boys, Bill Siddons, the many who adored Jim and for the people at Elektra who had worked so hard. The Doors were smart enough to know that most artists have a success cycle which is time-limited. You do as well as you can for as long as you can. An artist can influence his own cycle for good or bad. Jim had made this wrenching, violent move for reasons I'm not sure even he himself knew, although I thought that down deep it all made some kind of sense to him. Jim was now in another world. He had separated from the rest of us because he had to. We would survive, and I was certain that Miami wouldn't stop the group from recording, but the future certainly looked dark. Melancholy was the mood of the day.

PAUL ROTHCHILD: Promoters all over the country were canceling their shows as fast as the Doors could answer the telephone.

ROBBY KRIEGER: All the hall managers were alerted to us nasty boys.

VINCE TREANOR: We were the polluted, we were the untouchables, contagious.

JAC: And in the middle of all the confusion, the Doors were scheduled to go into the studio for their next album.

BRUCE BOTNICK: As Elektra started to grow, and there was not now just ten, twenty people, it was getting up into the hundred-plus, Jac couldn't spend the time with the artists that he used to, the real creative time. And Paul would get into a very protective mode with the Doors, because as Morrison got more out of control, Paul became the Doors in some respect. You have to understand, we made six Doors albums in a two-and-a-half year period. Very, very prodigious. And during the whole time with the Doors, Paul was the ringmaster of the circus, because we had every band known in the Sixties coming to the sessions, and everybody was getting high, everybody was juiced, it was a circus all the time. When I look back on it, it's amazing we made any records at all, and the only thing I can say about it is that I wasn't wrecked and Paul wasn't wrecked. Paul always had a very good viewpoint, he could stand aside from it, but he knew that without him there would be no records.

"Soft Parade" was a very, very tough album. We were going through hell. Jim was all over the place, and until that court thing in Miami was settled there was a real pall, a real lack of focus.

Paul was doing his best to keep the whole thing from drowning. We didn't have all the material that we wanted, and Paul, trying to make a better album, decided it was time to add horns and strings. I disagreed with the tack he was taking. I didn't feel it was true to the Doors. I had pretty heavy arguments with him.

And I remember on one of Jac's visits to LA, he and Paul got into a huge battle about concept.

JAC: I wanted to stick with the clean Doors sound as much as possible.

BRUCE BOTNCK: Paul's position was, "This is all I have, and so I have do something to make these songs work, and this is what I'm going do. You don't like it? That's tough. You want a record? You've got to let me finish it my way. If not, no record." I'd never seen Jac lose his cool before, but they got into a screaming argument. Nobody won.

JAC: "Soft Parade" is released in July 1969, goes gold, and the single, 'Touch Me,' with its horns blaring, shoots to the top of the charts.

Chapter 20
Cross-continental corporate commotions of 1969 ...
Uriah Heep and a dead mackerel ...
From Woodstock to Altamont ...
And a moment with Charles Manson

JAC: From the fall of 1968 onward, there were seismic rumblings at Elektra on both coasts, East and West. A commotion began in January 1969 at the New York office, which could not contain both Danny Fields and Bill Harvey.

DANNY FIELDS: Harvey was very strong, very mean, and he was cagey, crafty and cunning. He hated me and he wanted any excuse to have me out of there. There was a certain rumor going round the office that concerned him. Somehow it got back to Harvey. I didn't start it, and it was true anyway, but he came back from lunch, drunk as usual, called me into his office, and started hitting me in the head. I ran out into the hall and he kept following me and punching me in the head. I remember the date: January 20, 1969. Richard Nixon was inaugurated that very morning, my parents were hijacked to Cuba, and I was fired, all in the same day.

JAC: Later in the year on the West Coast, I decided that it was time to let David Anderle go. It was painful, and very complicated emotionally. David had done fine and subtle work and had helped greatly to burnish Elektra's glow, but he so identified now with the artists that his company perspective was lost. What an artist believes is good for them is not necessarily gospel, nor even always in their own best interests. David had trouble sorting this out and keeping me informed. He withdrew into himself, which was not going to get the job I needed done.

PAT FARALLA: I never really knew what transpired between Jac and David, and why David left. David made a funny remark once about himself being so tall and having so far to fall, should he fall. I often wondered what he meant. Was it a power struggle?

MICHAEL JAMES JACKSON: There was some jealousy on Jac's part, and some anger and egotism on David's part.

The way I saw Elektra on the West Coast, there was no way to separate a single individual out. David, Paul Rothchild, Bruce Botnick, John Haeny—they were a combination of loners and orphans, all of immense gifts, all uniquely fucked up, bound by mutual dysfunction, empowered by mutual love to achieve a common goal. There was individual fragility but communal strength and wonderful intention. Their gifts fit their gaps.

Jac wanted to be the creative source. His greatest creation was Elektra. He wore the cloak of the pioneer. Elektra's footprint was his footprint. He could say he was Elektra.

He also wanted to create a family experience. He created the environment for that to take place. He created the club, founded it, paid for it. But then in some subtle sense he wasn't invited to the party.

There was a kind of love between Jac and David. In a way Jac lived vicariously through David. You wanted Jac to be like David, you wanted the house to be complete. Jac wanted to be loved. But it was David who could sit and talk with artists, and artists on the label trusted that they were understood by David. The Stones come by and David and Jagger sit and talk for a couple of hours, where Jagger and Jac would never have talked like that.

BRUCE BOTNICK: Jac was into having open meetings with his LA staff. We'd go and have dinner down the street at the Lobster Barrel. He'd take about ten of us and we'd all sit around the table and Jac would say, "Tell me, what are you doing? How's it going? Been having any problems here?" It got to be a little too formal and stiff at times. It wasn't the Elektra gang going out and having a beer, because it started to become very divided, East Coast-West Coast. The company had its own personality on the West Coast. The West Coast was where it was all happening—we had the Doors, we had Judy Collins, and on and on. I felt there were energies within the West Coast to separate Jac out. He was the head of the company, but he wasn't here enough, and it's the old adage, if you're not here, you don't have anything to say about it.

MICHAEL JAMES JACKSON: David grew. He found his own feet. He liked the accolades, but he was uncomfortable if anything interfered with his self-perception as an artist. Elektra was growing, transitioning from small to large, yet it had to conform to the shoes Jac had made for himself. But there were musical opportunities that David wanted, and he couldn't have them because Jac didn't want them, wouldn't sign them. And enough of those things happened that you couldn't be sure if Jac was disagreeing on taste or disagreeing in order to be exerting power over David. So in a way David was caged by Jac. And the more difficult things were between Jac and David, the more withdrawn David became. He started to shut down. The last six months you could see this.

JAC: For all David's outward suavity and cool, he ate away at his own insides. A metaphor: In aviation, planes are equipped with a self-lubricating vacuum pump that powers the critical "blind flying" directional gyro and attitude indicator. These instruments lubricate themselves by very slowly eroding the material of the pump itself, and after a while it fails. David was like that pump—he took the day-to-day difficulties of the business and internalized them until he ran out of the substance needed to continue.

DAVID ANDERLE: I was hanging a lot, very much into the scene. I didn't want to come to the office every day. I didn't want to be responsible. And I was really loving producing—Delaney & Bonnie, the Bread demo, and I did a demo of Santana, which Jac at that time didn't get, didn't hear the rock and the Latin. I wanted to be an artist and a producer and go out. With all that, I was probably getting a bit sloppy around the office.

Jac summons me to New York. I go to his office and he fires me, tells me it's over and he's letting me go, and I remember being totally awestruck at how clean his desk was. How can a guy know so much, get so much business done, and have a desk as clean as that? There I was, sitting getting fired and just being awed by his desk.

I was sort of expecting it, in fact I was sort of wanting it, because I wanted to get on with my life and I didn't know how I was possibly going to leave Elektra. So that was OK. Then he said, "Let's go have lunch." We had a great time. Driving back to the office, he says, "Maybe you shouldn't leave." Because he remembered how much fun we had with each other, how much we liked each other. But he did exactly the right thing. It was definitely time, time for me. I said, "No, you fired me, I'm gonna stay fired, thanks."

JAC: Losing David was traumatic. Losing Paul Rothchild was even worse.

Paul had contributed enormously to the company. If you review the Elektra catalog, he was responsible as producer for a significant percentage of our early Sixties releases. He kept Jim Morrison on track, and delivered five gold or platinum Doors albums. All by itself that was a mountainous accomplishment and Paul carried a big work load on top of it.

I paid him a generous salary plus a producer's percentage, the standard two percent of the late Sixties. But it was Paul's sense that he wasn't sufficiently rewarded.

JOHN HAENY: Jac and Rothchild had an ongoing fight about money, Rothchild acting it out, picking on Jac in little ways, Jac picking back. They're standing in the doorway fighting and Jac stops the fight. "Paul," he says, "what is it that you want?" Paul says, "Jac, I want a million dollars." And Jac, instantly, very quiet, very gentle, very reflective, looks at Paul and says, "It's not enough, Paul. It's not enough." Classic. Embedded in that is a more profound thought, that the reality of life is that it isn't about money. When you don't have money it's about money, but when you've got money you realize it isn't about money, it's about making peace with life on an entirely different level.

JAC: After Paul's first two years at Elektra I had given him unparalleled freedom to record pretty much whatever he liked, subject only to my reasonable review. He never had absolute signing authority, even though he thought he did—I was too careful and probably too controlling to ever let that happen.

If I was dead set against an act, knowing deep in my gut it was a mistake, then Paul usually backed off. If I was ambivalent, Paul got to record it anyway—for example, Rhinoceros, a Rothchild-confected supergroup.

JANN WENNER: It was the heavy rock period, and everybody was losing their brains over supergroups.

JAC: Rhinoceros showed promise on paper but couldn't make it work in the studio. Like its namesake, the group was ponderous, and no amount of prodding or pushing or retakes was going to bring the ignition of life to a band that, despite flashes of brilliance, was a put-up job to begin with.

The blowup came over a much less consequential group than Rhinoceros. In fact, for the life of me I can't even remember their name. Paul insisted on signing them. Many superb producers are magical with bands assigned to them but that doesn't make them great A&R men. Paul's work with the Doors and others was brilliant, but he never signed a major act, Butterfield excepted. He fired blanks with Clear Light, Ars Nova and Rhinoceros—all ambitious signings of his—and I thought that the band he wanted now was not worth having on the label. I stood on my judgment, Paul stood on his dignity. For him it was a matter of principle. I wanted him to concede in this one instance. Normally, in the give and take of our relationship, it wouldn't have been a problem. But Paul was now a star, courted by other companies and with the usual gaggle of lawyers whispering sweet temptation into his ear. This ridiculous brouhaha between us led to him going.

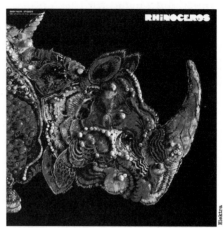

"Rhinoceros" ... an early supergroup

PAUL ROTHCHILD: Supposedly I could sign anything I wanted, as long as it lived up to Jac's conditions of being able to sell enough copies. Maybe only two or three albums that I've ever made haven't at least paid for themselves. Jac and I came to loggerheads over this one. Jac really dug in his heels and said, "No way." I said, "Are you breaking your promise?" He said, "You've got to give me this one, Paul." And I was so full of myself with my success that I wouldn't let it go.

The conversation got more and more heated, and finally Jac turned to Larry Harris. He says, "Larry, what should I do? I hate this confrontation with him. This guy's important to my company." And Larry says, "Let him go. You don't need producers any more. The bands will produce themselves." I said, "You're serious, aren't you?" He said, "Oh, yes. Producers are just a drain." And that's where I leave Elektra.

The one mistake I ever saw Jac make publicly—mean it, support it, defend it, even when it was obvious it was a mistake—was Larry Harris. Jac didn't stand on the side of wrong too often or for too long. He was usually very well placed in his judgment of the future, and about people. But Larry Harris he missed cold. I hated that man from the day he came. He was Uriah Heep alive and well at Elektra Records, with the personality of a dead mackerel. More than any other single factor, Larry Harris destroyed the spirit of Elektra. He put a wedge between Jac and everybody else who had been important to Jac up to that point. He created coastal rivalries that didn't exist, caused internecine fighting. And later he took a philosophy out into the industry at large which was so deadly a virus that its effects are still being felt today—that record companies could and should be run by attorneys and accountants.

JAC: It's a great story and far more interesting than the rather bland truth, in my memory, of sitting down with Paul and Irwin Russell at Dan Tana's restaurant in Hollywood trying to resolve an A&R issue, which is what I originally thought this was. My mistake was in not understanding that the problem went far deeper, to Paul's sense of self-worth. Had I made a gesture, financial or emotional, to show how valued he really was, I think we might have worked it out.

For any proposed album, casting the right producer was my most critical A&R decision. Out of this choice came magic or mayhem. I believed in a strong core of resident staff producers and we had them: Paul, Mark Abramson, David Anderle,

Peter Siegel, Russ Miller, and engineers who could double on the job like Bruce Botnick and John Haeny. Yet as the record industry grew, we could no longer maintain enough staff producers to handle the wide variety of music that presented itself. With more artists and different genres of music, we began to reach outside, the way a director would be selected for a film project. What had happened in film, with the shift in emphasis at the major studios from studio system to freelance, was now showing up in music. Producers found artists and became attached to the project. Though I wasn't necessarily thrilled with these structural changes, I recognized their inevitability and tried to work with them.

Paul's take on Larry is a catalog of frustrations and observations that he had accumulated over time and he tossed those, in his own mind, onto the small blaze already smoldering about the right to unilaterally sign acts. That having been said, his evaluation of Larry is shared by many, if not most, of the Elektra staff. Once Larry himself had gone, I agreed.

Paul had a great career, as he deserved to. He was a prodigious talent. As an independent he produced records that remain classics: Janis Joplin's "Pearl," and Bonnie Raitt at her best. And Paul continued with the Doors for Elektra as an independent, receiving healthy advances and a lifetime of royalties. We remained warm and devoted friends, and in 1992 we did another album together that recalled our best days. We had fun and laughed about the past. . . and the present.

JAC: 1969 seemed to race by. In August, Woodstock seized the imagination of the entire country—the high of all Sixties highs. Looking back in time, it's hard to imagine that there were only a few months separating the biggest coming together of music, peace and love in a farmer's field in upstate New York, from Altamont in December, the Rolling Stones concert at an auto race track in northern California, where Mick Jagger sang 'Sympathy For The Devil,' and in the name of security a Hell's Angel killed a member of the audience in full view of the stage and a film camera.

Not long before Altamont, at Elektra in LA we had our own brush with ultimate dreadfulness. We received a demo tape from Charles Manson.

RUSS MILLER: Elektra was a magnet for the weird. We'd have all kinds of people dropping by. The Doors were really the first punk artists, I mean they started it, and everybody was trying to copy them, and Elektra was the place where they would send this kind of music. So this guy comes in, he was representing Manson, he kept saying to me, "You gotta go to the ranch. Broads and smoke. I mean, it'd be great, you know? This guy's magnetic." I was curious, so I made a date to go out, but I had to do something with Jac that evening, and didn't.

Then the tape came to me. When I listened to it, I said, "This is crap." The worst of garage bands. It wasn't music, it was noise. All guitar noise. They were all whacking away there. It was totally violent. And soon after that the murders happened.

NINA HOLZMAN: After I don't know how many months of keeping our Mexican divorce secret, I told Jac, "You're living your life like you've always lived it, but I can't live like this, I'm going to tell people." He was very upset. So I started telling people, and together we told the children. Adam's response—he was eleven—was, "This is a joke, right?"

JAC: Simon Taub, who in the past had represented both Nina and me, urged Nina to get a California divorce because Mexican "quickies" were under scrutiny by US courts.

NINA HOLZMAN: It wasn't acrid, there weren't any fights, but there was real property involved, and I realized early on that I couldn't be negotiating with Jac, I had to let the attorney handle it.

In the depths of my gloom late in my marriage, I had this fantasy that the New Yorker would do a profile of Jac, and I would be able to tell them the real story, and it would be cathartic. But I don't have any big thing about what a terrible person Jac is, because he's not. And since then, he's always been a wonderful friend.

JAC: With Nina's decision to live in California, I no longer needed the large apartment in the Village, so I sold it and moved into something smaller and closer to the office. I was single, and record company presidents were becoming stars. We had our own groupies. A local underground newspaper assigned a piece to an "investigative reporter." Her assignment/assignation: to "get" every record company president and publish the results. I was inordinately fond of my review.

ELLEN SANDER: I was first introduced to Jac at a Judy Collins concert. Then I was in the office—I had been doing some writing for Elektra, artist bios—and Danny Fields said, "I think you're going to get a compliment. Jac really loves the last piece you did."

JAC: I admired Ellen's writing in the Saturday Review, and particularly her omnibus piece on the "Pantheon of Rock," a well-done primer for the uninitiated. And of course she had written the legendary piece on the Plaster Casters.

She invited me and some journalist friends to a private exhibition of the Plaster Casters' work. I arrived to see the reporter from Rolling Stone tape-measuring the significant dimensions of Jimi Hendrix.

Several days later Ellen phoned me about a rumor that I had a copy of the Beatles' yet-to-be-released album, "Let It Be." She was anxious, let's say desperate, to hear it. In fact I did have a master lacquer, given to David Anderle and me by Derek Taylor when we were in London at Apple Corps to discuss Delaney & Bonnie. I invited her to dinner.

ELLEN SANDER: He picked me up on his motor scooter. I was living on Third

Avenue between 35th and 36th Street, in a tiny apartment, and the doorbell was broken, the intercom wasn't working for me to talk back to him, and the elevator wouldn't come, so I had to run down the stairs, and he said, "Well, I thought you weren't home," and he was put off by that, and I tried to reassure him that I would never not be home for somebody to pick me up for a date, it was a technical problem—I was both there and not late.

JAC: Off we went to a candle-lit restaurant in the Village, one of those atmospheric places so thick with the vapor of romance and garlic that you don't even notice the marginal food.

ELLEN SANDER: Neither one of us had love on our agenda. Jac was not quite finished with his divorce from Nina, and I was very, very busy, not at all interested in keeping company with any one person. But I was curious and he was curious.

JAC: Before that evening I had no emotional interest in Ellen, but during dinner I found myself strongly attracted to her. She was beautiful, razor-sharp, full of opinions, and with an eclectic taste that paralleled my own.

ELLEN SANDER: And so we had a very romantic evening. I didn't taste my food. We were just talking and talking. I think we were just so overwhelmed with the attraction between us.

JAC: We scootered back to my apartment. I had promised to play her the record, and I hesitated to make any move until the promise was kept. I had a tape copy of the album cued and ready to go. I lit a few candles.

ELLEN SANDER: My memory is of walking in and he had candles lit. And it struck me, I guess he anticipated that we might be coming back here.

JAC: I rolled a joint and we settled back. When the final notes of 'Let It Be' had faded, I leaned over and kissed her.

When we awoke next morning Ellen said, "I thought it was very gentlemanly of you to wait until after I heard the album."

ELLEN SANDER: He called the office and said, "Pearl, I'm not coming in today." I heard her on the other line saying this, that, this, that, and he said, "That's all I have to say." And he hung up.

He never spent a night at my place. I kept my own apartment and my own phone number, but most of the time we spent together at his place.

We'd have dinner almost every night. And go to concerts. If it was going to be a mess we'd use the limo, but we'd go to the Fillmore East on the motor scooter, the little under-powered scooter. He got me a helmet, and we get off, and he's parking it, kicking the stand down, and a big black guy comes up and says, "Hey, man, you with the Hell's Angels?" And we both cracked up. We shared a love of music, to the same depth, certainly. One of the ways we communicated was to program tapes for each other. Jac would create these tapes, always beautifully segued, with themes weaving in and out. I started doing tapes for him as well.

Sometimes the tapes would be short. They'd be like three apologetic songs together, because we would have disagreements, or worse. I can't be dominated, I have that kind of a personality, I can't be bossed around. Although I've learned to handle it a lot better, at the time I was a raving brat, and we would come to loggerheads about things.

It usually worked out okay. Still, we had what could probably be characterized as a tumultuous relationship. We were very passionate about each other, we were very passionate about our own opinions, and we would have the clash of the titans. Off the scale. Especially on my part, because I come from a family of shouters.

And I was under a great deal of pressure. There really wasn't rock journalism before me and another half dozen people in the mid to late Sixties started writing it. I felt that I had a message to bring, more than a once-over-lightly on the product: it was the phenomenology of the politics and lifestyle changes that were opening up in the Sixties. And I had a lot of pressure from my contemporaries, none of whom liked me very much, and I always felt under pressure to perform. That was the load I was carrying for myself, in my early twenties, feeling terribly inexperienced and under-qualified, but having a great deal of feeling and certainty, too.

I tried to keep my own identity, but it was difficult. Jac was under a lot of pressure also and he was obviously working at a much higher level as far as the power he was dealing with, and even though I knew he admired my work, I felt that sometimes he belittled my work as well.

And of course I was the junior member by thirteen or fourteen years. It was a new experience. I didn't have that many relationships. I had married when I was nineteen or twenty, it lasted ten months, and I never knew what went wrong, so I was frightened to be in another relationship. But it wasn't as if I had a choice. I was very in love with Jac. He was my hero.

Chapter 21

Let the Synanon games begin ...
Encountering the self and other startlements ...
Kandy, Sandy and Stacy Keach

MARK ABRAMSON: I was very interested in alternative lifestyles, the idea of the Woodstock nation, talking it up a lot. There were enough of us who were thinking of that, and we met. I did an introduction: "Why don't we live communally? We have a lot of talent in this room, lots of energy, we've even got lots of money, we're all very successful, we've been there, so let's think of what else we can do with our lives." We went around the room, and everybody had an entirely different idea of what they wanted to do. Including, "I don't want to belong to any kind of group," or "I don't want to do anything," from "We should be politically active, support Chavez's grape strike," to "Let's go away and buy four hundred acres and make our whole commitment." Totally chaotic, and I'm pissed, because I had a very specific idea in mind. One person wrote me a letter saying she was very upset: "Why can't we be more politically active, why can't we help other people, why are we so selfish? In this age, when we really need to help each other, and black people are struggling for their lives, and the poor migrant workers, et cetera, and all you want to do is go off and live off the land and probably off those people." A typical late Sixties letter. Very disturbing.

So we decide to have another meeting, just for the people who are interested in alternative lifestyles, so we can be focused.

It's in Judy Collins's living room on West End Avenue, packed, there's got to be thirty people in the room, most of them people I've never seen before.

JUDY COLLINS: Here we were, this kind of upwardly mobile jumble of creative folks, mostly Upper West Side.

MARK ABRAMSON: And two very good-looking black guys with scarves around their necks. Very different from the rest of us, who were sniveling Jews and New York WASPs from the prairies and New England.

JUDY COLLINS: They were from Phoenix House, the drug rehabilitation center. I met them through Nancy and Tom Hoving. The Hovings had me to dinner, and there was this big articulate black man, Kandy Latson, who had escaped from Synanon.

MARK ABRAMSON: Synanon was a famous drug program in California which became a cult. The founder of it went on that kind of cult power trip. Dangerous. Guns all round, nobody leaves. These two guys, Kandy Latson and Sandy Jackson, escape at two in the morning. They come to New York, to Phoenix House, and start running programs there.

JUDY COLLINS: Nancy Hoving became friendly with Kandy. At dinner I told him—this big, articulate, sober man—that my friends and I, including Mark

Abramson and his wonderful wife Janet, were talking about buying some land together. He said, "Well, you wouldn't dream of doing anything like that without encountering each other." I said, "What on earth is that?" and invited him to the meeting, and Sandy came too.

MARK ABRAMSON: So I'm saying, "We're all here for the same thing." But somebody said, "Wait a minute, let's be democratic, why don't we go around the room and everybody say what they're interested in." And it's chaotic again. Even the people who were into alternative lifestyles at the first meeting were now not into alternative lifestyles at all; I was the only one.

It got around to these two black guys, and Kandy said, "I've never seen people so untogether. I heard you was comin' here to do somethin' real specific, and you're all over the place. You need to get it together. What you people need is encounter. You need to play the Synanon Game."

The Synanon Game—what the hell was that? There was something about the way these guys talked. Kandy was extremely good-looking, charismatic. People started asking them questions. They said, "Well, we don't want to tell you too much about it, it's the game, the Synanon Game. You get yourselves together, and what you want to do, you do it." It sounded really good. They said, "We'll have a group. And we'll run it, and you pay us, if that's what you want to do, because we're available and we'll be glad to do it."

A bunch of us said, "They're right. We're all over the place. Maybe that's what we should try."

A few weeks later we show up at somebody's apartment, to do this encounter group. Didn't know anything about it, scared to death. After that it was once a week.

JUDY COLLINS: It was a moveable feast, a different person's apartment every time.

MARK ABRAMSON: And different people would come and go. And then a lot more people came in. All kinds of people. Psychiatrists. You never knew who was going to show up.

Many were related outside the group. A lot of musicians, Judy's friends, people who worked for Judy, Judy's boyfriend at the time, Stacy Keach.

And eventually Jac. It had been going several months. Jac had been circling this interesting behavior, the way he did with drugs. He would ask us questions about the group. I think he was intrigued by it.

I remember talking to Judy: "Wouldn't the group be good for Jac? But would Jac be good for the group?" I was a little doubtful. I think Judy was positive that he should be included.

ELLEN SANDER: With me, Jac would go into the depth of our relationship to try to examine the power of the love we had, because he would feel so entirely different and at peace in a way that he told me he hadn't found before, and he was curious to understand the phenomenology of that. That's just the way his mind works. Everything has a technical reason which he theoretically can master. Maybe that's the dynamics of his searching. We're all searching for the mysteries of life and happiness and he apparently felt that it was a set of skills he could master, which on one level it is. On the other level, if you're going to have the authority in every situation that you're involved in, it's rather difficult to get to the central importance of interpersonal things. So that was always a dilemma.

Jac always had the authority in any situation in which he was involved. That was the basis for all of his relationships that I observed. Except ours, from time to time. It could be just very simple things, like, "I'm paying this person a lot of money. Does he really like me?" But as soon as Jac met this person and liked this person and admired this person, he would establish a relationship where he was in authority.

He wanted the depth of experience, but it was difficult for him to be vulnerable. Those two things competed and it puzzled him. Even though he would set up the situations, he would be puzzled about how people were responding to him.

JAC: Ellen is right. I was "in authority" in my relationships and preferred the safety of my chosen position, but at the same time I was aware that in shaping my interactions with people to such a model I was probably missing out on the juice of life.

When I was growing up, my parents routinely held up to me, as a paragon of ideal behavior, Zev Putterman, the son of the cantor at Park Avenue Synagogue. My mother would say in exasperation, "Why can't you be more like Zev?" Years later Zev got strung out on heroin, then found his way back through the Synanon Game. Zev was concrete evidence that encounter worked. On that basis alone I was intrigued. So I decided to try it.

My pace had been so frenetic that I was running ahead of who I was deep inside. In the small hours when there is no place to hide, I felt a big empty space at my core, rather like a partially inflated Macy's parade balloon that would have trouble staying aloft because it was not filled with its own authentic helium. For the first time I was really willing to look at my life.

ELLEN SANDER: Jac got me involved in the group. At first I flat out refused. I didn't like the sound of it. I was busy, I needed my time for more productive things. But when he kept saying it was very important for him . . . well, nobody wins many arguments with Jac. If something is important to him, he has a way of making it happen. So I eventually did join. Or I came to meetings. I never quite admitted that I joined. But I came to meetings in deference to him.

At the very first meeting, Judy attacked Jac, saying that she didn't think it was right that he make more money out of her records than she did. Which I thought was grossly unfair, to get him into that kind of a situation. She wanted to negotiate on a business level, but she was sitting in with it on an emotional level when he was trying to make himself emotionally available, with which he always had a difficult time.

MEL POSNER: Jac and Judy being in the same group therapy thing, it was insane.

JAC: I remember Stacy Keach, with the full force of his actor's intensity, assaulting me for not taking good enough care of Judy. That wasn't something to be argued out in front of people who had no direct involvement and didn't live the dynamic. I had two options; either scream at Stacy myself, or recognize that this was Stacy

Keach the actor doing Stacy Keach. And why did the group leaders allow professional performers to act out in an encounter group anyway? They had the skill to intimidate and few of us were capable of handling that. To attack could look synonymous with telling the truth, but it wasn't necessarily so.

JUDY COLLINS: I think it was a painful time for Jac. I don't think he had a lot of experience with people sitting around and being forthright with one another, and the kind of forthright that was happening was just very painful.

JAC: I was scared and vulnerable, but I stuck it out and learned—for one thing, learned to keep quiet, which was hard for me.

MARK ABRAMSON: The interesting thing was how many people had issues with Jac, over all kinds of stuff.

ELLEN SANDER: "Why do you think you're different than we are, Jac? Just because you have money?" People would say things like that to him. Or he would try to express some area of difficulty, and people would scoff at him: "Oh, you don't have any problems."

JAC: I felt like some poor little Japanese soldier hiding in his cave near the end of the war, emerging into the light and being vaporized by flame throwers. First the light, then zap!

BILL HARVEY: Apparently they ripped him up and down and really tore him apart.

JAC: After the first session, it felt like I had reached down my throat, grabbed my asshole and pulled myself inside out.

BILL HARVEY: He comes into my office and sits down, and he is visibly shaken: "Boy, they really said some terrible things about me." And I said, "For Christ's sake, what are you listening to that shit for? Look at you. Look at where you are. You're so far ahead of them it's not even funny. You're just somebody to shoot at, that's all. When you're on the top, they shoot at you." That made him feel a lot better.

JUDY COLLINS: Of course there was hostility. Under the guise of honestly revealing how we feel about each other, let's not pull any punches. If we are going to be revealing, let's also be, if it strikes our fancy, not just honest but mean.

MARK ABRAMSON: To see Jac be in the group and not be in the group was quite extraordinary. I think it highlighted that interpersonal—I don't know if it's an empathic lack. Judy and I would say, "OK, Jac, what's the problem? Why do we get into friction? Why is there somehow this feeling of discomfort?" And Jac says, "Whatever you want to do, that's fine." He would never cop to anything. It was very difficult to get him to open up about anything of his own. There was a lot of emotion, people would get very upset, people would cry in there, and Jac was still a closed book.

ELLEN SANDER: I remember Mark once saying to Jac, "I want to thank you, but I never think that I can. You've done so much for me, I want to tell you how much I love you and how grateful I am." And Jac withdrew from that. I'm sure it meant a lot to him, because I know how he loved Mark. I think that's maybe what he always wanted from Mark, but he didn't know how to respond. He didn't know how to handle that.

In the middle of this group time, Jac's father was dying. He had a stroke, and Jac was terrified. He would go to see his father in this condition, and he'd never take me, and he'd come home devastated—to know that he was losing his father without any possibility of reconciling. He used to weep. And he'd say, "I don't want to die like that." It frightened him.

Maybe that was one reason why Jac was in the group. But in the group he never said a word about it. To this day I don't really know why he was involved in that group, except that Jac was always searching.

Chapter 22

Overture to a competitor ...
The seductive smile of the conglomerateur ...
The eminently bearable elegance of
the executive dining room

JAC: What was I searching for at Elektra? I was at a point where I was looking for changes of substance and nuance at the label, and in my relationship to this new music business world in which we were now living.

At Atlantic, Ahmet and Nesuhi Ertegun and Jerry Wexler were a formidable threesome that worked smoothly together. I had always been a one-man band. But what if I took in somebody at my level? And if I did, who might that be? What about Clive Davis?

Clive was up from the streets, had earned his way into Harvard law school, then had done scut work for Columbia at an outside law firm. That was when we met and became friendly. He moved in-house, became Columbia's general counsel, and rose to be head of CBS Records.

Clive very smoothly took the reins of that large company machine from Goddard Lieberson, a record business deity known as God, revered for his lordly charm and his unerring taste—in one of his memorable coups, God decided that he would not only record the original cast album of a new Broadway musical but would also pick up the entire stage production investment of four hundred thousand dollars. The show was "My Fair Lady."

As for Clive, I never saw an attorney take so naturally to the music business. He had an insatiable curiosity, wanting to learn everything, quick to ask questions. The consummate student. At Monterey Pop he carried a portable radio tuned to Top 40, even taking it into the bathroom. His appetite for music was unquenchable.

By 1969 Clive was in full sail at Columbia. He looked good because he was good, and he had something that none of us at Elektra had: the experience of running a major label with all the resources of one of the best-staffed, most aggressive companies, with superb marketing, distribution and their own pressing facilities. If Clive could be persuaded to come to Elektra,

Holzman Family Archive

Clive Davis, Nina Holzman and Jac 1967

he would bring a proven ability to do the job. He knew the terrain. I expected that he would carry some of his best people with him, and I could see him making Elektra work even better.

Clive's style wasn't quite mine. Corporately, his style was, "I am the company." My manner was more, "We are the company." Musically, if I could summarize the difference between us in one sentence, it would be: I exercised taste first, then judgment; Clive exercised judgment first, then taste. No matter, it worked. He had a formidable pop song sense.

Clive was unhappy and surprisingly open about his compensation package at Columbia, so I approached him about coming to Elektra. We had dinner and discussed it in detail. I offered him a thirty percent stake over time and the opportunity to work in tandem, to merge our strengths. He thought about it but eventually declined. I think he was reluctant and perhaps wary of taking on a boutique label without the deep infrastructure of a CBS. Later he went on to do exactly that at Arista, but in 1969 he wasn't ready.

JAC: If I couldn't have Clive, I didn't want anyone else. Yet, the way the record business was developing, Elektra was going to have to change with it.

For years I had observed the parallels between motion pictures and records. Every major change that occurred in the record business was foretold through the evolution of the movie business: vertical and horizontal integration, consolidation of distribution, consolidation of exhibition (in the record business, read "retail"), offsite production, independent companies, and the rise of a new generation of packagers and gatekeepers, the producers, agents and lawyers.

A record selling in the hundreds of thousands was once a very big deal; now some were selling millions. Those numbers attracted the money-driven wanting in on the action.

Film was the old royalty; music was becoming the new royalty. The songs of the counter-culture had endowed music with a deeper resonance. Movie stars began hanging out with rock stars. And lawyers representing rock artists began to move on a level equivalent to the film entertainment lawyers—they became very powerful.

At Elektra we had been having a great run up to the end of the Sixties, showing higher profits in relations to our revenues than any other record company. If we were selling ten million dollars worth of records, we were making two and a half millions dollars, or twenty-five percent. That was serious money. We were doing very well, and so were our artists.

Regardless of how well we had done our job, the artists—and equally or more their managers and lawyers—were primarily interested in maximizing their profitability, and who could blame them.

The rub came when lawyers attempted to insinuate themselves, busting up existing arrangements if they thought they could hijack an artist and bring that artist to a situation that promised better money. Lawyers approached Elektra artists, offering to get them out of their contracts with us, spinning tales of million-dollar advances from a major label, less their cut, of course. It was unethical, time-consuming and personally painful. It was a venality I had never seen before.

DAVID BRAUN: I don't think Jac relished that. Jac was not the kind of guy who would pay you five million for an artist. First of all, I don't think he'd want to pay that kind of money. Because it was his own money. It's different when you're paying with CBS's money. Secondly, I think Jac's ego wouldn't go for it: "Why spend five million? I'd rather develop two hundred acts for the five million, and knowing my track record, half of them will work out." I think that was part of it too.

You see it in Michael Eisner at Disney, who's very much like Jac. Eisner does not pay the best salaries in town, but he gets the best product. He picks young people who are good, makes them into great executives, never overpays anybody. Jac was very much like that. Jac and Eisner really resemble each other a great deal.

Now, you wouldn't go to Jac with every artist. If you had a tonnage rock act, you'd go to Columbia and get big money and more royalties. If you didn't need a relationship with the company, you didn't go to Jac. And towards the late Sixties and early Seventies, the feeling developed among artists that all record companies were the same, it didn't make any difference with whom you went, they only wanted the money.

JAC: Each of the aggressive labels handled contracts and business affairs in a way that reflected their management style. Columbia was rigid. Mo Ostin and Warner Bros. rightly considered themselves an artist-oriented company, and whatever the artist wanted, within reason, the artist got. Elektra was somewhere in between, leaning toward Warners. From a legal standpoint, we did not want to have to go to an artist for every clearance, the withholding of which might later be used as leverage to stall the release of an album. This could be a negotiating ploy for something having nothing to do with the matter at hand. Yet we were always considerate of our artists, because I didn't want niggling discussions that didn't address my main concerns: the music and their career.

DAVID BRAUN: Jac's strength was the personal touch he offered the artist, selecting material and helping develop a career and being a kind of father.

JAC: Recording contracts were becoming terribly burdensome in their complexity. We might send a short amendment letter on some issue and the reply would be longer than the document submitted.

I liked simple, direct deals, but our simple, neat document was being obsoleted by the complexities of the brave new music world. And the more complex the negotiation, the more the artist was charged by the lawyer—and guess who was going to pay for it eventually?

And it slowed the process. Once, there had been a relatively clear road you traveled. Now you had to jump high hurdles daily.

Sue Roberts, our head of business affairs, kept special files, arranged by lawyer, containing detailed notes of the clauses they would or would not accept in their contracts. We knew not to present a draft that contained the "offending" language. This was just one symptom of a larger change. The MUSIC business—which was where I had started out and where I was happiest—was becoming the music BUSINESS.

JAC: Elektra was not one of the majors. We were a small, feisty company that had gotten bigger, and along the way we ran up against a problem that got bigger as we did: distribution.

I had identified distribution as a critical gating issue as early as 1963. By the end of the Sixties it had become a matter of survival, a choke point.

With independent distribution we had three customers—the distributor, the record retailer, and the individual record buyer, and we didn't control our connection to two of these.

STAN CORNYN: Independent distributors, to make a buck, would represent a hundred different labels. This is tough on those labels, and whether they got paid depended on all sorts of things—

JAC:—Like how hot you were at the moment.

STAN CORNYN: There was no guarantee that you got cash flow from independent distributors.

IRWIN RUSSELL: Someone was always going out of business or merging or not paying their bills.

JAC: We had to take charge of our distribution, but I couldn't afford to do it on my own.

Here were my options. I could take Elektra public, sell stock and raise capital to fund a distribution network and invite other labels to join me. Or I could make a strategic alliance which would guarantee control over distribution.

To float a trial balloon ahead of any potential stock offering, we hired a financial publicity firm. They immediately set up a major story in the Wall Street Journal. John O'Connor followed Elektra and me for two weeks and wrote a long, detailed, and enthusiastic piece: "Making Money and Music at Elektra." It yielded what we wanted—calls from several firms interested to be underwriters.

Initially attractive as the idea of a public offering was, the more I reflected on it the more problems I saw.

Federal law requires a high level of disclosure in a document called the 10-K. The 10-K dissects your company so thoroughly that your private information and trade secrets become

Well suited to going public

public property, available to everyone—how much cash you have, your revenues and profitability, key salaries, a tabulation of your biggest-selling artists. As a person who valued his relations with talent, I didn't want to deal with disclosure that would have been grist for the lawyers.

Then there were legal liability issues. Every time the principal of a public company utters anything in an open forum, you are on the record, and if your words don't coincide with the result there is an entire bar of lawyers drooling and ready to file a class action suit.

The distribution problem was not going to be solved by going public, so I came to the conclusion that an alliance, with distribution as the driving raison d'être, was the way to go.

I wanted to avoid any liaison with a major company that would have a predisposition to do things the way they had for the past twenty years. That ruled out RCA, Decca, Capitol and perhaps CBS. On the other hand there was Warner, which didn't have that baggage or inertia. There I could participate in creating the standards and practices that would guide our future.

As early as 1966, I had talked to the then-president of Warner Bros. Records, Mike Maitland, but I didn't feel any personal chemistry, and Mike only wanted to buy Elektra, which didn't suit me. Still, there were attractive aspects to an arrangement with Warner. I knew and appreciated Mo Ostin, who was running the Reprise label under the Warner umbrella. I had met Mo socially, and we delighted in each other's company and ideas. Over the years I would send Mo notes about odd items in the catalog and he'd always write back. We became trusted friends.

Then in 1969 Warner bought Atlantic. For many years, Atlantic had been running parallel with Elektra on its own musical track. Both labels had started from nothing, along with hundreds of other small companies two decades prior. Atlantic and Elektra were the two—really the only two from that time—that had survived the early Fifties and gone from strength to strength in the Sixties. The Ertegun brothers, Ahmet and Nesuhi, and Jerry Wexler, had learned to live together. Those guys were so different from each other that I wondered how one building, one company, could contain them. But they had done it, and done it well, none better. I respected that enormously, because I knew what a difficult and opinionated one-man band I was.

Atlantic's music was blues, R & B, Muscle Shoals, the Memphis Sound, jazz, and a different approach to pop than mine, all the way to Sonny and Cher. Warner and Reprise were conventional pop, the Everly Brothers, Trini Lopez, Sammy Davis, Dean Martin, Frank Sinatra, and also, courtesy of Mo and Lenny Waronker, the Kinks, Small Faces, and Jimi Hendrix. Arlo Guthrie and Joni Mitchell were as folky as Mo got.

Add Elektra to that mix, and it could be potent—we would bring a range of musical product they lacked, from Nonesuch to the Doors. And the combined size of the alliance would make a viable distribution network.

To create and feed a distribution organization would require an annual sales volume of close to a hundred million dollars. Warner Records and Atlantic combined were doing about seventy. Elektra was doing fifteen—close enough. Elektra would represent critical mass and a differentiated but coherent catalog.

MO OSTIN: Jac and I talked again about the situation.

JAC: Mo had recently replaced Mike Maitland at Warner.

MO OSTIN: We felt exactly the same way about distribution—that for a whole host of reasons, primarily that we would have much more clout in the marketplace and sell more records, we should have our own distribution.

When Jac said he was interested in merging, I felt strongly about it. Atlantic went along. I brought it to Steve Ross and said, "I want to buy this company."

JAC: Steve was the chairman of the Kinney Corporation, which had recently acquired Warner-7 Arts. Ted Ashley had run the Ashley Famous Agency which had previously been bought by Steve, and Ted had convinced him to acquire Warner-7 Arts and their record companies. I had known Ted for years, in fact Theo Bikel and I had introduced him to one of his wives. I had never met Steve.

One day I was in Mo's office, enjoying one of our regular schmoozes. Ahmet dropped by. He said, "Steve Ross is in Ted Ashley's office." Mo grabbed me by one arm and Ahmet got me by the other, and over we went.

Steve was silver-haired, suave, and very sure of himself. He had masterfully cobbled together Kinney—a curious mix of funeral parlors, office cleaning companies, parking lots, rental cars, real estate and magazine distribution—into a small public company. With the addition of the Ashley Famous Agency he had moved into entertainment and was now sitting atop Warner Bros. and their subsidiary record companies.

**Steve Ross,
master pitchman**

Steve pressed his master salesman button and talked about his vision for Kinney (soon to be renamed Warner Communications Inc.) as a full-spectrum entertainment company with serious interests in movies, music, publishing and whatever might come out of the new technologies. My ears perked.

I talked at length about domestic and international distribution. Steve asked if I would consider an acquisition, with a continuing participation, if Warner and Atlantic would commit to the distribution model we had discussed. I candidly told Steve that being with Mo and Ahmet, Nesuhi and Jerry would give Elektra added muscle and I couldn't think of better people with whom to cast my lot. I required only two additional understandings. Elektra would function with absolute autonomy; and if there were anti-trust problems with the Justice Department, Steve would have to deal with it. Under those conditions, I would seriously consider a sale or merger.

AHMET ERTEGUN: It was the wish, not only of the corporation, and of Jac, but also on our part—Mo Ostin and Joe Smith for the Warner's side, and the three of us from the Atlantic side, myself, Nesuhi, and Jerry—for Jac to come into the group. We respected him, we admired him, we were friends. We wanted it to happen.

JAC: Steve beamed his most glowing smile and said, "We'll get right back to you." And for six months I didn't hear a word. Not a word.

JAC: There were other people sniffing around Elektra, but Warner/Atlantic were the only suitors that interested me.

Whatever was to happen in the future, I wanted the company to appear solid. This meant creating value through our catalog, backed by audited financial statements. We had been having our books certified for a number of years, which most independent record companies didn't bother with, considering it an unnecessary expense. I wanted us to look clean and look good financially, and we did.

The company also needed to look its best physically and that meant another move, out and up. Though we now occupied one and a half floors at 1865 Broadway we were badly cramped. The new Gulf & Western building, to be constructed at 15 Columbus Circle, directly across the street and with unrestricted views, seemed perfect. What I didn't realize at the time was that Charles Bluhdorn, head honcho at Gulf & Western, felt competitive and antagonistic toward Steve Ross. Not that that would have made a difference.

MARTY RICHMOND: Jac had this odd quirk. Whenever Elektra moved he went to Europe and came back when the move was done, because he hated that turmoil.

JAC: I would take a roll of photos with a wide-angle lens, showing where each piece of furniture should be placed, each picture hung, and then leave town.

MARTY RICHMOND: He would have everything put in place in his new space so he could come back, sit down at his desk and not have to unpack a box, just keep going.

JAC: We signed a lease for a move-in date of June 1970. The new offices were going to be a mammoth and costly project, demanding meticulous planning and skilled execution. I turned to my brother, Keith.

KEITH HOLZMAN: I negotiated the lease. We watched the building go up literally from the point they excavated. I found the designer, Charles Winecoff, and worked with him, laying out the spaces, determining adjacencies, who needed what particular feature, and so on. And the decor. We spent a quarter of a million to design and furnish over ten thousand square feet of open space.

The elevator doors had Elektra logos covering the entire door. Every time the elevator stopped on our floor, the occupants knew we were there. In the reception area we had slide projectors with a little controller, projecting scenes of Elektra artists and events. For our lighting we made reflectors from record stampers that we got from our pressing plant, sixty to eighty of them, running along the entire hallway in the front part of the building.

We had a good working

15 Columbus Circle, entrance to office

archive, and a big mailroom—which was never big enough; mailrooms never are. The art department was big. In the center was a large pool table, and on top of that a ping-pong table covered with black material where we would lay out large jobs, album covers and all the ancillary materials.

We used specially milled wood elements throughout the office. Jac's office was rosewood on the inside, walnut on the outside, and the doors were multidimensional, carved wood, all Elektra logos.

The interior of the conference room was also wood-paneled. At the focus of the room, inlaid in the wood, was the Elektra logo, the stylized E that Bill Harvey had designed a few years earlier. Push a button in the projection room, and the pieces would separate and reveal a movie screen, which we used for slide and film projection during sales meetings.

The conference table was famous. One day I was sitting at the counter of a luncheonette under Rockefeller Center, playing around with ideas of hexagons and octagons, because I knew they would be part of the geometric scheme of the space. I was drawing and tearing up pieces of paper. The man sitting next to me was very intrigued. We struck up a conversation, and it turned out to be Robert Russell Bennett, the great orchestrator of the Rodgers and Hammerstein musicals and the famous World War II television documentary, "Victory at Sea." I realized that by taking three parallelograms you could form a hexagon, and by rearranging them you could get a long buffet table with odd, interesting angles at each end, and then be able to reform them into a hexagonal shape, with legs that, when they came together, would assume the same shape as the upper part of the table.

JAC: Details mattered. Keith's masterly table was a sweet, beautifully symmetrical design that said something about who we were. We did important business and had some great times at that table. We hired a cook for staff lunches, and to entertain prospective artists and their managers. At one lunch they could learn so much about the company and its people, feel the pulse. I had discovered early on that if you are pursuing people and deals, frequency of interaction is a key to

The elegant conference/lunch room.
The big "E" hides a projection screen.

success—and don't let them just see you, let them see the depth of the organization. Non-music guests would drop by, like Michael Korda, who shared his knowledge of the world of books and the problems of print publishing. We could feed the entire executive staff in-house, keeping them within the building and providing a healthy lunch that would energize them for the second half of the day. It was a perfect way to hold staff meetings and keep outside drinking down. Fridays were special because of interest in the dessert. If sales that week had been particularly good, there would be slices of fresh mango, no matter what the price or season.

Chapter 23

Ahmet's ten-million-dollar rug bazaar ...
First drafts and epitaphs ... Steve Ross's figurines ...
Warner Communications and Wile E. Coyote

JAC: Six months after my meeting with Steve Ross there was still no word from Kinney.

I was invited to keynote the National Association of Record Merchandisers convention in Miami on March 21, 1970, and while there I visited with Jerry Wexler, who kept a winter home in Florida. Jerry, as one of the three principals of Atlantic, had been dealing with Ross now for about a year. I said to him, "I had a terrific meeting with Steve and haven't heard a peep since. Other companies have been circling but I really don't want to do a deal elsewhere." Jerry promised to look into it.

About an hour later Mel Posner called. From the sound of his voice I could tell it was bad news. Hesitantly and with compassion Mel told me that my dad had died. Though it wasn't unexpected, it was still a shock and took a while to sink in. Just a few weeks earlier I had sat on his bed, holding his hand, and told him that I loved him. I don't know if he understood but I needed to say it anyway, for both of us.

Jerry handed me a stiff glass of brandy. I pulled myself together and grabbed the first flight to New York. George met the plane and drove Keith and me to my mother's apartment. The funeral service was held at a chapel owned by Kinney, which I thought ironic.

JAC: In late May, Ahmet Ertegun asked me to meet with him and Alan Cohen, Executive VP of Kinney, to move the merger talks forward. I've always felt safe with Irwin Russell at my side, so I asked him to join me at Kinney headquarters in Rockefeller Plaza. We were shown to Alan's office. Ahmet made the introductions and we got down to it with no time wasted.

Alan had an open face and a wide smile. Irwin and I liked him immediately. He was pleasant, smart, non-confrontational and had done his homework. I repeated the concerns I had expressed to Steve about distribution, autonomy and potential anti-trust problems with the Justice Department. Alan nodded his understanding and asked what we were looking for. Without a blink, I said, "$10,000,000."

I didn't think this was out of line for a company that was netting, pre-tax, $2,500,000 annually. I took my after-tax net earnings and multiplied them by a factor of between eight and ten, which was the conventional formula for valuing record companies (before the investment bankers got involved). Ahmet assumed his best bazaar bargaining manner, half horrified and half bemused, and began picking the company apart. Except for the Doors, Judy Collins, the singer-songwriters and Nonesuch, he didn't see that much value. To which Irwin said, "If that is the case, why are we here?" Ahmet continued to buy and sell a rug. He tried a counter offer of $8,000,000, and after a few hours we had worked him up $9,500,000, but still had no deal. So I said, "Why don't you gentlemen think about it because the number is not going to change. It's a fair number which you'll be able to pay out of our future cash flow"—which Alan Cohen knew all along. Elektra was the ideal acquisition, profitable and throwing off predictable cash. Steve would be buying cash flow and the belief that I would find other major artists.

Irwin and I left the building with a sense that Alan wanted to do the deal and was slightly embarrassed about Ahmet—or that perhaps they had planned to play good cop-bad cop from the beginning.

I was out of the office the next morning when Alan called. I dove into the quietest phone booth I could find, scrounged my pockets for change, and called back. Alan said, "Is it okay if we talk without your lawyer?" I said, "Fine." Alan continued, "I don't know record company values, maybe Ahmet is right, maybe you are, but the point is that we like you, we think we can do good things together, and it makes sense to bring Elektra into the group since your repertoire meshes nicely with Warner and Atlantic. We'll pay you the $10,000,000."

JAC: Nina received five percent of the company as part of our divorce settlement.

NINA HOLZMAN: When Jac was in the process of selling, he called me one day and said, "I need your stock in order to make the sale." And I had about thirty seconds of complete and utter power. Then I said, "Well, I'm not going to do anything to queer your deal." It all got straightened out.

JAC: The arrangement was a "follow-on," a go-along clause. Whatever I got, Nina would get five percent of. And of course, with my ninety percent of the company in play, I could be expected to try hard for a good price, and Nina would benefit from it in proportion. At $10,000,000, that was $500,000. I agreed to pay her $100,000 a year for five years, with a generous interest rate, so she would have a steady stream of principal and interest.

JAC: There was still something that Alan needed to work out and he needed my help in structuring the arrangement. In 1970, any acquisition of $10,000,000 or more automatically went to the Justice Department for review. Did I have any ideas? My thought had been to keep my publishing and the rights to the sound effects library, which were owned in a separate company, the Dyna Corporation. But I agreed to sell Dyna for $200,000 and Elektra for $9,800,000 in a deal that mixed cash with convertible debentures. The $10,000,000 was to be paid out, $1,000,000 on signing, $2,000,000 during the second year, plus $7,000,000 in notes, convertible to stock at $32 per share. At that time the stock was selling for around $24. If the stock price rose higher than the convert price, I could convert and I would see additional profit.

The next meeting was just Alan, Irwin, and myself, and we hammered out the fine points in a few hours.

In every merger there is a ritual called "due diligence" in which the seller's business, legal and financial representations are reviewed by the purchasing party.

Normally a process that takes several weeks, ours consisted of a succinct financial overview given by Jack Reinstein to the Kinney CFO. Our three years of financial certification had paid off. Alan Cohen accepted Irwin's word that all was in good order with legal title to the masters and that there was no pending litigation. It was the right gesture of confidence. I trusted Alan and he trusted us.

Along the way I briefly had second thoughts about distribution and the autonomy issue, so I met privately with Jerry Wexler. We reviewed Atlantic's sales experience at the Warner Bros.-owned branch in Los Angeles, the only such operation within the record group, which elsewhere was still handled by independents. Jerry's comment was a masterpiece of understatement: "The worst branch distribution is superior to the best independent distribution." And he eased my mind about the new partnership. "Jac," he said, "I would never let you get into something that's going to be bad for you. These are good people. Even Ahmet is impressed."

I had long admired my new business associates and I liked Alan Cohen and Steve Ross. Steve was always in awe of how quickly I got information and absorbed it, and I was equally in awe of how he dealt with numbers, how he could read a balance sheet. Steve could look at a wall of numbers and tell you, "That one's not right," and then tell you why. Steve was also fully committed to letting people do their own job. I only needed to see him once during the entire dealmaking process, when I was suffering through my moment of seller's remorse, and he sweetened the deal slightly to ease me over the hump.

The first draft of an agreement generally tells you if you really have a deal. If a draft comes in fairly reflecting what you have agreed to, it moves forward smoothly. If it comes back reading as if it was prepared by a bank, you have problems. The papers were nearly perfect. Irwin and I sailed through them in about two hours.

One open issue was our position in the hierarchy of Kinney's long-term debt structure. Frank Sinatra had sold his Reprise label to Warner in a similar deal and I was satisfied to be put on the same payment footing and schedule. A few other very minor points were cleaned up in a five-minute phone call.

A final quirk remained. We had agreed on stock options for me in the parent company, and a five-year employment contract at $200,000 per year, with a review at the end of three years. The quirk was in the employment paragraph which came back written for a three-year term with a two-year option on their part. Irwin puzzled over this for a moment and said, "I'm sure we can get it to five." I said "No. Maybe they'll forget to pick it up." In my mind—always in my mind—was my secret commitment to myself to be gone to Maui. In 1968 I had set a goal of five years on, which meant 1973. Selling to Warner in 1970 with a three-year term of employment also came out at 1973. If three years was enough to strengthen Elektra I might actually get to Maui on time, and have the option to either continue or move on with my life. I told Irwin to let it ride.

JAC: Within Elektra no one knew what was happening, not even my super-discreet secretary Pearl. My main concern was to get the agreement done quickly, to avoid leaks that might cause problems with artists and staff. Alan had promised to push the paperwork and we had seen the first drafts in about a week.

Then the phone began to ring. Abe Somer, who represented A&M and the

Doors, heard something. Abe was quick and smart and opportunistic, always looking out for himself. He said, "I hear you're selling the company to Steve Ross. It's the worst possible thing you can do. They don't have any money. Have you looked at their SEC documents? Kinney is on the verge of bankruptcy. I can get you a better deal"—which meant he wanted to represent the deal and take a piece for himself. I bit my tongue, listened, and said in a quiet but firm voice, "Abe, I'm not discussing this with you." He said, "Well, your artists are going to be very unhappy," and hung up.

Within three weeks, start to finish, we had the papers completed. Signing was on July 22, 1970. My set of documents weighed about four pounds and filled a substantial corrugated box. As we were leaving the Kinney building, with me clinging to my check, notes, and debentures, a security guard stopped us and refused to let me out until Alan and Steve vouched for me. "Now I understand your strategy," I said, straightfaced. "I could have gotten twice the amount, signed the papers and they would have never made it out of the building."

Steve took us for a celebratory lunch at Club 21.

Elektra joins Kinney/Warner Communications.
Irwin Russell, Jac

Alan Cohen

JAC: Ellen accompanied me to the signing ceremony wearing a clinging tangerine-colored summer smock.

ELLEN SANDER: I supported the sale to Kinney. Jac had considered taking Elektra public. I felt that a public company would be such an enormous burden it would preclude a family life. And from my perspective one of the reasons for doing the Kinney deal was for us to have more time together. But then when it actually happened, that became his interest rather than the family. The day he signed, we walked out of the meeting and Jac said, "I feel like I just got married"—with absolutely no sense of what effect that remark would have had on me.

JAC: The day before signing, I called all the staff into the Elektra conference room to tell them what was happening. I spoke for about five minutes, then took questions for another forty-five.

Our staff were mostly liberal-leaning people who abhorred the word "conglomerate," which had come to mean mindless acquisition for financial manipulation where nothing fit. They had lived in such a protected cocoon that any thought of outside scrutiny overrode common sense. I tried to assure them that we had a plan.

I called the key artists personally and most caught my enthusiasm, or at least said they did. I then had Pearl mail special letters we had prepared in advance to all artists, managers and attorneys informing them of the arrangement and that it would be business as usual, only better.

The women on the staff—with the exception of Tracey Sterne—were more willing than the men to be accepting. Mel Posner and Steve Harris were both enthusiastic. Steve just thought the idea made sense. Mel grasped the benefits in distribution and improved marketing. Jack Reinstein was pissed that I hadn't brought him into the negotiations, but with Irwin by my side that wasn't necessary, and it would have created problems with other key staff not privy to the talks.

Bill Harvey was the most contentious. He was petrified of losing control, and distrustful of the guarantee of autonomy that had been so willingly given by Steve Ross. Finally I just said, "Bill, it's a done deal, and I have watched out for you and the other key people. I will be dividing $1,000,000, pre-tax, among those who have the phantom stock options and were required to tender their "shares," and you, Mel Posner, Russ Miller and the others who have served." I made out thirty-two checks in all. The largest went to those with the longest service, who had made the biggest contribution. Bill and Mel each received between $75,000 and $100,000, and I gave Mel a sapphire Cartier watch in warm recognition of his years of service and the affection in which I held him.

When the word got out about this million-dollar distribution—the fact of it and the size of it—I was regarded by some in the business as a saint, by others as a holy fool, and by most entertainment-business lawyers as just plain crazy.

Chapter 24

Tranquility Base, but with sharp splinters …
Cannabis in Connecticut

JAC: Several months after completing my deal with Steve, I was introduced by a mutual friend to Charlie Bluhdorn, the honchissimo of Gulf & Western, the mega-corporation that was the master tenant in our new office building. Making conversation, my friend said, "And Jac just sold his company to Steve Ross." Bluhdorn exploded. He was furious that one of the few precious independent music companies was in the hands of a hated competitor. He screamed at me: "What are you doing in MY building?"

Aside from the chance of running into Charlie in the elevator, our new offices were splendid. And the new working arrangement with Warner was all I could have hoped for. But one insight from the encounter group was that if I wanted to work on myself, I needed some distance from the daily rat race—perhaps a retreat away from the city. Ellen wanted that too.

ELLEN SANDER: When we first got together, Jac asked me what my plans were and I said, "Well, I'm thinking of moving to LA." I said the people were friendlier, there was more space, you could live in nature and still be in the city. I had California fever. I was into, "I hate New York, I can't live through another winter like this one." Paul Simon had said in 'The Boxer'—"The New York City winters are bleeding me." And Jac would say, "Oh, the New York City winters are bleeding you?" After a few more months I said, "You know, I really am on my way to LA." Jac said, "Please don't put me under this kind of pressure. I can't leave New York. What can we do to make this work?" I said I really needed a place that had more space, where I didn't feel the urban pressure constantly. We came to the idea that a country house where we could spend long weekends would take care of my needs.

JAC: I told Bill Harvey I wanted a place north of the city, about an hour's commute, and would he keep his eyes open? A few days later Bill said, "I think I've found something that would be perfect for you, in South Salem, just a few miles east of the thruway." I made arrangements to see it the very next weekend.

George was out of town so I took the limo up myself, not knowing what to expect, but trusting Bill's enthusiasm and taste.

The land was forty-six glorious rolling acres with a driveway that ran a quarter mile from the main road to the house. The house itself was a barn, built in the latter part of the eighteenth century, dismantled and reassembled, turned inside out so that the weathered wood gave the interior a stunning patina of antiquity. The owners had lavished money and love on it. The living area was a huge, beamed, atrium-like space, with a peaked ceiling twenty-six feet high, with eight-foot-wide windows up top and sliding glass doors at ground level. There was a sunken brick area with built-in couches and an equipment cabinet. The fireplace was large enough for a matched set of Great Danes on either side and a yule log that could burn for a year, and the stone floors were heated. It was wonderful and livable.

ELLEN SANDER: I had a deadline and didn't go with Jac. When he came home that night he said, "It's really wonderful. I can't wait to bring you up there. It's an old barn." I said, "You want me to live in a barn?" He said, "No, no, it's all been redone. It's been turned inside out. There's heaters under the floor, you can walk around barefoot in the winter, there's a huge swimming pool. I really want this place, I love it, and I want you to see it as soon as possible." I just heard it in his voice. Jac doesn't take to rustic things, he's not Mr. Country Boy, this is something he's doing for me, and whatever it is, he loves it. I said, "Jac, I don't have to see it. Anything you love that much"—

And when I went up there the building was beautiful, the property was exquisite. It was like someone painted a picture out of my dream.

JAC: I bought it for $250,000, money from the sale. Ellen christened it 'Tranquility Base,' after the Apollo astronauts' first landing zone on the moon.

Marty Richmond had impressed me in Paxton days with his ability to get a wide range of tasks accomplished in good humor; he was responsible for winding down the project with as much style as could be salvaged under the circumstances. He was now at liberty, and I thought he would be the perfect choice to help me set up my new home in South Salem.

MARTY RICHMOND: Jac and Ellen had this huge king-sized bed built of thick wood beams, constructed by a friend of Ellen's and assembled in the room. No way anyone could move it after it was built. Jac put an English coat of arms over the top of it, four feet tall, five feet across, that he had found in some antique store in London. I hung it up for him, very carefully.

ELLEN SANDER: In the center of the living area we put a water bed and a hammock.

Jac at "Tranquility Base" South Salem, NY 1971

MARTY RICHMOND: One of the other bedrooms was turned into Jac's office, and another into Ellen's.

Ellen was on every company's list to get free records. After she started living there much of the time, the number of records arriving began increasing. The mailman would drive up and stack them on the porch. I think we were getting a thirty, fifty a day, six days a week. With all that, there's not enough time in the month to listen to them all. The stream of stuff was coming in bags, most of which she never opened. Some she would listen to. Sometimes she would literally throw them up the stairs, and the top three she'd listen to. Or the ones with red covers.

Jac Holzman

Jac, 10 lb. Hershey bar and cat "Moon"

JAC: I never saw so many records. The shipping containers alone would keep the fireplace going for days.

ELLEN SANDER: My room looked out over the pool. It was set into this beautifully manicured lawn. We kept it heated in the winter, there would be snow on the ground, the pool would be steaming, and ducks would be floating on the water, swimming around.

JAC: I loved to get loaded and run naked out to the pool, jump in and stay there until my skin shriveled.

MARTY RICHMOND: All night, every night, there was steam off the pool because it didn't have a cover. A propane truck was coming every week.

JAC: Marty and I built a small studio adjacent to the living room, where we could pre-record artists. Cables snaked under the part of the floor that was raised wood and were hooked into a McIntosh C-28 pre-amplifier, one of the best-sounding ever. Marty hung, God knows how, two Altec Voice of the Theater speakers in the northwest and northeast corners of the living room. They were supplemented by Bose reflecting speakers arranged strategically for either surround sound or quad playback, driven by 300-watt Crown amplifiers. It was a formidable battery of top-notch componentry.

MARTY RICHMOND: You could hear the music in Rhode Island.

JAC: Many weekends we invited guests. Sharing Tranquility added greatly to my enjoyment. With all the space inside and out, it was a wonderful place to entertain. I would come up from the city on a Thursday evening and go back on a Monday morning. Artists and friends would arrive late Friday or early Saturday and happily adjust to the quiet—sunbathing by the pool, reading, long walks.

Inside Tranquility

ANN PURTILL: It was like being at a friend's house that you had been to many times. Very relaxed, very informal.

JACLYN EASTON: It was a very pretty house. But that barn wood turned inside out, it was splinter city, so you could not go barefoot, and God forbid you should put your hand on a banister. There were tweezers in every room.

ELLEN SANDER: Paul Williams would come to visit us a lot with his writings and we would read them. Others that we would invite, the first thing they would do was just fall asleep. They would sleep the whole weekend, just be wiped out on the water bed or in their room.

MARTY RICHMOND: For those awake, the weekend would be food and music.

ANN PURTILL: There was a monastery-like refectory table.

JAC: Either Ellen or I would cook.

MARTY RICHMOND: Jac became a gourmet cook, doing Beef Wellington and all this Henry the Eighth kind of food—

JAC:—With a brief relapse onto a brown rice diet at one point. The meal might be followed by music pouring out of all the speakers, or a 16-millimeter print of a movie. One of my favorites, part of the deal with Warner, was a

Ellen Sander and Jac toke some "South Salem Sledgehammer"

set of Roadrunner-Wile E. Coyote cartoons, which I thought hysterical, especially if nudged in that direction by a friendly toke or two.

Ellen decided to grow some grass. I kidded her about it, saying that it would never flourish in the soil of New York State. But our land extended across in the direction of Ridgefield, up to the Connecticut border, and Connecticut used to be a tobacco-growing state. She found a sunny spot a quarter of a mile from any surveillance. I forgot about it until she walked in at the end of Indian summer with an armful of plants twice her height. She and Marty dried and prepared it. I smoked some, it was Connecticut-strength, and I passed out. I dubbed it "South Salem Sledgehammer."

For me, after twenty years of chasing the holy grail of music and business success, the house in the country was an oasis of serenity.

ELLEN SANDER: We had the encounter group over for a weekend. I was happy enough to be the hostess. It was more fun than anything. That was the most people we ever had up there. We just kept going at it, twenty-four hours a day. But then Kandy, who was supposed to be a recovered addict, had to be rushed to the hospital because he had been doing cocaine the whole time.

MARK ABRAMSON: Kandy was officially not using drugs, but he was. And he was still a con man. He was a wonderful person and taught me a lot, but he was bad news in many ways.

JUDY COLLINS: I came away thinking that kind of encounter, the deliberate attack to break down the ego, was destructive. And divisive. At the end of that time, none of us wanted to see each other, let alone contemplate owning any land together. It was very destructive.

JAC: I was pissed at Kandy's sneakiness and manipulation, but the group experience helped open me to myself and I decided to continue the personal work by different means. Many years later, in a long profile of me in Los Angeles Magazine, Merrill Shindler quoted a friend as saying, "Jac is obsessed with the perfect life." Merrill, with his reporter's cloak of confidentiality tightly wound around himself, would never tell me who said it, but it was intuitively correct, so right that it was one of those moments where you read something and your body shakes. I wanted to send that person, if it was a woman, a dozen silver roses, and if it was a man, perhaps a bottle of out-of-this-world 1945 Petrus Bordeaux. Other people obviously saw that obsessive perfectionism in me, and the encounter group enabled me for the first time to glimpse it in myself and begin to deal with it.

Chapter 25

Summer in the city, 1970 ...
Panhandlers, drunks, whales and nightingales ...
The cathedral's roar ... And Amazing Grace

JUDY COLLINS: In a funny way, one great thing did come out of the encounter group: 'Amazing Grace.' It was the one song that you could carry into any social environment. I first heard it from my Methodist grandmother and sang it at church, at school. Later, I often wound up an evening of folkie participation with it. And then it filtered its way into the encounter group, as a way to end the evening.

MARK ABRAMSON: Something very moving had happened in the group, and Judy said, "Why don't we sing a song?" We sang 'Amazing Grace,' and I said, "Judy, you've got to record that."

JUDY COLLINS: Mark and I were starting to put together a new album, which became "Whales And Nightingales." The whales came when I was doing "Peer Gynt" in Central Park with Stacy. Roger Payne, a whale researcher, came and brought me a tape of whale sounds, whale songs, and said, "I don't know what to do with these beautiful singers." I played them for Mark and Jac. On the way to Woodstock (which I went to despite not being invited to perform, the rap on me being that I was too much of a singer's singer), en route to Williamstown to see "The Cherry Orchard"—I played the tape in my car, and I thought, "I know what to do with this. I'm going to sing an old whaling song, 'Farewell To Tarwathie,' a capella, with the sound of the whales." And as we began to think of traditional things, 'Simple Gifts' came to mind. Then there was 'Nightingale I' and 'Nightingale II,' which I wrote, and Josh Rifkin did that beautiful arrangement, which I love so much—it's one of my favorites of anything I've written. And the next thought was 'Amazing Grace.'

JOSHUA RIFKIN: Judy asked me to work on one more record with her.

As I see Judy's early recordings, she was a bit dominated in the artistic process by the men with whom she was working. That's happened to so many people, and Judy is one of the most solid, independent women I know, and if this happened to her, it's nothing about her, it's an indication of the time and what the situation was like. But as I look back on it, she at least seemed to me to do what she was told. Certainly, when I was her arranger, in a way I was putting her in that position.

I think Judy was breaking out of that. Professional success, changing times—all of this was allowing her to do more of things that were always inside her, be stronger, grow a lot. None of this is to be taken as having at all a patronizing view of what she was before. These are struggles through which any performer, any artist, any human being—and in those days, particularly, any woman—would have been going. But this was giving her a different sense of her role in her records, a much more activist role, if you will. She was feeling more muscle, feeling able to take control more.

Which was a very salutary development, although it did not work in very salutary terms for our relationship at the time. You could say that the success we had had with our last project, "Wildflowers," had strengthened both of us, strengthened egos, character, abilities, but we could no longer quite mesh the way we had.

I didn't finish the album, and we never worked together again, in fact we never saw each other again. That said, I have a great fondness for Judy, and enormous respect, and I am glad that she has kind words for me in her autobiography.

JOHN HAENY: Putting that album together was a magical experience, one of the two best in my career. It was a brilliant record, on all levels, an enormously broad tapestry of music, big classical works, little folk works, esoteric works.

I was pretty much responsible for figuring out how to record. We did some test sessions in studios around town, including 'Amazing Grace,' where we had a whole bunch of folkies with a lot of acoustic guitars, and a big electric organ and basses and drums, and it was a wonderful evening and a musical disaster. Any time Judy tried anything with drums it was an absolute atrocity.

We had also test-recorded some small classical ensembles, in a big studio, and it was my impression that there was no one studio that would suit the various music types.

JUDY COLLINS: Mark and I decided that we were going to go out of the studios, and use sound situations that we thought were uniquely distinctive.

MARK ABRAMSON: I always liked those old days when Jac and I recorded in churches, or in any kind of hall that was acoustically right, or even cheap and convenient, like Judson Hall. John and I decided to record "Whales And Nightingales" all remote, but remote on a grander scale, since now we could afford to.

JOHN HAENY: We decided to pick locations that matched the emotional ambiance of the songs we were recording.

Mark and I spent weeks scouting locations. And then recording . . . What a time we had. We recorded out of a converted red truck, with bums, panhandlers and junkies all around us, during a hot steamy New York summer, and it was just the most vibrant experience imaginable.

For 'Simple Gifts' we went to Paul Harris, a keyboard player down in the Village—I had found his loft accidentally. We went to Carnegie Hall for 'Prothalamium.' We recorded Brel's 'Marieke' in the Manhattan Center, the seventh-floor ballroom where Capitol recorded all their great cast albums. We went to the library of a church—

MARK ABRAMSON: We figured that most people would not be conscious of what we were doing, but subconsciously it would have its effect.

JUDY COLLINS: If something is recorded someplace for a reason, then the reason will come through in the recording.

JOHN HAENY: Mark was a film maker at heart, and I always thought of music as a visual medium. So on this album we were moving from room to room, dissolving from one environment to another, like you would if you were montaging a film.

MARK ABRAMSON: In the final product we went to great lengths to actually cross-fade from one room to the next. There's no dead air between the tracks, just like Jac's earlier recordings. We let the ambient sound of the place we were in blend into the next one. If you listen with headphones, you can really hear this.

JOHN HAENY: After Jac had introduced us to Dolby we always recorded Judy with noise reduction. Without the tape noise, if you have the proper equipment to listen, at the end of the roar of a cathedral, you'll hear the chairs kind of squeaking as you enter the loft.

JUDY COLLINS: With 'Amazing Grace,' which I had always sung with friends, I said to Mark, "Let's open it up, get a bunch of friends together." Some of the people from the encounter group. My brother. Stacy. Josh and his girl friend. Susan Evans, who played drums for me, still does from time to time. John Cooke, Alistair Cooke's son, who had a fine voice. Not professional singers, just a whole gang of friends, really.

JAC: People that Judy or Mark knew, mostly white, mature, some music business people, but non-professional voices. And me.

JUDY COLLINS: I said to Mark and John, "Where to record? What's wonderful?" Mark had gone to Columbia and knew about St. Paul's chapel. He and John went up and took a look, and it was ideal, a beautiful, tiny little round-domed stone-tiled cathedral, green tile, with a stained glass window.

MARK ABRAMSON: There was just something about it, a spirit.

JUDY COLLINS: John set us up. For on-site recording, there was nobody better.

MARK ABRAMSON: It was partially the church, and then the way that John miked it, which was with a portable eight-track, a vocal mike tightly on Judy, close microphones, other microphones about sixty feet away, and then another set of microphones all the way to the back of the chapel, and up in the ceiling, that we could play with in the mixing, to get this incredibly full sound.

I was so frantic, so afraid that with all these people we were going to screw it up in some way. But it worked.

JAC: Everyone was grouped at the choir end, like a platoon of voices in a shower, but smoothed out and sounding great. The mood was joyous and affirming.

MARK ABRAMSON: It was almost heavenly, but not choir-like. It doesn't sound like a select choir. It's real down to earth. It was exciting, playing it back in the church, with all of those people, and everybody was just—"Jesus!" Then sitting in the van we had outside, listening to it, I knew we had something hair-raising.

JAC: I had been so impressed by 'Hey, Jude.' To me it was the Sistine Chapel of rock, and if I were in the dumps I would listen to it through headphones. Now there was 'Amazing Grace'—I was overcome by its purity, the sense of redemption in the words and the elegiac simplicity of the melody.

JUDY COLLINS: The rule that never held for me was that you had to have an up-tempo song on an album. 'Both Sides Now' is the closest thing to an up-tempo hit that I've ever had. 'Send In The Clowns' later on was completely out of left field. And 'Amazing Grace' is the farthest away.

MARK ABRAMSON: With every record, there's huge discussion about what the single should be. Jac told me 'Amazing Grace,' and I said, "You're kidding." It was the last thing I would have released as a single. It could have been a tremendous problem, because it was so long—

JAC:—A 'Light My Fire' all over again. And it was not rock and roll in any form.

JOHN HAENY: An a capella hymn? Are you serious?

JAC: I was considering 'Amazing Grace' as a wild card single when I was further nudged in that direction by Clive Selwood, our label manager in Europe. Elektra was completing a three-year contract with our licensee, Polygram, and Clive was trying to convince them to release 'Amazing Grace' as a Christmas record. Polygram thought the idea a tad far-fetched but at Clive's insistence did release it in mid-November, to massive holiday radio play, and it sold a million in England! The minute we knew the reaction in the UK we moved in the US, releasing the single in less than two days.

MARK ABRAMSON: 'Amazing Grace' certainly had an enormous impact. Far beyond sales. I remember George McGovern, when he was running for president against Nixon—Jac was a McGovern supporter, he had him in the office—McGovern came up to me and said, "I want to thank you for 'Amazing Grace.' It meant so much to me." It was Judy's recording that made that song an anthem for so many people.

Chapter 26

The police chief and the studio magician ...
Hendrix is one ... Joplin makes two ...
And a poet is evicted from the Morrison Hotel

JAC: All this time, Jim Morrison had been waiting to go to trial in Miami. And the Doors had another album to record, what became "Morrison Hotel." They were using the La Cienega studio.

BRUCE BOTNICK: Rolling Stone had printed a big picture of Jim with WANTED on it, and he taped it up in the control room. We drew a beard on it.

JAC: Jim was still the prankster he had always been.

BRUCE BOTNICK: On La Cienega in those days, every Tuesday night was gallery night—you could go gallery-hopping, walk up and down, have some wine and cheese.

PAUL ROTHCHILD: We were in the studio late with the Doors, less Jim, going over some arrangements.

BRUCE BOTNICK: In the console we had a little panel, with a sign that Fritz Richmond put there, DO NOT OPERATE EQUIPMENT, and under that panel we used to keep the dope. We had this one jar with KD on it, for Killer Destroyer. And we had things out, hashish and papers. We had the lights very dim—

PAUL ROTHCHILD:—All of a sudden the door opens and in comes Jim, dressed nicely, with some gentlemen in tuxedos and women in evening gowns. He had been at a function, picked them up and said, "I'm going to the studio to record. Would you like to come along?" These wealthy folks and political figures thought that would be a very good way to slum for the evening. Jim said to us, "Please continue, these are my friends."

BRUCE BOTNICK: One was Laurence Harvey, the movie actor. Paul said to me, "Do you recognize any of the others?" I turned around very casually. I said, "The man behind you is Thomas Redden, police chief of the city of Los Angeles." Paul said to the boys, "That's good, let's do another one," and he bent very professionally over the control board, and when he straightened up, everything was gone. Paul was a magician.

I'm looking over at Morrison, and he is in hysterics. He planned the whole thing.

HENRY DILTZ: My partner Gary Burden and I had done the Crosby, Stills and Nash album cover, and the Doors called us. Ray Manzarek said he had seen this place in downtown LA called Morrison Hotel. It was a flop house on Hope Street, with a sign that said "ROOMS FROM $2.50." The clerk at the desk wouldn't let us take pictures, but then he went to the elevator and the guys ran in and got into position in the easy chairs and I started snapping with a wide-angle lens, and then I went across the street with a telephoto, and they hit the mark, perfect.

Jim said, "Let's go get a drink." It's skid row, wino bars. We saw one called Hard Rock Café. We took pictures outside, and then inside, with the four Doors lined up on bar stools and these gentlemen behind them—this is before the days of "homeless," these are gentlemen who have left home.

After we finished Jim said, "Let's go to a couple more bars." He and I went, and he bought this old guy some beers, listened to him talk. Jim liked to do that. He would just look you in the eye and listen to you, with this bemused look, and he did it with this old guy, hardly said a word, just drinking in his life story.

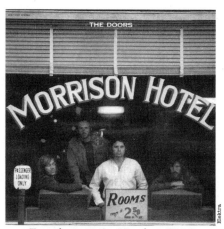

Transients at the Morrison Hotel
EKS-75007

The Hard Rock picture went on the back of the album. A year or so later they got a call from a guy in England: "We're starting a café over here. Would you mind if we use that name?" The beginning of the empire. And to this day, young kids ask me what covers I did, and I say Crosby, Stills and Nash, the Eagles, Jackson Browne, and on and on, and I say "Morrison Hotel," and they go, "Dude! You did "Morrison Hotel?" Whoa!" It's the one thing I can say that will get a reaction from young kids, all around the world.

JAC: The Doors' contract was coming to an end and we threw a lavish party for them at the New York Hilton, in the presidential suite, a duplex penthouse with a 360° view. Nearly everyone had gone home, and just as Pam and Jim were leaving she said, "Well, in case we're on Atlantic next year, thanks for the swell party." I died. Jim put her up to it. He was wearing his sly, "gotcha" smile as they shuffled out.

The Doors had promised me the right of first negotiation, which meant I would be the first to go up against their attorney, Abe Somer, who wasn't a fan of mine and who had very close ties to A&M Records. I had to devise a strategy that would defang Abe and give the boys what they deserved.

BILL SIDDONS: Abe was fiercely intelligent.

SUZANNE HELMS: He was another of the fastest thinkers I ever knew, up there with Jac.

BILL SIDDONS: When Abe went in to do the renegotiation, the first thing he did was have the label audited, to try to find out where they were stealing money from us, because all labels steal from artists, by definition.

Abe said to us, "Our settlement is anywhere from thirty to seventy percent, but fifty percent is a nice target. If you get half what you're asking for, half of what the auditors can come up with, that's a good settlement."

Jac gave him one hundred percent of the audit settlement—and gave the Doors their publishing back. Abe was flabbergasted.

JAC: Abe and I had been around the course before. After the Doors' second album he had advised them to go on strike, not to record again until I improved their royalty rate. I didn't take well to that approach and held out, not reacting. After the stalemate had gone on for several months the Doors dropped by one day, and we had a pleasant talk. They really wanted to go back into the studio, but Abe had told them not to until he got them more money. I said, "I have no objection to giving you more money. What I do object to is the way a lawyer interposed himself in my relationship with you. All you had to do was ask." I raised their royalty to seven percent.

Now, as part of our new contract for an additional album, I had increased the royalty again, to ten percent, and I gave them back the twenty-five percent of the publishing held by Elektra. The label had made a fortune with the Doors and they had given us a presence and credibility that we could and did use to attract and sign other artists. It was the right and proper thing for me to do.

BILL SIDDONS: It was amazing, a totally ballsy move by Jac. And to me, that's why Jac was a great man. He totally knew who he was dealing with, and he went, "I can either allow this lawyer to make me the Doors' enemy, or I can show them that I am their friend." Negotiations were over that day. There was no way we would go to another label or do anything else. It cost Jac millions of dollars, because that's what the Doors' catalog turned out to be worth. But it got him what he needed, which was to keep the Doors loyal to him.

I thought that really showed Jac's colors. He's El Supremo for a reason. I have always admired Jac Holzman for those kinds of moves, that I saw twenty different ways during my relationship of working with him. The guy knew what he was doing, and he ran a record company that had a lot of heart and soul and was founded on music first. It wasn't founded just on making him a millionaire.

ROBBY KRIEGER: At the time we didn't realize what a great guy Jac was. A guy who is able to succeed without screwing people. He's really the only guy I know who is a totally great businessman and totally generous.

JAC: The summer that Judy Collins recorded 'Amazing Grace,' Jim Morrison finally went on trial in Miami—August, 1970.

The proceedings were politically charged and painful, the verdict convoluted. Jim was found not guilty on the felony charge of lewd and lascivious behavior, and not guilty of a misdemeanor charge of public drunkenness, but guilty of a misdemeanor charge of profanity and a misdemeanor charge of indecent exposure. The judge sentenced him to sixty days of hard labor for profanity, and for indecent exposure six months of hard labor plus a $500 fine. He was expected to serve two months, with the other four months on probation, plus an additional two years probation. Jim remained free on bail pending appeal. In other words, it wasn't over and it wasn't going to be over any time soon.

ROBBY KRIEGER: Everything was coming down and going bad because of the Miami bullshit trip. But in a way I think Jim might have wanted that. He didn't like his image any more.

PAUL ROTHCHILD: He was unhappy with his role as a national sex symbol, and did everything in his power to obliterate that. He gained enormous weight, he grew a beard, he looked ugly.

STEVE HARRIS: My wife and I were going to have dinner with Jim and Pamela, and I was sitting in a back booth, and Jim walked in with Pam and I didn't recognize him. He walked by and someone said, "Isn't that Jim Morrison?" He had gotten very heavy, very jowly, and his hair even started receding.

MIRANDI BABITZ: I was so shocked when I saw him, because he was so fat and flabby and pale and strange-looking.

DIANE GARDINER: He was not comfortable in his skin any more. He was a changed person. He would simply sit in the corner in my apartment and watch people. The decline in him was amazing. Let's face it, he framed himself, he shocked himself.

MICHAEL FORD: He evicted himself from the Morrison Hotel.

JAC: While Jim was going through his ordeal by trial, Jimi Hendrix OD'd, in London, aged twenty-seven. In October, Janis Joplin OD'd, in the Landmark Hotel in Los Angeles, also twenty-seven. Jim was approaching his twenty-seventh birthday. He began to refer to himself as "number three."

Chapter 27

**These records don't spring fullblown
from Minerva's ear ...
Ahmet, Jac, Jerry, Joe, Mo, Nesuhi
and the baby mogul ...
Ertegun in pursuit of the Jagger ...
Icing on the cake in London**

MO OSTIN: With Warner Bros., Elektra and Atlantic—WEA—we were a powerful combination. We started our own domestic and international distribution, shifting from music licensing arrangements abroad to our own companies in England, France, Germany and Japan, and that was the beginning of Warner Communications becoming a very important big business. And for years and years the Number 1 profit center and cash generator was the record group. That was a very important turning point for us. And part of what enabled us to get into this vertical integration was that we were able to acquire Elektra. That was the swing factor.

MEL POSNER: For Jac, I think that the association with the Ahmet Erteguns and the Jerry Wexlers and the Mo Ostins was an important advance in his own mind. It was one thing to be a wealthy man; it's another to be accepted into that community. Jac wanted to be one of those guys. And now he was.

JAC: In 1969-1970 we had expanded our operations in New York with our new offices in the Gulf & Western Building. In 1970-1971 we enlarged our LA operation on La Cienega, with more office space and a second and bigger studio, which we called Studio A. But for me, more than impressive facilities and financial success, it was the smart people I was working with that was the measure of where I had come to.

BRUCE BOTNICK: Jac said, "This is going to be great."

JOE SMITH: Jac loves to be part of a fellowship. Elektra was a company run and controlled by Jac, and there weren't many people that he could feel were peers, that he could bounce things off of. Jac loved the relationship that Mo Ostin and I had—two people who could discuss things on the highest level, both policy makers. So he came into this group and I remember him hugging everybody, and we felt just like, "We're brothers, come in and join the fold."

JAC: I felt that I finally had found a home in the company of people I admired and of whom I was enormously fond. This crazy array of wild characters—

STAN CORNYN: Jerry Wexler, a delightful man, as outspoken people are, if you're not afraid of them. Very hip, tends to use patterns of obscure words. Loves to phrase.

MO OSTIN: He coined the term "rhythm and blues."

STAN CORNYN: And he was the traditionalist. For a long time he kept alive the Atlantic black tradition. One remembers with some delight that if anyone ever brought him an Atlantic single that had something like a string section on it, he would vituperate to the extreme, usually having to do with various synonyms for excrement.

Ahmet Ertegun—self-acknowledged as not being the office man. He considered his strength to be on a plane, in a hotel, in a café, or bar, or club, hanging out, connecting, relationships.

MO OSTIN: Ahmet can relate to artists as well as anybody I'm aware of.

STAN CORNYN: Mo I think of as being tremendous at the record business, and then maybe number two, oddly enough, David Geffen. Good record men. And I would put Nesuhi Ertegun there; he touched a lot of bases.

MO OSTIN: Fascinating man, Nesuhi. Everybody adored the guy. Very honest, spoke his mind, always up front about what he felt. He had a great sense of art as well as music. Really a very, very highly cultured individual. Incredible intellect. Studied at the Sorbonne. In terms of music, he covered the international world. He would find things abroad that were just fantastic. And he got along with artists.

STAN CORNYN: About Mo, the first thing that comes to mind is his engaging curiosity and respect for intelligent people. He knew how to gather talented people, listen to them, indulge them, support them, challenge them.

MO OSTIN: Joe Smith—very witty, incredibly funny, incredibly smart, also well educated.

STAN CORNYN: Joe Smith, Yale graduate; Mo Ostin, UCLA graduate with honors; Ahmet, St. John's College graduate. These weren't high school ruffians.

MO OSTIN: And Jerry Wexler I found very intellectual, with great perspective on things.

JAC: At the NARM convention in Miami in 1970 there was a famous exchange between Jerry (who vied with Joe Smith for best mouth in our music group), and an "over-his-belt" rack jobber whose face wore the life he had lived. This gentleman, whose experience with recordings was a fraction of Jerry's, rises and talks about records as if they are toothpaste or other drug store commodity. Jerry, in a response I will always cherish, says, "You're talking about music. People have to create these albums. They don't spring fullblown from Minerva's ear." Few in the auditorium get the classical reference, deliberately misquoted, except me, Ahmet (another St. John's College boy), and Joe. The rack jobber, with absolutely no notion of what Jerry is talking about, says, "No, no, Mr. Wexler, you don't understand. We sell eighty-five percent of what you make." And Jerry, smooth as can be, like the most beautiful return of a master tennis player, says, "And we make one hundred percent of what you sell." I am transported.

JOE SMITH: Our board meetings were tremendous fun, hilarious. Much of what was discussed was pedestrian, about distribution or manufacturing or something like that. Then we would get into something juicy, where we could assassinate characters, and then you saw the best and worst of everybody, just attacking constantly.

Once we were sitting with Ted Ashley. Ted was the ultimate agent. Warners had bought his agency, and that was the beginning of the whole Warner group. The name of an agent from William Morris came up. Jerry Wexler got up —

JAC: —Swelled up—

JOE SMITH: —And started to scream all this venom: "He's an agent, he's the lowest form of human being." He gave all the bad agent lines, and the blood was draining out of Ashley's face. Jac and I were next to Wexler, trying to sit him down, and he noticed this total silence, and he said to Jac and me, "I probably said something wrong."

Wexler was vicious, Ahmet was merciless, and I was always there to back them up, the vicious and the ferocious. The addition of David Geffen put a new edge on it, a little harder edge.

JAC: Geffen was not yet a division head within the music group and didn't attend all meetings, but he was clearly a rapidly rising star. Steve Ross was intrigued by David's quickness and similarity to himself, and Ahmet was hooked.

STAN CORNYN: Ahmet was probably entertained by the questions, by the intelligence, by the humor of David Geffen.

MO OSTIN: Geffen enters by starting a label with Ahmet at Atlantic called Asylum Records.

JOE SMITH: David sometimes can play district attorney. He was a challenger and a provoker. He could really shake you up.

JAC: Geffen could outsmart and outscream even Ahmet.

ALAN COHEN: David's absolutely blasphemous. Nothing's sacred or holy to him. Imagine—you're dealing with a bunch of people, basically nothing is sacred to them to begin with, that's the nature of the contemporary music business—and then you have Geffen, who'll almost say outrageous things just for the benefit of hearing them and seeing the reactions.

STAN CORNYN: And his focus, the intensity, the ambition to win.

MO OSTIN: Incredibly aggressive, so intense, and there was this amazing brilliance that comes from the guy. All of this—it had to really make you think, "Boy, this guy is a comer."

STAN CORNYN: David is consumed with the business he's in, like, "There's only so much fuel in this business, and once I have burned it by focusing the rays of my attention on it, and when there's nothing more combustible left, I'm bored, I'm going to move on."

ALAN COHEN: So you have David. And you have the drive and entrepreneurial attitude of Mo Ostin and Joe Smith, and of Ahmet—his greed, his singlemindedness, his combativeness. Nesuhi was unlike Ahmet, a much stabler and less volatile person. Ahmet was a very successful businessman, but he also had more of the impresario, the flakiness, what have you, all the different elements that you would expect of someone running a recording company with its origins in jazz.

DAVID BRAUN: Ahmet has a bit of a scoundrel in him.

ALAN COHEN: And then Jac. Jac always seemed to me to be more of a straight arrow than other people in the record business, emotionally much less outgoing, much more reserved. Jac was not a killer in the same way Ahmet and David were. His was a different direction, a different bent. I think the Nonesuch label typified Jac. He was a combination of Nonesuch and the Doors, if you will.

Jac had his own roster and niche. Elektra was a niche company, whereas Atlantic and Warners were both trying to be broad contemporary music companies.

JAC: Even though we were the boutique label within the group—and wanted to be—out of brute necessity we had to compete in marketing, sales, radio play. Warner and Atlantic had loud voices. Elektra had to make itself heard in that crowd.

Jac, Mo Ostin and Joe Smith (left to right)

ALAN COHEN: Of course there was competition. Warner, Atlantic, and Elektra—three separate competitive companies.

MO OSTIN: It was not unlike General Motors with Chevy and Buick and Pontiac and Cadillac. We fought and competed against another. Very, very hard.

ALAN COHEN: Bidding for the same artists. Nobody restricting their bidding. And they were making independent judgments. They were making tons of money, increasing and growing at a rapid rate. And doing their own things.

BOB ZACHARY: Jac would send me to England to find talent, and write me long memos, super-explicit instructions, what kind of cassette recorder to take, what kind of film, check at the police station to ask about street singers.

He had tremendous energy. My first trip to London, we flew overnight. I was twenty-five, he was fifteen years older than me. I was too excited to sleep on the plane. We got to the hotel and I crashed. Five minutes later the phone rings and Jac says, "Are you ready?" And in twenty-four hours I have met the Who, George Martin, Jane Asher, and gone to the Judy Collins concert at the Albert Hall.

JOE SMITH: We're brothers, but we're trying to beat each other's brains out all the time for an act.

MO OSTIN: We all killed for anything that we thought was worth signing.

ALAN COHEN: One of the great lines I remember from those meetings was Ahmet saying to Joe Smith, "Joe, I'm going over to Europe next week. Is there anything I can do for you?" And Joe said, "Ahmet, there's nothing you can do for me. I just ask you not to do anything *to* me."

JOE SMITH: We went head to head. We used to always battle for acts in England. This was open warfare.

We tried to establish some ground rules: whoever got there first had it. We would always sneak in. If we heard Atlantic was in there, we got in there, too. But Ahmet would trick you into announcing your dates, and then he would pre-date by a day. You would say, "I saw him on Thursday, January 10." And Ahmet would say, "Ah, I was there on Tuesday, January 8, so he's ours." So I suggested to Ahmet that his story should be that he used to date a woman in England and he made her promise that if she ever had a child that became a singer, that the child would sign with Atlantic Records—that even before the child was conceived, Ahmet had made his connection.

JAC: I would marvel at Ahmet. He had the stamina of a rhino, could work all day, party all night, lock his legs and fall asleep standing up for fifteen minutes, or cat-nap on a company plane, then wake and pick up in the middle of a sentence. During the last week of August, 1970, Ahmet and I were in London to discuss recording the Isle of Wight festival, the big European outdoor festival of the summer, featuring Jimi Hendrix (twelve days before he OD'd), the Who, Jethro Tull, Alvin Lee and Ten Years After, Emerson, Lake and Palmer, Joni Mitchell, Kris Kristofferson, Miles Davis, Tiny Tim, to name but a few, and the Doors, with the bearded and bulky Jim Morrison.

Ahmet and I are to meet at nine in the morning. He is at the Dorchester, and I spot the WEA limo outside, a stretch Daimler, with our loyal driver, Dennis Goodman, napping at the wheel. From this I deduce that Ahmet has been out late but is now in.

Ahmet is installed in the Oliver Messel suite, which he adores, but his mind is not on the Isle of Wight. Ahmet has been chasing Mick Jagger for over a year, trying to bring the Stones to Atlantic. He gets on the phone to Mick and recaps what a great evening they just shared, fabulous music, wonderful ladies, and isn't it time they sat down with Prince Rupert von Loewenstein, the Stones' manager, to cut a deal. By this time Ahmet felt that he had invested everything needed for Mick to make an informed decision. Mick says he will be happy to talk to Ahmet about the

Stones recording for Atlantic—just as soon as he has spoken to Clive Davis at Columbia. And Mick hangs up.

Ahmet goes ballistic. Before my eyes he is slowly, and uncharacteristically, coming unhinged, really pissed but struggling to regain control. Then a beatific calm smoothes the angry lines in his face and he picks up the phone, very deliberately dials, and says, "Mick, I can understand that you want to talk to Clive Davis, and you should. But I want you to know that I can only make one Stones-size deal this year, and it's either you"—long exquisitely-timed pause—"or Paul Revere and the Raiders." And he hangs up. Twenty seconds later the phone rings. We both know it's Mick, but Ahmet doesn't pick up. We go back to talking about the Isle of Wight.

Ahmet was the greatest poker player in the business. He loved the game and took more joy in it than anyone. And at WEA he had other people's money to play with and that made it particularly wonderful. He was serious about the music, but he went about the business of music cavalierly, in the best sense of that word, with a style unmatched to this day.

The Stones came to Atlantic. Of course.

JOE SMITH: Jac, who was the smartest of us all, took things more seriously than the rest of us and wasn't as quick on the trigger with humor. As a result, he would sometimes get caught in the crossfire.

Being rather formal in his way, he would present position papers on things that he had carefully researched, as he always does. We had short attention spans, there would be some jokes, and we could just attack him mercilessly, with the kind of humor that Ahmet can lay out and that I, on occasion, can be known to wield. Jac at first was very taken aback by our attitude, constantly in a position of having to step back—"Can't you guys ever be serious?" And Mo and I and Ahmet would just mock anger all the time.

There was this one meeting where Jac had been to England to do a review of our English operation, and he had slightly terrorized the English company, which was first of all a Warner company, and then Atlantic came in, and then Elektra.

Jac used to make notes on the things that he saw that were going wrong. Certainly not the best way for people to work, under the watchful eye of someone taking notes. We had heard about the discomfort there, and Jac came back to a meeting, really prepared. He had this report and as he was handing out copies he was prefacing it, saying, "As you probably know, I have been to England, and I am not very happy with our English company." He's about to set sail into his report when Ahmet said, "And, as you should probably know, man, our English company isn't very happy with you." So Jac immediately became defensive and it destroyed his whole posture.

JAC: I was pretty wrapped up in myself and these guys took some getting used to. After I had been in the group for about nine months, Ahmet and I were at a party in London and we sat down and talked, just friends, no attitude and no competition. It was Ahmet's way of finally allowing me to feel welcome. But there were still problems in England.

IAN RALFINI: I was running the company there, and it was very hard. I mean, Ahmet ran Atlantic, Mo and Joe ran Warners together, and Jac ran Elektra, completely autonomous. But in England everything was fed through this one company, WEA. Consequently, I'm there in the middle of all these people, who are coming at me every which way.

You've got Warners, with this—to me—easy music to understand, relate to, and decide on how to work. You've got Atlantic coming at me with R&B, and it's very different and has to be treated in a different way, and they've got a different kind of people. The Atlantic people that they chose didn't marry at all well with the Warners people, and also didn't marry terribly well with Elektra.

It was quite difficult at times to try to balance all that. Jac naturally wanted the attention for Judy Collins and the Doors and Bread and whoever. Ahmet wanted to make sure he had the best shot for Aretha Franklin. And there was Mo coming in with the James Taylors. You had very strong personalities. And I had to try to allocate resources because it was my staff working on all the records. There was no separation, there was no label manager identity. So we banged heads for a couple of years.

JAC: I thought the English setup was just dumb. The UK company decided to take what had been three highly individualistic labels that fiercely maintained their independence, and group them within a marketing wrapper called "The Kinney Collection." I went nuts. Ahmet, Mo and Joe didn't like it either, but I was so loud and contemptuous they let me take the heat. Ian was a great guy and a very skilled artist relations person. But I hated to see Elektra presented as anything other than singular.

IAN RALFINI: Jac had the smallest label. Elektra was this little gem. Very special, very attractive, a tremendous sort of prestige. But it wasn't a label that you found all over the charts all the time. It was like Jac's people, Jac's taste in music.

CLIVE SELWOOD: With Elektra acts we ran into a blank on radio, apart from one DJ, John Peel, who was on pirate radio. He would take Love and play it nonstop, and he did the same with the Incredible String Band, and the Doors. When they closed pirate radio down, John got a job on BBC Radio One, two hours a week, and that was the only time any kind of progressive music, Elektra music, got played.

JOE SMITH: Going into the Seventies, when we were Deep Purpling and Black Sabbathing and King Crimsoning and Led Zeppelining and all those things, Jac wasn't very visible in that, and hadn't chosen to be.

JAC: I wasn't into noise. If I didn't get the music, we didn't record it. At the same time, if I was going to be able to sign a major group in England, with Ahmet, Mo and Joe getting first crack at most everything that came through the UK office, I would have to find it myself, as surreptitiously as possible, and without any help from our English company.

IAN RALFINI: Elektra in England needed nurturing, but with the pressure on everybody there wasn't time to stop and do it. The three companies weren't of equal size, but in Jac's mind he was of equal size to the other executives, and therefore he wanted everything to be the same. He had to have strength. It was like he was fighting all of them on his own doorstep.

Every time he came to the office, it was always something he wasn't happy about. I mean, he let everybody know about it. Jac wanted it done his way. He was organized, he had his Filofax, and he laid it out. He was on top of everything. He would look at everything, the press releases, every piece of information that went out, and he followed through. He knew every detail, and he assumed that everybody else would know it too. Jac is a very intelligent person. He has a great vocabulary, and I'd know when he left the room that we had been castigated or praised.

We'd go to extreme lengths to get things right, really bent over backwards and tried, that's how sensitive we were to his needs. And unlike the other companies, it was always "him." With the others, it was, "I've got to satisfy Warners, I've got to satisfy Atlantic." With Jac, it was Jac. I remember one of the first things someone said to me: "When dealing with Jac, you have to remember you have to spell Jac with a C, Holzman with a Z, and you have to remember Elektra has a K."

We did a big promotion for Elektra at the Mayfair Hotel. We bought the restaurant for the evening, invited all the staff, DJs, everyone in the media. We flew some people in from America, Mel Posner, a lot of the Elektra staff. Nesuhi was there, representing WEA, and Phil Rose, managing director of WEA International. And Jac, of course.

We had ordered this enormous cake, about three feet by three and a foot high, with candles and a sugar Elektra butterfly. One side is the WEA logo, another is the Warner-Reprise logo, another the Atlantic logo, and finally the Elektra logo. The cake arrives. They put it down on the table, and Phil says, "Turn it around." So they turn it around. Phil says, "No, no, turn it around—get the Elektra logo in front." And would you believe, there was a WEA logo, an Atlantic logo, and two Warner-Reprise logos—and no Elektra logo!

I thought Phil, who is this very quiet Canadian, was going to have a heart attack. He was having a cholesterol problem and he was not eating cream or butter or eggs and all that . . . cake. But quickly he starts on the icing. He's eating like a pig. It was like this whole side of the cake was destroyed, and he was going to say the Elektra logo was on that side.

JAC: Poor Phil, the insult to his arteries was in vain. I cut the cake but never noticed the inscription.

Chapter 28

On a futon in Japan a song is heard,
the way it should be ...
One magic night at the Troub ...
New girl in town wakes up a star

JAC: The downside of working so hard and traveling so much was that it took me away from the music, especially at home in the US, so it was a double pleasure when I happened upon a great artist who seemed custom-made for Elektra.

CARLY SIMON: While I was growing up I did not want to be a singer, I did not want to be a star. I did not want to be in the public eye at all. From time to time, I wanted to be various things, from a spy to a nurse to a schoolteacher, to a professor's wife, where I would serve up the dinners.

I started singing with my sister Lucy, folk songs, just to make money for a summer vacation, and that turned into a semi-professional relationship, actually quite a professional relationship. I wouldn't say a lucrative one, but while I was in college we did sing together around the campuses of New England, for about two years. And then in the Village. We were the opening act for Woody Allen and Bill Cosby and Joan Rivers, all the wonderful comics who were testing out their new material. Shel Silverstein played there. We also opened for the Tarriers—Alan Arkin, Marshall Brickman. All these people went on to do good things.

You did have the feeling that you were in on something that was really beginning, a movement. It was exciting to be a part of that, in whatever small way. There was much more jamming than now, people just sitting around backstage and playing. People were so generous with their time. Theo Bikel would come into our dressing room and teach us songs. Buzzy Linhart, who was on the scene, so talented. I remember Phoebe Snow would come back and I'd teach her things.

Anyway, Lucy and I were the Simon Sisters, and we had a minor hit, 'Winken, Blinken and Nod.'

When Lucy married, I decided that we would not have a career anymore, and I was happy about that—not because I wanted a solo career, I didn't want a career at all. But I kept on getting somehow sucked into it. People would pay me a compliment, you see: "Wow, you have a great voice, you should make a record."

So I made a demo record. John Court introduced me to Albert Grossman, and then I met Bob Dylan, and the Band, and I made this record called "Carly and the Deacon." Albert Grossman had this image of me and this Southern deacon, and the deacon was probably going to be Richie Havens. They looked around for a suitable deacon and couldn't come up with one, so consequently I recorded a couple of tracks with Bob Dylan's engineer, Bob Johnston, with the Band playing.

One was a rewrite of a Dave Van Ronk song called 'Baby, Let Me Follow You Down.' Dylan rewrote the words for me the day before his motorcycle accident. He was pretty much out of it. I wonder what it would have been like the day after his accident? I never thought about that. Just before the accident was the time that he was most caressed and possessed by the various drugs that he was taking, and the effects on him were that he was pretty displaced. But it was a wonderful meeting, during which he gave me the lyrics that he had written for the Dave Van Ronk song. I fell in love with Robbie Robertson of the Band and we went into the studio and recorded.

And Bob Johnston said, "If you're nice to me, I'll make you a nice record." And I stood very calm and said, "I'm not that hungry." That was such a typical Hollywood casting couch routine that it was amazing to actually hear it come out of somebody's mouth.

But this was the end for me for quite a long time. I was frozen. Whatever Bob Johnston said to Albert Grossman, I was shelved. I wish I had those tapes. CBS owned the demo, and they never got put out. So I never heard them again.

Then I got an offer to sing with this group called Elephant's Memory. They were a bunch of very New York street-smart jazz hip people who had backed John Lennon for a time. And I had a very bad experience with them. Very bad.

They didn't like, as Albert Grossman didn't like, the fact that my parents had been wealthy and that I lived in a big house in Riverdale. Albert said to me, "On a one to ten scale as a woman, you're a nine." I said, "That's flattering, but where do I miss out?" Albert said, "You've had it too easy, you haven't suffered enough, you don't know what working for a living is like." And Elephant's Memory pretty much said, "Get off your fat ass and help us carry the speakers." I did have a fat ass at that point, by the way. But we didn't speak the same language at all, and the devastating part of it was that the management really screwed me.

I had never signed as a writer. I had signed something about performing with them, and they attached a writer's rider. And so later, after my first, second and third hit, they sued me. That was my experience with Elephant's Memory. Nothing good came out of it. Only that lawsuit. I'm sure that happens to a lot of people.

I didn't do more than five or six gigs with them. I left and went to work as a counselor at summer camp. There I met Jacob Brackman and we formed a very important friendship, which was to guide many of the things I did over the next ten years.

I was playing the guitar and singing for friends, and I sang at Jake's house. There were these Hollywood types—Jake was good friends with Jack Nicholson, Bob Rafelson and all those people. Jerry Brandt was over there one night at a party, and I sang a couple of my songs for him, and he said, "I'd love to manage you, and I'd love to put up money for you to do a demo."

So I did about five songs, with David Bromberg as the producer. Jerry took my tape to CBS, and Clive Davis heard it and threw it across the room and said, "What do I want with a Jewish New York girl?" That's what Jerry told me. And then he brought it to Jac.

From the time I was in high school, all the records I liked were on Elektra. I was very aware of the music industry. It was something that looked glamorous to me from outside, when I was in college. I always thought if I could ever make it in the music business I would want to be on Elektra. It was an appealing label. Elektra had Nonesuch, which was wonderful; I had a big library of Nonesuch records. And Elektra had artists that I liked. Theodore Bikel. Judy Henske—I loved Judy Henske. She was just kind of solidly earthy. Amazing. I remember her singing 'Wade in the Water,' and I adored that. I still have that record. And the Butterfield Band. And Judy Collins. I admired Judy Collins so much. She was one of the females I emulated, and I copied her songs, and the fact that she was on Elektra meant a lot to me, too. So Elektra had a standard. Elektra meant—if I get a book now and it's published by Knopf, it means that somebody there is checking their list. They're the third little pig, they're very careful about what they do and what they don't do, they have good taste, they seem to have values. And I had heard that Jac Holzman was terrific.

JAC: Carly's friend Jerry Brandt, who was sidelining into management, brought me a tape and said, "Look, I think this girl is rather unusual. Her name is Carly Simon." "Is she one of the Simon Sisters?" I asked. One of my favorite songs was a little lullaby called 'Winken, Blinken And Nod.'

In a few days I was to fly to Japan with my son Adam, who was then twelve, for Expo '70 in Osaka, and almost as an afterthought I tossed the cassette into my carry-on bag. The Walkman was not yet invented, so I lugged a rather cumbersome Sony cassette recorder, battery-driven, six heavy D cells. I'm isolated at Lake Hakone in a little ryokan, sleeping on a futon, it's four in the morning and I still haven't adjusted to the time difference, so I slip on the Carly Simon tape and listen through headphones. And whatever drowsiness I felt just evaporated. She is wonderful. Here I am in the Japanese countryside, and there's no phone at the inn. I don't even know how to dial a phone in this country. And I'm going to lose this artist! A few days later, I'm back in Tokyo, and I call Jerry and tell him that I love the tape and definitely want to work with Carly.

CARLY SIMON: So I went up to the Gulf & Western Building—it was an interesting building that swayed when you went to the top—and had my first meeting with Jac Holzman. He was very tall, with a leadership quality about him. His conversation was letter perfect. He wouldn't waste a word. It was almost as if you could read exactly what he was saying, in a letter. There's a very organized thing about him. You have the feeling that all his desk drawers are very neat and that every record and tape is catalogued. He was like a machine in a lot of ways, yet he had a very fluent imaginative style.

He took a strong role in the beginning of my career, very hands-on. The first thing was, he did not see me as a writer. Interestingly enough, Clive Davis doesn't see me as a writer, either. Clive Davis said only a couple of years ago that I was a singer, I wasn't really a writer. When I was inducted into the Songwriters Hall of Fame, I think he stopped saying that. But Jac at the beginning did not see me as a writer, either. And he said so.

He had heard my songs from the demo tape, and without hearing anything else he said, "I see you more as an interpretive singer," and "I'd like you to do songs of Tim Buckley," and he gave me various names of other people whose songs he wanted me to record—Tim Hardin, Paul Siebel, some Donovan songs. He played a lot of tunes for me.

I just went about my own business, writing my own songs. I think I was challenged by his saying that he didn't think I was a writer. Every time I wrote a song I would say, "What about this?" and he'd say, "Yes, that's good!" So he began to think of me in his own mind as a singer-songwriter, which I knew I already was, but he had to catch up with my vision. He simply had not heard what I could write, and that most of the material I sang of my own demonstrated a sincerity that was truer than when I interpreted the songs of others.

In my own mind I think I fashioned myself like a Carole King, because I wanted to be a writer more than anything else. I thought that maybe other artists would
hear my songs and want to do them. People say, "Are you a singer first or a writer
first?" Now I think I'm both first. And I don't always have to be the singer, I don't
always have to be the writer. And within my writing, I don't always have to be the
lyricist and I don't always have to be the composer. But then I didn't want to be an
interpretive singer, because if I'd been an interpretive singer and made an album, I
would have had to have gone out and promote it, and I didn't want to, because I
was too scared of getting on the stage. I hated to get onstage. I hadn't discussed this
with Jac. Or with Jerry Brandt. I almost hadn't discussed it with myself. It was
more panic.

JAC: Carly pulled together a fine group of songs, and now I had to select the right,
the most appropriate, producer. I had a hunch about Eddie Kramer who had
worked with Jimi Hendrix and who performed his magic at Electric Lady Studios,
on 8th street in the Village, a studio, literally underground, that he helped design.
Eddie was skilled at creating a rich, fat sound, each instrument or voice being heard
with its proper weight, and for her first album Carly needed the strength of a real
pro in the studio.

CARLY SIMON: Not all the songs had arrangements. A lot of them were head
arrangements—just get in the studio with a bunch of people and figure it out. I
would bring in other records. I was very big on James Taylor's sound at that point.
I brought in 'Sweet Baby James' and said, "I want the drums to sound like Russ
Kunkel on this track," or I would say I wanted a piano player that sounded like the
piano player on Judy Collins's record. I gave input, but I didn't know too much
about what I was doing. Eddie Kramer was producing, and he knew all the musicians. He had just done the Joe Cocker record, and I guess Jac thought he would be
good for me.

JAC: I went to several of the early sessions and they seemed to be getting on.

CARLY SIMON: But we had some wars and Jac was in Europe, so I called Keith.

KEITH HOLZMAN: About two weeks into the project Carly called, frustrated with
Eddie and the sessions. It wasn't fisticuffs or anything, just disagreements, and they
needed a buffer. I sped down to the studio and mediated, smoothed the waters,
held her hand, and got her through the remaining sessions plus attending all the
mix sessions.

STEVE HARRIS: I met Carly before she finished the album. David Steinberg was
friendly with her and we had talked about her and he said, "Why don't we go over
to her apartment?"
    She had a lovely flat on East 35th Street, right off Lexington Avenue. When I
walked in, I thought there was something about her, and I couldn't put my finger
on it. Sometimes she looked attractive, sometimes she didn't. We started talking

about the record. I hadn't heard it yet. She said, "Would you like to hear one of the songs?" She picked up her guitar and she sang the first cut on side one. And when she started to sing, her whole face changed, her whole manner shifted. She became absolutely beautiful and I thought, "If anything happens to this record, if we can get her out, working in front of an audience, this is going to be a killer."

JAC: The album was different from anything else I had been hearing and that buoyed me. The songs were sophisticated and openhearted, which is a rare combination. Some of the lyrics reminded me of Stephen Sondheim, with their keen sense of the crosscurrents of life and the human condition. Though Carly sang with a rock backing, her polished, well-bred voice was of a kind rarely heard in that context. Bill Harvey and I decided to give the album cover a soft, matte finish, a mark of substance and quality. The cover photo showed Carly wearing a lace dress with lace curtains behind her, sitting in a homey setting, legs gloriously akimbo, with a challenging look as if waiting for the world to finally pay attention to her.

Carly greets the world on her first album
EKS-74082

CARLY SIMON: Jac was the one who picked 'That's The Way I Always Heard It Should Be' for the single. It wasn't on the first demo tape. I had been asked to write the music for a TV documentary called "Who Killed Lake Erie?" a very early environmental documentary, and that became the melody for 'That's The Way I've Always Heard It Should Be.' Once I've got a melody in my head, I can't write words to it. For me, the words have to come first. So I had that melody for so long that I was blocked. I thought it would be fun to write some songs with Jake Brackman, so I gave it to him, and he came up with the lyrics. That's the first time that we ever collaborated. He was able to write from my point of view—that was what was so great about it.

We didn't know that it was going to be the single. But Jac did. I think it's terribly important when you put a song out—I don't think a lot of people are aware of this—that the song and the singer really match up, persona-wise. Because every song has a character of its own, and if the singer and the song are really closely interwoven, closely enmeshed in personality and essence, then it's probably going to catch on. At least it's going to be true. And when Jac picked 'That's The Way I Always Heard It Should Be'—that song was so much me. I can't really describe why. But Jac was able to see it. He was able to create a synthesis, or at least decide when it existed, and he was able to pick the songs that were most true to the artist. And so 'That's The Way I've Always Heard It Should Be' was a very smart choice, because it was introducing me to the public that wasn't aware of me, with a song that was unusual, that wasn't the typical single of the day. He took a chance on it.

STEVE HARRIS: The record came out in February of 1971. Carol Hall came out with a record at the same time, and Paul Siebel, and nothing much happened to the three albums. Nice word of mouth on Paul: "Isn't he wonderful?" Carol the same. Both great music, not good sales. Meanwhile I'm on the phone all over the place about Carly.

CARLY SIMON: I went off to Jamaica on a holiday and came back. The single was out, and Jac called me from California saying that Nina had been driving along the freeway and it had come on the radio and she had to pull off to the side because she was so moved by it. That meant a lot to him, that she had reacted so profoundly. And that was a sign that it was going to hit a lot of people in a very strong way.

It started moving up, slowly but steadily. Then I got a call from Steve, very excited. It was up around Number 25.

STEVE HARRIS: I'm promoting it. I'm on the phone. Now I need Carly in front of an audience, and I want to get her the right show, and I figure the best way to introduce her live is in Los Angeles. I heard about Elton John breaking big after his first night at the Troubadour.

JAC: I had been in London several months earlier, when Elton was still pretty much unknown in the US. I saw his album in several record stores, bought a copy, listened, and hightailed immediately over to Dick James to secure the US rights. Dick had a longstanding deal with Decca/MCA for release of his product through their Congress label, but he told me that if MCA didn't pick it up I could have it. I couldn't imagine that MCA would blow it, and they didn't.

This was when the Troubadour was really hot. The Elton John gig had just created a furor rarely seen in a town blasé about success. Radio stations took out paid ads thanking him for playing such a killer set and hailing his arrival. The irony was that another Elektra artist, David Ackles, was the headliner. Now, Elton was an over-the-top David Ackles fan and when he heard that David was on the same bill he was overjoyed.

STEVE HARRIS: I was pushing Carly. I called up Doug Weston, the owner of the Troub: "Who've you got coming in?" He reads me off about nine weeks worth of bookings. And when he got to Cat Stevens, I said, "That's the show, Doug. I want that show." Of course Carly would have to sign over everything to Doug, probably including her first-born child—that's how Doug was operating at the time. I called her: "Carly, Carly, we're going to do the Troubadour, and you're going to open April 6th."

CARLY SIMON: I was completely flustered, because it never occurred to me that this record was going to take off. I said I really couldn't do it, that I didn't really want to be a performer.

Well, I don't think they believed it at Elektra. They just thought I was hemming and hawing. The feedback was, "You can't not promote this record."

JAC: She had to be seen.

STEVE HARRIS: Carly says, "I have to perform? Let's talk." So I go over to her apartment. The realization had finally hit her. She says, "I can't go out there. I'm afraid to fly." I said, "So am I." And I really am. She says, "I haven't got a drummer." I said, "I'll work that out for you." Then she says, "I have to have a minor operation." I mean, she put all these roadblocks in the way. I said, "Look, we'll fly together. We'll both get loaded before we take off. I'll take fifty milligrams of valium, with some drinks." Carly says, "OK, I'll take five milligrams with a couple of Old-Fashioneds." Fine. Then she calls up again: "I can't do this job without a drummer." I said, "What kind of drummer do you want?" "Somebody who sounds like Russ Kunkel."

CARLY SIMON: Because I knew perfectly well that Russ Kunkel was on the road with James Taylor. So I thought he was not going to be available.

STEVE HARRIS: I call up Russ: "Russell, what are you doing April 6th through the 12th?" Russell says, "Nothing, James isn't working." I said, "Great, Carly Simon." He said, "Five hundred bucks." I called Carly and said, "I got you somebody who sounds just like Russ Kunkel." She says, "Oh, who?" You know, she was prepared to say, "Forget it, I can't do it." I said, "Russ Kunkel," and she screams and says, "Well, I guess I have to do it, don't I?"

CARLY SIMON: I made that huge step and said yes. We went into rehearsals, in my apartment.

STEVE HARRIS: Then Carly says, "Should I have the operation before or after the gig?" I said, "Look, I got you Russ Kunkel, I'll hold your hand on the plane, we'll work this out."

CARLY SIMON: So we flew, Steve and me, on valium. Five milligrams for me, which was a lot, forty for Steve—he really wanted to kind of float through the experience.

It was very exciting, but I tried very hard not to think about it. I tried to just let the minutes go by and soon it would be over. Because it was very scary.

STEVE HARRIS: We arrived two days early, and we were having a wonderful time, just terrific.

CARLY SIMON: It was so exciting to me, just driving in from the airport. I was a very East Coast person, never been west of New Jersey, and this was the first time I had seen a palm tree, if you can believe it. I remember being so amazed at the whole different color of it, the whole landscape. It was so un-East Coast and it seemed so dramatically far away. It was just thrilling. And I remember thinking, "Well, I can't be scared, this is a foreign land, these people won't even speak the same language. I don't have to be scared of them."

Steve was so giddy and giggly and fun, very eager to share and spill the beans and be naughty and scared with me. So alive. We stayed at the Continental Hyatt House on Sunset. He and I both had rooms with beds on platforms. His room was red with a crown over the bed. I was just amazed. I had hardly ever stayed in a hotel—I don't think I ever had. I was so provincial. It's very hard to call somebody provincial when they come from as sophisticated an environment as I did, but I was so backward in terms of my expansion into the world, this was a whole new world for me, and I was already twenty-five. How could I have lived that long and gone nowhere? I don't know.

We went up on the roof to the pool and we ordered drinks, and it seemed like the absolute most decadent thing that had ever happened to me—drinks on the roof! And I was trying very hard to get enough of a sunburn so that I would look like a California girl. This is my first time on the West Coast, and I wanted everything that the West Coast had, I wanted it all, including the sun. But it was April and it was quite cold, and I couldn't get the tan.

We went over to the Troubadour and had a rehearsal with Russ Kunkel, who was a kind of a demi-god to me, because I was already in love with James Taylor from a distance, that whole sound—I hadn't yet thought I was going to have his children. So I was rehearsing with Russ, and I was in awe of him, and somehow I didn't know how I was going to get through it, but I thought, "It's only six songs"— as an opening act I only had to prepare six songs. I had such a wonderful band. I loved Jimmy Ryan so much, and Andy Newmark. All of the guys were so great that I started to love being around musicians, the sensibility of the musician. This was my first real band experience. It was heavy. I loved it. And that's something I've never lost.

STEVE HARRIS: Then came the sound check. Jac knows sound, so I wanted him there if there were any technical problems. Jac found romance rewiring machines, as well as in the music and the artists. The sound check went fine.

JAC: The Troubadour had better than average acoustics and a good sound system which we augmented by bringing in our best studio mikes. Carly's voice was strong, and once we got the instruments balanced properly, blending her into the final mix would be easy.

There was not a moment of fear showing in the rehearsal. She seemed like such a pro.

CARLY SIMON: We went back to the Hyatt House and ordered room service, the first time I ever had room service, poor little rich kid. I think steak and french fries—I was eating meat in those days. Russ stayed and we watched a boxing match in my room, with Steve and Jimmy. It got to be that thing where I was hanging out with men who were musicians or in charge of my career and it was getting heady, and that's the first sign of life from me that there was going to be something about it that I really liked. And that evening was the opening.

STEVE HARRIS: I said to Carly, "I'll pick you up about seven." I knock on her door, and if you've ever held a kitten that's totally afraid, that was Carly. She was trembling, she couldn't focus, she was stuttering. She had a stuttering problem, and I saw that she stuttered every once in a while. What she said was, as a child she stuttered, and she knew which words she could say and which she couldn't, and she created a whole other vocabulary to avoid those words. Well, that day she was stuttering all over the place.

At the Troubadour she was so afraid. She went to the dressing room, tuned up, and said, "How many people are out there?" I said, "Carly, it's completely sold out." It was star-studded.

CARLY SIMON: There were a lot of A&M people because of Cat Stevens, and all the Elektra people. The Elektra publicity people had put a rose on every table, saying "Love from Carly and Elektra." That was quite a cool thing. They put a lot of energy behind me.

Carly ... clearly at ease

STEVE HARRIS: She said, "Can I go down and talk to everybody? Make friends with them?" I said, "No, you can't." She said, "Can we go for a walk?" I said, "Yes, we can." We walked down the stairs of the Troubadour, Elektra Records is all there, ready to cheer her on, and we walked arm in arm out the door and they think we've split forever, never to return.

We come back by the back door, up the stairs, and Carly looks at me and says, "After the show, if Jac Holzman comes backstage and tells me how wonderful I am, 'Carly, you were just fabulous, we're going to be behind you a hundred percent,' I'll know I failed. I'll know he's faking. I don't want to hear that, Steve. Don't let him come back and say that to me."

CARLY SIMON: That sounds just like me.

STEVE HARRIS: So—she goes on.

CARLY SIMON: I only had to do my six songs. I was singing and playing the piano, and the microphone kept slipping as I was singing into it, it kept veering off to the left and I'd follow it and play the piano at the same time and then I would swing it back like a typewriter and start again, and it would go further and further over to the left, and the audience was watching me do this. No stage manager, no Doug Weston, no Steve Harris or anybody, came up and tightened the mike, which was what should have happened. But that preoccupied me so much that it preoccupied me right out of fear, because I was too concerned with the mechanics of this microphone slipping. It was a wonderful thing. It was like a little angel, just doing something to distract me so that I wouldn't be afraid. Six songs, and 'That's The Way I Always Heard It Should Be' was the encore. And it was great.

STEVE HARRIS: She was wonderful, just wonderful. One of those magical nights that you knew she was going to wake up in the morning a star.

Everyone comes backstage to pay their greetings and salutations. Of course the first one is Jac. And of course he says, "Carly, you're wonderful. We think you're terrific. Everything you want, we're going to do for you." And Carly's looking at me like—

JAC: Well, she was wonderful! How do you think she would have felt if I said nothing?

STEVE HARRIS: Downstairs I talk with the press and I'm taking accolades for her, then I rush back up and she's sitting on the couch in the dressing room, and James Taylor is sitting on the floor.

CARLY SIMON: That was the night I met James. He had come to see Russ, I guess, and I can't imagine what Russ had said: "I'm working with this new girl singer "—

STEVE HARRIS: They're having this fabulous conversation. I can see the sparks flying. And there was a whole bunch of kids calling to her from the alleyway behind, so she took her guitar and opened up the window and played a song for them, and she was feeling no pain. Then she looked at the musicians and said, "Well, fellas, we've got a second show to do."

CARLY SIMON: You know, there are certain periods in your life when a lot of events seem to come together and they influence the rest of your life. The year I met Jake Brackman was very important for me. And then '71, right around April 6, was a confluence of a lot of people and energies which would change the rest of my life. Meeting James. And the big success at the Troub.

STEVE HARRIS: She was riding a crest. Everybody wanted her for press conferences. And she handled them so well, so intelligent and warm and charming. The stories were great. They couldn't get enough pictures of her. She was this remarkable looking young lady. Incredibly sexy. They were playing all the cuts from the album like they were singles, and it was really unifying her image, her songs, her personality, her looks, everything, The Woman Of The Seventies.

CARLY SIMON: I was the new girl in town. You can only be the new girl in town once. In that town, at least. I still haven't played Europe, so I can still be the new kid in town there. But LA was a big success. I never remember being so popular in my whole life as then. At Elektra too, of course. I certainly felt it there. Especially when you're breaking in as an artist, you have that feeling more than when you are established. Everybody's rooting for you, everybody's plugging for you in a way that they never will again. And it's such an exciting feeling.

As a result of the Troubadour I was asked to open for Cat Stevens at Carnegie Hall, and Kris Kristofferson at the Bitter End. I loved being the opening act. I liked it so much

"Anticipation," Carly's second album
EKS-75016

better than being the star.

April was the Troubadour, May was the Bitter End, June was Carnegie Hall. The single was about Number 20 when I played the Troub, and then the next two months really solidified it. It got to Number 10.

After the first album, Jac stopped telling me he didn't think I was a writer, and I was off to England to make my second record.

JAC: "Anticipation." It was to be produced by an old friend of mine, Paul Samwell-Smith, bass player for the original Yardbirds.

Carly is one of those artists whose incandescence burns brightest with a new producer for each album. After they have squeezed the juice out of each other, it's on to the next, rather like a holiday romance, which in some cases I'm sure it was.

Paul made a very caring and lovely record, beautifully crafted, giving the songs a frame of easy intimacy that helped the listener welcome them into his own life. "Anticipation" consolidated Carly's position as a writer-singer of enormous craft, imagination and honesty.

Approaching her third album, "No Secrets," I was prepared with fresh produc-er meat. This time I wanted a producer who had been born in the studio, with solid arranging skills, a person who would push Carly and not flinch when she pushed back, as I knew she would. My candidate was Richard Perry, whose lawyer was none other than my off-and-on nemesis, Abe Somer. Abe seemed surprised by my call but quickly warmed to the idea of matching Richard and Carly.

"No Secrets" EKS 75049

Carly went off to England, to record at Trident Studios. There were rumblings of problems between her and Richard, but from an ocean away I could do nothing unless there was an explosion needing my fire-fight-ing skills. I'm sure they drove each other nuts, but out of that combination came "You're So Vain," her million-selling, Number 1 single.

Chapter 29

A producer tears his hair ...
A storm rider walks away ... LA Woman, this is the end

JAC: When I gave the Doors back their publishing and paid the audit without contest, Elektra received in return an additional album at a royalty of ten percent. Paul Rothchild was slated to produce, as usual. I hadn't heard any of the tunes, but Bill Siddons thought the band was ready. I was praying it would be simple and go down easy, because I was sure Jim wouldn't make it through interminable sessions like "Soft Parade" and "Morrison Hotel." But "Morrison Hotel" had gone gold in two days, and the chance for one more album was enormously attractive. I'd deal with the future of the group after that.

BILL SIDDONS: Paul was a very exacting and professional producer, very demanding, didn't take any bullshit from anybody and was capable of provoking Jim into performing. But he was also a dictator, and his personality was so strong that it had begun to cause problems. And now they wanted to be in control of their own destiny.

"Morrison Hotel" was the record that killed them. Paul made a record that was a great bunch of songs, but so well produced and so perfect that I didn't feel them anymore. When I heard those songs live, they were a completely different experience, and I felt Paul lost what he was there to do. I was the guy that lived the live end of the business. They wouldn't go on stage without me being there. That was the part I lived, and then we'd get these records that I thought was a different band. It just wasn't what I thought the Doors to be, and I think it was because of Paul's mania for detail. Where I'd hear it and go, "Yeah, great!" he'd hear it and go, "Oh, no, the harmonic sibilance there was causing this to"—Who cares? Paul cared because he heard and understood. He was brilliant and totally knew the recording process, but took it to a point of refinement that lost the soul, and when I didn't hear the soul I knew he was the wrong guy.

ROBBY KRIEGER: Paul was the King of Slow. Not slow, but take after take. And we thought by that time we had earned the right to be able to pick our takes. Not to have to do eight million takes to make sure we got the perfect take.

BILL SIDDONS: The band developed all the songs. It was a real difficult process at that point, because there was a lot of distrust, a lot of arguing over who wrote what.

PAUL ROTHCHILD: Two months of rehearsals—boring as hell.

JAC: Paul heard all the songs and thought it might take another year, which I knew was both an exaggeration and an impossibility. You could sense that Jim was getting terminally itchy and the boys were on edge also.

PAUL ROTHCHILD: I had just finished the Janis Joplin album, completed after she died, which was a labor of love. I was very proud of it. And here I'm confronted by the Doors, and they're turning out shit. Two good songs, 'LA Woman' and 'Riders on the Storm,' and the rest is lounge music. Two weeks into production, I quit.

BRUCE BOTNICK: We were in the studio and the band was playing and he turned to me and put his head in his hand and he said, "I can't do this anymore."

PAUL ROTHCHILD: I quit because I had grown tired of dragging the Doors from one album to another, especially dragging an unwilling Jim through being a performer, and he had virtually dried up. It had been getting harder and harder, and more expensive, and less fun. Purely because of Jim. Two out of three times Jim would either not want to work or would go out into the studio drunk. He would intentionally disrupt things, pull things off course. Never fruitfully. Most of the energies were spent trying to get Jim coordinated with the group.

ROBBY KRIEGER: It was a question of how far out he would go. The further out he went, the more we would have to bend in his direction to keep it all together.

JAC: The band itself was never less than solidly consistent. The variable was Jim. Poor Rothchild tore his hair, what he had left of it, and did a hundred takes, and finally he just couldn't go to the well anymore. He was exhausted, and so were the Doors.

BRUCE BOTNICK: We went off to a restaurant down the street, and in the meantime Paul called Jac, and then he told the guys he couldn't do it, and we went back to the studio and he had gone home. And I know what he felt like. He was a free man.

JAC: There was no point in forcing an issue that couldn't be forced. I talked it over with Bruce and Bill Siddons and suggested that they and the group sort it out and I would support any reasonable idea they came up with. I had come to respect Bill's judgment highly, and I was certain that when it came to records that would be in the bins for years to come, the band wasn't about to slack off.

BRUCE BOTNICK: The boys said to me, "What are we gonna do?" I said, "We can make this album together."

We sat down and figured it out. I didn't want to go back into the Elektra studio. I thought, "Let's go to Sunset Sound and see if we can get some of the old magic back." But things had changed a lot there, it wasn't the same anymore. I said, "Where do you feel most comfortable?" They said, "Our rehearsal hall." I said, "That's what I think, too. Why don't I get the console and the eight-track that came down from Paxton. We've got all this gear, I'll take it across the street and build a control room."

And Jac said, "Fine." He didn't question it for a second. Here's the major act on the label, and he's trusting it to a twenty-three-year-old kid.

JAC: I wasn't a bit worried about Bruce. He had contributed brilliantly to every note the Doors had recorded. Robby's point about the band making its own choices was fair. They had more than earned the right.

BRUCE BOTNICK: It came together without much rehearsal, like a day or two. They felt, like I felt, free as well. Paul felt he was free, and we were now free of him. No reflection on Paul—it's just that, you do it long enough, and under that control, and now it was like school's out, and we just had a ball.

BILL SIDDONS: One day at rehearsal Jim drank thirty-six beers.

ADAM HOLZMAN: I went to some of the rehearsals. I was a little hippie at that point, wearing a headband. Jim was nice to me, he'd say, "Hi, how are you doing?" One day he showed up late, and he gave each of the guys in the band a dollar because he was late.

BRUCE BOTNICK: We recorded it live, really wanted to get back to the basics.

JAC: I never felt that returning to eight-track from sixteen-track was a step backward. You pick the tool you need to do the job, and eight-track was more than sufficient for an organic location recording, which is what this was. Fewer tracks meant fewer mikes and less problems with microphone phasing, always a consideration in ad hoc studios. The result was a return to the original Doors sound, before all the distractions of fame and fortune got in the way.

I purposefully stayed away from the sessions except for one evening. I walked across to the Doors office and rehearsal space and saw the desks pushed off to the side, heavy mover's quilts nailed to the walls, the windows covered, and Bruce, a floor above in Bill Siddons' office, with console, speaker and tape recorder, the bare minimum of everything. There was a lot of running up and down because Bruce was out of sight of the band, which probably was a plus. There were no visual clues. It was so spartan and so right.

JOHN DENSMORE: I think "LA Woman" is kind of like the first punk album. It's really raw and there are mistakes. But the concept was to just go for it—try to get in tune, but if the passion is there and you hit a few wrong notes, that's alright. Garages are where this music started, you know, let's not get too pristine.

BRUCE BOTNICK: We recorded the entire album and mixed it in ten days, and I remember the day we were supposed to start mixing it was the LA quake.

I finished the album and took it to play for Jac at Elektra with the Doors—without Morrison, who would never appear—and Jac sat there and wept.

JAC: I had been worried about the material because of Paul's negative comments, but the album knocked me out, song after song.

BILL SIDDONS: Jac listened to the whole album, and then said that 'Love Her Madly' is a Top 5 record, and 'Riders On The Storm' will get more FM airplay than any Doors LP cut, and song by song he ran down exactly what happened. The Doors said, "Wait a minute. We think 'The Changeling' is the single. That's what we want out, because that's the most credible musically." Jac sat there and looked at them like they were nuts and said, "It's not a hit. 'Love Her Madly' is a hit." And they said, "No." The meeting ended and he hadn't swayed them at all. It took about two weeks to get them to go with the obvious hit.

JAC: I wasn't sure there'd be another album ever, so I had Bill Harvey create a collector's cover. The Doors' faces were printed on clear film. The backing color of the inner sleeve could be changed and would affect the mood of the package. This is the first album on which Jim is bearded. His photo is on the right, no bigger, no smaller than the others, just another guy in the band.

RAY MANZAREK: "LA Woman" was the final record on our extended contract. At that point we were free to re-sign with Elektra, sign with another company, continue the band, break the band up, whatever we felt like doing. We were free and clear. And Jim had finished his obligations, as he felt, to the Doors.

He said, "Hey, you guys, I've got to take a break. I need some time off. This rock and roll is getting to me. I need to get away and find out who I am."

We all said, "Where are you going ?" Jim said, "Paris." What could be better? What better place for a poet, an artist, an American poet to go, than to Paris?

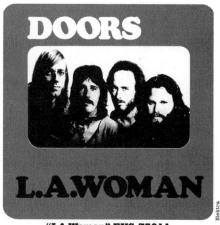

"LA Woman" EKS-75011

PAUL ROTHCHILD: I'd love to know whether Jim actually was searching for his medium, as so many people of great talent have done in the past. I think that perhaps rock was just the convenient medium, the popular one for art. To break through in our time, rock seemed to be the one. I think ultimately if he hadn't succeeded in rock he would have gone in a direction not unlike a Sam Shepard, where he would have been a playwright, an actor, a director. In another time Jim might have been a traveling troubadour, someone who went from town to town with a poem and a little bit of shtick, to entertain people.

But he was a haunted man. He was cursed by his own brilliance. He definitely had that poet's curse. He rode with madness. That was what chased him his whole life. He both explored it and fled from it.

About two weeks before he left for France—I hadn't seen him in six months— I was at the front desk filling out some paperwork. I heard the door open. I turned around and saw this large man entering. I didn't recognize him, turned back, finished my paperwork. Then I was tapped on the shoulder, and I turned around and this large person, who looked like Orson Welles' younger son, said, "Hi, Paul." I looked at him and I said to myself, "Holy fuck, this is Jim!" He had a huge beard, and was generally unrecognizable as a sex object. He had killed that part for sure.

DIANE GARDINER: By the time he went to Paris he looked like the old man from the mountain—not old, perhaps, but the middle-aged man from the mountain.

RUSS MILLER: We were having dinner. Jim was very quiet that night, saying good-bye to everyone. Jac was there, the other Doors, Bruce Botnick, Fred Myrow. Fred told me that Jim said he was never coming back.

JAC: There was a poignancy to that evening. Elektra had planned an office-warming party for six o'clock on Wednesday, March 3, 1971 to show off the expanded offices and our new Studio A. Jim had dropped by around seven-thirty, "to see," as he said, " what I helped pay for," and then we all went to dinner down the street at the Blue Boar. Jim, who was always fairly quiet in groups, was unusually so that evening, half there and half somewhere else. I could feel finality hanging in the air.

As we left the restaurant, we all said our goodbyes to him. We had enjoyed a lifetime together in the concentrated, blazing arc of rock and roll. Jim and I hugged each other, and then he turned somewhat awkwardly and walked away. I watched and wondered if I would ever see him again.

Chapter 30

The trick is not to bleed ...
A baby is born in Bolinas ... A poet dies in Paris ...
The song of the Nightbird ...
I knew it was gonna happen

ELLEN SANDER: Very early on, when Jac and I were dating, spending most of our time together, he would always ask these big questions. "What do you want out of life?" You ask a twenty-four-year-old woman, "What do you want to leave behind?" I told him my wish list, and it included children.

In 1969 we were driving up the Big Sur coast, staying at the Big Sur Inn, and during the night he took me to Esalen and we sat in the baths and he said, "I want to be the father of your child." He was very ardent about it, and we're sitting naked in these baths on this starry night. It was one of those romantic moments. I'll never forget it as long as I live. I was overjoyed, because until then I didn't know if this was going to be another love affair or the love of my life, and of course I was hoping for the latter.

When we moved into Tranquility, we went to the Westchester antique fair and Jac bought an antique cradle.

So the baby was an idea for a year, and then I got accidentally pregnant. I lost that baby, after only a few weeks. I was miserable. Six months later we were ready to try again. We spent the holiday season of 1970 very busy, until one night Jac said, "I think I got you that time. I'd like a son for my birthday."

But as the pregnancy went along, he would be very sharp and critical with me, provoke me into arguments—which was not difficult. I would try to say, "What's the problem? Can we work it out?" But he was just into a mode of being very difficult to get along with, treating me like he didn't like me any more.

JAC: Ellen was very picky, extremely competitive and it was a constant cat fight. Perhaps it was the pregnancy and, if so, I didn't understand that at the time.

MARTY RICHMOND: There were some times at Tranquility spent tippie-toeing, when either there had just been an incident or there was one about to happen, but I don't recall any real slambanger.

JAC: Unless you count the time that Ellen shied a cookbook at me.

ELLEN SANDER: We got to the point where I said, "Look, you know, I can't stand this anymore, and neither can you."

One day when we were in Los Angeles, he said, "Listen, I don't think it's going to work out with the two of us together." I just got in the car he had rented for me and started driving. I found myself a few hundred miles up the coast, called the rental company to say I was going to keep the car for a while, I didn't know how long, and I drove up the coast to Mendocino and back, and on my way back I made a down payment on a house in Bolinas.

JAC: I gave Ellen enough money to buy the house and start her life anew and, of course, agreed to support our child.

ELLEN SANDER: We went to Mexico, to some very luxurious tennis resort, and tried to reconcile, but I was too hurt. Jac has a way of doing something with finality, and no matter how good an idea it might or might not have been to reconcile at that point, I was unable to overcome my own response to that evening when he took care of business, said he would take responsibility for the child, but he didn't want to be with me anymore.

JAC: My memory of Mexico is that we were really saying our goodbyes to ourselves as a couple.

ELLEN SANDER: We're buying things there, and I saw a plate that you'd hang on the wall, very pretty, painted, and I asked Jac to buy it for me, and we both knew that I was buying it for my new home, it wasn't something that would be in Tranquility, it was a California piece.

So that's how that happened. I don't think either one of us handled it as well as we could have. I moved out in June of 1971.

JAC: That July 4 weekend I was at Tranquility with the usual gaggle of guests, and for some inexplicable reason I began telling all the stories I knew about Jim Morrison. I talked about Jim for hours, in the pool, at dinner, in the living room afterwards.

When I returned to the office on Monday morning, I received a call from Max Fink, Jim's lawyer. Max told me that Jim had died in Paris over the weekend and would be buried, as Max put it, in the cemetery of the poets, Père Lachaise. Bill Siddons was already on his way to see to the arrangements and deal with the local authorities.

I was dazed, disordered and dumbfounded. I sat at my desk staring at the wall, unable to move or say anything. Jim's death affected me more than the death of my dad or my grandparents, who had been along in years. It was more like losing someone whose presence in your life made a profound change after which nothing would ever be the same for you again.

Jim was twenty-seven, the same age as Jimi Hendrix and Janis Joplin when they died. I recalled their deaths and what a circus they had become. Elektra had to do better. We were not going to use this as an opportunity to ship records or any of that kind of sordid nonsense.

My guess was that we might have, at the outside, forty-eight hours to prepare. I called in Bill Harvey, told him the news and asked him to get on a plane to the West Coast and manage things from that end while I handled New York.

I knew the radio stations and press would be calling and I wanted to avoid interviews or questions to which I didn't have answers. I wrote out a statement in longhand, a personal reminiscence about what Jim's loss meant to me, to all of us at Elektra, to his friends, and to music. The media would get only the statement.

In the meantime we at Elektra had to keep the secret. It was not our place to tell anyone. That right belonged to Jim's family, or Pamela, or the Doors. Our job was keep it from turning into a tabloid craze, and in large measure we succeeded.

That same evening I had a dinner already planned with Carly Simon.

CARLY SIMON: I was to meet Jac at the Algonquin Hotel, and first I met Peter Beard for cocktails, and I had some kind of anxiety attack or something and fainted, and I was brought up to Peter's room and a doctor was called in, and then right after that Jac and I went to eat at a Japanese restaurant near the Algonquin. I was so absorbed in my own story, that I went on for fifteen minutes telling him about it. And he said, "Well, I've had a bad day too," and he told me Jim had died.

He was trying to keep it together. I would have been crumpled over in tears and having a fit. Jac's emotional expression takes a very different path from mine. He did-

Pat Faralla

Jim's grave at Père Lachaise before the commemorative stone was installed

n't cancel our dinner. He was controlled. But as much as you can imagine Jac out of control or losing it, he really was— running back and forth to the phone.

JAC: To share the news with Carly lightened the load and I knew I could count on her discretion.

On Wednesday evening I was still pretty upset and while I was listening to Alison Steele, the Nightbird, on WABC, the phone rang. Somehow Alison had found my unlisted home phone number. She asked me point blank if Jim was dead. We had had more than our forty-eight hours, we were ready, and I told her the truth. No details. I said, "Please play 'Riders On The Storm,' it's all in that song."

PAT FARALLA: Jim had written that death made angels of us all. To me, Jim was a fallen angel. His vision was his torment.

BILL SIDDONS: Jim moved to Paris to find out who he was creatively. He realized he had created a monster in the music world and didn't want to live it out anymore. The audience said, "Give me that again, and again." He didn't want to. He had left the band. He had felt controlled and manipulated by the band for quite a while, and there was a lot of animosity there, although no hostility. So he went to find a different muse.

Now, Jim may have died of a heart attack and he may have died of a drug overdose. He may have died of a heart attack induced by a drug overdose. But he didn't do drugs in the sense that he was an addict—he drank. He bought a drug, he found out what it did, he was done. If he died of a drug overdose it wasn't in the pursuit of pleasure, it was in pursuit of "break on through to the other side." He did everything to excess. It's only logical that this guy would kill himself for drugs if he experimented with them. Once, he bought an ounce of coke and did it in eight days. If he did that with heroin, it would have killed him, and that may be what happened to him. But not because he was a drug addict. If he happened to die of a drug overdose, he happened to die because he did something stupid. And he may have, but I don't know that he did.

ROBBY KRIEGER: For one thing, he was very sick when he went over to Paris. He was coughing up blood, that kind of stuff. So I think it would have been very easy for him, after a night of drinking, to take a snort, or couple of snorts of something and not know what it was. And then go into the bathtub, fall asleep and drown.

JAC: The last time Jim and I spent private time together was during the sessions for "LA Woman." We were sitting in a small bar near their rehearsal hall and Jim was pushing, trying to get me drunk. I wasn't foolish enough to match him beyond the first two. Jim chided me, "Jac, you've got to be more out there, on the edge." I said, "I understand, Jim, but the trick is to be out there and not to bleed."

BILL SIDDONS: To me, the consistency in Jim's persona was to push you far enough for you to get out of your shell and to become who you really were at the center. That's what he did to everybody. I had conversations with him where I had to get him to stop because he had taken my mind to places I didn't know how to handle.

He could be the biggest asshole in the world. And he could be one of the finest people you'd ever know. The guy who everybody perceived as nuts, arrogant, in fact was one of the most sensitive and highly developed minds I ever knew. There was a gentle, generous human soul there. And one of my more profound memories is his generosity.

FRANK LISCIANDRO: He regularly visited poets in Venice, and he always bought a number of copies of their books, and passed them out to his friends. He contributed money on an ongoing basis to the LA Art Squad, mural painters in Venice and Hollywood. They always needed funds for paint, scaffolding, just to have lunch. They would come to the office, bearded and longhaired, shabby clothes, and Jim would either empty out the petty cash or write them a check.

BILL SIDDONS: We were in a restaurant, some guy comes up, obviously just scratching by, and he's selling these little rings that he made out of the ends of spoons. Jim asked how many he'd sold, and the guy says, "Well, two today," and Jim said, "OK, I'll take the box." He continually did things like that.

PAUL ROTHCHILD: When I heard, I was sitting at home in Laurel Canyon, and Fritz Richmond came in. "Man," he said, "I've got bad news for you. We just heard down at Elektra. Jim died in Paris." And I had no feeling. I was numb. Then my first thought was, "Well, he finally made it over. I hope he's feeling good now."

There's a line from one of his poems I can't get out of my mind: "Out here, on the perimeter, there are no stars; out here we are stoned, immaculate." When you're on the cutting edge, there are no stars, no idols, because out there you're too high from the experience itself.

I think Jim spent every day trying to explore the frontiers. And one of the frontiers was death. Deep psychological explorations of death. He had a morbid curiosity about the other world. In Renaissance literature—and you hear this in old songs a great deal—the euphemism for orgasm, women would say, "I die, I die." Jim gets very deeply into sexual imagery and sexual exploration around the very words, "I die, I die." Playing with the ancient use of the word and bringing it to its new meaning. This again is going over to another world which is only partially reachable by the human mind. To him the exploration of death was another and maybe the ultimate high. 'The End' spells out how total his fascination was with dying. When you listen to that song, it's almost a love song to death. And the message is that this is not a bad thing. "Take comfort, my friend, who I love so much. This is the end of laughter, but also of soft lies." There's peace.

JAC: After the pain and the numbness and the confusion had washed away I was left with Jim's poetry and his songs. The road he was traveling had been mapped out, if only in his unconscious, and when you re-read his lyrics and poetry through the prism of his passing, it made some kind of off-kilter Homeric sense, rather like characters in the Iliad who are attracted to death as a passage to immortality. Jim understood this.

JAC: There was no one more into the Doors than Adam, and it was mutual. Jim would remember Adam's birthday, bring him a musical instrument, or just stop by and spend time with him.

NINA HOLZMAN: Adam ate and slept the music life, and Ray and Jim were enormous influences on him. When Jim died, we were very uneasy about the impact on Adam. It was summer, and Adam was away in camp. Jac and I each wrote to him. He didn't respond.

JAC: I was surprised when there was no call, no letter from him.

NINA HOLZMAN: The day came when we picked him up—

JAC: I asked why he hadn't called because we had been so concerned. He said, "No, I knew it was gonna happen."

NINA HOLZMAN: He knew Jim would never live to get older.

JAC: He said, "It's cool, because Jim's still with me, and I won't ever forget him. He's just gone to the place where he had to go." The wisdom of children.

JAC: Two and a half months after Jim died, and one week after my fortieth birthday, my child with Ellen was born.

ELLEN SANDER: I had a midwife and a Buddhist monk and some friends, and Paul Williams was my end-of-labor coach. While Jac and I were having our problems, Paul visited us at Tranquility. We were both very close to him and told him what was going on. Paul took me aside and said, "I know it's a difficult time. You didn't plan on raising a kid alone, but I know a lot of women who do it very successfully, and I know that you're going to be one of them, and I want to help." I said, "Help me have the baby." And he said, "I'd be pleased to." "Will you stand godfather?" And he said, "Yes."

I had the baby at home. Jac arranged to be in the area around the anticipated birth date. During childbirth he would call. I couldn't talk to him, I was busy. Paul would tell him how I was getting along.

He came the day after Marin was born. I'm lying on the bed with the baby, and Jac walks in the unlocked door and lies on the bed and picks him up, looks at him very carefully, and says, "Hello, pal." And then he just cried and cried.

I talked about this with Paul Rothchild once. "You know, I just never really understood that Jac and I never had a chance." And Paul's eyes filled with tears and he said, "I don't know what I can tell you that you don't already know." Perhaps, as loving as our intentions were, the times were against us in terms of our professional commitments. And our personal differences, he being in command and me being stubborn and defiant. It was difficult for me how authoritarian he was, and it was difficult for him how defiant I was. And neither one of us was always right. But we learned from each other, and we have this wonderful child whom we both adore.

Chapter 31

High tech, high performance, high mileage ...
Nashville cats... Pecan pie and watermelon in July ...
Flee ye from Mount Zion ...
Nearly a Sufi, almost a saint ... Taxi!

JAC: If my personal energy output at Elektra before the sale to Warner/Kinney was full out—and it always was—after the sale it was even higher. The extra load was partly WEA, and on top of that was technical work for the Warner Communications strategy group.

Steve Ross understood that with a vertically integrated record group and a film company he had a platform for building a communications empire. Within a few months of acquiring Elektra, he and Alan Cohen invited me to join a strategic planning team. Other members included Ted Ashley; Spencer Harrison, Ted's righthand man, a former broadcast attorney and consummate curmudgeon; and Peter Goldmark, one of my heroes, the co-inventor of the LP and now creating a research lab for Warner Communications. We were the think tank. Our charter was to figure out where to take the company. The invitation was unexpected but delightful. I could put my full range of knowledge and experience to work in a playpen bigger than anything I had ever imagined or could do on my own. The merger with Kinney/WCI was having unanticipated, heady benefits.

JOE SMITH: Jac had a talent for technical things. He read engineering journals voraciously, knew all about the innovations. He left us all in the dust with that.

JAC: We immediately honed in on cable TV as a splendid opportunity. I spent many engrossing hours brainstorming with Peter Goldmark. Though I wasn't as smart about technology as Peter, that didn't stop me from having arguments as an equal. We became very close friends. He gave me one of the three existing copies of the original LP. (Another is in the Smithsonian.)

I put in a lot of time on quad sound, which never took off in the Seventies but has now made a comeback in the late Nineties on the new DVD video discs as accompanying surround sound. And the laser disc—it was being worked on in Holland. In 1970 I flew over to see it, the first glass master, the only one of its kind in the world. I said to myself and anyone within our company who would listen—which wasn't everybody—"I've seen the future. The digital age is coming, and we will have a rare chance to reinvent the business, its economics and the means of delivering media and communications."

I loved the technology work. It was a game at a much higher level than the record business, and I was a player. It absorbed most of my time. I was flying all over the world, racking up hundreds of thousands of miles, and a sharply rising percentage of those were technology-driven, not music-driven, peaking at probably eighty-five percent technology to fifteen percent Elektra. One year I was in Japan every month for six months, and when I came home, I would have to work twice as hard.

PAUL ROTHCHILD: As Jac dealt with his success, which was coming at him with ever-increasing speed, he was at times short with people. The more successful Elektra became, the more demanding, brusque and inward Jac became. And the memo flow became more excessive. And after Elektra was sold and he got deeply involved in the gestalt of Warner—worldwide communications, corporate strategies—he was at his most inaccessible. I think it was because he was confronting his greatest challenges, and had little time for anything or anyone else.

JAC: Still, amid all the business hurlyburly and the technical brainbending, I kept my ears tuned for music to follow, and at a radio conference in Philadelphia I was led to take a walk down a country road.

During an off-the-record session people let down their hair and told the truth. Dick Clark talked very engagingly about early radio, the ethics (more precisely the non-ethics) of DJs and concert promoters. Next up was Michael Nesmith, ex-Monkee. He was so much more intelligent than the cute ersatz housebroken simian image—witty, articulate, and deeply concerned about how hard it was to get anything going on records in the early Seventies. I introduced myself and said, "You have interesting ideas. We should think about doing something together."

I invited him to Tranquility and we talked. Michael thought there was room for a West Coast record label featuring local country performers. West Coast country had been defined long before by Buck Owens, out of Bakersfield, and nothing fresh had happened since. There were fine natural country singers on the Coast. So—put together a simple studio and Michael would start producing records. Call the label Countryside, and release through Elektra and the WEA distribution system. It was a promising premise, a low-cost low-risk project—reminiscent of Paxton, but with the sizeable plus of being minus Frazier Mohawk, dope, and a gaggle of Cornish game hens.

I always thought of country music as a tributary of folk music. There were terrific writers in Nashville. From LA or New York it looked like a tough music community to enter. Someone would have to build and nurture those relationships. Russ Miller could do that and wanted to.

RUSS MILLER: One night Lonnie Mack came to my house in the Hollywood Hills with two albums under his arms. He said, "Put your ears between those speakers and smoke one of these and don't say anything." The first album was Roberta Flack. I freaked. The second was a Nashville singer-writer, Mickey Newbury, and I was so moved I cried.

Lonnie was a hero in Nashville. He said to me, "I've got some great friends there, great musicians." He introduced me to a lot of people, including Mickey, who was close to Kris Kristofferson, and he wrote songs for artists from Joan Baez and Buffy Sainte Marie to Ray Charles and Jerry Lee Lewis.

Mickey wouldn't come into town to see me, but he sent word to come out to his houseboat at Hendersonville. It was raining, and he welcomed me on board, and in the rain he sang. What an experience. We stayed up till about four in the morning, talking metaphysics, all kind of things. As I left, he shook my hand and said, "If you can get me off of Mercury, buy my contract out of there, I'll go with Elektra."

So I worked with Mickey. He wrote great songs and had interesting soulful ideas. He was the one who put together 'American Trilogy,' that Elvis Presley sang during his Vegas period: 'Battle Hymn Of The Republic,' 'Dixie,' and 'All My Trials, Lord,' the classic Northern song and the classic Southern song from the Civil War, and a song of black suffering.

Lonnie Mack also led me to Memphis, Tennessee, and Muscle Shoals, Alabama, and I was gathering up artists: Don Nix, Marlin Greene, and Marlin's wife Jeanie—

Lonnie Mack

she was white, but she sang black, she heard voices and truly believed she was the reincarnation of Mary Magdalene. Out of my Southern travels came a proposal from me to Jac: a tour, knock-down, boogie-woogie, bang-bang, funky great music, two drummers, black backup singers, Lonnie Mack's band and the band from Muscle Shoals, and Marlin and Jeanie and Don, and we would call it the Alabama State Troupers and the Mount Zion Choir and Band. Jac said, "Go for it."

I put everything together, and six days before the tour was supposed to start, with all the publicity cranking for Lonnie's new album, I'm visiting Jac at his house in the country, sitting in the sun, and Jac yells that Don Nix is on the phone, and what does Don tell me but Lonnie has disappeared.

I say to Jac, "Don't worry, I'll find him. We're friends. I'll get him back." I fly to Cincinnati where Lonnie lives. He's not there. I finally trace him to a place in Kentucky. He's w-a-y out in the country—he's a real country boy. I cross dirt roads, I ford streams. I finally come to a farmhouse, no electricity, and there's Lonnie's standing on the front steps. He says, "I'm not going back." I say, "How can you do this? We have a hundred thousand dollars tied up in this thing." He says, "I had this dream. I was running with my baby and my wife and the devil was after me and flames were coming out, and I woke up in a cold sweat and I walked over to the Bible in the motel there and the Bible was open to this text—'Flee ye from Mount Zion.'"

And that was it for Lonnie. I flew back to New York and walked into Jac's office, and Jac—I'll never forget this—took me in his arms and said, "Don't stop loving the artist, Russ. It's OK. We'll do something else. See who you can find."

I flew to Memphis and got this black blues guitar player, Furry Lewis, and he was great, he charmed the audiences. He was a heavy drinker. I'd hand him a bottle of Seagram's every day and shave him every morning. And the tour went on.

JAC: I went on the road with them. The publicity department had very authentic looking promotional shoulder patches made that said "Alabama State Troupers." In some of those roadhouses, with the boys at the bar barely able to sit their stools, and orthographically challenged anyway, not all that well equipped to distinguish between Troupers and Troopers, they thought we were the police.

RUSS MILLER: At that time the governor of Alabama was George Wallace, and when the tour was over he sent me a beautiful letter and a Confederate Civil War pistol.

JAC: Did we make any money? No. Was it fun to do? You bet. And the icing on the cake was how re-connected to the music I felt.

RUSS MILLER: In Nashville I was this freak from the West Coast, long hair, dressed like a cowboy and smoked dope, which was an acceptable thing in LA, while everybody down in Nashville was really hiding it.

Suddenly Jac and Mickey Newbury's publisher, Wesley Rose, decided that we should have a picnic to introduce Countryside in Nashville, a country picnic, and invite all the country-rooted people—watermelon, everything, at the lake, on the Fourth of July.

It was hot. Wesley Rose has sweat pouring down him, and there is Mike Nesmith and Mickey Newbury and Lonnie Mack, and Mel Posner. And Jac Holzman, president of Elektra Records, in a tank top. There's a picture of it someplace. I remember thinking, "What a culture clash."

At that time Nashville wasn't like it is today. We were staying at the Holiday Inn, and Jac—that night he nearly hit the fan: "You want to go to the movies?"

JAC: I wasn't much of a Nashville cat, but I loved the music. And there was nothing more seductive than spending an evening on Mickey's houseboat. His wife, Susan, just happened to bake the world's most sensuous all-Southern pecan pie. The lake, the quiet, the magnolia, a second piece of pie, Mickey singing—it doesn't get any better.

Jac and Mickey Newbury in the studio

JAC: In the early Seventies the Sixties singer-songwriter was an endangered species. They were either swallowed up in rock and roll, or off forming electric bands of their own. Carly Simon was of a differentiated species, but it was almost impossible for me to spot rarities, female or male. I simply didn't have the time anymore. It was Ann Purtill of our New York office who brought me Harry Chapin.

ANN PURTILL: I used to do reports for Jac of acts that I saw live that were of interest. These were called my hanging-out reports. I just typed them as if I was talking to Jac. He always said he liked them—I was listening with his ears, as he put it. I would do my report every Wednesday, after I had been out in the clubs on Tuesday night. Tuesday at the Gaslight or wherever was hoot night—it was still called that. I saw Bonnie Raitt; she was unsigned then. One night at the Bitter End I walked into a little ante-area and a woman smiled and said hello, because I have one of those faces that people think they know, and it was Lily Tomlin. I remember she did the rubber lady, the one who started out eating erasers and ended up with Goodyear tires.

After much badgering by a man named Fred Kewley, I went down to the Village Gate to see Harry Chapin.

FRED KEWLEY: Harry was opening solo for the family group, the Chapin Brothers. "Jacques Brel Is Alive And Well And Living In Paris" was playing from seven to nine, then we'd take over. We rented the Gate, $400 a week for five weeks, and continued on for nearly thirteen weeks. After expenses we cleared enough for bus fare for the musicians.

We were on the phone trying to stir up some action. We bugged and bugged and bugged the New York Times. Finally, at the second show, this guy came in with his girl friend. He was the writer. He was stoned out of his mind, drunker than a skunk. The show started and he fell asleep, put his head down on the table and was gone. He never even saw Harry, but his girl friend flipped. So Harry got a rave review from the girl friend, with the writer's byline. And it was placed in the Times where the lead story about this sniper or hijacker started on page one, went to page twenty-three, and where that story ended the Harry Chapin review began. There were a lot of lucky things like that.

About the eighth week or so, Ann Purtill came down. She was the first one who heard something.

ANN PURTILL: It was the best thing I had ever seen unsigned. It started out in the darkened room with Harry singing, 'Could You Put Your Light On, Please,' and slowly bringing the lights up. His background singer, John Wallace, could sing very high falsetto, very low bass. There was a cello underscoring the songs. Harry didn't have a very good voice, but it didn't matter. When they finished, Harry said, "I have a new song, we've never done it before, so bear with us." Then he sang 'Taxi.' And I just went, "Aaah . . ."

FRED KEWLEY: She dragged Jac down. The first time he didn't like it. We changed songs so he would come back. Ann kept pushing him. The second time he came down was the night before Clive Davis was coming from CBS. Jac liked Harry that time.

JAC: I asked Ann to arrange for Harry and his band to go into the studio and do a tape, one take of everything, so I could find my way into the music. Out in LA I'd often drive the Pacific Coast Highway at night, looking at the ocean and listening to music with a stereo unit and big headphones. I had been a bit lukewarm about Harry. He wasn't an impressive singer, but you could tell he believed every word he wrote. And in the process of listening without interruptions in a beautiful setting I came to understand and love the songs and knew that this was the kind of artist who belonged on Elektra. We made an offer.

Negotiations were well underway—and then Harry disappeared from my radar screen. I called his house on Long Island repeatedly and could never get hold of him. His wife, Sandy, would say, "He's out running on the beach." Mike Mayer, Elektra's East Coast attorney, couldn't get hold of Harry's attorney either, and they were close friends. Something weird was going on.

Indeed. Atlantic, Elektra's stablemate label, was chasing Harry. And Clive Davis at Columbia had got hold of my demo tape.

Clive was trying to convince Harry that he should be on the label of legends—Bob Dylan, Paul Simon—and that was a damned good argument. Clive trotted out computer runs showing how many records Paul sold, how many Bob sold, and predicted that Harry's numbers would be in that range.

Since the Doors, any artist that I truly went after I had been able to sign. I didn't want to lose now, and not this artist. It became something of a crusade.

FRED KEWLEY: We had been hoping for $5,000. Jac made an offer, about $15,000. Clive flipped and offered $20,000. Jac upped to $25,000. Clive went to $30,000. Jac upped that. In between those jumps, we committed definitely to both of them.

ANN PURTILL: Finally I said to Jac, "Do you have a memo of understanding with him?" and Jac said, "No, just a handshake." And I said, "Fuck it, don't sign him. I don't want to do business with him. He's not a man of his word. He has no honor."

JAC: Harry calls and says he has to talk to me. I was on my way to the West Coast, so we met in the Admiral's Club at the airport. Harry and Fred told me they had decided to go with Columbia, and I was miserable for the entire flight.

Arriving at the office the next morning, I played the tape for Mickey Kapp, the son of Dave Kapp, who was now VP of administration for the west coast Elektra office. Mickey had A&R chops and years of experience. When the tape had finished, Mickey turned to me and said, "Jac, that sure is a tough one to lose."

I was having lunch with Joel Friedman, head of the WEA distribution network, and I told him the story of Clive Davis and the computer printouts. Joel says, "Hmmm. Would you like to see an authentic CBS run?" Within hours it's messengered to me, and the numbers Clive has been quoting to Harry are exactly double what is on the printout.

Armed with new data—also known as the facts—I start calling again. Harry was still "running on the beach" (at 10pm?). Eventually I got to Fred and said, "I'm coming in early Sunday morning, and I'll bang on doors, I'll haunt you guys until somebody talks to me."

JAC: I couldn't get there any earlier than Sunday, because on the Saturday night there was an Elektra party in LA to celebrate my friend Cyrus Faryar's first album.

Cyrus was the product of one of those romance-novel marriages: English show-girl-Persian diplomat. He was a sexy devil, between handsome and beautiful, with beckoning dark eyes and an effortless baritone voice that came out, speaking or singing, as smoothly and sweetly as some sort of rare fragrant Middle-Eastern unguent topping from a tube—attar of Faryar.

OONA AUSTIN: Oh, Cyrus . . . Nearly a sufi, almost a saint.

JAC: Cyrus and his friends lived, somewhat communally, at a place called the Farm, just over the hill from Hollywood toward Burbank and up a treacherous little road off Barham Boulevard. It was one of the scenes where you could drop by any time, and among my favorite spots to spend an evening. John Sebastian dwelled for a spell in the yard in a tie-dye tent of his own creation.

HENRY DILTZ: Tie-Dye Annie taught John how to tie-dye, and he tie-dyed everything he owned, every piece of clothing, every pillow case, the sheets that lined the inside of his tent.

JAC: There was a nice little studio in the house, built by a journeyman carpenter named Harrison Ford. That was where Cyrus recorded his album, gentle songs that felt like warm ocean breezes, under the guidance of his friend Ron Jacobs, a powerhouse Boss Jock of Southern California rock radio. Ron also produced "A Child's Garden Of Grass" for Elektra—

CYRUS FARYAR:—On which I was the voice of the Indian guru.

HENRY DILTZ: All the Farm ladies worked on the party—Renais, Lynn, Annie, Oona.

Cyrus Faryar in full bloom EKS-75068

OONA AUSTIN: I was there as a complete born-again Cyrus person.

CYRUS FARYAR: A great tent was erected over the driveway, which was then carpeted in oriental rugs.

OONA AUSTIN: We made a hundred-fifty pillows.

HENRY DILTZ: A ton of pillows.

CYRUS FARYAR: Bigger than your head, bigger than your body.

JAC: And the ladies appeared that night in all their best makeup and finery.

OONA AUSTIN: We were there for the love of Cyrus, worshipping Cyrus.

BILL ALEXANDER: It was an Arabian Nights scene.

JAC: There were caftans all round.

ALLEN DAVIAU: Marrakesh meets hippie tie-dye psychedelia.

HENRY DILTZ: Very tasteful. Not your Hog Farm hippies.

ANTON GREENE: The party menu was planned by Jack Poet, loosely based on the Shah of Iran's great party. Hummus. Stuffed grape leaves. Stuffing the quail eggs with caviar was meticulous work. None of us had done it before. We were in the kitchen it seemed for days. The caviar was real beluga, and we sneaked a little along the way, licking the finger.

HENRY DILTZ: I had taken the cover photo for Cyrus's album, Cyrus in profile in the desert, and for the party the picture was reproduced on the wall in flowers, huge, no expense spared.

JAC: Invitations went out to perhaps a hundred people, and two hundred turned up.

ALLEN DAVIAU: Music business hondlers, Laurel Canyon creatures, friends and lovers.

CYRUS FARYAR: We had a glorious time, rejoicing in one another. I sang the album for everyone, and it was over. We had spent the entire promotion budget. It was like fireworks. For one night I promoted myself, and then disappeared into invisibility. To this day I have the tin in which the caviar came and which now holds guitar picks.

JAC: I was having a wonderful time. I didn't want to leave. But I had to be on the red-eye to New York in the big game hunt for Harry Chapin.

Deep in the night, somewhere over the heartland, I decided to offer to produce Harry myself. I had been away from the studio far too long and I was curious if I could still hack it.

At the airport at six in the morning, George Graves met me with the limo and drove me to Long Island. In civilized fashion I knocked, not banged, on the door. Harry and Fred were both there. I walked in, and turned into a manic terrier with Harry's trouser cuff in my teeth. Nothing was going to make me let go. Forget that they were signing with Columbia, act as if there was no doubt that Harry would record for Elektra, ignore all evidence to the contrary.

I said I would fly Harry and the band to LA in the Warner company jet—equipment and ladies and dogs and cats. I offered to produce; we would do the album together, go into the studio and stay until we got it right. I took a leaf out of my book of the Doors and promised to release no other album in that month.

Then I showed them the real CBS numbers. Harry happily collapsed. He said, "We'll do it. Let me call Clive." And as light began to peek over the transoms of the East Coast he made the call, and Harry Chapin was an Elektra artist.

CLIVE DAVIS: That was a wonderful, valuable lesson that I've attempted to use myself, after I started Arista. A terrific example of where, with not only tenacity but with imagination, a small company with an extremely imaginative, tasteful head—which is really what Jac has always been—was able to win out in competition with a large company, where I personally established an equally strong connection with the artists.

Jac came up with things that a large company could never match. No other artist being released at the same time—with the size of the Columbia roster it's inconceivable, just by the nature of the obligation to release product, that you could ever match such a commitment. Also, a trade advertising commitment, in which a small company does not have to rationalize it to other artists, who say, "Why is this artist getting something as compared to other artists?" So, Jac very imaginatively thought of at least two different areas that a company like Columbia could not possibly match.

JAC: An independent enjoys greater flexibility in its actions. We pinpoint exactly what needs to be done rather than take the more scatter shot approach of the majors. An independent rises and falls on its senses, its feel of the audience, on its judgment and taste, intuition, and, of course, luck. Without much margin for error we dance on a tightrope over the moat that is home to the crocodiles.

Harry Chapin

David Gahr

ANN PURTILL: The day Jac signed Harry was my birthday. Harry and the band took me out to dinner and bought me a bicycle.

JAC: I hadn't produced a record in years. My ass was on the line.

FRED KEWLEY: Jac acted like it was his first project. He put in eighteen-hour days.

JAC: My going into the studio with Harry created problems with other artists. Judy Collins, for one, admired Harry's songs and his politics, but there was some light scratching. I was willing to pay that price.

This was the first record scheduled for our big new and improved Studio A. No studio ever works right the first time, there are always little things that go wrong, but you can't anticipate these snags until you put the facility through its paces during real sessions. We had some minor breakdowns but soon things settled in.

Harry was an extraordinarily fast study. He had the kind of rapid assimilation and facility that Bill Clinton has—in fact he was like Clinton in many ways. He quickly figured how a studio worked, which was important because the more he knew the more he could conceive of doing. During breaks the band would be taking fifteen minutes and Harry would sit in a corner writing a new song. We talked a great deal about the difference between craft and art. Harry had craft down pat; I was pushing him for more art. After several weeks of pressure-cooker days that went on till we dropped, we became close friends.

When the album was finished, mixed and ready, we sat around the studio listening to it, trying to forget all the tension that went into its making. I thought we had done very well. But the studio can be a very deceptive place. Everything sounds fat and happy coming through those enormous speakers, but how will it sound on a home stereo? How do you take great sound and stuff it through a car radio? Most studios would check a final mix through a set of smallish speakers, surrogates for the home system. I went one step further. I had gotten hold of a little AM transmitter to which we attached a wire coat hanger for an antenna. It had a range of about a hundred yards. We tuned to an open space on the AM band, which was tough considering the crowded spectrum in Los Angeles, transmitted the mix illegally over the air, and then ran outside and jumped into our cars and listened. Me being me, I went from car radio to car radio. That was the final test.

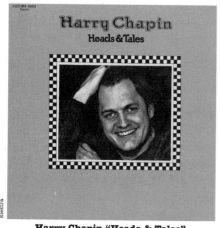

Harry Chapin "Heads & Tales"
EKS-75023

JAC: 'Taxi' was the single —the touching story of a guy whose dreams of flying, being an ace pilot, have come down to driving a cab, hacking. Late at night he picks up a fare, and by chance it is a girl he once knew, whose dreams of becoming a star have come down to hooking.

It was one of the alltime singer-songwriter songs. It was also outrageously long for conventional airplay: 6:37. We had another 'Light My Fire' problem.

KEITH HOLZMAN: I think we put on the record label 4:69 or some bizarre time that didn't exist, pretending it was shorter than it was.

JAC: With the Warner jet, the hotels, and all the studio time, the album cost about forty thousand to make. The packaging was expensive, and there was a fund for tour support. All told we had well over a hundred thousand invested. We had to sell a lot of records. We did.

GEORGE STEELE: Harry was involved. He wanted to know the marketing strategies, what the promotions were, what the process was. There were forty other projects on the line, but he wanted to make sure he was Number 1 in your heart, so he would work at it. He knew how to work the room at Elektra better than any other artist.

JAC: He got everyone to go out of their way for him, and it wasn't artifice. He genuinely cared.

JACLYN EASTON: He was a great guy, a conflict resolver. At Tranquility, Adam put milk in my soup and I was militant. Harry said, "Mmm, I love milk soup! Jaclyn, can I have some?"

KEITH HOLZMAN: Harry and his four brothers volunteered for our softball team. Mel Posner got us into the music league. We had the most anemic team in America, the Elektra Butterflies. Most of us could barely lift a pen to sign our names. Harry and his brothers were great athletes, and we started winning.

JAC: Harry had tremendous energy and he was brilliant at promotion. He could do the softest of hard sells nonstop and forever. We'd put him in a room and give him a phone and he would call every DJ in America, every program director. We gave him endless lists. We had little notes: this DJ loves the Dodgers, this one is an Orioles fan, and Harry would have these really nice conversations, not bringing up the record unless they did, but imprinting himself indelibly upon their hearts and minds.

MITCHELL FINK: After he had a hit with 'Taxi,' he and Sandy had a party at his house and gave out plaques to people who believed in him before—the Harry Chapin Early Believers Club. He was very appreciative.

KEITH HOLZMAN: And he went out and toured like crazy. These were the times when we knew touring was absolutely essential, and a lot of acts didn't want to do it.

FRED KEWLEY: There wasn't anything we wouldn't do on a last-minute basis—if we get four days' notice to go to El Paso to open for the Temptations, we're there.

MITCHELL FINK: When an artist is on the road, usually there's a field guy who meets them—someone from the Philadelphia market; or maybe someone from artist relations in the record company goes with them. In this case it was the president of the company, it was Jac. That was the first time I had been exposed to a record company president who would put himself totally on the line for an artist— I mean, who believed in that artist to such a degree that he was, in fact, like a road manager. When Harry walked up to the stage that night, Jac was walking in front of him, kind of almost an advance man, or a roadie, and just in that spirit. Jac Holzman was there as someone who was on the road with Harry Chapin. I'll never forget that.

JAC: We presented our artists and new releases to our WEA marketing and sales staff at our annual conventions. These were very important meetings.

For the weekend event we held in Palm Springs in 1972, we chartered an American Airlines 727 from New York. On final approach the stewardess's announcement was: "Ladies and gentlemen, thank you for choosing American and would you please extinguish whatever it is that you have been smoking." Definitely a music business charter in the early Seventies.

On Friday evening we showcased the Doors. After Jim died, I had re-signed Ray, Robby and John, to a multi-record deal, my way of showing them that it wasn't all Jim and saying thank you, with Warner's money.

Their first album, "Other Voices," was released in October 1971, and to launch the record and the new reality, we put on a Carnegie Hall concert. Carnegie Hall was big enough to hold the crowd and small enough to go three-quarters of the way back toward intimacy. With Ray doing most of the singing, the Doors wowed the sell-out audience of soaked-in-brine Doors fanatics. At Palm Springs they played another killer set at the restaurant atop the tramway overlooking the city.

During dinner, some kids who had snuck in to hear them were found hiding in a serving cabinet behind the bar. Security was called, the police were called; and when the cops came piling off the tram car the paranoid among us were sure it was a bust, and we were treated to a performance-art spectacle, a frieze of promotion men feigning not to be tossing baggies over the railing and down the slopes of Mt. San Jacinto.

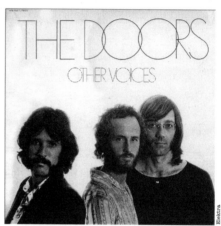

For the closing Saturday banquet we showcased both Carly Simon and Harry Chapin live. Harry opened. Being Harry, he had been working the house all day like a seasoned pol, and the audience was primed and ready. He more than lived up to his billing.

The Doors "Other Voices" EKS-75017

STEVE HARRIS: Harry was a hard act to follow.

JAC: Carly had flown in separately, and the airline lost her bags—

CARLY SIMON:—Not my guitar. But all my clothes. I had this beautiful American Indian chamois dress that I wore on stage. Gone. My jewelry. Gone. All I had was my handbag. And I had nothing to wear, because I came in, like, a nightgown, because I was traveling at night; it was like a muumuu with a monk's hood. But the thing that killed me was my journal. It was a black leather notebook with looseleaf pages, Gucci, that somebody had given to me. My whole first smell of success, my opening at the Troubadour, that whole year, was all in my journal. And it had all my lyrics up until that time, all the different versions of all the songs. There was an earlier version of 'You're So Vain'—it was like a year before it actually came out, because that's a song I wrote originally called 'Bless You, Ben' and it was completely different. But I did have the line, "You're so vain, you probably think this song is about you." All gone. I was sick.

JAC: What a theft of memory. Despite everything, and in a dress hastily bought on the spot with Steve's wife, Nicole, Carly gave a wonderful performance. I was the MC. I said, "Remember our success last year with Carly. Harry Chapin is this year's

Carly Simon." And Carly said—she was so quick, so smart and funny—"Harry, if you're this year's Carly Simon you must have had some very interesting boy friends these past twelve months."

STEVE HARRIS: And then she sang her ass off and the audience went crazy.

GEORGE STEELE: Those conventions were very powerful. I remember one where Bill Harvey's visual presentation was computerized slides, with the music synchronized. The logo for our Elektra singles was a caterpillar, and as the lights went down and the room hushed and the music came up, the caterpillar went through a metamorphosis and became a butterfly. Beautiful job. And as the various artists came up on the screen with their music, there was some magic that came into that room full of jaded salespeople. A hush, a stillness, as the message of the songs unfolded. It was spiritual. It was mystical. It was overpowering. People left in awe. That was Elektra.

Chapter 32

In pursuit of a Queen ...
Glam slam, thank you ma'am ...
Fugue of a record man ... A hot tub in Muir Woods

JAC: There were moments like that when everything came together—and always through the music. The business of music was less and less to my taste.

Some record companies were abdicating their responsibility to find talent to the new gatekeepers, the lawyers and the managers. They were not just packaging artists with producers, they were making label deals—take a producer and an act, and that's the beginning of a new label.

These deals carry a high cost. The company funds one hundred percent of the money, paying advances to the artists, all the marketing, tour support, and, most critical, contributing their valuable staff time while also paying for the executive staff of the label imprint. You are fronting all the money and most of the effort, and if it succeeds you have a fifty percent equity ownership. These deals were onerous—and very few of them, Asylum excepted, worked out. But they were now the fashion. Again, it's a parallel to the motion picture companies: all the bad news of the movie business coming to roost in the record business. Except for Countryside, we never made those kinds of deals.

People at the record companies were becoming removed from the record-making process, or at least less essential to it. Which would take a lot of the fun out of it for me. We were no longer fulltime record makers; we were becoming bankers and distributors, exercising our artistic judgment less. So-called street smarts were now acing out taste. The production entity could require the company to issue an album. If we didn't like it, were we going to substitute our judgment for the producer's? No—as a choice of evils we would have to issue it anyway. It was not my kind of record making and I avoided it like the plague it was.

JAC: Which is not to say that great music didn't come our way from production companies. Jack Nelson of Trident Audio Productions in London paid me a visit.

JACK NELSON: A casual meeting, a little fishing expedition. I had a couple of hours between planes. Jac was a fan of our work. I was carrying a sample tape of what Trident could do, so that people could hear our studio sound and also the groups we had under management. I was going to see if we could license some bands to Elektra.

Trident was probably the foremost studio of its time in England. It was a beehive of activity because of the engineers and the sound. Everybody from the Beatles and the Stones recorded there. Elton John—that's where he made his first six or seven albums. David Bowie. Cat Stevens was with Trident. One of Jac's English signings, Lindisfarne, recorded there. Carly Simon made her 'You're So Vain' album there.

I had a group called Queen. I had been shopping them for almost a year, and now I was signing them to EMI in England and I was in the process of signing them to CBS in North America. Jac said, "I'd like to hear them." I said, "OK, but I'm already in my third revision of the CBS contract."

JAC: Jack gave me the Queen tapes, a complete album, two full 10-inch reels. I listened to them at Tranquility, first through the speakers, then through headphones. It was so beautifully recorded and performed; everything was there, like a perfectly cut diamond landing on your desk.

JACK NELSON: Queen reminded me of the makeup of the Beatles. Each guy was so totally the opposite of the others, the four points of the compass. Freddie Mercury was the lead vocalist. He composed on keyboards, and he was classically trained. Very complex guy, incredibly talented. Brian May was a rock and roll guitarist and he brought that influence. Also incredibly talented, scatterbrained as they come, and yet as focused as they come. He had a degree in infrared astronomy. John Deacon was the bass player. He brought the solid bit, as bass players do, grounded them. He had a first-class honors degree in electronics. Roger Meddows-Taylor, the drummer, had a double degree. They were probably the smartest band in the business. And totally diverse personalities—we could get into an airport and one would stop, one would go right, one would go left, and one would go straight ahead. But it made a great creative force. When they got together in the middle, with the stacked vocals, that center was amazing.

JAC: I was knocked out. 'Keep Yourself Alive,' 'Liar,' 'The Night Comes Down'—all great songs in a sumptuous production that felt like the purest ice-cream poured over a real rock and roll foundation. I wanted Queen and CBS wanted Queen—this was going to be Harry Chapin times two, Clive Davis and me duking it out again.

JACK NELSON: I flew back to England over the weekend, and on Monday I get a call from Jac: "I love this band." And then another call from him in LA. And maybe a week or two later another call from him in Japan: "I'm really serious." I do my calculations and realize it's the middle of the night in Japan, so I guess he was.

Negotiations with CBS had stalled over something inconsequential in the grand scheme of things, half a point or something. Also I had had a conversation with Clive Davis that was very unsettling. Clive and his A&R staff hadn't really listened to the music like Jac had. The might of CBS was very attractive. However, if you studied your history, you saw that they weren't particularly good as far as rock and roll was concerned. And the fact that one of their A&R guys called Queen one of the best country bands he had heard in a long time made me extremely nervous.

Jac was pursuing us heavily, without being obnoxious about it—it wasn't the bullshit that we knew too well in the business. He called me again, from Australia, I think: "I've got to have them." I said, "You know, if you're really serious, I'll put on a gig and you come over and see them."

JAC: I flew to London, listened to them at the gig Jack had set up at the Marquee in Soho, and was dreadfully disappointed. I saw nothing on stage to match the power I had heard on the tape. But the music was there. I wrote them a long memo, four or five pages single-spaced, with my thoughts and suggestions. Then I sent Mel

Queen

Posner to follow up on my visit to discuss marketing. Then a will-of-the-wisp passionate lady from our artist relations department, Jeannie Theis, who was a real fan of their music. And always more ideas and memos—the Holzman wear-them-down, frequency-of-interaction method.

And I had yet to unleash another potent persuader, the no-nonsense Elektra contract. By contrast, the CBS standard contract was a thing of wonder for CBS, but for artists it was desperation—thirty pages or more, the first sixteen pages protecting CBS and on page seventeen a tiny paragraph about what the artist might receive if all the planets were properly in conjunction.

JACK NELSON: Everybody told me I was crazy to go with Elektra, that they were a great folk label, but Queen was the farthest thing from folk. I looked at Arthur Lee and Love, and the Doors, which was totally different from what Jac had done in the past. Also, his knowledge of Queen's music and his enthusiasm for it. My brain kept saying, "Is he a great merchandiser, can he promote the stuff?" In the end, against popular advice, I said, "To heck with it, we're going for Elektra."

We got the contract done quickly. Certain things I had to have, take it or leave it. Jac didn't give me Elektra Records for Queen, but we came to a very fair deal. I always felt you'd never get sold down the river with Jac. And from then on, everyone at Elektra did what they said they were going to do, and that's a miracle for our business.

JAC: I was a believer. I wrote an internal memo to staff saying, "I have seen the future of pop music, and it is a band called Queen." And the group took the com-ments in my memos about staging and per-formance, far beyond my expectations. By the time of their huge hit single, 'Bohemian Rhapsody'—another seven-and-a-half-minute wonder, by the way—their stage theatrics were phenomenal. Freddie was extraordinarily flamboyant, a great glam rocker. I have rarely seen a band work so hard, have such success, and remain so nice. They were very special people. And when they were in full flight they sold millions and millions of records. All by itself, my signing of Queen more than compensated Steve Ross for what he had paid for Elektra.

"Queen II" EKS-75082

JAC: Queen would have been unimaginable in the Fifties or mid-Sixties. Rock and roll had begun with short singles on AM radio. By the early Seventies it had flowered, lyrically and stylistically, moving in as many directions as there were talented writers and performers.

In the first half of the Sixties, British groups—the Beatles and especially the Stones, then others like the Animals and Eric Clapton—had taught young Americans lessons from American roots music. In the second half of the decade, garage bands, building on the instrumental riffs of West Coast surf bands like the Beach Boys and the Ventures, created very tight, AM-oriented pop-rock-punkish records. They were a category of their own, and I thought it would be wonderful to assemble a representative survey of these groups.

I asked Lenny Kaye, a guitarist and rock historian (later of the Patti Smith band), to help me. We assembled a two-record album with thirty tracks featuring the Electric Prunes, 13th Floor Elevator, Amboy Dukes, Blues Magoos, the Vagrants, the Magic Mushrooms, the Seeds, the Standells, the Chocolate Watch Band and

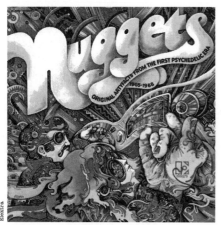

Elektra

"Nuggets" 7E-2006

twenty-one—count 'em—more. In an interview years later, Lenny said that he thought the groups we picked reflected the yearning of a teenager aching to play in a band.

This was no K-TEL bargain TV ragbag, but a serious study. Already I could sense that we were on the cusp of a time when doctoral candidates would be writing dissertations on the history of rock. I didn't have any designs on a degree; I just wanted to get there first. The only title that seemed roomy enough to contain the whole idea was "Nuggets—Original Artyfacts From The First Psychedelic Era 1965-1968." The album created an enormous stir, as much for its concept of an archeological dig into the recent past as for its contents. Harold Bronson and Richard Foos, who founded the celebrated Rhino Records label in 1978, credit "Nuggets" and the Elektra style as the starting point.

What Elektra had begun with the Stooges was furthered by "Nuggets" and would influence the Ramones and others right through to the subterranean revival of retro-punk in the Eighties.

JAC: During my busy, busy times with WEA distributing, WEA International and the strategic planning group, Queen was a rare opportunity, as Harry Chapin had been. I was too busy to produce Harry's second album. With everything else on my plate, I simply wasn't able to pay as much attention to the label, and I suffered and Elektra suffered too.

The Seventies were impatient to push the Sixties into the past. And Elektra and I were drifting apart. There were things going down that I didn't know about, and wouldn't have liked if I had known, and I should have.

STEVE HARRIS: I saw something I didn't like. Jac had to do a lot of traveling, and he might not have seen a lot of things that I saw going on. I really believe some people got hired because of their good drug contacts. It was to the extent that it was unprofessional.

BOB ZACHARY: Elektra was shifting from dope smoking to coke snorting.

FRITZ RICHMOND: In the studio at La Cienega there would be cocaine in quantity. People wouldn't be singing on the records, but they would show up because they knew the coke was going to be there. You know those cigars that come in a glass tube that's about as big around as your finger? Well, one of those would arrive half full of cocaine. Walk over to the new building, walk down the hall where all the gold records were and take somebody that was thought to be somewhat stodgy, like Carly Simon or Judy Collins, take their gold record, lay it on top of the grand piano in the studio and cover it with a layer of cocaine. Someone would chop it up and then spin it out in a giant spiral, approximating the grooves of the record, and straws would be handed out, and on the word Go, six or eight people would start honking this coke in spirals until it disappeared.

LENNY KAYE: As drugs became less smart, when that Sixties sense of LSD's promise, and the whole pot thing, became subsumed by the Seventies—all of a sudden, Jac was less comfortable in that environment too.

JOHN VAN HAMMERSVELD: The drugs broke the scene down and took the people with it. You can go from '61 with a group of people, and by the time you get to '74 or so—you can watch them, they go through these different drugs and the whole thing changes.

JUDY JAMES: When speed came to Laurel Canyon, that's when we had to start locking our doors.

JAC: The familiar was turning unfamiliar, in many ways—unfamiliar behaviors, unfamiliar people. Elektra had been on both coasts since the mid-Sixties, and that was fun—my Chinese banquet table east and west. Now there was security at both locations, Gulf & Western and La Cienega. There were over a hundred people on staff, and there was a lot of bloat in that number, probably twenty too many. Who were they? And what was I to them? One morning I walked up from the garage into the La Cienega offices, and somebody I had never seen in my life, so full of himself, from the Seventies hot-shit heights of working for Elektra, stopped me and rudely demanded to know who I was and what I was doing there.

Further down that bad road, I was at a sales conference in New York, and the comedian they had hired to provide laughs leered at Carly's photo on her latest album and said, "Now, there are two critical points about this album," and he pointed to her nipples. I got up and walked out, in something approaching a trance, upset and too tired to fight. The dynamic was about to shift and that shift would bring with it excesses and insensitivities that would take what I considered a calling and convert it into a career path. What I had fought for, to keep the music ahead of the money, would change. The galoots would be coming to the party.

JAC: Feeling very cut up, not knowing where I belonged, I had to squeeze moments of personal life through the cracks, get away whenever I could.

JANN WENNER: Jac and I used to go to Aspen together, to ski and hang out and have fun. I have one particular memory of playing Monopoly with him there. We were pretty rusty, we both wanted to win this thing, and it got pretty tense. We were friends, and he would always tell me what was going on. I had Rolling Stone up and running, and during those days if you had a little youth company, everybody was poaching all the time. Jac would say, "Don't ever sell. I don't know of anybody who sold a small company who has ever been happy after that." He had lost this formative big thing in his life, and he was never going to duplicate that experience. I think he hadn't anticipated how much that meant to him. He took it pretty hard, and I don't blame him.

BRUCE BOTNICK: After Jac sold the company, he would call up at night and talk for hours. It was a rough time for him. The company wasn't his any more, he was divorced from Nina, he had separated from Ellen, and he had pangs of loneliness— a double whammy.

JAC: Although the decision to merge the company made enormous sense, it still left me feeling disconnected emotionally, and without a family or someone to love I felt disoriented, afraid and out of my element. Elektra was truly mine only if I continued to contribute to it with full energy, and when I chose to leave, as I had planned to do, I knew it would be lost to me forever. The decision to go was the right one for me. The changes in the music business climate were going against my grain. My juices were sapped. But leaving was an emotional sea change that would take a long time to reconcile myself to.

MO OSTIN: I think Jac could adapt himself to any time in the music business if he wanted to.

JAC: The question was—did I want to?

LENNY KAYE: The great trick in pop culture is to make a million dollars doing what you love. It's not that hard making a million doing something you don't like doing, or it's not hard to do something you like and make two dollars from it. I think Jac had it really nice, especially in the late Sixties, leading the artistic vanguard and putting gold records on the wall from it. That's a great thing. Then there comes a time when either the art drives you or the money drives you. I think he came up with a choice where he could put those gold records on the wall, but the art was becoming more an empty exercise in sussing out popular taste. Some of the art wasn't getting through, and sometimes you just get sick of the bullshit.

PAUL WILLIAMS: Even though Jac does have this genius for money and business, there are other things that he cared about tremendously, and being sucked up into the headlong plunge of the record industry in the early Seventies was not fitting with the Jac Holzman who was my brother out there on the front lines of consciousness expansion. Consciously or unconsciously, Jac didn't want to be sucked up into the unstoppable, the forces that were bigger than him, of what the fucking record business became in the Seventies. That was distasteful to him. He made the choice not to be a billionaire.

LENNY KAYE: If I can indulge in a little amateur psychologizing, I think Jac never really wanted to have a standard music business company. He wanted to have one that furrowed out things that were a bit arcane.

We can work these metaphors: I think he had a scientific sensibility in music, where he was almost like a sociologist visiting far-off New Guinea, bringing back these exotic specimens, and sometimes, like exotic specimens will, they will run amok in civilization, unleashing weird plagues. So it's an interesting dichotomy, and like most dichotomies, when you blend these disparate instincts together, you get an intriguing personality and certainly an adventurous record label that has the seeds of its own dissolution in it. Sooner or later, you start getting spun, one against the other. And I think Jac was not only feeling these pressures, but feeling the drift of the music business which was becoming more business than music.

He enjoyed odd bands, and when it seemed like it was either these odd bands were killing themselves or it was the music business as usual, I don't think he found his place in it. He really did like art that was somewhat white, that was articulate and intellectual, art made for the New York Times. And if it spilled over into complete excess on the one hand, or if it spilled over on the other hand to kind of formulaic Top 40 stuff, he really wasn't interested. His sense of control, maybe, matched his sense of adventure. Later, what might he have done with a Patti Smith? Would he have discovered the Talking Heads? They might have been the perfect Jac group. But that was several years on. I guess at the time he came to feel disengaged from what he was doing.

JAC: I had a way of disengaging that I particularly enjoyed. I would drive the Pacific Coast Highway to Muir Woods, north of San Francisco, to visit Roger Somers. Roger had this small community, in a wonderful sylvan setting, little craft houses that people lived in, or came to at weekends. It was yet another gift from Kim von Tempski, the purser on the President Roosevelt, who had first brought me to Roger's.

BILL ALEXANDER: Roger was a carpenter-builder. He was whitehaired, but he would be up at four in the morning on projects, wearing out a couple of shifts of vigorous younger workmen. He always had the energy of ten. He was creatively wild.

FRED WILLIAMS: The first time I met Roger was in Sausalito. He leaped on me, wrapped his legs and arms around me, kissed me on the mouth, held out his hand and said, "Watch," and blood came out the back of his hand.

JAC: I always brought music with me. Business I left behind. Roger had built a hot tub big enough for ten. He played the saxophone slightly better than Jack Benny pretended to play the violin. As the moon shone through the woods, Roger would tootle, like the Pied Piper, and people would come from all over the property, near naked, and walk to the hot tub, single file. We would all be loaded. On hashish at Roger's I would vibrate like a tuning fork. We would get in the tub and talk and do what people do in hot tubs. Then, one by one, we would curl up into a tight ball, and the others would twirl you around underwater until you couldn't hold your breath any longer. I loved being curled and spun around, like a child from another dimension.

BILL ALEXANDER: Roger was a creative artist, an architectural and design genius. He built Neil Young's touring bus, a fantasy of redwood filigree arpeggios, an adult play pen. He also built a limo for a crazy mufti type who went to Maui with it—it had a built-in hot tub.

JAC: I had Maui on my mind, always and increasingly. I bought land in Hana, five acres by the ocean, deliriously beautiful, gave Roger a design commission, and let his creativity loose on a model for a house.

Roger's conception, which he showed me in a full-on colored rendering and model, looked like a starfish with three points. It was set in the middle of the property with the ocean frothing below and several miles of mountain rising into the clouds.

The northern point was the entrance and you came down a long, rather narrow hallway into the main communal body of the house which contained the living room with fireplace, kitchen, dining area and tiny alcoves where you could be private.

Then, to the southwest, a similar long hall which led into the master bedroom suite, bathroom, outdoor

Model of Hana house... unbuilt

Holzman Family Archive

shower, hot tub—connected to but away from the hub of the house. To the southeast, a matching starfish point which was to be my office.

All of this was open to the air and covered with a roof, rather like a dinosaur skin crafted by Frank Lloyd Wright. Totally unusual and totally divine.

And then one day I called Roger and said, "I'm not going to build it."

I would have been replicating my life on the mainland. Too much bigness, too sumptuous, and needing people to constantly maintain it. I felt as if I might lose myself just as I was ready to find me.

Regrouping, I opted for something on a much smaller scale, simpler, lighter—a home right on the beach just outside Lahaina, where I could sling my hammock and feel the trade winds. I gave Roger carte blanche to make the six hundred-foot interior over completely, and he went to work with his craftsman's feel for wood and his unflagging energy.

Simple living in paradise

Chapter 33

**Options ... Can I change your mind? ...
The mogul had to say something ...
An evening with friends at Tavern on the Green**

JAC: Meanwhile, back at the office, Ahmet Ertegun and David Geffen had each re-made their deals with Steve Ross.

DAVID GEFFEN: I had made a deal to sell my record company, Asylum, to Warner Communications, a stock deal. I got the stock at $40 a share. In six months it had crashed to $8. I got completely fucked on that deal. At the same time my company had gone through the roof. I was very unhappy.

JAC: And so we come to 1973. This is five years from 1968, when I had briefly gone on the lam, sitting at Lahaina on Maui looking out at the sea, making a promise to myself to be gone from the business in five years. 1973 was my private target date for exiting. Hawai'i was calling.

When Cyrus Faryar, who had lived his young life in Hawai'i, recorded his second album, we called it "Islands," and for the back cover photo we used a snapshot I had taken of my hammock by the ocean at sunset. For me that was a mind-picture, a ruling image.

Under my agreement with Warner, 1973 was the last of my three years' obligation at Elektra. Then there was a two-year option period. If the option was picked up, I would have to serve another two years, to 1975, and it felt like a prison sentence.

If the option was not picked up, I would be a free man. The date for the exercise of the option was July 22, and no notification came. My legal address was at Tranquility Base in South Salem, and I had Marty Richmond checking the mail daily. One key person within the music group knew that the New York office had forgotten the paperwork, and he was torn between his friendship for me and his fiduciary duty to the company. I held my breath. What continued to happen was. . . nothing. I gave it a respectable interval, way past the option date, exhaled gratefully, and wrote Steve a note saying that I had other plans for my life.

When we met to talk, the first thing Steve said was, "Can I change your mind?" I said no, this was something I was committed to and there was no turning back. He then said, "Well, you can do anything you want now, that's not a problem. But I have a problem. The technology area is too important to let go, and nobody around here knows how to screw in a light bulb. We want you close to the company. Let me keep your compensation going, and you just act for us as a consultant in technology." Fine, as long as I could do it from Maui. We worked out the details rapidly and cordially. I was free of my excess burden and also had something worth doing in a field I loved and found challenging. Hawai'i was mid-ocean between the mainland and Japan, to which I traveled frequently. I was already on the board of Pioneer Electronics (the first American to serve on the board of a major Japanese corporation) whom I had put in the cable hardware and LaserDisc businesses while a member of the strategic planning team. Perfect. I could have a foot of my own choosing in two worlds of my choosing, at a level of involvement and energy which would keep me from boredom without coming close to using me up.

For twenty-three years Elektra had been my life. Everything in me told me that that cycle had played itself out, had come to a natural end. To me the Seventies did not look musically promising. But my record company had to be looked after. To me the solution was obvious: David Geffen. David at Asylum was artist-oriented. Elektra was an artist-oriented label. So—move Asylum out of Atlantic, put it with Elektra, and have David oversee both labels.

Steve Ross saw the virtue in the idea at once, and brought it up at the next meeting of the record company heads in LA on August 9. I hadn't discussed it with David because, knowing David, it wouldn't have been a secret any longer, and I didn't want premature rumors of my departure causing unnecessary turmoil within the company. At the LA meeting David was—angry would be too strong a word, let's say upset, pissed off at not being consulted. But David was very ambitious, and the way I saw things I was making it possible for him to take his next step toward wherever he saw himself going.

The public announcement of the change came in New York, at a press conference at Club 21. Steve Ross made it official: I would continue with Warner Communications as senior vice-president and chief technologist, and David would move with Asylum from Atlantic to Elektra. Ahmet Ertegun lightheartedly said that he hated to lose the Asylum billing.

The news hit hard at Elektra, particularly among some who had been with me the longest.

ANN PURTILL: Judy Collins got on the phone to Jac and started crying and screaming at him, and he came and got me and said: "I can't get her to calm down."

JAC: Judy didn't talk to me for several years.

CARLY SIMON: It was devastating. It was like I was a child of divorce—my father was leaving me and now I had David Geffen as a stepfather.

JAC: David's executive style was very different. All sorts of scuttlebutt began to leak from Elektra: David hurrying in with a raincoat over his head to avoid being seen; David behind closed doors, on the phone shouting loud enough to be heard in the halls, then suddenly coming out and screaming at someone; David's psychiatrist making house calls at the office. Insecurity rampant in the corridors. All this might or might not have been merely smoke. The harsher substance of the situation was that David almost immediately declared Elektra to be a disaster area and took an axe to the artist roster.

STAN CORNYN: I have found this phenomenon to be the case: if you look at any transition of power, the year of transition is viewed by the person who's leaving as the best year ever, and by the person coming in as saying, "The company was a shambles, they were in terrible shape." That's a judgment call. The manipulations of David coming in seemed to tumble very quickly onto the tabletop, and it seems to me that there was a measured change that happened at that point. Well, with David coming in, you would expect a change.

JANN WENNER: The Geffen thing was a painful period for Jac, seeing what became of it all. And David, he looks to be a tough person to take over your company.

DAVID GEFFEN: Candidly, Elektra wasn't doing well when I took over. I kept most of Jac's staff, although frankly a lot of the people who were there were not very good. My desire not to fire people got in the way of putting the best people in place, and I was hard-pressed to make the kinds of changes that I thought were necessary. I dropped a huge amount of artists. I kept, I think, a total of ten or twelve and dropped everybody else. Let's put it this way: Over time, eighty percent of everything you sign turns out to be shit. That's pretty much the industry average, or maybe even worse than that. And it was the same at Elektra. It was the same with Vanguard. It was the same at Columbia or Warner Bros. or Reprise, but people tend to pat themselves on the back for their good things and forget about their bad things.

As for technical excellence, Jac makes a lot of that because it interested him, but I'm not sure what you think technical excellence does in the record business. You hire engineers. Engineers are like bringing in a plumber to fix your toilet. Let me put it this way: if I was deaf I'd still be a great record executive, because I had a nose and a sense for it.

Building Asylum Records was an accident that turned out to be fortuitous. Taking over Elektra Records was something I did because I wanted to make sure I didn't lose all my money in Warner Communications stock. The success rate of Asylum Records in 1973 was higher than any record company in history. And putting the two companies together revitalized Elektra Records bigtime. It was really heading to oblivion in 1973. I don't think Jac likes to look at it that way, but that's the way it was. You know, I love Jac. Jac is a very dry guy, a very tough man and I've had difficult times with Jac, and he was very upset with the idea that after I took over Elektra I talked about how I had to drop all these artists and resurrect the company. He was offended by these things. It was simply the truth.

I was not a person who would say I was in this for the music. I used to be offended by people who would tell me they were in it for the music, who were just trying to make tons and tons of money. It's all self-serving crap, one way or the other. Jac took the money and left, so what can I tell you? I think Jac got a very poor price for it. We can simply look at where I am in the world today and where Jac is.

JAC: David was interviewed by Time magazine and said, in essence, most of the above. Ahmet ran into David and asked why he had given that interview, because from Ahmet's perspective it wasn't true. David shrugged, "Well, they called me and I had to say something."

David always hankered to be a mogul, a power in the world of entertainment, and he got his wish. I wanted something far more personal and less public, and with an eye to my well-being, not just my wallet.

My $10,000,000 for Elektra stacked up well next to the $17,000,000 paid for

Atlantic, when you take into account that Atlantic was twice our size. If I had approached Steve just the right way and committed to two additional years, I could have had my deal remade, but Steve had paid me a fair price. Far more important than the money—indeed decisive—was the gift of a moment of time, to change the way I lived.

Making records had been my entire life. Starting in 1965, I had enjoyed my biblical seven fatted years of good fortune. My confidence in my instincts had grown. By 1973 the only thing I had never done was walk away from it all, and my instinct was screaming, "It's time to go."

I was happy to leave with the affection of my artists and the good opinion of people in the business whom I respected.

JOE SMITH: Jac started Elektra with a love for the music and an IQ very high on the charts. And he had an ongoing influence. The company's origins and success make for textbook reading in the music business. On a short, short list you've got to look at Jac.

AHMET ERTEGUN: Artists liked Jac because of his straightforwardness and his intelligence. He didn't record things just because they would sell. What was different about Jac was that he had the same dedication as people who had jazz labels. He was more interested in recording things that he thought were worthwhile, of intrinsic value, with people that he liked. He was one of the most reputable people, a man of integrity, honesty and dedication to art. Very few people in my business have that. He gave the business a better look. I was proud to be associated with him.

CLIVE DAVIS: Jac was a major learning experience for me. I have tremendous admiration for his standards of excellence at every stage of his career.

JUDY COLLINS: He had a sensibility that extended itself from one end of the business to the other. He could look at a project and make it make business sense. And he could also walk into the recording studio and pick the right phrase. I don't think anyone can do both anymore.

NESUHI ERTEGUN: Jac was a very special person, a visionary, a pioneer, in the forefront. And personally a brilliant producer. He proved it over and over again, through the years, with the records he made with much less means than the biggest companies. Jac's music survives because he had more than good taste, he really did the best to bring out the best from his artists and wouldn't accept anything else. After thirty years those records are still in the catalogs, still selling very well.

BHASKAR MENON: A large number of the artists on Elektra were not passing hit single artists. They are artists who had a career arc and had something to say that transcended a hit record. Jac had a rare ability to see and foster that. He combined that insight with a really extraordinary shrewd knowledge and judgment of the business. In that respect, in a whole generation that had some extraordinarily gifted and talented people in it, I would say he is without peer.

MO OSTIN: Jac was a consummate record man who had incredibly broad experience and ability. I mean, he could produce records, he could engineer records, he could promote records, he could bargain records, he could conduct the business on a first-rate basis. To me, he, more than any other record executive that I'm aware of, including all the guys who were in the room at WEA, had all the attributes, all the pieces.

JACKSON BROWNE: There's an aspect to the music business—bottom line, nuts and bolts, money—so much falls away and you're left with just that, it's just a business. But Jac's spirit was always more grand and generous and adventurous. He understood that everybody should get well paid for what they do, but that the real treasure is the doing of the work that matters to you. He always seemed to go for fostering the creative, recording the original, trying to figure out how to capture things. And at the same time he was recording obscure music from all over the world, out of left field—send these guys to faraway places with a Nagra, capture the festival music and put it out on Nonesuch.

Nonesuch records—they were everyone's secret possession, like the secret lore. On Ridpath everyone would roll a big fat joint and put on "Music Of Bulgaria" and say, "Listen to this." It was like the first time I tried acid—"Wow! I didn't know this was going on! How long has this been going on?" He had this adventurous spirit, the spirit of someone documenting his time. He had started with folk, moved to electric folk, and white blues, and singer-songwriters, and on to rock and roll, with enormous commercial success for Elektra. He won the lottery with the Doors. The Sixties coin of the realm was people making a new order of things. Jac did this on a huge scale, involving business and finance. He took what was a fortune then, and he made these eclectic records with people who ordinarily would not be signed. So Jac was this sort of mystic purveyor of all these things, kind of like the Wizard of Oz. There were legends about him.

CARLY SIMON: It was the best feeling I ever had in the music business. And I think an era died when he left. It became so corporate. It seemed like Graham crackers or things that had nothing to do with the music business were in charge. Jac should start a new record label right now. Tell him I said so. Tell him that I'd be there in a second and come running.

RUSS MILLER: The day Jac left, the butterfly died.

JAC: Mel Posner asked me to save the evening of Wednesday, August 22nd. I smelled a party. I was already feeling the post-partum blues, but it would be sweet to have my time at Elektra wrapped up with a bow on it, and to publicly thank everyone I had worked with for their skills, their loyalty, their devotion.

This would be the greatest turning of a page in my life, just a few weeks shy of my forty-second birthday. I had much to look back on, and enormous good fortune to celebrate. So much music history had been written since I started. Hundreds of independent labels that had been born in hope had passed away. Elektra had stayed afloat and ridden the rapids of enormous change, and that was rare. From the time of my beginnings only Elektra, Atlantic and Vanguard made it into the Seventies with their founders at the helm, and in a few years Vanguard would not be a company, just a collection of masters to be sold.

I had followed the music. We had touched so many lives, left so many marks, some powerful, some subtle, all traceable, many indelible. Our artists were seeded and cultivated at the company. It was a proud roster of the famous and talented as well as the talented and not so famous: Jean Ritchie, Frank Warner, Ed McCurdy, Sabicas, Phil Ochs, the Toms—Rush and Paxton; Joseph Spence, Tim Buckley, Theodore Bikel, Judy Collins, Carly Simon, Queen, Harry Chapin, David Ackles, Jean Redpath, Lord Buckley, the Incredible String Band, the Stooges, Earth Opera, Paul Siebel, Carol Hall, Bread, Koerner Ray & Glover, the Holy Modal Rounders, Paul Butterfield, Delaney & Bonnie, Lonnie Mack, and the Doors. Their records entertained and they reverberate still.

Nonesuch brought a freshness to the recording of classical and world music, very much like Elektra's impact on popular culture. We were the early explorers of electronic and synthesizer music, the music of Bulgaria and the Indonesian gamelan, now routinely heard in hundreds of films. Composers whose repertoire had lain ignored were relaunched on Nonesuch and none more touching than Scott Joplin.

All these sounds were in my ears and in my heart on the night of August 22nd. It was a storybook New York evening, warm but not hot, the sky cloudless and a very deep blue-black. You could even see some stars. George, my driver of many years, wheeled us over to the Tavern on the Green in Central Park, a festive setting, aglow with little Tivoli lights twinkling through the trees. The largest party room had been reserved. The Warner company jet had been shuttling back and forth, bringing people in from the West Coast. Many of the Elektra artists were there, alongside people who had sustained me at every point in my musical life, all the way back to Anne and Frank Warner, who had fed me Brunswick stew in my scuffling Village days. The Warners' son Jeff had been in the fourth grade in the Village with Harry Chapin; Frank had played for the schoolkids, and that was the first time Harry ever heard folk music. The room was filled with these human connections, linkages of lives braided with mine.

I ate very little of my dinner. Just before dessert, Mel Posner—Mel, who had been with me all the way, from stock boy to senior executive, through days rough and smooth—made a short speech. He presented me, on behalf of the company, with a crystal ball to divine the future and a sextant to guide my path. I had no words prepared, just trusting to the moment. I spoke, finding faces, speaking of them and to them. What I wanted to communicate was love and gratitude. When I could say no more I stepped into the crowd and said my personal farewells to everyone in the room.

The evening ended. George drove me home. We had traveled many miles together, George and I; this was our last.

Chapter 33 ⅓

JAC: There was business to wind up at corporate headquarters in New York, and farewells to say in London. With everything taken care of, on November 11th I boarded Pan Am Flight 1 to Hawai'i. Every minute of the five hours from the West Coast was a blessed mental and emotional separation. I landed at Honolulu and shuttled to the inter-island terminal. After the cool dryness of the plane, the smell of flowers and the richness of the warm island air wrapped me in a welcoming breeze. I caught Hawaiian Flight 818 to Maui.

Taking a cab from Kahului airport, I found myself on the same road across the isthmus I had traveled five years before. I was happy to be alone with my thoughts and remember a promise made to myself, and kept.

I reached the home that Roger Somers had crafted for me to my heart's yearning. There are moments in a life where you look on something new for the first time and you know, to a certainty, whether it is right or wanting. It was so right.

I strolled around to the ocean side and stood on the lanai, listening to the gentle lapping of the waves. The sliding door was unlocked. I took a deep breath and walked into the rest of my life.

Acknowledgments

First—a retrospective Thank You to the multitudes who helped to make Elektra Records what it was in the Jac Holzman years. Their names constitute a roll call that sounds through the pages of this book.

Grateful thanks to the many who took time and trouble to sit for interviews, and often to respond to follow-up questions. Their names appear in the cast of characters.

Life slips away, and a number of people of great importance to Jac's Elektra years are no longer with us. Prime among them are Jim Morrison and Paul Rothchild. We have done our best to give them a presence on the page. Jim lives and moves in the words of a great number of others. As for Paul, his wife Terry and his son Dan speak about him, along with Elektra co-workers and artists. Joe Smith kindly gave us permission to use Paul's thoughts from interviews Joe recorded for his oral history of popular music, Off The Record. And Paul spoke at length in 1990 with Sandy Gibson, who conducted a number of the early interviews for Jac's nationally syndicated radio special "The Doors—From The Inside." We have quoted Paul selectively from these transcripts, as well as others interviewed by Sandy (Bill Harvey for one—another important figure at Elektra who is now gone). Sandy's interviews are a big contribution.

Pearl Goodman transcribed most of the interview tapes, working long hours at her lifelong high level of conscientious accuracy, grounded in her personal knowledge of people and events. JoAnna Linn gave the final manuscript her careful scrutiny.

Maricel Pagulayan and later Tracy Blair were cheerfully efficient office managers for the project, with the invaluable added extra of being able to remain blessedly calm and good-tempered in the face of random irruptions of Murphy's Law and the inexorable onset of deadlines. Tracy's skillful scans of all the images and her dedicated production follow-through were a godsend.

Jac's children—Marin, Jaclyn and Adam—and his brother Keith all made thoughtful suggestions, and the book is richer for their active interest.

Ray Randolph, with his specialist knowledge of Boss Radio in Sixties LA, helped verify some important dates and authenticate some arcane teenage language of the times.

Andy Finney, who has been the BBC's resident expert on all things Elektra, painstakingly compiled the discography, without which this book would be the poorer.

Sylvia Rhone and Gary Casson of Elektra graciously granted permission to use the company's trademarks and album cover art.

We have benefited greatly from the contributions of the Doors and Danny Sugerman, including their permission to quote lyrics and their help locating photos.

Every effort has been made to credit photos correctly. If errors or omissions remain, we would appreciate being informed so that correct attribution can be made in any future edition.

Finally, to all those who asked for this book and supported us along the way, our gratitude.

Jac Holzman — Cenan Daws

Discography

Elektra Records 1951-1973

Compiled by Andy Finney

This discography details all the albums released or recorded during Jac Holzman's Elektra years from Spring 1951 to Fall 1973. Only the most significant releases contain a complete listing of song titles. A fuller discography is available on our "Follow The Music" website at *www.followthemusic.com*

Elektra EKLP 1 [Mono] - Released in 1952 - 12-inch LP
New Songs - Georgianna Bannister (Soprano) and John Gruen (Piano)
Produced by Jac Holzman

Da Neight Sich Die Stunde (1); Wenn Es Nur Einmal So Ganz Stille Wäre (1); Lösch Mir Die Augen Aus (1); Was Wirst Du Ton Gott, Wenn Ich Sterbe? (1); Die Sirenen; Hälfte Des Lebens; It Is At Moments After I Have Dreamed (2); Spring Is Like A Perhaps Hand (2); The Moon Is Hiding (2); O By The By (2); Intimité (3); Fleurs Qui Tombez (3); O Reves (3); A Peine M'as-Tu Dit (3); Pour Une Parole Timide (3)

Note: First Elektra LP. The songs are grouped on the sleeve and label. Group 1 is 'Vier Stundenbuch Lieder' by Rilke, group 2 is four songs by e e cummings and group 3 are 'Chansons De Geishas' by anonymous Japanese poets.

Elektra EKLP 2 [Mono] - Released in 1952 - 10-inch LP
Jean Ritchie Singing The Traditional Songs Of Her Kentucky Mountain Family - Jean Ritchie
Produced by Jac Holzman and Edward Tatnall Canby

O Love Is Teasin'; Jubilee; Black Is The Color; A Short Life Of Trouble; One Morning In May; One Morning In May (another version); Old Virginny; Skin And Bones; The Little Devils; My Boy Willie; Hush Little Baby; Gypsum Davy; The Cuckoo; The Cuckoo (another version); Little Cory; Keep Your Garden Clean

Elektra EKLP 3 [Mono] - Released in 1952 - 10-inch LP
American Folk Songs And Ballads - Frank Warner
Produced by Jac Holzman

Keep Your Hand On The Plow; Hold My Hand, Lord Jesus; Lord Lovel; Battle Of Bull Run; The Unreconstructed Rebel; He's Got The Whole World In His Hand; The Days Of Forty-Nine; Gilgary Mountain; Blue Mountain Lake; Tom Dooley

Elektra EKL 4 [Mono] - 10-inch LP
British Traditional Ballads In America - Shep Ginandes

Elektra EKL 5 [Mono] - Released in 1953 - 10-inch LP
Voices Of Haiti - Various Artists
Produced by Jac Holzman

The recordings were made during ceremonials near Croix-Des-Missions and Pationville in Haiti by Maya Deren.

Elektra EKL 6 [Mono] - 10-inch LP

Turkish And Spanish Folksongs - Cynthia Gooding
Produced by Jac Holzman

Elektra EKL 7 [Mono] - Released in 1953 - 10-inch LP
American Folksongs For Children - Shep Ginandes

Elektra EKL 8 [Mono] - Released in 1953 - 10-inch LP
Mexican Folk Songs - Cynthia Gooding
Produced by Jac Holzman

Elektra EKL 9 [Mono] - Released in 1953 - 10-inch LP
French Traditional Songs - Shep Ginandes

Elektra EKL 10 [Mono] - Released in 1953 - 10-inch LP
O Lovely Appearance Of Death - Hally Wood
Produced by Jac Holzman

Elektra EKL 11 [Mono] - Released in 1953 - 10-inch LP
The Queen Of Hearts - English Folksongs - Cynthia Gooding
Produced by Jac Holzman

Elektra EKL 12 [Mono] - Released in 1953 - 10-inch LP
Folk Songs From The Southern Appalachians - Tom Paley

Elektra EKL 13 [Mono] - Released in 1954 - 10-inch LP
Songs And Ballads Of America's Wars - Frank Warner
Produced by Jac Holzman

Elektra EKL 14 [Mono] - Released in 1954 - 10-inch LP
Folk Blues - Sonny Terry
Produced by Jac Holzman

Elektra EKL 15 [Mono] - 10-inch LP
City Blues - Sonny Terry
Produced by Jac Holzman

Elektra EKL 16 [Mono] - Released in 1955 - 10-inch LP
Badmen And Heroes - Ed McCurdy, Jack Elliott and Oscar Brand
Produced by Jac Holzman

Captain Kidd; Charles Guiteau; Jesse James; Billy The Kid; Quantrell; Robin Hood And The Bold Pedlar; Bold Turpin; Pretty Boy Floyd; Jim Fisk

Elektra EKL 17 [Mono] - Released in 1954 - 10-inch LP
Italian Folk Songs - Cynthia Gooding
Produced by Jac Holzman

Elektra EKL 18 [Mono] - Released in 1954 - 10-inch LP
Pirate Songs And Ballads - Dick Wilder
Produced by Jac Holzman

Elektra EKL 21 [Mono] - Released in 1954 - 10-inch LP
Folk Songs-Once Over Lightly - Alan Arkin
Produced by Jac Holzman

Note: An alternative title for this album was "Folksongs (And 2 1/2 That Aren't) Once over Lightly."

Elektra EKL 22 [Mono] - Released in 1954 - 10-inch LP
Courting Songs - Jean Ritchie and Oscar Brand

Produced by Jac Holzman

Elektra EKL 23 [Mono] - 10-inch LP
Nova Scotia Folk Music - Recorded by Diane Hamilton

Elektra EKL 24 [Mono] - 10-inch LP
Sin Songs - Pro and Con - Ed McCurdy
Produced by Jac Holzman

Elektra EKL 25 [Mono] - Released in 1954 - 10-inch LP
Kentucky Mountain Songs - Jean Ritchie
Produced by Jac Holzman

Cedar Swamp; Nottamun Town; The Hangman Song; Sister Phoebe; False Sir John; Dulcimer Pieces: Shady Grove, Old King Cole, Skip To My Lou; Batchelor's Hall; The Girl I Left Behind; Jemmy Taylor-O; Killy Krankie; The Lonesome Dove; Old Woman and Pig; The Little Sparrow; Goin' To Boston

---

Elektra EKL 26 [Mono] - Released in 1954 - 10-inch LP
Old Airs From Ireland, Scotland and England - Susan Reed
Produced by Jac Holzman

At The Foot Of Yonder's Mountain; The Pretty Girl Milking Her Cow; The Leprechaun; He Moved Through The Fair; Bendemeer's Stream; Irish Famine Song; Wraggle Taggle Gypsies; Seventeen Come Sunday; The Foggy Dew; I Know My Love; Must I Go Bound; The Boreens of Derry; Wailie, Wailie

---

Elektra EKL 27 [Mono] - 10-inch LP
Goin' Down The Road - Clarence Cooper
Produced by Jac Holzman

Elektra EKL 30 [Mono] - Released in 1955 - 10-inch LP
Festival In Haiti - Jean Léon Destiné and Ensemble
Produced by Jac Holzman

Elektra EKL 32 [Mono] - Released in 1955 - 10-inch LP
Folksongs Of Israel - Theodore Bikel
Produced by Jac Holzman

Dodi Li; Mi Barechev; Hechalil; Ptsach Bazemer; Karev Yom; Shech Abrek; Sissoo Vessimchoo; El Ginat Egoz; Shomer Mah Milel; Hana'ava Babanot; Ana Pana' Dodech; Shim'oo Shim'oo; Lyla Lyla

---

Elektra EKL 701 [Mono] - Released in 1955
The Story Of John Henry & Ballads, Blues And Other Songs - Josh White
Produced by Jac Holzman

The Story Of John Henry; Black Girl; Free And Equal Blues; Live The Life; Sam Hall; Where Were You Baby; Delia's Gone; Run, Mona, Run; You Don't Know My Mind

Note: Double 10-inch album, 'John Henry' takes up one of the two discs. Later issued as a single 12-inch disc on EKL 123.

Elektra EKL 102 [Mono] - Released in 1956
Josh At Midnight - Josh White
Produced by Jac Holzman

St. James Infirmary; Raise A Rukus; Scandalize My Name; Jesus Gonna Make Up My Dyin' Bed; Timber (Jerry The Mule); Jelly, Jelly; One Meat Ball; Joshua Fit The Battle Of Jericho; Don't Lie Buddy; Number Twelve Train; Peter; Takin' Names

Note: Issued in UK on Bounty Label.

Elektra EKL 103 [Mono] - Released in 1956
Los Gitanillos De Cadiz - Los Gitanillos de Cadiz

Elektra EKL 104 [Mono] - Released in 1956
Songs Of Montmartre - Suzanne Robert

Elektra EKL 105 [Mono] - Released in 1956
An Actor's Holiday - Theodore Bikel
Produced by Jac Holzman

Elektra EKL 107 [Mono]
Faithful Lovers And Other Phenomena - Cynthia Gooding

Elektra EKL 108 [Mono]
Blood Booze 'n Bones - Ed McCurdy
Produced by Jac Holzman

Darlin' Cory; Josie; The Dublin Murder Ballad; Four Nights Drunk; Cowboy's Lament; Kentucky Moonshiner; No More Booze; Farewell To Grog; Portland County Jail; Banks Of The Ohio; John Hardy; The Pig And The Inebriate; Stackerlee; Lamkins; Yo Ho Ho; Lulu; The Drunkard's Doom

---

Elektra EKL 109 [Mono] EKS 7109 [Stereo]
A Young Man And A Maid (AKA: Love Songs Of Many Lands) - Theodore Bikel and Cynthia Gooding
Produced by Jac Holzman

Where Does It Lead (C+T); A Meidl In Di Yoren (T); Sur la Route (C+T); Laredo (C+T); Greensleeves (C); Ro'e Vero'a (C+T); Auprès De Ma Blonde (C); As I Roved Out (C+T); Mi Jacalito (C+T); Coplas (C+T); Katherine Jaffrey (C); Hej Pada Pada (T); Well Met, Pretty Maid (C+T); La Ballade Du Chercheur D'Or (T); Western Wind (C); Proschay (C+T)

Elektra EKL 110 [Mono] - Released in 1956
When Dalliance Was In Flower 1 - Ed McCurdy
Produced by Jac Holzman

Go Bring Me A Lass; The Trooper; A Young Man And A Maid; A Wanton Trick; There Was A Knight; Two Maidens Went Milking One Day; A Lusty Young Smith; Tom And Doll; A Riddle; A Maiden Did A-Bathing Go; The Jolly Tinker; Old Fumbler; The Three Travelers; Kitt Hath Lost Her Key; To A Lady; The Four Able Physicians; Sylvia The Fair

---

Elektra EKL 112 [Mono]
Songs Of The Old West - Ed McCurdy
Produced by Jac Holzman

Elektra EKL 113 [Mono] - Released in 1957
Tenderly - Norene Tate
Produced by Jac Holzman

Note: Jazz album.

Elektra EKL 114 [Mono] - Released in 1957
Josh, Ballads And Blues - Josh White
Produced by Jac Holzman

Midnight Special; Miss Otis Regrets; Halleleu; Woman Sure Is A Curious Critter; Prison Bound Blues; Gloomy Sunday; Ball And Chain Blues; One For My Baby; Jim Crow Train; Told My Captain; So Soon In The Mornin'; Bury My Body

Elektra EKL 115 [Mono] - Released in 1957
The New York Jazz Quartet
Produced by Jac Holzman

Features Herbie Mann on flute.

Elektra EKL 116 [Mono] - Released in 1957
Susan Reed - Susan Reed
Produced by Jac Holzman

Black Is The Color; The Old Woman; I'm Sad And I'm Lonely; Drill, Ye Tarriers; Greensleeves; Go Away From My Window; A Mighty Ship; Mother I Would Marry; Barbara Allen; Michie Banjo; Zelime; Gué Gué; The Soldier And The Lady; Molly Malone; Three White Gulls; Venezuela; If I Had A Ribbon Bow; Miss Bailey; Danny Boy

Elektra EKL 117 [Mono] EKS 7117 [Stereo] - Released in 1957
Sabicas Vol 1 - Sabicas
Produced by Leonard Ripley

Bulerias; Farruca; Fandango; Solea Por Bulerias; Granadina; Soleares; Seguiriva; Malaguena; Alegrias; Taranta

Elektra EKL 118 [Mono] - Released in 1957
The New York Jazz Quartet Goes Native - The New York Jazz Quartet
Produced by Jac Holzman

Elektra EKL 119 [Mono] - Released in 1957
An Evening At L'Abbaye - Gordon Heath And Lee Payant

Another Man Done Gone; Chanson De La Mariée; The Youth Of The Heart; Black Girl; Big Rock Candy Mountain; Jacob's Ladder; J'ai Un Long Voyage A Faire; We Will Break Bread Together; Hill An' Gully; Au Claire De La Lune; The Foggy, Foggy Dew; Little David; The Spinning Wheel; Le Roy A Fait Battre Tambour; Scarborough Fair; Linstead Market; L'Occasion Manquée

Elektra EKL 120 [Mono] - Released in 1957
The Jazz Messengers - The Jazz Messengers
Produced by Jac Holzman

Note: Features Art Blakey on drums.

Elektra EKL 121 [Mono] - Released in 1957
Sabicas Vol 2 - Sabicas
Produced by Leonard Ripley

Elektra EKL 122 [Mono] - Released in 1957
Courtin's A Pleasure (Courting And Other Folk Songs Of The South Appalacians) - Jean Ritchie, Oscar Brand (1-10) and **Tom Paley** (11-20)
Produced by Jac Holzman

Note: The Ritchie and Brand tracks come from EKL 22 and the Paley tracks come from EKL 12.

Elektra EKL 123 [Mono] - Released in 1957
25th Anniversary Album - Josh White
Produced by Jac Holzman

The Story Of John Henry; Black Girl; Free And Equal Blues; Live The Life; Sam Hall; Where Are You Baby; Delia's Gone; Run Mona Run; You Don't Know My Mind

Note: This is a single 12-inch edition of the double 10-inch EKL 701.

Elektra EKL 124 [Mono] - Released in 1957
Sin Songs - Pro And Con - Ed McCurdy
Produced by Jac Holzman

Note: EKLP 24 with extra tracks.

Elektra EKL 125 [Mono] - Released in 1957
Songs Of Her Kentucky Mountain Family - Jean Ritchie
Produced by Jac Holzman

Note: This disc combines tracks from the 10-inch albums EKLP 2 and EKLP 25

Elektra EKL 126 [Mono] - Released in 1957
Susan Reed Sings Old Airs - Susan Reed
Produced by Jac Holzman

The Golden Vanity; Go Tell Aunt Rhody; The Pretty Girl Milking Her Cow; Must I Go Bound; The Leprechaun; He Moved Through The Fair; Bendermeer's Stream; Irish Famine Song; Wraggle Taggle Gypsies; Seventeen Come Sunday; I Know My Love; The Foggy Dew; At The Foot Of Yonder Mountain; Wailie Wailie; The Boreens Of Derry; Jennie Jenkins; Peter Gray; Come Follow

Note: This includes tracks from EKLP 26.

Elektra EKL 127 [Mono] - Released in 1957
Mr Calypso! - Lord Foodoos and His Calypso Band

Elektra EKL 128 [Mono] - Released in 1957
Turkish, Spanish And Mexican Folk Songs - Cynthia Gooding
Produced by Jac Holzman

Note: This album takes tracks from EKLP 6 (Turkish And Spanish Folk Songs) and EKLP 8 (Mexican Folk Songs).

Elektra EKL 129 [Mono]
Badmen, Heroes And Pirate Songs - Ed McCurdy, Oscar Brand, Jack Elliott and Dick Wilder
Produced by Jac Holzman

Bold Turpin; Pretty Boy Floyd; Jim Fisk; Jesse James; Robin Hood And The Bold Pedlar; Charles Guiteau; Billy The Kid; Quantrell; The Bold Princess Royal; The Romantic Pirate; Henry Martyn; The Female Warrior; Captain Kidd; The Female Smuggler; High Barbaree; Bold Manning

Note: This album combines tracks from EKLP 16 (Badmen And Heroes) and EKLP 18 (Pirate Songs And Ballads).

Elektra EKL 130 [Mono] - Released in 1957
Festival In Haiti - Jean Léon Destiné

Elektra EKL 131 [Mono] - Released in 1958
**Queen Of Hearts - Early English Folk Songs -
Cynthia Gooding**
Produced by Jac Holzman

Note: Most of these tracks are also on EKLP 11.

Elektra EKL 132 [Mono] - Released in 1958
Folk Songs Of Israel - Theodore Bikel
Produced by Jac Holzman

Dodili; Hehali L; Ana Pana; Orcha Bamidbar; Shech
Abram Yom; Shomer Ma Milel; Uziyah; Shir Habokrim;
El Ginat; Barechev; Shim'u Shim'u; Hana'ava Babanot;
S Kerem; Ptsach Bazemer; Aclayla

Note: This album uses tracks from EKLP 32 plus additional titles.

Elektra EKL 133 [Mono] - Released in 1958
Shep Ginandes Sings Folksongs - Shep Ginandes

Elektra EKL 134 [Mono]
**Four French Horns Plus Rhythm - Four French
Horns Plus Rhythm**
Produced by Jac Holzman

Note: Jazz album

Elektra EKL 135 [Mono] - Released in 1958
Glenn Yarbrough - Glenn Yarbrough
Produced by Jac Holzman

Rich Gal, Poor Gal; Spanish Is A Loving Tongue; Hey,
Jim Along; Johnny I Hardly Knew You; All My Sorrows;
Hard Ain't It Hard; All Through The Night; Here We
Go Baby; Turtle Dove; Goodbye My Lover; One More
River; Sailor's Grave; Wasn't That A Mighty Day; House
Of The Rising Sun; This Land Is Your Land

Elektra EKL 136 [Mono] - Released in 1957
Vibe-Rant - Teddy Charles
Produced by Jac Holzman

Old Devil Moon; Skylark; No More Nights; How Deep
Is The Ocean; Arlene; Blues Become Elektra

Note: Jazz album

Elektra EKL 137 [Mono] - Released in 1958
Of Maids And Mistresses - Tom Kines

Elektra EKL 138 [Mono] - Released in 1959
Delta Rhythm Boys Sing - Delta Rhythm Boys

Elektra EKL 139 [Mono] EKS 7139 [Stereo]
**Original Trinidad Steel Band - Original Trinidad
Steel Band**
Produced by Jac Holzman

Elektra EKL 140 [Mono] - Released in 1958
When Dalliance Was In Flower 2 - Ed McCurdy
Produced by Jac Holzman and Leonard Ripley

Uptails All; Tottingham Frolic; A Young Man; A
Tradesman; A Tenement To Let; The Playhouse Saint;
The Merchant And The Fiddler's Wife; A Virgin's

Meditation; Would You Have A Young Virgin?; The
Jolly Miller; Of Chloe And Celia; A Lady So Frolic And
Gay; My Thing Is My Own; The Jolly Pedlar's Pretty
Thing; Phillis; To Bed To Me

Elektra EKL 141 [Mono] EKS 7141 [Stereo] - Released in
1958
Jewish Folk Songs - Theodore Bikel
Produced by Jac Holzman

Der Rebe Elimetech; Di Yontevdike Teyg; Sha Shtil; Di
Ban; Kum Aher Du Filozof; Di Mezinke; A Sudenyu;
Achtsik Er Un Zibetsik Zi; Di Mame Lz Gegangen;
Margaritkelech; Mu Asapru; Lomir Zich Iberbeten;
Homeentashin; A Chazn Oyf Shabes; Reyzl;
Tumbalalayka

Elektra EKL 142 [Mono] - Released in 1958
Off-Beat Folk Songs - The Shanty Boys
Produced by Jac Holzman

Elektra EKL 143 [Mono] - Released in 1958
**English And American Folksongs - Marilyn Child
and Glenn Yarbrough**
Produced by Jac Holzman

Elektra EKL 144 [Mono]
**Gene And Francesca Sing Songs Of Many Lands -
Gene And Francesca**
Produced by Jac Holzman

Elektra EKL 145 [Mono]
Sabicas Vol 3 - Sabicas
Produced by Jac Holzman and Leonard Ripley

Elektra EKL 146 [Mono] EKS 7146 [Stereo]
Shalom - Oranim Zabar
Produced by Jac Holzman

Elektra EKL 147 [Mono] - Released in 1958
Unholy Matrimony - Paul Clayton

Elektra EKL 148 [Mono]
The Many Sides Of Sandy Paton - Sandy Paton
Produced by Jac Holzman

Elektra EKL 149 [Mono] EKS 7149 [Stereo]
Festival Gitana - Sabicas
Produced by Leonard Ripley

Elektra EKL 150 [Mono] EKS 7150 [Stereo]
Songs Of A Russian Gypsy - Theodore Bikel
Produced by Jac Holzman

Beryuzoviye Kalyechka; Yekhali Tsigane; Dve Gitari;
Kagda Ya Pyann; Svyetit Myesats; Kak Stranno;
Nichevo; Chto Mnye Gorye; Dyen I Noch; Metyelitsa;
Snilsya Mnye Sad; Karobushka; Karabli; Sudarinya

Elektra EKL 151 [Mono] - Released in 1958
**Our Singing Heritage Vol 1 - Peggy Seeger, Paul
Clayton, Pat Foster and George Pegram**
Produced by Jac Holzman

Elektra EKL 152 [Mono]
Our Singing Heritage Vol 2
Produced by Jac Holzman

Elektra EKL 153 [Mono] - Released in 1958
Our Singing Heritage Vol 3 - Frank Warner

Produced by Jac Holzman

Elektra EKL 154 [Mono]
Erik Darling - Erik Darling
Produced by Jac Holzman

Elektra EKL 155 [Mono] - Released in 1958
Bobby Burns' Merry Muses - Paul Clayton
Produced by Jac Holzman

Nine Inch Will Please A Lady; Our Jock's Broke
Yesterday; How Can I Keep My Maidenhead?; Who
Will Mow Me Now?; Johnnie Scott; John Anderson My
Jo; Tommie Makes My Tail Toddle; Tweedmouth Town;
Would You Do That?; Ellibanks; Beware Of The
Ripples; Duncan Macleerie; Muirland Meg; No Hair On
It; Copper Of Dundee; Who The Devil Can Hinder The
Wind To Blow; Lassie Gathering Nuts; The Thrusting
Of It; My Bonnie Highland Lad; The Patriarch; Duncan
Davison; Know Ye Not Our Bess; Auntie Jean; A Hole
To Hide It In; Can You Labour Lea

Elektra EKL 156 [Mono] EKS 7156 [Stereo]
On The Road To Elath - Oranim Zabar
Produced by Jac Holzman and Mark Abramson

Elektra EKL 157 [Mono] - Released in 1958
The Folk Singers - Folk Singers

Elektra EKL 158 [Mono] EKS 7158 [Stereo] - Released in
1958
Chain Gang Songs - Josh White
Produced by Jac Holzman

Trouble; 'Twas On A Monday; Going Home Boys; Nine
Foot Shovel; Crying Who And Crying You; Dip Your
Fingers In The Water; Old Ship Of Zion; Mary Had A
Baby; Did You Ever Love A Woman; Every Time I Feel
The Spirit

Elektra EKL 159 [Mono] EKS 7159 [Stereo]
Cuadro Flamenco - Cuadro Flamenco

Note: Reissued as Nonesuch 2002 in 1965.

Elektra EKL 160 [Mono] EKS 7160 [Stereo]
When Dalliance Was In Flower 3 - Ed McCurdy
Produced by Jac Holzman

Yeoman Of Kent; Shepherd; Old Brass To Mend; Celia;
As I Walked In The Woods; Merry Wedding; Whilst
Alexis Lay Prest; How Happy's The Miller; Hive Of
Bees; Sound Of Country Lass; She Rose To Let Me In;
Country Wake; Pollycock; When Flora Had On Her
New Gown; Spinning Wheel; End

Elektra EKL 161 [Mono] EKS 7161 [Stereo]
**Folk Songs From Just About Everywhere - Theodore
Bikel and Geula Gill**
Produced by Jac Holzman and Mark Abramson

Pollerita; Ah Si Mon Moine; Shir Hanoar; Din Plaiurile
Romaniei; Rozhinkes Mit Mandlen; Darogoy Dalnoyu;
Yerakina; Oleana; Erets Zavat Khalav; Viva Jujuy; Ayil
Ayil; Azizam; Peixe Vivo; Shney Khaverim

Elektra EKL 162 [Mono] EKS 7162 [Stereo]
Catches And Glees - Randolph Singers

Elektra EKL 163 [Mono]

Songs For The Wee Folk - Susan Reed

Elektra EKL 164 [Mono]
**Love And War Between The Sexes - Gene and
Francesca**

Elektra EKL 165 [Mono] EKS 7165 [Stereo]
More Jewish Folk Songs - Theodore Bikel
Produced by Jac Holzman

Hulyet Hulyet Kinderlech; Lomir Alle Zingen; A Zemer;
A Fidler; Drei Techterlech; Der Becher; Kinder Yorn;
Dona Dona; Unter A Kleyn Beymele; Der Fisher; Drei
Yingelech; Papir Iz Doch Veis; Az Der Rebbe Zingt; Di
Zun Vet Arunter Geyn

Elektra EKL 166 [Mono] EKS 7166 [Stereo]
Around The Campfire - Oranim Zabar
Produced by Jac Holzman and Mark Abramson

Al Tira; Erev Shel Shoshanim; Hora Oz; Gozi Li;
Shim'oo Shim'oo Esh All; Dayagim; Va Yven; Chi Dot;
David Melech; Leylot Bich'na'an; Eretz Zavat

Elektra EKL 167 [Mono] EKS 7167 [Stereo] - Released in
1959
**Gold Coast Saturday Night - Saka Acquaye And His
African Ensemble**
Produced by Jac Holzman

Sugar Soup; Down The Congo; Saturday Night; Drum
Festival; Concomba; Beyond Africa; Congo Beat;
Echoes Of The African Forest; Bus Conductor; Ebony;
Kenya Sunset; Awuben; Akudonno

Note: High Life music from Ghana.

Elektra EKL 168 [Mono] EKS 7168 [Stereo]
**The Wild Blue Yonder - Oscar Brand featuring the
Roger Wilco Four**
Produced by Jac Holzman

Save A Fighter Pilot's Ass; Come And Join The Air
Force; Give Me Operations; Itazuke Tower; Sidi
Slimane; Army Air Force Heaven; Bless 'em All; Glory
Flying Regulations; God Damned Reserves; Barnacle
Bill The Pilot; Fighter Pilot's Lament; I Wanted Wings;
Poor Co-Pilot; Cigarettes And Sake; Wreck Of The Old
Ninety-Seven; Let's Have A Party

Elektra EKL 169 [Mono] EKS 7169 [Stereo]
Every Inch A Sailor - Oscar Brand
Produced by Jac Holzman

Elektra EKL 170 [Mono] - Released in 1959
Son Of Dalliance - Ed McCurdy
Produced by Jac Holzman

A Petition; Character Of A Mistress; Rapture; The
Miller's Daughter; I Dreamed My Love; The
Presbyterian Wedding; A Lamentable Case; The Way To
Win Her; She Lay All Naked; A Pleasant Ballad; A
Maiden's Delight; The Vine; Three Birds; The
Fornicator

Elektra EKL 171 [Mono] - Released in 1959
A Concert With Hillel And Aviva - Hillel and Aviva
Produced by Jac Holzman

Elektra EKL 172 [Mono]

Jean Shepherd And Other Foibles - Jean Shepherd
Produced by Jac Holzman

Note: A comedy album.

Elektra EKL 173 [Mono] EKS 7173 [Stereo]
Donkey Debka! - Young Israel Sings - Ron and Nama
Produced by Jac Holzman

Elektra EKL 174 [Mono] EKS 7174 [Stereo]
Tell It To The Marines - Oscar Brand
Produced by Jac Holzman

Honey Baby; Call Out The Corps; Man In The Moon; Reserves Lament; Wake Island; Dinky Die; Gee But I Wanna Go Home; United States Marines; Moving On; Pua Pua; Cuts And Guts; Old Number Nine; Bless 'Em All; Marines Hymn

Elektra EKL 175 [Mono] EKS 7175 [Stereo] - Released in 1959
Bravo Bikel! - Theodore Bikel
Produced by Jac Holzman and Mark Abramson

Proschay; Buffalo Boy; Doce Cascabeles; Mul Har Sinai; Two Brothers; Harmonicas; Mot'l; Le Caissier; Barnyards O'Delgatty; Digging The Weans; Coplas; Sano Duso; Chemdat I; Kretchma; Nitchevo Nitchevo Nitchevo

Elektra EKL 176 [Mono] EKS 7176 [Stereo] - Released in 1959
Hairy Jazz - Shel Silverstein
Produced by Jac Holzman and Mark Abramson

I'm Satisfied With My Girl; Go Back Where You Got It Last Night; Broken Down Mama; Somebody Else Not Me; Good Whiskey; I Wonder Who's Kissing Her Now; Who Walks In; Kitchen Man; Sister Kate; A Good Man Is Hard to Find; Pass Me By Just Like You Never Knowed Me; Ragged but Right

Note: Shel Silverstein later made his name as the writer behind Dr Hook and the Medicine Show. He contributed sleeve notes to many Elektra albums of this period.

Elektra EKL 177 [Mono] EKS 7177 [Stereo]
Ski Songs - Bob Gibson
Produced by Jac Holzman and Mark Abramson

Celebrated Skier; In This White World; Super Skier; My Highlands Lassie; Bend In His Knees; Talking Skier; Ski Patrol; Skiin' In The Mornin'; Super Skier's Last Race; What'll We Do; Skol To The Skier

Elektra EKL 178 [Mono] EKS 7178 [Stereo]
Out Of The Blue, Songs Of A Fighting Airforce - Oscar Brand and the Roger Wilco 5
Produced by Jac Holzman

Flying Fortress; Will You Go Boom Today; I Learned About Flying From That; Lee's Hoochie; Air Force Ground Crew; It's A Shyme; Pilot's Heaven; Pilot Of Renown; Yankee Dollar; Prettiest Ship; In Flight Refueling; New Guinea Strafers; Stand To Your Glasses; Our Bomber Files 10,000 Miles; Airman's Toast

Elektra EKL 179 [Mono]

The World In My Arms - Anita Ellis
Produced by Jac Holzman and Mark Abramson

Elektra EKL 180 [Mono] EKS 7180 [Stereo] - Released in 1961
The Limeliters - Limeliters
Produced by Jac Holzman and Mark Abramson

The Hammer Song; Battle At Gandessa; Charlie, The Midnight Marauder; Zhankoye; When I First Came To This Land; Malaguena Salerosa; The Bear Chase; The Burro; Gari Gari; John Henry, the Steel Driving Man; Take My True Love By The Hand; Lonesome Traveler

Elektra EKL 181 [Mono]
The Exciting Artistry Of Will Holt - Will Holt

Elektra EKL 182 [Mono]
We Sing Of The Sea - Seafarers Chorus

Elektra EKL 183 [Mono] EKS 7183 [Stereo] - Released in 1960
Boating Songs And All That Bilge - Oscar Brand and the Sea Wolves
Produced by Jac Holzman and Mark Abramson

Elektra EKL 184 [Mono]
Presenting Joyce Grenfell - Joyce Grenfell
Produced by Jac Holzman

Hello Song; Life And Literature; Thought For Today; Two Songs My Mother Taught Me; Nursery School; Life Story; I Like Life; Time To Waste; Three Brothers; Artist's Room; Mediocre Waltz; Committee

Note: A unique English comedienne and actress, Joyce Grenfell made her name with monologues about the trials of looking after children. Her role, repeated often in films, was a dotty school mistress.

Elektra EKL 185 [Mono] EKS 7185 [Stereo]
Songs Of Russia Old And New - Theodore Bikel
Produced by Jac Holzman

Elektra EKL 186 [Mono] EKS 7186 [Stereo]
Hora! Songs And Dances Of Israel - Oranim Zabar
Produced by Jac Holzman and Mark Abramson

Nayeem; Hineh Ma Tov; In Hashachar; Harmonica; Itee Milvanon; Krakowiak; Hora Mechona; Dodi Li; Bat Hareem; Mechol Ovadia; El Ginat Egoz; Vedaveed

Elektra EKL 187 [Mono] EKS 7187 [Stereo] - Released in 1960
Sabra - The Young Heart Of Israel - Ron and Nama
Produced by Jac Holzman and Mark Abramson

Elektra EKL 188 [Mono] EKS 7188 [Stereo] - Released in 1960
Sports Car Songs For Big Wheels - Oscar Brand

Elektra EKL 189 [Mono] EKS 7189 [Stereo]
Newport Folk Festival 1960 - Various Artists (Oscar Brand, Will Holt, Oranim-Zabar, Theo Bikel)

Talking Atomic Blues; Great Selchie Of Shule Skerry; Horse With A Union Label; Three Jovial Huntsmen; Edward Ballad; MTA; Bukhara; Russian Spoof; Ayil Ayil; Al Harim; Mi Caballo; Three Jolly Rogues; Eres Alta; Galveston Flood

Elektra EKL 190 [Mono] EKS 7190 [Stereo] - Released in 1960
Spook Along With Zacherley - Zacherley
Produced by Jac Holzman and Mark Abramson

Note: Also issued on Crestview records in 1963 under the title "Zacherley's Monster Gallery", CRV 803.

Elektra EKL 191 [Mono] EKS 7191 [Stereo]
Caledonia - MacPherson Singers and Dancers of Scotland

Elektra EKL 192 [Mono] EKS 7192 [Stereo]
Goin' Places - Casey Anderson

Elektra EKL 193 [Mono] EKS 7193 [Stereo]
Spirituals And Blues - Josh White
Produced by Jac Holzman and Mark Abramsom

Southern Exposure; Red Sun; Silicosis Blues; Black Snake; Things About Coming My Way; My Way; I've Got That Pure Religion; Nobody Knows The Trouble I've Seen; I Know King Jesus; Just A Closer Walk With Thee; I Don't Intend To Die In Egypt

Elektra EKL 194 [Mono] EKS 7194 [Stereo]
Balalaika - Sasha Polinoff and His Russian Gypsy Orchestra
Produced by Jac Holzman and Mark Abramson

Elektra EKL 195 [Mono]
Will Failure Spoil Jean Shepherd? - Jean Shepherd
Produced by Jac Holzman and Mark Abramson

Note: Comedy album.

Elektra EKL 196 [Mono] EKS 7196 [Stereo]
The Dudaim - Dudaim
Produced by Jac Holzman and Mark Abramson

Note: Israeli folk songs

Elektra EKL 197 [Mono] EKS 7197 [Stereo]
Yes I See - Bob Gibson
Produced by Jac Holzman and Mark Abramson

Yes I See; Springhill Mine Disaster; Well, Well, Well; You Can Tell The World; Copper Kettle; John Henry; Gilgarry Mountain; Motherless Children; Daddy Roll 'Em; Trouble In Mind; By And By; Blues Around My Head

Elektra EKL 198 [Mono] EKS 7198 [Stereo]
Up In The Air - Songs for The Madcap Airman - Oscar Brand
Produced by Jac Holzman

Teterboro Tower; Loaded Down; Gooney Bird; When I First Set Out To Fly; A and E Mechanics; Light Planes On Parade; Checklist Song; Line Boy; Plane Talk; Roving Flyer; From The Cab Docket; Passenger's Lament; Masters Of The Air

Elektra EKL 199 [Mono] EKS 7199 [Stereo]
Go To Blazes - Peter Myers and Ronnie Cass

Elektra EKL 200 [Mono] EKS 7200 [Stereo]
From Bondage To Freedom - Theodore Bikel
Produced by Jac Holzman and Mark Abramson

Elektra EKL 201 [Mono] EKS 7201 [Stereo]
A Town Hall Concert - Oranim Zabar And Geula Gil
Produced Mark Abramson

Elektra EKL 202 [Mono] EKS 7202 [Stereo]
Pulsating Rhythms Of Paraguay - Los Chiriguanos

Elektra EKL 203 [Mono] EKS 7203 [Stereo]
The House I Live In - Josh White
Produced by Jac Holzman

Good Morning Blues; Johnny Has Gone For A Soldier; Waltzing Matilda; When I Lay Down And Die; Mean Mistreater; Blind Man Stood On The Road; Freedom Road; Man Who Couldn't Walk Around; T B Blues; House I Live In

Elektra EKL 204 [Mono] EKS 7204 [Stereo]
For Doctors Only - Oscar Brand
Produced by Jac Holzman

How To Be A Doctor; Appendectomy Country-Style; Ort Gyn; Charming White Caps; Television Doctors; Miracle Drugs; My First Day At Med School; Old G P; Here Comes The AMA; Conventional Behaviour; Surgery; Doctor's Wife; Medical Life Calypso; Conquest Of Disease

Elektra EKL 205 [Mono] - Released in 1961
A Treasure Chest Of American Folk Song - Ed McCurdy
Produced by Jac Holzman

Who Is The Man; The Two Sisters; Yorkshire Bite; Frog's Courtship; Gypsy Laddie; Andrew Bardine; Lord Randal; The Paw Paw Patch; In Old Virginny; Boll Weevil; Hunters Of Kentucky; Derby Ram; The Squirrel; Black Is The Color; Rock About, My Saro Jane; Down In The Valley; Across The Western Ocean; Paddy Works On The Railway; My Pretty Little Pink; Lane County Bachelor; Careless Love; Bury Me Beneath The Willow; Gently, Fair Jenny; Simple Gifts; Wondrous Love; John Brown's Body; There Was An Old Soldier; Jesse James; The Cowboy's Dream; Roving Gambler; James Whaland; Clinch Mountain; Willy The Weeper; Hard Travelin'

Note: A double album (Bonus Pak). This solidly-packed double splits four areas of American folk tradition across the four sides: New England, The South, O Pioneers! and A Song for Occupations.

Elektra EKL 206 [Mono] EKS 7206 [Stereo]
The Whole World Dances - Geula Gill (Oranim Zabar)

Elektra EKL 207 [Mono] EKS 7207 [Stereo] - Released in 1961
Gibson And Camp At The Gate Of Horn - Bob Gibson and Bob Camp
Produced by Jac Holzman and Mark Abramson

Skillet Good And Greasy; Old Blue; St. Claire's Defeat; I'm Gonna Tell God; Two In The Middle; Civil War Trilogy (1st Battalion, Yes I See, Two Brothers); Daddy Roll 'Em; The Thinking Man; Wayfaring Stranger; Chicago Cops; Betty And Dupree

Note: Bob Camp later changed his name to Hamilton

Camp and is well known as an actor.

Elektra EKL 208 [Mono] EKS 7208 [Stereo]
The Virtuoso Guitars Of Presti And Lagoya - Presti and Lagoya
Produced by Jac Holzman

Elektra EKL 209 [Mono] EKS 7209 [Stereo] - Released in 1962
A Maid Of Constant Sorrow - Judy Collins
Produced by Jac Holzman

Maid Of Constant Sorrow; Prickilie Bush; Wild Mountain Thyme; Tim Evans; Sailor's Life; Bold Fenian Men; Wars Of Germany; O Daddy Be Gay; I Know Where I'm Going; John Riley; Pretty Saro; The Rising Of The Moon

---

Elektra EKL 210 [Mono] EKS 7210 [Stereo]
A Harvest Of Israeli Folksongs - Theodore Bikel
Produced by Jac Holzman

Ken Yovdu; Ha'avoda; Havu Lanu Yayin; Tsei'i Lach; Shuva Elay; Erev Ba; Migdalor; Emek; Plyus; Arava Ho Arava; Layla Al Hakfar; Simchu Na; Shabat Shalom; Avigayil; Har Vakar

---

Elektra EKL 211 [Mono] EKS 7211 [Stereo]
Empty Bed Blues - Josh White
Produced by Jac Holzman

Empty Bed Blues; Mother On That Train; Bottle Up And Go; Backwater Blues; Baby Baby Blues; Lord Have Mercy; Home In That Rock; Paul And Silas; His Eye Is On The Sparrow; That Suits Me

---

Elektra EKL 212 [Mono] EKS 7212 [Stereo] - Released in 1962
Fastest Balalaika In The West - Sasha Polinoff and His Russian Gypsy Orchestra
Produced by Jac Holzman and Mark Abramson

Elektra EKL 213 [Mono]
The Best Of Dalliance - Ed McCurdy
Produced by Jac Holzman

Go Bring Me A Lass; Lusty Young Smith; The Trooper; When Flora Had On Her New Gown; Uptails All; The Shepherd; Four Able Physicians; Hive Of Bees; Yeoman Of Kent; Lady So Frolic And Gay; A Riddle; Three Birds; Sylvia The Fair; Playhouse Saint; Sound Country Lass; Young Man And A Maid; Jolly Tinker; A Wanton Trick; Jolly Miller; She Lay All Naked; A Trades Man; A Petition; Tottingham Frolic; Character Of A Mistress; The Vine; Country Wake; Pleasant Ballad; The End

Note: 'Bonus Pak' double album.

Elektra EKL 214 [Mono]
Scottish Ballad Book - Jean Redpath

Elektra EKL 215 [Mono]
Bob Grossman - Bob Grossman
Produced by Jac Holzman

Elektra EKL 216 [Mono] - Released in 1963
The Travelers 3 - Travelers 3
Produced by Jac Holzman

Elektra EKL 217 [Mono] EKS 7217 [Stereo]
Folk Banjo Styles - Eric Weissberg, Marshall Brickman, Tom Paley and Art Rosenbaum
Produced by Jac Holzman

Elektra EKL 218 [Mono]
Treasury Of Spanish And Mexican Folk Songs - Cynthia Gooding

Note: 'Bonus Pak' double album.

Elektra EKL 219 [Mono]
Sing Along In Hebrew - Maccabee Singers

Elektra EKL 220 [Mono] EKS 7220 [Stereo]
The Poetry And Prophecy Of The Old Testament - Theodore Bikel
Produced by Jac Holzman and Mark Abramson

Elektra EKL 221 [Mono]
French And Italian Folksongs - Cynthia Gooding and Yves Tessier

---

Elektra EKL 222 [Mono] EKS 7222 [Stereo] - Released in 1962
Golden Apples Of The Sun - Judy Collins
Produced by Jac Holzman and Mark Abramson

Golden Apples Of The Sun; Bonnie Ship The Diamond; Little Brown Dog; Twelve Gates To The City; Christ Child Lullaby; Great Selchie Of Shule; Tell Me Who I'll Marry; Fannerio; Crow On The Cradle; Lark In The Morning; Sing Hallelujah; Shule Aroon

---

Elektra EKL 223 [Mono]
A Treasury Of Folk Songs for Children

Note: 'Bonus Pak' double album.

Elektra EKL 224 [Mono]
Songs Of Love Lilt And Laughter - Jean Redpath

Day We Went To Rothesay; Caller O'u; Mouth Music; Wae's Me For Prince Charlie; Mcfarlane O' The Sprots O'bur; Nicky Tams; Song Of The Seals; Peat Fire Flame; Love Is Teasin'; Lewis Bridal Song; Paddy McGinty's Goat; Tae The Weavers; Kirk Swaree; She Moved Through The Fair

---

Elektra EKL 225 [Mono] EKS 7225 [Stereo]
The Best Of Bikel - Theodore Bikel

Dodi Li; Ma Guitare Et Moi; Beryuzoviye Kalyechke; Unter A Kleyn Beymele; Rue; Pollerita; Hel Pada Pada; Plylis; Hulyet, Hulyet, Kinderlech; One Sunday Morning; Yamshchik Gani-Ka K Yaru; Managwani Mpulele; Kum Aher Du Filozof; Ken Yovdu; Padrushka Milaya

---

Elektra EKL 226 [Mono]
Open House - Travelers 3

Elektra EKL 227 [Mono] EKS 7227 [Stereo]
Ole La Mano - Juan Serrano

Bulerias; Tarantas; Seoul Rlyas; Granadinas; Aires De Huelva; Zambra; Alegrias; Zapateado; Soleares

---

Elektra EKL 228 [Mono] EKS 7228 [Stereo]
A Snow Job For Skiers - Oscar Brand
Produced by Jac Holzman and Mark Abramson

Elektra EKL 229 [Mono]
Treasury Of Music Of The Renaissance - La Société De Musique D'Autrefois

Note: 'Bonus Pak' double album.

Elektra EKL 230 [Mono] EKS 7230 [Stereo]
Theodore Bikel On Tour - Theodore Bikel
Produced by Jac Holzman and Mark Abramson

Polyushka; She Was Poor But She Was Honest; J'ai Perdu Le Do; Ti N'avto; Que Bonita; Hassade Netse; Az A Sze P; Tshiribim; El Burro; Doina (Peulita); Pakom Pakom; Zvyozdochka; Yankele; Three Translation Professors; Chapt Un Nemt

Elektra EKL 231 [Mono] EKS 7231 [Stereo] - Released in 1963
Judy Henske - Judy Henske
Produced by Mark Abramson

Low Down Alligator; Empty Bed Blues; Ballad Of Little Romy; Wade In The Water; Hooka Tooka; I Know You Rider; Lily Langtree; Lilac Wine; Love Henry; Every Night When The Sun Goes In; Salvation Army Song

Elektra EKL 232 [Mono] EKS 7232 [Stereo] - Released in 1963
Back Porch Bluegrass - Dillards
Produced by James Dickson

Old Joseph; Somebody Touched Me; Polly Vaughn; Banjo In The Hollow; Dooley; Lonesome Indian; Ground Hog; Old Home Place; Hickory Hollow; Old Man At The Mill; Doug's Tune; Rainin' Here This Mornin'; Cold Trailin'; Reuben's Train; Duelin' Banjo

Note: 'Duelin' Banjo' is the famous 'Dueling Banjos' tune from the movie "Deliverance".

Elektra EKL 233 [Mono] EKS 7233 [Stereo]
Dián And The Greenbriar Boys - Dián and the Greenbriar Boys

Elektra EKL 234 [Mono] EKS 7234 [Stereo]
Art Of The Koto - The Music Of Japan - Kimio Eto
Produced by Mark Abramson and Jac Holzman

Sakura, Sakura (Cherry Blossoms); Yuki No Genso (Snow Fantasy); Hachidan No Shirabe (Variations In Eight Steps); Three Children's Songs; Yaciyo Jishi (Lion Of Eight Thousand Generations); Izumi (A Spring)

Note: Classical stringed instrument from Japan

Elektra EKL 235 [Mono] EKS 7235 [Stereo]
Flamenco Fenomenon - Juan Serrano

Elektra EKL 236 [Mono]
Live! Live! Live! - Travelers 3

Elektra EKL 237 [Mono] EKS 7237 [Stereo]
Songs Fore Golfers - Oscar Brand
Produced by Jac Holzman

Elektra EKL 238 [Mono] EKS 7238 [Stereo] - Released in 1963
New Dimensions In Banjo And Bluegrass - Eric Weissberg and Marshall Brickman

Note: Later reissued on Warner Bros (BS 2683) with the addition of 'Dueling Banjos' as the 'Soundtrack' of the movie of the same name.

Elektra EKL 239 [Mono] EKS 7239 [Stereo] - Released in 1964
Where I'm Bound - Bob Gibson
Produced by Jac Holzman and Mark Abramson

Where I'm Bound; The Waves Roll Out; 12-String Guitar Rag; Wastin' Your Time; The New Frankie And Johnnie Song; Foghorn; Baby I'm Gone Again; Farewell My Honey, Cindy Jane; Some Old Woman; Stella's Got A New Dress; The Town Crier's Song; What You Gonna Do; Betsy From Pike; Fare Thee Well

Elektra EKL 240 [Mono] - Released in 1963
Blues Rags And Hollers - Koerner, Ray & Glover
Produced by Paul Nelson

Linin' Track; Ramblin' Blues; It's All Right; Hangman; Down To Louisiana; Bugger Burns; Creepy John; Sun's Wail; One Kind Favor; Go Down Ol' Hannah; Good Time Charlie; Banjo Thing; Stop That Thing; Snaker's Here; Low Down Rounder; Jimmy Bell

Note: Elektra licensed these recordings from Audiophile Records (their original catalog number was Audiophile AP-78 released June 1963). Re-released on CD by Red House Records (RHR CD 76) in Feb 1995. The CD includes the whole of the album as recorded in stereo. The orginal recordings were rather long to be cut effectively onto vinyl so Jac had to snip a couple of tracks out and issue the LP in mono. The ones that originally got away were: 'Ted Mack Rag', 'Dust My Broom', 'Too Bad' and 'Mumblin' Word'.

Elektra EKL 241 [Mono] EKS 7241 [Stereo] - Released in 1964
High Flying Bird - Judy Henske
Produced by Jac Holzman

High Flying Bird; Buckeye Jim; Till The Real Thing Comes Along; Oh, You Engineer; Baltimore Oriole; Columbus Stockade; Blues Chase Up A Rabbit; Lonely Train; Duncan And Brady; God Bless The Child; Good Old Wagon; You Are Not My First Love; Charlotte Town

Elektra EKL 242 [Mono] EKS 7242 [Stereo]
Cough - Army Songs Out Of The Barracks Bag - Oscar Brand and the Short Arms
Produced by Jac Holzman

Enemy Generals On Parade; Hinky Die; Hearse Song; Man Behind The Armor-Plate; Ballad Of Anzio; Paratrooper Song; Benny Havens; Quartermaster Corps; We're Moving On; Caisson Song; Infiltration Course; Messkit Song; Goddamn Reserves; Shannadore

Elektra EKL 243 [Mono] EKS 7243 [Stereo] - Released in 1964
Judy Collins No: 3 - Judy Collins
Produced by Mark Abramson and Jac Holzman

Anathea; Bullgine Run; Farewell; Hey Nelly Nelly; Ten O'Clock All Is Well; The Dove; Masters Of War; In The Hills Of Shiloh; The Bells Of Rhymney; Deportee (Plane Wreck At Los Gatos); Settle Down; Come Away

Melinda; Turn! Turn! Turn! (To Everything There Is A Season)

Note: 'Turn! Turn! Turn!' bears the credit Ecclesiastes/Seeger: Pete always did credit his sources. Looking closer on the credits you find that Jim McGuinn is listed as arranger for almost the whole album and plays second guitar and banjo.

Elektra EKL 244 [Mono]
20th Century Music For Guitar - Rey De La Torre

Elektra EKL 245 [Mono] EKS 7245 [Stereo] - Released in 1964
Adventures For 12 String, 6 String And Banjo - Dick Rosmini
Produced by Jac Holzman and Mark Abramson

Elektra EKL 246 [Mono] EKS 7246 [Stereo] - Released in 1964
The Even Dozen Jug Band - Even Dozen Jug Band
Produced by Paul Rothchild

Take Your Fingers Off It; Come On In; Mandolin King Rag; Overseas Stomp; Evolution Mama; The Even Dozens; I Don't Love Nobody; Rag Mama; France Blues; On The Road Again; Original Colossal Drag Rag; All Worn Out; Lonely One In This Town; Sadie Green

Note: UK release on Bounty BY6023. This band included some people who later went on to 'greater' things, John Sebastian, Maria Muldaur (as Maria D'Amato), Steve Katz, Stefan Grossman and Joshua Rifkin.

Elektra EKL 247 [Mono]
The Songs Of Fred Engelberg - Fred Engelberg

Elektra EKL 248 [Mono] EKS 7248 [Stereo]
Tear Down The Walls - Vince Martin and Fred Neil
Produced by Paul Rothchild

I Know You Rider; Red Flowers; Tear Down The Walls; Weary Blues; Toy Balloon; Baby; Morning Dew; I'm A Drifter; Linin' Track; Wild Child In A World Of Trouble; Dade County Jail; I Got 'em; Lonesome Valley

---

Elektra EKL 249 [Mono] EKS 7249 [Stereo]
The Patriot Game - The Irish Ramblers
Produced by Jac Holzman

Note: Sleeve credits say 'The Irish Ramblers would like to express their appreciation to Jim McGuinn for his help in preparing these songs for recording'.

Elektra EKL 250 [Mono] EKS 7250 [Stereo]
A Folksinger's Choice - Theodore Bikel

Elektra EKL 251- 263 [Mono] **EKS 7251-7263** [Stereo]
Authentic Sound Effects Vol 1-13
Produced by Jac Holzman

Elektra EKL 264 [Mono] EKS 7264 [Stereo] - Released in 1964
The Blues Project - Various Artists
Produced by Paul Rothchild and Jac Holzman

Dave Ray: Fixin' To Die; Eric Von Schmidt: Blow Whistle Blow; John Koerner: My Little Woman; Geoff Muldaur: Ginger Man; Dave Van Ronk: Bad Dream Blues; Ian Buchanan: Winding Boy; Danny Kalb: I'm Troubled; Mark Spoelstra: France Blues; Dave Van Ronk: Don't You Leave Me Here; Geoff Muldaur: Devil Got My Woman; John Koerner: Southbound Train; Geoff Muldaur: Downtown Blues; Dave Ray: Leavin' Here Blues; Danny Kalb: Hello Baby Blues; Mark Spoelstra: She's Gone; Dave Ray: Slappin' On My Black Cat Bone

Note: Bob Landy, who appears on this album playing 'Treble Piano' on the track 'Downtown Blues', is really Bob Dylan. This album generously points the listener to many other blues recordings, including John Hammond's debut on Vanguard.

Elektra EKL 265 [Mono] EKS 7265 [Stereo] - Released in 1964
Live!!! Almost!!! - Dillards
Produced by Jim Dickson

Elektra EKL 266 [Mono]
Jean Carignan - Jean Carignan

Note: French-Canadian fiddler

Elektra EKL 267 [Mono] EKS 7267 [Stereo] - Released in 1964
Lots More Blues, Rags And Hollers - Koerner, Ray & Glover
Produced by Jac Holzman and Paul Rothchild with the assistance of Paul Nelson

Black Dog; Whomp Bom; Black Betty; Honey Bee; Crazy Fool; Keep Your Hands Off Her; Duncan And Brady; Fine Soft Land; Red Cross Store; Lady Day; Freeze To Me, Mama; Ted Mack Rag; Fannin Street; Love Bug; Can't Get My Rest At Night; What's The Matter With The Mill

---

Elektra EKL 268 [Mono] EKS 7268 [Stereo]
Ian Campbell Folk Group - Ian Campbell Folk Group

Elektra EKL 269 [Mono] EKS 7269 [Stereo] - Released in 1964
All The News That's Fit To Sing - Phil Ochs

One More Parade; The Thresher; Talking Vietnam; Lou Marsh; Power And The Glory; Celia; The Bells; Automation Song; Ballad Of William Worthy; Knock On The Door; Talking Cuban Crisis; Bound For Glory; Too Many Martyrs; What's That I Hear

---

Elektra EKL 270 [Mono] EKS 7270 [Stereo]
Swing Hallelujah - The Christian Tabernacle Church

Elektra EKL 271 [Mono]
Library Of Congress Recordings - Woody Guthrie
Produced and edited by Jac Holzman

Lost Train Blues; Railroad Blues; Rye Whiskey; Old Joe Clark; Beaumont Rag; Greenback Dollar; Boll Weevil Song; So Long It's Been Good To Know You; Talking Dust Bowl Blues; Do-Re-Mi; Hard Times; Pretty Boy Floyd; They Laid Jesus Christ In His Grave; Jolly Banker; I Ain't Got No Home; Dirty Overalls; Chain Around My Leg; Worried Man Blues; Lonesome Valley; Walkin' Down That Railroad Line; Goin' Down That Road Feelin' Bad; Dust Storm Disaster; Foggy Mountain Top; Dust Pneumonia Blues; California Blues; Dust

Bowl Refugees; Will Rogers Highway; Los Angeles New Year's Flood

Note: Boxed set of three records with a booklet. Also used number 272.

___

Elektra EKL 273 [Mono]
Happy All The Time - Joseph Spence
Produced by Fritz Richmond

Out On The Rollin' Sea; Bimini Gal; We Shall Be Happy; Crow; Diamond On Earth; Uncle Lou/No Lazy Man; How I Love Jesus; Conch Ain't Got No Bone; I Am Living On The Hallelujah

___

Elektra EKL 274 [Mono] EKS 7274 [Stereo]
Laddie Lie Near Me - Jean Redpath

___

Elektra EKL 275 [Mono] EKS 7275 [Stereo]
Bravo Serrano! - Juan Serrano

___

Elektra EKL 276 [Mono] EKS 7276 [Stereo]
Old Time Banjo Project - Various Artists
Produced by Paul Rothchild

___

Elektra EKL 277 [Mono] EKS 7277 [Stereo] - Released in 1964
Ramblin' Boy - Tom Paxton
Produced by Paul Rothchild

A Job Of Work; A Rumblin' In The Land; When Morning Breaks; Daily News; What Did You Learn In School Today; The Last Thing On My Mind; Harper; Fare Thee Well, Cisco; I Can't Help But Wonder Where I'm Bound; High Sheriff Of Hazard; My Lady's A Wild Flying Dove; Standing On The Edge Of Town; I'm Bound For The Mountains and The Sea; Goin' To The Zoo; Ramblin' Boy

Note: Some songs are so strong that they single-handedly overshadow a body of work. Tom Paxton's 'Last Thing On My Mind' was such a song, and from that moment on there were few 1960s folk clubs where someone didn't get up and sing it, or 'Bottle Of Wine' or some other Paxton composition. In the longer term however, it's his children's songs that may persist for decades. What we risk forgetting is his wonderful sense of humor.

___

Elektra EKL 278 [Mono] EKS 7278 [Stereo]
Paths Of Victory - Hamilton Camp

Guess I'm Doin' Fine; Girl Of The North Country; Walkin' Down The Line; A Satisfied Mind; Pride Man; Get Together; Innisfree; Long Time Gone; Only A Hobo; Irish Poetry; Lonely; Tomorrow Is A Long Time; Paths Of Victory

___

Elektra EKL 279 [Mono]
The Iron Muse - Various Artists
Produced by A. L. Lloyd

Note: Licensed from Topic Records in the UK with a booklet giving notes on the songs, written by A. L. (Bert) Lloyd. In the mid-60s, the era of the oppressed worker seemed as much a part of British industry's past as the grimy and foggy urban view on the cover of this album. Then came the miner's strike in the 80s and the Blackleg Miner didn't seem so outdated after all.

___

Elektra EKL 280 [Mono] EKS 7280 [Stereo] - Released in 1965
Judy Collins Concert - Judy Collins
Produced by Jac Holzman and Mark Abramson

Winter Sky; The Last Thing on my Mind; Tear Down The Walls; Bonnie Boy Is Young; Me And My Uncle; Wild Rippling Water; The Lonesome Death of Hattie Carroll; My Ramblin' Boy; Red-Winged Blackbird; Coal Tattoo; Cruel Mother; Bottle of Wine; Medger Evers Lullaby; Hey, Nelly, Nelly

___

Elektra EKL 281 [Mono] EKS 7281 [Stereo]
Yiddish Theatre And Folk Songs - Theodore Bikel
Produced by Jac Holzman and Mark Abramson

___

Elektra EKL 282 [Mono]
Music Of Bulgaria - Ensemble Of Bulgarian Republic

Chope Dance; Theodora Is Dozing; Mother Has Decided To Marry Me; The Moon Shines; Trio Of Bagpipes; A Young Girl At Parting; Niagol Talks To Milka; The Bird Has Come; Fida Is Sleepy; Bre Pretrounko; Come To Supper Tonight, Rada; Bulgarian Suite; Rank Weeds; Stoyan Comes Back To Constanti; The Drums Roll; They Are Going Across The Fore; Theodora Have You Had Supper

___

Elektra EKL 283 [Mono] EKS 7283 [Stereo] - Released in 1965
Five And Twenty Questions - Mark Spoelstra
Produced by Paul Rothchild

___

Elektra EKL 284 [Mono] EKS 7284 [Stereo] - Released in 1965
Snaker's Here - Dave 'Snaker' Ray

Julie Ann Johnson; Go My Bail; Rock Me; Bull Frog Blues; Old Country Rock; Rambling On My Mind; Broke Down Engine; Blind Lemon; Last Fair Deal Gone Down; Saddle Up My Pony; Brownsville Blues; Becky Dean; Yellow Woman's Door Bells; Killing Me By Degrees; 'Fore Day Worry Blues; Rising Sun Blues; Need My Help Someday

___

Elektra EKL 285 [Mono] EKS 7285 [Stereo] - Released in 1965
Pickin' And Fiddlin' - Dillards with Byron Berline
Produced by Jim Dickson

Note: Just as it says, this is an album of fingerbusters and demonstrations of the devil's elbow at work.

___

Elektra EKL 286 [Mono] EKS 7286 [Stereo]
Classical Music Of Japan - Various Artists

___

Elektra EKL 287 [Mono] EKS 7287 [Stereo] - Released in 1965
I Ain't Marching Anymore - Phil Ochs

I Ain't Marching Anymore; In The Heat Of The Summer; Draft Dodger Rag; That's What I Want To Hear; That Was The President; Iron Lady; The Highwayman; Links On The Chain; Hills Of West Virginia; The Men Behind The Guns; Talking Birmingham Jam; Ballad Of The Carpenter; Days Of Decision; Here's To The State Of Mississippi

___

Elektra EKL 288 [Mono] EKS 7288 [Stereo] - Released in 1965

Tom Rush - Tom Rush
Produced by Paul Rothchild

Long John; If Your Man Gets Busted; Do-Re-Mi; Milk
Cow Blues; The Cuckoo; Black Mountain Blues; Poor
Man; Solid Gone; When She Wants Good Lovin'; I'd
Like To Know; Jelly Roll Baker; Windy Bill; Panama
Limited

Elektra EKL 289 [Mono] EKS 7289 [Stereo] - Released in
1965
**Kathy And Carol - Kathy Larisch and Carol
McComb**

Sprig Of Thyme; George Collins; The Blacksmith; Fair
Beauty Bright; Green Rocky Road; The Grey Cock;
Wondrous Love; Carter's Blues; Lady Maisry; Brightest
And Best; Gold Watch And Chain; Just A Hand To
Hold

Elektra EKL 290 [Mono] EKS 7290 [Stereo] - Released in
1965
Spider Blues - John Koerner
Produced by Jac Holzman

Good Luck Child; I Want To Be Your Partner; Nice
Legs; Spider Blues; Corrina; Shortnin' Bread; Ramblin'
And Tumblin'; Delia Holmes; Need A Woman; I Want
To Do Something; Baby Don't Come Back; Hal C Blake;
Things Ain't Right; Rent Party Rag

Elektra EKL 291 [Mono] EKS 7291 [Stereo]
**Corrie Folk Trio With Paddie Bell - Corrie Folk Trio
with Paddie Bell**

Lock The Door Lariston; O'er The Water; Bungle Rye;
Doodle Let Me Go; The Singing Games; Singin' Bird;
Queen Mary, Queen Mary; The Jug O' Punch; Coorie
Doon; Blow, Ye Winds In The Morning; Bothwell
Castle; The Itinerant Cobbler; Fine Flowers In The
Valley; The Lass O'Fyvie

Elektra EKL 292 [Mono] EKS 7292 [Stereo]
The String Band Project - Various Artists
Produced by Paul Rothchild

Hallelujah To The Lamb; Burial Of Wild Bill; All
Around The Mountain; Shoot The Turkey Buzzard;
Been All Around This World; Cocaine; Baldheaded End
Of The Broom; Jealous; What Will I Do For My
Money's; I Got A Gal In Baltimore; Sugar Hill; Chilly
Winds; Bagtime Annie; Red Rocking Chair; Billy In The
Low Ground; Train On The Island; Ever See A Devil;
Oncle Joe; Goodbye Miss Liza Jane; Single Girl; Stoney
Point

Elektra EKL 293 [Mono] EKS 7293 [Stereo] - Released in
1965
Bleecker And MacDougal - Fred Neil
Produced by Paul Rothchild

Bleecker And MacDougal; Blues On The Ceiling; Sweet
Mama; Little Bit Of Rain; Country Boy; Other Side To
This Life; Mississippi Train; Travellin' Shoes; The Water
is Wide; Yonder Comes the Blues; Candy Man; Handful
of Gimme; Gone Again

Note: Reissued as EKS 74073 with the title 'Little Bit of
Rain' and with a different sleeve.

Elektra EKL 294 [Mono] EKS 7294 [Stereo] - Released in
1965
**The Paul Butterfield Blues Band - The Paul
Butterfield Blues Band**
Produced by Paul Rothchild with the assistance of
Mark Abramson

Born in Chicago; Shake Your Moneymaker; Blues with
a Feeling; Thank You Mr. Poobah; I Got My Mojo
Working; Mellow Down Easy; Screamin'; Our Love is
Drifting; Mystery Train; Last Night; Look Over Yonders
Wall

Note: This album came from the third sessions because
the earlier recordings were not judged good enough by
Paul Rothchild. In 1995 Rhino Records, in their
Elektra Traditions series, released those tracks as 'The
Original Lost Elektra Sessions' (R2 73505). According
to Paul Rothchild's sleeve notes for the CD, Elektra had
already pressed 10,000 copies of the album, which Jac
agreed to junk at Paul's recommendation.

Elektra EKL 295 [Mono] EKS 7295 [Stereo]
**Tom Paley And Peggy Seeger - Tom Paley and Peggy
Seeger**

Elektra EKL 296 [Mono]
Negro Folklore Texas State Prison - Various Artists

Elektra EKL 297 [Mono] EKS 7297 [Stereo]
Sounds Of Japan - Actuality Sounds
Produced by Mark Abramson

Elektra EKL 298 [Mono] EKS 7298 [Stereo] - Released in
1965
Ain't That News - Tom Paxton
Produced by Paul Rothchild

Ain't That News; Willing Conscript; Lyndon Johnson
Told The Nation; Hold On To Me Babe; The Name Of
The Game Is Stud; Bottle Of Wine; The Natural Girl
For Me; Goodman Schwerner And Chaney; We Didn't
Know; Buy A Gun For Your Son; Every Time; Georgie
On The Freeways; Sully's Pail; I'm The Man That Built
The Bridges

Elektra EKL 299 [Mono] EKS 7299 [Stereo] - Released in
1965
Singer-Songwriter Project - Various Artists
Produced by Jac Holzman

Richard Fariña: House Un-American Blues Activity
Dream; Richard Fariña: Birmingham Sunday; Richard
Fariña: Bold Marauder; Patrick Sky: Too Many Times;
Patrick Sky: Talking Socialized Anti-Undertaker Blues;
Patrick Sky: Many A Mile; Bruce Murdoch: Rompin'
Rovin' Days; Bruce Murdoch: Down In Mississippi;
Bruce Murdoch: Farewell My Friend; Bruce Murdoch:
Try 'n' Ask; Dave Cohen: I Like To Sleep Late In The
Morning; Dave Cohen: It's Alright With Me; Dave
Cohen: Don't Get Caught In A Storm

Note: Some copies of this album are missing two tracks
... despite what it says on the labels! David Cohen also
recorded as David Blue and Richard Fariña is listed as
Dick Fariña on the front cover. Sky and Fariña
appeared courtesy of Vanguard, for whom they recorded.

Elektra EKL 300 [Mono] EKS 7300 [Stereo] - Released in

1965
Judy Collins Fifth Album - Judy Collins
Produced by Mark Abramson and Jac Holzman

Pack Up Your Sorrows; The Coming Of The Roads; So
Early, Early In The Spring; Tomorrow Is A Long Time;
Daddy You've Been On My Mind; Thirsty Boots; Mr
Tambourine Man; Lord Gregory; In The Heat Of The
Summer; Early Morning Rain; Carry It On; It Isn't Nice

Elektra EKL 301 [Mono]
Library Of Congress Recordings - Leadbelly
Edited by Jac Holzman

Mr. Tom Hughes Town; De Kalb Blues; Take A Whiff
On Me; The Medicine Man; I'm Sorry Mama; Square
Dances Sooky Jump; Dance Calls, Dance Steps; Gwine
Dig A Hole; Tight Like That; Green Corn; Becky Dean;
Prison Singing; Midnight Special; Medley; I Ain't
Gonna Ring Dem Yellow; Rock Island Line; Governor
Pat Neff; Irene (Part I, Part II); Governor OK Allen; Git
On Board; Medley: Hallelujah; Joining The Church;
Backslider; Fare You Well; Amazing Grace; Must I Be
Carried To The Sky; Flowered Beds Of Ease; Down In
The Valley To Pray; Let It Shine On Me; Run Sinners;
Ride On; Monologue: The Blues; Thirty Days In The
Workhouse; Fo' Day Worry Blues; Matchbox Blues; You
Don't Know My Mind; Got A Gal In Town With;
Alberta; Take Me Back; Henry Ford Blues; Ella Speed;
Billy The Weaver; Frankie and Albert; If It Wasn't For
Dicky; Mama Did You Bring Me An; The Bourgeois
Blues; Howard Hughes; Scottsboro Blues; The
Hindenburg Disaster; Turn Yo' Radio On; The
Roosevelt Song

Note: Boxed set of three discs with booklet. Also used
number 302.

Elektra EKL 303 [Mono]
**Maxwell Street Jimmy Davis - Maxwell Street
Jimmy Davis**

Elektra EKL 304 [Mono] EKS 7304 [Stereo] - Released in
1966
**The Promise Of The Day - Corrie Folk Trio with
Paddle Bell**

Elektra EKL 305 [Mono] EKS 7305 [Stereo] - Released in
1965
**The Return Of Koerner, Ray & Glover - Koerner, Ray
& Glover**
Produced by Jac Holzman and Paul Rothchild with the
assistance of Paul Nelson

Elektra EKL 306 [Mono] EKS 7306 [Stereo]
The Baroque Beatles Book - Joshua Rifkin
Produced by Mark Abramson assisted by Paul
Rothchild

I Want To Hold Your Hand; You're Going to Lose that
Girl; I'll Cry Instead; Things We Said Today; You've
Got To Hide Your Love Away; Ticket To Ride; Hold Me
Tight; Please Please Me; In They Came Jorking; Help;
I'll Be Back; Eight Days A Week; She Loves You; Thank
You Girl; Hard Day's Night

Note: Joshua Rifkin was later to find fame by bringing
Scott Joplin's rags to serious attention on the
Nonesuch label. This disc takes Lennon/McCartney
songs and takes them back 400 years or so. The name

given on the sleeve to the ensemble performing this is
'Baroque Ensemble of the Merseyside
Kammermusikgesellschaft'.

Elektra EKL 307 [Mono] EKS 7307 [Stereo] - Released in
1966
State Of Mind - Mark Spoelstra

Elektra EKL 308 [Mono] EKS 7308 [Stereo] - Released in
1966
Take A Little Walk With Me - Tom Rush
Produced by Mark Abramson

You Can't Tell A Book By The Cover; Who Do You
Love; Love's Made A Fool Of You; Too Much Monkey
Business; Money Honey; On The Road Again; Joshua
Gone Barbados; Statesboro Blues; Turn Your Money
Green; Sugar Babe; Galveston Flood

Note: Tom Rush finds electricity! This album is a little
gem of an example of the cross-over from folk to rock.

Elektra EKL 309 [Mono] EKS 7309 [Stereo] - Released in
1966
The Rights Of Man - Ian Campbell Folk Group

Elektra EKL 310 [Mono] EKS 7310 [Stereo] - Released in
1966
Phil Ochs In Concert - Phil Ochs

I'm Going To Say It Now; Bracero; Ringing Of
Revolution; Is There Anybody Here?; Canons Of
Christianity; There But For Fortune; Cops Of The
World; Santo Domingo; Changes; Love Me, I'm A
Liberal; When I'm Gone

Elektra EKL 311 [Mono] EKS 7311 [Stereo] - Released in
1966
Light Of Day - Pat Kilroy
Produced by Peter K. Siegel

Elektra EKL 312 [Mono] EKS 7312 [Stereo] - Released in
1967
How To Play Electric Bass - Harvey Brooks
Produced by Bill Szymczyk and Harvey Brooks

Note: After tuning your instrument, you could play
along with Harvey on six tunes. The tracks were on
the disc three times: with a simple bass line, an
advanced bass line and finally no bass line. Instruction
booklet included but bring your own bass guitar.

Elektra EKL 313 [Mono] EKS 7313 [Stereo] - Released in
1966
**Elektra Library Of Authentic Sound Effects - Sound
Effects**
Produced by Jac Holzman

Note: Boxed set of three discs. Catalog number was
313/4.

Elektra EKL 315 [Mono] EKS 7315 [Stereo] - Released in
1966
East-West - Paul Butterfield Blues Band
Produced by Mark Abramson and Paul Rothchild

Walkin' Blues; Get Out of My Life Woman; I Got A
Mind To Give Up; All These Blues; Work Song; Mary,
Mary; Two Trains Running; Never Say No; East-West

Elektra EKL 316 [Mono] EKS 7316 [Stereo] - Released in 1966
Oliver Smith - Oliver Smith

Elektra EKL 317 [Mono] EKS 7317 [Stereo] - Released in 1966
Outward Bound - Tom Paxton
Produced by Paul Rothchild

Leaving London; Don't You Let Nobody Turn You; My Son John; The King Of My Backyard; One Time And One Time Only; Is This Any Way To Run An Airline; All The Way Home; I Followed Her Into The West; This World Goes 'Round And 'Round; Talking Pop Art; When You Get Your Ticket; I Believe I Do; Outward Bound

Note: Tom Paxton's unsuccessful foray into folk/rock was on a single version of 'One Time and One Time Only' released in the UK. He disowns it in the sleeve notes to this album which includes a more subtle and suitable arrangement of the song.

Elektra EKL 319 [Mono] EKS 7319 [Stereo] - Released in 1967
Fine Soft Land - Dave 'Snaker' Ray

Alabama Women; Young Man; Crying Shame; Got To Live; West Egg Rag; How You Want Your Rolling Done; Highway 51; Tribute; Baby Please Don't Go; Kid Man Blues; Death Valley Blues; If I Get Lucky; Married Woman Blues; Look Over Yonder's Wall; You Can't Go; Born To Surrender

---

Elektra EKL 321 [Mono] EKS 7321 [Stereo] - Released in 1967
Frost And Fire - Watersons

Note: Licensed from Topic Records, UK (12T136).

Elektra EKL 322 [Mono] EKS 7322 [Stereo] - Released in 1966
The Incredible String Band - Incredible String Band

Maybe Someday; October Song; When The Music Starts To Play; Schaeffer's Jig; Womankind; The Tree; Whistle Tune; Dandelion Blues; How Happy I Am; Empty Pocket Blues; Smoke Shovelling Song; Can't Keep Me Here; Good As Gone; Footsteps Of The Heron; Niggertown; Everything's Fine Right Now

Note: The original UK issue (EUK 254) has a different sleeve than the US version, although the CD reverts to the UK cover.

Elektra EKL 324 [Mono] EKS 7324 [Stereo]
How To Play Blues Guitar - Stefan Grossman

Elektra EKL 325 [Mono] EKS 7325 [Stereo]
The Bauls Of Bengal - The Bauls Of Bengal
Produced by John Court

Note: The word Baul means 'Afflicted with the wind disease', that is 'mad'. The Bauls are wandering musicians who dress in both Hindu and Moslem clothes.

Elektra EKL 326 [Mono] EKS 7326 [Stereo]
Songs Of The Earth - Theodore Bikel and The Pennywhistlers

Elektra EKL 4001 [Mono] EKS 74001 [Stereo] - Released in 1966
Love - Love
Produced by Jac Holzman and Mark Abramson

My Little Red Book; Can't Explain; A Message To Pretty; My Flash On You; Softly To Me; Mo Matter What You Do; Emotions; You I'll Be Following; Gazing; Hey Joe; Signed D C; Colored Balls Falling; Mushroom Clouds; And More

Note: Having been unsuccessful in signing the Lovin' Spoonful, Jac found Arthur Lee and Love to catapult Elektra into the 60s rock scene. The band gave Elektra their first hit single ('My Little Red Book') and are fondly remembered in England if not everywhere else. A two-CD retrospective was also released in 1995 in Rhino Records' Elektra Traditions series (R2 73500).

Elektra EKL 4002 [Mono] EKS 74002 [Stereo] - Released in 1966
What's Shakin' - Various Artists

Paul Butterfield Blues Band: Spoonful; Paul Butterfield Blues Band: Off The Wall; Paul Butterfield Blues Band: Lovin' Cup; Paul Butterfield Blues Band: Good Morning Little Schoolgirl; Paul Butterfield Blues Band: One More Mile; Eric Clapton And The Powerhouse: I Want To Know; Eric Clapton And The Powerhouse: Cross Roads; Eric Clapton and The Powerhouse: Steppin' Out; Lovin' Spoonful: Good Time Music; Lovin' Spoonful: Almost Grown; Lovin' Spoonful: Don't Bank On It Baby; Lovin' Spoonful: Searchin'; Al Kooper: Can't Keep From Crying Sometimes; Tom Rush: I'm In Love Again

Note: A collection of tracks without another home ... such as the Spoonful tracks. Eric Clapton's band 'The Powerhouse' includes Steve Winwood (under the alias Steve Anglo) on vocals and Jack Bruce on bass. This disc has also (erroneously) appeared in lists as EKS 7304.

Elektra EKL 4003 [Mono] EKS 74003 [Stereo] - Released in 1966
David Blue - David Blue

Note: David Blue also recorded as David Cohen.

Elektra EKL 4004 [Mono] EKS 74004 [Stereo] - Released in 1966
Tim Buckley - Tim Buckley
Produced by Paul Rothchild and Jac Holzman

I Can't See You; Wings; Song Of The Magician; Strange Street Affair Under Blue; Valentine Melody; Aren't You The Girl; Song Slowly Song; It Happens Every Time; Song For Jainie; Grief In My Soul; She Is; Understand Your Man

[Also released on CD]

Elektra EKL 4005 [Mono] EKS 74005 [Stereo] - Released in 1967
Da Capo - Love
Produced by Paul Rothchild with Jac Holzman

Stephanie Knows Who; Orange Skies; Que Vida; Seven And Seven Is; The Castle; She Comes In Colors; Revelation

Note: Surprisingly, 'The Castle' was used for several years by BBC Television as the theme for a Holiday magazine programme. 'Stephanie Knows Who' was covered by The Move and, at first, it was rumored that the Rolling Stones were covering 'She Comes in Colours'. This turned out to be a reference to a completely different song on their 'Satanic Majesties' album. [Also released on CD]

Elektra EKL 4006 [Mono] EKS 74006 [Stereo] - Released in 1966
Beatle Country - The Charles River Valley Boys
Produced by Paul Rothchild and Peter K. Siegel

I've Just Seen A Face; Baby's In Black; I Feel Fine; Yellow Submarine; Ticket To Ride; And Your Bird Can Sing; What Goes On; Norwegian Wood; Paperback Writer; She's A Woman; I Saw Her Standing There; Help!

Note: It seems that Lennon and McCartney wrote some fine country tunes. 'I've Just Seen a Face' works particularly well as bluegrass.

Elektra EKL 4007 [Mono] EKS 74007 [Stereo] - Released in 1967
The Doors - The Doors
Produced by Paul Rothchild

Break On Through (To The Other Side); Soul Kitchen; The Crystal Ship; Twentieth Century Fox; Alabama Song (Whisky Bar); Light My Fire; Back Door Man; I Looked At You; End Of The Night; Take It As It Comes; The End

[Also released on CD]

Elektra EKS 74008 [Stereo] - Released in 1967
Sea Drift - Dusk 'Til Dawn Orchestra conducted by Mort Garson
Produced by Alex Hassilev

Sea Drift; Sand Castles; The Lonely Surfer; The Sea Of Love; Sea Cricket; Big Sur; Mediterranée; Our Secret Cove; Underwater Fantasy; Tropica; The Pink Seagull; Across The Sea And Far Away

Note: This is mood music recorded in the UK.

Elektra EKL 4009 [Mono] EKS 74009 [Stereo] - Released in 1967
The Zodiac Cosmic Sounds - Composed, arranged and conducted by Mort Garson, words by Jacques Wilson, spoken by Cyrus Faryar
Produced by Jac Holzman

Aries (The Fire-Fighter); Taurus (The Voluptuary); Gemini (The Cool Eye); Cancer (The Moon Child); Leo (The Lord of Lights); Virgo (The Perpetual Perfectionist); Libra (The Flower Child); Scorpio (The Passionate Hero); Sagittarius (The Versatile Daredevil); Capricorn (The Uncapricious Climber); Aquarius (The Lover of Life); Pisces (The Peace Piper)

Note: The voice on this album is Cyrus Faryar and the electronic instruments are played by Paul Beaver.

Elektra EKS 74010 [Stereo] - Released in 1967
The 5000 Spirits Or The Layers Of The Onion -

Incredible String Band
Produced by Joe Boyd

Chinese White; No Sleep Blues; Painting Box; The Mad Hatter's Song; Little Cloud; The Eyes Of Fate; Blues For The Muse; The Hedgehog's Song; First Girl I Loved; You Know What You Could Be; My Name Is Death; Gently Tender; Way Back In The 1960's

Note: UK release on EUK 257. [Also released on CD]

Elektra EKS 74011 [Stereo] - Released in 1967
Clear Light - Clear Light
Produced by Paul Rothchild

Black Roses; Sand; A Child's Smile; The Street Singer; The Ballad Of Freddie And Larry; With All In Mind; Mr Blue; Think Again; They Who Have Nothing; How Many Days Have Passed; Night Sounds Loud

Note: The B-Side of the single 'Black Roses' is an extra track, 'She's Ready to be Free', which was featured on the Soundtrack of the Movie 'The President's Analyst'.

Elektra EKL 4012 [Mono] EKS 74012 [Stereo] - Released in 1968
Wildflowers - Judy Collins
Produced by Mark Abramson

Michael from Mountains; Since You Asked; Sisters of Mercy; Priests; A Ballata of Francesco Landini; Both Sides Now; La Chanson Des Vieux Amants (The Song Of Old Lovers); Sky Fell; Albatross; Hey, That's No Way to Say Goodbye

Note: All arrangements but one were by Joshua Rifkin.

Elektra EKL 4013 [Mono] EKS 74013 [Stereo] - Released in 1967
Forever Changes - Love
Produced by Arthur Lee with Bruce Botnick

Alone Again Or; A House is Not a Motel; Andmoreagain; The Daily Planet; Old Man; The Red Telephone; Maybe The People Would Be The Times Or Between Clark And Hilldale; Live And Let Live; The Good Humor Man He Sees Everything Like This; Bummer In The Summer; You Set the Scene

Note: Quintessential Love ... and for some people this is the best album ever made. [Also released on CD]

Elektra EKL 4014 [Mono] EKS 74014 [Stereo] - Released in 1968
Strange Days - The Doors
Produced by Paul Rothchild

Strange Days; You're Lost Little Girl; Love Me Two Times; Unhappy Girl; Horse Latitudes; Moonlight Drive; People Are Strange; My Eyes Have Seen You; I Can't See Your Face In My Mind; When The Music's Over

[Also released on CD]

Elektra EKL 4015 [Mono] EKS 74015 [Stereo] - Released in 1967
The Resurrection Of Pigboy Crabshaw - Paul Butterfield Blues Band
Produced by John Court

One More Heartache; Driftin' And Driftin' (Driftin' Blues); I Pity The Fool; Born Under A Bad Sign; Run Out Of Time; Double Trouble; Drivin' Wheel; Droppin' Out; Tollin' Bells

---

Elektra EKS 74016 [Stereo] - Released in 1968
Earth Opera - Earth Opera
Produced by Peter K. Siegel

The Red Sox Are Winning; As It Is Before; Dreamless; To Care At All; Home Of The Brave; The Child Bride; Close Your Eyes And Shut The Door; Time And Again; When You Were Full Of Wonder; Death By Fire

---

Elektra EKS 74017 [Stereo] - Released in 1968
Steve Noonan - Steve Noonan

Elektra EKL 4018 [Mono] EKS 74018 [Stereo] - Released in 1968
The Circle Game - Tom Rush
Produced by Arthur Gorson

Tin Angel; Something In The Way She Moves; Urge For Going; Sunshine Sunshine; The Glory Of Love; Shadow Dream Song; The Circle Game; So Long; Rockport Sunday; No Regrets

Note: This is the album with 'No Regrets' on it ... possibly Tom Rush's finest hour. [Also released on CD]

Elektra EKL 4019 [Mono] EKS 74019 [Stereo] - Released in 1968
Morning Again - Tom Paxton
Produced by Peter K. Siegel

Jennifer's Rabbit; Mr Blue; Victoria Dines Alone; The Hooker; So Much For Winning; Talking Vietnam Pot Luck Blues; Clarissa Jones; Morning Again; A Thousand Years; Now That I've Taken My Life

---

Elektra EKS 74020 [Stereo] - Released in 1968
Ars Nova - Ars Nova
Produced by Paul Rothchild

Elektra EKL 4021 [Mono] EKS 74021 [Stereo] - Released in 1968
The Hangman's Beautiful Daughter - Incredible String Band
Produced by Joe Boyd

Note: UK release on EUK 258. [Also released on CD]

Elektra EKS 74022 [Stereo] - Released in 1968
David Ackles - David Ackles
Produced by David Anderle and Russ Miller

The Road To Cairo; When Love Is Gone; Sonny Comes Home; Blue Ribbons; What A Happy Day; Down River; Laissez Faire; Lotus Man; His Name Is Andrew; Be My Friend

---

Elektra EKL 4023 [Mono] EKS 74023 [Stereo] - Released in 1968
Eclection - Eclection
Produced by Ossie Byrne

Elektra EKL 4024 [Mono] EKS 74024 [Stereo] - Released in 1968
Waiting For The Sun - The Doors

Produced by Paul Rothchild

Hello, I Love You; Love Street; Not To Touch The Earth; Summer's Almost Gone; Wintertime Love; The Unknown Soldier; Spanish Caravan; My Wild Love; We Could Be So Good Together; Yes, The River Knows; Five to One

[Also released on CD]

Elektra EKL 4025 [Mono] EKS 74025 [Stereo] - Released in 1968
In My Own Dream - Butterfield Blues Band
Produced by John Court

Last Hope's Gone; Mine To Love; Get Yourself Together; Just To Be With You; Morning Blues; Drunk Again; In My Own Dream

---

Elektra EKS 74026 [Stereo] - Released in 1968
The Moray Eels Eat The Holy Modal Rounders - The Holy Modal Rounders
Produced by Frazier Mohawk

Bird Song; One Will Do For Now; Take-Off Artist Song; Werewolf; Interlude; Dame Fortune; Mobile Line; The Duji Song; My Mind Capsized; The S T P Song; Interlude Two; Half A Mind; The Pledge

Note: 'Bird Song' was used on the soundtrack of "Easy Rider," which is where most people first heard it.

Elektra EKS 74027 [Stereo] - Released in 1967
In My Life - Judy Collins
Produced by Mark Abramson

Tom Thumb's Blues; Hard Lovin' Loser; Pirate Jenny; Suzanne; La Colombe; Marat/Sade; I Think It's Going to Rain Today; Sunny Goodge Street; Liverpool Lullaby; Dress Rehearsal Rag; In My Life

Note: Also released as EKS 7320. [Also released on CD]

Elektra EKS 74028 [Stereo] - Released in 1967
Goodbye And Hello - Tim Buckley
Produced by Jerry Yester

No Man Can Find The War; Carnival Song; Pleasant Street; Hallucinations; I Never Asked To Be Your Mountain; Once I Was; Phantasmagoria In Two; Knight-Errant; Goodbye And Hello; Morning Glory

Note: Also issued as EKS 7318. Some UK copies did not have the gatefold sleeve with lyrics. [Also released on CD]

Elektra EKS 74029 [Stereo] - Released in 1968
The Marble Index - Nico
Produced by Frazier Mohawk

Prelude; Lawns Of Dawns; No One Is There; Ari's Song; Facing The Wind; Julius Caesar (Momento Hodié); Frozen Warnings; Evening Of Light

Note: Arrangements by John Cale.

Elektra EKS 74030 [Stereo] - Released in 1969
Rhinoceros - Rhinoceros
Produced by Paul Rothchild

When You Say You're Sorry; Same Old Way; Apricot Brandy; That Time Of The Year; You're My Girl (I don't want to Discuss it); I Need Love; I've Been There; Belbuekus; Along Comes Tomorrow; I Will Serenade You

Note: 'Apricot Brandy' was used at least twice by BBC Radio as a signature/theme tune for two totally different programmes.

Elektra EKS 74031 [Stereo] - Released in 1969
Early Morning Blues And Greens - Diane Hildebrand
Produced by David Anderle and Russ Miller

Jan's Blues; Thumbin'; From Rea Who Died Last Summer; There's A Coming Together; And It Was Good; Gideon; Early Morning Blues And Greens; The Reincarnation Of Emmalina Stearns; You Wonder Why You're Lonely; Come Looking For Me; Given Time

Note: The title track was covered by the Monkees.

Elektra EKL 4032 [Mono] EKS 74032 [Stereo] - Released in 1968
Have A Marijuana - David Peel and the Lower East Side
Produced by Peter K. Siegel

Mother Where Is My Father?; I Like Marijuana; Here Comes A Cop; I've Got Some Grass; Happy Mother's Day; Up Against The Wall; I Do My Bawling In The Bathroom; Alphabet Song (The); Show Me The Way To Get Stoned; We Love You

Note: This is possibly the only album you will ever hear where the artists sing the credits. It was recorded 'Live on the Streets of New York'.

Elektra EKL 4033 [Mono] EKS 74033 [Stereo] - Released in 1969
Who Knows Where the Time Goes - Judy Collins
Produced by David Anderle

Hello, Hooray; Story Of Isaac; My Father; Someday Soon; Who Knows Where The Time Goes; Poor Immigrant; First Boy I Loved; Bird On The Wire; Pretty Polly

---

Elektra EKS 74034 [Stereo] - Released in 1968
Transformer - David Stoughton

Elektra EKS 74035 [Stereo] - Released in 1968
Wheatstraw Suite - Dillards
Produced by Rodney Dillard and Jimmy Hilton

Elektra EKL 4036 [Mono] EKS 74036 [Stereo] - Released in 1968
Wee Tam - Incredible String Band

Job's Tears; Puppies; Beyond The Sea; Yellow Snake; Log Cabin Home In The Sky; You Get Brighter; Half-Remarkable Question; Air; Ducks On A Pond

Note: Wee Tam and The Big Huge were also available as a double with the number EKS 74036/7.

Elektra EKS 74037 [Stereo] - Released in 1968
The Big Huge - Incredible String Band

Maya; Greatest Friend; Son Of Noah's Brother; Lordly Nightshade; Mountain Of God; Cousin Caterpillar; Iron Stone; Douglas Traherne Harding; Circle Is Unbroken

Note: Wee Tam and the Big Huge were also available as a double with the number EKS 74036/7.

Elektra EKS 74038 [Stereo] - Released in 1969
Great American Eagle Tragedy - Earth Opera
Produced by Peter K. Siegel

Home To You; Mad Lydia's Waltz; Alfie Finney; Sanctuary From The Law; All Winter Long; American Eagle Tragedy; Roast Beef Love; Its Love

---

Elektra EKS 74039 [Stereo] - Released in 1969
Accept No Substitute (The Original Delaney And Bonnie) - Delaney and Bonnie and Friends
Produced by Delaney for DelBon Productions

Get Ourselves Together; Someday; The Ghetto; When The Battle Is Over; Dirty Old Man; Love Me A Little Bit Longer; I Can't Take It Much Longer; Do Right Woman - Do Right Man; Soldiers Of The Cross; The Gift Of Love

---

Elektra EKS 74040 [Stereo] - Released in 1969
Glad I'm In The Band - Lonnie Mack

Why; Save Your Money; Old House; Too Much Trouble; In The Band; Let Them Talk; Memphis; Sweat And Tears; Roberta; Stay Away From My Baby; She Don't Come Here Anymore

---

Elektra EKS 74041 [Stereo] - Released in 1967
Running, Jumping, Standing Still - 'Spider' John Koerner and Willie Murphy
Produced by Frazier Mohawk

Red Palace; I Ain't Blue; Bill And Annie; Old Brown Dog; Running, Jumping, Standing Still; Sidestep; Magazine Lady; Friends And Lovers; Sometimes I Can't Help Myself; Good Night

Note: CD re-issue on Red House Records RHR 63 in Feb 1994.

Elektra EKS 74042 [Stereo] - Released in 1969
Kick Out The Jams - MC5
Produced by Jac Holzman and Bruce Botnick

Ramblin' Rose; Kick Out The Jams; Come Together; Rocket Reducer No 62 (Rama Lama Fa Fa Fa); Borderline; Motor City Is Burning; I Want You Right Now; Starship

Note: Recorded live at Russ Gibb's Grande Ballroom, Detroit, Oct. 30-31, 1968.

Elektra EKS 74043 [Stereo] - Released in 1969
The Things I Notice Now - Tom Paxton
Produced by Peter K. Siegel

Elektra EKS 74044 [Stereo] - Released in 1969
Bread - Bread
Produced by Bread

Dismal Day; London Bridge; Could I; Look At Me; The Last Time; Any Way You Want Me; Move Over; Don't

Shut Me Out; You Can't Measure The Cost; Family Doctor; It Don't Matter To Me; Friends And Lovers

Note: CD reissue in 1995 in the Elektra Traditions series from Rhino.

Elektra EKS 74045 [Stereo] - Released in 1968
Happy Sad - Tim Buckley
Produced by Jerry Yester and Zal Yanovsky

Strange Feelin'; Buzzin' Fly; Love from Room 109 At The Islander (On Pacific Coast Highway); Dream Letter; Gypsy Woman; Sing a Song for You

[Also released on CD]

Elektra EKS 74047 [Stereo]
The Best Of Lord Buckley - Lord Buckley
Produced by Jim Dickson

The Nazz; Gettysburg Address; The Hip Gahn; Jonah And The Whale; Marc Antony's Funeral Oration; Nero

Note: Hip jive talk from the man who did it best. Originally released on Vaya Records 1951 on two albums, also released as Crestview CRV 801 in 1963. CD released on Discovery Records #71001.

Elektra EKS 74048 [Stereo] - Released in 1968
Bamboo - Bamboo
Produced by Allan Emig

Note: Band includes Dave Ray.

Elektra EKS 74049 [Stereo] - Released in 1969
Four Sail - Love
Produced by Arthur Lee

August; Your Friend And Mine - Neil's Song; Good Times; I'm With You; Singing Cowboy; Dream; Robert Montgomery; Nothing; Talking In My Sleep; Always See Your Face

Note: Reissued on CD by Thunderbolt Records (CDTB 047) in the UK. 'Your Friend And Mine' is listed as 'You're Friends Of Mine' on the Thunderbolt release.

Elektra EKS 74050 [Stereo] - Released in 1969
Whatever's Right - Lonnie Mack

Untouched By Human Love; I Found A Love; Share Your Love With Me; Teardrops On Your Letter; Baby What You Want Me To Do; Mt Healthy Blues; What Kind Of World Is This; My Babe; Gotta Be An Answer; Things Have Gone To Pieces

Elektra EKS 74051 [Stereo] - Released in 1969
The Stooges - The Stooges
Produced by John Cale

1969; I Wanna Be Your Dog; We Will Fall; No Fun; Real Cool Time; Ann; Not Right; Little Doll

Note: Featuring Iggy Pop who is credited as Iggy Stooge.

Elektra EKS 74052 [Stereo] - Released in 1969
Matthew, Mark, Luke And John - Methuselah
Produced by Kenny Young

Note: This British band later changed their name to Amazing Blondel.

Elektra EKS 74053 [Stereo] - Released in 1969
Keep On Moving - Butterfield Blues Band
Produced by Jerry Ragavoy

Love March; No Amount Of Loving; Morning Sunrise; Losing Hand; Walking By Myself; Except You; Love Disease; Where Did My Baby Go; All In A Day; So Far So Good; Buddy's Advice; Keep On Moving

Elektra EKS 74054 [Stereo] - Released in 1970
Copperfields - Dillards

Elektra EKS 74055 [Stereo] - Released in 1969
Recollections - Judy Collins
Produced by Mark Abramson

Pack Up Your Sorrows; Tomorrow Is A Long Time; Early Morning Rain; Anathea; Turn! Turn! Turn! (To Everything There Is A Season); Daddy You've Been On My Mind; Mr. Tambourine Man; Winter Sky; The Last Thing On My Mind; The Bells Of Rhymney; Farewell

Elektra EKS 74056 [Stereo] - Released in 1969
Satin Chickens - Rhinoceros
Produced by David Anderle (The Frog)

Note: 'Satin Doll' is the Duke Ellington number.

Elektra EKS 74057 [Stereo] - Released in 1969
Changing Horses - Incredible String Band

Big Ted; White Bird; Dust Be Diamonds; Sleepers Awake; Mr And Mrs; Creation

Elektra EKS 74058 [Stereo] - Released in 1970
Revisited - Love

My Little Red Book; Softly To Me; Hey Joe; Signed D C; 7 and 7 Is; Orange Skies; Your Mind And We Belong Together; She Comes In Colors; Alone Again Or; And More Again; Your Friend And Mine (Neil's Song); You Set The Scene; Good Times

Note: Includes the last Love A-side 'Your Mind And We Belong Together', which was not any of their main albums.

Elektra EKS 74059 [Stereo]
Partyin' - Wild Thing

Note: The one album Jac would like the world to forget.

Elektra EKS 74060 [Stereo] - Released in 1970
Subway To The Country - David Ackles
Produced by Russ Miller

Main Line Saloon; That's No Reason To Cry; Candy Man; Out On The Road; Cabin On The Mountain; Woman River; Inmates Of The Institution; Subway To The Country

Note: Some copies also included a radio station promotion single with an interview.

Elektra EKS 74061 [Stereo] - Released in 1970
I Looked Up - Incredible String Band

Black Jack Davy; Letter; Pictures In A Mirror; This Moment; When You Find Out Who You Are; Fair As You

---

Elektra EKL 4062 [Mono] EKS 74062 [Stereo] - Released in 1971
Classic Rush - Tom Rush

On The Road Again; The Cuckoo; Who Do You Love; Joshua Gone Barbados; Shadow Dream Song; Urge For Going; Galveston Flood; Love's Made A Fool Of You; No Regrets/Rockport Sunday; Something In The Way She Moves; The Circle Game

---

Elektra EKS 74063 [Stereo] - Released in 1969
Roxy - Roxy

Love Love Love; Sing A Song; New York City; Somebody Told You; Love For A Long Time; Windy Day; You Got A Lot Of Style; I Got My Friends; Yesterday's Song; Rock And Roll Circus

Note: Not to be confused with Roxy Music. The sleeve of this album is notable because it includes a photo of famed Elektra album cover designer William S Harvey.

Elektra EKS 74064 [Stereo] - Released in 1970
Woodsmoke And Oranges - Paul Siebel
Produced by Peter K. Siegel

She Made Me Lose My Blues; Miss Cherry Lane; Nashville Again; The Ballad Of Honest Sam; Then Came The Children; Louise; Bride 1945; My Town; Any Day Woman; Long Afternoons

---

Elektra EKS 74065 [Stereo] - Released in 1971
Relics Of The Incredible String Band (UK release) - Incredible String Band
Produced by Joe Boyd, Witchseason Productions

Way Back In The 1960's; Painting Box; First Girl I Loved; Everything's Fine Right Now; Koeeoaddi There; Chinese White; No Sleep Blues; The Minotaur's Song; October Song; My Name Is Death; A Very Cellular Song; Nightfall

Note: Single album release in the UK. The sleeve lists the UK String Band albums as EKS 7254, 7257 and 7258 rather than EUKS with the same numbers, which is an error as these numbers were sound effects discs.

Elektra EKS 74065 [Stereo] - Released in 1970
Disguised As A Normal Person - David Steinberg
Produced by George Sherman

Note: Comedy album recorded live at the Bitter End in New York. This is a rare album to bear the credit Production Supervisor Keith Holzman.

Elektra EKS 74066 [Stereo] - Released in 1970
Tom Paxton 6 - Tom Paxton
Produced by Milton Okun

Elektra EKS 74067 [Stereo]
Crabby Appleton - Crabby Appleton

Elektra EKS 74068 [Stereo] - Released in 1969
Renaissance - Renaissance
Produced by Paul Samwell-Smith

Kings & Queens; Innocence; Island; Wanderer; Bullet

Note: Released in UK on Island Records ILPS 9114.

Elektra EKS 74069 [Stereo] - Released in 1970
The American Revolution - David Peel and the Lower East Side
Produced by Peter K. Siegel

The Lower East Side; The Pledge Of Allegiance; Legalize Marijuana; Oink, Oink; I Want To Get High; I Want To Kill You; Girls Girls Girls; Hey, Mr. Draft Board; God

---

Elektra EKS 74070 [Stereo] - Released in 1970
Gulliver - Gulliver

Elektra EKS 74071 [Stereo] - Released in 1970
Fun House - The Stooges
Produced by Don Gallucci

Down On The Street; Loose; T V Eye; Dirt; 1970; Fun House; L A Blue

Note: Featuring Iggy Pop. [Also released on CD]

Elektra EKS 74072 [Stereo] - Released in 1970
Suite Steel - Various Artists
Produced by John Boylan

Elektra EKS 74073 [Stereo]
Little Bit Of Rain - Fred Neil
Produced by Paul Rothchild

Note: Originally issued as EKS 7293 under the title 'Bleeker And MacDougal' and with a different sleeve.

Elektra EKS 74074 [Stereo] - Released in 1970
Lorca - Tim Buckley
Produced by Dick Kunc

Lorca; Anonymous Proposition; I Had A Talk With My Woman; Driftin'; Nobody Walkin'

Note: Tim Buckley's 'difficult' album. [Also released on CD]

Elektra EKS 74075 [Stereo] - Released in 1970
Better Times Are Coming - Rhinoceros
Produced by Guy Draper

Elektra EKS 74076 [Stereo] - Released in 1970
On The Waters - Bread
Produced by David Gates, James Griffin and Robb Royer

Why Do You Keep Me Waiting; Make It With You; Blue Satin Pillow; Look What You've Done; I Am That I Am; Been Too Long On The Road; I Want You With Me; Coming Apart; Easy Love; In The Afterglow; Call On Me; The Other Side Of Life

Note: CD reissue in 1995 in the Elektra Traditions series from Rhino. [Also released on CD]

Elektra EKS 74077 [Stereo] - Released in 1970
For Collectors Only - Lonnie Mack

Wham; I'll Keep You Happy; Suzie Q; Farther On

Down Road; Bounce; Where There's A Will; Chicken Pickin; Baby What's Wrong; Down In The Dumps; Down And Out; Satisfied; Memphis; Why

Note: Reissued classics from Lonnie, including the seminal 'Memphis' instrumental.

Elektra EKS 74078 [Stereo]
If I Be Your Lady - Carol Hall
Produced by Keith Holzman

If I Be Your Lady; Why Be Lonely; Baby If We Had Time; Who Will Dance With The Blind; It's Been A Long Time Comin'; Miss McKinley; Let Me Be Lucky This Time; Crooked Clock; Goodbye Jasper; Ceiling Song; Crazy Marinda; Jenny Rebecca; Ain't Love Easy

Elektra EKS 74079 [Stereo] - Released in 1971
13 - The Doors

Light My Fire; People Are Strange; Back Door Man; Moonlight Drive; Crystal Ship; Roadhouse Blues; Touch Me; Love Me Two Times; You're Lost, Little Girl; Hello, I Love You; Land Ho; Wild Child; Unknown Soldier

Elektra EKS 74080 [Stereo]
Right On Be Free - Voices Of East Harlem

Elektra EKS 74081 [Stereo] - Released in 1971
Jack-Knife Gypsy - Paul Siebel
Produced by Robert W. Zachary

Jasper And The Miners; If I Could Stay; Jack-Knife Gypsy; Prayer Song; Legend Of Captain's Daughter; Chips Are Down; Pinto Pony; Hillbilly Child; Uncle Dudley; Miss Jones; Jeremiah's Song

Elektra EKS 74082 [Stereo] - Released in 1971
Carly Simon - Carly Simon
Produced by Eddie Kramer for Jerry Brandt/Brandtworks Records Inc

That's The Way I've Always Heard It Should Be; Alone; One More Time; The Best Thing; Just A Sinner; Dan, My Fling; Another Door; Reunions; Rolling Down The Hills; The Love's Still Growing

Note: Also issued in Quad as EQ 4082.

Elektra EKS 74083 [Stereo]
Farquahr - Farquahr

Elektra EKS 74084 [Stereo] - Released in 1970
Formerly Anthrax - Show Of Hands
Produced by Russ Miller

Note: This band was once called Anthrax ... hence the album title.

Elektra EKS 74085 [Stereo]
Radio Free Nixon - David Frye

Note: David Frye was the comedian who 'did' Richard Nixon. The radio jingles on this album come authentically from the Dallas heartland of radio jingledom. The 'Hail To The Chief ...Dick Nixon' jingle is a showstopper.

Elektra EKS 74086 [Stereo] - Released in 1971
Manna - Bread
Produced by David Gates, together with James Griffin and Robb Royer

Let Your Love Go; Take Comfort; Too Much Love; If; Be Kind To Me; He's A Good Lad; She Was My Lady; Live In Your Love; What A Change; I Say Again; Come Again; Truckin'

Note: CD reissue in 1995 in the Elektra Traditions series from Rhino. Some copies of this, probably just in Europe, have the prefix EKX which may well mean 'extra cost' because of the intricate sleeve.

Elektra EKS 74087 [Stereo]
Strange Locomotion - Siren

Relaxing With Bonnie Lou; Some Dark Day; Lillian; Stride; I'm All Aching; Strange Locomotion; Lonesome Ride; Fetch Me My Woman; Hot Potato; Soon; Squeeze Me

Note: Based on the UK release on Dandelion and jointly labeled 'Dandelion'. A notable inclusion on this version is 'The Stride', which was originally credited to Coyne-Clague, the band's earlier name.

Elektra EKS 74088 [Stereo] - Released in 1971
Beautiful People - New Seekers

One; All Right My Love; Ain't Love Easy; Blackberry Way; When There's No Love Left; Your Song; Look What They've Done To My Song, Ma; Cincinnati; Eighteen Carat Friend; Beautiful People; I'll Be Home; Never Ending Song Of Love

Elektra EKS 74089 [Stereo] - Released in 1971
Rat On - Swamp Dogg

Elektra EKS 74091 [Stereo] - Released in 1971
Crow Dog's Paradise - Henry and Leonard Crow Dog with Al Running
Produced by Peter K. Siegel of Burmese Records Inc

4 Peyote Songs (Leonard); Wolakota (Peace Song) (Henry); Jesus, Light Of The World (L); Song For Him Who Do Not Return (H); Gourd Dance (H); 2 Peyote Songs (L); Hanblechia Song to the Universe (H); Leonard Crow Dog Talks About Peyote and The Native American Church; 4 Peyote Songs (L)

Elektra EKS 74092 [Stereo]
The Rainbow Band - Rainbow Band

Elektra EKS 74093 [Stereo] - Released in 1971
Smiling Men With Bad Reputations - Mike Heron

Elektra EKS 74094 [Stereo] - Released in 1971
Death Walks Behind You - Atomic Rooster

Death Walks Behind You; Vug; Tomorrow Night; Seven Streets; Sleeping For Years; I Can't Take No More; Nobody Else; Gershatzer

Note: Licensed from B&C Records in the UK.

Elektra EKS 74095 [Stereo]
Bring America Home - Timber

Elektra EKS 74096 [Stereo] - Released in 1971
The Quinaimes Band - Quinaimes Band

Elektra EKS 74097 [Stereo] - Released in 1971
Uncle Dirty Primer - Uncle Dirty

Note: Adult comedian, recorded at Sam Hood's Village Gaslight in December 1970.

Elektra EKS 74098 [Stereo]
Wackering Heights - Wackers
Produced by Gary Usher

Travelin' Time; Body Go Round; Don't Be Cruel; Country Queen; Strangers; Don't Put Down The Singer; I Don't Want My Love Refused; White House; I Like; On The Way Up; Such A Good Thing; No Place For The Children

Elektra EKS 74099 [Stereo] - Released in 1971
Nicely Out Of Tune - Lindisfarne
Produced by John Anthony

Lady Eleanor; Road To Kingdom Come; Winter Song; Turn A Deaf Ear; Clear White Light, Part II; We Can Swing Together; Float Me Down The River; Down; Nothing But The Marvellous; Scarecrow Song

Note: Licensed from Charisma Records in the UK but remixed and with a more sophisticated sleeve than the original UK release.

Elektra EKS 74100 [Stereo] - Released in 1971
The House On The Hill - Audience
Produced by Gus Dudgeon

Indian Summer; You're Not Smilin'; Jackdaw; It Brings A Tear; Raviole; Nancy; I Had A Dream; I Put A Spell On You; The House On The Hill

Elektra EKS 74101 [Stereo] - Released in 1971
Living By The Days - Don Nix

Elektra EKS 74102 [Stereo] - Released in 1972
The Hills Of Indiana - Lonnie Mack

Elektra EKS 74103 [Stereo] - Released in 1971
Mary Called Jeanie Greene - Jeanie Greene

Elektra/Dandelion EKS 74104 [Stereo] - Released in 1971
Songs For The Gentle Man - Bridget St John
Produced by Ron Geesin

Note: Licensed from Dandelion Records in the UK and jointly labeled 'Dandelion'.

Elektra EKS 74105 [Stereo] - Released in 1971
Cyrus - Cyrus Faryar

Softly Through The Darkness; I Think He's Hiding; Sweet Believer; Evergreen (Earth Anthem); Rattle's Dream; New Beginnings; Companion; Brother, Friend; Springtime Bouquet; Kingdom

Note: The voice of the Zodiac (EKS 74009) goes solo.

Elektra EKS 74106 [Stereo]
Rotten To The Core - Crabby Appleton

Elektra EKS 74107 [Stereo] - Released in 1971
Frisco Mabel Joy - Mickey Newbury
Produced by Dennis Linde

An American Trilogy; How Many Times; Future's Not What It Used To; Mobile Blue; Frisco Depot; You're Not My Same Sweet Baby; Remember The Good; Swiss Cottage Place; How I Love Them Old Songs

Note: Also released in Quad as EQ-4107.

Elektra EKS 74108 [Stereo]
New Colours - New Seekers

Tonight; Too Many Trips To Nowhere; Wanderer's Song; Boom-Town; Evergreen; Move Me Lord; Nickel Song; Lay Me Down; No Man's Land; Sweet Louise; Good Old Fashioned

Elektra EKS 74109 [Stereo] - Released in 1971
In Hearing Of - Atomic Rooster

Breakthrough; Break The Ice; Decision/Indecision; Spoonful Of Bromide; Devil's Answer; Black Snake; Head In The Sky; Rock; Price

Note: Licensed from B&C Records in the UK.

Elektra EKS 74112 [Stereo] - Released in 1971
Liquid Acrobat As Regards The Air - Incredible String Band

Talking Of The End; Dear Old Battlefield; Cosmic Boy; Worlds They Rise And Fall; Evolution Rag; Painted Chariot; Adam and Eve; Red Hair; Here Till Here Is There; Tree; Jigs; Darling Belle

Note: UK Release on Island ILPS 9172.

Elektra EKS 74115 [Stereo]
I'd Like To Teach The World To Sing - New Seekers

Tonight; Too Many Trips To Nowhere; Wanderer's Song; Boom-Town; Evergreen; I'd Like To Teach The World To Sing; Nickel Song; Lay Me Down; No Man's Land; Sweet Louise; Good Old Fashioned Music; Child Of Mine

Note: The title song was used by Coca-Cola as their advertising song with the words changed to 'I'd Like to buy the World a Coke'.

Elektra EKS 75005 [Stereo] - Released in 1969
The Soft Parade - The Doors
Produced by Paul Rothchild

Tell all the People; Touch Me; Shaman's Blues; Do It; Easy Ride; Wild Child; Runnin' Blue; Wishful Sinful; The Soft Parade

[Also released on CD]

Elektra EKS 75006 [Stereo]
I Am The President - David Frye

Note: David Frye was the comedian who did Richard Nixon impressions.

Elektra EKS 75007 [Stereo] - Released in 1970

Morrison Hotel - The Doors
Produced by Paul Rothchild

Roadhouse Blues; Waiting For The Sun; You Make Me
Real; Peace Frog; Blue Sunday; Ship Of Fools; Land Ho!;
The Spy; Queen Of The Highway; Indian Summer;
Maggie M'Gill

[Also released on CD]

Elektra EKS 75008 [Stereo]
The Best Of Josh White - Josh White
Produced by Jac Holzman ('occasional selections' by
Mark Abramson)

Free And Equal Blues; Where Were You, Baby?; You
Don't Know My Mind; Sam Hall; Run, Mona, Run;
Timber; Takin' Names; St James Infirmary; One Meat
Ball; Peter; Jelly, Jelly; Jesus Gonna Make Up My Dyin'
Bed; Halleleu; Prison Bound Blues; Midnight Special;
Told My Captain; Going Home Boys; Trouble; Silicosis
Blues; Southern Exposure; Empty Bed Blues; The Story
Of John Henry

Note: Double album.

Elektra EKS 75010 [Stereo] - Released in 1971
Whales And Nightingales - Judy Collins
Produced by Mark Abramson

Song For David; Sons Of; The Patriot Game;
Prothalamium; Golden Thread; Gene's Song; Farewell
To Tarwathie; Time Passes Slowly; Marieke; Nightingale
I; Nightingale II; Simple Gifts; Amazing Grace

Note: 'Amazing Grace' became a worldwide hit. This
album also contains the sounds of Humpback Wales
singing on 'Farewell to Tarwathie', courtesy of Dr
Roger Payne.

Elektra EKS 75011 [Stereo] - Released in 1971
L.A. Woman - The Doors
Produced by Bruce Botnick and the Doors

The Changeling; Love Her Madly; Been Down So Long;
Cars Hiss By My Window; L A Woman; L'America;
Hyacinth House; Crawling King Snake; The Wasp
(Texas Radio And The Big Beat); Riders On The Storm

Note: Early copies of this album have a multi-part
sleeve with a clear window in the front. [Also released
on CD]

Elektra EKS 75012 [Stereo] - Released in 1971
A Child's Garden Of Grass - Various Artists
Produced by Ron Jacobs for Watermark Inc

History Of Marijuana; Acquiring Marijuana/General
Effects; Creativity; Physical Effects; Psychological
Effects; Time And Space; Getting Hung-Up; Funniness;
Meditation; Eating Food; Listening To Music; Making
Love; Physical Games

Note: From the book of the same name.

Elektra EKS 75013 [Stereo]
**Sometimes I Just Feel Like Smilin' - Paul Butterfield
Blues Band**
Produced by Paul Rothchild

Play On; One Thousand Ways; Pretty Woman; Little
Piece Of Dying; Song For Lee; Trainman; Night Child;
Drowned In My Own Tears; Blind Leading The Blind

Elektra EKS 75014 [Stereo] - Released in 1972
Living - Judy Collins
Produced by Mark Abramson

Joan Of Arc; Four Strong Winds; Vietnam Love Song;
Innisfree (The Lake Of Innisfree); Song For Judith
(Open The Door); All Things Are Quite Silent; Easy
Times; Chelsea Morning; Famous Blue Raincoat; Just
Like Tom Thumb's Blues

Elektra EKS 75015 [Stereo] - Released in 1972
Baby I'm - A Want You - Bread
Produced by David Gates

Mother Freedom; Baby I'm - A Want You; Down On
My Knees; Everything I Own; Nobody Like You; Diary;
Dream Lady; Daughter; Games of Magic; This Isn't
What the Governmeant; Just Like Yesterday; I Don't
Love You

Note: Also available in Quad as EQ 5015.

Elektra EKS 75016 [Stereo] - Released in 1971
Anticipation - Carly Simon
Produced by Paul Samwell-Smith for Silven
Productions Ltd

Anticipation; Legend in Your Own Time; Our First Day
Together; The Girl You Think You See; Summer's
Coming Around Again; Share the End; The Garden;
Three Days; Julie Through the Glass; I've Got to Have
You

Elektra EKS 75017 [Stereo]
Other Voices - The Doors

In The Eyes Of The Sun; Variety Is The Spice Of Life;
Ships W/Sails; Tightrope Ride; Down On The Farm; I'm
Horny I'm Stoned; Wandering Musician; Hang On To
Your Life

Note: The Doors without Jim.

Elektra EKS 75018 [Stereo] - Released in 1972
Beads And Feathers - Carol Hall
Produced by Russ Miller

Carnival Man; Sandy; Thank You Babe; Hello My Old
Friend; Uncle Malcolm; Sunday Lady; Nana; Hard
Times Lovin; My House; Charlie's Waiting For The
Snow; I Never Thought Anything Like This Would
Happen

Elektra EKS 75019 [Stereo]
Kongos - John Kongos
Produced by Gus Dudgeon

Elektra EKS 75020 [Stereo] - Released in 1971
Bernie Taupin - Bernie Taupin

Birth; The Greatest Discovery; Flatters (A Beginning);
Brothers Together; Rowston Manor; End Of A Day; To
A Grandfather; Solitude; Conclusion; When The Heron
Wakes; Like Summer Tempests; Today's Hero; Sisters Of
The Cross; Brothers Together Again; Verses After Dark;
La Petite Marionette; Ratcatcher; The Visitor

Note: Elton John's lyricist read his poetry on this album and was accompanied by some famous friends including Caleb Quaye, Davey Johnstone and Shawn Phillips.

Elektra EKS 75021 [Stereo]
Fog On The Tyne - Lindisfarne

Elektra EKS 75022 [Stereo]
Road Show - Alabama State Troupers (Don Nix, Jeanie Greene, Furry Lewis ...)
Produced by Don Nix

Furry's Blues; Brownsville; I'm Black; A Chicken Ain't Nothin But A Bird; Will The Circle Be Unbroken; Amos Burke; Mighty Time; Jesus On The Mainline; Mary Louise; Yes I Do Understand; Opening (Part I); Opening (Part II); Living In The Country; Joa-Bim; Dixie; Heavy Makes You Happy; Iuka; Asphalt Outlaw Hero; Olena; My Father's House; Going Down

Note: Double live album.

Elektra EKS 75023 [Stereo] - Released in 1972
Heads & Tales - Harry Chapin
Produced by Jac Holzman

Could You Put Your Light On, Please; Greyhound; Everybody's Lonely; Sometime, Somewhere Wife; Empty; Taxi; Any Old Kind of Day; Dogtown; Same Sad Singer

Note: Jac Holzman was so excited by Harry's talent that he climbed back into the producer's chair one last time.

Elektra EKS 75024 [Stereo] - Released in 1972
J F Murphy And Salt - JF Murphy and Salt
Produced by Eddie Kramer for Remarkable Productions Inc

Elektra EKS 75025 [Stereo] - Released in 1972
Hot Wacks - Wackers
Produced by Gary Usher

Elektra EKS 75026 [Stereo] - Released in 1972
Lunch - Audience
Produced by Gus Dudgeon

Elektra EKS 75027 [Stereo] - Released in 1972
Ronee Blakley - Ronee Blakley
Produced by Robert W. Zachary

Dues; Sleepin' Sickness Blues; Attachment; Down To The River; Gabriel; I Lied; Along The Shore; Fred Hampton; Cock O' The Walk; Bluebird; Graduation Tune

Elektra EKS 75028 [Stereo] - Released in 1972
Tiptoe Past The Dragon - Marlin Greene

Elektra EKS 75029 [Stereo] - Released in 1972
Motorcycle Mama - Sailcat
Produced by Pete Carr

Elektra EKS 75030 [Stereo] - Released in 1972
Colors Of the Day - The Best Of Judy Collins - Judy Collins
Produced by Mark Abramson

Someday Soon; Since You Asked; Both Sides Now; Sons Of; Suzanne; Farewell to Tarwathie; Who Knows Where The Time Goes; Sunny Goodge Street; My Father; Albatross; In My Life; Amazing Grace

Note: This album was entitled 'Amazing Grace' in the UK. It was also available in Quad as EQ-5030.

Elektra EKS 75031 [Stereo] - Released in 1972
Aztec Two-Step - Aztec Two-Step
Produced by Jerry Yester

Elektra EKS 75032 [Stereo] - Released in 1972
American Gothic - David Ackles
Produced by Bernie Taupin

American Gothic; Love's Enough; Ballad Of The Ship Of State; One Night Stand; Oh, California!; Another Friday Night; Family Band; Midnight Carousel; Waiting For The Moving Van; Blues For Billy Whitecloud; Montana Song

[Also released on CD]

Elektra EKS 75033 [Stereo] - Released in 1972
Jubal - Jubal

Elektra EKS 75034 [Stereo] - Released in 1972
Circles - New Seekers

Elektra EKS 75036 [Stereo] - Released in 1972
Ship - The Ship
Produced by David Gates

Elektra EKS 75037 [Stereo] - Released in 1973
There's An Innocent Face - Curt Boettcher

Note: Curt had been a member of the Association and Millennium and was a demon vocal arranger.

Elektra EKS 75038 [Stereo] - Released in 1972
Full Circle - The Doors

Get Up And Dance; 4 Billion Souls; Verdilac; Hardwood Floor; Good Rockin'; The Mosquito; The Piano Bird; It Slipped My Mind; The Peking King and The New York Queen

Elektra EKS 75039 [Stereo] - Released in 1972
Made In England - Atomic Rooster

Elektra EKS 75040 [Stereo] - Released in 1972
Casey Kelly - Casey Kelly
Produced by Richard Sanford Orshoff

Elektra EKS 75041 [Stereo] - Released in 1972
Goodthunder - Goodthunder

Elektra EKS 75042 [Stereo] - Released in 1972
Sniper And Other Love Songs - Harry Chapin
Produced by Fred Kewley

Sunday Morning Sunshine; Sniper; And The Baby Never Cries; Burning Herself; Barefoot Boy; Better Place To Be; Circle; Woman Child; Winter Song

Elektra EKS 75043 [Stereo] - Released in 1972
Dingly Dell - Lindisfarne

Elektra EKS 75044 [Stereo] - Released in 1972
In Search Of Amelia Earhart - Plainsong
Produced by Sandy Robertson

For The Second Time; Yo Yo Man; Louise; Call The
Tune; Diesel On My Tail; Amelia Earhart's Last Flight;
I'll Fly Away; True Story Of Amelia Earhart; Even The
Guiding Light; Side Roads; Raider

Note: Featuring Ian Matthews

Elektra EKS 75045 [Stereo] - Released in 1972
Sweet Salvation - Sweet Salvation

Elektra EKS 75046 [Stereo] - Released in 1972
Shredder - Wackers
Produced by Mark Abramson

Elektra EKS 75047 [Stereo] - Released in 1972
Guitar Man - Bread
Produced by David Gates

Welcome To The Music; The Guitar Man; Make It By
Yourself; Aubrey; Fancy Dancer; Sweet Surrender;
Tecolote; Let Me Go; Yours For Life; Picture In Your
Mind; Don't Tell Me No; Didn't Even Know Her Name

Note: The lead guitar on 'Guitar Man' was Larry
Knechtel.

Elektra EKS 75048 [Stereo] - Released in 1972
Portland - Gary Ogan and Bill Lamb

Elektra EKS 75049 [Stereo] - Released in 1972
No Secrets - Carly Simon
Produced by Richard Perry

The Right Thing To Do; The Carter Family; You're So
Vain; His Friends are More than Fond of Robin; We
Have No Secrets; Embrace Me, You Child; Waited so
Long; It Was So Easy; Night Owl; When You Close
Your Eyes

Note: Also in Quad as EQ 5049

Elektra EKS 75050 [Stereo] - Released in 1973
Veronique Sanson - Veronique Sanson

Amoureuse; Tout Est Cassé Tout Est Mort; L'Irreparable;
Louis; Mariavah; Pour Les Michel; Pour Qui; Green
Green Green; I Needed Nobody; Bahia; C'est Le
Moment; Birds Of Summer

Note: European copies have a different sleeve from US
copies and the album was released in Europe in two
versions (one with more French than the other) but
with the same catalog number.

Elektra EKS 75051 [Stereo] - Released in 1973
Best Of The New Seekers - New Seekers

Look What They've Done To My Song, Ma; Beautiful
People; Nickel Song; Blackberry Way; A Perfect Love;
Never Ending Song Of Love; I'd Like To Teach World
To Sing; Tonight; Evergreen; Circles; Beg, Steal Or
Borrow; Dance, Dance, Dance

Note: Also available in Quad on EQ-5051.

Elektra EKS 75052 [Stereo] - Released in 1973
Dana Cooper - Dana Cooper

Elektra EKS 75053 [Stereo] - Released in 1973
True Stories & Other Dreams - Judy Collins
Produced by Mark Abramson and Judy Collins

Cook With Honey; So Begins The Task; Fishermen
Song; The Dealer (Down And Losin'); Secret Gardens;
Holly Ann; The Hostage; Song for Martin; Ché

Elektra EKS 75054 [Stereo] - Released in 1973
Special Delivery - Billy Mernit

Elektra EKS 75055 [Stereo] - Released in 1973
Heaven Help The Child - Mickey Newbury
Produced by Russ Miller, Marlin Greene and Dennis
Linde

Heaven Help The Child; Good Morning Dear;
Sunshine; Sweet Memories; Why You Been Gone So
Long; Cortelia Clark; Song For Susan; San Francisco
Mabel Joy

Note: 'Frisco Mabel Joy' was produced by Bob
Beckham.

Elektra EKS 75056 [Stereo] - Released in 1973
Best Of Bread - Bread
Produced by David Gates

Make it With You; Too Much Love; If; Let Your Love
Go; Everything I Own; Been Too Long On The Road;
Baby I'm - A Want You; Down On My Knees; It Don't
Matter To Me; Mother Freedom; Look What You've
Done; Truckin'

Note: Also released in Quad as EQ-5056

Elektra EKS 75057 [Stereo] - Released in 1973
Homegrown - Don Agrati

Elektra EKS 75058 [Stereo] - Released in 1973
Intergalactic Trot - Star Drive

Note: Also released in Quad as EQ-5058.

Elektra EKS 75059 [Stereo] - Released in 1973
Capital City Rockets - Capital City Rockets

Elektra EKS 75060 [Stereo] - Released in 1973
Fancy Dancer - Courtland Pickett
Produced by Pete Carr

Elektra EKS 75061 [Stereo] - Released in 1973
Valley Hi - Ian Matthews

Elektra EKS 75062 [Stereo] - Released in 1973
Dennis Linde - Dennis Linde
Produced by Dennis Linde

Elektra EKS 75063 [Stereo] - Released in 1973
Music Is Your Mistress - Linda Hargrove

Elektra EKS 75064 [Stereo] - Released in 1973
Queen - Queen
Produced by John Anthony, Roy Baker and Queen

Keep Yourself Alive; Doing All Right; Great King Rat;
My Fairy King; Liar; Night Comes Down; Modern

Times Rock 'n' Roll; Son And Daughter; Jesus; Seven Seas Of Rhye

Note: Early US copies of this album had a gold embossed cover.

Elektra EKS 75065 [Stereo] - Released in 1973
Short Stories - Harry Chapin
Produced by Paul Leka

Short Stories; WOLD; Song for Myself; Song Man; Changes; They Call Her Easy; Mr Tanner; Mail Order Annie; There's a Lot of Lonely People Tonight; Old College Avenue

---

Elektra EKS 75066 [Stereo] - Released in 1973
First - David Gates
Produced by David Gates

Sail Around The World; Sunday Rider; Soap (I Use The); Suite: Clouds, Rain; Help Is On The Way; Ann; Do You Believe He's Comin'; Sight & Sound; Lorilee

Note: There's a note on the sleeve of this LP that says 'This album is dedicated to Jac Holzman, I shall miss him'.

Elektra EKS 75067 [Stereo] - Released in 1973
Dennis Coulson - Dennis Coulson

Elektra EKS 75068 [Stereo] - Released in 1973
Islands - Cyrus Faryar

Bright Island; On The Sea; So We Sailed; Dolphins; Good Feeling; Livin' In A Land O' Sunshine; Ghosts; Paradise; At Sunset

---

Elektra EKS 75070 [Stereo] - Released in 1973
Jobriath - Jobriath

Take Me I'm Yours; Be Still; World Without End; Space Clown; Earthling; Movie Queen; I'm a Man; Inside; Morning Star Ship; Rock Of Ages; Blow Away

---

Elektra EKS 75071 [Stereo] - Released in 1973
Painter - Painter
Produced by Danny Lowe

West Coast Woman; Tell Me Why; Song For Sunshine; Goin' Home To Rock 'n' Roll; Space Truck; Kites and Gliders; Oh! You; Slave Driver; For You; Crazy Feeling; Going Down The Road

---

Elektra EKS 75073 [Stereo] - Released in 1973
Skymonters With Hamid Hamilton Camp - Skymonters

Gypsy; Kings; Steal Away; Disaster; All I Need; Long River; Time; Shadows On The Wall; Laksmi's Song; The Dalang

---

Elektra EKS 75074 [Stereo] - Released in 1973
IV - Atomic Rooster

All Across The Country; Save Me; Voodoo In You/Jackie Avery; Moods; Take One Toke; Can't Find A Reason; Ear In The Snow; What You Gonna Do/Chris Farlowe

Note: Licensed from B&C Records in the UK.

Elektra EKL 9001 [Mono] - Released in 1964
The Folk Box - Various Artists
Produced by Jac Holzman

Cynthia Gooding: Greensleeves; Ian Campbell Folk Group: Down In The Coal Mine; Ewan MacColl: Geordie; Irish Ramblers: Whiskey In The Jar; Susan Reed: Irish Famine Song; Ed McCurdy: Gypsy Laddie; Jean Redpath: Tae The Weavers; African Traveling Song; Navajo Night Chant; Gene Bluestein: Skada At America; New Lost City Ramblers: When First Unto This Country; Susan Reed: Springfield Mountain; Ed McCurdy: Good Old Colony Times; Oscar Brand: Jefferson And Liberty; Pete Seeger: Darling Cory; Jack Elliott: Jesse James; Leadbelly: Rock Island Line; Woody Guthrie: Oregon Trail; Erik Darling: Swannanda Tunnel; Ed McCurdy: Kentucky Moonshine; Alabama School Children: Green Green Rocky Road; Leadbelly: Pick A Bale Of Cotton; Seafarers Chorus: Haul On The Bowline; Pete Seeger: Paddy Works On The Railway; Harry Jackson: I Ride An Old Paint; Cisco Houston: Zebra Dun; Horace Sprott: Field Holler; Koerner, Ray & Glover: Linin' Track; Willer Turner: Now Your Man Done Gone; Josh White: Timber; Negro Prisoners: Grizzly Bear; Marilyn Child & Glenn Yarbrough: Mary Had A Baby; Josh White: Jesus Gonna Make Up My Dyin Bed; Blind Willie Johnson: Dark Was The Night; Judy Collins: Twelve Gates To The City; Theodore Bikel: A Zemer; Glenn Yarbrough: Wayfaring Stranger; Ed McCurdy: Simple Gifts; Leadbelly: Meetin' At The Building; Bob Gibson: You Can Tell the World; Christian Tabernacle Church: Down By The Riverside Willy Clancy: Sligo Reel/Mountain Road; Eric Weissberg: Old Joe Clark; Clarence Ashley: Coo Coo Bird; Tom Paley: Shady Grove; Eric Weissberg & Marshall Brickman: Flop-Eared Mule; Jean Ritchie: Nottamun Town; Doc Watson and others: Amazing Grace; Doc Watson: Cripple Creek; The Dillards: Pretty Polly; George Pegram & Walter Parham: Yellow Rose Of Texas; Dián And The Greenbriar Boys: Green Corn; The Dillards: Old Man At The Mill; Sonny Terry: Lost John; Big Bill Broonzy: I Wonder When I'll Get To Be Called a Man; Leadbelly: Black Snake Moan; Blind Lemon Jefferson: See That My Grave Is Kept Clean; Hally Wood: House Of The Rising Sun; Mark Spoelstra: France Blues; New Lost City Ramblers: Carter Blues; Dave Ray: Slappin' On My Black Cat Bone; Dave Van Ronk: Don't Leave Me Here; Josh White: Southern Exposure; Ed McCurdy: John Brown's Body; Frank Warner: Virginia's Bloody Soil; Judy Collins: Two Brothers; Judy Collins: Masters of War; Theodore Bikel: Blow The Candles Out; Jean Redpath: Love Is Teasin'; Clarence Ashley and Doc Watson: Sally Ann; Jean Ritchie: Little Devils; Limeliters: The Hammer Song; Woody Guthrie: This Land Is Your Land; Pete Seeger, Almanac Singer With Audience: Which Side Are You On?; New Lost City Ramblers: No Depression In Heaven; Woody Guthrie: Talking Dust Bowl; Big Bill Broonzy: Black Brown And White; Oscar Brand: Talking Atomic Blues; Hamilton Camp: Girl From The North Country; Judy Collins: The Dove; Tom Paxton: High Sheriff Of Hazard; Phil Ochs: The Thresher; Pete Seeger: We Shall Overcome

Side 1: Songs Of The Old World And Migration To The New
Side 2: Settling, Exploring And Growing In The New World

Side 3: Work Songs
Side 4: Many Worshippers, One God
Side 5: Country Music - From Ballads To Bluegrass
Side 6: Nothing But The Blues
Side 7: Of War, Love And Hope
Side 8: Broadsides, Topical Songs, Protest Songs

Note: A boxed set of 4 discs with a 48 page booklet ,
put together by Robert Shelton with the assistance of
Folkways Records. This box was issued in the UK as
EUK 2512/2.

Elektra EKS 79002 [Stereo] - Released in 1970
Absolutely Live - The Doors
Produced by Paul Rothchild

Who Do You Love; Alabama' Song; Backdoor Man;
Love Hides; Five To One; Build Me A Woman; When
The Music's Over; Close To You; Universal Mind; Break
On Thru #2; Celebration Of The Lizard; Soul Kitchen

Note: Double album.

Elektra [Mono] - Released in 1973
**The Elektra Story (Project) - BBC Radio London
'Fresh Garbage' Series**
Produced by Andy Finney

Note: This was a radio program presented by Andy
Finney and Bob Harris. A hundred or so copies were
pressed by Elektra in the UK onto a double LP package.

Elektra 60381 [Stereo] - Released in 1984
**Bleecker And MacDougal (The Folk Scene Of The
1960's) [The Jac Holzman Years] - Various Artists**
Edited by Lenny Kaye

Fred Neil: Bleecker and MacDougal; Mark Spoelstra:
White Winged Dove; Bruce Murdoch: Rompin' Rovin'
Days; Dave Van Ronk: Don't You Leave Me Here; Geoff
Muldaur: Ginger Man; Eric von Schmidt: Blow Whistle
Blow; Hamilton Camp: Girl from the North Country;
Patrick Sky: Many a Mile; Josh White: One Meat Ball;
Josh White: Johnny Has Gone for a Soldier; Josh
White: Free and Equal Blues; The Even Dozen Jug
Band: On The Road Again; Danny Kalb: Hello Baby
Blues; Koerner, Ray & Glover: Good Time Charlie;
Koerner, Ray & Glover: Titanic; Koerner, Ray & Glover:
John Hardy; Oscar Brand: Talking Atomic Blues; Oscar
Brand: Great Selchie of Shule Skerry; Will Holt: M T A;
Tom Paley & Peggy Seeger: Who's Going to Shoe Your
Pretty Little Foot; Tom Paley: Buck Dancer's Choice;
Tom Paley: Cuckoo (The); Eric Weissberg: Devil's
Dream; Eric Weissberg: Nine Hundred Miles; Dick
Rosmini: Nine Hundred Miles to Go; Dick Rosmini:
Picker's Medley; The Limeliters: If I Had A Hammer;
The Limeliters: Lonesome Traveller; Glenn Yarbrough:
House of the Rising Sun; Erik Darling: Pretty Polly; Erik
Darling: Salty Dog; The Folksingers: Peter Gray; The
Travellers 3: Marcella Wahine; The Travellers 3: Sinner
Man; Judy Henske: Wade in the Water; Tom Paxton: I
Can't Help But Wonder Where I'm Bound; Tom
Paxton: What did you Learn in School Today; Tom
Paxton: The Last Thing on my Mind; Tom Paxton:
Daily News; Tom Paxton: Ramblin' Boy; Tom Paxton:
Lyndon Johnson Told The Nation; Tom Paxton: Bottle
Of Wine; Phil Ochs: Power And The Glory; Phil Ochs: I
Ain't Marchin' Anymore; Phil Ochs: Here's To The
State Of Mississippi; Phil Ochs: Changes; Phil Ochs:
Love Me I'm A Liberal; Phil Ochs: When I'm Gone;

Judy Collins: Maid Of Constant Sorrow; Judy Collins:
Fannerio; Judy Collins: The Bells Of Rhymney; Judy
Collins: Daddy You've Been On My Mind; Tom Rush:
Urge For Going; Tom Rush: Panama Limited; Fred Neil:
Blues On The Ceiling; Fred Neil: Other Side To This
Life; Fred Neil: A Little Bit of Rain; Richard Fariña:
House Un-American Blues Activity Dream; Richard
Fariña: Birmingham Sunday; David Blue: Midnight
Through Morning; David Blue: So Easy She Goes By

Elektra 60383 [Stereo] - Released in 1984
**Crossroads (White Blues in the 1960's) [The Jac
Holzman Years] - Various Artists**
Edited by Lenny Kaye

Koerner, Ray & Glover: Linin' Track; Koerner, Ray &
Glover: Hangman; Koerner, Ray & Glover: One Kind
Favor; Koerner, Ray & Glover: Banjo Thing; Koerner,
Ray & Glover: Jimmy Bell; Koerner, Ray & Glover:
Corrina; Koerner, Ray & Glover: Fannin Street;
Koerner, Ray & Glover: Black Dog; Koerner, Ray &
Glover: Poor Howard; Koerner, Ray & Glover: Black
Betty; Koerner, Ray & Glover: Broke Down Engine;
Koerner, Ray & Glover: Rent Party Rag; Koerner, Ray &
Glover: Don't Let Right Hand Know What Your Left
Hand Do; Koerner, Ray & Glover: Can't Get My Rest At
Night; Dave Van Ronk: Bad Dream Blues; Geoff
Muldaur: Downtown Blues; Mark Spoelstra: France
Blues; Danny Kalb: I'm Troubled; Al Kooper: Can't
Keep From Crying Sometimes; Tom Rush: You Can't
Tell a Book by the Cover; The Lovin' Spoonful: Good
Time Music; The Lovin' Spoonful: Almost Grown; The
Lovin' Spoonful: Searchin'; The Lovin' Spoonful: Don't
Bank on it Baby; Eric Clapton & the Powerhouse:
Steppin' Out; Eric Clapton & the Powerhouse:
Crossroads; Eric Clapton & the Powerhouse: I Want to
Know; The Paul Butterfield Blues Band: Born in
Chicago; The Paul Butterfield Blues Band: Shake your
Money-Maker; The Paul Butterfield Blues Band: Blues
with a Feeling; The Paul Butterfield Blues Band: I Got
My Mojo Working; The Paul Butterfield Blues Band:
Mellow Down Easy; The Paul Butterfield Blues Band:
Look Over Yonder's Wall; The Paul Butterfield Blues
Band: Good Morning Little Schoolgirl; The Paul
Butterfield Blues Band: Walkin Blues; The Paul
Butterfield Blues Band: I Got A Mind To Give Up
Living; The Paul Butterfield Blues Band: Work Song;
The Paul Butterfield Blues Band: Pity the Fool

Note: Boxed set of 3 LPs in series 'The Jac Holzman
Years' with booklet.

Elektra 60402 [Stereo] - Released in 1985
**O Love Is Teasin' (Anglo-American Mountain
Balladry) - Various Artists**
Edited by Lenny Kaye

Tom Paley: Shady Grove; Tom Paley: The Miller's Song;
Tom Paley: Old Grey Goose; Tom Paley: Jackaro; Tom
Paley: The Girl On The Greenbriar Shore; Tom Paley:
Little Maggie; Tom Paley: Banjo Pieces; Tom Paley:
Pretty Polly Susan Reed: Barbara Allen; Ed McCurdy:
The Two Sisters; Cynthia Gooding: The Cherry Tree
Carol; Ellen Stekert: Froggie Went A-Courtin'; Lori
Holland: Gypsy Lover; Susan Reed: The Golden Vanity;
Ed McCurdy: Lord Randal; Shep Ginandes: The Wife of
Usher's Well; Susan Reed: The Foggy Dew; Ed
McCurdy: The Derby Ram; Myra Ross: John Riley;
Cynthia Gooding: The Lass From The Low Countrie;
Peggy Seeger: Love Henry (Young Hunting); George

Pegram: Little Old Log Cabin In The Lane; Susan Reed: At The Foot Of Yonders Mountain; Jean Ritchie: O Love Is Teasin'; Jean Ritchie: Black Is The Color; Jean Ritchie: Jubilee; Jean Ritchie: Old Virginny; Jean Ritchie: Skin And Bones; Jean Ritchie: The Little Devils; Jean Ritchie: The Cuckoo Version I; Jean Ritchie: The Cuckoo Version II; Jean Ritchie: Cedar Swamp; Jean Ritchie: Nottamun Town; Jean Ritchie: The Hangman's Song; Jean Ritchie: Sister Phoebe; Jean Ritchie: False Sir John; Jean Ritchie: Dulcimer Pieces: Shady Grove, Old King Cole, Skip To My Lou; Jean Ritchie: Batchelor's Hall; Jean Ritchie: One Morning In May; Jean Ritchie: Jemmy Taylor-O; Jean Ritchie: Killy Krankie; Jean Ritchie: Old Woman And Pig; Jean Ritchie: Hush Little Baby; Jean Ritchie: The Little Sparrow; Jean Ritchie: Goin' To Boston; Oscar Brand And Jean Ritchie: Hey Little Boy; Oscar Brand and Jean Ritchie: I Wonder When I Shall be Married; Oscar Brand and Jean Ritchie: The Keys Of Canterbury; Oscar Brand and Jean Ritchie: Young Man Who Wouldn't Hoe Corn (A); Oscar Brand and Jean Ritchie: Hog Drivers; Oscar Brand and Jean Ritchie: Lazy John; Oscar Brand and Jean Ritchie: My Good Old Man; Oscar Brand and Jean Ritchie: Paper of Pins; Oscar Brand and Jean Ritchie: No Sir

Note: Boxed set of 3 LPs in series 'The Jac Holzman Years' with booklet.

Elektra 60403 [Stereo] - Released in 1985
Elektrock (The Sixties) - Various Artists
Edited by Lenny Kaye

The Holy Modal Rounders: Bird Song; The Beefeaters (Byrds): Please Let Me Love You; The Beefeaters (Byrds): Don't Be Long; Luke And The Apostles: Been Burnt; Ars Nova: March Of The Mad Duke's Circus; Clear Light: Black Roses; Clear Light: Mr Blue; Earth Opera: The Red Sox Are Winning; Earth Opera: Home To You; Eclection: Nevertheless; David Peel and the Lower East Side: I Like Marijuana; Wild Thing: In A Gadda-Da-Vida; Roxy: Rock And Roll Circus; Crabby Appleton: Go Back; Rhinoceros: Apricot Brandy; Rhinoceros: I Need Love; Gulliver (featuring Daryl Hall): Christine; Voices of East Harlem: Right On Be Free; Delaney & Bonnie: Someday; Delaney & Bonnie: Get Ourselves Together; The Stalk-Forrest Group: Arthur Comics; Nico: Frozen Warnings; The Butterfield Blues Band: East-West; The Incredible String Band: Way Back In The 1960s; Love: My Little Red Book; Love: Hey Joe; Love: Signed D C; Love: Seven And Seven Is; Love: She Comes In Colors; Love: Alone Again Or; Love: Andmoreagain; Love: Singing Cowboy; Tim Buckley: Aren't You The Girl; Tim Buckley: Strange Street Affair Under Blue; Tim Buckley: I Can't See You; Tim Buckley: No Man Can Find The War; Tim Buckley: Pleasant Street; Tim Buckley: Dream Letter; Tim Buckley: Morning Glory; The MC5: Kick Out The Jams; The MC5: Come Together; The MC5: Motor City Is Burning; The MC5: Rambin' Rose; The MC5: Starship; The Stooges: 1969; The Stooges: I Wanna Be Your Dog; The Stooges: No Fun; The Stooges: T V Eye; The Stooges: 1970

Note: Boxed set of 4 LPs in series 'The Jac Holzman Years' with booklet.

Elektra 5E 502 [Stereo] - Released in 1978
An American Prayer - Jim Morrison: Music by the Doors

Produced by John Haeny, John Densmore, Robbie Krieger, Frank Lisciandro and Ray Manzarek

Awake; Ghost Song; Dawn's Highway/New Born Awakening; To Come of Age; Black Polished Chrome/Latino Chrome; Angels and Sailors/Stoned Immaculate; Curses, Invocations; American Night; Roadhouse Blues; Lament; The Hitchhiker; An American Prayer (The End, Albinoni Adagio)

Note: Posthumous post-dubbing by the remaining Doors over poetry tapes recorded in the early Seventies by Jim. [Also released on CD]

Elektra 7E 2006 [Stereo] - Released in 1973
Nuggets - Artyfacts Of The First Psychedelic Era - Various Artists
Edited by Lenny Kaye and Jac Holzman

Electric Prunes: I Had Too Much To Dream Last Night; Standells: Dirty Water; Strangeloves: Night Time; Knickerbockers: Lies; Vagrants: Respect; Mouse: A Public Execution; Blues Project: No Time Like The Right Time; Shadows Of Knight: Oh Yeah; Seeds: Pushin' Too Hard; Barbarians: Moulty; Remains: Don't Look Back; Magicians: Invitation To Cry; Castaways: Liar Liar; Thirteenth Floor Elevators: You're Gonna Miss Me; Count Five: Psychotic Reaction; Leaves: Hey Joe; Michael And The Messengers: Just Like Romeo And Juliet; Cryan Shames: Sugar And Spice; Amboy Dukes: Baby Please Don't Go; Blues Magoos: Tobacco Road; Chocolate Watch Band: Let's Talk About Girls; Mojo Men: Sit Down I Think I Love You; Third Rail: Run Run Run; Sagittarius: My World Fell Down; Nazz: Open My Eyes; Premiers: Farmer John; Magic Mushrooms: It's-A-Happening

Note: Double album. UK release was short two tracks for which clearance was not obtained: Seeds (Pushing Too Hard) + AN Other.

Elektra CC 1 [Mono] - Released in 1958
Morse Code Course
Produced by Jac Holzman

Note: 12 progressive recorded lessons on a 12-inch LP intended as an aid to acquiring skill in sending and receiving International Morse Code.

Elektra EB 1 [Stereo] - Released in 1968
Elektra's Best: Volume 1, 1966 through 1968 - Various Artists

Tim Buckley: Morning Glory; Paul Butterfield Blues Band: Born In Chicago; Paul Butterfield Blues Band: In My Own Dream; Judy Collins: Both Sides Now; Judy Collins: Suzanne; Judy Collins: Someday Soon; David Ackles: Down River; The Doors: Light My Fire; The Doors: Hello, I Love You; The Doors: Touch Me; The Dillards: Listen To The Sound; Earth Opera: Home To You; Diane Hildebrand: Early Morning Blues And Greens; Love: Seven And Seven Is; Love: Alone Again Or; Incredible String Band: First Girl I Loved; Incredible String Band: Air; Lonnie Mack: Why; Lonnie Mack: Save Your Money; 'Spider' John Koerner and Willie Murphy: Magazine Lady; Tom Rush: No Regrets; Hold Modal Rounders: Bird Song; Tom Paxton: Mister Blue; Rhinoceros: I Need Love; Rhinoceros: Apricot Brandy; Zodiac Cosmic Sounds: Aquarius; Baroque Beatles Book: You've Got to Hide Your Love

Away/Ticket to Ride

Note: A double album for radio station use.

Elektra S3 10 [Stereo] - Released in 1971
Garden Of Delights - Various Artists

Butterfield Blues Band: Play On; Carly Simon: Alone; 'Spider' John Koerner and Willie Murphy: Magazine Lady; Paul Siebel: She Made Me Lose My Blues; Don Nix: Three Angels; Carol Hall: If I Be Your Lady; Tim Buckley: Wings; Bread: London Bridge; Beefeaters: Please Let Me Love You; Love: Hey Joe; Clear Light: Mr Blue; Crabby Appleton: Peace by Peace; Show Of Hands: Moondance; The Stooges: Down on the Street; The Voices of East Harlem: Right On, Be Free; Joshua Rifkin: Scott Joplin's 'Maple Leaf Rag'; Even Dozen Jug Band: Come On In; Josh White: Jesus Gonna Make Up My Dyin' Bed; Lonnie Mack: Lay It Down; Lord Buckley: The Nazz; The New Seekers: Blackberry Way; Farquahr: Start Living; Rhinoceros: Apricot Brandy; Swamp Dogg: Creepin' Away; Roxy: Listen To The Music; The Wackers: Travellin' Time; Diane Hildebrand: Early Morning Blues And Greens; The Rainbow Band: Rama Rama; Siren: The Stride; Incredible String Band: Blackjack Davy; Lindisfarne: Lady Eleanor; Audience: It Brings A Tear; Atomic Rooster: Nobody Else; Renaissance: Island; Timber: Bring America Home; The Quinames Band: Green Rolling Hills Of West Virginia; Judy Collins: Coming Of The Roads; David Ackles: Subway To The Country; Jeanie Green: Like A Road Leading Home; Earth Opera: Home To You

Note: This compilation may have been for radio station use but it boasts copious liner notes which were a DJ's dream. Jac and Keith Holzman put it together to celebrate the 17th anniversary of the first sampler LP: Elektra's 'A Folk Music Sampler' of 1954.

Elektra SMP 2 [Mono] - Released in 1956
Folk Festival - Various Artists

Ed McCurdy: Josie; Jean Léon Destiné and Ensemble: Declaration Paysanne; Clarence Cooper: Erie Canal; Cynthia Gooding and Theodore Bikel: Coplas; Ed McCurdy: Robin Hood And The Bold Pedlar; Theodore Bikel: Ptsach Bazemer; Jean Ritchie: Nottamun Town; Cynthia Gooding: Bella Regazza; Josh White: John Henry; Los Gitanillos De Cadiz: Sevillanas; Susan Reed: Must I Go Bound; Theodore Bikel: Mangwani Mpulele; Alan Arkin: Crawdad Song; Suzanne Robert: Le Moulin De La Galette; Cynthia Gooding: The Derby Ram; Gordon Heath and Lee Payant: Au Clair De La Lune; Jean Ritchie and Oscar Brand: Keys Of Canterbury; The Funmakers: My Ain House

---

Elektra SMP 3 [Mono] - Released in 1957
Folk Pops 'n Jazz Sampler - Various Artists
Edited by Jac Holzman

Josh White: Midnight Special; Cynthia Gooding: Lass Of The Low Countrie; Clarence Cooper: Nine Hundred Miles; Ed McCurdy: Sacramento; Sabicas: Soleares; Susan Reed: Black Is The Color; Glenn Yarbrough: Hard, Ain't It Hard; The New York Jazz Quartet: Coo Coo Calypso; Four French Horns: Come Rain Or Come Shine; The Jazz Messengers: Ugh!; Norene Tate: The Wail; The New York Jazz Quartet: Blue Chips; Teddy Charles: Skylark

Note: The actual order of the three musical categories varied depending on whether you looked at the front, back or spine of the cover. In the sleeve note Jac explains how the origins of folk and jazz are similar and that the apparently diverse album is, in fact, homogenous.

Elektra SMP 5 [Mono]
Folk Sampler Five - Various Artists

A Maid Goin' To Comber; Bulerias; Nine Foot Shovel; Hora Heachzut; Mary Had A Baby; Beryuzoviye Kalyechke; Swannanda Tunnel; Steel Merengue; Kum Aher Du Filozof; Johnson Boys; Ankaranin Tasina Bak; Michael Row The Boat Ashore; Il Est Petit; Which Is The Properest Day To; Stay Away From The Girls; Day-O

Elektra SMP 6 [Mono]
The Folk Scene - Various Artists

Bowling Green; Red Sun; Gypsy Laddie; Pretty Saro; Talking Dust Bowl; Flop-Eared Mule; Grizzly Bear; Bonnie Highland Laddie; Greenland Fisheries; One Sunday Morning; Lowlands Of Holland; Gilgary Mountain; Daily Growing; Squid Jiggin' Ground

---

Elektra SMP 7 [Mono] [Stereo]
Sound Effects Sampler - Sound Effects

Machine Guns; Telephone Rings Five Times; Plate Glass Smashing; Ping Pong; Fire Engine Passes With Bell; Steam Locomotive; Jet Fighter Flyby; Bacon Frying; Ethereal Space Sounds; Pile Driver; Niagara Falls; IBM Electric Typewriter; News Presses; High Speed; Hacksaw; Prize Fight; Large Arena; Car Skid and Crash; Pop Bottle Sequence; Steamship Blast; Surf; Cricket Background; Pinball Machine; Bowling Sequence; Shooting Gallery; Dentist's Drill; Tea Kettle Sequence; Grandfather Clock Strikes Twelve; Trolley Car; Gong; Seven Strokes; Carousel; Stage Coach Passes; Tire Pump; Coal Truck Unloading

Note: Stereo album had number SMP-7-ST.

Elektra SMP 8 [Mono] [Stereo] - Released in 1965
Folksong '65 - Various Artists

Tom Rush: Long John; Judy Collins: So Early, Early In The Morning; Koerner, Ray & Glover: Linin' Track; Hamilton Camp: Girl Of The North Country; Dick Rosmini: 900 Miles; Tom Paxton: The Last Thing On My Mind; Paul Butterfield: Born In Chicago; Kathy and Carol: Fair Beauty Bright; Mark Spoelstra: White Winged Dove; Fred Neil: Blues On The Ceiling; Bruce Murdoch: Rompin' Rovin' Days; Phil Ochs: Power And The Glory

Note: Stereo number is S-78

Dandelion D9 101 [Stereo] - Released in 1970
Ask Me No Questions - Bridget St John
Produced by John Peel

To B Without A Hitch; Autumn Lullaby; Curl Your Toes; Like Never Before; The Curious Crystals Of Unusual Purity; Bare Feet And Hot Pavements; I Like To Be With You In The Sun; Lizard-Long-Tongue Boy; Hello Again (Of Course); Many Happy Returns; Broken

Faith; Ask Me No Questions

Note: Licensed from the Dandelion label in the UK.
John Martyn plays second guitar on parts of this.

Dandelion D9 102 [Stereo]
I'm Back And I'm Proud - Gene Vincent

Rockin' Robin; In The Pines; Be Bop A Lula; Rainbow
At Midnight; Black Letter; White Lightning; Sexy
Ways; Ruby Baby; Lotta Lovin; Circle Never Broken;
Number Nine Lonesome Whistle; Scarlet Ribbons

Note: The energetic original rocker makes his comeback and final album: courtesy of the Dandelion label
in the UK.

Dandelion D9 103 [Stereo]
Soundtrack - Principal Edwards Magic Theatre

Enigmatic Insomniac Machine; Sacrifice; Death Of Don
Quixote; Third Sonnet; To A Broken Guitar; Pinky A
Mystery Cycle

Note: Licensed from the Dandelion label in the UK.

Dandelion D9 104 [Stereo]
Siren - Siren

Ze Ze Ze Ze Ze; Get Right Church; Rock Me Baby; Wake
Up My Children; Wasting My Time; Sixteen Women;
First Time I Saw Your Face; Gardener Man; And I
Wonder; The War Is Over; Asylum; Bertha Lee; I
Wonder Where

Note: Licensed from the Dandelion label in the UK.
Siren features Kevin Coyne. The UK versions of both
Siren albums were released in the UK as a single CD in
1994 on See For Miles Records SEECD 413.

Countryside CM 101 [Stereo]
Pure Country - Garland Frady

A Good Love Is Like A Good Song; Silver Moon;
Orange Silk Blouse; I Still Miss Someone; Brand New
Tennessee Waltz; You Be You; I Can See Clearly Now;
Drivin' Down That Lonesome Road; Teach Your
Children; Bar-Rooms Have Found You

Countryside CM 102 [Stereo] - Released in 1973
Velvet Hammer In A Cowboy Band - Red Rhodes
Produced by Michael Nesmith for Countryside

Crippled Lion; Poinciana; Lothario In A; Jay's Tune;
Dana's Waltz; Lunar Nova; Lonesome; Great American
Thunder Turkey; Steel Guitar Waltz

Elektra EUK 253 [Mono] - Released in 1966
A Cold Wind Blows - Various Artists
Produced by Joe Boyd

Cyril Tawney: Five Foot Flirt; Alasdair Clayre, Peggy
Seeger and Martin Carthy: Hawthorne Berries; Matt
McGinn, David Speirs: Get Up, Get Out; Johnny
Handle: Dust; Alasdair Clayre, Peggy Seeger: Tiny
Newman; Matt McGinn, David Speirs: The Champagne
Flows; Johnny Handle: The Trepanner Song; Cyril
Tawney: Monday Morning; Matt McGinn, David
Speirs: Mr Rising Price; Johnny Handle: Fill Up The
Pints Again; Alasdair Clayre: Old Man's Song; Matt

McGinn, David Speirs: I've Packed Up My Bags; Cyril
Tawney: Sammy's Bar; Johnny Handle: The Old Pubs;
Alasdair Clayre, Peggy Seeger: A Cold Wind Blows;
Matt McGinn: Jeannie Gallacher; Johnny Handle:
Because It Wouldn't Pay; Cyril Tawney: The Oggie Man

Elektra EUK 254 [Mono] - Released in 1966
The Incredible String Band - Incredible String Band
Produced by Joe Boyd

Maybe Someday; October Song; When The Music
Starts To Play; Schaeffer's Jig; Womankind; The Tree;
Whistle Tune; Dandelion Blues; How Happy I Am;
Empty Pocket Blues; Smoke Shovelling Song; Can't
Keep Me Here; Good As Gone; Footsteps Of The
Heron; Niggertown; Everything's Fine Right Now

Note: Original UK release.

Elektra EUK 255 [Mono] - Released in 1967
Alasdair Clayre - Alasdair Clayre
Produced by Joe Boyd and Alasdair Clayre

The Invisible Backwards-Facing Grocer Who Rose To
Fame; Snow; Adam And The Beasts; Lighterman; Night
Song; Tied To The Line; The Professor And The Girl; A
Gentle Easy-Flowing River; The Formless Maid; The
Wayward Way; Irish Girl; Lament For A Writer; Old
Couple Walking; Lullaby And Come Afloat

Elektra EUK 256 [Mono] [Stereo] - Released in 1967
AMMMusic - AMM
Produced by Harry Davis and Jac Holzman

Later During A Flaming Riviera Sunset; After Rapidly
Circling The Plaza

Note: Improvised music using both conventional
instruments and 'found' sounds. The group included
Cornelius Cardew and there is a photo of Jac on the
sleeve.

Elektra EKL 5000 [Mono]
**The Golden Apple - Original New York Cast of the
early Fifties musical, based on the legend of Helen
of Troy**

Note: Released by arrangement with RCA.

Elektra EKL 5001 [Mono]
**The Folk Song Kit/How To Play Folk Guitar - Lee
Hays**

Elektra EKL 5002 [Mono]
Dramatic Cue Mood Music 1- Dramatic Cue Music
Produced by Jac Holzman

Elektra EKL 5003 [Mono]
**Dramatic Cue and Mood Music 2 - Dramatic Cue
Music**
Produced by Jac Holzman

Elektra EKL 5004 [Mono]
**Dramatic Cue and Mood Music 3 - Dramatic Cue
Music**
Produced by Jac Holzman

Index